...in's Guide to
CAR COLLECTING

Prepared by the experts at

Sports Car Market

motorbooks

Thanks

I would like to dedicate this 2nd edition of Keith Martin's Guide to car Collecting to my uncle, Virgil McDowell, who, during his long and productive life, was a constant source of encouragement to me, and to my first and always best dance teacher, Judy Massee at Reed College, for teaching me that no dream was too big. My editor at the New York Times, Jim Cobb, continues to both mentor me as a writer and as an editor, and has helped me become a much more thoughtful editor for the contributors to Sports Car Market and Corvette Market.

In a larger sense, I want to thank everyone who has been a part of Sports Car Market, and now Corvette Market, for the past twenty-two years. Each article written, each auction report filed, have added to the cumulative knowledge of the collector car market that all culminate in this book.

The project-meister who has brought this book together is our Operations Manager, Jennifer Davis-Shockley. Undeterred by the birth of her daughter, Keelin, midway through the project, she relentlessly herded all the wild gerbils that made up the *Keith Martin's Guide to Car Collecting, Second Edition*, team and got them to deliver their stories on time. The artistic Merlin who shaped all of this into the visually appetizing package you've now got on your desk is our Art Director, Kirsten Onoday, who accomplished this while concurrently finishing up monthly editions of Sports Car Market and Corvette Market. Stefan Lombard, the Managing Editor of both SCM and CM, played the role of the all-star utility infielder. Simply put, he did everything necessary to make this book happen, from chasing down stories to assigning copyediting to final proofing, all while juggling the multiple unfamiliar balls of fatherhood to a new daughter, Hazel. The final two members of the primary team were Executive Editor Paul Duchene, who assigned and edited the editorial contributions, and Jim Pickering, our Auction Editor, who made sure we had the right cars, with the correct results, in this book. I'm very lucky to have such a hard-working group here, which includes the rest of the SCM and CM staff, and this book represents the culmination of months of work on their part.

On the family side, my daughter Alexandra, who is heading off to college this fall, and my son Bradley, who at the age of two is just beginning to develop expertise riding his tricycle, both bring joy and a constant sense of exploration to my life. My wife Wendie is both intellectually supportive and fiscally wise as she helps drive my career forward—while at the same time sharing my passion for all things motorized. —*Keith Martin*

This edition published in 2009 by MBI Publishing Company and Motorbooks, an imprint of MBI Publishing Company, 400 First Avenue North, Suite 300, Minneapolis, MN 55401 USA

Motorbooks titles are also available at discounts in bulk quantity for industrial or sales-promotional use. For details write to Special Sales Manager at MBI Publishing Company, 400 First Avenue North, Suite 300, Minneapolis, MN 55401 USA.

To find out more about our books, visit us online at www.motorbooks.com.

ISBN-13: 978-0-7603-3749-3

Editor: Paul Duchene
Designed by: Kirsten Onoday

Printed in China

About the Author

Keith Martin has been involved with the collector car hobby for more than forty years. As a writer, publisher, television commentator and enthusiast, he is constantly on the go, meeting collectors and getting involved in their activities throughout the world.

He founded the monthly Sports Car Market magazine twenty-two years ago, and it has developed into the authoritative informed voice of the collector car hobby. His second publication, Corvette Market magazine, launched in 2008, brings the same intellectual vigor and analysis to the Corvette marketplace as Sports Car Market does to exotics and classics.

The website for Sports Car Market, www.sportscarmarket.com, contains the world's largest and most informative database of collectible cars, with more than 60,000 cars listed with serial numbers, photos, and descriptive and valuation details. It includes a graphical display of value trends over time for any marque in the database, a unique tool for collectors.

His Keith Martin on Collecting series, published by Motorbooks International, includes books on Ferrari, Jaguar, Alfa Romeo, Porsche, and English sports cars. His Keith Martin on Car Collecting sold out, necessitating this updated second edition.

In a partnership with Road & Track, Martin has developed instant-access, downloadable "Buyer's Guides" for more than 50 of the most popular collectible cars. These guides are available on the websites of the New York Times, Road & Track and Collector Car Traderonline, as well as Sports Car Market and Corvette Market.

Martin's columns on collecting and reviews of exotic cars, including the Ford GT and the Bentley Continental GT, have appeared in the New York Times.

He has hosted numerous television specials, and was most recently featured on "Appraise My Car," shown on Discovery HD Theater. As a commentator, emcee and judge, he has been involved with Pebble Beach, Amelia Island, Meadow Brook, and Concorso Italiano, among other events.

He is the chairman of the Meguiar's Collector Car Person of the Year Award Committee, is on the Board of Trustees of the LeMay Museum and the Hagerty-founded Collectors Foundation, and has served on the faculty of the Collier Museum symposium on connoisseurship.

Martin brings an eclectic background to his passion for cars. His academic background includes the study of intellectual history at Reed College, in Portland, Oregon, and study as a dance major at the Juilliard School in New York City. He founded the first professional ballet company in Oregon, Ballet Oregon, was awarded an Oregon Art's Commission Individual Artist's Fellowship for new choreography, and was director of dance for the Portland Opera.

Martin, his wife Wendie, and their three teen-aged children Tyler, Alexandra, and Andrew, and their son Bradley, born in May of 2007, live in Portland, Oregon.

Table of Contents

INTRODUCTION

Keith Martin.. 7

What is Car Collecting? 8

Collecting Strategies 10

Collector Car Auction Companies 14

BY THE NUMBERS

Introduction 24

2008–09

Million-Dollar Sales in 2008–09 25

Top 1,000 Sales in 2008–09 by Price............ 30

Top 1,000 Sales in 2008–09 by Marque 53

Top 5 Sales per Marque in 2008–09 76

Top 100 Muscle Car Sales 88

Top 100 Corvette Sales 91

History

All-Time Top 10 Sales 94

Sales Results by Vehicle Era........................ 96

MARKET REPORTS

Introduction.............................. 100

Ferraris 101

British.............................. 105

Porsches 109

Muscle Cars 113

Corvettes 117

Pre-War Classics 121

Modern Day Supercars 125

BEST BETS & WORST

Introduction.............................. 129

Getting Started

Why Buy a Collector Car?...................... 130

Starting Out: Buying Your First
Collector Car.............................. 131

Nine Exotics You Can Afford 133

Fun Collectible Cars Under $25,000 138

Italian

Eight Italian Sports Cars
for the First-Time Collector 141

Eight Ferraris for Under $100,000.............. 145

Five Best Ferraris Over $1,000,000........... 148

12-Cylinder Ferraris You Can Afford 151

The Ferrari Market Today:
What's Really Going On............................ 154

British

English Convertibles Combining
Value and Fun 156

How to Buy a Jaguar E-type 159

Why Provenance Can Add 50%
to the Price 161

German

Entry-Level 356 and 911 Porsches 163

Porsches That Are on an Upward Trend 165

Five Porsches to Avoid............................ 167

American

Buying Your First Collectible Muscle Car.. 169

How to Buy the Best Cobra and Tiger........ 171

Nine Muscle Car Sleepers.......................... 173

How to Determine Legitimacy
in a Muscle Car 177

Corvettes

The Z-Code Option:
What Does It Mean? 179

Top Ten Corvette Options for
Increased Value 185

Market Makers: Historical Corvettes
from the GM Fleet 187

Eight Corvettes to Run Away From 190

BUYING & SELLING SMART

Introduction 192

What It's Worth

Does "Spare Parts Included"
Really Matter 193

The Relationship Between
Condition and Price................................... 195

Why One High Sale Doesn't
Mean All Cars are Worth More 197

Buying and Selling

Buying Collector Cars Online..................... 199

What "Everything Works" Really Means ... 201

Buying Techniques That Work.................... 203

Modify, Restore, or Preserve?.................... 205

Avoiding Taxes on the Sale of
Your Collector Car 207

What "No Reserve" Really Means 209

Tax Consequences of Selling Your Car....... 211

When the High Bidder at an Auction
Won't Pay Up... 213

Finances

What is Collector Car Insurance? 215

What is an Agreed Value Policy?................ 217

How to Finance a Collector Car.................. 219

Settling Insurance Claims 220

You and the Law

Lemon Laws.. 222

The Ferrari Enzo Crash in Los Angeles...... 224

"As Is" Disclosures 227

VIN Plate Transfers.................................... 229

Track Day Insurance 231

Barn Finds

The Famous Portuguese Barn Find............. 233

Unrestored 1911 Oldsmobile Sells for
$1.65 Million 235

RESTORATION TODAY

Introduction 237

Restoration Types:
Street, Show, and Race.............................. 238

Restoring Your Dream Car......................... 240

Odometer Replacement and Value............. 242

Restoration to True Concours Standard 244

Seven Ways to Make Your British Car
More Reliable... 246

PRICE GUIDE

Introduction... 248

Price Guide.. 249

RESOURCES

Introduction 272

Clubs 273

Glossary of Car Terms 281

Contributors

The Sports Car Market and Corvette Market gang is a close-knit, hard-working group of enthusiasts. This book is the result of all of them working together for long hours, day and night, to share their insights on collecting with you.

GARY ANDERSON is the co-founder of the Austin-Healey Concours Registry, which created restoration standards and judging guidelines now in use around the world. He is the co-author of the best-selling book *Austin-Healey 100/100-6/3000.* He is the editor and publisher of MC2, the magazine for classic and new Minis, and has recently published the book *Motoring—Getting the Maximum from Your New MINI.* His "English Patient" column appears monthly in SCM.

MILES C. COLLIER is a practicing artist, investor, philanthropist, and noted authority on vintage automobiles. Collier worked for his family's Collier Enterprises until retirement in 1995. He then attended the New York Studio School of Drawing, Painting, and Sculpture, where he studied for three years with the noted Graham Nickson. Collier currently serves as chairman of the Board of Trustees of Eckerd College.

COLIN COMER estimates he had owned over 50 cars by the age of 20. A career in the automotive world was inevitable, and Comer founded his own business, working out of his garage after hours restoring and selling collector cars. Today, Colin's Classic Automobiles enjoys a loyal following and is regarded as one of the premier classic car dealerships in the nation. His column "Domestic Affairs" appears monthly in SCM.

JOHN DRANEAS is a Portland, Oregon, attorney who has practiced primarily in the tax and business area since 1977. Draneas is an active SCCA racer, organizes the Sunriver Exotic Car show, served for two years as president of the Oregon Region of the Porsche Club of America, and chaired PCA's 2006 Parade held in Portland. He drives a 1980 Porsche 911 Targa every day and also owns a 1959 Porsche 356A Coupe, a 1957 Alfa Giulietta Spider, a 1983 Ferrari 308 GTSi, and a Lotus Elise.

TOM GLATCH has been contributing stories and photographs to automotive publications since 1983. He is particularly interested in automotive design and history, as well as architecture, music, and computing. He has been assisted by his wife, Kelly, since they met in 1992. Though they live on the "frozen tundra" of Elm Grove, Wisconsin, with their two children, son Sean (9) and daughter Keara (14), the top is down on their 2001 Chrysler Sebring convertible from late March through October.

DONALD OSBORNE is a native New Yorker, and has contributed to SCM since 1993. Osborne's operatic career as a baritone culminated with his solo debut at the Metropolitan Opera. He is a marketing specialist and recently started Automotive Valuation Services as a certified auto appraiser. His particular automotive interest lies in Italian cars, but anything strange or bizarre with almost no actual resale value has a way of finding its way into his garage.

ROB SASS was pre-ordained to accumulate strange collector cars. His first-ever car ride, on the way home from the hospital, was in the back seat of his dad's 1959 Hillman Minx. Sass served as assistant attorney general for the state of Missouri and then as a partner in a St. Louis law firm before deciding his billable hours requirement terminally interfered with his old car affliction. His stable of affordable classics has included a TVR 280i, a Triumph TR250, an early Porsche 911S, and a Daimler SP250. He currently owns a 1967 E-type convertible and a 1967 Maserati Mistral coupe. He has written for Business Week and the New York Times, and has been SCM's "Affordable Classics" columnist for two years.

JIM SCHRAGER writes for SCM as well as the Porsche 356 Registry, and is author of the best selling book, *Buying, Driving, and Enjoying the Porsche 356.* In his spare time, he teaches business strategy at the University of Chicago Graduate School of Business. Schrager is married with two sons and works hard to keep his fleet of about 15 vintage Porsches on the road. His monthly column, "Porsche Gesprach," has appeared in SCM for the last decade.

MICHAEL SHEEHAN has been SCM's featured columnist for all things Ferrari since 1998. He's written hundreds of articles, not only for *Sports Car Market*, but for *Cavallino*, the *Ferrari Market Letter*, and numerous other Ferrari publications. Sheehan bought his first Ferrari, a 250 PF coupe, for $2,000 in 1972. He has raced extensively in several professional series and is currently a Ferrari broker at his business, www .Ferraris-online.com. He is the father of twins Mick and Colleen.

JOHN L. STEIN served as the editor of Corvette Quarterly, the award-winning official journal for Corvette, from 1998 to 2005 and remains the only independent editor to have led GM's halo magazine. Stein has driven every generation of Corvette, from the original 1953 model up through the 2008 Pratt & Miller C6RS, and tested or raced them at Daytona, Laguna Seca, Sebring, and other tracks. His favorite Corvette experience may just be sneaking through the woods at Le Mans in 2000 to watch the factory C5-R racers assault La Sarthe for the first time, their yellow headlights searing the night and their guttural scream quaking the marrow.

THE SCM/CM TEAM
Editorial: Yael Abel, Steve Ahlgrim, John Apen, Carl Bomstead, Diane Brandon, Marshall Buck, B. Mitchell Carlson, Paul Duchene, Martin Emmison, Dan Grunwald, Kristen Hall-Geisler, Paul Hardiman, Jérôme Hardy, Simon Kidston, Chip Lamb, Stefan Lombard, John Lucas, Raymond Milo, Norm Mort, Bill Neill, Dale Novak, Kirsten Onoday, Jim Pickering, Steve Serio, Thor Thorson
Administration: Mary Artz, Jennifer Davis-Shockley, Nikki Nalum, Bill Woodard
Internet: Jerret Kinsman, Bryan Wolfe
Sales: Ted Alfano, Cody Wilson

Introduction

What a pleasant phone call it was when Zack Miller of MBI, the publisher of the first edition of *Keith Martin's Guide to Car Collecting*, requested an updated and revised second edition of the book. In this book, you'll find not only the nuggets of information that made the first edition so popular, but new sections and updated information that reflect everything we have learned in the interim. If you are new to *Keith Martin's Guide to Car Collecting*, you'll be surprised by the wealth of knowledge contained here. If you already own the first edition, you should add this edition to your library, as all the sales data is new, along with much of the content.

Photo: John Vincent

The collector car market is a part of the economy at large, and there is no question that it is challenged. However, in this book we report on some record-breaking sales, as well as discuss segments of the market that have simply plummeted. *Keith Martin's Guide to Car Collecting* is the only place you'll find frank discussions of these topics, along with actual data to back up our conclusions.

However, some aspects of car collecting—those on the human side—have not changed a bit. All of us who love buying, driving, and selling old cars will always have a continual stream of them passing through our lives. In the past 24 months, the Sports Car Market and Corvette Market stables have included a variety of cars, each of which offered a different driving experience, from a vintage Mini Cooper S to an Iso Rivolta.

Keith Martin's Guide to Car Collecting is dedicated to all of us who are afflicted with an incurable and insatiable passion for cars. If we could, we'd eat our breakfast cereal out of a headlight bucket, use valve pushrods as chopsticks at lunch, and have dinner served in an aluminum engine sump. Our idea of a perfect day is one spent at a swapmeet, kicking tires and filling a tote wagon with useless bits that will stay in our garage until we sell them at the next swapmeet. The very best car in the world is the one we are about to buy, and there is no pain worse than saying goodbye to one you own.

With this book, we are creating a one-stop resource directory for the 21st-century collector. Through the relentless compilation of data in the Sports Car Market magazine database, we can bring you up-to-date auction results from around the world. By scouring our database, we have come up with the top 1,000 sales of 2008–09. You'll also find the top sellers by marque, as well as all the cars that sold for over $1,000,000.

You'll get expert advice from leaders in the field, ranging from authority Miles Collier, who offers a strategy for smart collecting, to legal specialist John Draneas, who explains what to do if the high bidder at an auction won't pay up.

In the end, reading this book should be like sitting down with a bunch of fellow gearheads, with everyone getting to tell his favorite story. Some will be about muscle cars, others about sports cars. Some will brag about classics like Duesenbergs, others about modern exotics like Lamborghinis.

Just as you would in a clubhouse, you'll find opinions you think are brilliant, and others with which you vehemently disagree. Our goal is that you'll find some new nugget of information on every page of this second edition of *Keith Martin's Guide to Car Collecting*.

Cars have been good to me and brought me over 40 years of pleasure (and some pain as well). Most importantly, they've been the reason I've met literally thousands of fellow enthusiasts, all of whom have had something to teach me.

With this book, I'm hoping to give back to the car community some of that accumulated wisdom, and offer you new tools that will help you get even more enjoyment out of your own collectible cars in the year ahead.

Keith Martin
Portland, Oregon

What Is Car Collecting?

It's important to understand the difference between a collection of cars and an accumulation of cars

by Donald Osborne

The theme here seems to be Ferrari...

When many people think of the term "car collecting," they might conjure up an image of celebrities such as Jay Leno, Jerry Seinfeld, Ralph Lauren, or Reggie Jackson. Or perhaps they think of the palatial garages of wealthy owners, where dozens of super-valuable cars—each one more perfect than the next—have been subjected to restorations costing hundreds of thousands, if not millions, of dollars.

While that is certainly a part of the car collecting scene, it is of course far from the mainstream. Thousands of people across the country and indeed around the world are a part of the car collecting hobby in much more modest ways, proof that it's not necessary to own a fleet of cars to be "a collector." You can regard yourself as a collector even if you only have one collectible car, and even if that car doesn't happen to be

running at the time. What all car collectors have in common is a passion for the automobiles that interest them and a desire to own, use, and enjoy those cars, and to share that deep feeling with other like-minded souls.

But what is collecting all about? Research, research, and more research. Asking and answering questions is how it begins:

• What is it?
• When was it made?
• How many were made?
• What is the correct equipment for the year and model?
• How much is it worth?
• What are the clubs or groups for my type of car?

Research is a key part of collecting. Finding out all the details about the car in which you have an interest is for some even more of a pleasure than the actual purchase or use of the car.

Whether it consists of a single car, a few, or a hundred, a collection should have a reason for being. Jorge Luis Borges, an Argentine writer, poet, philosopher, and rare book collector, expressed it well, writing: "I believe that collecting books, but, for that matter, collecting anything, begins as an act of love. We collect what we love, but more precisely we collect what we believe represents us. As we collect, we make a statement about ourselves."

This is why it's important to understand what differentiates a "collection" of cars from an "accumulation" of cars, which could just as easily be found in a dealer's showroom or auction tent. Collections can be made up of cars from a single marque, of a specific body style, from a particular country. They can be comprised of cars that competed with each other when new, of cars of distinctive design, of cars that made engineering breakthroughs, of cars that were complete market failures, or perhaps of cars made the year the collector was born.

Once you've decided on the car or cars of your dreams, done the research to find out more about it, and met and chatted with the folks who already own one, you can begin the process of acquiring the object of your affection. It doesn't matter if you find your car at a leading international auction, an online auction web site, in the small ads in your local paper, or sitting in a driveway around the corner with a sign in the window. What is important is that you buy what you love and what you know about.

For some collectors, the hunt for a car is as thrilling as owning it—perhaps it's looking for the exact make, model, and color you owned when you were 16. Or the car your father or grandfather used for your first driving lesson. Or maybe it's the car the coolest guy or the prettiest girl drove when you were in high school. It could be the last missing piece to complete a list of cars you made 20 years ago. Finding the right car can be the work of a lifetime.

As mentioned earlier, a collection doesn't have to be of many cars. There are plenty of people who are best described as "serial" collectors. Those are people who might make a "wish list" of the cars they want to own eventually and who work their way through that list one car at a time, buying and enjoying a car for a few years then selling it to buy the next. This is also a good way to proceed if you're new to the hobby. Start with a car you know a lot about, which has a good availability of repair and replacement parts, is easily maintained either by yourself or by a good local mechanic, has a strong and active club for support, and of course which fits your budget comfortably. Every one of the big collectors started small. Though it might be tempting to buy a bunch of "restorable" cars to jumpstart a collection, nothing will be more frustrating than to look out at a beautiful day imagining what it would be like to drive an old car while your pile of old cars remains just that, rusting heap of parts in your garage or storage room.

Even if you do want to own every Porsche ever made but only have a one-car garage and a limited budget, there's another part of car collecting that can help you fulfill your dream. There's no reason why you can't find a single affordable example, and instead of filling a warehouse with the rest, collect scale models instead. It can be just as challenging to find rare and unusual miniatures of the cars you love. But in doing so, you'll be able to assemble a collection that can be housed on shelves in your den or on the walls of your single garage for a fraction of what it would cost to own even two of the real thing.

Another final important part of car collecting is participating in shows, cruise-ins, tours, rallies, and vintage racing. Using your old car rather than locking it away in a garage has become more important than ever to collectors. It also helps to drive the market and determines why many people buy the cars they do. It's useful once again to turn to the words of J.L. Borges to sum it all up: "Finally, I realize that my collection, and really all collections, are time machines. The books we have are the surest way to travel across time, and to give us a direct image of what the past looked like."

Every time we sit in our old cars, we share a bit of the lives they've already led and give them another chapter for their future. ♦

Collecting one car at a time isn't a bad way to go, either

Collecting Strategies

Intelligence coupled with emotion creates a collection that evokes understanding, appreciation, and delight in others

by Miles Collier

Collier's McLaren F1

How is it that of two collectors with equal resources and dedication, one becomes a major figure and the other does not? For any given level of resources (income, time, and contacts), a collector is capable of rising to the level that his senses and understanding permit. Sensibility and expertise make the difference between connoisseurship and mere accumulation. The uncanny ability to distinguish the very good from the good, the fine from the ordinary, is a trait of all great collectors.

Beyond even sensibility and taste, good collecting requires establishing criteria that focus the collection and give it intelligible structure. Simultaneously, the collection must be about passion, with a true love for—and understanding of—the object. Similar to much successful creativity elsewhere, the formal, syntactical structure of the collection needs to be counterbalanced by the sheer emotionality of the collector's passion. It is the emotion of the collector that causes him to incorporate the idiosyncratic cars that no expert would dare suggest. It is this willingness to consciously break the formal criteria that gives the collection its savor. Intelligence coupled

with emotion is the necessary ingredient required to create a collection that evokes understanding, appreciation, and delight in others. If we are to aspire to significant collections, we must harness our "animal spirits" with understanding and sensibility for the object, and we must have knowledge of basic collecting strategies.

Almost all collections are built with a mixture of strategies, and provided the mix is used consciously, the results can be gratifying. Let us now review the characteristics and properties of six common approaches to collecting.

Nostalgic Collecting Strategy

One common strategy almost universally present in collections is the nostalgic/opportunistic strategy. Despite the title, it is essentially a non-strategy. The nostalgic collecting approach of pure emotionality probably represents the normal starting point for most collectors. It is an "extensive" strategy, being unbounded by any constraint, and usually is without focus. As one collector said, "You kind of just buy."

The nostalgic/opportunist strategy is founded in the

hobbyist point of view and takes its direction from areas of deep subjectivity, summed up by the phrase: "I don't know much about cars, but I know what I like." Such collections, while scratching an emotional itch, tend to be excessively repetitive, unfocused, or of very uneven quality. They tend to develop into a hodgepodge of objects that, upon the subsequent development of the collector's taste and experience, require substantial if not total revision. The ultimate size and quality of collections built this way is based on happenstance and the product of the collector's initial obsession. Such collections, being directionless, are limited only by the collector's ambition, appetite, and the capacity to support his activity.

The collector's first great step forward in collecting is the incorporation of cars not directly related to his personal experience. The result of that developmental step is commonly a conversion to a vertical strategy.

Vertical Collecting Strategy

One element of automobile collecting we often take for granted is the extreme complexity of the subject matter, the very complexity that makes the collectible car such a rich and satisfying object. Unfortunately, this complexity also means that the nascent collector must master a great deal of information relating to automotive technology, maintenance, history, original model configuration, subtle variations in specification, etc., that strongly affect value.

As often as not, as the collector's experience grows, the nostalgic/opportunistic strategy, given time to mature, develops a theme either as a primary focus or as a secondary or subsidiary focus by turning from an extensive to an intensive (focused and bounded) strategy. The most logical and simple vertical theme involves a concentration on one marque. Such an approach cuts through time along the production continuum of one maker. Organizing the collection about the chronological sequence of models, vertical strategies are often concerned with "completeness" and the filling out of sets.

Advantages:

• Reduces the collectible universe to a manageable size.
• The collector can master one marque in great detail relatively easily.
• Allows a focus on individual quality, the thing that distinguishes one example of a make/model from another.
• Good strategy for someone who wants to collect definitive examples, therefore good for sharpening the eye and developing connoisseurship skills.
• Easier to know "where the bodies are buried," to get deal flow, and be able to rate the quality of that flow.
• Easier to master the maintenance and restoration technology and sources for research material.

Disadvantages:

• The market for other makes can move away in terms of real dollars, creating a lost opportunity never to be recaptured.
• The marque's collecting scope may be limited with few

models and a short history.
• Collection can become self-limiting or hermetic, and the collector parochial in his views.
• After years of collecting, the collector may find his real interest lies elsewhere.

Horizontal Collecting Strategy

Another collecting alternative that can be extensive or intensive in scope is an approach based on collecting within a horizontal slice of time. By limiting the area requiring mastery to a band of time, the collector once more can focus his research to a manageable body of knowledge. For example, he might choose to collect American convertibles of the late 1950s. In so doing, he creates collecting criteria that cut across a series of marques, but is restricted by upper and lower temporal boundaries as well as specific car types.

Advantages:

The horizontal strategy enjoys many of the same advantages as the vertical strategy. In addition, however, it opens collectors to:
• Seeing market value changes across a broader spectrum of cars. Seeing the bigger picture reduces the danger of being left out in the cold by rapid market shifts.
• Serendipity. The collector may find he is more interested in cars of type "x" than type "y."

Disadvantages:

Horizontal strategies make it more difficult to connect to sources, as typically more than one make of automobile is involved. As cars are normally studied, supported, and even sourced by marque, the research, acquisition, and conservation challenges increase. Consequently, to move from Ferrari to Aston Martin is a harder task than shifting from Ferrari road cars to Ferrari Grand Prix cars.

Implied Horizontal Strategy

As a collection grows and encompasses more than one make, multiple vertical themes may emerge. The accretion of multiple vertical themes can begin to place a number of cars within the same time period. At some point, sufficient contemporaneous cars exist to make the further pursuit of one or more horizontal strategies a practical reality.

Understanding one marque makes cross-correlating to another make via their common world automotive history much easier. This process is analogous to learning a new language. The more languages you already speak, the easier it is to learn the next due to commonalities. A cross-correlating horizontal strategy may have less validity when two marques are wholly unrelated, i.e. Lotus and Duesenberg, as distinct from Duesenberg and Isotta-Fraschini, or more naturally yet, Duesenberg and Packard.

Thematic Collecting Strategy

Thematic approaches, being intensive in nature, are

related to vertical strategies, but have a more random pattern to the connections. Thematic collections are not confined to one make or even a few makes or time slices. Consider the high performance sports car as a theme. Such a collection might start at the turn of the century and terminate with, say, the McLaren F1.

Execution of such a theme becomes a function of judgment and taste, open to debate, argument and differences of opinion. For example, is the 540K Mercedes a required element on the continuum of high performance sports cars? Comparing experts' thoughts on the proper constituents of this sports car-themed collection would be instructive, especially if the judgments came from driving experience in addition to research.

Indeed, the Collier Museum, in Naples, Florida, exhibits such a theme in the sports cars of Briggs Cunningham. It is one of our four themed collections in the museum. Obviously the particular selection of cars is open to personal idiosyncrasies (the emotional/expressive element referred to earlier). For example, not all would agree with the selection of the Lotus Elite as a worthy addition to the sports car collection. In this type of collecting, the issue turns on finding the "right" object, as identified by the particular collector through thorough research. In the history of the sports car example, the identity of the individual automobile, allowing for condition, would be less critical to the quality of the collection than the absolutely right make and model. By contrast, the individual car *is* critical to a racing-based theme, where the history of each individual car chosen becomes significant (e.g. Jorgensen Eagle Indy car).

With the thematic strategy, the requirement for broader expertise becomes more important. This collecting approach requires a large investment in research and analysis. Fortunately, such research elements are logically connected by development of the theme in question. A thematic strategy will push every collector into unknown areas outside his comfort zone, where his intellect must serve as a guide to his emotion. The focus of such a strategy lies in finding the appropriate make, model, and example to do justice to the theme. If the car in question is very rare, such a requirement makes the search an exercise in patience and focus, to say nothing of pocketbook capacity. Consider for example, a collection based on the history of the Grand Prix car, which sooner or later would require an example of a pre-war Mercedes or Auto-Union.

Relational Collecting Strategy

At first this strategy looks like the nostalgic/opportunistic strategy. Similar to that strategy, it is extensive, being neither bounded nor otherwise thematically constrained. However, the relationship between objects is no longer inchoate, arising out of the collector's psychic stew, but explicit and carefully conceived.

Consider the Ford Model T–Rolls-Royce Dyad

FORD	ROLLS-ROYCE
1908-27	1907-26
Mass/quality	Class/quality
12.8 million	7,900
Mass production	Artisanal
Completely integrated manufacturing	Integrated manufacturing
Industry Standard/ Paradigm	Industry Standard/ Paradigm
Internationally built for a world market	Internationally built for a world market
Declining demand due to obsolescence.	Failure to see the one-model business strategy was no longer working

What car might we add to create a triad? Let's consider the McLaren F1:
- One-model strategy
- About 100 built (class/quality)
- Artisanal but cutting edge technology
- Non-integrated manufacturing
- Industry standard/paradigm
- U.K.-built for a world market
- Not obsolete—production stopped due to declining demand

The connectivity among these cars could be through history, technology, significance, and so on. The linkages may not be obvious to the casual observer unless explained, but the key is that the linkages are made through similarities and not differences. In the Ford–Rolls example above, the Model T becomes a "surprise" object, hardly the thing that would be suggested by a slew of experts for a "calendar collection" of great classic automobiles. The relational approach represents a highly intellectualized step in collecting. In relational collecting, to a great extent, the intellect controls the direction in which the collector's emotions run.

The process of connecting emotionally appealing cars is akin to creating a crossword puzzle. The appropriate car linking several others must be found by inference and through relationships to other cars in the collection. It should be apparent that the successful implementation of relational collecting requires an almost encyclopedic knowledge of automotive history and collectible cars.

Because of the cross connections in relational collecting, the problem of filling out a series, or completing a theme, never applies. Right from the beginning, the collection is always "complete." A collection carefully constructed in this way,

Few modern supercars hold real sway over collectors

incorporating both the collector's love of the objects and his consummate research to create a web of connections, would be intensely exciting for connoisseur and casual enthusiast alike.

Before we conclude, we should consider one important dichotomy among car collectors. This particular trait, whether the collector is contemplative or experiential in his collecting nature, determines many characteristics of his collection.

The experiential collector's primary interaction with his collection is through his kinesthetic senses. He drives his cars and indeed has little use or regard for cars he cannot use. This is not to say that he doesn't appreciate his car's technology, beauty, and historic importance; indeed he does. But to this collector, use is paramount.

The contemplative collector, by contrast, interacts with his collection through his intellect. As such, while this collector may enjoy driving his cars, operation is not the key requirement to his collecting. Indeed, some of his cars may not even run. This great and fundamental divide has important implications.

The need to drive every car limits the size of the experiential collection. In addition, the variety of cars, their condition, and practicality all need to be limited if the operating constraint is to be fulfilled. For example, highly fragile or delicate cars, whether due to condition or design, are inappropriate and not usually collected. More prone to seeing his collection, not only as a repository of historic objects, but also as an assemblage of sporting or competition equipment, the experiential collector's maintenance and service costs will tend to be much higher per vehicle than the contemplative collector's.

Where a user's collection is limited in size, a contemplative collection is unbounded by practical considerations, and often features "museum-type" or other impractical vehicles. Contemplative collectors are much more focused on filling out sets, or collecting according to some idea. In fact, contemplative collectors are probably closer in their sensibilities to collectors in other antiquarian fields.

Conclusion

Human nature being what it is, the strategies discussed above probably have a greater chance of guiding a collection after it has been begun. A strategic collecting plan represents a way to bring structure, editing, and refinement to a group of objects perhaps assembled with a lack of sufficient temperance, but an admirable amount of zeal. The sooner we as collectors can bring focus to our collections, the more we can increase our engagement with these objects in an appropriate way, and the better we can become at preserving our automotive heritage. ♦

Auction Company Roundup

At the end of the day, the job of these companies is to bring buyers and sellers together

Artcurial Briest-Poulain-F.Tajan

Artcurial Briest-Poulain-F.Tajan is the premier French auction house and has the expertise to set up classic and sports car auctions three to four times a year among the one hundred auctions usually organized by the company. Artcurial addresses every specialty (modern and contemporary art, furniture and *objets d'art*, old masters, etc.).

Artcurial has been a leader in this field for many years, and with a turnover of $11.9m in 2008 (around 10% of entire sales volume), the classic and sports cars department is keeping its head up in spite of the tough times the economy has experienced in the past few months.

Their dynamism and willingness to explore new territory allow them to stay in a leading position in the market, as well as to select even more quality products. They also put their heart into auctions, such as in Sochaux, when they sold cars from the Peugeot estate, or in Deauville at he Concours d'Elegance which was so famous in the Années Folles.

Don't miss their yearly rendezvous, the prestige auction in February jointly with Rétromobile, and the Luxe Sport & Collection sales in April and November.

For more information, visit www.artcurial.com.

Barrett-Jackson Auction Company

Since 1971, the Barrett-Jackson Auction Company has been the barometer of values and trends in the collector car industry. Craig Jackson and his team continue to produce the industry's biggest events, when measured any number of ways.

The success of the company's long-running Scottsdale event has even spawned smaller, yet equally thriving auctions in West Palm Beach and Las Vegas. With unique bidders and consignors attending the new venues, each auction has patterned itself into a distinct piece of the complex but well-planned Barrett-Jackson puzzle.

In addition to the auctions, the puzzle—or better yet

Artcurial

domain—includes multi-year TV contracts with SPEED, an extensive merchandise offering, collector car insurance, and interactive Internet options that have yet to be matched in the industry. And with leaders like Jackson and company president Steve Davis, it's unlikely they're done "breaking the mold" to grow the hobby.

With the economic crisis at a climax in fall 2008, the collector car industry, like most markets, faced unseen challenges, even for lifers like Jackson and Davis.

Barrett-Jackson was preparing for its inaugural Las Vegas auction in October when consignment efforts were revised to include a broad range of entry-level and mid-range cars. This approach provided modest buys for regular collectors, as well as opportunities for new members of the hobby. The diverse offering paid off in Las Vegas as Barrett-Jackson exceeded expectations by selling over 500 vehicles for just under $30m. Of the 1,200 registered bidders, more than 50% were first-timers.

Previous 2008 totals of $88m in Scottsdale (January) and $23m in Palm Beach (March), brought Barrett-Jackson's 2008 auction total to more than $140m. In addition, each 2008 auction broke attendance records, as roughly 398,000 people enjoyed the automotive lifestyle events. Barrett-Jackson also remained a devoted supporter of charities nationwide, helping raise more than $6.7m for various organizations in 2008.

In January 2009, with the economy still in flux, Barrett-Jackson again offered a mix of rare, pristine cars and more attainable vehicles. Sales totaled $63m and the growth of the hobby was evident as first-time bidders accounted for nearly 70% of the transactions. While the newcomers snatched up the extensive offering of cars in the $50k–$150k range, premium vehicles continued to shine. Stars of the 2009 Scottsdale auction included a 1929 Ford 4-AT-E Tri-Motor airplane that sold for $1.2m and a 1955 Ford Thunderbird that fetched $660k.

Barrett-Jackson returned to the East Coast in April 2009 and recorded more than $20m in sales at the fairgrounds in Palm Beach. Top sales included $500k for the "Project American Heroes" 1969 Chevrolet Camaro RS/SS custom and $253k for a classic 1934 Auburn 1250 Salon Cabriolet.

Moving forward, Barrett-Jackson plans to continue expanding the hobby by participating in more grassroots events and finding new ways to reach potential collectors to educate them about the industry. With transparent auction processes and a set of iron-clad company ethics, Barrett-Jackson instills a comfort level among bidders and consignors that can't be matched. It's that comfort, mixed with the exhilarating experience of attending the automotive lifestyle event, that keeps Barrett-Jackson at the forefront of the hobby.

For more information, visit www.barrett-jackson.com.

Bonhams Europe

Founded in 1793, Bonhams is one of the world's oldest and largest auctioneers of fine art and antiques. One of the few surviving Georgian London auction houses, Bonhams was founded by Thomas Dodd, an antique print dealer, and Walter Bonham, a book specialist. Expanded into antiques during the 1850s, Bonhams is active in over 70 categories embracing the spectrum of fine art, antiques, and collectibles.

The present company was formed by the merger in November 2001 of Bonhams & Brooks and Phillips, Son & Neale. In August 2002, the company acquired Butterfields, the principal firm of auctioneers on the U.S. West Coast, and in August 2003, Goodmans, a leading Australian fine art and antiques auctioneer with salerooms in Sydney.

The Bonhams Motoring Department is the largest auction house to hold scheduled auction sales of classic and vintage motor cars and car memorabilia and has a worldwide network of motoring-specific representatives.

Bonhams is prominent in the auction of classic Aston Martin, Rolls-Royce, Jaguar, Ferrari, Maserati, and Bugatti motor cars.

For more information, visit www.bonhams.com.

Bonhams & Butterfields

Butterfields started in 1865 when William Butterfield turned in his sheriff's badge for an auctioneer's gavel. The doors to Marble Head Auctioneers, on what is now the site of

Barrett-Jackson

Branson

Bonhams & Butterfields

San Francisco's Transamerica Pyramid, first catered to thriving Gold Rush Californians. As the city became more prosperous, Butterfield adapted his business accordingly.

Mr. Fred R. Butterfield, William's son, joined the firm in 1914 and Reeder Butterfield, Fred's son, in 1935. One of his biggest contributions was the development of the European and Asian markets—both in acquiring consigned goods and in attracting collectors from those continents. In August 2002, Butterfields was acquired by Bonhams, creating a united company specializing in the appraisal and sale of fine art, antiques, and objects in all collecting categories. Bonhams and Butterfields is part of the third largest auction house in the world, and they hold annual collector car sales in Brookline, Massachusetts, Greenwich, Connecticut, Carmel Valley, California, and Los Angeles.

For more information, visit www.butterfields.com.

Bonhams & Goodman

Bonhams & Goodman, incorporating Bonhams & Bruce and Dalia Stanley, is the largest Australian-owned, internationally operated fine art auction house.

The company employs 20 full-time specialists and consultants covering Australian and international art, fine Ab-

original paintings and artifacts, fine jewelry, collectors cars, sport and entertainment collectibles, and decorative arts and objects.

Goodmans Auctioneers joined the Bonhams group of companies in September 2003, Tim D. Goodman having been a key figure in the industry in Australia and New Zealand since 1971.

In June 2005, Bonhams & Goodman completed its merger with Theodore Bruce of Adelaide, Australia's oldest auction house, founded in 1878.

In October 2005, Bonhams & Goodman acquired Stanley & Co., one of Sydney's most prominent boutique auction businesses, and Dalia Stanley joined Bonhams & Goodman as a Senior Specialist.

In May 2008, Bonhams & Goodman announced its acquisition of Leonard Joel, one of the last of the old Australian auction houses in private family ownership.

For more information, visit www.bonhamsandgoodman.com.au.

The Branson Auction

Established in 1981, The Branson Auction has been offering quality "Service to the Collector" for 30 years, with bi-annual sales now held at the new Branson/Hilton Convention Center. With an earned reputation for excellence in the caliber and diversity of its consignments and attentive, personal customer service, the Branson Auction offers buyers and sellers an excellent venue within an eight-hour drive of 50% of America's population.

The latest addition servicing Branson's 8 million annual visitors is the opening of the new Branson Airport, with daily flights from Dallas, Atlanta, and Milwaukee, and hub connections nationwide. This, combined with the great variety of entertainment, accommodations, and dining experiences, makes the location ideal for collectors and most accommodating for their families.

The Branson Auction offers the individual as well as major collectors the opportunity to showcase their automobiles in a spectacular setting with a history of exciting results, as well as offering appraisal services, collection management and estate services.

For more information, visit www.bransonauction.com.

Gooding & Company

The official auction house for the Pebble Beach Concours d'Elegance, Southern California-based Gooding & Company provides unparalleled service for those in the collector car market, offering a range of services, including private and estate sales, appraisals, and collection management.

Gooding & Company has been chosen to sell several of the automotive auction world's finest collections, including the prestigious Dr. Peter and Susan Williamson Bugatti Collection, which sold in 2008 for more than $15.5m, the Richard J. Solove Rolls-Royce Collection, which sold for $14.3m in 2007, and the Otis Chandler Collection, which sold for $36m in 2006, the highest recorded single-day automotive collection sale in history.

Gooding & Company's team of talented specialists have a particular expertise in rare, unusual, and high-value automobiles and regularly advise many of the world's top collectors on developing and maintaining their collections.

The auction house started broadcasting its auctions via live webcast on Goodingco.com last year, a popular feature for international bidders and consignors who are unable to physically attend the events. In 2008, Gooding & Company reached new heights with combined automotive auction sales totaling more than $85.2m from 185 lots.

During the 2008 Pebble Beach Concours d'Elegance auction, Gooding & Company captured $64.2m in sales from a total of 140 lots, which included 20 cars that sold for more than $1m each and five cars that sold for more than $2m each.

The remarkable offerings included some of the world's most spectacular automobiles, top private and estate collections, and rare vintage racing cars, such the 1937 Bugatti Type 57SC Atalante coupe that sold for a stunning $7.92m—a record for the highest price ever paid for an automobile at a North American auction.

At this record-breaking event, Gooding & Company auctioned chassis 001 of the 2009 Bugatti Veyron 16.4 Grand Sport benefiting the Pebble Beach Company Foundation, which delivered an impressive $3.19m. Bugatti collectors continued to swoon over Dr. Peter and Susan Williamson's collection of twelve significant Bugattis—the world's finest collection of Bugattis ever to come to auction. A portion of the $15.5m proceeds were donated to the Dartmouth-Hitchcock Medical Center and the Dartmouth Medical School.

In January 2008, the inaugural Gooding & Company Scottsdale Auction was a stunning success, with a grand total of more than $21m from 64 cars, of which seven cars sold for more than $1m individually. World-record sales were set for an Alfa Romeo 6C 1750 GS Spyder ($1.54m) and the Rolls-Royce Phantom II Streamline Saloon ($852,500). Gooding & Company's star car, the 1959 Ferrari 250 GT LWB California Spyder, sold for $3.3m, the highest price paid above all other auction house results during the Scottsdale auction week.

For more information, visit www.goodingco.com.

Gooding

H&H

of collector cars—one of the first collector car auctions in the United States.

In 1964, the Leake family hired Park-Bernet (later to become Sotheby's) to conduct a one-day auction on the Leake site in Muskogee, Oklahoma. Considered a smashing success by everyone, this one event set the stage for a museum on this site and the annual collector car auction based in Tulsa.

Forty-five years later, the auction company has sold more than 31,000 cars and currently operates auctions in Tulsa, Oklahoma City, Dallas, Houston, and San Antonio, which was added to the line-up in 2009.

In 2008, Leake's total sales for Dallas, Tulsa, and Oklahoma City hit $23 million. (The Houston auction was cancelled due to Hurricane Ike.)

Leake is on track for a successful 2009, despite the readjustment of the market. Cars prices have dipped slightly, but are still a safe investment as the market rebounds. Sales for the Tulsa show exceeded $12m, surpassing the $10m goal. During this auction, a 1936 Lincoln once owned by Howard Hughes sold for $1m.

Leake also added the San Antonio show, which resulted in $1.8m during its first one-day auction. And the Houston auction was expanded from a one-day auction to a two-day auction to accommodate nearly 500 cars.

Leake was aggressive in 2009 with online marketing and advertising, as well as Internet bidding. The new generation of car buyers is Internet savvy, so Leake has made it a priority to find new ways to connect with the up and coming collectors and buyers and stay ahead of this emerging trend.

For more information, visit www.leakecarauction.com.

H&H Classic Auctions Ltd.

H&H is dynamically dedicated to the historic collector motor car market and is the largest specialist auction house of historic motor cars in Europe.

Simon Hope and Mark Hamilton felt strongly that the established auction houses were not serving the historic motorcar customer adequately and launched H&H Classic Auctions Limited in 1993. As directors and long-term historic motorcar enthusiasts, they felt the high commissions and other charges levied did not equate to the standard of service delivered. Using a combination of experience of the people, the motorcars, and the market, and upon their in-depth knowledge of the auction industry, both were convinced they could provide a better all-round service with competitive charges.

The H&H ethos still runs true today. The company has offered some of the world's best motorcars—both race and roadgoing—achieving world-record prices in the process, and still offers to both buyers and sellers a standard of service that is unrivalled.

As hands-on enthusiasts, the H&H team vigorously supports the historic motorcar movement in all its forms, and the display unit can be seen at all major events around England.

For more information, visit www.classic-auctions.com.

Leake Auction Company

Before car collecting was a business, before collector cars became a hobby, back when "old" cars were considered junk, that is when the passion for the "old junkers" took hold of Jim Leake, Sr. Finding these old cars and stockpiling them brought about one important stage in the evolution

Leake

Mecum

Mecum High Performance Auctions

During 2008 and early 2009, the collector car market stabilized and vehicle prices returned to 2004–05 levels. Mecum believes this a trend that will continue, and although economic conditions are tough right now, the company will prosper.

Throughout the last several years, Mecum has had strong growth and ended 2008 with $55m in sales.

In the first half of 2009, all Mecum auctions were successful, with the best spring sale (the Original Spring Classic, May 13–17), and at $34m, the largest auction in the history of the company. The Spring Classic has been one of the top five auctions in the country for dollar volume and one of the top three for total number of cars consigned and auctioned. Although Mecum's June 2009 Corvette auction was off a little, they still had some strong individual sales. Overall, Mecum remains optimistic about collector/investment grade cars for 2009 and 2010.

For 22 years, Mecum Auction has specialized in the sale of classic and collector cars and now offers more than 5,000 vehicles per year. As high-performance and collector car auction specialists, they deliver quality cars, customer service, and high-energy auctions to the collector car crowd.

It all began in 1988, with the first auction at the Rockford Airport in Rockford, Illinois, with approximately 250 cars. By the early 1990s, Mecum developed its own clientele by offering Corvettes, Camaros, and Chevelles when the rest of the market was selling Packards and Model As. The company slogan, "Nobody Sells More Muscle Than Mecum, Nobody,"

defines its leadership in the muscle car segment.

At one point, Mecum held 28 auctions a year, but it made the decision to grow vertically, with fewer auctions, right at the time the muscle car market took off. Now, Mecum hosts ten auctions each year. In spring 2008, the company sold its 50,000th car.

While the muscle car market has really become part of Mecum's DNA, they are continually expanding to bring all makes and models to auction. With the launch of the new Mecum Monterey Auction in August 2009, the expert team can use its knowledge and skills at selling exotic sports cars, classics, and other high-end collector vehicles to help customers find the perfect car.

The Mecum team is committed to serving consignors and bidders by delivering the best results for the lowest commissions—Mecum currently charges just a 6% buyer/seller fee, which is several percentage points less than other industry auction companies. And Mecum has made the commitment to make sure sellers leave the auction with a check.

For more information, visit www.mecum.com.

RM Auctions

Celebrating its 30th anniversary in 2009, preeminent international auction house, RM Auctions, is the leader in the investment-grade collector car market. Headquartered in Ontario, Canada, with offices across the U.S. and in London, England, RM has experienced impressive growth, facilitated record-breaking auctions—including the sale of five of the

RM

top ten most valuable motorcars sold at auction—and created a global network of clients and partners over the past three decades.

In addition to the auction division, the RM group boasts its own dedicated restoration shop—RM Auto Restoration—which is widely regarded as one of North America's leading automobile restoration facilities, earning accolades at the world's top concours events.

Each year, RM hosts an enviable roster of collector car events in a variety of prestigious settings. From Phoenix, Arizona, and Monterey, California, to Hershey, Pennsylvania, and Amelia Island, Florida, the events span the North American continent. In 2007, through an alliance with Sotheby's, RM entered the European market, establishing annual auction events in Maranello, Italy, and London, England.

Despite the economic climate of 2008–09, RM events worldwide achieved strong results and sales percentages, indicating a stable market for quality collector cars. While some segments of the market experienced minor price adjustments, it was an expected result of the overall economy.

The passion for the collector car hobby remains at an all-time high, with RM's catalog events continuing to attract strong international interest and record bidder registrations as discerning collectors from around the world seek out alternative investments. Worthy of mention are new and expanding markets in Russia and Asia, with an increasing level of interest in both regions.

Beyond the highly successful North American auctions, RM continued its record-breaking streak in Europe in 2008 and 2009, building upon the success of the inaugural Maranello and London events and firmly placing its stamp on the European collector car market. The 2009 Ferrari Leggenda e Passione event saw RM, in association with Sotheby's, break its own world record for the most expensive motorcar ever to be sold at auction with the sale of a legendary 1957 Ferrari 250 Testa Rossa for an impressive $12.4m. This represents $1.5m over the previous world record set at the same sale in 2008.

"RM's vertically integrated range of services, from restoration to private treaty sales, auctions, and financial services, coupled with our expert team of car specialists, established annual calendar of events, and international footprint, provides us with an unsurpassed perspective on the global collector car market," says Ian Kelleher, President and Chief Operating Officer of RM Auctions.

RM's future plans include continued growth through the presentation of private and single-vendor collection sales to solidify its reputation as specialists in this area of the market. Two such events took place the second half of 2009—the distinguished Nick Alexander Woody Collection in August, and the single-owner Icons of Speed & Style, which was held inSeptember.

Additionally, RM expanded its reach in the collector car hobby with the launch of an exclusive online auction on August 9, 2009. Designed to provide a convenient and credible means of conducting business over the Internet (each lot will be accompanied by extensive photography, comprehensive condition reports, and guaranteed good titles) this new collector car auction experience offers valued clients a cyberspace alternative to RM's traditional auction venues and complements the company's existing calendar of annual events.

For more information, visit www.rmauctions.com.

Russo and Steele

"For enthusiasts, by enthusiasts," Russo and Steele specializes strictly in European sports cars, American muscle cars, hot rods, and custom automobiles.

Created to provide a highly targeted alternative in the world of collector car auctions, Russo and Steele was launched in Scottsdale, Arizona, in 2001. The unique format established a one-of-a-kind, highly personal and visceral experience in an intimate environment, known as Russo and Steele's "Auction in the Round." This style encourages an interactive auction block that generates excitement with a sense of urgency and the personal emotion that live auction events are all about.

The buyers are right on the floor with the car—no separation. With a ground-level auction block and elevated platform seating 360 degrees around the stage, a virtual "boxing ring" or "coliseum" effect funnels buyers directly to the epicenter of the action.

Now celebrating its tenth anniversary, Russo and Steele has solidly maintained the coveted position of being one of the top three auction companies in the United States. The combination of steady growth and reputation has earned a loyal following of some of the world's most discriminating and savvy enthusiasts.

Russo and Steele is a lifestyle, and in an effort to improve the integrity of the hobby, the company made a fundamental transition to an "All Reserve All The Time" format. Every automobile sold at a Russo and Steele auction has a reasonable market-value reserve, creating the only true and honest representation of the current marketplace.

The ultimate venues of Scottsdale in January and Monterey in August represent the pinnacle of auction environments, and are the preeminent destinations for car enthusiasts worldwide. The culmination of Russo and Steele's loyal clientele, premier venues, and All Reserve format is directly responsible for the company's enduring success.

For more information, visit www.russoandsteele.com.

Shannons Auctions

Shannons is Australia's leading classic vehicle auction house, and is a division of Shannons Insurance, the country's largest insurer of collectible vehicles.

Since 1981, Shannons has sold over 4,000 classic vehicles through successful auctions around Australia. The company typically holds a total of eight classic auctions in Melbourne and Sydney each year, plus two national auctions associated with major motor shows.

In 2008, Shannons put around 500 classic vehicles to auction in these events, generating in excess of $6.6m in total sales, with over 70% of all vehicles sold.

As well as being a major player in the Australian collectible vehicle market, Shannons's expertise in historical and special-issue number plates is highly sought after, with the company chosen by the major government licensing authorities in Victoria, New South Wales, and Tasmania to host special auctions for heritage and numerical number plate sales. The most recent of these in 2006 and in June 2009 generated sales of $3.18m and $1.86m, respectively.

Shannons has also staged very successful automobilia sales on behalf of leading collectors in recent years.

Shannons has continued its focus on motoring enthusiasts throughout the current global financial crisis, enjoying considerable success in marketing rare and unique vehicles with realistic reserve prices to a still-buoyant collector market.

For more information, visit www.shannons.com.au.

Russo and Steele

Shannons

Silver Auctions

Silver Auctions began in 1979 in Spokane, Washington, when the owner, Mitch Silver, was still holding a full-time position as a college administrator at Eastern Washington University. Silver now produces 15 auctions per year, including estate sales. Their annual Hot August Nights event in Reno, Nevada, is widely recognized as one of the nation's premier collector car events.

Silver Auctions offers real buyers and sellers real cars and real deals. Presenting a comfortable and personalized environment is an alternative many auction attendees prefer. Silver's expertise and reputation is focused on just that. Whether this is your first-time collector vehicle purchase or you are an experienced buyer, Silver delivers mainstream, desirable, and rare examples with an average selling price of $20k, and most sales fall in the $8k–$100k range.

"We are not the million-dollar store,

but we are on top of the 4-speed, big-block, chrome, fins, and custom car store," says Mitch Silver.

There are many transactions that roll in under the $100k end of the auction market, and Silver is an excellent example of this success. You can expect to see a range of vehicles at each sale, including muscle cars, outstanding originals, vintage cars of the 1940s, '50s, and '60s, and of course, street rods and customs.

Silver typically realizes $22m in annual sales, and 2008 proved to be a great year for the company, as sales totaled over $25m, with a sell-through rate of around 50% overall.

For 2009, Silver has observed that vehicle prices have pretty much stayed the same, with a slight drop of around 5% on most cars. They are just selling slightly fewer cars overall. The difference has really come from buyers exercising caution with their cash. Many buyers who would regularly purchase two or three cars are purchasing just one instead.

Having been involved in the collector car auction business for 30 years, Silver has seen the market and economy go up and down many times. To date, it has always come back strong and aggressive out of the past downturns.

Mitch Silver and his customers are still buying good cars to add to their collections. Those people who are not buying now are missing some exceptional opportunities.

For more information, visit www.silverauctions.com.

Worldwide Auctioneers

Formed by two passionate automobile enthusiasts, Worldwide Auctioneers reflects the background of its principals, both of whom grew up in the auction business.

Rod Egan and John Kruse have each held management/partnership positions at leading auction companies throughout North America, refining their trade working with some of the best collector car enthusiasts and owners in the industry.

The company takes great pride in having an astute owner

Silver

Worldwide

as Chief Auctioneer, enabling an intimate knowledge of each car far in advance of the auction and a uniquely comfortable and essential level of communication with both buyer and seller from the auction block itself. With an emphasis on integrity, quality, and expertise, the team at Worldwide Auctioneers is committed to making the customer experience a positive and productive one, a mission that has helped it grow into one of the leading auction houses in the world of vintage motorcars.

With three strategically located auctions in 2008, Worldwide Auctioneers produced some spectacular results throughout the year. The Houston Classic Auction in May saw 87% of the 115 lots successfully sell, with a venerable 1914 Rolls-Royce Skiff Torpedo attracting the highest sale at $1.1m. August witnessed the launch of the inaugural Auburn Auction, held on the grounds of the company's new U.S. headquarters in Indiana. An extraordinary 1959 Ferrari Superamerica Series III SWB made history when it sold for an impressive $2.53m.

In November, at the Hilton Head Sports & Classic Car Auction, over 100 automobiles representing all makes and eras went under the hammer, with the top sale going to the headline car, a rare 1942 Alfa Romeo 6C 2500 Sport Cabriolet.

The common factor in Worldwide's success at all venues has been attention to detail, both when it comes to quality of the motorcars offered and total commitment its customers' satisfaction.

Worldwide Auctioneers's 2009 calendar again encompassed the Houston Classic Auction in May and the Auburn Auction in September, complementing the famous Auburn-Cord-Duesenberg Festival, traditionally held over that same Labor Day weekend. The early part of the year also saw the sale of two exciting private collections, each offered entirely without reserve. These "one-off" collection auctions nicely augment Worldwide's schedule of existing auctions, as well as confidential estate planning and private treaty sales, making the company a complete service and solution provider for the collector.

In the words of Rod Egan, Managing Partner and Chief Auctioneer, "At Worldwide, we are first and foremost car people. Worldwide Auctioneers continues to grow in both stature and reputation, and we look forward to continued relationships in the hobby. There is no place we'd rather be."

For more information, visit www.wwgauctions.com. ♦

By The Numbers

Lists tell a story all their own. Without flowery prose or exaggerating adjectives, lists just roll out numbers, one after the next.

And in this case, it is our list of Million-Dollar Sales that heads the category. After all, what better place to begin examining the market than with the "best of the best." That's followed by a host of other lists as we examine the results in the Sports Car Market Platinum database from a variety of perspectives.

This section is a kind of "Do-it-Yourself" analysis of the market. Look at all the numbers, think about what types of cars are selling for what kinds of dollars, and put together your own picture of what's happening in the collector car market today.—*Keith Martin*

In This Section

2008–09

Million-Dollar Sales in 2008-09 25

Top 1,000 Sales in 2008-09 by Price 30

Top 1,000 Sales in 2008-09 by Marque 53

Top 5 Sales per Marque in 2008-09 76

Top 100 Muscle Car Sales...................................88

Top 100 Corvette Sales..91

History

All-Time Top 10 Sales...94

Sales Results by Vehicle Era 96

Welcome to the Million-Dollar Club

Despite an economic downturn, great cars still brought great prices at sales around the world.*

1957 Ferrari 250 Testa Rossa—$12,402,500

Rank	Model	Sold Price	Lot #	Auction Location	Date
1	1957 Ferrari 250 Testa Rossa	$12,402,500	237	RM, Maranello, ITA	5/17/09
2	1961 Ferrari 250 GT SWB California Spyder	$10,894,400	328	RM, Maranello, ITA	5/18/08
3	1937 Bugatti Type 57SC Atalante Coupe	$7,920,000	27	Gooding, Pebble Beach, CA	8/17/08
4	1964 Ferrari 250 LM Sports Racer	$6,979,225	339A	RM, Maranello, ITA	5/18/08
5	1960 Jaguar XKE E2A Prototype Sports Racer	$4,957,000	364	Bonhams & Butterfields, Carmel Valley, CA	8/15/08
6	1960 Ferrari 250 GT LWB California Spyder	$4,950,000	78	Gooding, Scottsdale, AZ	1/17/09
7	1939 Talbot-Lago T150C SS Teardrop Coupe	$4,847,000	330	Bonhams & Butterfields, Carmel Valley, CA	8/15/08
8	1961 Ferrari 250 GT SWB Berlinetta	$4,510,000	447	RM, Monterey, CA	8/16/08
9	1937 Bugatti Type 57S Atalante Coupe	$4,408,575	142	Bonhams, Paris, FRA	2/7/09
10	1955 Jaguar XKD-type Sports Racer	$4,378,343	523	Bonhams, Sussex, UK	7/11/08
11	1958 Ferrari 250 GT LWB California Spyder	$3,659,838	337	RM, Maranello, ITA	5/18/08
12	1959 Ferrari 250 GT LWB California Spider	$3,630,000	133	Gooding, Pebble Beach, CA	8/17/08
13	1955 Ferrari 121 LM Sports Racer	$3,544,796	205	Bonhams, Gstaad, CHE	12/20/08
14	1937 Talbot-Lago T150C SS Teardrop Coupe	$3,520,000	23	Gooding, Scottsdale, AZ	1/17/09
15	1928 Mercedes-Benz 26/120/180 S-Type Roadster	$3,360,375	155	Bonhams, Paris, FRA	2/9/08
16	1959 Ferrari 250 GT LWB California Spyder	$3,300,000	44	Gooding, Scottsdale, AZ	1/19/08

Sales from the SCM Platinum Database, recorded between 1/1/2008 and 6/15/2009

1937 Bugatti Type 57SC Atalante Coupe—$7,920,000

Rank	Model	Sold Price	Lot #	Auction Location	Date
17	1932 Bugatti Type 55 Super Sport Roadster	$3,251,125	147	Bonhams, Monte Carlo, MCO	5/10/08
18	1971 Ferrari 512M Group 5 Prototype Racer	$3,234,275	317	RM, Maranello, ITA	5/18/08
19	2009 Bugatti Veyron 16.4 Grand Sport	$3,190,000	134	Gooding, Pebble Beach, CA	8/17/08
20	1956 Ferrari 250 GT Tour de France Coupe	$3,176,250	232	RM, Maranello, ITA	5/17/09
21	1913 Bugatti Type 18 Sports 2-Seater "Black Bess"	$3,131,475	114	Bonhams, Paris, FRA	2/7/09
22	1932 Daimler 40/50 Double Six Sport Saloon	$2,970,000	39	Gooding, Scottsdale, AZ	1/17/09
23	1959 Ferrari 250 GT LWB California Spyder	$2,911,563	234	RM, Maranello, ITA	5/17/09
24	1931 Duesenberg Model J Convertible Coupe by Murphy	$2,640,000	241	RM, Amelia Island, FL	3/8/08
25	1938 Alfa Romeo 6C 2300 B Mille Miglia	$2,585,000	116	Gooding, Pebble Beach, CA	8/17/08
26	1959 Ferrari 410 Superamerica Series III SWB Coupe	$2,530,000	50	Worldwide, Auburn, IN	8/30/08
27	1944 Vickers-Supermarine Spitfire Mk IX Fighter Plane	$2,522,275	390	Bonhams, Hendon, UK	4/20/09
28	1933 Rolls-Royce Phantom II Special Town Car	$2,310,000	453	RM, Monterey, CA	8/16/08
29	1931 Bentley 8-Liter Open Tourer by Harrison	$2,200,000	263	RM, Amelia Island, FL	3/8/08
30	1950 Ferrari 166 MM Berlinetta Le Mans	$2,200,000	42	Gooding, Pebble Beach, CA	8/17/08
31	2006 Maserati MC12 Corsa	$2,194,318	252	Coys, Monte Carlo, MCO	5/10/08

BY THE NUMBERS

Rank	Model	Sold Price	Lot #	Auction Location	Date
32	1961 Aston Martin DB4GT Coupe	$2,115,820	345	Bonhams, Newport Pagnell, UK	5/17/08
33	1945 Supermarine Spitfire Mk XIV Fighter Plane	$2,088,240	10	Bonhams & Goodman, Annesbrook, NZL	9/14/08
34	1967 Ferrari 275 GTB/4 Coupe	$2,042,700	327	RM, Maranello, ITA	5/18/08
35	1936 Mercedes-Benz 540K Special Cabriolet	$2,035,000	144	RM, Phoenix, AZ	1/18/08
36	1934 Packard Twelve Coupe	$2,035,000	163	RM, Phoenix, AZ	1/18/08
37	1923 Miller 122 Supercharged	$2,035,000	240	RM, Tustin, CA	6/14/08
38	1967 Ferrari 275 GTB/4 Berlinetta	$1,925,000	434	RM, Monterey, CA	8/16/08
39	1929 Bugatti Type 43 Grand Sport	$1,924,875	120	Bonhams, Paris, FRA	2/9/08
40	1969 Matra MS650 Prototype Racer	$1,922,933	39	Artcurial, Paris, FRA	2/8/09
41	1963 Chevrolet Corvette "Rondine" Concept Car	$1,760,000	1304	Barrett-Jackson, Scottsdale, AZ	1/20/08
42	1929 Duesenberg Model J Dual Cowl Phaeton	$1,760,000	136	RM, Phoenix, AZ	1/18/08
43	1934 Ford Model 40 Special Speedster	$1,760,000	252	RM, Amelia Island, FL	3/8/08
44	1930 Duesenberg Model J Dual Cowl Phaeton	$1,760,000	441	RM, Monterey, CA	8/16/08
45	1931 Bentley 4½ Liter Blower	$1,760,000	114	Gooding, Pebble Beach, CA	8/17/08
46	1932 Bugatti Type 55 Roadster	$1,760,000	30	Gooding, Pebble Beach, CA	8/17/08
47	1963 Shelby Cobra 289 Competition	$1,732,500	152	RM, Phoenix, AZ	1/18/08
48	1962 Ferrari 250 GTL Lusso Competition	$1,702,250	315	RM, Maranello, ITA	5/18/08
49	1933 Duesenberg Model SJ Phaeton	$1,688,500	242	RM, Hershey, PA	10/10/08
50	1961 Ferrari 400 Superamerica Coupe Aerodinamica	$1,650,000	452	RM, Monterey, CA	8/16/08
51	1911 Rambler 7-Passenger Touring	$1,620,000	2764	Kruse, Scottsdale, AZ	1/25/09
52	1932 Alfa Romeo 6C 1750 Gran Sport Spyder	$1,540,000	70	Gooding, Scottsdale, AZ	1/19/08
53	1913 Isotta Fraschini 100-120 hp Tipo KM 4 4-Seat Torpedo Tourer	$1,492,000	316	Bonhams & Butterfields, Carmel Valley, CA	8/15/08
54	1971 Ferrari 365 GTS/4 Daytona Spyder	$1,489,469	311	RM, Maranello, ITA	5/18/08
55	1973 Ferrari 365 GTB/4 Daytona Spyder	$1,485,000	435	RM, Monterey, CA	8/16/08
56	1962 Chevrolet Corvette 327/360 Gulf Oil Race Car	$1,485,000	121	Gooding, Pebble Beach, CA	8/17/08
57	1966 Ford GT40 Mk1	$1,465,000	443	RM, Monterey, CA	8/16/08
58	1927 Bugatti Type 35B Grand Prix	$1,457,500	25	Gooding, Pebble Beach, CA	8/17/08
59	1967 Ferrari 275 GTB/4	$1,430,000	56	Gooding, Pebble Beach, CA	8/17/08
60	1929 Duesenberg Model J Convertible Coupe	$1,413,500	457	RM, Monterey, CA	8/16/08
61	1936 Lagonda LG45R Rapide Sports-Racing 2-Seater	$1,382,000	310	Bonhams & Butterfields, Carmel Valley, CA	8/15/08

BY THE NUMBERS

1959 Ferrari 410 Superamerica Series III SWB Coupe—$2,530,000

1929 Bugatti Type 43 Grand Sport—$1,924,875

Rank	Model	Sold Price	Lot #	Auction Location	Date
62	1929 Duesenberg Model J Dual Cowl Phaeton	$1,375,000	9	Gooding, Scottsdale, AZ	1/17/09
63	1966 Ferrari 275 GTB/6C Coupe	$1,375,000	160	RM, Phoenix, AZ	1/18/08
64	1967 Ferrari 275 GTB/4 Berlinetta	$1,375,000	466	RM, Monterey, CA	8/16/08
65	1965 Ferrari 275 GTB Alloy Long-Nose	$1,375,000	119	Gooding, Pebble Beach, CA	8/17/08
66	1914 Stutz Series E Bearcat	$1,375,000	45	Gooding, Pebble Beach, CA	8/17/08
67	1937 Bentley 4¼-Liter Fixed Head Sport Coupe	$1,320,000	62	Gooding, Scottsdale, AZ	1/17/09
68	1941 Chrysler Thunderbolt LeBaron	$1,320,000	140	RM, Phoenix, AZ	1/18/08
69	1963 Ferrari 400 Superamerica Coupe	$1,320,000	14	Gooding, Scottsdale, AZ	1/19/08
70	1931 Alfa Romeo 6C 1750 Gran Sport Spyder	$1,320,000	44	Gooding, Pebble Beach, CA	8/17/08
71	2004 Ferrari Enzo Coupe	$1,319,244	318	RM, Maranello, ITA	5/18/08
72	1990 Ferrari F40 LM Competition Coupe	$1,302,075	234	Bonhams, Monte Carlo, MCO	5/18/09
73	1971 Ferrari 365 GTS/4 Daytona Spyder	$1,290,000	40	Gooding, Scottsdale, AZ	1/19/08
74	1936 Mercedes-Benz 500K Cabriolet A	$1,286,875	162	Bonhams, Paris, FRA	2/9/08
75	2003 Ferrari Enzo Coupe	$1,265,000	61	Gooding, Scottsdale, AZ	1/17/09
76	1930 Alfa Romeo 6C 1750 Spyder	$1,265,000	137	Gooding, Pebble Beach, CA	8/17/08
77	1969 Ferrari 365 GTS Convertible	$1,265,000	8	Gooding, Pebble Beach, CA	8/17/08
78	1969 Ferrari 365 GTS Spyder	$1,239,225	108	Bonhams, Monte Carlo, MCO	5/10/08
79	1966 Shelby Cobra 427 S/C Roadster	$1,234,900	F248.1	Mecum, Indianapolis, IN	5/17/09

1963 Chevrolet Corvette Z06 Yenko "Gulf One" Race Car—$1,113,000

1914 Stutz Series E Bearcat—$1,375,000

2003 Ferrari Enzo Coupe—$1,191,575

Rank	Model	Sold Price	Lot #	Auction Location	Date
80	1929 Ford 4-AT-E Tri-Motor Airplane	$1,210,000	1307	Barrett-Jackson, Scottsdale, AZ	1/18/09
81	1932 Packard Model 904 Custom Eight Convertible Victoria	$1,210,000	50	Gooding, Scottsdale, AZ	1/19/08
82	1929 Duesenberg Model J Convertible Berline by LeBaron	$1,210,000	257	RM, Amelia Island, FL	3/8/08
83	1925 Rolls-Royce Phantom I Barker Boattail	$1,210,000	131	Gooding, Pebble Beach, CA	8/17/08
84	2003 Ferrari Enzo Coupe	$1,191,575	341	RM, Maranello, ITA	5/18/08
85	1904 Thomas Model 27 Racer	$1,188,000	775	Kruse, Phoenix, AZ	1/27/08
86	1963 Ferrari 250 GTL Lusso Coupe	$1,174,553	319	RM, Maranello, ITA	5/18/08
87	1967 Ferrari 275 GTB/4 Coupe	$1,155,000	62	Gooding, Scottsdale, AZ	1/19/08
88	1972 Ferrari 365 GTB/4 Daytona Spyder	$1,127,500	467	RM, Monterey, CA	8/16/08
89	1963 Chevrolet Corvette Z06 Yenko "Gulf One" Race Car	$1,113,000	S110	Mecum, Kissimmee, FL	1/24/09
90	1930 Alfa Romeo 6C 1750 Gran Sport Spyder	$1,107,000	352	Bonhams & Butterfields, Carmel Valley, CA	8/15/08
91	1936 Duesenberg Model J Clear Vision Sedan	$1,100,000	42	Gooding, Scottsdale, AZ	1/19/08
92	2009 Chevrolet Corvette ZR-1 Coupe	$1,100,000	1316	Barrett-Jackson, Scottsdale, AZ	1/20/08
93	1928 Duesenberg Model J Dual Cowl Phaeton	$1,100,000	1311	Barrett-Jackson, Scottsdale, AZ	1/20/08
94	1966 Ferrari 275 GTB/2 Alloy Coupe	$1,096,563	233	RM, Maranello, ITA	5/17/09
95	1954 Porsche 550 Spyder	$1,090,841	234	Coys, Monte Carlo, MCO	5/10/08
96	1933 Isotta Fraschini Tipo 8A Dual Cowl Phaeton	$1,089,000	43	Gooding, Scottsdale, AZ	1/17/09
97	1936 Lincoln Model K "Howard Hughes" Boattail Speedster	$1,080,000	496	Leake, Tusla, OK	6/14/09
98	1935 Alfa Romeo 6C 2300 Pescara Spyder	$1,079,681	55	H&H, Cheltenham, UK	2/27/08
99	2006 Pagani Zonda F Clubsport Coupe	$1,079,471	437	Coys, London, UK	3/12/09
100	1929 Cord L-29 Hayes Coupe	$1,078,000	141	Gooding, Pebble Beach, CA	8/17/08
101	1930 Duesenberg Model J Convertible Coupe	$1,072,500	247	RM, Amelia Island, FL	3/14/09
102	1914 Rolls-Royce 40/50hp Silver Ghost Skiff Torpedo	$1,072,500	81	Worldwide, Houston, TX	5/3/08
103	1966 Shelby Cobra 427 Competition Roadster	$1,060,000	F246	Mecum, Indianapolis, IN	5/17/09
104	2008 Maserati MC12 Corsa	$1,058,750	203	RM, Maranello, ITA	5/17/09
105	1936 Mercedes-Benz 500K Cabriolet B	$1,045,000	112	Gooding, Pebble Beach, CA	8/17/08
106	1907 Thomas Flyer Model 36 60hp	$1,028,500	127	Gooding, Pebble Beach, CA	8/17/08
107	1971 Ferrari 365 GTS/4 Daytona Spyder	$1,023,000	162	Gooding, Pebble Beach, CA	8/17/08
108	1948 Tucker 48 Sedan	$1,017,500	449	RM, Monterey, CA	8/16/08
109	1965 Ferrari 275 GTB/6C Berlinetta	$1,012,000	430	RM, Monterey, CA	8/16/08

The 1,000 Most Expensive Cars of 2008–09

Of the more than 20,000 collector cars sold at auction in 2008–09, this group represents the top 5%, arranged by price.*

Rank	Model	Sold Price	Lot #	Auction Location	Date
1	1957 Ferrari 250 Testa Rossa	$12,402,500	237	RM, Maranello, ITA	5/17/09
2	1961 Ferrari 250 GT SWB California Spyder	$10,894,400	328	RM, Maranello, ITA	5/18/08
3	1937 Bugatti Type 57SC Atalante Coupe	$7,920,000	27	Gooding, Pebble Beach, CA	8/17/08
4	1964 Ferrari 250 LM Sports Racer	$6,979,225	339A	RM, Maranello, ITA	5/18/08
5	1960 Jaguar XKE E2A Prototype Sports Racer	$4,957,000	364	Bonhams & Butterfields, Carmel Valley, CA	8/15/08
6	1960 Ferrari 250 GT LWB California Spyder	$4,950,000	78	Gooding, Scottsdale, AZ	1/17/09
7	1939 Talbot-Lago T150C SS Teardrop Coupe	$4,847,000	330	Bonhams & Butterfields, Carmel Valley, CA	8/15/08
8	1961 Ferrari 250 GT SWB Berlinetta	$4,510,000	447	RM, Monterey, CA	8/16/08
9	1937 Bugatti Type 57S Atalante Coupe	$4,408,575	142	Bonhams, Paris, FRA	2/7/09
10	1955 Jaguar XKD-type Sports Racer	$4,378,343	523	Bonhams, Sussex, UK	7/11/08
11	1958 Ferrari 250 GT LWB California Spyder	$3,659,838	337	RM, Maranello, ITA	5/18/08
12	1959 Ferrari 250 GT LWB California Spider	$3,630,000	133	Gooding, Pebble Beach, CA	8/17/08
13	1955 Ferrari 121 LM Sports Racer	$3,544,796	205	Bonhams, Gstaad, CHE	12/20/08
14	1937 Talbot-Lago T150C SS Teardrop Coupe	$3,520,000	23	Gooding, Scottsdale, AZ	1/17/09
15	1928 Mercedes-Benz 26/120/180 S-type Roadster	$3,360,375	155	Bonhams, Paris, FRA	2/9/08
16	1959 Ferrari 250 GT LWB California Spyder	$3,300,000	44	Gooding, Scottsdale, AZ	1/19/08
17	1932 Bugatti Type 55 Super Sport Roadster	$3,251,125	147	Bonhams, Monte Carlo, MCO	5/10/08
18	1971 Ferrari 512M Group 5 Prototype Racer	$3,234,275	317	RM, Maranello, ITA	5/18/08
19	2009 Bugatti Veyron 16.4 Grand Sport	$3,190,000	134	Gooding, Pebble Beach, CA	8/17/08
20	1956 Ferrari 250 GT Tour de France Coupe	$3,176,250	232	RM, Maranello, ITA	5/17/09
21	1913 Bugatti Type 18 Sports 2-Seater "Black Bess"	$3,131,475	114	Bonhams, Paris, FRA	2/7/09
22	1932 Daimler 40/50 Double Six Sport Saloon	$2,970,000	39	Gooding, Scottsdale, AZ	1/17/09
23	1959 Ferrari 250 GT LWB California Spyder	$2,911,563	234	RM, Maranello, ITA	5/17/09
24	1931 Duesenberg Model J Convertible Coupe by Murphy	$2,640,000	241	RM, Amelia Island, FL	3/8/08
25	1938 Alfa Romeo 6C 2300 B Mille Miglia	$2,585,000	116	Gooding, Pebble Beach, CA	8/17/08
26	1959 Ferrari 410 Superamerica Series III SWB Coupe	$2,530,000	50	Worldwide, Auburn, IN	8/30/08
27	1944 Vickers-Supermarine Spitfire Mk IX Fighter Plane	$2,522,275	390	Bonhams, Hendon, UK	4/20/09
28	1933 Rolls-Royce Phantom II Special Town Car	$2,310,000	453	RM, Monterey, CA	8/16/08
29	1931 Bentley 8-Liter Open Tourer by Harrison	$2,200,000	263	RM, Amelia Island, FL	3/8/08
30	1950 Ferrari 166 MM Berlinetta Le Mans	$2,200,000	42	Gooding, Pebble Beach, CA	8/17/08
31	2006 Maserati MC12 Corsa	$2,194,318	252	Coys, Monte Carlo, MCO	5/10/08
32	1961 Aston Martin DB4GT Coupe	$2,115,820	345	Bonhams, Newport Pagnell, UK	5/17/08
33	1945 Supermarine Spitfire Mk XIV Fighter Plane	$2,088,240	10	Bonhams & Goodman, Annesbrook, NZL	9/14/08

Sales from the SCM Platinum Database, recorded between 1/1/2008 and 6/15/2009

#12—1959 Ferrari 250 GT LWB California Spyder

#21—1913 Bugatti Type 18 Sports 2-Seater "Black Bess"

#28—1933 Rolls-Royce Phantom II Special Town Car

Rank	Model	Sold Price	Lot #	Auction Location	Date
34	1967 Ferrari 275 GTB/4 Coupe	$2,042,700	327	RM, Maranello, ITA	5/18/08
35	1936 Mercedes-Benz 540K Special Cabriolet	$2,035,000	144	RM, Phoenix, AZ	1/18/08
36	1923 Miller 122 Supercharged	$2,035,000	240	RM, Tustin, CA	6/14/08
37	1934 Packard Twelve Coupe	$2,035,000	163	RM, Phoenix, AZ	1/18/08
38	1967 Ferrari 275 GTB/4 Berlinetta	$1,925,000	434	RM, Monterey, CA	8/16/08
39	1929 Bugatti Type 43 Grand Sport	$1,924,875	120	Bonhams, Paris, FRA	2/9/08
40	1969 Matra MS650 Prototype Racer	$1,922,933	39	Artcurial, Paris, FRA	2/8/09
41	1963 Chevrolet Corvette "Rondine" Concept Car	$1,760,000	1304	Barrett-Jackson, Scottsdale, AZ	1/20/08
42	1931 Bentley 4½-Liter Blower	$1,760,000	114	Gooding, Pebble Beach, CA	8/17/08
43	1932 Bugatti Type 55 Roadster	$1,760,000	30	Gooding, Pebble Beach, CA	8/17/08
44	1929 Duesenberg Model J Dual Cowl Phaeton	$1,760,000	136	RM, Phoenix, AZ	1/18/08
45	1930 Duesenberg Model J Dual Cowl Phaeton	$1,760,000	441	RM, Monterey, CA	8/16/08
46	1934 Ford Model 40 Special Speedster	$1,760,000	252	RM, Amelia Island, FL	3/8/08
47	1963 Shelby Cobra 289 Competition Roadster	$1,732,500	152	RM, Phoenix, AZ	1/18/08
48	1962 Ferrari 250 GTL Lusso Competition	$1,702,250	315	RM, Maranello, ITA	5/18/08
49	1933 Duesenberg Model SJ Phaeton	$1,688,500	242	RM, Hershey, PA	10/10/08
50	1961 Ferrari 400 Superamerica Coupe Aerodinamica	$1,650,000	452	RM, Monterey, CA	8/16/08
51	1911 Rambler 7-Passenger Touring	$1,620,000	2764	Kruse, Scottsdale, AZ	1/25/09
52	1932 Alfa Romeo 6C 1750 Gran Sport Spyder	$1,540,000	70	Gooding, Scottsdale, AZ	1/19/08
53	1913 Isotta Fraschini 100-120 hp Tipo KM 4 4-Seat Torpedo Tourer	$1,492,000	316	Bonhams & Butterfields, Carmel Valley, CA	8/15/08
54	1971 Ferrari 365 GTS/4 Daytona Spyder	$1,489,469	311	RM, Maranello, ITA	5/18/08
55	1962 Chevrolet Corvette 327/360 Gulf Oil Race Car	$1,485,000	121	Gooding, Pebble Beach, CA	8/17/08
56	1973 Ferrari 365 GTB/4 Daytona Spyder	$1,485,000	435	RM, Monterey, CA	8/16/08
57	1966 Ford GT40 Mk1	$1,465,000	443	RM, Monterey, CA	8/16/08
58	1927 Bugatti Type 35B Grand Prix	$1,457,500	25	Gooding, Pebble Beach, CA	8/17/08
59	1967 Ferrari 275 GTB/4	$1,430,000	56	Gooding, Pebble Beach, CA	8/17/08
60	1929 Duesenberg Model J Convertible Coupe	$1,413,500	457	RM, Monterey, CA	8/16/08
61	1936 Lagonda LG45R Rapide Sports Racing 2-Seater	$1,382,000	310	Bonhams & Butterfields, Carmel Valley, CA	8/15/08
62	1929 Duesenberg Model J Dual Cowl Phaeton	$1,375,000	9	Gooding, Scottsdale, AZ	1/17/09
63	1966 Ferrari 275 GTB/6C Coupe	$1,375,000	160	RM, Phoenix, AZ	1/18/08
64	1967 Ferrari 275 GTB/4 Berlinetta	$1,375,000	466	RM, Monterey, CA	8/16/08
65	1965 Ferrari 275 GTB Alloy Long-Nose	$1,375,000	119	Gooding, Pebble Beach, CA	8/17/08
66	1914 Stutz Series E Bearcat	$1,375,000	45	Gooding, Pebble Beach, CA	8/17/08
67	1931 Alfa Romeo 6C 1750 Gran Sport Spyder	$1,320,000	44	Gooding, Pebble Beach, CA	8/17/08
68	1937 Bentley 4¼-Liter Fixed Head Sport Coupe	$1,320,000	62	Gooding, Scottsdale, AZ	1/17/09
69	1941 Chrysler Thunderbolt LeBaron	$1,320,000	140	RM, Phoenix, AZ	1/18/08
70	1963 Ferrari 400 Superamerica Coupe	$1,320,000	14	Gooding, Scottsdale, AZ	1/19/08
71	2004 Ferrari Enzo Coupe	$1,319,244	318	RM, Maranello, ITA	5/18/08
72	1990 Ferrari F40 LM Competition Coupe	$1,302,075	234	Bonhams, Monte Carlo, MCO	5/18/09
73	1971 Ferrari 365 GTS/4 Daytona Spyder	$1,290,000	40	Gooding, Scottsdale, AZ	1/19/08
74	1936 Mercedes-Benz 500K Cabriolet A	$1,286,875	162	Bonhams, Paris, FRA	2/9/08
75	1930 Alfa Romeo 6C 1750 Spyder	$1,265,000	137	Gooding, Pebble Beach, CA	8/17/08
76	2003 Ferrari Enzo Coupe	$1,265,000	61	Gooding, Scottsdale, AZ	1/17/09
77	1969 Ferrari 365 GTS Convertible	$1,265,000	8	Gooding, Pebble Beach, CA	8/17/08

BY THE NUMBERS

#40—1969 Matra MS650 Prototype Racer

#46—1934 Ford Model 40 Special Speedster

#53—1913 Isotta Fraschini 100-120 hp Tipo KM 4 4-Seat Torpedo Tourer

#79—1966 Shelby Cobra 427 S/C Roadster

#102—1914 Rolls-Royce 40/50hp Silver Ghost Skiff Torpedo

#120—1964 Porsche 904 GTS Coupe

Rank	Model	Sold Price	Lot #	Auction Location	Date
78	1969 Ferrari 365 GTS Spyder	$1,239,225	108	Bonhams, Monte Carlo, MCO	5/10/08
79	1966 Shelby Cobra 427 S/C Roadster	$1,234,900	F248.1	Mecum, Indianapolis, IN	5/17/09
80	1929 Duesenberg Model J Convertible Berline by LeBaron	$1,210,000	257	RM, Amelia Island, FL	3/8/08
81	1929 Ford 4-AT-E Tri-Motor Airplane	$1,210,000	1307	Barrett-Jackson, Scottsdale, AZ	1/18/09
82	1932 Packard Model 904 Custom Eight Convertible Victoria	$1,210,000	50	Gooding, Scottsdale, AZ	1/19/08
83	1925 Rolls-Royce Phantom I Barker Boattail	$1,210,000	131	Gooding, Pebble Beach, CA	8/17/08
84	2003 Ferrari Enzo Coupe	$1,191,575	341	RM, Maranello, ITA	5/18/08
85	1904 Thomas Model 27 Racer	$1,188,000	775	Kruse, Phoenix, AZ	1/27/08
86	1963 Ferrari 250 GTL Lusso Coupe	$1,174,553	319	RM, Maranello, ITA	5/18/08
87	1967 Ferrari 275 GTB/4 Coupe	$1,155,000	62	Gooding, Scottsdale, AZ	1/19/08
88	1972 Ferrari 365 GTB/4 Daytona Spyder	$1,127,500	467	RM, Monterey, CA	8/16/08
89	1963 Chevrolet Corvette Z06 Yenko "Gulf One" Race Car	$1,113,000	S110	Mecum, Kissimmee, FL	1/24/09
90	1930 Alfa Romeo 6C 1750 Gran Sport Spyder	$1,107,000	352	Bonhams & Butterfields, Carmel Valley, CA	8/15/08
91	2009 Chevrolet Corvette ZR-1 Coupe	$1,100,000	1316	Barrett-Jackson, Scottsdale, AZ	1/20/08
92	1936 Duesenberg Model J Clear Vision Sedan	$1,100,000	42	Gooding, Scottsdale, AZ	1/19/08
93	1928 Duesenberg Model J Dual Cowl Phaeton	$1,100,000	1311	Barrett-Jackson, Scottsdale, AZ	1/20/08
94	1966 Ferrari 275 GTB/2 Alloy Coupe	$1,096,563	233	RM, Maranello, ITA	5/17/09
95	1954 Porsche 550 Spyder	$1,090,841	234	Coys, Monte Carlo, MCO	5/10/08
96	1933 Isotta Fraschini Tipo 8A Dual Cowl Phaeton	$1,089,000	43	Gooding, Scottsdale, AZ	1/17/09
97	1936 Lincoln Model K "Howard Hughes" Boattail Speedster	$1,080,000	496	Leake, Tulsa, OK	6/14/09
98	1935 Alfa Romeo 6C 2300 Pescara Spyder	$1,079,681	55	H&H, Cheltenham, UK	2/27/08
99	2006 Pagani Zonda F Clubsport Coupe	$1,079,471	437	Coys, London, UK	3/12/09
100	1929 Cord L-29 Hayes Coupe	$1,078,000	141	Gooding, Pebble Beach, CA	8/17/08
101	1930 Duesenberg Model J Convertible Coupe	$1,072,500	247	RM, Amelia Island, FL	3/14/09
102	1914 Rolls-Royce 40/50hp Silver Ghost Skiff Torpedo	$1,072,500	81	Worldwide, Houston, TX	5/3/08
103	1966 Shelby Cobra 427 Competition Roadster	$1,060,000	F246	Mecum, Indianapolis, IN	5/17/09
104	2008 Maserati MC12 Corsa	$1,058,750	203	RM, Maranello, ITA	5/17/09
105	1936 Mercedes-Benz 500K Cabriolet B	$1,045,000	112	Gooding, Pebble Beach, CA	8/17/08
106	1907 Thomas Flyer Model 36 60hp	$1,028,500	127	Gooding, Pebble Beach, CA	8/17/08
107	1971 Ferrari 365 GTS/4 Daytona Spyder	$1,023,000	162	Gooding, Pebble Beach, CA	8/17/08
108	1948 Tucker 48 Sedan	$1,017,500	449	RM, Monterey, CA	8/16/08
109	1965 Ferrari 275 GTB/6C Berlinetta	$1,012,000	430	RM, Monterey, CA	8/16/08
110	1962 Lotus 25 Formula 1 Single-Seater	$988,524	58	Bonhams & Goodman, Sydney, AUS	11/16/08
111	1965 Ferrari 500 Superfast Coupe	$983,125	223	RM, Maranello, ITA	5/17/09
112	1967 Ferrari 275 GTB/4 Coupe	$981,551	207	Bonhams, Gstaad, CHE	12/20/08
113	1966 Shelby Cobra 427 Roadster	$962,500	248	RM, Monterey, CA	8/16/08
114	1938 Mercedes-Benz 540K Sport Cabriolet	$946,000	90	Gooding, Scottsdale, AZ	1/17/09
115	1967 Ferrari 275 GTB/4 Coupe	$918,500	167	RM, Phoenix, AZ	1/16/09
116	1925/31 Bugatti Type 35A/51 Grand Prix	$907,500	35	Gooding, Pebble Beach, CA	8/17/08
117	1966 Ferrari 275 GTB/6C Coupe	$907,500	218	RM, Maranello, ITA	5/17/09
118	1972 Lamborghini Miura P400 SV	$891,000	433	RM, Monterey, CA	8/16/08
119	1951 Ferrari 340 America Coupe	$889,813	322	RM, Maranello, ITA	5/18/08
120	1964 Porsche 904 GTS Coupe	$888,465	326	Bonhams, Sussex, UK	9/19/08
121	1910 Mercedes 45hp 4-Seat Tourabout	$887,000	873	Bonhams & Butterfields, Owls Head, ME	9/27/08

#124—1939 Bugatti Type 57C Atalante Coupe

#143—1933 Duesenberg Model J Franay Touring

#147—1935 Avions Voisin C25 Aerodyne

Rank	Model	Sold Price	Lot #	Auction Location	Date
122	1930 Alfa Romeo 6C 1750 Series IV Grand Sport Spyder	$880,000	77	Worldwide, Houston, TX	5/3/08
123	1929 Bentley 4½-Liter Tourer	$880,000	135	RM, Phoenix, AZ	1/18/08
124	1939 Bugatti Type 57C Atalante Coupe	$880,000	32	Gooding, Pebble Beach, CA	8/17/08
125	1954 Dodge Firearrow III Sports Coupe Concept Car	$880,000	170	RM, Phoenix, AZ	1/16/09
126	1936 Hispano-Suiza J12 Convertible Victoria	$880,000	47	Gooding, Scottsdale, AZ	1/17/09
127	1967 Shelby GT500 Convertible	$874,500	F248	Mecum, Indianapolis, IN	5/17/09
128	1929 Duesenberg Model J Convertible Coupe	$858,000	152	RM, Phoenix, AZ	1/16/09
129	1955 Mercedes-Benz 300SL Coupe	$852,500	445	RM, Monterey, CA	8/16/08
130	1933 Rolls-Royce Phantom II Streamline Saloon	$852,500	72	Gooding, Scottsdale, AZ	1/19/08
131	1961 Ferrari 250 GT PF SII Cabriolet	$851,125	338	RM, Maranello, ITA	5/18/08
132	1929 Duesenberg Model J Clear Vision Sedan	$836,000	34	Gooding, Scottsdale, AZ	1/17/09
133	1930 Invicta 4½-Liter S-type Tourer "Scimitar"	$834,302	539	Bonhams, Sussex, UK	7/11/08
134	1913 Rolls-Royce 40/50hp Silver Ghost Roi-des-Belges Tourer	$832,000	836	Bonhams & Butterfields, Owls Head, ME	9/27/08
135	1967 Shelby Cobra 427 Roadster	$829,250	S654	Russo and Steele, Monterey, CA	8/16/08
136	1952 Alfa Romeo 6C 2500 Sport Cabriolet Ville d'Este	$825,000	38	Worldwide, Houston, TX	5/3/08
137	1937 Delage D8-120 Aerosport Coupe	$825,000	132	RM, Phoenix, AZ	1/16/09
138	1950 Ferrari 166/195 Inter Coupe	$800,058	333	RM, Maranello, ITA	5/18/08
139	1969 Chevrolet Camaro RS ZL1 Coupe	$800,000	S99	Mecum, Indianapolis, IN	5/18/08
140	1912 Rolls-Royce 40/50hp Silver Ghost Tourer	$797,500	27	Gooding, Scottsdale, AZ	1/17/09
141	1966 Porsche 906 Endurance Racing Coupe	$782,325	256	Bonhams, Monte Carlo, MCO	5/18/09
142	1966 Shelby Cobra 427 Roadster	$781,000	SP79	RM, Ft. Lauderdale, FL	2/17/08
143	1933 Duesenberg Model J Franay Touring Sedan	$777,600	581	Cox, Branson, MO	4/18/09
144	1964 Ferrari 250 GT/L Lusso Berlinetta	$770,000	440	RM, Monterey, CA	8/16/08
145	1955 Mercedes-Benz 300SL Coupe	$770,000	469	RM, Monterey, CA	8/16/08
146	1997 Ferrari F310B Formula One	$766,013	316	RM, Maranello, ITA	5/18/08
147	1935 Avions Voisin C25 Aerodyne	$757,178	8	Artcurial, Paris, FRA	2/9/08
148	1990 Ferrari F40 Coupe	$753,500	446	RM, Monterey, CA	8/16/08
149	1941 Chrysler Newport LeBaron	$748,000	141	RM, Phoenix, AZ	1/18/08
150	1929 Duesenberg J Convertible Coupe by Murphy	$748,000	234	RM, Rochester, MI	8/2/08
151	1967 Chevrolet Corvette L88 Competition Convertible	$744,000	355	Bonhams & Butterfields, Carmel Valley, CA	8/15/08
152	1969 Shelby GT500 Convertible	$742,500	1287	Barrett-Jackson, Scottsdale, AZ	1/20/08
153	1929 Duesenberg Model J Derham Convertible Coupe	$742,500	40	Worldwide, Auburn, IN	8/30/08
154	1953 Ferrari 212 Inter Coupe	$742,500	456	RM, Monterey, CA	8/16/08
155	1957 Mercedes-Benz 300SL Roadster	$742,500	172	RM, Phoenix, AZ	1/18/08
156	1955 Mercedes-Benz 300SL Coupe	$737,383	229	Coys, Monte Carlo, MCO	5/10/08
157	1937 Bugatti Type 57C Coupe	$731,500	17	Gooding, Scottsdale, AZ	1/19/08
158	1934 Bugatti Type 57 Cabriolet	$726,000	36	Gooding, Pebble Beach, CA	8/17/08
159	1956 Ferrari Europa GT	$715,000	48	Gooding, Pebble Beach, CA	8/17/08
160	1934 ERA A-type Prototype Single Seater	$713,979	560	Bonhams, Sussex, UK	7/11/08
161	1963 Ferrari 250 GTL Lusso	$704,000	37	Gooding, Scottsdale, AZ	1/17/09
162	1957 Mercedes-Benz 300SL Roadster	$704,000	164	Gooding, Pebble Beach, CA	8/17/08
163	1954 Packard Panther-Daytona Roadster Concept Car	$700,000	277	RM, Amelia Island, FL	3/14/09
164	1930 Cadillac 452A V16 Roadster	$693,000	128	Gooding, Pebble Beach, CA	8/17/08
165	1932 Auburn V12 Boattail Speedster	$687,500	126	Gooding, Pebble Beach, CA	8/17/08

BY THE NUMBERS

Rank	Model	Sold Price	Lot #	Auction Location	Date
166	1941 Chrysler Newport Dual Cowl Phaeton	$687,500	270	RM, Amelia Island, FL	3/14/09
167	1967 Shelby Cobra 427 Roadster	$687,500	1281.1	Barrett-Jackson, Scottsdale, AZ	1/20/08
168	1937 BMW 328 Roadster	$685,100	134	Bonhams, Monte Carlo, MCO	5/10/08
169	1966 Shelby Cobra 427 Roadster	$675,000	264	RM, Amelia Island, FL	3/14/09
170	1968 Ferrari 330 GTS Convertible	$671,000	130	Gooding, Pebble Beach, CA	8/17/08
171	1931 Avions Voisin C14 Chartre	$667,000	323	Bonhams & Butterfields, Carmel Valley, CA	8/15/08
172	1954 Chrisman Bonneville Coupe	$660,000	235	RM, Tustin, CA	6/14/08
173	1932 Chrysler CL Imperial Convertible Roadster by LeBaron	$660,000	240	RM, Rochester, MI	8/2/08
174	1955 Ford Thunderbird Convertible "Production #1"	$660,000	1295	Barrett-Jackson, Scottsdale, AZ	1/18/09
175	1963 Ford Thunderbird Italien Concept Car	$660,000	1306	Barrett-Jackson, Scottsdale, AZ	1/20/08
176	1955 Mercedes-Benz 300SL Coupe	$660,000	S705	Russo and Steele, Scottsdale, AZ	1/18/09
177	1911 Oldsmobile Autocrat Racing Car "Yellow Peril"	$660,000	260	RM, Amelia Island, FL	3/14/09
178	1932 Packard Twin Six Coupe Roadster	$660,000	143	RM, Phoenix, AZ	1/18/08
179	1967 Shelby Cobra 427 Roadster	$660,000	1301	Barrett-Jackson, Scottsdale, AZ	1/20/08
180	1955 Mercedes-Benz 300SL Coupe	$647,800	323	Coys, Essen, DEU	3/29/08
181	1989 Ferrari F40 Valeo Coupe	$646,855	330	RM, Maranello, ITA	5/18/08
182	1966 Aston Martin DB6 Short Chassis Volante	$642,510	30	H&H, Harrogate, UK	4/16/08
183	1964 Cooper Monaco King Cobra Sports Racer	$636,000	F237	Mecum, Indianapolis, IN	5/17/09
184	1931 Cadillac 452A V16 Sport Phaeton	$632,500	13	Gooding, Scottsdale, AZ	1/17/09
185	1969 Chevrolet Camaro RCR Series 3 Coupe	$632,500	1303	Barrett-Jackson, Scottsdale, AZ	1/20/08
186	1910 Pierce-Arrow Model 48 SS	$632,500	145	Gooding, Pebble Beach, CA	8/17/08
187	Robosaurus Car Crushing Robot	$632,500	1307	Barrett-Jackson, Scottsdale, AZ	1/20/08
188	1963 Ferrari 250 GT/L Lusso	$627,000	106	Gooding, Pebble Beach, CA	8/17/08
189	1938 Cadillac V16 Convertible Coupe	$616,000	158	RM, Anaheim, CA	6/29/08
190	1984 Ferrari 288 GTO Coupe	$616,000	4	Gooding, Scottsdale, AZ	1/17/09
191	1952 Glöckler-Porsche Roadster	$616,000	159	RM, Phoenix, AZ	1/18/08
192	1930 Hispano-Suiza H6C Boattail Speedster	$616,000	129	Gooding, Pebble Beach, CA	8/17/08
193	1991 Ferrari F40 Coupe	$612,810	339	RM, Maranello, ITA	5/18/08
194	1906 American Tourist Roi-des-Belges Touring Car	$612,000	854	Bonhams & Butterfields, Owls Head, ME	9/27/08
195	1968 Aston Martin DB6 Mk I Volante	$606,620	304	Bonhams, Newport Pagnell, UK	5/17/08
196	1931 Chrysler CG Imperial Dual Cowl Phaeton	$605,000	28	Gooding, Scottsdale, AZ	1/17/09
197	1963 Ferrari 250 GT/L Lusso Coupe	$605,000	212	RM, Maranello, ITA	5/17/09
198	2008 Ford Mustang Shelby GT500 KR Coupe	$605,000	1300	Barrett-Jackson, Scottsdale, AZ	1/20/08
199	1955 Mercedes-Benz 300SL Coupe	$605,000	66	Gooding, Scottsdale, AZ	1/19/08
200	1954 Mercedes-Benz 300SL Coupe	$605,000	61	Gooding, Pebble Beach, CA	8/17/08
201	1965 Shelby Cobra 289 Roadster	$605,000	438	RM, Monterey, CA	8/16/08
202	1958 Ferrari 250 GT Ellena Coupe	$595,788	309	RM, Maranello, ITA	5/18/08
203	1966 Ferrari 275 GTS Convertible	$595,788	325	RM, Maranello, ITA	5/18/08
204	1961 Mercedes-Benz 300SL Roadster	$594,000	43	Gooding, Pebble Beach, CA	8/17/08
205	1932 Stutz DV-32 Super Bearcat	$594,000	151	RM, Phoenix, AZ	1/16/09
206	1955 Mercedes-Benz 300SL Coupe	$588,500	151	RM, Phoenix, AZ	1/18/08
207	1964 Shelby Cobra 289 Roadster	$583,000	6	Gooding, Scottsdale, AZ	1/19/08
208	1961 Mercedes-Benz 300SL Roadster	$577,500	1283.1	Barrett-Jackson, Scottsdale, AZ	1/20/08
209	1956 Mercedes-Benz 300SL Coupe	$577,500	150	Gooding, Pebble Beach, CA	8/17/08
210	1966 Bizzarrini Strada 5300 Coupe	$572,000	S648	Russo and Steele, Monterey, CA	8/16/08

#172—1954 Chrisman Bonneville Coupe

#176—1955 Mercedes-Benz 300SL Coupe

#195—1968 Aston Martin DB6 Mk I Volante

Rank	Model	Sold Price	Lot #	Auction Location	Date
211	1955 Lancia Aurelia B24S Spyder America	$572,000	118	Gooding, Pebble Beach, CA	8/17/08
212	1927 Bentley Speed Six 2-Seater and Dickey	$568,000	354	Bonhams & Butterfields, Carmel Valley, CA	8/15/08
213	1959 Mercedes-Benz 300SL Roadster	$567,716	445	Coys, London, UK	7/5/08
214	1935 Auburn 851SC Boattail Speedster	$566,500	262	RM, Amelia Island, FL	3/14/09
215	1965 Ferrari 275 GTS Spider	$562,380	221	Bonhams, Gstaad, CHE	12/20/08
216	1929 Bentley 6½-Liter Sedanca Coupe	$561,000	146	Gooding, Pebble Beach, CA	8/17/08
217	1956 Mercedes-Benz 300SL Coupe	$557,225	153	Bonhams, Monte Carlo, MCO	5/10/08
218	1951 Ferrari 195 Inter Coupe	$557,100	310	RM, Maranello, ITA	5/18/08
219	1962 Mercedes-Benz 300SL Roadster	$556,500	S158	Mecum, Kissimmee, FL	1/24/09
220	1956 Ferrari 250 GT Boano Coupe	$552,063	226	RM, Maranello, ITA	5/17/09
221	1970 Plymouth Superbird Custom Replica	$551,100	1289	Barrett-Jackson, Scottsdale, AZ	1/18/09
222	1954 Bentley R-type Continental Fastback	$550,000	479	RM, Monterey, CA	8/16/08
223	2006 Chevrolet Monte Carlo NASCAR Jeff Gordon	$550,000	1274	Barrett-Jackson, Scottsdale, AZ	1/18/09
224	1971 Chevrolet Corvette ZR2 Convertible	$550,000	S107	Mecum, St. Charles, IL	6/28/08
225	1964 Ferrari 250 GTL Lusso Coupe	$550,000	178	RM, Phoenix, AZ	1/16/09
226	1967 Ferrari 330 GTC Speciale	$550,000	49	Gooding, Scottsdale, AZ	1/19/08
227	1956 Mercedes-Benz 300SL Coupe	$550,000	96	Gooding, Scottsdale, AZ	1/17/09
228	1981 Porsche 935/78 Moby Dick Race Car	$550,000	451	RM, Monterey, CA	8/16/08
229	1963 Shelby Cobra 289 Roadster	$550,000	143	Gooding, Pebble Beach, CA	8/17/08
230	1912 Rolls-Royce 40/50hp Silver Ghost Roi-des-Belges Tourer	$546,975	219	Bonhams, Northamptonshire, UK	6/13/09
231	1963 Ferrari 250 GTL Lusso	$546,100	153	Coys, Padua, ITA	10/25/08
232	1960 Mercedes-Benz 300SL Roadster	$545,000	58	Worldwide, Auburn, IN	8/30/08
233	1956 Mercedes-Benz 300SL Coupe	$535,000	252	RM, Rochester, MI	8/2/08
234	1936 Auburn 852SC Boattail Speedster	$533,500	423	RM, Monterey, CA	8/16/08
235	1985 Ferrari 288 GTO Coupe	$529,375	204	RM, Maranello, ITA	5/17/09
236	1966 Gurney Eagle AAR Indy Car	$528,000	225	RM, Tustin, CA	6/14/08
237	1958 Mercedes-Benz 300SL Roadster	$528,000	432	RM, Monterey, CA	8/16/08
238	1970 Aston Martin DB6 Mk II Volante Convertible	$526,125	322	Bonhams, Sussex, UK	9/19/08
239	1970 Chevrolet Chevelle SS 454 LS6 Convertible	$525,000	S103	Mecum, Indianapolis, IN	5/18/08
240	1971 Ferrari 365 GTB/4 Daytona Comp Replica	$524,847	213	Coys, Monte Carlo, MCO	5/10/08
241	2007 Blastolene B-702 Custom Roadster	$522,500	1310	Barrett-Jackson, Scottsdale, AZ	1/20/08
242	1926/41 Bugatti Type 35/Miller V8	$522,500	29	Gooding, Pebble Beach, CA	8/17/08
243	1996 Buick Custom "Blackhawk"	$522,500	1303	Barrett-Jackson, Scottsdale, AZ	1/18/09
244	1931 Cadillac V16 Sport Phaeton	$522,500	251	RM, Amelia Island, FL	3/8/08
245	1962 Chaparral 1 Sports Racer	$522,500	460	RM, Monterey, CA	8/16/08
246	1911 Rolls-Royce 40/50hp Silver Ghost Roi-des-Belges	$522,500	43	Worldwide, Auburn, IN	8/30/08
247	1964 Ferrari 250 GT Lusso	$521,275	143	Bonhams, Paris, FRA	2/9/08
248	1967 Bizzarrini 5300 GT Strada Alloy	$517,000	124	Gooding, Pebble Beach, CA	8/17/08
249	1933 Rolls-Royce Phantom II Short Chassis Continental Sedanca Coupe	$512,122	327	Coys, Essen, DEU	3/29/08
250	1938 BMW 328 Roadster	$507,600	265	Bonhams, Monte Carlo, MCO	5/18/09
251	1931 Bentley 8-Liter Sedanca deVille	$506,900	651	Bonhams, London, UK	12/1/08
252	1912 Speedwell Model 12-H Speed Car	$506,000	10	Gooding, Pebble Beach, CA	8/17/08
253	1955 Lancia Aurelia B24 Spyder America	$505,600	334	Coys, Essen, DEU	3/29/08
254	1967 Chevrolet Camaro Yenko Coupe	$504,000	S105	Mecum, Indianapolis, IN	5/18/08

#218—1951 Ferrari 195 Inter Coupe

#224—1971 Chevrolet Corvette ZR2 Convertible

#248—1967 Bizzarrini 5300 GT Strada Alloy

#271—1905 Sunbeam 12/14hp 5-Seat Side-Entrance Tonneau

#284—1965 Alfa Romeo TZ Berlinetta

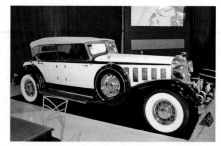

#290—1933 Chrysler CL Imperial Sport Phaeton by LeBaron

Rank	Model	Sold Price	Lot #	Auction Location	Date
255	1969 Chevrolet Camaro ZL1 Coupe	$504,000	S109	Mecum, Indianapolis, IN	5/18/08
256	2003 Ferrari 575 GTC Competizione	$500,175	239	Bonhams, Monte Carlo, MCO	5/18/09
257	1969 Chevrolet Camaro RS/SS Custom "Project American Heroes"	$500,000	369.1	Barrett-Jackson, Palm Beach, FL	4/11/09
258	1976 Lagonda V8 Series I Saloon	$498,820	320	Bonhams, Newport Pagnell, UK	5/17/08
259	1969 Dodge Charger 2-Door Hardtop "General Lee"	$495,000	1321	Barrett-Jackson, Scottsdale, AZ	1/20/08
260	1934 Bugatti Type 59 3.3-Liter Supercharged Grand Prix	$495,000	50	Worldwide, Houston, TX	5/3/08
261	1930 Isotta Fraschini 8A Transformable Torpedo	$495,000	176	RM, Phoenix, AZ	1/18/08
262	1958 Mercedes-Benz 300SL Roadster	$495,000	NR26	RM, Ft. Lauderdale, FL	2/17/08
263	1934 Packard Twelve Model 1107 5-Passenger Touring	$495,000	65	Worldwide, Auburn, IN	8/30/08
264	1964 Shelby Cobra 289 Roadster	$495,000	S708	Russo and Steele, Scottsdale, AZ	1/18/09
265	1960 Watson Indy Roadster	$495,000	234	RM, Tustin, CA	6/14/08
266	1961 Mercedes-Benz 300SL Roadster	$492,800	207	Coys, Monte Carlo, MCO	5/10/08
267	1960 Mercedes-Benz 300SL Roadster	$489,375	170	Bonhams, Paris, FRA	2/9/08
268	1970 Lamborghini Miura P400 S Series II Coupe	$484,273	577	Bonhams, Sussex, UK	7/11/08
269	1937 Cord 812 SC Convertible Coupe	$484,000	180	RM, Phoenix, AZ	1/16/08
270	1990 Ferrari 641/2 F1	$484,000	235	RM, Maranello, ITA	5/17/08
271	1905 Sunbeam 12/14hp 5-Seat Side-Entrance Tonneau	$482,130	535	Bonhams, Hendon, UK	4/21/08
272	1931 Delage D8 4-Seat Sports Tourer	$480,500	136	Bonhams, Monte Carlo, MCO	5/10/08
273	1972 Porsche 911 2.7 RS Prototype	$480,000	359	Bonhams & Butterfields, Carmel Valley, CA	8/15/08
274	1959 Mercedes-Benz 300SL Roadster	$478,500	1292	Barrett-Jackson, Scottsdale, AZ	1/20/08
275	1957 Mercedes-Benz 300SL Roadster	$477,945	175	Bonhams, Paris, FRA	2/7/09
276	1955 OSCA MT4 Roadster	$477,945	116	Bonhams, Paris, FRA	2/7/09
277	1935 Cadillac V16 Imperial Convertible Sedan	$473,000	148	RM, Phoenix, AZ	1/16/09
278	1959 Ferrari 250 GT LWB California Spyder Replica	$472,082	231	Coys, Birmingham, UK	1/10/09
279	1910 Peerless Victoria	$469,000	844	Bonhams & Butterfields, Owls Head, ME	9/27/08
280	1953 Ferrari 212 Inter Europa Vignale Coupe	$468,875	229	RM, Maranello, ITA	5/17/09
281	1930 Isotta Fraschini 8A Convertible Sedan by Castagna	$467,500	253	RM, Rochester, MI	8/2/08
282	1955 Mercedes-Benz 300SL Coupe	$467,500	164	RM, Phoenix, AZ	1/16/09
283	1965 Shelby Cobra 289 Mk II Roadster	$467,500	185	RM, Phoenix, AZ	1/16/09
284	1965 Alfa Romeo TZ Berlinetta	$465,735	325	Bonhams, Sussex, UK	9/19/08
285	1961 Aston Martin DB4 SIII Coupe	$464,963	21	Artcurial, Paris, FRA	2/9/08
286	1935 Bugatti Type 57 Stelvio Cabriolet	$464,963	12	Artcurial, Paris, FRA	2/9/08
287	1969 Lamborghini Miura P400 S Coupe	$464,963	39	Artcurial, Paris, FRA	2/9/08
288	1958 Mercedes-Benz 300SL Roadster	$464,963	28	Artcurial, Paris, FRA	2/9/08
289	1965 Shelby GT350 Fastback	$462,000	1293	Barrett-Jackson, Scottsdale, AZ	1/20/08
290	1933 Chrysler CL Imperial Sport Phaeton by LeBaron	$462,000	167	RM, Anaheim, CA	6/29/08
291	1960 Meskowski Bowes Seal Fast Special	$462,000	223	RM, Tustin, CA	6/14/08
292	1969 Aston Martin DB6 Volante	$455,700	325	Bonhams, Newport Pagnell, UK	5/17/08
293	1958 Aston Martin DB4 Series I Coupe	$454,925	138	Bonhams, Monte Carlo, MCO	5/10/08
294	1963 Pontiac Catalina "Swiss Cheese" 2-Door Hardtop	$451,500	S88	Mecum, St. Charles, IL	10/5/08
295	1941 Lincoln Continental Hardtop	$451,000	39	Gooding, Scottsdale, AZ	1/19/08
296	1935/41 Miller Ford Winfield V8	$451,000	251	RM, Tustin, CA	6/14/08
297	1925 Bugatti Type 30 Tourer	$449,500	125	Bonhams, Paris, FRA	2/9/08
298	1967 Chevrolet Camaro RS/SS Nickey Coupe	$446,250	S97	Mecum, St. Charles, IL	10/5/08

#309—1973 Citroën DS23 ie Cabriolet

#317—1929 Ruxton Prototype Muller Front
Drive Roadster

#334—1935 Delage D8-85 Clabot Roadster

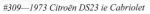

Rank	Model	Sold Price	Lot #	Auction Location	Date
299	1931 Maserati Tipo 8C-2800 2-Seat Competition Car	$445,605	308	Bonhams, Sussex, UK	9/19/08
300	1966 Ferrari 275 GTS Convertible	$445,500	279	RM, Amelia Island, FL	3/14/09
301	2008 Dodge Challenger SRT8 Coupe #001	$440,000	1331	Barrett-Jackson, Scottsdale, AZ	1/20/08
302	1935 Rolls-Royce Phantom II	$440,000	1312	Barrett-Jackson, Scottsdale, AZ	1/20/08
303	1966 Alfa Romeo Giulia TZ-1 Coupe	$440,000	33	Gooding, Scottsdale, AZ	1/17/09
304	1932 Bugatti Type 46 Sports Sedan	$440,000	31	Gooding, Pebble Beach, CA	8/17/08
305	1953 Cadillac Eldorado Convertible	$440,000	247	RM, Dallas, TX	4/19/08
306	1970 Plymouth Hemi 'Cuda 2-Door Hardtop	$440,000	S704	Russo and Steele, Scottsdale, AZ	1/18/09
307	1934 Rolls-Royce Phantom II Continental	$440,000	30	Gooding, Scottsdale, AZ	1/17/09
308	1969 Chevrolet Corvette L88 Convertible	$435,750	S91	Mecum, St. Charles, IL	6/28/08
309	1973 Citroën DS23 ie Cabriolet	$435,375	123	Bonhams, Paris, FRA	2/7/09
310	1928 Bugatti Type 37A Grand Prix	$434,500	59	Worldwide, Houston, TX	5/3/08
311	1934 Bentley 3½-Liter Sports Tourer	$429,000	110	Gooding, Pebble Beach, CA	8/17/08
312	1992 Ferrari F40 Coupe	$429,000	200	RM, Phoenix, AZ	1/16/09
313	1920 Rolls-Royce Silver Ghost Roadster	$429,000	107	Gooding, Pebble Beach, CA	8/17/08
314	1971 Ferrari 365 GTB/4 Daytona Coupe	$425,694	36	Artcurial, Paris, FRA	6/28/08
315	1973 Porsche 911 2.7 RS Coupe	$425,575	131	Bonhams, Paris, FRA	2/9/08
316	1971 Ferrari 365 GTB/4 Daytona	$425,563	336	RM, Maranello, ITA	5/18/08
317	1929 Ruxton Prototype Muller Front Drive Roadster	$423,500	1313	Barrett-Jackson, Scottsdale, AZ	1/20/08
318	1970 Lamborghini Miura S Coupe	$423,500	S655	Russo and Steele, Monterey, CA	8/16/08
319	1955 Lancia Aurelia B24 Spyder America	$420,750	55	H&H, Sparkford, UK	10/12/08
320	1934 Bugatti Type 57 Stelvio Convertible	$419,500	281	Bonhams & Butterfields, Greenwich, CT	6/7/09
321	1956 Ford F100 Custom Cab Pickup	$418,000	232	RM, Tustin, CA	6/14/08
322	1936 Bugatti Type 57 Galibier Coupe	$416,877	16	Artcurial, Paris, FRA	6/28/08
323	1962 Aston Martin DB4 Series IV Vantage	$413,820	37	H&H, Harrogate, UK	4/16/08
324	1969 Chevrolet Corvette L88 Coupe	$412,500	S714	Russo and Steele, Scottsdale, AZ	1/20/08
325	2009 Ford Mustang FR500 CJ Prototype #1	$412,500	1333.1	Barrett-Jackson, Scottsdale, AZ	1/18/09
326	1967 Lamborghini Miura P400 Coupe	$412,500	437	RM, Monterey, CA	8/16/08
327	1933 Packard Super Eight Convertible Victoria	$412,500	247	RM, Amelia Island, FL	3/8/08
328	1962 Pontiac Catalina Super Duty 2-Door Hardtop	$412,500	SN825	Russo and Steele, Scottsdale, AZ	1/18/09
329	2005 Saleen S7 Twin Turbo Coupe	$412,500	1305	Barrett-Jackson, Scottsdale, AZ	1/18/09
330	1930 Sampson Miller U16 Special	$412,500	247	RM, Tustin, CA	6/14/08
331	1960 Aston Martin DB4 Coupe	$409,577	316	Coys, Essen, DEU	3/29/08
332	1989 Ferrari F40 Coupe	$409,374	223	Coys, Birmingham, UK	1/10/09
333	1925 Bentley 3-Liter 100mph Supersports Brooklands 2-Seater	$409,220	624	Bonhams, London, UK	12/1/08
334	1935 Delage D8-85 Clabot Roadster	$407,000	30	Worldwide, Auburn, IN	8/30/08
335	1970 Ford Mustang Boss 302 TransAm Race Car	$407,000	87	Gooding, Scottsdale, AZ	1/17/09
336	1955 Lancia Aurelia B24S Spyder America	$406,995	176	Bonhams, Paris, FRA	2/7/09
337	1970 Dodge Hemi Coronet R/T Convertible	$404,250	S108	Mecum, Indianapolis, IN	5/18/08
338	1952 Fitch-Whitmore Le Mans Special Roadster	$403,000	269	Bonhams & Butterfields, Greenwich, CT	6/7/09
339	1937 Cord 812 Supercharged Phaeton	$401,500	S713	Russo and Steele, Scottsdale, AZ	1/18/09
340	1927 Bugatti Type 40 Roadster	$399,244	12	Artcurial, Paris, FRA	6/28/08
341	1950 Ferrari 195 Inter Ghia Coupe	$398,750	224	RM, Maranello, ITA	5/17/09
342	1970 Chevrolet Chevelle 454 LS6 Convertible	$397,500	S126	Mecum, Indianapolis, IN	5/17/09
343	1938 Indy Blue Crown Special Race Car	$397,500	F256	Mecum, Indianapolis, IN	5/17/09

BY THE NUMBERS

Top 1,000 Sales in 2008–09 by Price

Rank	Model	Sold Price	Lot #	Auction Location	Date
344	1966 Pontiac GTO Monkeemobile	$396,000	1297	Barrett-Jackson, Scottsdale, AZ	1/20/08
345	1936 Auburn 852 Boattail Speedster	$396,000	146	RM, Phoenix, AZ	1/18/08
346	1936 Bugatti Type 57 Pillarless Coupe	$396,000	18	Gooding, Scottsdale, AZ	1/17/09
347	1939 Bugatti Type 57C Galibier Sport	$396,000	34	Gooding, Pebble Beach, CA	8/17/08
348	1977 Lamborghini Countach LP400 Coupe	$396,000	161	Gooding, Pebble Beach, CA	8/17/08
349	1963 Meskowski Sheraton-Thompson Dirt Championship Car	$396,000	252	RM, Tustin, CA	6/14/08
350	1971 Plymouth 'Cuda 2-Door Hardtop	$396,000	F515	Russo and Steele, Scottsdale, AZ	1/20/08
351	1934 Bugatti Type 57 Sports Sedan	$395,643	165	Bonhams, Paris, FRA	2/7/09
352	1991 Ferrari F40 Coupe	$393,250	236	RM, Maranello, ITA	5/17/09
353	1964 Aston Martin DB5 Coupe	$391,020	326	Bonhams, Newport Pagnell, UK	5/17/08
354	1971 Dodge Hemi Challenger R/T 2-Door Hardtop	$390,500	F520	Russo and Steele, Scottsdale, AZ	1/18/09
355	1972 Ferrari 365 GTB/4 Daytona Coupe	$390,500	S646	Russo and Steele, Monterey, CA	8/16/08
356	1961 Rolls-Royce Silver Cloud II DHC	$387,129	171	Bonhams, Paris, FRA	2/7/09
357	2010 Chevrolet Camaro Coupe 1st Production	$385,000	1316	Barrett-Jackson, Scottsdale, AZ	1/18/09
358	1961 Ferrari 250 GT SII Cabriolet	$385,000	81	Gooding, Scottsdale, AZ	1/17/09
359	1966 Ferrari 275 GTS Convertible	$385,000	194	RM, Phoenix, AZ	1/16/09
360	1936 Packard Twelve Convertible Victoria	$385,000	256	RM, Rochester, MI	8/2/08
361	1917 Pierce-Arrow Model 48 Touring Car	$385,000	267	RM, Hershey, PA	10/10/08
362	1962 Ferrari 250 GTO Replica	$383,925	211	Coys, Monte Carlo, MCO	5/10/08
363	1987 Ferrari F1-87 Formula One	$383,006	343	RM, Maranello, ITA	5/18/08
364	1969 Lamborghini Miura P400 Coupe	$381,627	219	Coys, Monte Carlo, MCO	5/10/08
365	1963 Porsche 356 Carrera 2 Convertible	$381,000	249	Bonhams & Butterfields, Greenwich, CT	6/7/09
366	1955 Lancia Aurelia B24 Spyder America	$380,025	236	Coys, Monte Carlo, MCO	5/18/09
367	1957 Ferrari 250 GT Ellena Coupe	$378,125	209	RM, Maranello, ITA	5/17/09
368	1935 Packard 12 Convertible	$378,000	U50	Mecum, Indianapolis, IN	5/18/08
369	1971 Plymouth Hemi 'Cuda 2-Door Hardtop	$378,000	S175	Mecum, Indianapolis, IN	5/18/08
370	1970 Pontiac GTO Judge Ram Air IV Convertible	$378,000	S113	Mecum, Indianapolis, IN	5/18/08
371	1923 Rolls-Royce 40/50hp Silver Ghost "Salamanca"	$377,586	539	Bonhams, Hendon, UK	4/21/08
372	1964 Ford Galaxie 500 "Tobacco King" Rocket Car	$376,000	S139	Mecum, Indianapolis, IN	5/18/08
373	1965 Aston Martin DB5 4.2 Coupe	$375,990	340	Bonhams, Newport Pagnell, UK	5/9/09
374	1959 Ferrari 250 GT Series II Cabriolet	$375,000	125	RM, Phoenix, AZ	1/16/09
375	1933 Rolls-Royce Phantom II Continental Sedanca Coupe	$375,000	192	RM, Phoenix, AZ	1/16/09
376	1969 Ferrari 365 GTC/S Spyder Conversion (Graypaul)	$374,889	579	Bonhams, Sussex, UK	7/11/08
377	1972 Ferrari 365 GTB/4 Daytona Coupe	$374,000	171	RM, Phoenix, AZ	1/18/08
378	1935 Pierce-Arrow 12 Convertible Coupe	$374,000	158	RM, Phoenix, AZ	1/18/08
379	1978/79 Lotus 79 Formula 1 Single-Seater	$373,442	61	Bonhams & Goodman, Sydney, AUS	11/16/08
380	1966 Ferrari 275 GTS Convertible	$371,520	125	Bonhams, Paris, FRA	2/7/09
381	1966 Maserati Mistral 4000 Spyder	$369,675	126	Bonhams, Monte Carlo, MCO	5/10/08
382	1973 Ferrari 365 GTB/4 Daytona Spyder Conversion	$368,500	S656	Russo and Steele, Monterey, CA	8/16/08
383	1961 Mercedes-Benz 300SL Roadster	$368,500	20	Gooding, Scottsdale, AZ	1/17/09
384	1912 Peerless Model 36 7-Passenger Touring Car	$368,500	464	RM, Monterey, CA	8/16/08
385	1970 Abarth SE10	$366,520	209	Coys, Monte Carlo, MCO	5/10/08
386	1971 Ferrari 365 GTB/4 Daytona Coupe	$366,265	105	Bonhams, Monte Carlo, MCO	5/10/08
387	1929 Rolls-Royce Phantom I Convertible Sedan	$364,500	220	Bonhams & Butterfields, Greenwich, CT	6/8/08
388	1962 Aston Martin DB4 Convertible	$364,363	339	Bonhams, Newport Pagnell, UK	5/9/09

#355—1972 Ferrari 365 GTB/4 Daytona Coupe

#370—1970 Pontiac GTO Judge Ram Air IV Convertible

#381—1966 Maserati Mistral 4000 Spyder

Rank	Model	Sold Price	Lot #	Auction Location	Date
389	1990 Ferrari F40 GTM Berlinetta	$363,950	597	Bonhams, Sussex, UK	7/11/08
390	1973 Ferrari 365 GTB/4 Daytona	$363,400	322	Coys, Essen, DEU	3/29/08
391	1967 Shelby GT500 Fastback	$363,000	1318	Barrett-Jackson, Scottsdale, AZ	1/20/08
392	1937 Cord 812 Supercharged Phaeton	$363,000	48	Gooding, Scottsdale, AZ	1/19/08
393	1972 Ferrari 365 GTB/4 Daytona Coupe	$363,000	1	Gooding, Pebble Beach, CA	8/17/08
394	1976 Lamborghini Countach LP400 Periscopo	$363,000	S651	Russo and Steele, Monterey, CA	8/16/08
395	1931 Ruxton Model C Roadster	$363,000	239	RM, Rochester, MI	8/2/08
396	1984 Peugeot 205 Turbo 16 Group B Rally	$359,586	67	Artcurial, Paris, FRA	6/14/09
397	1921 Avions Voisin OC1 Presidential Coupe	$359,000	321	Bonhams & Butterfields, Carmel Valley, CA	8/15/08
398	1955 Aston Martin DB2/4 Mk II Drophead Coupe	$358,680	335	Bonhams, Newport Pagnell, UK	5/17/08
399	1965 Aston Martin DB5 Coupe	$358,680	310	Bonhams, Newport Pagnell, UK	5/17/08
400	1968 Aston Martin DB6 Volante	$357,876	227	Coys, Brands Hatch, UK	5/25/08
401	1971 Chevrolet Corvette ZR2 Coupe	$357,500	1290	Barrett-Jackson, Scottsdale, AZ	1/20/08
402	1969 Ford Mustang Boss 429 Fastback	$357,500	1269	Barrett-Jackson, Scottsdale, AZ	1/20/08
403	1913 Locomobile Model M-48 3-4 Passenger Baby Tonneau	$357,500	245	RM, Hershey, PA	10/10/08
404	1949 Ferrari 166 Inter Touring Coupe	$355,438	225	RM, Maranello, ITA	5/17/09
405	1965 Chevrolet Chevelle SS Z16 2-Door Hardtop Prototype	$355,100	S122	Mecum, Indianapolis, IN	5/17/09
406	1935 Bentley 3½-Liter Vanden Plas Tourer	$353,766	128	Coys, Nürburgring, DEU	8/9/08
407	1932 Ford Custom Roadster "Rollin Stone"	$352,000	1262	Barrett-Jackson, Scottsdale, AZ	1/20/08
408	1970 Lamborghini Miura P400 S Coupe	$352,000	272	RM, Monterey, CA	8/16/08
409	1934 Packard 1108 Twelve Sport Phaeton	$352,000	56A	Gooding, Scottsdale, AZ	1/17/09
410	1915 Stutz Model 4-F Bulldog Demi-Tonneau	$352,000	29	Gooding, Scottsdale, AZ	1/17/09
411	1904 Société Manufacturiere d'Armes 24/30hp Open Drive Landaulette	$351,450	530	Bonhams, Hendon, UK	4/21/08
412	1942 Alfa Romeo 6C 2500 Sport Cabriolet	$345,400	69	Worldwide, Hilton Head, SC	11/1/08
413	1905 Gardner-Serpollet 18hp Type L Steamer with Tulip Phaeton Coachwork	$345,100	320	Bonhams, Hendon, UK	4/20/09
414	1933 Alfa Romeo 6C 1750 6th Series Supercharged Gran Sport Cabriolet	$342,683	226	Bonhams, Gstaad, CHE	12/20/08
415	1940 Alfa Romeo 6C 2500 Sport Cabriolet by Graber	$341,000	482	RM, Monterey, CA	8/16/08
416	1969 Chevrolet Chevelle 2-Door Hardtop	$341,000	S711	Russo and Steele, Scottsdale, AZ	1/20/08
417	1971 Plymouth Hemi 'Cuda 2-Door Hardtop	$341,000	F518	Russo and Steele, Scottsdale, AZ	1/18/09
418	2008 Ferrari 612 Scaglietti	$340,450	306	RM, Maranello, ITA	5/18/08
419	1970 Ferrari 365 GTB/4 Daytona Coupe	$339,376	317	Coys, Ascot, UK	10/4/08
420	1967 Chevrolet Corvette 427/400 Convertible	$336,000	S73	Mecum, St. Charles, IL	6/28/08
421	1919/20 Rolls-Royce 40/50hp Silver Ghost Alpine Eagle	$335,819	224	Bonhams, Northamptonshire, UK	6/21/08
422	1941 Chrysler Town & Country 9-Passenger Estate Wagon	$335,500	148	RM, Anaheim, CA	6/29/08
423	1973 Porsche 911 Carrera RS Touring	$332,281	115	Coys, Nürburgring, DEU	8/9/08
424	1988 Porsche 959 Coupe	$331,784	349	Coys, Essen, DEU	3/29/08
425	1965 Ferrari 250 GTO Replica (330 GT)	$331,135	586	Bonhams, Sussex, UK	7/11/08
426	1964 Aston Martin DB5 Coupe	$330,876	338	Coys, London, UK	3/3/08
427	1956 Ferrari 250 GT Berlinetta Prototipo	$330,057	208	Bonhams, Gstaad, CHE	12/20/08
428	1939 Cadillac V16 Convertible Coupe	$330,000	161	RM, Phoenix, AZ	1/18/08
429	2007 Chevrolet Monte Carlo NASCAR "Tony Stewart"	$330,000	1012	Barrett-Jackson, Scottsdale, AZ	1/20/08
430	1947 Chrysler Town & Country Sedan "Big Red"	$330,000	191	RM, Phoenix, AZ	1/16/09
431	1969 Ford Mustang Boss 429 Fastback	$330,000	1329	Barrett-Jackson, Scottsdale, AZ	1/20/08

#394—1976 Lamborghini Countach LP400 Periscopo

#403—1913 Locomobile Model M-48-3 4-Passenger Baby Tonneau

#422—1941 Chrysler Town & Country 9-Passenger Estate Wagon

#433—1967 Lamborghini Miura P400 Coupe

#451—1958 Dual Ghia Convertible

#457—1970 Chevrolet Chevelle 454 LS6 2-Door Hardtop

Rank	Model	Sold Price	Lot #	Auction Location	Date
432	2006 Ford Mustang GT Coupe "Funkmaster Flex"	$330,000	774.4	Barrett-Jackson, Las Vegas, NV	10/18/08
433	1967 Lamborghini Miura P400 Coupe	$330,000	73	Gooding, Pebble Beach, CA	8/17/08
434	1933 Marmon Sixteen Convertible Sedan	$330,000	156	RM, Phoenix, AZ	1/16/09
435	1970 Maserati Ghibli Spyder	$330,000	S662	Russo and Steele, Monterey, CA	8/16/08
436	1942 Packard One-Eighty Convertible Victoria by Darrin	$330,000	237	RM, Rochester, MI	8/2/08
437	1936 Packard Super Eight Roadster	$330,000	57	Gooding, Pebble Beach, CA	8/17/08
438	1913 Peerless Model 48-Six Roadster	$330,000	465	RM, Monterey, CA	8/16/08
439	1929 Rolls-Royce Phantom I Ascot Sport Phaeton	$330,000	129	RM, Phoenix, AZ	1/16/09
440	1913 Stevens-Duryea Model C 5-Passenger Touring Car	$330,000	269	RM, Rochester, MI	8/2/08
441	1935 Avions Voisin C25 Clairière Berline	$330,000	35	Gooding, Scottsdale, AZ	1/17/09
442	1969 Chevrolet Chevelle COPO 2-Door Hardtop	$328,600	S124	Mecum, Indianapolis, IN	5/17/09
443	1955 Chevrolet Corvette Duntov EX-87 Test Mule	$328,600	F208	Mecum, Indianapolis, IN	5/17/09
444	1934 Bugatti Type 57 Double Cabriolet Stelvio	$326,000	213	Bonhams & Butterfields, Greenwich, CT	6/8/08
445	1930 Cadillac V16 Convertible Coupe by Fleetwood	$324,500	238	RM, Rochester, MI	8/2/08
446	1969 Ferrari 365 GTC	$324,500	448	RM, Monterey, CA	8/16/08
447	1917 Pierce-Arrow Four-Passenger Touring Car	$324,500	170	RM, Phoenix, AZ	1/18/08
448	1969 Chevrolet Corvette 427/430 L88 Convertible	$323,300	S142	Mecum, Kissimmee, FL	1/24/09
449	1934 Auburn Twelve Salon Phaeton Sedan	$319,000	154	RM, Phoenix, AZ	1/16/09
450	1969 Chevrolet Camaro ZL1 COPO Coupe	$319,000	1277.1	Barrett-Jackson, Scottsdale, AZ	1/18/09
451	1958 Dual-Ghia Convertible	$319,000	63	Worldwide, Hilton Head, SC	11/1/08
452	1957 Dual-Ghia Convertible	$319,000	257	RM, Dallas, TX	4/19/08
453	1971 Ferrari 365 GTB Daytona Coupe	$319,000	S705	Russo and Steele, Scottsdale, AZ	1/20/08
454	1908 Packard Model 30 Touring Car	$319,000	17	Gooding, Pebble Beach, CA	8/17/08
455	1927 Rolls-Royce Phantom I Playboy Roadster	$319,000	145	RM, Anaheim, CA	6/29/08
456	1926 Rolls-Royce Silver Ghost Piccadilly Roadster	$319,000	163	Gooding, Pebble Beach, CA	8/17/08
457	1970 Chevrolet Chevelle 454 LS6 2-Door Hardtop	$318,000	S127	Mecum, Indianapolis, IN	5/17/09
458	1970 Plymouth Hemi Superbird 2-Door Hardtop	$318,000	S180.1	Mecum, Indianapolis, IN	5/17/09
459	1938 Jaguar SS 100 Roadster	$317,250	235	Coys, Essen, DEU	4/4/09
460	1970 Maserati Ghibli Spyder	$315,700	114	Worldwide, Houston, TX	5/3/08
461	1964 Aston Martin DB5 Coupe	$315,560	324	Bonhams, Newport Pagnell, UK	5/17/08
462	1994 Bugatti EB110 GT Coupe	$315,115	135	Bonhams, Monte Carlo, MCO	5/10/08
463	1913 Pierce-Arrow 48-B 7-Passenger Touring	$315,000	847	Bonhams & Butterfields, Owls Head, ME	9/27/08
464	1923 Rolls-Royce 40/50hp Silver Ghost Pall Mall Dual Cowl Phaeton	$315,000	862	Bonhams & Butterfields, Owls Head, ME	9/27/08
465	1958 Ferrari 250 GT Coupe	$314,916	302	RM, Maranello, ITA	5/18/08
466	1961 Maserati 3500 GT Spyder	$314,906	213	Bonhams, Gstaad, CHE	12/20/08
467	1967 Aston Martin DB6 Vantage Volante	$314,863	67	Bonhams & Goodman, Sydney, AUS	11/16/08
468	1948 Cisitalia 202 Nuvolari MM Spyder	$313,925	123	Bonhams, Paris, FRA	2/9/08
469	1969 Ferrari 365 GTB/4 Daytona Spyder Conversion	$313,925	146	Bonhams, Paris, FRA	2/9/08
470	1937 Jaguar SS 100 2½-Liter Roadster	$313,925	124	Bonhams, Paris, FRA	2/9/08
471	1931 Auburn 8-98 Speedster	$313,500	129	RM, Phoenix, AZ	1/18/08
472	1941 Chrysler Town & Country Barrel Back Estate Wagon	$313,500	132	RM, Phoenix, AZ	1/18/08
473	1937 Cord 812 SC Phaeton	$313,500	150	RM, Phoenix, AZ	1/18/08
474	1994 Jaguar XJ 220 Coupe	$313,500	1291	Barrett-Jackson, Scottsdale, AZ	1/20/08
475	1949 MG TC Race Roadster	$313,500	819	Barrett-Jackson, Las Vegas, NV	10/18/08

#482—1964 Lamborghini 350 GT Coupe

#488—1959 Cadillac Eldorado Seville 3-Position Cabriolet

#494—1965 Shelby GT350 Fastback "Final Prototype"

Rank	Model	Sold Price	Lot #	Auction Location	Date
476	1962 Rolls-Royce Silver Cloud II DHC	$313,500	164	RM, Phoenix, AZ	1/18/08
477	1968 Lamborghini Miura P400 Coupe	$313,200	234	Coys, Monte Carlo, MCO	5/18/09
478	2005 Mercedes-Benz SLR McLaren Coupe	$309,258	554	Bonhams, Sussex, UK	7/11/08
479	1951 Allard J2 Roadster	$300,000	67	Gooding, Pebble Beach, CA	8/17/08
480	1969 Iso Grifo Coupe	$308,000	157	RM, Phoenix, AZ	1/18/08
481	1971 Lamborghini Miura P400 S Coupe	$308,000	133	RM, Phoenix, AZ	1/16/09
482	1964 Lamborghini 350 GT Coupe	$308,000	57	Gooding, Scottsdale, AZ	1/19/08
483	1912 Pierce-Arrow Model 66-QQ 5-Passenger Touring Car	$308,000	250	RM, Amelia Island, FL	3/14/09
484	1934 Riley MPH Roadster	$308,000	64	Gooding, Pebble Beach, CA	8/17/08
485	1962 Rolls-Royce Silver Cloud II	$302,621	23	Artcurial, Paris, FRA	2/9/08
486	1937 BMW 328 Cabriolet	$302,500	245	RM, Amelia Island, FL	3/14/09
487	1930 Cadillac V16 Sport Phaeton	$302,500	138	RM, Phoenix, AZ	1/18/08
488	1959 Cadillac Eldorado Seville 3-Position Cabriolet	$302,500	257	RM, Monterey, CA	8/16/08
489	1911 Locomobile Model M-48 7-Passenger Touring	$302,500	142	RM, Phoenix, AZ	1/18/08
490	1973 Porsche 911 2.7 RS Coupe	$302,500	S659	Russo and Steele, Monterey, CA	8/16/08
491	1936 Jaguar SS 100 Roadster	$300,960	66	H&H, Buxton, UK	11/26/08
492	1932 Talbot 105 Fox & Nicholl Team Car	$300,960	42	H&H, Buxton, UK	11/26/08
493	1963 Chevrolet Corvette 327/360 Z06 Coupe	$300,000	142	Gooding, Pebble Beach, CA	8/17/08
494	1965 Shelby GT350 Fastback "Final Prototype"	$299,450	F240	Mecum, Indianapolis, IN	5/17/09
495	1908 Stanley Model M 5-Passenger Touring	$298,500	864	Bonhams & Butterfields, Owls Head, ME	9/27/08
496	1928 Hispano-Suiza H6B Sedanca deVille	$297,975	118	Bonhams, Paris, FRA	2/9/08
497	1950 Talbot-Lago T26 Record Grand Sport Cabriolet	$297,975	109	Bonhams, Paris, FRA	2/9/08
498	1931 Cadillac V16 Roadster	$297,000	26	Gooding, Scottsdale, AZ	1/19/08
499	1969 Chevrolet Camaro Yenko COPO Coupe	$297,000	1278	Barrett-Jackson, Scottsdale, AZ	1/18/09
500	1959 Chrysler Imperial Crown Convertible	$297,000	350A	RM, Anaheim, CA	6/29/08
501	1929 Graham-Paige Dual Cowl Phaeton	$297,000	146	RM, Phoenix, AZ	1/16/09
502	1937 Alvis 4.3-Liter Short Chassis Vanden Plas Tourer	$295,020	89	H&H, Buxton, UK	4/16/09
503	1970 Chevrolet Chevelle SS 454 LS6 Convertible	$294,000	S111	Mecum, Indianapolis, IN	5/18/09
504	1936 Auburn 852 Supercharged Boattail Speedster	$291,500	81	Worldwide, Seabrook, TX	5/2/09
505	1937 Cord 812 SC Phaeton	$291,500	261	RM, Amelia Island, FL	3/8/08
506	1993 Jaguar XJ 220 Coupe	$291,500	1281	Barrett-Jackson, Scottsdale, AZ	1/20/08
507	1931 Packard Deluxe Eight Sport Phaeton	$291,500	459	RM, Monterey, CA	8/16/08
508	1938 Jaguar SS 100 3½-Liter Roadster	$289,275	337	Bonhams, Hendon, UK	4/20/08
509	1969 Ford Mustang Boss 429 Fastback	$288,750	S101	Mecum, Indianapolis, IN	5/18/08
510	1915 Van Blerck 17-Liter Roadster	$288,200	18	Worldwide, Houston, TX	5/3/08
511	1963 Aston Martin DB5 Vantage-spec Coupe	$287,382	550	Bonhams, Sussex, UK	7/11/08
512	1970 Ferrari 365 GTB/4 Daytona Coupe	$287,375	227	RM, Maranello, ITA	5/17/09
513	1969 Ford Mustang Boss 429 Fastback	$287,280	2481	Leake, Tulsa, OK	6/8/08
514	1970 Plymouth Hemi 'Cuda 2-Door Hardtop	$286,200	S170	Mecum, Indianapolis, IN	5/17/09
515	1970 Plymouth Hemi Superbird 2-Door Hardtop	$286,200	S90.1	Mecum, Indianapolis, IN	5/17/09
516	1989 Chevrolet Corvette DR-1 Convertible	$286,000	1218	Barrett-Jackson, Scottsdale, AZ	1/18/09
517	1973 Ferrari 365 GTB/4 Daytona Coupe	$286,000	17	Gooding, Scottsdale, AZ	1/17/09
518	1938 Packard Twelve Coupe Roadster	$286,000	259	RM, Amelia Island, FL	3/14/09
519	1964 Aston Martin DB5 4.2 Coupe	$284,635	327	Bonhams, Newport Pagnell, UK	5/9/09

Top 1,000 Sales in 2008–09 by Price

Rank	Model	Sold Price	Lot #	Auction Location	Date
520	1907 Packard 30hp Gentleman's Roadster	$284,200	852	Bonhams & Butterfields, Owls Head, ME	9/27/08
521	1966 Lamborghini 350 GT Coupe	$283,800	S710	Russo and Steele, Scottsdale, AZ	1/20/08
522	1961 Aston Martin DB4 Series IV Coupe	$283,220	329	Bonhams, Newport Pagnell, UK	5/17/08
523	1960 Aston Martin DB4 SIII Coupe	$282,025	136	Bonhams, Paris, FRA	2/9/08
524	c.1990/91 Lister-Jaguar "Knobbly" Competition Sports 2-Seater	$282,000	343	Bonhams & Butterfields, Carmel Valley, CA	8/15/08
525	1938 Packard Model 120 Darrin Convertible	$282,000	222	Bonhams & Butterfields, Greenwich, CT	6/7/09
526	1911 Stoddard Dayton Model 11K 50hp Roadster	$282,000	856	Bonhams & Butterfields, Owls Head, ME	9/27/08
527	1937 Bugatti Type 57 Sports Saloon	$281,624	34	H&H, Surrey, UK	6/8/08
528	1969 Chevrolet Camaro Yenko Coupe	$280,900	S128	Mecum, Indianapolis, IN	5/17/09
529	1963 Ferrari 330 America	$280,871	303	RM, Maranello, ITA	5/18/08
530	1936 Mercedes-Benz 230B Cabriolet	$280,717	133	Coys, Nürburgring, DEU	8/9/08
531	1956 Chevrolet Bel Air 2-Door Hardtop Custom	$280,500	1256	Barrett-Jackson, Scottsdale, AZ	1/20/08
532	1952 Delahaye 235 Drophead Coupe	$280,500	208	RM, Phoenix, AZ	1/16/09
533	1970 Plymouth 'Cuda 2-Door Hardtop	$280,500	S706	Russo and Steele, Scottsdale, AZ	1/20/08
534	1972 Ferrari 365 GTB/4 Daytona Coupe	$279,285	140	Bonhams, Paris, FRA	2/7/09
535	1939 Jaguar SS 100 Roadster	$279,285	154	Bonhams, Paris, FRA	2/7/09
536	1938 BMW 327 Roadster	$278,569	167	Coys, Nürburgring, DEU	8/9/08
537	1996 Cadillac Fleetwood Presidential Series Limo	$275,000	1328	Barrett-Jackson, Scottsdale, AZ	1/20/08
538	2004 Chevrolet Monte Carlo SS NASCAR #8	$275,000	S696	Russo and Steele, Scottsdale, AZ	1/18/09
539	1959 Chevrolet Corvette 283/290 FI Competition Convertible	$275,000	260	RM, Amelia Island, FL	3/8/08
540	1931 Chrysler CG Imperial Dual Cowl Phaeton	$275,000	1271	Barrett-Jackson, Scottsdale, AZ	1/18/09
541	2008 Dodge Viper SRT-10 50th Anniversary Hurst Coupe	$275,000	1328	Barrett-Jackson, Scottsdale, AZ	1/18/09
542	1963 Dual-Ghia L6.4 Coupe	$275,000	258	RM, Dallas, TX	4/19/08
543	1954 Hudson Italia Coupe	$275,000	290	RM, Amelia Island, FL	3/14/09
544	1933 Packard 1005 Twelve Touring	$275,000	49	Gooding, Scottsdale, AZ	1/17/09
545	1906 Reo Model A 16hp	$275,000	132	Gooding, Pebble Beach, CA	8/17/08
546	1980 Ferrari Pinin Prototipo	$272,360	220	RM, Maranello, ITA	5/18/08
547	1967 Lamborghini 400 GT 2+2 Coupe	$271,000	358	Bonhams & Butterfields, Carmel Valley, CA	8/15/08
548	1969 Chevrolet Camaro Coupe	$270,600	F516	Russo and Steele, Scottsdale, AZ	1/20/08
549	1955 Chevrolet Corvette Roadster	$270,000	753	Kruse, Phoenix, AZ	1/27/08
550	1936 Cord 810 Phaeton	$269,500	136	Gooding, Pebble Beach, CA	8/17/08
551	1947 Ford Model 71 Sportsman	$269,500	67A	Gooding, Scottsdale, AZ	1/19/08
552	1969 Ford Mustang Boss 429 Fastback	$269,500	1280	Barrett-Jackson, Scottsdale, AZ	1/20/08
553	1970 Ford Mustang Boss 429 Fastback	$269,500	1319	Barrett-Jackson, Scottsdale, AZ	1/20/08
554	1938 Packard Twelve Custom Limousine	$269,500	1553	Barrett-Jackson, Scottsdale, AZ	1/20/08
555	1970 Plymouth Hemi 'Cuda 2-Door Hardtop	$269,500	1254.1	Barrett-Jackson, Scottsdale, AZ	1/20/08
556	1912 Renault Type CB Coupe de Ville	$269,500	139	RM, Phoenix, AZ	1/18/08
557	1934 Rolls-Royce Phantom II Sedanca DeVille	$269,500	165	Gooding, Pebble Beach, CA	8/17/08
558	1951 Bugatti Type 101 Coach	$269,265	119	Bonhams, Paris, FRA	2/9/08
559	1959 Aston Martin DB Mk III Convertible	$267,375	125	Bonhams, Monte Carlo, MCO	5/10/08
560	1962 Bentley S3 Continental Flying Spur Sedan	$267,375	109	Bonhams, Monte Carlo, MCO	5/10/08
561	1963 Ferrari 250 GTE 2+2 Series III Coupe	$267,375	168	Bonhams, Monte Carlo, MCO	5/10/08
562	1905 Léon Bollée 45/50hp 8.3-Liter Double Chain-Drive Roi-des-Belges Tourer	$265,505	519	Bonhams, Sussex, UK	7/11/08

#524—.1990/91 Lister-Jaguar "Knobbly" Competition Sports 2-Seater

#543—1954 Hudson Italia Coupe

#556—1912 Renault Type CB Coupe de Ville

Rank	Model	Sold Price	Lot #	Auction Location	Date
563	1933 Ford-Auburn Roadster Special	$265,500	350	Bonhams & Butterfields, Carmel Valley, CA	8/15/08
564	1956 Jaguar XK 140 DHC	$265,135	72	Brightwells, Herefordshire, UK	7/2/08
565	1957 Chevrolet Corvette 283/283 FI Convertible	$265,000	S138	Mecum, Kissimmee, FL	1/24/09
566	1970 Dodge Challenger R/T 440/6 Convertible	$265,000	S181	Mecum, Indianapolis, IN	5/18/08
567	1935 Auburn 851 Boattail Speedster	$264,000	6	Gooding, Scottsdale, AZ	1/17/09
568	1962 Bentley S2 Continental	$264,000	258	RM, Hershey, PA	10/10/08
569	1929 Bugatti Type 44 Dual-Cowl Phaeton	$264,000	28	Gooding, Pebble Beach, CA	8/17/08
570	1953 Buick Skylark Convertible	$264,000	137	RM, Phoenix, AZ	1/18/08
571	1953 Chevrolet Corvette Roadster	$264,000	182	RM, Phoenix, AZ	1/18/08
572	1937 Cord 812 Coupe	$264,000	134	RM, Phoenix, AZ	1/18/08
573	1971 Ferrari 365 GTB/4 Daytona Spyder Conversion	$264,000	162	RM, Phoenix, AZ	1/18/08
574	1934 Packard Super Eight Convertible Victoria	$264,000	149	RM, Phoenix, AZ	1/16/09
575	1926 Rolls-Royce Springfield Silver Ghost	$264,000	56A	Gooding, Scottsdale, AZ	1/19/08
576	1964 Aston Martin DB5 Coupe	$262,007	34	Artcurial, Paris, FRA	2/8/09
577	1989 Aston Martin V8 Vantage Volante "X Pack" Convertible	$261,660	308	Bonhams, Newport Pagnell, UK	5/17/08
578	2003 Saleen S7 Coupe	$260,700	805.1	Barrett-Jackson, Las Vegas, NV	10/18/08
579	1937 Mercedes-Benz Type 320 Cabriolet B	$260,000	370	Bonhams & Butterfields, Carmel Valley, CA	8/15/08
580	1970 Plymouth 'Cuda 440/6 Convertible	$260,000	S178	Mecum, Indianapolis, IN	5/18/08
581	1938 Packard Twelve Coupe Roadster	$259,600	424	RM, Monterey, CA	8/16/08
582	1990 Tyrell Cosworth F1 Single-Seater	$258,720	259	Coys, Monte Carlo, MCO	5/10/08
583	1957 AC Ace Bristol Roadster	$258,500	1289	Barrett-Jackson, Scottsdale, AZ	1/20/08
584	1953 Allard J2X Roadster	$258,500	68	Gooding, Scottsdale, AZ	1/17/09
585	1969 Chevrolet Camaro RS/SS NASCAR Pace Car Convertible	$258,500	F524	Russo and Steele, Scottsdale, AZ	1/18/09
586	1955 Chevrolet "Newmad" Street Rod Wagon	$258,500	201	RM, Phoenix, AZ	1/16/09
587	1934 Packard Eight Convertible Sedan	$258,500	156	RM, Phoenix, AZ	1/18/08
588	1958 Porsche 356A Speedster	$258,500	138	Gooding, Pebble Beach, CA	8/17/08
589	1934 Bugatti Type 57 Ventoux	$256,500	230	Coys, Monte Carlo, MCO	5/18/09
590	1952 Mercedes-Benz 300S Cabriolet	$255,750	237	RM, Amelia Island, FL	3/14/09
591	1953 Cunningham C-3 Cabriolet	$255,000	252	RM, Amelia Island, FL	3/14/09
592	2004 Koenigsegg CC8S Coupe	$254,560	617	Bonhams, London, UK	12/1/08
593	1969 Lamborghini 400 GT Coupe	$254,100	F517	Russo and Steele, Scottsdale, AZ	1/20/08
594	1999 Prost-Peugeot AP02 F1 Single-Seater	$253,918	46	Artcurial, Paris, FRA	2/9/08
595	1955 Mercedes-Benz 300Sc Coupe	$253,000	1283	Barrett-Jackson, Scottsdale, AZ	1/20/08
596	1950 Allard J2 Roadster	$253,000	169	RM, Phoenix, AZ	1/16/09
597	1934 Auburn 1250 Salon Cabriolet	$253,000	669.1	Barrett-Jackson, Palm Beach, FL	4/11/09
598	1969 Ford Mustang Coupe	$253,000	F518	Russo and Steele, Scottsdale, AZ	1/20/08
599	1933 Lagonda 3-Liter Tourer	$253,000	24	Gooding, Scottsdale, AZ	1/19/08
600	1963 Maserati 3500 GTi Spyder	$253,000	35	Gooding, Scottsdale, AZ	1/19/08
601	1953 Nash-Healey Roadster	$253,000	27	Gooding, Scottsdale, AZ	1/19/08
602	1953 Oldsmobile Fiesta Convertible	$253,000	246	RM, Dallas, TX	4/19/08
603	1932 Packard 903 Deluxe Eight Coupe Roadster	$253,000	40	Worldwide, Seabrook, TX	5/2/09
604	1960 Plymouth Fury Convertible	$253,000	242	RM, Dallas, TX	4/19/08
605	1970 Plymouth Hemi Road Runner Superbird 2-Door Hardtop	$253,000	29	Worldwide, Houston, TX	5/3/08

#574—1934 Packard Super Eight Convertible Victoria

#578—2003 Saleen S7 Coupe

#591—1953 Cunningham C-3 Cabriolet

#605—1970 Plymouth Hemi Road Runner Superbird 2-Door Hardtop

#618—1955 Aston Martin DB2/4 Drophead Coupe

#624—1938 Lagonda LG6 Drophead Coupe

Rank	Model	Sold Price	Lot #	Auction Location	Date
606	1920 Stutz Bearcat Roadster	$253,000	60	Worldwide, Auburn, IN	8/30/08
607	1954 Arnolt-Bristol Bolide Roadster	$252,787	125	Coys, Nürburgring, DEU	8/9/08
608	1955/57 Lister Sports Racer	$252,684	76	H&H, Buxton, UK	7/23/08
609	1928/1945 Alfa Romeo 1,500cc Supercharged Race Car	$252,623	62	Bonhams & Goodman, Sydney, AUS	11/16/08
610	1969 Chevrolet Chevelle Yenko 2-Door Hardtop	$252,000	S80	Mecum, Indianapolis, IN	5/18/08
611	1974 Citroën SM "Opera" Sedan	$250,905	122	Bonhams, Paris, FRA	2/7/09
612	1969 Chevrolet Camaro Yenko Coupe	$250,000	S173	Mecum, St. Charles, IL	10/5/08
613	1960 Maserati 3500 GT Spyder	$250,000	S758	Russo and Steele, Scottsdale, AZ	1/18/09
614	1953 Chevrolet Corvette Roadster	$249,900	S109	Mecum, Kissimmee, FL	1/26/08
615	1953 Aston Martin DB2 Vantage Coupe	$249,550	173	Bonhams, Monte Carlo, MCO	5/10/08
616	1970 Maserati Ghibli Spyder	$249,000	312	Bonhams & Butterfields, Carmel Valley, CA	8/15/08
617	1965 McLaren-Elva M1A Chevrolet Sports Racer	$249,000	224	Bonhams & Butterfields, Greenwich, CT	6/8/08
618	1955 Aston Martin DB2/4 Drophead Coupe	$248,003	598	Bonhams, Sussex, UK	7/11/08
619	1969 Ford Mustang Boss 429 Fastback	$248,000	83	Worldwide, Houston, TX	5/3/08
620	1959 Pontiac Catalina Convertible "Pink Lady"	$247,500	1314	Barrett-Jackson, Scottsdale, AZ	1/20/08
621	1971 Dodge Hemi Challenger R/T 2-Door Hardtop	$247,500	S702	Russo and Steele, Scottsdale, AZ	1/18/09
622	2010 Ferrari F430 Coupe	$247,500	221A	RM, Maranello, ITA	5/17/09
623	1927 Ford Roadster Shadow Rods XL 27	$247,500	S661	Russo and Steele, Monterey, CA	8/16/08
624	1938 Lagonda LG6 Drophead Coupe	$247,500	264	RM, Amelia Island, FL	3/8/08
625	1968 Shelby GT500 KR Convertible	$247,500	S722	Russo and Steele, Scottsdale, AZ	1/20/08
626	1965 Shelby GT350 Fastback	$247,500	269	RM, Monterey, CA	8/16/08
627	1930 Rolls-Royce Phantom II Experimental	$246,882	451	Coys, London, UK	7/5/08
628	1967 Chevrolet Corvette 427/435 Convertible	$246,750	X9	Mecum, St. Charles, IL	6/28/08
629	1931 Rolls-Royce Phantom II Continental Touring Sedan	$246,420	636	Bonhams, London, UK	12/1/08
630	1968 Shelby GT500 KR Convertible	$246,100	S114	Mecum, Indianapolis, IN	5/18/08
631	1970 Plymouth Hemi 'Cuda 2-Door Hardtop	$244,125	S177	Mecum, Indianapolis, IN	5/18/08
632	1934 Mercedes-Benz 290 Cabriolet A	$243,810	111	Bonhams, Paris, FRA	2/7/09
633	1914 Peugeot 145S Torpedo Tourer	$243,000	561	Cox, Branson, MO	4/18/09
634	1937 Bentley 4¼-Liter All-Weather Thrupp & Maberly Tourer	$242,457	416	Coys, London, UK	7/5/08
635	1902 Clément Twin-Cylinder 9hp 4-Seater Rear-Entrance Tonneau	$242,250	301	Bonhams, London, UK	10/31/08
636	1935 Buick 67C Custom Convertible	$242,000	1276.1	Barrett-Jackson, Scottsdale, AZ	1/20/08
637	1958 Chevrolet Corvette 283/240 Convertible	$242,000	990.1	Barrett-Jackson, Scottsdale, AZ	1/20/08
638	1934 Bugatti Type 57 Galibier Sedan	$242,000	670	RM, Novi, MI	4/27/08
639	1954 Buick Skylark Convertible	$242,000	121	RM, Phoenix, AZ	1/18/08
640	1937 Cord 812 SC Sportsman Convertible Coupe	$242,000	63	Worldwide, Auburn, IN	8/30/08
641	1933 Lincoln Model KB Dual Cowl Phaeton	$242,000	235	RM, Hershey, PA	10/10/08
642	1957 Mercedes-Benz 300SL Roadster	$242,000	69	Gooding, Scottsdale, AZ	1/17/09
643	1910 Mitchell Model S Touring Car	$242,000	12	Gooding, Pebble Beach, CA	8/17/08
644	1930 Packard Custom Eight Roadster	$242,000	131	RM, Phoenix, AZ	1/18/08
645	1935 Packard Twelve Convertible Sedan	$242,000	336	RM, Anaheim, CA	6/29/08
646	1970 Plymouth 'Cuda 2-Door Hardtop	$242,000	S720	Russo and Steele, Scottsdale, AZ	1/20/08
647	1957 Pontiac Bonneville Convertible	$242,000	110	RM, Phoenix, AZ	1/18/08
648	1967 Shelby GT500 Fastback	$242,000	S715	Russo and Steele, Scottsdale, AZ	1/20/08
649	1963 Urgo/Kuzma Sprint Car	$242,000	242	RM, Tustin, CA	6/14/08

#656—1965 Chevrolet Chevelle Z16

#665—1966 Lotus 39 Tasman Series Single-Seater

#677—1959 Cadillac Eldorado Biarritz Convertible

Rank	Model	Sold Price	Lot #	Auction Location	Date
650	1970 Plymouth Hemi 'Cuda 2-Door Hardtop	$241,150	S113	Mecum, Indianapolis, IN	5/17/09
651	1965 Aston Martin DB5 Coupe	$240,279	358	Bonhams, Sussex, UK	9/19/08
652	1961 Aston Martin DB4 Series II Coupe	$240,100	321	Bonhams, Newport Pagnell, UK	5/17/08
653	1963 Aston Martin DB4 Series V Vantage Coupe	$240,100	307	Bonhams, Newport Pagnell, UK	5/17/08
654	1986 Aston Martin V8 Vantage Zagato Coupe	$240,100	316	Bonhams, Newport Pagnell, UK	5/17/08
655	1973 Porsche 911 2.7 RS Coupe	$238,950	227	Coys, Monte Carlo, MCO	5/18/09
656	1965 Chevrolet Chevelle Z16	$238,875	S112	Mecum, Kissimmee, FL	1/26/08
657	1967 Ford GT40 Mk II Coupe	$238,500	F257	Mecum, Indianapolis, IN	5/17/09
658	1964 Mercury Comet Caliente A/FX 2-Door Hardtop	$238,500	S109	Mecum, Indianapolis, IN	5/17/09
659	1922 Mercer Series 5 Raceabout	$238,000	840	Bonhams & Butterfields, Owls Head, ME	9/27/08
660	1928 Rolls-Royce Phantom Ascot Tourer	$238,000	224	Bonhams & Butterfields, Greenwich, CT	6/7/09
661	1903 Winton Runabout	$238,000	859	Bonhams & Butterfields, Owls Head, ME	9/27/08
662	1948 Ford Sportsman Convertible Coupe	$236,500	143	RM, Anaheim, CA	6/29/08
663	1938 Packard Twelve Collapsible Touring Cabriolet	$236,500	246	RM, Hershey, PA	10/10/08
664	1938 Bentley 4¼-Liter MX Vanden Plas Tourer	$236,056	225	Coys, Brands Hatch, UK	5/25/08
665	1966 Lotus 39 Tasman Series Single-Seater	$234,317	59	Bonhams & Goodman, Sydney, AUS	11/16/08
666	1965 Aston Martin DB5 Coupe	$233,755	420	Coys, London, UK	3/12/09
667	1963 Chevrolet Corvette 327/360 Z06 Coupe	$233,625	B34	Mecum, Indianapolis, IN	4/5/08
668	1969 Ferrari 246 GT Dino Coupe	$231,725	141	Bonhams, Monte Carlo, MCO	5/10/08
669	1935 Mercedes-Benz 200 W21 40hp Landaulet	$231,725	159	Bonhams, Monte Carlo, MCO	5/10/08
670	1944 Volkswagen Schwimmwagen Amphibious	$231,725	163	Bonhams, Monte Carlo, MCO	5/10/08
671	1969 Chevrolet Camaro COPO Coupe	$231,000	F459	Russo and Steele, Hollywood, FL	3/30/08
672	1968 Shelby GT500 KR Convertible	$231,000	1278	Barrett-Jackson, Scottsdale, AZ	1/20/08
673	1931 Cadillac 452A V16 All-Weather Phaeton	$231,000	19	Worldwide, Seabrook, TX	5/2/09
674	1932 Cadillac 452B V16 All-Weather Phaeton	$231,000	22	Gooding, Scottsdale, AZ	1/17/09
675	1956 Cadillac Eldorado Convertible	$231,000	SP68	RM, Ft. Lauderdale, FL	2/17/08
676	1947 Cadillac Series 75 7-Passenger Imperial Sedan	$231,000	264	RM, Dallas, TX	4/19/08
677	1959 Cadillac Eldorado Biarritz Convertible	$231,000	232	RM, Rochester, MI	8/2/08
678	1968 Chevrolet Corvette L88 Coupe	$231,000	S6	Mecum, St. Charles, IL	6/28/08
679	1990 Chevrolet Corvette ZR-1 Coupe (w/5 others)	$231,000	S32	Mecum, St. Charles, IL	6/28/08
680	1971 Dodge Hemi Challenger 2-Door Hardtop	$231,000	32	Worldwide, Houston, TX	5/3/08
681	1969 Ford Mustang Fastback	$231,000	S700	Russo and Steele, Scottsdale, AZ	1/20/08
682	1970 Ford Mustang Boss 429 Fastback	$231,000	231	RM, Monterey, CA	8/16/08
683	1966 Lamborghini 400 GT Interim Coupe	$231,000	72	Gooding, Pebble Beach, CA	8/17/08
684	1934 Packard Super Eight 1104 Touring	$231,000	32	Gooding, Scottsdale, AZ	1/19/08
685	1936 Packard Twelve Dual Cowl Sport Phaeton	$231,000	249	RM, Hershey, PA	10/10/08
686	1972 Ferrari 365 GTB/4 Daytona Spyder Conversion	$229,047	227	Bonhams, Gstaad, CHE	12/20/08
687	1929 Rolls-Royce Phantom II Imperial Cabriolet	$227,000	253	Bonhams & Butterfields, Greenwich, CT	6/7/09
688	1959 Lotus 16 Formula 2 Single-Seater	$226,994	56	Bonhams & Goodman, Sydney, AUS	11/16/08
689	1954 Rolls-Royce Silver Dawn Custom Sedan	$225,500	794	Barrett-Jackson, Las Vegas, NV	10/18/08
690	1969 Chevrolet Camaro COPO Coupe	$225,250	S149	Mecum, Indianapolis, IN	5/17/09
691	1950 Jaguar XK 120 Alloy Open Two Seater	$225,000	461	RM, Monterey, CA	8/16/08
692	1966 Citroën DS21 "Palm Beach" Cabriolet	$222,525	117	Bonhams, Paris, FRA	2/7/09
693	1950 Maserati A6 1500 Coupe	$222,250	175	Coys, Padua, ITA	10/25/08

Top 1,000 Sales in 2008–09 by Price

Rank	Model	Sold Price	Lot #	Auction Location	Date
694	1959 Cadillac Eldorado Convertible	$221,400	2488	Leake, Tulsa, OK	6/8/08
695	1970 Plymouth Hemi 'Cuda 2-Door Hardtop	$220,500	U106	Mecum, Indianapolis, IN	5/18/08
696	1967 Chevrolet Corvette 427/435 Convertible	$220,000	1267	Barrett-Jackson, Scottsdale, AZ	1/20/08
697	2005 Ford Mustang FR500C Racer	$220,000	1288	Barrett-Jackson, Scottsdale, AZ	1/20/08
698	1970 Plymouth Superbird 2-Door Hardtop	$220,000	1021	Barrett-Jackson, Scottsdale, AZ	1/20/08
699	1969 Shelby GT500 Fastback	$220,000	1329.1	Barrett-Jackson, Scottsdale, AZ	1/20/08
700	1950 Allard J2 Roadster	$220,000	S721	Russo and Steele, Scottsdale, AZ	1/20/08
701	1954 Buick Skylark Convertible	$220,000	267	RM, Dallas, TX	4/19/08
702	1957 Cadillac Eldorado Brougham	$220,000	263	RM, Dallas, TX	4/19/08
703	1959 Chevrolet Corvette 283/245 Convertible	$220,000	1019	Barrett-Jackson, Scottsdale, AZ	1/18/09
704	1970 Chevrolet Chevelle Convertible	$220,000	S701	Russo and Steele, Scottsdale, AZ	1/20/08
705	1937 Cord 812 SC Convertible Coupe	$220,000	238	RM, Amelia Island, FL	3/8/08
706	1932 Ford Deluxe Boyd Coddington Custom Coupe	$220,000	1282	Barrett-Jackson, Scottsdale, AZ	1/18/09
707	1993 Jaguar XJ 220 Coupe	$220,000	1290	Barrett-Jackson, Scottsdale, AZ	1/18/09
708	1923 Oldsmobile Custom Touring Roadster	$220,000	397.2	Barrett-Jackson, Scottsdale, AZ	1/18/09
709	1936 Packard Twelve Coupe Roadster	$220,000	SP138	RM, Ft. Lauderdale, FL	2/8/09
710	1916 Packard Twin Six 1-35 Touring Car	$220,000	18	Gooding, Scottsdale, AZ	1/19/08
711	1909 Packard Model 18 Runabout	$220,000	72	Worldwide, Houston, TX	5/3/08
712	1967 Plymouth Barracuda West Coast Customs 2-Door Hardtop	$220,000	1306.2	Barrett-Jackson, Scottsdale, AZ	1/18/09
713	1958 Porsche 356 1600 Speedster	$220,000	183	RM, Phoenix, AZ	1/18/08
714	1956 Porsche 356A 1600S Speedster	$220,000	240	RM, Amelia Island, FL	3/8/08
715	1932 Reo Royale Convertible Coupe	$220,000	286	RM, Amelia Island, FL	3/14/09
716	1966 Shelby GT350 Fastback	$220,000	1271.1	Barrett-Jackson, Scottsdale, AZ	1/18/09
717	1966 Shelby GT350 Fastback	$220,000	F509	Russo and Steele, Scottsdale, AZ	1/20/08
718	1968 Shelby GT500 Convertible	$220,000	SP47	RM, Ft. Lauderdale, FL	2/17/08
719	1908 White Model L Touring Car	$220,000	13	Gooding, Pebble Beach, CA	8/17/08
720	1961 Aston Martin DB4 Coupe	$219,725	42	H&H, Buxton, UK	7/23/08
721	1967 Ferrari 330 GTC Coupe	$218,900	56	H&H, Cheltenham, UK	2/27/08
722	1970 Dodge Challenger 2-Door Hardtop	$217,800	S696	Russo and Steele, Scottsdale, AZ	1/20/08
723	1953 Lancia Aurelia B20GT Coupe	$217,465	146	Bonhams, Monte Carlo, MCO	5/10/08
724	1964 Ford Galaxie 2-Door Hardtop	$217,300	S130	Mecum, Kissimmee, FL	1/24/09
725	1968 Shelby GT500 KR Convertible	$217,250	SP41	RM, Ft. Lauderdale, FL	2/17/08
726	1955 Mercedes-Benz 300S Coupe	$216,775	129	Bonhams, Paris, FRA	2/9/08
727	1967 Shelby GT500 E "Gone in 60 Seconds"	$216,700	1317	Barrett-Jackson, Scottsdale, AZ	1/18/09
728	1956 AC Ace Roadster	$216,000	229	Bonhams & Butterfields, Greenwich, CT	6/8/08
729	1912 Benz 14/30 PS Touring	$216,000	752	Kruse, Phoenix, AZ	1/27/08
730	1959 Cadillac Series 62 Convertible	$216,000	2469	Leake, Oklahoma City, OK	2/23/08
731	1966 Rolls-Royce Silver Cloud III DHC	$215,641	212	Coys, Monte Carlo, MCO	5/18/09
732	1934 Bugatti Type 57 Ventoux Coach	$215,108	110	Bonhams, Paris, FRA	2/7/09
733	1971 Dodge Hemi Charger R/T 2-Door Hardtop	$215,000	S173	Mecum, Indianapolis, IN	5/18/08
734	1953 Buick Skylark Convertible	$214,500	1260	Barrett-Jackson, Scottsdale, AZ	1/20/08
735	1970 Chevrolet Chevelle LS6 COPO SS 2-Door Hardtop	$214,500	1279.1	Barrett-Jackson, Scottsdale, AZ	1/20/08
736	1957 Chevrolet Corvette LS7 Custom Convertible	$214,500	1276	Barrett-Jackson, Scottsdale, AZ	1/20/08
737	1969 Ford Mustang Boss 429 Fastback	$214,500	803.1	Barrett-Jackson, Las Vegas, NV	10/18/08

#700—1950 Allard J2 Roadster

#714—1956 Porsche 356A 1600S Speedster

#721—1967 Ferrari 330 GTC Coupe

Rank	Model	Sold Price	Lot #	Auction Location	Date
738	1950 Jaguar XK 120 Roadster	$214,500	S657	Russo and Steele, Hollywood, FL	3/30/08
739	1970 Plymouth Superbird 2-Door Hardtop	$214,500	1277.1	Barrett-Jackson, Scottsdale, AZ	1/20/08
740	1968 Shelby GT500 KR Custom Fastback	$214,500	1270	Barrett-Jackson, Scottsdale, AZ	1/20/08
741	1928 Bugatti Type 35B Replica	$214,500	246	RM, Tustin, CA	6/14/08
742	1957 Buick Model 70 Roadmaster Convertible	$214,500	44	Worldwide, Houston, TX	5/3/08
743	1931 Cadillac 370-A V12 Dual Cowl Sport Phaeton	$214,500	27	Worldwide, Seabrook, TX	5/2/09
744	1963 Ferrari 250 GT California Spyder Replica	$214,500	265	RM, Monterey, CA	8/16/08
745	1970 Ford Mustang Boss 429 Fastback	$214,500	F513	Russo and Steele, Scottsdale, AZ	1/18/09
746	1937 Ford Woody Custom Station Wagon	$214,500	238	RM, Tustin, CA	6/14/08
747	1901 Packard Model C Runabout	$214,500	9	Gooding, Pebble Beach, CA	8/17/08
748	1947 Talbot-Lago T26 Record Cabriolet	$214,500	239	RM, Monterey, CA	8/16/08
749	1950 Jaguar XK 120 Roadster	$214,080	218	Bonhams, Sussex, UK	8/9/08
750	1972 Mercedes-Benz 280SE 3.5 Convertible	$213,900	104	Bonhams, Monte Carlo, MCO	5/10/08
751	1934 Packard Twelve 5-Passenger Phaeton	$211,750	251	RM, Amelia Island, FL	3/14/09
752	1948 Delahaye 135 M Pennock Cabriolet	$211,457	20	Artcurial, Paris, FRA	2/8/09
753	1963 Maserati 3500 GT Spyder	$211,200	48	Worldwide, Hilton Head, SC	11/1/08
754	1957 Lancia Aurelia B24S Convertible	$211,140	255A	Bonhams, Monte Carlo, MCO	5/18/09
755	1970 Ford Mustang Boss 429 Fastback	$210,940	F239	Mecum, Indianapolis, IN	5/17/09
756	1959 AC Ace Bristol Roadster	$210,813	518	Bonhams, Sussex, UK	7/11/08
757	1968 Shelby GT500 KR Fastback	$210,600	733	Kruse, Hershey, PA	10/11/08
758	1964 Aston Martin DB4 SV Coupe	$210,198	239	Coys, Brands Hatch, UK	5/24/09
759	1963 Ferrari 250 Testa Rossa Replica	$209,937	232	Bonhams, Gstaad, CHE	12/20/08
760	1965 Aston Martin DB5 Sports Coupe	$209,444	139	Bonhams, Monte Carlo, MCO	5/10/08
761	1962 Lincoln Continental Sedan "John F. Kennedy"	$209,000	812	Barrett-Jackson, Las Vegas, NV	10/18/08
762	1938 Packard 16th Series Twelve Convertible Victoria	$209,000	801	Barrett-Jackson, Las Vegas, NV	10/18/08
763	1967 Shelby GT500 Fastback	$209,000	659	Barrett-Jackson, West Palm Beach, FL	3/30/08
764	1929 Cadillac 341B Eight Sport Dual Cowl Phaeton	$209,000	47	Worldwide, Auburn, IN	8/30/08
765	1994 Chevrolet Lumina NASCAR Winston Cup Car	$209,000	221	RM, Tustin, CA	6/14/08
766	1958 Dual-Ghia Convertible	$209,000	254	RM, Amelia Island, FL	3/14/09
767	1970 Ford Mustang Boss 429 Fastback	$209,000	1319	Barrett-Jackson, Scottsdale, AZ	1/18/09
768	1941 Lincoln Continental Coupe	$209,000	151	RM, Anaheim, CA	6/29/08
769	1958 Oldsmobile J-2 Super 88 Convertible	$209,000	24	Worldwide, Houston, TX	5/3/08
770	1939 Packard Super Eight Transformable Town Car by Franay	$209,000	187	RM, Anaheim, CA	6/29/08
771	1930 Packard Seventh Series Deluxe Eight Model 745 Roadster	$209,000	38	Worldwide, Auburn, IN	8/30/08
772	1937 Bentley 4¼-Liter Sedanca Coupe	$208,023	326	Coys, Essen, DEU	3/29/08
773	1989 Aston Martin V8 Vantage Volante	$207,760	338	Bonhams, Newport Pagnell, UK	5/17/08
774	1969 Dodge Daytona 2-Door Hardtop	$206,700	S154	Mecum, Kissimmee, FL	1/24/09
775	1964 Ford Fairlane Thunderbolt Drag Racer	$206,700	S134	Mecum, Kissimmee, FL	1/24/09
776	1969 Ford Mustang Boss 429 Fastback	$206,700	S110	Mecum, Indianapolis, IN	5/17/09
777	1970 Ford Mustang Boss 429 Fastback	$206,700	n/a	MidAmerica, St. Paul, MN	5/10/08
778	1970 Oldsmobile 442 W-30 Convertible	$206,700	1789	G. Potter King, Atlantic City, NJ	3/2/08
779	1968 Lamborghini 400 GT 2+2 Coupe	$205,802	42	H&H, Surrey, UK	6/8/08
780	1970 Ford Mustang Boss 429 Fastback	$205,700	816	Barrett-Jackson, Las Vegas, NV	10/18/08

#738—1950 Jaguar XK 120 Roadster

#754—1957 Lancia Aurelia B24S Convertible

#770—1939 Packard Super Eight Transformable Town Car by Franay

#784—1968 Citroën DS21 Convertible

#797—1969 Lamborghini Islero Coupe

#805—1954 Buick Skylark Convertible

Rank	Model	Sold Price	Lot #	Auction Location	Date
781	1959 Arnolt-Bristol Deluxe Competition Roadster	$205,521	143	Coys, Nürburgring, DEU	8/9/08
782	1931 Rolls-Royce Phantom II Continental Close-Coupled Sports Saloon	$205,400	342	Coys, Essen, DEU	3/29/08
783	1963 Shelby Cobra 289 Roadster	$205,400	345	Coys, Essen, DEU	3/29/08
784	1968 Citroën DS21 Convertible	$205,216	40	Artcurial, Paris, FRA	2/9/08
785	1954 Talbot-Lago T26 Grand Sport Coupe	$205,000	362	Bonhams & Butterfields, Carmel Valley, CA	8/15/08
786	1973 Ferrari 246 GTS Dino Spyder	$204,270	332	RM, Maranello, ITA	5/18/08
787	2001 Rolls-Royce Corniche Convertible	$204,045	333	Bonhams, Sussex, UK	9/19/08
788	1972 Ferrari 365 GTB/4 Daytona Coupe	$203,745	231	Bonhams, Oxford, UK	3/8/09
789	1970 Chevrolet Chevelle LS6 SS Convertible	$203,500	1324	Barrett-Jackson, Scottsdale, AZ	1/20/08
790	1969 Ford Mustang 428 SCJ Convertible	$203,500	1333	Barrett-Jackson, Scottsdale, AZ	1/20/08
791	1974 Lincoln Batmobile Replica	$203,500	994	Barrett-Jackson, Scottsdale, AZ	1/20/08
792	1955 Mercedes-Benz 300SL Gullwing Custom Replica	$203,500	1322	Barrett-Jackson, Scottsdale, AZ	1/20/08
793	1931 Auburn 8-98 Cabriolet	$203,500	130	RM, Phoenix, AZ	1/18/08
794	1953 Buick Skylark Convertible	$203,500	245	RM, Dallas, TX	4/19/08
795	Deco Rides Bugnotti Roadster	$203,500	38	Gooding, Scottsdale, AZ	1/17/09
796	1936 Jenson-Ford Tourer	$203,500	183	RM, Anaheim, CA	6/29/08
797	1969 Lamborghini Islero Coupe	$203,500	21	Gooding, Pebble Beach, CA	8/17/08
798	1947 Steyr-Allard Alloy Monoposto	$203,500	1304	Barrett-Jackson, Scottsdale, AZ	1/18/09
799	1974 Ferrari 246 GTS Dino Spyder	$202,834	240	Coys, Brands Hatch, UK	5/25/08
800	1936 Lincoln Model K Brunn Cabriolet	$202,500	494	Leake, Tulsa, OK	6/14/09
801	1970 Dodge Challenger 440 Convertible	$201,400	S190	Mecum, Indianapolis, IN	5/17/09
802	1936 Bentley 4¼-Liter Drophead Coupe	$200,836	608	Bonhams, London, UK	12/1/08
803	1966 Iso Grifo GL Coupe	$200,401	248	Coys, Essen, DEU	4/4/09
804	1958 Lancia Aurelia B24S Convertible	$200,273	144	Bonhams, Paris, FRA	2/7/09
805	1954 Buick Skylark Convertible	$200,200	62	Worldwide, Auburn, IN	8/30/08
806	1960 Bentley S2 Continental Flying Spur	$200,100	128	Bonhams, Paris, FRA	2/9/08
807	1946 Delahaye 135M Cabriolet	$200,100	108	Bonhams, Paris, FRA	2/9/08
808	1967 Lamborghini 400 GT Coupe	$200,019	371	Bonhams, Sussex, UK	9/19/08
809	2006 Chevrolet Monte Carlo NASCAR Jimmie Johnson #48	$200,000	672	Barrett-Jackson, Palm Beach, FL	4/11/09
810	1936 AC 16/90 Competition	$199,902	22	Artcurial, Paris, FRA	2/8/09
811	1931 Cadillac V16 Convertible Sedan	$199,800	400	Leake, Tulsa, OK	6/14/09
812	1967 Baja Boot Off Road Racing Buggy	$199,500	346	Bonhams & Butterfields, Carmel Valley, CA	8/15/08
813	1948 Ford Sportsman Convertible Coupe	$199,100	SP133	RM, Ft. Lauderdale, FL	2/8/09
814	1963 Aston Martin DB5 Mk I Coupe	$198,263	305	Bonhams, Newport Pagnell, UK	5/9/09
815	1988 Peugeot 405 Turbo 16 Grand Raid	$198,139	60	Artcurial, Paris, FRA	6/14/09
816	1988 Peugeot Oxia Concept	$198,139	45	Artcurial, Paris, FRA	6/14/09
817	1958 Chevrolet Corvette 283/290 FI Convertible	$198,000	1272	Barrett-Jackson, Scottsdale, AZ	1/20/08
818	1967 Chevrolet Corvette 427/435 Coupe	$198,000	1327	Barrett-Jackson, Scottsdale, AZ	1/20/08
819	1949 Alfa Romeo 6C 2500 Super Sport Coupe	$198,000	174	RM, Phoenix, AZ	1/16/09
820	1934 Brewster Ford Town Car	$198,000	253	RM, Amelia Island, FL	3/8/08
821	1927 Bugatti Type 38 Roadster	$198,000	33	Gooding, Pebble Beach, CA	8/17/08
822	1958 Buick Limited Convertible	$198,000	128	RM, Phoenix, AZ	1/18/08
823	1959 Cadillac Eldorado Biarritz Convertible	$198,000	SP73	RM, Ft. Lauderdale, FL	2/17/08
824	1931 Cadillac Series 370 V12 Dual Cowl Sport Phaeton	$198,000	28	Worldwide, Houston, TX	5/3/08

#828—1937 Cord 812 Supercharged Phaeton

#840—1921 Rolls-Royce 45/50hp Silver Ghost
Salamanca Cabriolet

#848—1989 Aston Martin V8 Vantage Volante X-Pack
Convertible

Rank	Model	Sold Price	Lot #	Auction Location	Date
825	1953 Chevrolet Corvette Roadster	$198,000	278	RM, Amelia Island, FL	3/14/09
826	1989 Chevrolet Corvette ZR-1 Coupe	$198,000	1230.4	Barrett-Jackson, Scottsdale, AZ	1/18/09
827	1955 Chevrolet Nomad Custom Wagon	$198,000	1255	Barrett-Jackson, Scottsdale, AZ	1/18/09
828	1937 Cord 812 Supercharged Phaeton	$198,000	56	Worldwide, Seabrook, TX	5/2/09
829	1936 Cord 810 Convertible Phaeton	$198,000	52	Worldwide, Auburn, IN	8/30/08
830	1967 Ferrari 330 GTC Coupe	$198,000	59	Gooding, Scottsdale, AZ	1/19/08
831	1969 Ford Mustang Boss 429 Fastback Drag Car	$198,000	1283	Barrett-Jackson, Scottsdale, AZ	1/18/09
832	1966 Ford Mustang Convertible	$198,000	SP65	RM, Ft. Lauderdale, FL	2/8/09
833	1927 Hudson Super Six Supercharged Sports Tourer	$198,000	276	RM, Amelia Island, FL	3/14/09
834	1960 Mercedes-Benz 220SE Convertible	$198,000	24	Gooding, Pebble Beach, CA	8/17/08
835	1949 Mercury Eight Station Wagon	$198,000	174	RM, Anaheim, CA	6/29/08
836	1940 Packard 120 Station Wagon	$198,000	53	Gooding, Scottsdale, AZ	1/17/09
837	1938 Packard Twelve Convertible Victoria	$198,000	152	RM, Anaheim, CA	6/29/08
838	1970 Plymouth Hemi 'Cuda 2-Door Hardtop	$198,000	1262	Barrett-Jackson, Scottsdale, AZ	1/18/09
839	1933 Lagonda M45 Tourer	$197,580	609	Bonhams, London, UK	12/1/08
840	1921 Rolls-Royce 45/50hp Silver Ghost Salamanca Cabriolet	$197,483	212	Bonhams, Northamptonshire, UK	6/21/08
841	1969 Citroën DS21 Convertible	$196,765	152	Bonhams, Paris, FRA	2/9/08
842	1913 National Model 40 Series V Type N3 Semi-Racing Roadster	$196,200	508	Bonhams & Butterfields, Brookline, MA	10/4/08
843	1979 Ferrari 512 BB Coupe	$195,759	305	RM, Maranello, ITA	5/18/08
844	1958 AC Ace Bristol Roadster	$195,437	82	H&H, Buxton, UK	6/10/09
845	1970 Chevrolet Chevelle LS6 SS Coupe	$195,250	1254	Barrett-Jackson, Scottsdale, AZ	1/20/08
846	1926 Rolls-Royce 40/50hp Berwick Sedan	$195,098	142	Bonhams, Paris, FRA	2/9/08
847	1953 Oldsmobile 98 Fiesta Convertible	$195,000	72	Worldwide, Seabrook, TX	5/2/09
848	1989 Aston Martin V8 Vantage Volante X-Pack Convertible	$194,941	328	Bonhams, Newport Pagnell, UK	5/9/09
849	1965 Chevrolet Chevelle Z16 2-Door Hardtop	$194,700	660	Barrett-Jackson, West Palm Beach, FL	3/30/08
850	1965 Aston Martin DB5 Coupe	$194,700	354	Coys, Ascot, UK	10/4/08
851	1936 Cadillac Series 90 V16 Convertible Sedan	$194,000	512	Bonhams & Butterfields, Brookline, MA	10/4/08
852	1935 BMW 319 Sport	$193,879	324	Coys, Essen, DEU	3/29/08
853	1968 Shelby GT350 Convertible	$193,600	SP51	RM, Ft. Lauderdale, FL	2/17/08
854	1954 Jaguar XK 120SE Coupe	$192,960	212	Bonhams, Sussex, UK	8/9/08
855	1932 Ford Ardun Special Roadster	$192,920	S103	Mecum, Indianapolis, IN	5/17/09
856	1965 Aston Martin DB6 Mk I 4.2 Vantage Coupe	$192,668	305	Bonhams, Newport Pagnell, UK	5/17/09
857	1960 Chevrolet Corvette 283/290 FI Convertible	$192,500	1045	Barrett-Jackson, Scottsdale, AZ	1/20/08
858	1954 Chevrolet Corvette Roadster	$192,500	1259	Barrett-Jackson, Scottsdale, AZ	1/20/08
859	2003 Hummer H2 Custom Convertible	$192,500	1309.1	Barrett-Jackson, Scottsdale, AZ	1/20/08
860	1968 Shelby GT500 KR Fastback	$192,500	1555	Barrett-Jackson, Scottsdale, AZ	1/20/08
861	1931 Cadillac V12 5-Passenger Phaeton by Fleetwood	$192,500	249	RM, Rochester, MI	8/2/08
862	1937 Cadillac V16 Custom Imperial Cabriolet by Fleetwood	$192,500	233	RM, Rochester, MI	8/2/08
863	1963 Chevrolet Corvette 327/360 Z06 Coupe	$192,500	287	RM, Amelia Island, FL	3/14/09
864	1968 Chevrolet Corvette 427/435 L89 Coupe	$192,500	F513	Russo and Steele, Scottsdale, AZ	1/20/08
865	1969 Chevrolet Camaro Coupe	$192,500	71	Gooding, Pebble Beach, CA	8/17/08
866	1967 Ferrari 330 GTC Coupe	$192,500	34	Worldwide, Houston, TX	5/3/08
867	1938 Lincoln Model K Convertible Victoria	$192,500	426	RM, Monterey, CA	8/16/08
868	1955 Mercedes-Benz 300Sc Coupe	$192,500	1284	Barrett-Jackson, Scottsdale, AZ	1/18/09

Rank	Model	Sold Price	Lot #	Auction Location	Date
869	1930 Packard 740 Custom Eight Sport Phaeton	$192,500	84	Gooding, Scottsdale, AZ	1/17/09
870	1934 Packard Eight Coupe Roadster	$192,500	188	RM, Phoenix, AZ	1/18/08
871	1967 Shelby GT500 E Fastback	$192,500	1343	Barrett-Jackson, Scottsdale, AZ	1/18/09
872	1903 Toledo 12hp Touring Car	$192,500	11	Gooding, Pebble Beach, CA	8/17/08
873	1960 Porsche 356B 1600 Roadster	$191,800	335	Bonhams & Butterfields, Carmel Valley, CA	8/15/08
874	1930 Invicta 4½-Liter Type A Tourer	$191,196	123	Bonhams & Goodman, Melbounre, AUS	3/13/08
875	1971 Lancia Fulvia 1600HF Coupe	$191,166	52	Artcurial, Paris, FRA	6/28/08
876	1935 Riley "Dobbs Special" 2-Liter Offset Monoposto	$191,124	568	Bonhams, Sussex, UK	7/11/08
877	1968 Chevrolet Camaro SS 396 Convertible	$190,800	S117	Mecum, Indianapolis, IN	5/17/09
878	1970 Chevrolet Chevelle 396 Convertible	$190,800	S125	Mecum, Indianapolis, IN	5/17/09
879	1983 Lancia 037 Stradale Coupe	$190,728	129	Bonhams, Monte Carlo, MCO	5/10/08
880	1958 Ferrari 250 GT Coupe	$189,750	487	RM, Monterey, CA	8/16/08
881	1968 Shelby GT500 KR Convertible	$189,200	1238.1	Barrett-Jackson, Scottsdale, AZ	1/20/08
882	2004 SSC Aero SC/8T Prototype	$189,200	671	Barrett-Jackson, West Palm Beach, FL	3/30/08
883	1970 Chevrolet Corvette ZR1 Coupe	$189,000	S108	Mecum, St. Charles, IL	6/28/08
884	1931 Packard 840 Roadster	$189,000	566	Cox, Branson, MO	4/18/09
885	1993 Jaguar XJ 220 Coupe	$188,664	339	Coys, London, UK	3/3/08
886	1931 Studebaker President Four Seasons Roadster	$188,100	SP176	RM, Ft. Lauderdale, FL	2/17/08
887	1967 Chevrolet Corvette 427/435 Convertible	$188,000	S135	Mecum, Kissimmee, FL	1/26/08
888	1965 Ferrari 330 GT 2+2	$187,380	231	Coys, Monte Carlo, MCO	5/18/09
889	1969 Chevrolet Camaro Coupe	$187,000	1269.1	Barrett-Jackson, Scottsdale, AZ	1/20/08
890	1965 Chevrolet Chevelle Malibu SS 2-Door Hardtop	$187,000	1315	Barrett-Jackson, Scottsdale, AZ	1/20/08
891	1958 Chevrolet Corvette LS2 Custom Convertible	$187,000	788	Barrett-Jackson, Las Vegas, NV	10/18/08
892	1958 DeSoto Firesweep Convertible	$187,000	1252	Barrett-Jackson, Scottsdale, AZ	1/20/08
893	1970 Plymouth Hemi 'Cuda 2-Door Hardtop	$187,000	804.2	Barrett-Jackson, Las Vegas, NV	10/18/08
894	1967 Shelby GT500 E Supersnake Fastback	$187,000	804.1	Barrett-Jackson, Las Vegas, NV	10/18/08
895	1934 Buick Series 90 Convertible Coupe	$187,000	137	RM, Phoenix, AZ	1/16/09
896	1954 Buick Skylark Convertible	$187,000	SP68	RM, Ft. Lauderdale, FL	2/8/09
897	1999 Lamborghini Diablo VT Roadster	$187,000	8	Gooding, Scottsdale, AZ	1/19/08
898	1930 Packard 745 4-Passenger Phaeton	$187,000	199	RM, Phoenix, AZ	1/16/09
899	1938 Packard Touring Sedan by Brunn	$187,000	SP170	RM, Ft. Lauderdale, FL	2/17/08
900	1936 Packard Eight Phaeton	$187,000	278	RM, Amelia Island, FL	3/8/08
901	1938 Packard Twelve Brunn Touring Cabriolet	$187,000	671	RM, Novi, MI	4/27/08
902	1934 Packard Model 1104 Super Eight Convertible Victoria	$187,000	268	RM, Rochester, MI	8/2/08
903	1932 Studebaker President Four-Seasons	$187,000	23	Gooding, Pebble Beach, CA	8/17/08
904	2001 Bentley Continental T Short Chassis Coupe	$186,300	263A	Bonhams, Monte Carlo, MCO	5/18/09
905	1980 BMW M1 Coupe	$186,300	242	Bonhams, Monte Carlo, MCO	5/18/09
906	1967 Shelby GT500 Fastback	$185,500	F226	Mecum, Indianapolis, IN	5/17/09
907	1967 Shelby GT500 Fastback	$185,500	F249	Mecum, Indianapolis, IN	5/17/09
908	1960 Aston Martin DB4 Series II	$185,133	226	Bonhams, Oxford, UK	3/8/09
909	1963 Aston Martin DB4 Series V Vantage Coupe	$184,975	331	Bonhams, Newport Pagnell, UK	5/9/09
910	1970 Plymouth Superbird 2-Door Hardtop	$184,800	649.1	Barrett-Jackson, West Palm Beach, FL	3/30/08
911	1969 Chevrolet Baldwin Motion Roadster	$184,800	F514	Russo and Steele, Scottsdale, AZ	1/20/08
912	1969 Chevrolet Camaro Coupe	$184,800	F520	Russo and Steele, Scottsdale, AZ	1/20/08
913	1970 Oldsmobile 442 W30 Convertible	$184,800	S716	Russo and Steele, Scottsdale, AZ	1/18/09

#872—1903 Toledo 12hp Touring Car

#879—1983 Lancia 037 Stradale Coupe

#907—1967 Shelby GT500 Fastback

Rank	Model	Sold Price	Lot #	Auction Location	Date
914	1970 Dodge Challenger 2-Door Hardtop	$184,250	S663	Russo and Steele, Hollywood, FL	3/30/08
915	1970 Chevrolet Chevelle SS 454 LS6 2-Door Hardtop	$184,250	SP36	RM, Ft. Lauderdale, FL	2/17/08
916	1911 Stanley Steamer 10hp Model 63 Toy Tonneau	$184,250	241	RM, Hershey, PA	10/10/08
917	1970 Dodge Challenger 440/6 2-Door Hardtop	$183,750	S183	Mecum, Indianapolis, IN	5/18/08
918	1970 Chevrolet Chevelle Convertible	$183,700	1274.1	Barrett-Jackson, Scottsdale, AZ	1/20/08
919	1969 Ford Mustang Boss 429 Custom Fastback	$183,700	1270.1	Barrett-Jackson, Scottsdale, AZ	1/18/09
920	1952 Citroën 11 Normale Traction Roadster	$183,425	135	Bonhams, Paris, FRA	2/9/08
921	1972 Ferrari 246 GTS Dino Spyder	$183,425	145	Bonhams, Paris, FRA	2/9/08
922	1928 Auburn 115S Boattail Speedster	$183,000	226	Bonhams & Butterfields, Greenwich, CT	6/7/09
923	1928 Rolls-Royce Phantom I Derby Speedster	$183,000	317	Bonhams & Butterfields, Carmel Valley, CA	8/15/08
924	1908 Sharp Arrow Runabout	$183,000	866	Bonhams & Butterfields, Owls Head, ME	9/27/08
925	1972 Ford Escort RS1600 Mk I Coupe	$181,685	328	Bonhams, Stoneleigh Park, UK	3/15/08
926	1957 Chevrolet Bel Air Custom Convertible	$181,500	1333.1	Barrett-Jackson, Scottsdale, AZ	1/20/08
927	1969 Chevrolet Chevelle COPO 2-Door Hardtop	$181,500	1279	Barrett-Jackson, Scottsdale, AZ	1/20/08
928	1958 Chevrolet Corvette 283/270 Convertible	$181,500	1231.1	Barrett-Jackson, Scottsdale, AZ	1/20/08
929	1969 Dodge Hemi Charger 500 2-Door Hardtop	$181,500	1270.1	Barrett-Jackson, Scottsdale, AZ	1/20/08
930	1918 Le Bestioni Boattail Speedster	$181,500	813	Barrett-Jackson, Las Vegas, NV	10/18/08
931	1970 Plymouth Superbird 2-Door Hardtop	$181,500	1268	Barrett-Jackson, Scottsdale, AZ	1/20/08
932	1967 Shelby GT500 Fastback	$181,500	789.4	Barrett-Jackson, Las Vegas, NV	10/18/08
933	1953 Cadillac Eldorado Convertible	$181,500	SP70	RM, Ft. Lauderdale, FL	2/17/08
934	1939 Cadillac V16 Convertible Sedan	$181,500	33	Worldwide, Auburn, IN	8/30/08
935	2007 Chevrolet Monte Carlo NASCAR Tony Stewart	$181,500	1575	Barrett-Jackson, Scottsdale, AZ	1/18/09
936	1955 Chrysler C-300 2-Door Hardtop	$181,500	144	RM, Anaheim, CA	6/29/08
937	1947 Chrysler C39 New Yorker Town & Country Convertible	$181,500	332	RM, Anaheim, CA	6/29/08
938	1936 Cord 810 Convertible Coupe	$181,500	139	RM, Phoenix, AZ	1/16/09
939	1930 Cord L-29 Cabriolet	$181,500	187	RM, Phoenix, AZ	1/16/09
940	1967 Ferrari 330 GTC	$181,500	S642	Russo and Steele, Monterey, CA	8/16/08
941	1969 Ford Mustang Boss 429 Fastback	$181,500	S641	Russo and Steele, Monterey, CA	8/16/08
942	1967 Ghia 450 SS Convertible	$181,500	1264	Barrett-Jackson, Scottsdale, AZ	1/18/09
943	1948 Hudson Commodore Eight Convertible	$181,500	266	RM, Dallas, TX	4/19/08
944	1961 Jaguar XK 150 3.8 Coupe	$181,500	428	RM, Monterey, CA	8/16/08
945	1967 Lamborghini 400 GT 2+2 Coupe	$181,500	425	RM, Monterey, CA	8/16/08
946	1972 Mercedes-Benz 280SE 3.5 Convertible	$181,500	50	Gooding, Scottsdale, AZ	1/17/09
947	1933 Pierce-Arrow Twelve Convertible Sedan	$181,500	150	RM, Phoenix, AZ	1/16/09
948	2006 Ford GT Hennessey Heritage Edition	$181,260	F234	Mecum, Indianapolis, IN	5/17/09
949	1956 Lincoln Premiere Convertible	$181,125	U45	Mecum, Indianapolis, IN	5/18/08
950	1964 Chevrolet Corvette Z06 Coupe	$180,600	S87	Mecum, St. Charles, IL	6/28/08
951	1970 Pontiac GTO Judge Ram Air IV "Tin Indian" 2-Door Hardtop	$180,200	S116	Mecum, Indianapolis, IN	5/17/09
952	1966 Shelby GT350 H Fastback	$180,200	n/a	Tom Mack, Concord, NC	4/5/08
953	1969 Ferrari 365 GTC Coupe	$180,185	530	Bonhams, Sussex, UK	7/11/08
954	1967 Chevrolet Corvette 427/435 Convertible	$178,750	SP91	RM, Ft. Lauderdale, FL	2/17/08
955	1957 Oldsmobile Starfire 98 Convertible	$178,750	256	RM, Dallas, TX	4/19/08
956	1934 Packard Super Eight Coupe Roadster	$178,750	145	RM, Phoenix, AZ	1/16/09
957	1967 Ferrari 206 GT Dino Coupe	$178,736	323	RM, Maranello, ITA	5/18/08

#916—1911 Stanley Steamer 10hp Model 63 Toy Tonneau

#925—1972 Ford Escort RS1600 Mk I Coupe

#946—1972 Mercedes-Benz 280SE 3.5 Convertible

#973—1969 Dodge Charger Daytona

#980—1939 Packard Twelve All-Weather Cabriolet by Brunn

#994—2001 Ferrari 550 Barchetta

Rank	Model	Sold Price	Lot #	Auction Location	Date
958	2005 Ferrari F360 GTC Racer	$178,736	342	RM, Maranello, ITA	5/18/08
959	1965 Aston Martin DB5 Coupe	$178,200	458	Coys, London, UK	7/5/08
960	1953 Buick Skylark Convertible	$178,200	476	Leake, Tulsa, OK	6/14/09
961	1966 Chevrolet Corvette 427/425 Convertible	$178,200	F503	Russo and Steele, Scottsdale, AZ	1/20/08
962	c.1953 Rolls-Royce Silver Wraith 4½-Liter Limousine	$178,020	146	Bonhams, Paris, FRA	2/7/09
963	1967 Lamborghini 400 GT Coupe	$177,998	591	Bonhams, Sussex, UK	7/11/08
964	1970 Monteverdi 375/S Series II Coupe	$177,998	534	Bonhams, Sussex, UK	7/11/08
965	1972 Ferrari 246 GT Dino Coupe	$177,800	123	Coys, Padua, ITA	10/25/08
966	1955 AC Ace Roadster	$177,650	19	H&H, Sparkford, UK	10/12/08
967	1977 Holden LX Torana A9X Sedan	$177,560	52	Shannons, Melbourne, AUS	3/10/08
968	1968 Shelby GT500 KR Convertible	$177,100	F521	Russo and Steele, Scottsdale, AZ	1/20/08
969	1931 Auburn 8-98 Boattail Speedster	$176,000	263	RM, Rochester, MI	8/2/08
970	1967 Chevrolet Corvette 427/430 Convertible	$176,000	1247	Barrett-Jackson, Scottsdale, AZ	1/18/09
971	1989 Chevrolet Corvette ZR-1 Coupe "Snake Skinner"	$176,000	396.1	Barrett-Jackson, Scottsdale, AZ	1/18/09
972	1959 Chevrolet Corvette 283/290 FI Convertible	$176,000	1238	Barrett-Jackson, Scottsdale, AZ	1/20/08
973	1969 Dodge Charger Daytona	$176,000	S687	Russo and Steele, Scottsdale, AZ	1/20/08
974	1957 Dual-Ghia Convertible	$176,000	168	RM, Phoenix, AZ	1/16/09
975	1957 Dual-Ghia Convertible	$176,000	486	RM, Monterey, CA	8/16/08
976	1954 Kaiser-Darrin Roadster	$176,000	1254	Barrett-Jackson, Scottsdale, AZ	1/18/09
977	1954 Kaiser-Darrin Roadster	$176,000	957	Barrett-Jackson, Scottsdale, AZ	1/20/08
978	1935 MG K-type to K3 Supercharged Specification	$176,000	167	RM, Phoenix, AZ	1/18/09
979	1939 Packard Model 1708 Convertible Sedan	$176,000	SP142	RM, Ft. Lauderdale, FL	2/8/09
980	1939 Packard Twelve All-Weather Cabriolet by Brunn	$176,000	236	RM, Rochester, MI	8/2/08
981	1934 Packard Twelve Formal Sedan	$176,000	260	RM, Rochester, MI	8/2/08
982	1931 Packard 840 Dual Cowl Phaeton	$176,000	53	Worldwide, Auburn, IN	8/30/08
983	1968 Shelby GT500 KR Fastback	$176,000	1338	Barrett-Jackson, Scottsdale, AZ	1/20/08
984	1968 Shelby GT500 KR Fastback	$176,000	224	RM, Dallas, TX	4/19/08
985	1969 Aston Martin DB6 Coupe	$175,420	342	Bonhams, Newport Pagnell, UK	5/17/08
986	1974 Ferrari 246 GTS Dino Spyder	$175,203	320	Coys, Ascot, UK	10/4/08
987	1937 Cord 812 SC Phaeton	$175,000	235	RM, Amelia Island, FL	3/14/09
988	2004 Ford Mustang GT Convertible Concept	$175,000	655	Barrett-Jackson, Palm Beach, FL	4/11/09
989	2004 Ford Mustang GT Coupe Concept	$175,000	655.1	Barrett-Jackson, Palm Beach, FL	4/11/09
990	1953 Cadillac Eldorado Convertible	$174,900	F254	Mecum, Kissimmee, FL	1/24/09
991	1970 Plymouth Hemi 'Cuda 2-Door Hardtop	$174,300	C39	Mecum, Indianapolis, IN	4/12/08
992	1937 Lagonda LG45 Drophead Coupe	$174,240	38	H&H, Harrogate, UK	4/16/08
993	1974 Ferrari 365 GT4 BB Coupe	$173,938	207	RM, Maranello, ITA	5/17/09
994	2001 Ferrari 550 Barchetta	$173,938	205	RM, Maranello, ITA	5/17/09
995	1954 Buick Skylark Convertible	$173,880	2477	Leake, Tulsa, OK	6/8/08
996	1961 Aston Martin DB4 Competition Coupe	$173,622	528	Bonhams, Sussex, UK	7/11/08
997	1973 Porsche 911 2.7 RS Touring Coupe	$173,552	226A	Bonhams, Silverstone, UK	7/26/08
998	1939 Alvis Speed 25 Tourer	$173,250	236	RM, Amelia Island, FL	3/14/09
999	1967 Chevrolet Corvette 427/435 Convertible	$173,250	X10	Mecum, St. Charles, IL	6/28/08
1000	1969 Dodge Daytona 440 2-Door Hardtop	$173,250	S108	Mecum, St. Charles, IL	10/5/08

The 1,000 Top Sellers, Arranged by Marque and Price

The easiest way to see which marques take up the most real estate in our list of big sellers.*

Model	Sold Price	Lot #	Auction Location	Date
1970 Abarth SE10	$366,520	209	Coys, Monte Carlo, MCO	5/10/08
1957 AC Ace Bristol Roadster	$258,500	1289	Barrett-Jackson, Scottsdale, AZ	1/20/08
1956 AC Ace Roadster	$216,000	229	Bonhams & Butterfields, Greenwich, CT	6/8/08
1959 AC Ace Bristol Roadster	$210,813	518	Bonhams, Sussex, UK	7/11/08
1936 AC 16/90 Competition	$199,902	22	Artcurial, Paris, FRA	2/8/09
1958 AC Ace Bristol Roadster	$195,437	82	H&H, Buxton, UK	6/10/09
1955 AC Ace Roadster	$177,650	19	H&H, Sparkford, UK	10/12/08
1938 Alfa Romeo 6C 2300 B Mille Miglia	$2,585,000	116	Gooding, Pebble Beach, CA	8/17/08
1932 Alfa Romeo 6C 1750 Gran Sport Spyder	$1,540,000	70	Gooding, Scottsdale, AZ	1/19/08
1931 Alfa Romeo 6C 1750 Gran Sport Spyder	$1,320,000	44	Gooding, Pebble Beach, CA	8/17/08
1930 Alfa Romeo 6C 1750 Spyder	$1,265,000	137	Gooding, Pebble Beach, CA	8/17/08
1930 Alfa Romeo 6C 1750 Gran Sport Spyder	$1,107,000	352	Bonhams & Butterfields, Carmel Valley, CA	8/15/08
1935 Alfa Romeo 6C 2300 Pescara Spyder	$1,079,681	55	H&H, Cheltenham, UK	2/27/08
1930 Alfa Romeo 6C 1750 Series IV Gran Sport Spyder	$880,000	77	Worldwide, Houston, TX	5/3/08
1952 Alfa Romeo 6C 2500 Sport Cabriolet Ville d'Este	$825,000	38	Worldwide, Houston, TX	5/3/08
1965 Alfa Romeo TZ Berlinetta	$465,735	325	Bonhams, Sussex, UK	9/19/08
1966 Alfa Romeo Giulia TZ-1 Coupe	$440,000	33	Gooding, Scottsdale, AZ	1/17/09
1942 Alfa Romeo 6C 2500 Sport Cabriolet	$345,400	69	Worldwide, Hilton Head, SC	11/1/08
1933 Alfa Romeo 6C 1750 6th Series Supercharged Gran Sport Cabriolet	$342,683	226	Bonhams, Gstaad, CHE	12/20/08
1940 Alfa Romeo 6C 2500 Sport Cabriolet by Graber	$341,000	482	RM, Monterey, CA	8/16/08
1928/1945 Alfa Romeo 1,500-cc Supercharged Race Car	$252,623	62	Bonhams & Goodman, Sydney, AUS	11/16/08
1949 Alfa Romeo 6C 2500 Super Sport Coupe	$198,000	174	RM, Phoenix, AZ	1/16/09
1951 Allard J2 Roadster	$308,000	67	Gooding, Pebble Beach, CA	8/17/08
1953 Allard J2X Roadster	$258,500	68	Gooding, Scottsdale, AZ	1/17/09
1950 Allard J2 Roadster	$253,000	169	RM, Phoenix, AZ	1/16/09
1950 Allard J2 Roadster	$220,000	S721	Russo and Steele, Scottsdale, AZ	1/20/08
1937 Alvis 4.3-Liter Short Chassis Vanden Plas Tourer	$295,020	89	H&H, Buxton, UK	4/16/09
1939 Alvis Speed 25 Tourer	$173,250	236	RM, Amelia Island, FL	3/14/09
1906 American Tourist Roi-des-Belges Touring Car	$612,000	854	Bonhams & Butterfields, Owls Head, ME	9/27/08
1954 Arnolt-Bristol Bolide Roadster	$252,787	125	Coys, Nürburgring, DEU	8/9/08
1959 Arnolt-Bristol Deluxe Competition Roadster	$205,521	143	Coys, Nürburgring, DEU	8/9/08
1961 Aston Martin DB4GT Coupe	$2,115,820	345	Bonhams, Newport Pagnell, UK	5/17/08
1966 Aston Martin DB6 Short Chassis Volante	$642,510	30	H&H, Harrogate, UK	4/16/08

Sales from the SCM Platinum Database, recorded between 1/1/2008 and 6/15/2009

1956 AC Ace Roadster

1949 Alfa Romeo 6C 2500 Super Sport Coupe

1937 Alvis 4.3-Liter Short Chassis Vanden Plas Tourer

Model	Sold Price	Lot #	Auction Location	Date
1968 Aston Martin DB6 Mk I Volante	$606,620	304	Bonhams, Newport Pagnell, UK	5/17/08
1970 Aston Martin DB6 Mk II Volante Convertible	$526,125	322	Bonhams, Sussex, UK	9/19/08
1961 Aston Martin DB4 SIII Coupe	$464,963	21	Artcurial, Paris, FRA	2/9/08
1969 Aston Martin DB6 Volante	$455,700	325	Bonhams, Newport Pagnell, UK	5/17/08
1958 Aston Martin DB4 Series I Coupe	$454,925	138	Bonhams, Monte Carlo, MCO	5/10/08
1962 Aston Martin DB4 Series IV Vantage	$413,820	37	H&H, Harrogate, UK	4/16/08
1960 Aston Martin DB4 Coupe	$409,577	316	Coys, Essen, DEU	3/29/08
1964 Aston Martin DB5 Coupe	$391,020	326	Bonhams, Newport Pagnell, UK	5/17/08
1965 Aston Martin DB5 4.2 Coupe	$375,990	340	Bonhams, Newport Pagnell, UK	5/9/09
1962 Aston Martin DB4 Convertible	$364,363	339	Bonhams, Newport Pagnell, UK	5/9/09
1955 Aston Martin DB2/4 Mk II Drophead Coupe	$358,680	335	Bonhams, Newport Pagnell, UK	5/17/08
1965 Aston Martin DB5 Coupe	$358,680	310	Bonhams, Newport Pagnell, UK	5/17/08
1968 Aston Martin DB6 Volante	$357,876	227	Coys, Brands Hatch, UK	5/25/08
1964 Aston Martin DB5 Coupe	$330,876	338	Coys, London, UK	3/3/08
1964 Aston Martin DB5 Coupe	$315,560	324	Bonhams, Newport Pagnell, UK	5/17/08
1967 Aston Martin DB6 Vantage Volante	$314,863	67	Bonhams & Goodman, Sydney, AUS	11/16/08
1963 Aston Martin DB5 Vantage-spec Coupe	$287,382	550	Bonhams, Sussex, UK	7/11/08
1964 Aston Martin DB5 4.2 Coupe	$284,635	327	Bonhams, Newport Pagnell, UK	5/9/09
1961 Aston Martin DB4 Series IV Coupe	$283,220	329	Bonhams, Newport Pagnell, UK	5/17/08
1960 Aston Martin DB4 SIII Coupe	$282,025	136	Bonhams, Paris, FRA	2/9/08
1959 Aston Martin DB Mk III Convertible	$267,375	125	Bonhams, Monte Carlo, MCO	5/10/08
1964 Aston Martin DB5 Coupe	$262,007	34	Artcurial, Paris, FRA	2/8/09
1989 Aston Martin V8 Vantage Volante X-Pack Convertible	$261,660	308	Bonhams, Newport Pagnell, UK	5/17/08
1953 Aston Martin DB2 Vantage Coupe	$249,550	173	Bonhams, Monte Carlo, MCO	5/10/08
1955 Aston Martin DB2/4 Drophead Coupe	$248,003	598	Bonhams, Sussex, UK	7/11/08
1965 Aston Martin DB5 Coupe	$240,279	358	Bonhams, Sussex, UK	9/19/08
1961 Aston Martin DB4 Series II Coupe	$240,100	321	Bonhams, Newport Pagnell, UK	5/17/08
1963 Aston Martin DB4 Series V Vantage Coupe	$240,100	307	Bonhams, Newport Pagnell, UK	5/17/08
1986 Aston Martin V8 Vantage Zagato Coupe	$240,100	316	Bonhams, Newport Pagnell, UK	5/17/08
1965 Aston Martin DB5 Coupe	$233,755	420	Coys, London, UK	3/12/09
1961 Aston Martin DB4 Coupe	$219,725	42	H&H, Buxton, UK	7/23/08
1964 Aston Martin DB4 SV Coupe	$210,198	239	Coys, Brands Hatch, UK	5/24/09
1965 Aston Martin DB5 Sports Coupe	$209,444	139	Bonhams, Monte Carlo, MCO	5/10/08
1989 Aston Martin V8 Vantage Volante	$207,760	338	Bonhams, Newport Pagnell, UK	5/17/08
1963 Aston Martin DB5 Mk I Coupe	$198,263	305	Bonhams, Newport Pagnell, UK	5/9/09
1989 Aston Martin V8 Vantage Volante X Pack Convertible	$194,941	328	Bonhams, Newport Pagnell, UK	5/9/09
1965 Aston Martin DB5 Coupe	$194,700	354	Coys, Ascot, UK	10/4/08
1965 Aston Martin DB6 Mk I 4.2 Vantage Coupe	$192,668	305	Bonhams, Newport Pagnell, UK	5/17/08
1960 Aston Martin DB4 Series II	$185,133	226	Bonhams, Oxford, UK	3/8/09
1963 Aston Martin DB4 Series V Vantage Coupe	$184,975	331	Bonhams, Newport Pagnell, UK	5/9/09
1965 Aston Martin DB5 Coupe	$178,200	458	Coys, London, UK	7/5/08
1969 Aston Martin DB6 Coupe	$175,420	342	Bonhams, Newport Pagnell, UK	5/17/08
1961 Aston Martin DB4 Competition Coupe	$173,622	528	Bonhams, Sussex, UK	7/11/08
1932 Auburn V12 Boattail Speedster	$687,500	126	Gooding, Pebble Beach, CA	8/17/08
1935 Auburn 851SC Boattail Speedster	$566,500	262	RM, Amelia Island, FL	3/14/09
1936 Auburn 852SC Boattail Speedster	$533,500	423	RM, Monterey, CA	8/16/08

1964 Aston Martin DB5 Coupe

1964 Aston Martin DB5 Coupe

1970 Aston Martin DB6 Mk II Volante

1935 Auburn 851 Boattail Speedster

1931 Avions Voisin C14 Chartre

1925 Bentley 3-Liter 100mph Supersports Brooklands 2-Seater

Model	Sold Price	Lot #	Auction Location	Date
1936 Auburn 852 Boattail Speedster	$396,000	146	RM, Phoenix, AZ	1/18/08
1934 Auburn Twelve Salon Phaeton Sedan	$319,000	154	RM, Phoenix, AZ	1/16/09
1931 Auburn 8-98 Speedster	$313,500	129	RM, Phoenix, AZ	1/18/08
1936 Auburn 852 Supercharged Boattail Speedster	$291,500	81	Worldwide, Seabrook, TX	5/2/09
1935 Auburn 851 Boattail Speedster	$264,000	6	Gooding, Scottsdale, AZ	1/17/09
1934 Auburn 1250 Salon Cabriolet	$253,000	669.1	Barrett-Jackson, Palm Beach, FL	4/11/09
1931 Auburn 8-98 Cabriolet	$203,500	130	RM, Phoenix, AZ	1/18/08
1928 Auburn 115S Boattail Speedster	$183,000	226	Bonhams & Butterfields, Greenwich, CT	6/7/09
1931 Auburn 8-98 Boattail Speedster	$176,000	263	RM, Rochester, MI	8/2/08
1935 Avions Voisin C25 Aerodyne	$757,178	8	Artcurial, Paris, FRA	2/9/08
1935 Avions Voisin C25 Clairière Berline	$330,000	35	Gooding, Scottsdale, AZ	1/17/09
1931 Avions Voisin C14 Chartre	$667,000	323	Bonhams & Butterfields, Carmel Valley, CA	8/15/08
1921 Avions Voisin OC1 Presidential Coupe	$359,000	321	Bonhams & Butterfields, Carmel Valley, CA	8/15/08
1967 Baja Boot Off Road Racing Buggy	$199,500	346	Bonhams & Butterfields, Carmel Valley, CA	8/15/08
1931 Bentley 8-Liter Open Tourer by Harrison	$2,200,000	263	RM, Amelia Island, FL	3/8/08
1931 Bentley 4½-Liter Blower	$1,760,000	114	Gooding, Pebble Beach, CA	8/17/08
1937 Bentley 4¼-Liter Fixed Head Sport Coupe	$1,320,000	62	Gooding, Scottsdale, AZ	1/17/09
1929 Bentley 4½-Liter Tourer	$880,000	135	RM, Phoenix, AZ	1/18/08
1927 Bentley Speed Six 2-Seater and Dickey	$568,000	354	Bonhams & Butterfields, Carmel Valley, CA	8/15/08
1929 Bentley 6½-Liter Sedanca Coupe	$561,000	146	Gooding, Pebble Beach, CA	8/17/08
1954 Bentley R-type Continental Fastback	$550,000	479	RM, Monterey, CA	8/16/08
1931 Bentley 8-Liter Sedanca deVille	$506,900	651	Bonhams, London, UK	12/1/08
1934 Bentley 3½-Liter Sports Tourer	$429,000	110	Gooding, Pebble Beach, CA	8/17/08
1925 Bentley 3-Liter 100mph Supersports Brooklands 2-Seater	$409,220	624	Bonhams, London, UK	12/1/08
1935 Bentley 3½-Liter Vanden Plas Tourer	$353,766	128	Coys, Nürburgring, DEU	8/9/08
1962 Bentley S3 Continental Flying Spur Sedan	$267,375	109	Bonhams, Monte Carlo, MCO	5/10/08
1962 Bentley S2 Continental	$264,000	258	RM, Hershey, PA	10/10/08
1937 Bentley 4¼-Liter All-Weather Thrupp & Maberly Tourer	$242,457	416	Coys, London, UK	7/5/08
1938 Bentley 4¼-Liter MX Vanden Plas Tourer	$236,056	225	Coys, Brands Hatch, UK	5/25/08
1937 Bentley 4¼-Liter Sedanca Coupe	$208,023	326	Coys, Essen, DEU	3/29/08
1936 Bentley 4¼-Liter Drophead Coupe	$200,836	608	Bonhams, London, UK	12/1/08
1960 Bentley S2 Continental Flying Spur	$200,100	128	Bonhams, Paris, FRA	2/9/08
2001 Bentley Continental T Short Chassis Coupe	$186,300	263A	Bonhams, Monte Carlo, MCO	5/18/09
1912 Benz 14/30 PS Touring	$216,000	752	Kruse, Phoenix, AZ	1/27/08
1966 Bizzarrini Strada 5300 Coupe	$572,000	S648	Russo and Steele, Monterey, CA	8/16/08
1967 Bizzarrini 5300 GT Strada Alloy	$517,000	124	Gooding, Pebble Beach, CA	8/17/08
2007 Blastolene B-702 Custom Roadster	$522,500	1310	Barrett-Jackson, Scottsdale, AZ	1/20/08
1937 BMW 328 Roadster	$685,100	134	Bonhams, Monte Carlo, MCO	5/10/08
1938 BMW 328 Roadster	$507,600	265	Bonhams, Monte Carlo, MCO	5/18/09
1937 BMW 328 Cabriolet	$302,500	245	RM, Amelia Island, FL	3/14/09
1938 BMW 327 Roadster	$278,569	167	Coys, Nürburgring, DEU	8/9/08
1935 BMW 319 Sport	$193,879	324	Coys, Essen, DEU	3/29/08
1980 BMW M1 Coupe	$186,300	242	Bonhams, Monte Carlo, MCO	5/18/09
1934 Brewster Ford Town Car	$198,000	253	RM, Amelia Island, FL	3/8/08
1937 Bugatti Type 57SC Atalante Coupe	$7,920,000	27	Gooding, Pebble Beach, CA	8/17/08

Top 1,000 Sales in 2008–09 by Marque

1932 Bugatti Type 55 Roadster

1994 Bugatti EB110 GT Coupe

1953 Buick Skylark Convertible

Model	Sold Price	Lot #	Auction Location	Date
1937 Bugatti Type 57S Atalante Coupe	$4,408,575	142	Bonhams, Paris, FRA	2/7/09
1932 Bugatti Type 55 Super Sport Roadster	$3,251,125	147	Bonhams, Monte Carlo, MCO	5/10/08
2009 Bugatti Veyron 16.4 Grand Sport	$3,190,000	134	Gooding, Pebble Beach, CA	8/17/08
1913 Bugatti Type 18 Sports 2-Seater "Black Bess"	$3,131,475	114	Bonhams, Paris, FRA	2/7/09
1929 Bugatti Type 43 Grand Sport	$1,924,875	120	Bonhams, Paris, FRA	2/9/08
1932 Bugatti Type 55 Roadster	$1,760,000	30	Gooding, Pebble Beach, CA	8/17/08
1927 Bugatti Type 35B Grand Prix	$1,457,500	25	Gooding, Pebble Beach, CA	8/17/08
1925/31 Bugatti Type 35A/51 Grand Prix	$907,500	35	Gooding, Pebble Beach, CA	8/17/08
1939 Bugatti Type 57C Atalante Coupe	$880,000	32	Gooding, Pebble Beach, CA	8/17/08
1937 Bugatti Type 57C Coupe	$731,500	17	Gooding, Scottsdale, AZ	1/19/08
1934 Bugatti Type 57 Cabriolet	$726,000	36	Gooding, Pebble Beach, CA	8/17/08
1926/41 Bugatti Type 35/Miller V8	$522,500	29	Gooding, Pebble Beach, CA	8/17/08
1934 Bugatti Type 59 3.3-Liter Supercharged Grand Prix	$495,000	50	Worldwide, Houston, TX	5/3/08
1935 Bugatti Type 57 Stelvio Cabriolet	$464,963	12	Artcurial, Paris, FRA	2/9/08
1925 Bugatti Type 30 Tourer	$449,500	125	Bonhams, Paris, FRA	2/9/08
1932 Bugatti Type 46 Sports Sedan	$440,000	31	Gooding, Pebble Beach, CA	8/17/08
1928 Bugatti Type 37A Grand Prix	$434,500	59	Worldwide, Houston, TX	5/3/08
1934 Bugatti Type 57 Stelvio Convertible	$419,500	281	Bonhams & Butterfields, Greenwich, CT	6/7/09
1936 Bugatti Type 57 Galibier Coupe	$416,877	16	Artcurial, Paris, FRA	6/28/08
1927 Bugatti Type 40 Roadster	$399,244	12	Artcurial, Paris, FRA	6/28/08
1936 Bugatti Type 57 Pillarless Coupe	$396,000	18	Gooding, Scottsdale, AZ	1/17/09
1939 Bugatti Type 57C Galibier Sport	$396,000	34	Gooding, Pebble Beach, CA	8/17/08
1934 Bugatti Type 57 Sports Sedan	$395,643	165	Bonhams, Paris, FRA	2/7/09
1934 Bugatti Type 57 Double Cabriolet Stelvio	$326,000	213	Bonhams & Butterfields, Greenwich, CT	6/8/08
1994 Bugatti EB110 GT Coupe	$315,115	135	Bonhams, Monte Carlo, MCO	5/10/08
1937 Bugatti Type 57 Sports Saloon	$281,624	34	H&H, Surrey, UK	6/8/08
1951 Bugatti Type 101 Coach	$269,265	119	Bonhams, Paris, FRA	2/9/08
1929 Bugatti Type 44 Dual-Cowl Phaeton	$264,000	28	Gooding, Pebble Beach, CA	8/17/08
1934 Bugatti Type 57 Ventoux	$256,500	230	Coys, Monte Carlo, MCO	5/18/09
1934 Bugatti Type 57 Galibier Sedan	$242,000	670	RM, Novi, MI	4/27/08
1934 Bugatti Type 57 Ventoux Coach	$215,108	110	Bonhams, Paris, FRA	2/7/09
1928 Bugatti Type 35B Replica	$214,500	246	RM, Tustin, CA	6/14/08
1927 Bugatti Type 38 Roadster	$198,000	33	Gooding, Pebble Beach, CA	8/17/08
1996 Buick Custom "Blackhawk"	$522,500	1303	Barrett-Jackson, Scottsdale, AZ	1/18/09
1953 Buick Skylark Convertible	$264,000	137	RM, Phoenix, AZ	1/18/08
1935 Buick 67C Custom Convertible	$242,000	1276.1	Barrett-Jackson, Scottsdale, AZ	1/20/08
1954 Buick Skylark Convertible	$242,000	121	RM, Phoenix, AZ	1/18/08
1954 Buick Skylark Convertible	$220,000	267	RM, Dallas, TX	4/19/08
1953 Buick Skylark Convertible	$214,500	1260	Barrett-Jackson, Scottsdale, AZ	1/20/08
1957 Buick Model 70 Roadmaster Convertible	$214,500	44	Worldwide, Houston, TX	5/3/08
1953 Buick Skylark Convertible	$203,500	245	RM, Dallas, TX	4/19/08
1954 Buick Skylark Convertible	$200,200	62	Worldwide, Auburn, IN	8/30/08
1958 Buick Limited Convertible	$198,000	128	RM, Phoenix, AZ	1/18/08
1934 Buick Series 90 Convertible Coupe	$187,000	137	RM, Phoenix, AZ	1/16/09
1954 Buick Skylark Convertible	$187,000	SP68	RM, Ft. Lauderdale, FL	2/8/09

Model	Sold Price	Lot #	Auction Location	Date
1953 Buick Skylark Convertible	$178,200	476	Leake, Tulsa, OK	6/14/09
1954 Buick Skylark Convertible	$173,880	2477	Leake, Tulsa, OK	6/8/08
1930 Cadillac 452A V16 Roadster	$693,000	128	Gooding, Pebble Beach, CA	8/17/08
1931 Cadillac 452A V16 Sport Phaeton	$632,500	13	Gooding, Scottsdale, AZ	1/17/09
1938 Cadillac V16 Convertible Coupe	$616,000	158	RM, Anaheim, CA	6/29/08
1931 Cadillac V16 Sport Phaeton	$522,500	251	RM, Amelia Island, FL	3/8/08
1935 Cadillac V16 Imperial Convertible Sedan	$473,000	148	RM, Phoenix, AZ	1/16/09
1953 Cadillac Eldorado Convertible	$440,000	247	RM, Dallas, TX	4/19/08
1939 Cadillac V16 Convertible Coupe	$330,000	161	RM, Phoenix, AZ	1/18/08
1930 Cadillac V16 Convertible Coupe by Fleetwood	$324,500	238	RM, Rochester, MI	8/2/08
1930 Cadillac V16 Sport Phaeton	$302,500	138	RM, Phoenix, AZ	1/18/08
1959 Cadillac Eldorado Seville 3-Position Cabriolet	$302,500	257	RM, Monterey, CA	8/16/08
1931 Cadillac V16 Roadster	$297,000	26	Gooding, Scottsdale, AZ	1/19/08
1996 Cadillac Fleetwood Presidential Series Limo	$275,000	1328	Barrett-Jackson, Scottsdale, AZ	1/20/08
1931 Cadillac 452A V16 All-Weather Phaeton	$231,000	19	Worldwide, Seabrook, TX	5/2/09
1932 Cadillac 452B V16 All-Weather Phaeton	$231,000	22	Gooding, Scottsdale, AZ	1/17/09
1956 Cadillac Eldorado Convertible	$231,000	SP68	RM, Ft. Lauderdale, FL	2/17/08
1947 Cadillac Series 75 7-Passenger Imperial Sedan	$231,000	264	RM, Dallas, TX	4/19/08
1959 Cadillac Eldorado Biarritz Convertible	$231,000	232	RM, Rochester, MI	8/2/08
1959 Cadillac Eldorado Convertible	$221,400	2488	Leake, Tulsa, OK	6/8/08
1957 Cadillac Eldorado Brougham	$220,000	263	RM, Dallas, TX	4/19/08
1959 Cadillac Series 62 Convertible	$216,000	2469	Leake, Oklahoma City, OK	2/23/08
1931 Cadillac 370-A V12 Dual Cowl Sport Phaeton	$214,500	27	Worldwide, Seabrook, TX	5/2/09
1929 Cadillac 341B Eight Sport Dual Cowl Phaeton	$209,000	47	Worldwide, Auburn, IN	8/30/08
1931 Cadillac V16 Convertible Sedan	$199,800	400	Leake, Tulsa, OK	6/14/09
1959 Cadillac Eldorado Biarritz Convertible	$198,000	SP73	RM, Ft. Lauderdale, FL	2/17/08
1931 Cadillac Series 370 V12 Dual Cowl Sport Phaeton	$198,000	28	Worldwide, Houston, TX	5/3/08
1936 Cadillac Series 90 V16 Convertible Sedan	$194,000	512	Bonhams & Butterfields, Brookline, MA	10/4/08
1931 Cadillac V12 5-Passenger Phaeton by Fleetwood	$192,500	249	RM, Rochester, MI	8/2/08
1937 Cadillac V16 Custom Imperial Cabriolet by Fleetwood	$192,500	233	RM, Rochester, MI	8/2/08
1953 Cadillac Eldorado Convertible	$181,500	SP70	RM, Ft. Lauderdale, FL	2/17/08
1939 Cadillac V16 Convertible Sedan	$181,500	33	Worldwide, Auburn, IN	8/30/08
1953 Cadillac Eldorado Convertible	$174,900	F254	Mecum, Kissimmee, FL	1/24/09
1962 Chaparral 1 Sports Racer	$522,500	460	RM, Monterey, CA	8/16/08
1963 Chevrolet Corvette "Rondine" Concept Car	$1,760,000	1304	Barrett-Jackson, Scottsdale, AZ	1/20/08
1962 Chevrolet Corvette 327/360 Gulf Oil Race Car	$1,485,000	121	Gooding, Pebble Beach, CA	8/17/08
1963 Chevrolet Corvette Z06 Yenko "Gulf One" Race Car	$1,113,000	S110	Mecum, Kissimmee, FL	1/24/09
2009 Chevrolet Corvette ZR-1 Coupe	$1,100,000	1316	Barrett-Jackson, Scottsdale, AZ	1/20/08
1969 Chevrolet Camaro RS ZL1 Coupe	$800,000	S99	Mecum, Indianapolis, IN	5/18/08
1967 Chevrolet Corvette L88 Competition Convertible	$744,000	355	Bonhams & Butterfields, Carmel Valley, CA	8/15/08
1969 Chevrolet Camaro RCR Series 3 Coupe	$632,500	1303	Barrett-Jackson, Scottsdale, AZ	1/20/08
2006 Chevrolet Monte Carlo NASCAR Jeff Gordon	$550,000	1274	Barrett-Jackson, Scottsdale, AZ	1/18/09
1971 Chevrolet Corvette ZR2 Convertible	$550,000	S107	Mecum, St. Charles, IL	6/28/08
1970 Chevrolet Chevelle SS 454 LS6 Convertible	$525,000	S103	Mecum, Indianapolis, IN	5/18/08
1967 Chevrolet Camaro Yenko Coupe	$504,000	S105	Mecum, Indianapolis, IN	5/18/08

1930 Cadillac V16 Convertible Coupe by Fleetwood

1962 Chaparral 1 Sports Racer

1969 Chevrolet Camaro RS ZL1 Coupe

Top 1,000 Sales in 2008–09 by Marque

Model	Sold Price	Lot #	Auction Location	Date
1969 Chevrolet Camaro ZL1 Coupe	$504,000	S109	Mecum, Indianapolis, IN	5/18/08
1969 Chevrolet Camaro RS/SS Custom "Project American Heroes"	$500,000	369.1	Barrett-Jackson, Palm Beach, FL	4/11/09
1967 Chevrolet Camaro RS/SS Nickey Coupe	$446,250	S97	Mecum, St. Charles, IL	10/5/08
1969 Chevrolet Corvette L88 Convertible	$435,750	S91	Mecum, St. Charles, IL	6/28/08
1969 Chevrolet Corvette L88 Coupe	$412,500	S714	Russo and Steele, Scottsdale, AZ	1/20/08
1970 Chevrolet Chevelle 454 LS6 Convertible	$397,500	S126	Mecum, Indianapolis, IN	5/17/09
2010 Chevrolet Camaro Coupe 1st Production	$385,000	1316	Barrett-Jackson, Scottsdale, AZ	1/18/09
1971 Chevrolet Corvette ZR2 Coupe	$357,500	1290	Barrett-Jackson, Scottsdale, AZ	1/20/08
1965 Chevrolet Chevelle SS Z16 2-Door Hardtop Prototype	$355,100	S122	Mecum, Indianapolis, IN	5/17/09
1969 Chevrolet Chevelle 2-Door Hardtop	$341,000	S711	Russo and Steele, Scottsdale, AZ	1/20/08
1967 Chevrolet Corvette 427/400 Convertible	$336,000	S73	Mecum, St. Charles, IL	6/28/08
2007 Chevrolet Monte Carlo NASCAR "Tony Stewart"	$330,000	1012	Barrett-Jackson, Scottsdale, AZ	1/20/08
1969 Chevrolet Chevelle COPO 2-Door Hardtop	$328,600	S124	Mecum, Indianapolis, IN	5/17/09
1955 Chevrolet Corvette Duntov EX-87 Test Mule	$328,600	F208	Mecum, Indianapolis, IN	5/17/09
1969 Chevrolet Corvette 427/430 L88 Convertible	$323,300	S142	Mecum, Kissimmee, FL	1/24/09
1969 Chevrolet Camaro ZL1 COPO Coupe	$319,000	1277.1	Barrett-Jackson, Scottsdale, AZ	1/18/09
1970 Chevrolet Chevelle 454 LS6 2-Door Hardtop	$318,000	S127	Mecum, Indianapolis, IN	5/17/09
1963 Chevrolet Corvette 327/360 Z06 Coupe	$300,000	142	Gooding, Pebble Beach, CA	8/17/08
1969 Chevrolet Camaro Yenko COPO Coupe	$297,000	1278	Barrett-Jackson, Scottsdale, AZ	1/18/09
1970 Chevrolet Chevelle SS 454 LS6 Convertible	$294,000	S111	Mecum, Indianapolis, IN	5/18/08
1989 Chevrolet Corvette DR-1 Convertible	$286,000	1218	Barrett-Jackson, Scottsdale, AZ	1/18/09
1969 Chevrolet Camaro Yenko Coupe	$280,900	S128	Mecum, Indianapolis, IN	5/17/09
1956 Chevrolet Bel Air 2-Door Hardtop Custom	$280,500	1256	Barrett-Jackson, Scottsdale, AZ	1/20/08
2004 Chevrolet Monte Carlo SS NASCAR #8	$275,000	S696	Russo and Steele, Scottsdale, AZ	1/18/09
1959 Chevrolet Corvette 283/290 FI Competition Convertible	$275,000	260	RM, Amelia Island, FL	3/8/08
1969 Chevrolet Camaro Coupe	$270,600	F516	Russo and Steele, Scottsdale, AZ	1/20/08
1955 Chevrolet Corvette Roadster	$270,000	753	Kruse, Phoenix, AZ	1/27/08
1957 Chevrolet Corvette 283/283 FI Convertible	$265,000	S138	Mecum, Kissimmee, FL	1/24/09
1953 Chevrolet Corvette Roadster	$264,000	182	RM, Phoenix, AZ	1/18/08
1969 Chevrolet Camaro RS/SS NASCAR Pace Car Convertible	$258,500	F524	Russo and Steele, Scottsdale, AZ	1/18/09
1955 Chevrolet Newmad Street Rod Wagon	$258,500	201	RM, Phoenix, AZ	1/16/09
1969 Chevrolet Chevelle Yenko 2-Door Hardtop	$252,000	S80	Mecum, Indianapolis, IN	5/18/08
1969 Chevrolet Camaro Yenko Coupe	$250,000	S173	Mecum, St. Charles, IL	10/5/08
1953 Chevrolet Corvette Roadster	$249,900	S109	Mecum, Kissimmee, FL	1/26/08
1967 Chevrolet Corvette 427/435 Convertible	$246,750	X9	Mecum, St. Charles, IL	6/28/08
1958 Chevrolet Corvette 283/240 Convertible	$242,000	990.1	Barrett-Jackson, Scottsdale, AZ	1/20/08
1965 Chevrolet Chevelle Z16	$238,875	S112	Mecum, Kissimmee, FL	1/26/08
1963 Chevrolet Corvette 327/360 Z06 Coupe	$233,625	B34	Mecum, Indianapolis, IN	4/5/08
1969 Chevrolet Camaro COPO Coupe	$231,000	F459	Russo and Steele, Hollywood, FL	3/30/08
1968 Chevrolet Corvette L88 Coupe	$231,000	S6	Mecum, St. Charles, IL	6/28/08
1990 Chevrolet Corvette ZR-1 Coupe (w/5 others)	$231,000	S32	Mecum, St. Charles, IL	6/28/08
1969 Chevrolet Camaro COPO Coupe	$225,250	S149	Mecum, Indianapolis, IN	5/17/09
1967 Chevrolet Corvette 427/435 Convertible	$220,000	1267	Barrett-Jackson, Scottsdale, AZ	1/20/08

1967 Chevrolet Corvette 427/400 Convertible

1969 Chevrolet Camaro RS/SS NASCAR Pace Car Convertible

1958 Chevrolet Corvette 283/240 Convertible

1965 Chevrolet Chevelle Z16 2-Door Hardtop

1968 Chevrolet Corvette 427/435 L89 Coupe

1989 Chevrolet Corvette ZR-1 Coupe "Snake Skinner"

Model	Sold Price	Lot #	Auction Location	Date
1959 Chevrolet Corvette 283/245 Convertible	$220,000	1019	Barrett-Jackson, Scottsdale, AZ	1/18/09
1970 Chevrolet Chevelle Convertible	$220,000	S701	Russo and Steele, Scottsdale, AZ	1/20/08
1970 Chevrolet Chevelle LS6 COPO SS 2-Door Hardtop	$214,500	1279.1	Barrett-Jackson, Scottsdale, AZ	1/20/08
1957 Chevrolet Corvette LS7 Custom Convertible	$214,500	1276	Barrett-Jackson, Scottsdale, AZ	1/20/08
1994 Chevrolet Lumina NASCAR Winston Cup Car	$209,000	221	RM, Tustin, CA	6/14/08
1970 Chevrolet Chevelle LS6 SS Convertible	$203,500	1324	Barrett-Jackson, Scottsdale, AZ	1/20/08
2006 Chevrolet Monte Carlo NASCAR Jimmie Johnson #48	$200,000	672	Barrett-Jackson, Palm Beach, FL	4/11/09
1958 Chevrolet Corvette 283/290 FI Convertible	$198,000	1272	Barrett-Jackson, Scottsdale, AZ	1/20/08
1967 Chevrolet Corvette 427/435 Coupe	$198,000	1327	Barrett-Jackson, Scottsdale, AZ	1/20/08
1953 Chevrolet Corvette Roadster	$198,000	278	RM, Amelia Island, FL	3/14/09
1989 Chevrolet Corvette ZR-1 Coupe	$198,000	1230.4	Barrett-Jackson, Scottsdale, AZ	1/18/09
1955 Chevrolet Nomad Custom Wagon	$198,000	1255	Barrett-Jackson, Scottsdale, AZ	1/18/09
1970 Chevrolet Chevelle LS6 SS Coupe	$195,250	1254	Barrett-Jackson, Scottsdale, AZ	1/20/08
1965 Chevrolet Chevelle Z16 2-Door Hardtop	$194,700	660	Barrett-Jackson, West Palm Beach, FL	3/30/08
1960 Chevrolet Corvette 283/290 FI Convertible	$192,500	1045	Barrett-Jackson, Scottsdale, AZ	1/20/08
1954 Chevrolet Corvette Roadster	$192,500	1259	Barrett-Jackson, Scottsdale, AZ	1/20/08
1963 Chevrolet Corvette 327/360 Z06 Coupe	$192,500	287	RM, Amelia Island, FL	3/14/09
1968 Chevrolet Corvette 427/435 L89 Coupe	$192,500	F513	Russo and Steele, Scottsdale, AZ	1/20/08
1969 Chevrolet Camaro Coupe	$192,500	71	Gooding, Pebble Beach, CA	8/17/08
1968 Chevrolet Camaro SS 396 Convertible	$190,800	S117	Mecum, Indianapolis, IN	5/17/09
1970 Chevrolet Chevelle 396 Convertible	$190,800	S125	Mecum, Indianapolis, IN	5/17/09
1970 Chevrolet Corvette ZR1 Coupe	$189,000	S108	Mecum, St. Charles, IL	6/28/08
1967 Chevrolet Corvette 427/435 Convertible	$188,000	S135	Mecum, Kissimmee, FL	1/26/08
1969 Chevrolet Camaro Coupe	$187,000	1269.1	Barrett-Jackson, Scottsdale, AZ	1/20/08
1965 Chevrolet Chevelle Malibu SS 2-Door Hardtop	$187,000	1315	Barrett-Jackson, Scottsdale, AZ	1/20/08
1958 Chevrolet Corvette LS2 Custom Convertible	$187,000	788	Barrett-Jackson, Las Vegas, NV	10/18/08
1969 Chevrolet Baldwin Motion Roadster	$184,800	F514	Russo and Steele, Scottsdale, AZ	1/20/08
1969 Chevrolet Camaro Coupe	$184,800	F520	Russo and Steele, Scottsdale, AZ	1/20/08
1970 Chevrolet Chevelle SS 454 LS6 2-Door Hardtop	$184,250	SP36	RM, Ft. Lauderdale, FL	2/17/08
1970 Chevrolet Chevelle Convertible	$183,700	1274.1	Barrett-Jackson, Scottsdale, AZ	1/20/08
1957 Chevrolet Bel Air Custom Convertible	$181,500	1333.1	Barrett-Jackson, Scottsdale, AZ	1/20/08
1969 Chevrolet Chevelle COPO 2-Door Hardtop	$181,500	1279	Barrett-Jackson, Scottsdale, AZ	1/20/08
1958 Chevrolet Corvette 283/270 Convertible	$181,500	1231.1	Barrett-Jackson, Scottsdale, AZ	1/20/08
2007 Chevrolet Monte Carlo NASCAR Tony Stewart	$181,500	1575	Barrett-Jackson, Scottsdale, AZ	1/18/09
1964 Chevrolet Corvette Z06 Coupe	$180,600	S87	Mecum, St. Charles, IL	6/28/08
1967 Chevrolet Corvette 427/435 Convertible	$178,750	SP91	RM, Ft. Lauderdale, FL	2/17/08
1966 Chevrolet Corvette 427/425 Convertible	$178,200	F503	Russo and Steele, Scottsdale, AZ	1/20/08
1967 Chevrolet Corvette 427/430 Convertible	$176,000	1247	Barrett-Jackson, Scottsdale, AZ	1/18/09
1989 Chevrolet Corvette ZR-1 Coupe "Snake Skinner"	$176,000	396.1	Barrett-Jackson, Scottsdale, AZ	1/18/09
1959 Chevrolet Corvette 283/290 FI Convertible	$176,000	1238	Barrett-Jackson, Scottsdale, AZ	1/20/08
1967 Chevrolet Corvette 427/435 Convertible	$173,250	X10	Mecum, St. Charles, IL	6/28/08
1954 Chrisman Bonneville Coupe	$660,000	235	RM, Tustin, CA	6/14/08
1941 Chrysler Thunderbolt LeBaron	$1,320,000	140	RM, Phoenix, AZ	1/18/08
1941 Chrysler Newport LeBaron	$748,000	141	RM, Phoenix, AZ	1/18/08
1941 Chrysler Newport Dual Cowl Phaeton	$687,500	270	RM, Amelia Island, FL	3/14/09

1947 Chrysler Town & Country Sedan Big Red

1936 Cord 810 Convertible Phaeton

1952 Delahaye 235 Drophead Coupe

Model	Sold Price	Lot #	Auction Location	Date
1932 Chrysler CL Imperial Convertible Roadster by LeBaron	$660,000	240	RM, Rochester, MI	8/2/08
1931 Chrysler CG Imperial Dual Cowl Phaeton	$605,000	28	Gooding, Scottsdale, AZ	1/17/09
1933 Chrysler CL Imperial Sport Phaeton by LeBaron	$462,000	167	RM, Anaheim, CA	6/29/08
1941 Chrysler Town & Country Nine-Passenger Estate Wagon	$335,500	148	RM, Anaheim, CA	6/29/08
1947 Chrysler Town & Country Sedan Big Red	$330,000	191	RM, Phoenix, AZ	1/16/09
1941 Chrysler Town & Country Barrel Back Estate Wagon	$313,500	132	RM, Phoenix, AZ	1/18/08
1959 Chrysler Imperial Crown Convertible	$297,000	350A	RM, Anaheim, CA	6/29/08
1931 Chrysler CG Imperial Dual Cowl Phaeton	$275,000	1271	Barrett-Jackson, Scottsdale, AZ	1/18/09
1955 Chrysler C-300 2-Door Hardtop	$181,500	144	RM, Anaheim, CA	6/29/08
1947 Chrysler C39 New Yorker Town & Country Convertible	$181,500	332	RM, Anaheim, CA	6/29/08
1948 Cisitalia 202 Nuvolari MM Spyder	$313,925	123	Bonhams, Paris, FRA	2/9/08
1973 Citroën DS23 ie Cabriolet	$435,375	123	Bonhams, Paris, FRA	2/7/09
1974 Citroën SM "Opera" Sedan	$250,905	122	Bonhams, Paris, FRA	2/7/09
1966 Citroën DS21 "Palm Beach" Cabriolet	$222,525	117	Bonhams, Paris, FRA	2/7/09
1968 Citroën DS21 Convertible	$205,216	40	Artcurial, Paris, FRA	2/9/08
1969 Citroën DS21 Convertible	$196,765	152	Bonhams, Paris, FRA	2/9/08
1952 Citroën 11 Normale Traction Roadster	$183,425	135	Bonhams, Paris, FRA	2/9/08
1902 Clément Twin-Cylinder 9hp 4-Seater Rear-Entrance Tonneau	$242,250	301	Bonhams, London, UK	10/31/08
1964 Cooper Monaco King Cobra Sports Racer	$636,000	F237	Mecum, Indianapolis, IN	5/17/09
1929 Cord L-29 Hayes Coupe	$1,078,000	141	Gooding, Pebble Beach, CA	8/17/08
1937 Cord 812 SC Convertible Coupe	$484,000	180	RM, Phoenix, AZ	1/16/09
1937 Cord 812 Supercharged Phaeton	$401,500	S713	Russo and Steele, Scottsdale, AZ	1/18/09
1937 Cord 812 Supercharged Phaeton	$363,000	48	Gooding, Scottsdale, AZ	1/19/08
1937 Cord 812 SC Phaeton	$313,500	150	RM, Phoenix, AZ	1/18/08
1937 Cord 812 SC Phaeton	$291,500	261	RM, Amelia Island, FL	3/8/08
1936 Cord 810 Phaeton	$269,500	136	Gooding, Pebble Beach, CA	8/17/08
1937 Cord 812 Coupe	$264,000	134	RM, Phoenix, AZ	1/18/08
1937 Cord 812 SC Sportsman Convertible Coupe	$242,000	63	Worldwide, Auburn, IN	8/30/08
1937 Cord 812 SC Convertible Coupe	$220,000	238	RM, Amelia Island, FL	3/8/08
1937 Cord 812 Supercharged Phaeton	$198,000	56	Worldwide, Seabrook, TX	5/2/09
1936 Cord 810 Convertible Phaeton	$198,000	52	Worldwide, Auburn, IN	8/30/08
1936 Cord 810 Convertible Coupe	$181,500	139	RM, Phoenix, AZ	1/16/09
1930 Cord L-29 Cabriolet	$181,500	187	RM, Phoenix, AZ	1/16/09
1937 Cord 812 SC Phaeton	$175,000	235	RM, Amelia Island, FL	3/14/09
1953 Cunningham C-3 Cabriolet	$255,000	252	RM, Amelia Island, FL	3/14/09
1932 Daimler 40/50 Double Six Sport Saloon	$2,970,000	39	Gooding, Scottsdale, AZ	1/17/09
1939 Deco Rides Bugnotti Roadster	$203,500	38	Gooding, Scottsdale, AZ	1/17/09
1937 Delage D8-120 Aerosport Coupe	$825,000	132	RM, Phoenix, AZ	1/16/09
1931 Delage D8 4-Seat Sports Tourer	$480,500	136	Bonhams, Monte Carlo, MCO	5/10/08
1935 Delage D8-85 Clabot Roadster	$407,000	30	Worldwide, Auburn, IN	8/30/08
1952 Delahaye 235 Drophead Coupe	$280,500	208	RM, Phoenix, AZ	1/16/09
1948 Delahaye 135 M Pennock Cabriolet	$211,457	20	Artcurial, Paris, FRA	2/8/09
1946 Delahaye 135M Cabriolet	$200,100	108	Bonhams, Paris, FRA	2/9/08

Model	Sold Price	Lot #	Auction Location	Date
1958 DeSoto Firesweep Convertible	$187,000	1252	Barrett-Jackson, Scottsdale, AZ	1/20/08
1954 Dodge Firearrow III Sports Coupe Concept Car	$880,000	170	RM, Phoenix, AZ	1/16/09
1969 Dodge Charger 2-Door Hardtop "General Lee"	$495,000	1321	Barrett-Jackson, Scottsdale, AZ	1/20/08
2008 Dodge Challenger SRT8 Coupe #001	$440,000	1331	Barrett-Jackson, Scottsdale, AZ	1/20/08
1970 Dodge Hemi Coronet R/T Convertible	$404,250	S108	Mecum, Indianapolis, IN	5/18/08
1971 Dodge Hemi Challenger R/T 2-Door Hardtop	$390,500	F520	Russo and Steele, Scottsdale, AZ	1/18/09
2008 Dodge Viper SRT-10 50th Anniversary Hurst Coupe	$275,000	1328	Barrett-Jackson, Scottsdale, AZ	1/18/09
1970 Dodge Challenger R/T 440/6 Convertible	$265,000	S181	Mecum, Indianapolis, IN	5/18/08
1971 Dodge Hemi Challenger R/T 2-Door Hardtop	$247,500	S702	Russo and Steele, Scottsdale, AZ	1/18/09
1971 Dodge Hemi Challenger 2-Door Hardtop	$231,000	32	Worldwide, Houston, TX	5/3/08
1970 Dodge Challenger 2-Door Hardtop	$217,800	S696	Russo and Steele, Scottsdale, AZ	1/20/08
1971 Dodge Hemi Charger R/T 2-Door Hardtop	$215,000	S173	Mecum, Indianapolis, IN	5/18/08
1969 Dodge Daytona 2-Door Hardtop	$206,700	S154	Mecum, Kissimmee, FL	1/24/09
1970 Dodge Challenger 440 Convertible	$201,400	S190	Mecum, Indianapolis, IN	5/17/09
1970 Dodge Challenger 2-Door Hardtop	$184,250	S663	Russo and Steele, Hollywood, FL	3/30/08
1970 Dodge Challenger 440/6 2-Door Hardtop	$183,750	S183	Mecum, Indianapolis, IN	5/18/08
1969 Dodge Hemi Charger 500 2-Door Hardtop	$181,500	1270.1	Barrett-Jackson, Scottsdale, AZ	1/20/08
1969 Dodge Charger 2-Door Hardtop	$176,000	S687	Russo and Steele, Scottsdale, AZ	1/20/08
1969 Dodge Daytona 440 2-Door Hardtop	$173,250	S108	Mecum, St. Charles, IL	10/5/08
1958 Dual-Ghia Convertible	$319,000	63	Worldwide, Hilton Head, SC	11/1/08
1957 Dual-Ghia Convertible	$319,000	257	RM, Dallas, TX	4/19/08
1963 Dual-Ghia L6.4 Coupe	$275,000	258	RM, Dallas, TX	4/19/08
1958 Dual-Ghia Convertible	$209,000	254	RM, Amelia Island, FL	3/14/09
1957 Dual-Ghia Convertible	$176,000	168	RM, Phoenix, AZ	1/16/09
1957 Dual-Ghia Convertible	$176,000	486	RM, Monterey, CA	8/16/08
1931 Duesenberg Model J Convertible Coupe by Murphy	$2,640,000	241	RM, Amelia Island, FL	3/8/08
1929 Duesenberg Model J Dual Cowl Phaeton	$1,760,000	136	RM, Phoenix, AZ	1/18/08
1930 Duesenberg Model J Dual Cowl Phaeton	$1,760,000	441	RM, Monterey, CA	8/16/08
1933 Duesenberg Model SJ Phaeton	$1,688,500	242	RM, Hershey, PA	10/10/08
1929 Duesenberg Model J Convertible Coupe	$1,413,500	457	RM, Monterey, CA	8/16/08
1929 Duesenberg Model J Dual Cowl Phaeton	$1,375,000	9	Gooding, Scottsdale, AZ	1/17/09
1929 Duesenberg Model J Convertible Berline by LeBaron	$1,210,000	257	RM, Amelia Island, FL	3/8/08
1936 Duesenberg Model J Clear Vision Sedan	$1,100,000	42	Gooding, Scottsdale, AZ	1/19/08
1928 Duesenberg Model J Dual Cowl Phaeton	$1,100,000	1311	Barrett-Jackson, Scottsdale, AZ	1/20/08
1930 Duesenberg Model J Convertible Coupe	$1,072,500	247	RM, Amelia Island, FL	3/14/09
1929 Duesenberg Model J Convertible Coupe	$858,000	152	RM, Phoenix, AZ	1/16/09
1929 Duesenberg Model J Clear Vision Sedan	$836,000	34	Gooding, Scottsdale, AZ	1/17/09
1929 Duesenberg J Convertible Coupe by Murphy	$748,000	234	RM, Rochester, MI	8/2/08
1929 Duesenberg Model J Derham Convertible Coupe	$742,500	40	Worldwide, Auburn, IN	8/30/08
1933 Duesenberg Model J Franay Touring Sedan	$777,600	581	Cox, Branson, MO	4/18/09
1934 ERA A-type Prototype Single Seater	$713,979	560	Bonhams, Sussex, UK	7/11/08
1957 Ferrari 250 Testa Rossa	$12,402,500	237	RM, Maranello, ITA	5/17/09
1961 Ferrari 250 GT SWB California Spyder	$10,894,400	328	RM, Maranello, ITA	5/18/08
1964 Ferrari 250 LM Sports Racer	$6,979,225	339A	RM, Maranello, ITA	5/18/08
1960 Ferrari 250 GT LWB California Spyder	$4,950,000	78	Gooding, Scottsdale, AZ	1/17/09

1954 Dodge Firearrow III Sports Coupe Concept Car

1957 Dual-Ghia Convertible

1929 Duesenberg Model J Derham Convertible Coupe

Top 1,000 Sales in 2008–09 by Marque

Model	Sold Price	Lot #	Auction Location	Date
1961 Ferrari 250 GT SWB Berlinetta	$4,510,000	447	RM, Monterey, CA	8/16/08
1958 Ferrari 250 GT LWB California Spyder	$3,659,838	337	RM, Maranello, ITA	5/18/08
1959 Ferrari 250 GT LWB California Spider	$3,630,000	133	Gooding, Pebble Beach, CA	8/17/08
1955 Ferrari 121 LM Sports Racer	$3,544,796	205	Bonhams, Gstaad, CHE	12/20/08
1959 Ferrari 250 GT LWB California Spyder	$3,300,000	44	Gooding, Scottsdale, AZ	1/19/08
1971 Ferrari 512M Group 5 Prototype Racer	$3,234,275	317	RM, Maranello, ITA	5/18/08
1956 Ferrari 250 GT Tour de France Coupe	$3,176,250	232	RM, Maranello, ITA	5/17/09
1959 Ferrari 250 GT LWB California Spyder	$2,911,563	234	RM, Maranello, ITA	5/17/09
1959 Ferrari 410 Superamerica Series III SWB Coupe	$2,530,000	50	Worldwide, Auburn, IN	8/30/08
1950 Ferrari 166 MM Berlinetta Le Mans	$2,200,000	42	Gooding, Pebble Beach, CA	8/17/08
1967 Ferrari 275 GTB/4 Coupe	$2,042,700	327	RM, Maranello, ITA	5/18/08
1967 Ferrari 275 GTB/4 Berlinetta	$1,925,000	434	RM, Monterey, CA	8/16/08
1962 Ferrari 250 GTL Lusso Competition	$1,702,250	315	RM, Maranello, ITA	5/18/08
1961 Ferrari 400 Superamerica Coupe Aerodinamica	$1,650,000	452	RM, Monterey, CA	8/16/08
1971 Ferrari 365 GTS/4 Daytona Spyder	$1,489,469	311	RM, Maranello, ITA	5/18/08
1973 Ferrari 365 GTB/4 Daytona Spyder	$1,485,000	435	RM, Monterey, CA	8/16/08
1967 Ferrari 275 GTB/4	$1,430,000	56	Gooding, Pebble Beach, CA	8/17/08
1966 Ferrari 275 GTB/6C Coupe	$1,375,000	160	RM, Phoenix, AZ	1/18/08
1967 Ferrari 275 GTB/4 Berlinetta	$1,375,000	466	RM, Monterey, CA	8/16/08
1965 Ferrari 275 GTB Alloy Long-Nose	$1,375,000	119	Gooding, Pebble Beach, CA	8/17/08
1963 Ferrari 400 Superamerica Coupe	$1,320,000	14	Gooding, Scottsdale, AZ	1/19/08
2004 Ferrari Enzo Coupe	$1,319,244	318	RM, Maranello, ITA	5/18/08
1990 Ferrari F40 LM Competition Coupe	$1,302,075	234	Bonhams, Monte Carlo, MCO	5/18/09
1971 Ferrari 365 GTS/4 Daytona Spyder	$1,290,000	40	Gooding, Scottsdale, AZ	1/19/08
2003 Ferrari Enzo Coupe	$1,265,000	61	Gooding, Scottsdale, AZ	1/17/09
1969 Ferrari 365 GTS Convertible	$1,265,000	8	Gooding, Pebble Beach, CA	8/17/08
1969 Ferrari 365 GTS Spyder	$1,239,225	108	Bonhams, Monte Carlo, MCO	5/10/08
2003 Ferrari Enzo Coupe	$1,191,575	341	RM, Maranello, ITA	5/18/08
1963 Ferrari 250 GTL Lusso Coupe	$1,174,553	319	RM, Maranello, ITA	5/18/08
1967 Ferrari 275 GTB/4 Coupe	$1,155,000	62	Gooding, Scottsdale, AZ	1/19/08
1972 Ferrari 365 GTB/4 Daytona Spyder	$1,127,500	467	RM, Monterey, CA	8/16/08
1966 Ferrari 275 GTB/2 Alloy Coupe	$1,096,563	233	RM, Maranello, ITA	5/17/09
1971 Ferrari 365 GTS/4 Daytona Spyder	$1,023,000	162	Gooding, Pebble Beach, CA	8/17/08
1965 Ferrari 275 GTB/6C Berlinetta	$1,012,000	430	RM, Monterey, CA	8/16/08
1965 Ferrari 500 Superfast Coupe	$983,125	223	RM, Maranello, ITA	5/17/09
1967 Ferrari 275 GTB/4 Coupe	$981,551	207	Bonhams, Gstaad, CHE	12/20/08
1967 Ferrari 275 GTB/4 Coupe	$918,500	167	RM, Phoenix, AZ	1/16/09
1966 Ferrari 275 GTB/6C Coupe	$907,500	218	RM, Maranello, ITA	5/17/09
1951 Ferrari 340 America Coupe	$889,813	322	RM, Maranello, ITA	5/18/08
1961 Ferrari 250 GT PF SII Cabriolet	$851,125	338	RM, Maranello, ITA	5/18/08
1950 Ferrari 166/195 Inter Coupe	$800,058	333	RM, Maranello, ITA	5/18/08
1964 Ferrari 250 GT/L Lusso Berlinetta	$770,000	440	RM, Monterey, CA	8/16/08
1997 Ferrari F310B Formula One	$766,013	316	RM, Maranello, ITA	5/18/08
1990 Ferrari F40 Coupe	$753,500	446	RM, Monterey, CA	8/16/08
1953 Ferrari 212 Inter Coupe	$742,500	456	RM, Monterey, CA	8/16/08

1959 Ferrari 250 GT LWB California Spyder

1990 Ferrari F40 LM Competition Coupe

1966 Ferrari 275 GTB/6C Coupe

1984 Ferrari 288 GTO Coupe

1950 Ferrari 195 Inter Ghia Coupe

1969 Ferrari 365 GTC/S Spyder Conversion

Model	Sold Price	Lot #	Auction Location	Date
1956 Ferrari Europa GT	$715,000	48	Gooding, Pebble Beach, CA	8/17/08
1963 Ferrari 250 GTL Lusso	$704,000	37	Gooding, Scottsdale, AZ	1/17/09
1968 Ferrari 330 GTS Convertible	$671,000	130	Gooding, Pebble Beach, CA	8/17/08
1989 Ferrari F40 Valeo Coupe	$646,855	330	RM, Maranello, ITA	5/18/08
1963 Ferrari 250 GT/L Lusso	$627,000	106	Gooding, Pebble Beach, CA	8/17/08
1984 Ferrari 288 GTO Coupe	$616,000	4	Gooding, Scottsdale, AZ	1/17/09
1991 Ferrari F40 Coupe	$612,810	339	RM, Maranello, ITA	5/18/08
1963 Ferrari 250 GT/L Lusso Coupe	$605,000	212	RM, Maranello, ITA	5/17/09
1958 Ferrari 250 GT Ellena Coupe	$595,788	309	RM, Maranello, ITA	5/18/08
1966 Ferrari 275 GTS Convertible	$595,788	325	RM, Maranello, ITA	5/18/08
1965 Ferrari 275 GTS Spider	$562,380	221	Bonhams, Gstaad, CHE	12/20/08
1951 Ferrari 195 Inter Coupe	$557,100	310	RM, Maranello, ITA	5/18/08
1956 Ferrari 250 GT Boano Coupe	$552,063	226	RM, Maranello, ITA	5/17/09
1964 Ferrari 250 GTL Lusso Coupe	$550,000	178	RM, Phoenix, AZ	1/16/09
1967 Ferrari 330 GTC Speciale	$550,000	49	Gooding, Scottsdale, AZ	1/19/08
1963 Ferrari 250 GTL Lusso	$546,100	153	Coys, Padua, ITA	10/25/08
1985 Ferrari 288 GTO Coupe	$529,375	204	RM, Maranello, ITA	5/17/09
1971 Ferrari 365 GTB/4 Daytona Comp Replica	$524,847	213	Coys, Monte Carlo, MCO	5/10/08
1964 Ferrari 250 GT Lusso	$521,275	143	Bonhams, Paris, FRA	2/9/08
2003 Ferrari 575 GTC Competizione	$500,175	239	Bonhams, Monte Carlo, MCO	5/18/09
1990 Ferrari 641/2 F1	$484,000	235	RM, Maranello, ITA	5/17/09
1959 Ferrari 250 GT LWB California Spyder Replica	$472,082	231	Coys, Birmingham, UK	1/10/09
1953 Ferrari 212 Inter Europa Vignale Coupe	$468,875	229	RM, Maranello, ITA	5/17/09
1966 Ferrari 275 GTS Convertible	$445,500	279	RM, Amelia Island, FL	3/14/09
1992 Ferrari F40 Coupe	$429,000	200	RM, Phoenix, AZ	1/16/09
1971 Ferrari 365 GTB/4 Daytona Coupe	$425,694	36	Artcurial, Paris, FRA	6/28/08
1971 Ferrari 365 GTB/4 Daytona	$425,563	336	RM, Maranello, ITA	5/18/08
1989 Ferrari F40 Coupe	$409,374	223	Coys, Birmingham, UK	1/10/09
1950 Ferrari 195 Inter Ghia Coupe	$398,750	224	RM, Maranello, ITA	5/17/09
1991 Ferrari F40 Coupe	$393,250	236	RM, Maranello, ITA	5/17/09
1972 Ferrari 365 GTB/4 Daytona Coupe	$390,500	S646	Russo and Steele, Monterey, CA	8/16/08
1961 Ferrari 250 GT SII Cabriolet	$385,000	81	Gooding, Scottsdale, AZ	1/17/09
1966 Ferrari 275 GTS Convertible	$385,000	194	RM, Phoenix, AZ	1/16/09
1962 Ferrari 250 GTO Replica	$383,925	211	Coys, Monte Carlo, MCO	5/10/08
1987 Ferrari F1-87 Formula One	$383,006	343	RM, Maranello, ITA	5/18/08
1957 Ferrari 250 GT Ellena Coupe	$378,125	209	RM, Maranello, ITA	5/17/09
1959 Ferrari 250 GT Series II Cabriolet	$375,000	125	RM, Phoenix, AZ	1/16/09
1969 Ferrari 365 GTC/S Spyder Conversion (Graypaul)	$374,889	579	Bonhams, Sussex, UK	7/11/08
1972 Ferrari 365 GTB/4 Daytona Coupe	$374,000	171	RM, Phoenix, AZ	1/18/08
1966 Ferrari 275 GTS Convertible	$371,520	125	Bonhams, Paris, FRA	2/7/09
1973 Ferrari 365 GTB/4 Daytona Spyder Conversion	$368,500	S656	Russo and Steele, Monterey, CA	8/16/08
1971 Ferrari 365 GTB/4 Daytona Coupe	$366,265	105	Bonhams, Monte Carlo, MCO	5/10/08
1990 Ferrari F40 GTM Berlinetta	$363,950	597	Bonhams, Sussex, UK	7/11/08
1973 Ferrari 365 GTB/4 Daytona	$363,400	322	Coys, Essen, DEU	3/29/08
1972 Ferrari 365 GTB/4 Daytona Coupe	$363,000	1	Gooding, Pebble Beach, CA	8/17/08

Top 1,000 Sales in 2008–09 by Marque

1971 Ferrari 365 GTB Daytona Coupe

1969 Ferrari 246 GT Dino Coupe

1966 Ford GT40 Mk 1

Model	Sold Price	Lot #	Auction Location	Date
1949 Ferrari 166 Inter Touring Coupe	$355,438	225	RM, Maranello, ITA	5/17/09
2008 Ferrari 612 Scaglietti	$340,450	306	RM, Maranello, ITA	5/18/08
1970 Ferrari 365 GTB/4 Daytona Coupe	$339,376	317	Coys, Ascot, UK	10/4/08
1965 Ferrari 250 GTO Replica (330 GT)	$331,135	586	Bonhams, Sussex, UK	7/11/08
1956 Ferrari 250 GT Berlinetta Prototipo	$330,057	208	Bonhams, Gstaad, CHE	12/20/08
1969 Ferrari 365 GTC	$324,500	448	RM, Monterey, CA	8/16/08
1971 Ferrari 365 GTB Daytona Coupe	$319,000	S705	Russo and Steele, Scottsdale, AZ	1/20/08
1958 Ferrari 250 GT Coupe	$314,916	302	RM, Maranello, ITA	5/18/08
1969 Ferrari 365 GTB/4 Daytona Spyder Conversion	$313,925	146	Bonhams, Paris, FRA	2/9/08
1970 Ferrari 365 GTB/4 Daytona Coupe	$287,375	227	RM, Maranello, ITA	5/17/09
1973 Ferrari 365 GTB/4 Daytona Coupe	$286,000	17	Gooding, Scottsdale, AZ	1/17/09
1963 Ferrari 330 America	$280,871	303	RM, Maranello, ITA	5/18/08
1972 Ferrari 365 GTB/4 Daytona Coupe	$279,285	140	Bonhams, Paris, FRA	2/7/09
1980 Ferrari Pinin Prototipo	$272,360	220	RM, Maranello, ITA	5/18/08
1963 Ferrari 250 GTE 2+2 Series III Coupe	$267,375	168	Bonhams, Monte Carlo, MCO	5/10/08
1971 Ferrari 365 GTB/4 Daytona Spyder Conversion	$264,000	162	RM, Phoenix, AZ	1/18/08
2010 Ferrari F430 Coupe	$247,500	221A	RM, Maranello, ITA	5/17/09
1969 Ferrari 246 GT Dino Coupe	$231,725	141	Bonhams, Monte Carlo, MCO	5/10/08
1972 Ferrari 365 GTB/4 Daytona Spyder Conversion	$229,047	227	Bonhams, Gstaad, CHE	12/20/08
1967 Ferrari 330 GTC Coupe	$218,900	56	H&H, Cheltenham, UK	2/27/08
1963 Ferrari 250 GT California Spyder Replica	$214,500	265	RM, Monterey, CA	8/16/08
1963 Ferrari 250 Testa Rossa Replica	$209,937	232	Bonhams, Gstaad, CHE	12/20/08
1973 Ferrari 246 GTS Dino Spyder	$204,270	332	RM, Maranello, ITA	5/18/08
1972 Ferrari 365 GTB/4 Daytona Coupe	$203,745	231	Bonhams, Oxford, UK	3/8/09
1974 Ferrari 246 GTS Dino Spyder	$202,834	240	Coys, Brands Hatch, UK	5/25/08
1967 Ferrari 330 GTC Coupe	$198,000	59	Gooding, Scottsdale, AZ	1/19/08
1979 Ferrari 512 BB Coupe	$195,759	305	RM, Maranello, ITA	5/18/08
1967 Ferrari 330 GTC Coupe	$192,500	34	Worldwide, Houston, TX	5/3/08
1958 Ferrari 250 GT Coupe	$189,750	487	RM, Monterey, CA	8/16/08
1965 Ferrari 330 GT 2+2	$187,380	231	Coys, Monte Carlo, MCO	5/18/09
1972 Ferrari 246 GTS Dino Spyder	$183,425	145	Bonhams, Paris, FRA	2/9/08
1967 Ferrari 330 GTC	$181,500	S642	Russo and Steele, Monterey, CA	8/16/08
1969 Ferrari 365 GTC Coupe	$180,185	530	Bonhams, Sussex, UK	7/11/08
1967 Ferrari 206 GT Dino Coupe	$178,736	323	RM, Maranello, ITA	5/18/08
2005 Ferrari F360 GTC Racer	$178,736	342	RM, Maranello, ITA	5/18/08
1972 Ferrari 246 GT Dino Coupe	$177,800	123	Coys, Padua, ITA	10/25/08
1974 Ferrari 246 GTS Dino Spyder	$175,203	320	Coys, Ascot, UK	10/4/08
1974 Ferrari 365 GT4 BB Coupe	$173,938	207	RM, Maranello, ITA	5/17/09
2001 Ferrari 550 Barchetta	$173,938	205	RM, Maranello, ITA	5/17/09
1972 Ferrari 246 GT Dino Coupe	$172,662	310	Coys, Essen, DEU	3/29/08
1952 Fitch-Whitmore Le Mans Special Roadster	$403,000	269	Bonhams & Butterfields, Greenwich, CT	6/7/09
1934 Ford Model 40 Special Speedster	$1,760,000	252	RM, Amelia Island, FL	3/8/08
1966 Ford GT40 Mk1	$1,465,000	443	RM, Monterey, CA	8/16/08
1929 Ford 4-AT-E Tri-Motor Airplane	$1,210,000	1307	Barrett-Jackson, Scottsdale, AZ	1/18/09
1955 Ford Thunderbird Convertible "Production #1"	$660,000	1295	Barrett-Jackson, Scottsdale, AZ	1/18/09

Model	Sold Price	Lot #	Auction Location	Date
1963 Ford Thunderbird Italien Concept Car	$660,000	1306	Barrett-Jackson, Scottsdale, AZ	1/20/08
2008 Ford Mustang Shelby GT500 KR Coupe	$605,000	1300	Barrett-Jackson, Scottsdale, AZ	1/20/08
1956 Ford F100 Custom Cab Pickup	$418,000	232	RM, Tustin, CA	6/14/08
2009 Ford Mustang FR500 CJ Prototype #1	$412,500	1333.1	Barrett-Jackson, Scottsdale, AZ	1/18/09
1970 Ford Mustang Boss 302 TransAm Race Car	$407,000	87	Gooding, Scottsdale, AZ	1/17/09
1964 Ford Galaxie 500 "Tobacco King" Rocket Car	$376,000	S139	Mecum, Indianapolis, IN	5/18/08
1969 Ford Mustang Boss 429 Fastback	$357,500	1269	Barrett-Jackson, Scottsdale, AZ	1/20/08
1932 Ford Custom Roadster "Rollin Stone"	$352,000	1262	Barrett-Jackson, Scottsdale, AZ	1/20/08
1969 Ford Mustang Boss 429 Fastback	$330,000	1329	Barrett-Jackson, Scottsdale, AZ	1/20/08
2006 Ford Mustang GT Coupe "Funkmaster Flex"	$330,000	774.4	Barrett-Jackson, Las Vegas, NV	10/18/08
1969 Ford Mustang Boss 429 Fastback	$288,750	S101	Mecum, Indianapolis, IN	5/18/08
1969 Ford Mustang Boss 429 Fastback	$287,280	2481	Leake, Tulsa, OK	6/8/08
1947 Ford Model 71 Sportsman	$269,500	67A	Gooding, Scottsdale, AZ	1/19/08
1969 Ford Mustang Boss 429 Fastback	$269,500	1280	Barrett-Jackson, Scottsdale, AZ	1/20/08
1970 Ford Mustang Boss 429 Fastback	$269,500	1319	Barrett-Jackson, Scottsdale, AZ	1/20/08
1969 Ford Mustang Coupe	$253,000	F518	Russo and Steele, Scottsdale, AZ	1/20/08
1969 Ford Mustang Boss 429 Fastback	$248,000	83	Worldwide, Houston, TX	5/3/08
1927 Ford Roadster Shadow Rods XL 27	$247,500	S661	Russo and Steele, Monterey, CA	8/16/08
1967 Ford GT40 Mk II Coupe	$238,500	F257	Mecum, Indianapolis, IN	5/17/09
1948 Ford Sportsman Convertible Coupe	$236,500	143	RM, Anaheim, CA	6/29/08
1969 Ford Mustang Fastback	$231,000	S700	Russo and Steele, Scottsdale, AZ	1/20/08
1970 Ford Mustang Boss 429 Fastback	$231,000	231	RM, Monterey, CA	8/16/08
2005 Ford Mustang FR500C Racer	$220,000	1288	Barrett-Jackson, Scottsdale, AZ	1/20/08
1932 Ford Deluxe Boyd Coddington Custom Coupe	$220,000	1282	Barrett-Jackson, Scottsdale, AZ	1/18/09
1964 Ford Galaxie 2-Door Hardtop	$217,300	S130	Mecum, Kissimmee, FL	1/24/09
1969 Ford Mustang Boss 429 Fastback	$214,500	803.1	Barrett-Jackson, Las Vegas, NV	10/18/08
1970 Ford Mustang Boss 429 Fastback	$214,500	F513	Russo and Steele, Scottsdale, AZ	1/18/09
1937 Ford Woody Custom Station Wagon	$214,500	238	RM, Tustin, CA	6/14/08
1970 Ford Mustang Boss 429 Fastback	$210,940	F239	Mecum, Indianapolis, IN	5/17/09
1970 Ford Mustang Boss 429 Fastback	$209,000	1319	Barrett-Jackson, Scottsdale, AZ	1/18/09
1964 Ford Fairlane Thunderbolt Drag Racer	$206,700	S134	Mecum, Kissimmee, FL	1/24/09
1969 Ford Mustang Boss 429 Fastback	$206,700	S110	Mecum, Indianapolis, IN	5/17/09
1970 Ford Mustang Boss 429 Fastback	$206,700	n/a	MidAmerica, St. Paul, MN	5/10/08
1970 Ford Mustang Boss 429 Fastback	$205,700	816	Barrett-Jackson, Las Vegas, NV	10/18/08
1969 Ford Mustang 428 SCJ Convertible	$203,500	1333	Barrett-Jackson, Scottsdale, AZ	1/20/08
1948 Ford Sportsman Convertible Coupe	$199,100	SP133	RM, Ft. Lauderdale, FL	2/8/09
1969 Ford Mustang Boss 429 Fastback Drag Car	$198,000	1283	Barrett-Jackson, Scottsdale, AZ	1/18/09
1966 Ford Mustang Convertible	$198,000	SP65	RM, Ft. Lauderdale, FL	2/8/09
1932 Ford Ardun Special Roadster	$192,920	S103	Mecum, Indianapolis, IN	5/17/09
1969 Ford Mustang Boss 429 Custom Fastback	$183,700	1270.1	Barrett-Jackson, Scottsdale, AZ	1/18/09
1972 Ford Escort RS1600 Mk I Coupe	$181,685	328	Bonhams, Stoneleigh Park, UK	3/15/08
1969 Ford Mustang Boss 429 Fastback	$181,500	S641	Russo and Steele, Monterey, CA	8/16/08
2006 Ford GT Hennessey Heritage Edition	$181,260	F234	Mecum, Indianapolis, IN	5/17/09
2004 Ford Mustang GT Convertible Concept	$175,000	655	Barrett-Jackson, Palm Beach, FL	4/11/09
2004 Ford Mustang GT Coupe Concept	$175,000	655.1	Barrett-Jackson, Palm Beach, FL	4/11/09

1964 Ford Galaxie 500 "Tobacco King" Rocket Car

1969 Ford Mustang Coupe

1937 Ford Woody Custom Station Wagon

Top 1,000 Sales in 2008–09 by Marque

Model	Sold Price	Lot #	Auction Location	Date
1933 Ford-Auburn Roadster Special	$265,500	350	Bonhams & Butterfields, Carmel Valley, CA	8/15/08
1905 Gardner-Serpollet 18hp Type L Steamer with Tulip Phaeton Coachwork	$345,100	320	Bonhams, Hendon, UK	4/20/09
1967 Ghia 450 SS Convertible	$181,500	1264	Barrett-Jackson, Scottsdale, AZ	1/18/09
1952 Glöckler-Porsche Roadster	$616,000	159	RM, Phoenix, AZ	1/18/08
1929 Graham-Paige Dual Cowl Phaeton	$297,000	146	RM, Phoenix, AZ	1/16/09
1966 Gurney Eagle AAR Indy Car	$528,000	225	RM, Tustin, CA	6/14/08
1936 Hispano-Suiza J12 Convertible Victoria	$880,000	47	Gooding, Scottsdale, AZ	1/17/09
1930 Hispano-Suiza H6C Boattail Speedster	$616,000	129	Gooding, Pebble Beach, CA	8/17/08
1928 Hispano-Suiza H6B Sedanca deVille	$297,975	118	Bonhams, Paris, FRA	2/9/08
1977 Holden LX Torana A9X Sedan	$177,560	52	Shannons, Melbourne, AUS	3/10/08
1954 Hudson Italia Coupe	$275,000	290	RM, Amelia Island, FL	3/14/09
1927 Hudson Super Six Supercharged Sports Tourer	$198,000	276	RM, Amelia Island, FL	3/14/09
1948 Hudson Commodore Eight Convertible	$181,500	266	RM, Dallas, TX	4/19/08
2003 Hummer H2 Custom Convertible	$192,500	1309.1	Barrett-Jackson, Scottsdale, AZ	1/20/08
1938 Indy Blue Crown Special Race Car	$397,500	F256	Mecum, Indianapolis, IN	5/17/09
1930 Invicta 4½-Liter S-type Tourer "Scimitar"	$834,302	539	Bonhams, Sussex, UK	7/11/08
1930 Invicta 4½-Liter Type A Tourer	$191,196	123	Bonhams & Goodman, Melbounre, AUS	3/13/08
1969 Iso Grifo Coupe	$308,000	157	RM, Phoenix, AZ	1/18/08
1966 Iso Grifo GL Coupe	$200,401	248	Coys, Essen, DEU	4/4/09
1913 Isotta Fraschini 100-120 hp Tipo KM 4 4-Seat Torpedo Tourer	$1,492,000	316	Bonhams & Butterfields, Carmel Valley, CA	8/15/08
1933 Isotta Fraschini Tipo 8A Dual Cowl Sports Phaeton	$1,089,000	43	Gooding, Scottsdale, AZ	1/17/09
1930 Isotta Fraschini 8A Convertible Sedan by Castagna	$467,500	253	RM, Rochester, MI	8/2/08
1930 Isotta Fraschini 8A Transformable Torpedo	$495,000	176	RM, Phoenix, AZ	1/18/08
1960 Jaguar XKE E2A Prototype Sports Racer	$4,957,000	364	Bonhams & Butterfields, Carmel Valley, CA	8/15/08
1955 Jaguar XKD-type Sports Racer	$4,378,343	523	Bonhams, Sussex, UK	7/11/08
1938 Jaguar SS 100 Roadster	$317,250	235	Coys, Essen, DEU	4/4/09
1937 Jaguar SS 100 2½-Liter Roadster	$313,925	124	Bonhams, Paris, FRA	2/9/08
1994 Jaguar XJ 220 Coupe	$313,500	1291	Barrett-Jackson, Scottsdale, AZ	1/20/08
1993 Jaguar XJ 220 Coupe	$291,500	1281	Barrett-Jackson, Scottsdale, AZ	1/20/08
1938 Jaguar SS 100 3½-Liter Roadster	$289,275	337	Bonhams, Hendon, UK	4/20/09
1939 Jaguar SS 100 Roadster	$279,285	154	Bonhams, Paris, FRA	2/7/09
1956 Jaguar XK 140 DHC	$265,135	72	Brightwells, Herefordshire, UK	7/2/08
1950 Jaguar XK 120 Alloy Open Two Seater	$225,000	461	RM, Monterey, CA	8/16/08
1993 Jaguar XJ 220 Coupe	$220,000	1290	Barrett-Jackson, Scottsdale, AZ	1/18/09
1950 Jaguar XK 120 Roadster	$214,500	S657	Russo and Steele, Hollywood, FL	3/30/08
1950 Jaguar XK 120 Roadster	$214,080	218	Bonhams, Sussex, UK	8/9/08
1954 Jaguar XK 120SE Coupe	$192,960	212	Bonhams, Sussex, UK	8/9/08
1993 Jaguar XJ 220 Coupe	$188,664	339	Coys, London, UK	3/3/08
1961 Jaguar XK 150 3.8 Coupe	$181,500	428	RM, Monterey, CA	8/16/08
1936 Jenson-Ford Tourer	$203,500	183	RM, Anaheim, CA	6/29/08
1954 Kaiser-Darrin Roadster	$176,000	1254	Barrett-Jackson, Scottsdale, AZ	1/18/09
1954 Kaiser-Darrin Roadster	$176,000	957	Barrett-Jackson, Scottsdale, AZ	1/20/08
2004 Koenigsegg CC8S Coupe	$254,560	617	Bonhams, London, UK	12/1/08
1936 Lagonda LG45R Rapide Sports Racing 2-Seater	$1,382,000	310	Bonhams & Butterfields, Carmel Valley, CA	8/15/08

1966 Gurney Eagle AAR Indy Car

1930 Invicta 4½-Liter S-type Tourer "Scimitar"

1955 Jaguar XKD-type Sports Racer

1937 Lagonda LG45 Drophead Coupe

1969 Lamborghini Miura P400 S Coupe

1955 Lancia Aurelia B24S Spyder America

Model	Sold Price	Lot #	Auction Location	Date
1976 Lagonda V8 Series I Saloon	$498,820	320	Bonhams, Newport Pagnell, UK	5/17/08
1933 Lagonda 3-Liter Tourer	$253,000	24	Gooding, Scottsdale, AZ	1/19/08
1938 Lagonda LG6 Drophead Coupe	$247,500	264	RM, Amelia Island, FL	3/8/08
1933 Lagonda M45 Tourer	$197,580	609	Bonhams, London, UK	12/1/08
1937 Lagonda LG45 Drophead Coupe	$174,240	38	H&H, Harrogate, UK	4/16/08
1972 Lamborghini Miura P400 SV	$891,000	433	RM, Monterey, CA	8/16/08
1970 Lamborghini Miura P400 S Series II Coupe	$484,273	577	Bonhams, Sussex, UK	7/11/08
1969 Lamborghini Miura P400 S Coupe	$464,963	39	Artcurial, Paris, FRA	2/9/08
1970 Lamborghini Miura S Coupe	$423,500	S655	Russo and Steele, Monterey, CA	8/16/08
1967 Lamborghini Miura P400 Coupe	$412,500	437	RM, Monterey, CA	8/16/08
1977 Lamborghini Countach LP400 Coupe	$396,000	161	Gooding, Pebble Beach, CA	8/17/08
1969 Lamborghini Miura P400 Coupe	$381,627	219	Coys, Monte Carlo, MCO	5/10/08
1976 Lamborghini Countach LP400 Periscopo	$363,000	S651	Russo and Steele, Monterey, CA	8/16/08
1970 Lamborghini Miura P400 S Coupe	$352,000	272	RM, Monterey, CA	8/16/08
1967 Lamborghini Miura P400 Coupe	$330,000	73	Gooding, Pebble Beach, CA	8/17/08
1968 Lamborghini Miura P400 Coupe	$313,200	234	Coys, Monte Carlo, MCO	5/18/09
1971 Lamborghini Miura P400 S Coupe	$308,000	133	RM, Phoenix, AZ	1/16/09
1964 Lamborghini 350 GT Coupe	$308,000	57	Gooding, Scottsdale, AZ	1/19/08
1966 Lamborghini 350 GT Coupe	$283,800	S710	Russo and Steele, Scottsdale, AZ	1/20/08
1967 Lamborghini 400 GT 2+2 Coupe	$271,000	358	Bonhams & Butterfields, Carmel Valley, CA	8/15/08
1969 Lamborghini 400 GT Coupe	$254,100	F517	Russo and Steele, Scottsdale, AZ	1/20/08
1966 Lamborghini 400 GT Interim Coupe	$231,000	72	Gooding, Pebble Beach, CA	8/17/08
1968 Lamborghini 400 GT 2+2 Coupe	$205,802	42	H&H, Surrey, UK	6/8/08
1969 Lamborghini Islero Coupe	$203,500	21	Gooding, Pebble Beach, CA	8/17/08
1967 Lamborghini 400 GT Coupe	$200,019	371	Bonhams, Sussex, UK	9/19/08
1999 Lamborghini Diablo VT Roadster	$187,000	8	Gooding, Scottsdale, AZ	1/19/08
1967 Lamborghini 400 GT 2+2 Coupe	$181,500	425	RM, Monterey, CA	8/16/08
1967 Lamborghini 400 GT Coupe	$177,998	591	Bonhams, Sussex, UK	7/11/08
1955 Lancia Aurelia B24S Spyder America	$572,000	118	Gooding, Pebble Beach, CA	8/17/08
1955 Lancia Aurelia B24 Spyder America	$505,600	334	Coys, Essen, DEU	3/29/08
1955 Lancia Aurelia B24 Spyder America	$420,750	55	H&H, Sparkford, UK	10/12/08
1955 Lancia Aurelia B24S Spyder America	$406,995	176	Bonhams, Paris, FRA	2/7/09
1955 Lancia Aurelia B24 Spyder America	$380,025	236	Coys, Monte Carlo, MCO	5/18/09
1953 Lancia Aurelia B20GT Coupe	$217,465	146	Bonhams, Monte Carlo, MCO	5/10/09
1957 Lancia Aurelia B24S Convertible	$211,140	255A	Bonhams, Monte Carlo, MCO	5/18/09
1958 Lancia Aurelia B24S Convertible	$200,273	144	Bonhams, Paris, FRA	2/7/09
1971 Lancia Fulvia 1600HF Coupe	$191,166	52	Artcurial, Paris, FRA	6/28/08
1983 Lancia 037 Stradale Coupe	$190,728	129	Bonhams, Monte Carlo, MCO	5/10/09
1918 Le Bestioni Boattail Speedster	$181,500	813	Barrett-Jackson, Las Vegas, NV	10/18/08
1905 Léon Bollée 45/50hp 8.3-Liter Double Chain-Drive Roi-des-Belges Tourer	$265,505	519	Bonhams, Sussex, UK	7/11/08
1936 Lincoln Model K "Howard Hughes" Boattail Speedster	$1,080,000	496	Leake, Tulsa, OK	6/14/09
1941 Lincoln Continental Hardtop	$451,000	39	Gooding, Scottsdale, AZ	1/19/08
1933 Lincoln Model KB Dual Cowl Phaeton	$242,000	235	RM, Hershey, PA	10/10/08
1962 Lincoln Continental Sedan "John F. Kennedy"	$209,000	812	Barrett-Jackson, Las Vegas, NV	10/18/08

BY THE NUMBERS

Top 1,000 Sales in 2008–09 by Marque

1938 Lincoln Model K Convertible Victoria

1970 Maserati Ghibli Spyder

1936 Mercedes-Benz 500K Cabriolet B

Model	Sold Price	Lot #	Auction Location	Date
1941 Lincoln Continental Coupe	$209,000	151	RM, Anaheim, CA	6/29/08
1974 Lincoln Batmobile Replica	$203,500	994	Barrett-Jackson, Scottsdale, AZ	1/20/08
1936 Lincoln Model K Brunn Cabriolet	$202,500	494	Leake, Tulsa, OK	6/14/09
1938 Lincoln Model K Convertible Victoria	$192,500	426	RM, Monterey, CA	8/16/08
1956 Lincoln Premiere Convertible	$181,125	U45	Mecum, Indianapolis, IN	5/18/08
1955/57 Lister Sports Racer	$252,684	76	H&H, Buxton, UK	7/23/08
c.1990/91 Lister-Jaguar "Knobbly" Competition Sports 2-Seater	$282,000	343	Bonhams & Butterfields, Carmel Valley, CA	8/15/08
1913 Locomobile Model M-48-3 4-Passenger Baby Tonneau	$357,500	245	RM, Hershey, PA	10/10/08
1911 Locomobile Model M-48 7-Passenger Touring	$302,500	142	RM, Phoenix, AZ	1/18/08
1962 Lotus 25 Formula 1 Single-Seater	$988,524	58	Bonhams & Goodman, Sydney, AUS	11/16/08
1978/79 Lotus 79 Formula 1 Single-Seater	$373,442	61	Bonhams & Goodman, Sydney, AUS	11/16/08
1966 Lotus 39 Tasman Series Single-Seater	$234,317	59	Bonhams & Goodman, Sydney, AUS	11/16/08
1959 Lotus 16 Formula 2 Single-Seater	$226,994	56	Bonhams & Goodman, Sydney, AUS	11/16/08
1933 Marmon Sixteen Convertible Sedan	$330,000	156	RM, Phoenix, AZ	1/16/09
2006 Maserati MC12 Corsa	$2,194,318	252	Coys, Monte Carlo, MCO	5/10/08
2008 Maserati MC12 Corsa	$1,058,750	203	RM, Maranello, ITA	5/17/09
1931 Maserati Tipo 8C-2800 2-Seat Competition Car	$445,605	308	Bonhams, Sussex, UK	9/19/08
1966 Maserati Mistral 4000 Spyder	$369,675	126	Bonhams, Monte Carlo, MCO	5/10/08
1970 Maserati Ghibli Spyder	$330,000	S662	Russo and Steele, Monterey, CA	8/16/08
1970 Maserati Ghibli Spyder	$315,700	114	Worldwide, Houston, TX	5/3/08
1961 Maserati 3500 GT Spyder	$314,906	213	Bonhams, Gstaad, CHE	12/20/08
1963 Maserati 3500 GTi Spyder	$253,000	35	Gooding, Scottsdale, AZ	1/19/08
1960 Maserati 3500 GT Spyder	$250,000	S758	Russo and Steele, Scottsdale, AZ	1/18/09
1970 Maserati Ghibli Spyder	$249,000	312	Bonhams & Butterfields, Carmel Valley, CA	8/15/08
1950 Maserati A6 1500 Coupe	$222,250	175	Coys, Padua, ITA	10/25/08
1963 Maserati 3500 GT Spyder	$211,200	48	Worldwide, Hilton Head, SC	11/1/08
1969 Matra MS650 Prototype Racer	$1,922,933	39	Artcurial, Paris, FRA	2/8/09
1965 McLaren-Elva M1A Chevrolet Sports Racer	$249,000	224	Bonhams & Butterfields, Greenwich, CT	6/8/08
1910 Mercedes 45hp 4-Seat Tourabout	$887,000	873	Bonhams & Butterfields, Owls Head, ME	9/27/08
1928 Mercedes-Benz 26/120/180 S-type Roadster	$3,360,375	155	Bonhams, Paris, FRA	2/9/08
1936 Mercedes-Benz 540K Special Cabriolet	$2,035,000	144	RM, Phoenix, AZ	1/18/08
1936 Mercedes-Benz 500K Cabriolet A	$1,286,875	162	Bonhams, Paris, FRA	2/9/08
1936 Mercedes-Benz 500K Cabriolet B	$1,045,000	112	Gooding, Pebble Beach, CA	8/17/08
1938 Mercedes-Benz 540K Sport Cabriolet	$946,000	90	Gooding, Scottsdale, AZ	1/17/09
1955 Mercedes-Benz 300SL Coupe	$852,500	445	RM, Monterey, CA	8/16/08
1955 Mercedes-Benz 300SL Coupe	$770,000	469	RM, Monterey, CA	8/16/08
1957 Mercedes-Benz 300SL Roadster	$742,500	172	RM, Phoenix, AZ	1/18/08
1955 Mercedes-Benz 300SL Coupe	$737,383	229	Coys, Monte Carlo, MCO	5/10/08
1957 Mercedes-Benz 300SL Roadster	$704,000	164	Gooding, Pebble Beach, CA	8/17/08
1955 Mercedes-Benz 300SL Coupe	$660,000	S705	Russo and Steele, Scottsdale, AZ	1/18/09
1955 Mercedes-Benz 300SL Coupe	$647,800	323	Coys, Essen, DEU	3/29/08
1955 Mercedes-Benz 300SL Coupe	$605,000	66	Gooding, Scottsdale, AZ	1/19/08
1954 Mercedes-Benz 300SL Coupe	$605,000	61	Gooding, Pebble Beach, CA	8/17/08
1961 Mercedes-Benz 300SL Roadster	$594,000	43	Gooding, Pebble Beach, CA	8/17/08

Model	Sold Price	Lot #	Auction Location	Date
1955 Mercedes-Benz 300SL Coupe	$588,500	151	RM, Phoenix, AZ	1/18/08
1961 Mercedes-Benz 300SL Roadster	$577,500	1283.1	Barrett-Jackson, Scottsdale, AZ	1/20/08
1956 Mercedes-Benz 300SL Coupe	$577,500	150	Gooding, Pebble Beach, CA	8/17/08
1959 Mercedes-Benz 300SL Roadster	$567,716	445	Coys, London, UK	7/5/08
1956 Mercedes-Benz 300SL Coupe	$557,225	153	Bonhams, Monte Carlo, MCO	5/10/08
1962 Mercedes-Benz 300SL Roadster	$556,500	S158	Mecum, Kissimmee, FL	1/24/09
1956 Mercedes-Benz 300SL Coupe	$550,000	96	Gooding, Scottsdale, AZ	1/17/09
1960 Mercedes-Benz 300SL Roadster	$545,000	58	Worldwide, Auburn, IN	8/30/08
1956 Mercedes-Benz 300SL Coupe	$535,000	252	RM, Rochester, MI	8/2/08
1958 Mercedes-Benz 300SL Roadster	$528,000	432	RM, Monterey, CA	8/16/08
1958 Mercedes-Benz 300SL Roadster	$495,000	NR26	RM, Ft. Lauderdale, FL	2/17/08
1961 Mercedes-Benz 300SL Roadster	$492,800	207	Coys, Monte Carlo, MCO	5/10/08
1960 Mercedes-Benz 300SL Roadster	$489,375	170	Bonhams, Paris, FRA	2/9/08
1959 Mercedes-Benz 300SL Roadster	$478,500	1292	Barrett-Jackson, Scottsdale, AZ	1/20/08
1957 Mercedes-Benz 300SL Roadster	$477,945	175	Bonhams, Paris, FRA	2/7/09
1955 Mercedes-Benz 300SL Coupe	$467,500	164	RM, Phoenix, AZ	1/16/09
1958 Mercedes-Benz 300SL Roadster	$464,963	28	Artcurial, Paris, FRA	2/9/08
1961 Mercedes-Benz 300SL Roadster	$368,500	20	Gooding, Scottsdale, AZ	1/17/09
2005 Mercedes-Benz SLR McLaren Coupe	$309,258	554	Bonhams, Sussex, UK	7/11/08
1936 Mercedes-Benz 230B Cabriolet	$280,717	133	Coys, Nürburgring, DEU	8/9/08
1937 Mercedes-Benz Type 320 Cabriolet B	$260,000	370	Bonhams & Butterfields, Carmel Valley, CA	8/15/08
1952 Mercedes-Benz 300S Cabriolet	$255,750	237	RM, Amelia Island, FL	3/14/09
1955 Mercedes-Benz 300Sc Coupe	$253,000	1283	Barrett-Jackson, Scottsdale, AZ	1/20/08
1934 Mercedes-Benz 290 Cabriolet A	$243,810	111	Bonhams, Paris, FRA	2/7/09
1957 Mercedes-Benz 300SL Roadster	$242,000	69	Gooding, Scottsdale, AZ	1/17/09
1935 Mercedes-Benz 200 W21 40hp Landaulet	$231,725	159	Bonhams, Monte Carlo, MCO	5/10/08
1955 Mercedes-Benz 300S Coupe	$216,775	129	Bonhams, Paris, FRA	2/9/08
1972 Mercedes-Benz 280SE 3.5 Convertible	$213,900	104	Bonhams, Monte Carlo, MCO	5/10/08
1955 Mercedes-Benz 300SL Gullwing Custom Replica	$203,500	1322	Barrett-Jackson, Scottsdale, AZ	1/20/08
1960 Mercedes-Benz 220SE Convertible	$198,000	24	Gooding, Pebble Beach, CA	8/17/08
1955 Mercedes-Benz 300Sc Coupe	$192,500	1284	Barrett-Jackson, Scottsdale, AZ	1/18/09
1972 Mercedes-Benz 280SE 3.5 Convertible	$181,500	50	Gooding, Scottsdale, AZ	1/17/09
1922 Mercer Series 5 Raceabout	$238,000	840	Bonhams & Butterfields, Owls Head, ME	9/27/08
1964 Mercury Comet Caliente A/FX 2-Door Hardtop	$238,500	S109	Mecum, Indianapolis, IN	5/17/09
1949 Mercury Eight Station Wagon	$198,000	174	RM, Anaheim, CA	6/29/08
1960 Meskowski Bowes Seal Fast Special	$462,000	223	RM, Tustin, CA	6/14/08
1963 Meskowski Sheraton-Thompson Dirt Championship Car	$396,000	252	RM, Tustin, CA	6/14/08
1949 MG TC Race Roadster	$313,500	819	Barrett-Jackson, Las Vegas, NV	10/18/08
1935 MG K-type to K3 Supercharged Specification	$176,000	167	RM, Phoenix, AZ	1/18/08
1923 Miller 122 Supercharged	$2,035,000	240	RM, Tustin, CA	6/14/08
1935/41 Miller Ford Winfield V8	$451,000	251	RM, Tustin, CA	6/14/08
1910 Mitchell Model S Touring Car	$242,000	12	Gooding, Pebble Beach, CA	8/17/08
1970 Monteverdi 375/S Series II Coupe	$177,998	534	Bonhams, Sussex, UK	7/11/08
1953 Nash-Healey Roadster	$253,000	27	Gooding, Scottsdale, AZ	1/19/08

1957 Mercedes-Benz 300SL Roadster

1922 Mercer Series 5 Raceabout

1949 MG TC Race Roadster

Model	Sold Price	Lot #	Auction Location	Date
1913 National Model 40 Series V Type N3 Semi-Racing Roadster	$196,200	508	Bonhams & Butterfields, Brookline, MA	10/4/08
1911 Oldsmobile Autocrat Racing Car "Yellow Peril"	$660,000	260	RM, Amelia Island, FL	3/14/09
1953 Oldsmobile Fiesta Convertible	$253,000	246	RM, Dallas, TX	4/19/08
1923 Oldsmobile Custom Touring Roadster	$220,000	397.2	Barrett-Jackson, Scottsdale, AZ	1/18/09
1958 Oldsmobile J-2 Super 88 Convertible	$209,000	24	Worldwide, Houston, TX	5/3/08
1970 Oldsmobile 442 W-30 Convertible	$206,700	1789	G. Potter King, Atlantic City, NJ	3/2/08
1953 Oldsmobile 98 Fiesta Convertible	$195,000	72	Worldwide, Seabrook, TX	5/2/09
1970 Oldsmobile 442 W30 Convertible	$184,800	S716	Russo and Steele, Scottsdale, AZ	1/18/09
1957 Oldsmobile Starfire 98 Convertible	$178,750	256	RM, Dallas, TX	4/19/08
1970 Oldsmobile 442 W30 Convertible	$173,250	668	Barrett-Jackson, Palm Beach, FL	4/11/09
1955 OSCA MT4 Roadster	$477,945	116	Bonhams, Paris, FRA	2/7/09
1934 Packard Twelve Coupe	$2,035,000	163	RM, Phoenix, AZ	1/18/08
1932 Packard Model 904 Custom Eight Convertible Victoria	$1,210,000	50	Gooding, Scottsdale, AZ	1/19/08
1954 Packard Panther-Daytona Roadster Concept Car	$700,000	277	RM, Amelia Island, FL	3/14/09
1932 Packard Twin Six Coupe Roadster	$660,000	143	RM, Phoenix, AZ	1/18/08
1934 Packard Twelve Model 1107 5-Passenger Touring	$495,000	65	Worldwide, Auburn, IN	8/30/08
1933 Packard Super Eight Convertible Victoria	$412,500	247	RM, Amelia Island, FL	3/8/08
1936 Packard Twelve Convertible Victoria	$385,000	256	RM, Rochester, MI	8/2/08
1935 Packard 12 Convertible	$378,000	U50	Mecum, Indianapolis, IN	5/18/08
1934 Packard 1108 Twelve Sport Phaeton	$352,000	56A	Gooding, Scottsdale, AZ	1/17/09
1942 Packard One-Eighty Convertible Victoria by Darrin	$330,000	237	RM, Rochester, MI	8/2/08
1936 Packard Super Eight Roadster	$330,000	57	Gooding, Pebble Beach, CA	8/17/08
1908 Packard Model 30 Touring Car	$319,000	17	Gooding, Pebble Beach, CA	8/17/08
1931 Packard Deluxe Eight Sport Phaeton	$291,500	459	RM, Monterey, CA	8/16/08
1938 Packard Twelve Coupe Roadster	$286,000	259	RM, Amelia Island, FL	3/14/09
1907 Packard 30hp Gentleman's Roadster	$284,200	852	Bonhams & Butterfields, Owls Head, ME	9/27/08
1938 Packard Model 120 Darrin Convertible	$282,000	222	Bonhams & Butterfields, Greenwich, CT	6/7/09
1933 Packard 1005 Twelve Touring	$275,000	49	Gooding, Scottsdale, AZ	1/17/09
1938 Packard Twelve Custom Limousine	$269,500	1553	Barrett-Jackson, Scottsdale, AZ	1/20/08
1934 Packard Super Eight Convertible Victoria	$264,000	149	RM, Phoenix, AZ	1/16/09
1938 Packard Twelve Coupe Roadster	$259,600	424	RM, Monterey, CA	8/16/08
1934 Packard Eight Convertible Sedan	$258,500	156	RM, Phoenix, AZ	1/18/08
1932 Packard 903 Deluxe Eight Coupe Roadster	$253,000	40	Worldwide, Seabrook, TX	5/2/09
1930 Packard Custom Eight Roadster	$242,000	131	RM, Phoenix, AZ	1/18/08
1935 Packard Twelve Convertible Sedan	$242,000	336	RM, Anaheim, CA	6/29/08
1938 Packard Twelve Collapsible Touring Cabriolet	$236,500	246	RM, Hershey, PA	10/10/08
1934 Packard Super Eight 1104 Touring	$231,000	32	Gooding, Scottsdale, AZ	1/19/08
1936 Packard Twelve Dual Cowl Sport Phaeton	$231,000	249	RM, Hershey, PA	10/10/08
1936 Packard Twelve Coupe Roadster	$220,000	SP138	RM, Ft. Lauderdale, FL	2/8/09
1916 Packard Twin Six 1-35 Touring Car	$220,000	18	Gooding, Scottsdale, AZ	1/19/08
1909 Packard Model 18 Runabout	$220,000	72	Worldwide, Houston, TX	5/3/08
1901 Packard Model C Runabout	$214,500	9	Gooding, Pebble Beach, CA	8/17/08
1934 Packard Twelve 5-Passenger Phaeton	$211,750	251	RM, Amelia Island, FL	3/14/09
1938 Packard 16th Series Twelve Convertible Victoria	$209,000	801	Barrett-Jackson, Las Vegas, NV	10/18/08

1955 OSCA MT4 Roadster

1942 Packard One-Eighty Convertible Victoria by Darrin

1909 Packard Model 18 Runabout

BY THE NUMBERS

1940 Packard 120 Station Wagon

1917 Pierce-Arrow Model 48 Touring Car

1970 Plymouth Hemi 'Cuda 2-Door Hardtop

Model	Sold Price	Lot #	Auction Location	Date
1939 Packard Super Eight Transformable Town Car by Franay	$209,000	187	RM, Anaheim, CA	6/29/08
1930 Packard Seventh Series Deluxe Eight Model 745 Roadster	$209,000	38	Worldwide, Auburn, IN	8/30/08
1940 Packard 120 Station Wagon	$198,000	53	Gooding, Scottsdale, AZ	1/17/09
1938 Packard Twelve Convertible Victoria	$198,000	152	RM, Anaheim, CA	6/29/08
1930 Packard 740 Custom Eight Sport Phaeton	$192,500	84	Gooding, Scottsdale, AZ	1/17/09
1934 Packard Eight Coupe Roadster	$192,500	188	RM, Phoenix, AZ	1/18/08
1930 Packard 745 4-Passenger Phaeton	$187,000	199	RM, Phoenix, AZ	1/16/09
1938 Packard Touring Sedan by Brunn	$187,000	SP170	RM, Ft. Lauderdale, FL	2/17/08
1936 Packard Eight Phaeton	$187,000	278	RM, Amelia Island, FL	3/8/08
1938 Packard Twelve Brunn Touring Cabriolet	$187,000	671	RM, Novi, MI	4/27/08
1934 Packard Model 1104 Super Eight Convertible Victoria	$187,000	268	RM, Rochester, MI	8/2/08
1934 Packard Super Eight Coupe Roadster	$178,750	145	RM, Phoenix, AZ	1/16/09
1939 Packard Model 1708 Convertible Sedan	$176,000	SP142	RM, Ft. Lauderdale, FL	2/8/09
1939 Packard Twelve All-Weather Cabriolet by Brunn	$176,000	236	RM, Rochester, MI	8/2/08
1934 Packard Twelve Formal Sedan	$176,000	260	RM, Rochester, MI	8/2/08
1931 Packard 840 Dual Cowl Phaeton	$176,000	53	Worldwide, Auburn, IN	8/30/08
1932 Packard 903 Super 8 Coupe Roadster	$172,800	493	Leake, Tulsa, OK	6/14/09
1931 Packard 840 Roadster	$189,000	566	Cox, Branson, MO	4/18/09
2006 Pagani Zonda F Clubsport Coupe	$1,079,471	437	Coys, London, UK	3/12/09
1910 Peerless Victoria	$469,000	844	Bonhams & Butterfields, Owls Head, ME	9/27/08
1912 Peerless Model 36 7-Passenger Touring Car	$368,500	464	RM, Monterey, CA	8/16/08
1913 Peerless Model 48-Six Roadster	$330,000	465	RM, Monterey, CA	8/16/08
1984 Peugeot 205 Turbo 16 Group B Rally	$359,586	67	Artcurial, Paris, FRA	6/14/09
1914 Peugeot 145S Torpedo Tourer	$243,000	561	Cox, Branson, MO	4/18/09
1988 Peugeot 405 Turbo 16 Grand Raid	$198,139	60	Artcurial, Paris, FRA	6/14/09
1988 Peugeot Oxia Concept	$198,139	45	Artcurial, Paris, FRA	6/14/09
1910 Pierce-Arrow Model 48 SS	$632,500	145	Gooding, Pebble Beach, CA	8/17/08
1917 Pierce-Arrow Model 48 Touring Car	$385,000	267	RM, Hershey, PA	10/10/08
1935 Pierce-Arrow 12 Convertible Coupe	$374,000	158	RM, Phoenix, AZ	1/18/08
1917 Pierce-Arrow Four-Passenger Touring Car	$324,500	170	RM, Phoenix, AZ	1/18/08
1913 Pierce-Arrow 48-B 7-Passenger Touring	$315,000	847	Bonhams & Butterfields, Owls Head, ME	9/27/08
1912 Pierce-Arrow Model 66-QQ 5-Passenger Touring Car	$308,000	250	RM, Amelia Island, FL	3/14/09
1933 Pierce-Arrow Twelve Convertible Sedan	$181,500	150	RM, Phoenix, AZ	1/16/09
1970 Plymouth Superbird Custom Replica	$551,100	1289	Barrett-Jackson, Scottsdale, AZ	1/18/09
1970 Plymouth Hemi 'Cuda 2-Door Hardtop	$440,000	S704	Russo and Steele, Scottsdale, AZ	1/18/09
1971 Plymouth 'Cuda 2-Door Hardtop	$396,000	F515	Russo and Steele, Scottsdale, AZ	1/20/08
1971 Plymouth Hemi 'Cuda 2-Door Hardtop	$378,000	S175	Mecum, Indianapolis, IN	5/18/08
1971 Plymouth Hemi 'Cuda 2-Door Hardtop	$341,000	F518	Russo and Steele, Scottsdale, AZ	1/18/09
1970 Plymouth Hemi Superbird 2-Door Hardtop	$318,000	S180.1	Mecum, Indianapolis, IN	5/17/09
1970 Plymouth Hemi 'Cuda 2-Door Hardtop	$286,200	S170	Mecum, Indianapolis, IN	5/17/09
1970 Plymouth Hemi Superbird 2-Door Hardtop	$286,200	S90.1	Mecum, Indianapolis, IN	5/17/09
1970 Plymouth 'Cuda 2-Door Hardtop	$280,500	S706	Russo and Steele, Scottsdale, AZ	1/20/08
1970 Plymouth Hemi 'Cuda 2-Door Hardtop	$269,500	1254.1	Barrett-Jackson, Scottsdale, AZ	1/20/08
1970 Plymouth 'Cuda 440/6 Convertible	$260,000	S178	Mecum, Indianapolis, IN	5/18/08

1970 Plymouth Superbird 2-Door Hardtop

1963 Pontiac Catalina "Swiss Cheese"

1966 Porsche 906 Endurance Racing Coupe

Model	Sold Price	Lot #	Auction Location	Date
1960 Plymouth Fury Convertible	$253,000	242	RM, Dallas, TX	4/19/08
1970 Plymouth Hemi Road Runner Superbird 2-Door Hardtop	$253,000	29	Worldwide, Houston, TX	5/3/08
1970 Plymouth Hemi 'Cuda 2-Door Hardtop	$244,125	S177	Mecum, Indianapolis, IN	5/18/08
1970 Plymouth 'Cuda 2-Door Hardtop	$242,000	S720	Russo and Steele, Scottsdale, AZ	1/20/08
1970 Plymouth Hemi 'Cuda 2-Door Hardtop	$241,150	S113	Mecum, Indianapolis, IN	5/17/09
1970 Plymouth Hemi 'Cuda 2-Door Hardtop	$220,500	U106	Mecum, Indianapolis, IN	5/18/08
1970 Plymouth Superbird 2-Door Hardtop	$220,000	1021	Barrett-Jackson, Scottsdale, AZ	1/20/08
1967 Plymouth Barracuda West Coast Customs 2-Door Hardtop	$220,000	1306.2	Barrett-Jackson, Scottsdale, AZ	1/18/09
1970 Plymouth Superbird 2-Door Hardtop	$214,500	1277.1	Barrett-Jackson, Scottsdale, AZ	1/20/08
1970 Plymouth Hemi 'Cuda 2-Door Hardtop	$198,000	1262	Barrett-Jackson, Scottsdale, AZ	1/18/09
1970 Plymouth Hemi 'Cuda 2-Door Hardtop	$187,000	804.2	Barrett-Jackson, Las Vegas, NV	10/18/08
1970 Plymouth Superbird 2-Door Hardtop	$184,800	649.1	Barrett-Jackson, West Palm Beach, FL	3/30/08
1970 Plymouth Superbird 2-Door Hardtop	$181,500	1268	Barrett-Jackson, Scottsdale, AZ	1/20/08
1970 Plymouth Hemi 'Cuda 2-Door Hardtop	$174,300	C39	Mecum, Indianapolis, IN	4/12/08
1963 Pontiac Catalina "Swiss Cheese" 2-Door Hardtop	$451,500	S88	Mecum, St. Charles, IL	10/5/08
1962 Pontiac Catalina Super Duty 2-Door Hardtop	$412,500	SN825	Russo and Steele, Scottsdale, AZ	1/18/09
1966 Pontiac GTO Monkeemobile	$396,000	1297	Barrett-Jackson, Scottsdale, AZ	1/20/08
1970 Pontiac GTO Judge Ram Air IV Convertible	$378,000	S113	Mecum, Indianapolis, IN	5/18/08
1959 Pontiac Catalina Convertible "Pink Lady"	$247,500	1314	Barrett-Jackson, Scottsdale, AZ	1/20/08
1957 Pontiac Bonneville Convertible	$242,000	110	RM, Phoenix, AZ	1/18/08
1970 Pontiac GTO Judge Ram Air IV "Tin Indian" 2-Door Hardtop	$180,200	S116	Mecum, Indianapolis, IN	5/17/09
1954 Porsche 550 Spyder	$1,090,841	234	Coys, Monte Carlo, MCO	5/10/08
1964 Porsche 904 GTS Coupe	$888,465	326	Bonhams, Sussex, UK	9/19/08
1966 Porsche 906 Endurance Racing Coupe	$782,325	256	Bonhams, Monte Carlo, MCO	5/18/09
1981 Porsche 935/78 Moby Dick Race Car	$550,000	451	RM, Monterey, CA	8/16/08
1972 Porsche 911 2.7 RS Prototype	$480,000	359	Bonhams & Butterfields, Carmel Valley, CA	8/15/08
1973 Porsche 911 2.7 RS Coupe	$425,575	131	Bonhams, Paris, FRA	2/9/08
1963 Porsche 356 Carrera 2 Convertible	$381,000	249	Bonhams & Butterfields, Greenwich, CT	6/7/09
1973 Porsche 911 Carrera RS Touring	$332,281	115	Coys, Nürburgring, DEU	8/9/08
1988 Porsche 959 Coupe	$331,784	349	Coys, Essen, DEU	3/29/08
1973 Porsche 911 2.7 RS Coupe	$302,500	S659	Russo and Steele, Monterey, CA	8/16/08
1958 Porsche 356A Speedster	$258,500	138	Gooding, Pebble Beach, CA	8/17/08
1973 Porsche 911 2.7 RS Coupe	$238,950	227	Coys, Monte Carlo, MCO	5/18/09
1958 Porsche 356 1600 Speedster	$220,000	183	RM, Phoenix, AZ	1/18/08
1956 Porsche 356A 1600S Speedster	$220,000	240	RM, Amelia Island, FL	3/8/08
1960 Porsche 356B 1600 Roadster	$191,800	335	Bonhams & Butterfields, Carmel Valley, CA	8/15/08
1973 Porsche 911 2.7 RS Touring Coupe	$173,552	226A	Bonhams, Silverstone, UK	7/26/08
1999 Prost-Peugeot AP02 F1 Single-Seater	$253,918	46	Artcurial, Paris, FRA	2/9/08
1911 Rambler 7-Passenger Touring	$1,620,000	2764	Kruse, Scottsdale, AZ	1/25/09
1912 Renault Type CB Coupe de Ville	$269,500	139	RM, Phoenix, AZ	1/18/08
1906 Reo Model A 16hp	$275,000	132	Gooding, Pebble Beach, CA	8/17/08
1932 Reo Royale Convertible Coupe	$220,000	286	RM, Amelia Island, FL	3/14/09
1934 Riley MPH Roadster	$308,000	64	Gooding, Pebble Beach, CA	8/17/08
1935 Riley "Dobbs Special" 2-Liter Offset Monoposto	$191,124	568	Bonhams, Sussex, UK	7/11/08

Model	Sold Price	Lot #	Auction Location	Date
Robosaurus Car Crushing Robot	$632,500	1307	Barrett-Jackson, Scottsdale, AZ	1/20/08
1933 Rolls-Royce Phantom II Special Town Car	$2,310,000	453	RM, Monterey, CA	8/16/08
1925 Rolls-Royce Phantom I Barker Boattail	$1,210,000	131	Gooding, Pebble Beach, CA	8/17/08
1914 Rolls-Royce 40/50hp Silver Ghost Skiff Torpedo	$1,072,500	81	Worldwide, Houston, TX	5/3/08
1933 Rolls-Royce Phantom II Streamline Saloon	$852,500	72	Gooding, Scottsdale, AZ	1/19/08
1913 Rolls-Royce 40/50hp Silver Ghost Roi-des-Belges Tourer	$832,000	836	Bonhams & Butterfields, Owls Head, ME	9/27/08
1912 Rolls-Royce 40/50hp Silver Ghost Tourer	$797,500	27	Gooding, Scottsdale, AZ	1/17/09
1912 Rolls-Royce 40/50hp Silver Ghost Roi-des-Belges Tourer	$546,975	219	Bonhams, Northamptonshire, UK	6/13/09
1911 Rolls-Royce 40/50hp Silver Ghost Roi-des-Belges	$522,500	43	Worldwide, Auburn, IN	8/30/08
1933 Rolls-Royce Phantom II Short Chassis Continental Sedanca Coupe	$512,122	327	Coys, Essen, DEU	3/29/08
1935 Rolls-Royce Phantom II	$440,000	1312	Barrett-Jackson, Scottsdale, AZ	1/20/08
1934 Rolls-Royce Phantom II Continental	$440,000	30	Gooding, Scottsdale, AZ	1/17/09
1920 Rolls-Royce Silver Ghost Roadster	$429,000	107	Gooding, Pebble Beach, CA	8/17/08
1961 Rolls-Royce Silver Cloud II DHC	$387,129	171	Bonhams, Paris, FRA	2/7/09
1923 Rolls-Royce 40/50hp Silver Ghost "Salamanca"	$377,586	539	Bonhams, Hendon, UK	4/21/08
1933 Rolls-Royce Phantom II Continental Sedanca Coupe	$375,000	192	RM, Phoenix, AZ	1/16/09
1929 Rolls-Royce Phantom I Convertible Sedan	$364,500	220	Bonhams & Butterfields, Greenwich, CT	6/8/08
1919/20 Rolls-Royce 40/50hp Silver Ghost Alpine Eagle	$335,819	224	Bonhams, Northamptonshire, UK	6/21/08
1929 Rolls-Royce Phantom I Ascot Sport Phaeton	$330,000	129	RM, Phoenix, AZ	1/16/09
1927 Rolls-Royce Phantom I Playboy Roadster	$319,000	145	RM, Anaheim, CA	6/29/08
1926 Rolls-Royce Silver Ghost Piccadilly Roadster	$319,000	163	Gooding, Pebble Beach, CA	8/17/08
1923 Rolls-Royce 40/50hp Silver Ghost Pall Mall Dual Cowl Phaeton	$315,000	862	Bonhams & Butterfields, Owls Head, ME	9/27/08
1962 Rolls-Royce Silver Cloud II DHC	$313,500	164	RM, Phoenix, AZ	1/18/08
1962 Rolls-Royce Silver Cloud II	$302,621	23	Artcurial, Paris, FRA	2/9/08
1934 Rolls-Royce Phantom II Sedanca DeVille	$269,500	165	Gooding, Pebble Beach, CA	8/17/08
1926 Rolls-Royce Springfield Silver Ghost	$264,000	56A	Gooding, Scottsdale, AZ	1/19/08
1930 Rolls-Royce Phantom II Experimental	$246,882	451	Coys, London, UK	7/5/08
1931 Rolls-Royce Phantom II Continental Touring Sedan	$246,420	636	Bonhams, London, UK	12/1/08
1928 Rolls-Royce Phantom Ascot Tourer	$238,000	224	Bonhams & Butterfields, Greenwich, CT	6/7/09
1929 Rolls-Royce Phantom II Imperial Cabriolet	$227,000	253	Bonhams & Butterfields, Greenwich, CT	6/7/09
1954 Rolls-Royce Silver Dawn Custom Sedan	$225,500	794	Barrett-Jackson, Las Vegas, NV	10/18/08
1966 Rolls-Royce Silver Cloud III DHC	$215,641	212	Coys, Monte Carlo, MCO	5/18/09
1931 Rolls-Royce Phantom II Continental Close-Coupled Sports Saloon	$205,400	342	Coys, Essen, DEU	3/29/08
2001 Rolls-Royce Corniche Convertible	$204,045	333	Bonhams, Sussex, UK	9/19/08
1921 Rolls-Royce 45/50hp Silver Ghost Salamanca Cabriolet	$197,483	212	Bonhams, Northamptonshire, UK	6/21/08
1926 Rolls-Royce 40/50hp Berwick Sedan	$195,098	142	Bonhams, Paris, FRA	2/9/08
1928 Rolls-Royce Phantom I Derby Speedster	$183,000	317	Bonhams & Butterfields, Carmel Valley, CA	8/15/08
c.1953 Rolls-Royce Silver Wraith 4½-Liter Limousine	$178,020	146	Bonhams, Paris, FRA	2/7/09
1929 Ruxton Prototype Muller Front Drive Roadster	$423,500	1313	Barrett-Jackson, Scottsdale, AZ	1/20/08
1931 Ruxton Model C Roadster	$363,000	239	RM, Rochester, MI	8/2/08
2005 Saleen S7 Twin Turbo Coupe	$412,500	1305	Barrett-Jackson, Scottsdale, AZ	1/18/09
2003 Saleen S7 Coupe	$260,700	805.1	Barrett-Jackson, Las Vegas, NV	10/18/08

1911 Rolls-Royce 40/50hp Silver Ghost Roi-des-Belges

1962 Rolls-Royce Silver Cloud II DHC

1931 Ruxton Model C Roadster

Model	Sold Price	Lot #	Auction Location	Date
1930 Sampson Miller U16 Special	$412,500	247	RM, Tustin, CA	6/14/08
1908 Sharp Arrow Runabout	$183,000	866	Bonhams & Butterfields, Owls Head, ME	9/27/08
1963 Shelby Cobra 289 Competition Roadster	$1,732,500	152	RM, Phoenix, AZ	1/18/08
1966 Shelby Cobra 427 S/C Roadster	$1,234,900	F248.1	Mecum, Indianapolis, IN	5/17/09
1966 Shelby Cobra 427 Competition Roadster	$1,060,000	F246	Mecum, Indianapolis, IN	5/17/09
1966 Shelby Cobra 427 Roadster	$962,500	248	RM, Monterey, CA	8/16/08
1967 Shelby GT500 Convertible	$874,500	F248	Mecum, Indianapolis, IN	5/17/09
1967 Shelby Cobra 427 Roadster	$829,250	S654	Russo and Steele, Monterey, CA	8/16/08
1966 Shelby Cobra 427 Roadster	$781,000	SP79	RM, Ft. Lauderdale, FL	2/17/08
1969 Shelby GT500 Convertible	$742,500	1287	Barrett-Jackson, Scottsdale, AZ	1/20/08
1967 Shelby Cobra 427 Roadster	$687,500	1281.1	Barrett-Jackson, Scottsdale, AZ	1/20/08
1966 Shelby Cobra 427 Roadster	$675,000	264	RM, Amelia Island, FL	3/14/09
1967 Shelby Cobra 427 Roadster	$660,000	1301	Barrett-Jackson, Scottsdale, AZ	1/20/08
1965 Shelby Cobra 289 Roadster	$605,000	438	RM, Monterey, CA	8/16/08
1964 Shelby Cobra 289 Roadster	$583,000	6	Gooding, Scottsdale, AZ	1/19/08
1963 Shelby Cobra 289 Roadster	$550,000	143	Gooding, Pebble Beach, CA	8/17/08
1964 Shelby Cobra 289 Roadster	$495,000	S708	Russo and Steele, Scottsdale, AZ	1/18/09
1965 Shelby Cobra 289 Mk II Roadster	$467,500	185	RM, Phoenix, AZ	1/16/09
1965 Shelby GT350 Fastback	$462,000	1293	Barrett-Jackson, Scottsdale, AZ	1/20/08
1967 Shelby GT500 Fastback	$363,000	1318	Barrett-Jackson, Scottsdale, AZ	1/20/08
1965 Shelby GT350 Fastback "Final Prototype"	$299,450	F240	Mecum, Indianapolis, IN	5/17/09
1968 Shelby GT500 KR Convertible	$247,500	S722	Russo and Steele, Scottsdale, AZ	1/20/08
1965 Shelby GT350 Fastback	$247,500	269	RM, Monterey, CA	8/16/08
1968 Shelby GT500 KR Convertible	$246,100	S114	Mecum, Indianapolis, IN	5/18/08
1967 Shelby GT500 Fastback	$242,000	S715	Russo and Steele, Scottsdale, AZ	1/20/08
1968 Shelby GT500 KR Convertible	$231,000	1278	Barrett-Jackson, Scottsdale, AZ	1/20/08
1969 Shelby GT500 Fastback	$220,000	1329.1	Barrett-Jackson, Scottsdale, AZ	1/20/08
1966 Shelby GT350 Fastback	$220,000	1271.1	Barrett-Jackson, Scottsdale, AZ	1/18/09
1966 Shelby GT350 Fastback	$220,000	F509	Russo and Steele, Scottsdale, AZ	1/20/08
1968 Shelby GT500 Convertible	$220,000	SP47	RM, Ft. Lauderdale, FL	2/17/08
1968 Shelby GT500 KR Convertible	$217,250	SP41	RM, Ft. Lauderdale, FL	2/17/08
1967 Shelby GT500 E "Gone in 60 Seconds"	$216,700	1317	Barrett-Jackson, Scottsdale, AZ	1/18/09
1968 Shelby GT500 KR Custom Fastback	$214,500	1270	Barrett-Jackson, Scottsdale, AZ	1/20/08
1968 Shelby GT500 KR Fastback	$210,600	733	Kruse, Hershey, PA	10/11/08
1967 Shelby GT500 Fastback	$209,000	659	Barrett-Jackson, West Palm Beach, FL	3/30/08
1963 Shelby Cobra 289 Roadster	$205,400	345	Coys, Essen, DEU	3/29/08
1968 Shelby GT350 Convertible	$193,600	SP51	RM, Ft. Lauderdale, FL	2/17/08
1968 Shelby GT500 KR Fastback	$192,500	1555	Barrett-Jackson, Scottsdale, AZ	1/20/08
1967 Shelby GT500 E Fastback	$192,500	1343	Barrett-Jackson, Scottsdale, AZ	1/18/09
1968 Shelby GT500 KR Convertible	$189,200	1238.1	Barrett-Jackson, Scottsdale, AZ	1/20/08
1967 Shelby GT500 E Supersnake Fastback	$187,000	804.1	Barrett-Jackson, Las Vegas, NV	10/18/08
1967 Shelby GT500 Fastback	$185,500	F226	Mecum, Indianapolis, IN	5/17/09
1967 Shelby GT500 Fastback	$185,500	F249	Mecum, Indianapolis, IN	5/17/09
1967 Shelby GT500 Fastback	$181,500	789.4	Barrett-Jackson, Las Vegas, NV	10/18/08
1966 Shelby GT350 H Fastback	$180,200	n/a	Tom Mack, Concord, NC	4/5/08

1966 Shelby Cobra 427 Competition Roadster

1966 Shelby Cobra 427 Roadster

1967 Shelby GT500 Fastback

1939 Talbot-Lago T150C SS Teardrop Coupe

1948 Tucker 48 Sedan

1960 Watson Indy Roadster

Model	Sold Price	Lot #	Auction Location	Date
1968 Shelby GT500 KR Convertible	$177,100	F521	Russo and Steele, Scottsdale, AZ	1/20/08
1968 Shelby GT500 KR Fastback	$176,000	1338	Barrett-Jackson, Scottsdale, AZ	1/20/08
1968 Shelby GT500 KR Fastback	$176,000	224	RM, Dallas, TX	4/19/08
1904 Société Manufacturiere d'Armes 24/30hp Open Drive Landaulette	$351,450	530	Bonhams, Hendon, UK	4/21/08
1912 Speedwell Model 12-H Speed Car	$506,000	10	Gooding, Pebble Beach, CA	8/17/08
1936 Jaguar SS 100 Roadster	$300,960	66	H&H, Buxton, UK	11/26/08
2004 SSC Aero SC/8T Prototype	$189,200	671	Barrett-Jackson, West Palm Beach, FL	3/30/08
1911 Stanely Steamer 10 Horsepower Model 63 Toy Tonneau	$184,250	241	RM, Hershey, PA	10/10/08
1908 Stanley Model M 5-Passenger Touring	$298,500	864	Bonhams & Butterfields, Owls Head, ME	9/27/08
1913 Stevens-Duryea Model C 5-Passenger Touring Car	$330,000	269	RM, Rochester, MI	8/2/08
1947 Steyr-Allard Alloy Monoposto	$203,500	1304	Barrett-Jackson, Scottsdale, AZ	1/18/09
1911 Stoddard Dayton Model 11K 50hp Roadster	$282,000	856	Bonhams & Butterfields, Owls Head, ME	9/27/08
1931 Studebaker President Four Seasons Roadster	$188,100	SP176	RM, Ft. Lauderdale, FL	2/17/08
1932 Studebaker President Four-Seasons	$187,000	23	Gooding, Pebble Beach, CA	8/17/08
1914 Stutz Series E Bearcat	$1,375,000	45	Gooding, Pebble Beach, CA	8/17/08
1932 Stutz DV-32 Super Bearcat	$594,000	151	RM, Phoenix, AZ	1/16/09
1915 Stutz Model 4-F Bulldog Demi-Tonneau	$352,000	29	Gooding, Scottsdale, AZ	1/17/09
1920 Stutz Bearcat Roadster	$253,000	60	Worldwide, Auburn, IN	8/30/08
1905 Sunbeam 12/14hp 5-Seat Side-Entrance Tonneau	$482,130	535	Bonhams, Hendon, UK	4/21/08
1945 Supermarine Spitfire Mk XIV Fighter Plane	$2,088,240	10	Bonhams & Goodman, Annesbrook, NZL	9/14/08
1932 Talbot 105 Fox & Nicholl Team Car	$300,960	42	H&H, Buxton, UK	11/26/08
1939 Talbot-Lago T150C SS Teardrop Coupe	$4,847,000	330	Bonhams & Butterfields, Carmel Valley, CA	8/15/08
1937 Talbot-Lago T150C SS Teardrop Coupe	$3,520,000	23	Gooding, Scottsdale, AZ	1/17/09
1950 Talbot-Lago T26 Record Grand Sport Cabriolet	$297,975	109	Bonhams, Paris, FRA	2/9/08
1947 Talbot-Lago T26 Record Cabriolet	$214,500	239	RM, Monterey, CA	8/16/08
1954 Talbot-Lago T26 Grand Sport Coupe	$205,000	362	Bonhams & Butterfields, Carmel Valley, CA	8/15/08
1904 Thomas Model 27 Racer	$1,188,000	775	Kruse, Phoenix, AZ	1/27/08
1907 Thomas Flyer Model 36 60hp	$1,028,500	127	Gooding, Pebble Beach, CA	8/17/08
1903 Toledo 12hp Touring Car	$192,500	11	Gooding, Pebble Beach, CA	8/17/08
1948 Tucker 48 Sedan	$1,017,500	449	RM, Monterey, CA	8/16/08
1990 Tyrell Cosworth F1 Single-Seater	$258,720	259	Coys, Monte Carlo, MCO	5/10/08
1963 Urgo/Kuzma Sprint Car	$242,000	242	RM, Tustin, CA	6/14/08
1915 Van Blerck 17-Liter Roadster	$288,200	18	Worldwide, Houston, TX	5/3/08
1944 Vickers-Supermarine Spitfire Mk IX Fighter Plane	$2,522,275	390	Bonhams, Hendon, UK	4/20/09
1944 Volkswagen Schwimmwagen Amphibious	$231,725	163	Bonhams, Monte Carlo, MCO	5/10/08
1960 Watson Indy Roadster	$495,000	234	RM, Tustin, CA	6/14/08
1908 White Model L Touring Car	$220,000	13	Gooding, Pebble Beach, CA	8/17/08
1903 Winton Runabout	$238,000	859	Bonhams & Butterfields, Owls Head, ME	9/27/08

BY THE NUMBERS

Marque by Marque, the Top Five

From AC to Zimmer, here's a look at the high sellers from each manufacturer.*

Model	Sold Price	Lot #	Auction Location	Date
AC				
1957 Ace Bristol Roadster	$258,500	1289	Barrett-Jackson, Scottsdale, AZ	1/20/08
1956 Ace Roadster	$216,000	229	Bonhams & Butterfields, Greenwich, CT	6/8/08
1959 Ace Bristol Roadster	$210,813	518	Bonhams, Sussex, UK	7/11/08
1936 16/90 Competition	$199,902	22	Artcurial, Paris, FRA	2/8/09
1958 Ace Bristol	$195,437	82	H&H, Buxton, UK	6/10/09
Alfa Romeo				
1938 6C 2300 B Mille Miglia	$2,585,000	116	Gooding, Pebble Beach, CA	8/17/08
1932 6C 1750 Gran Sport Spyder	$1,540,000	70	Gooding, Scottsdale, AZ	1/19/08
1931 6C 1750 Gran Sport Spyder	$1,320,000	44	Gooding, Pebble Beach, CA	8/17/08
1930 6C 1750 Spyder	$1,265,000	137	Gooding, Pebble Beach, CA	8/17/08
1930 6C 1750 Gran Sport Spyder	$1,107,000	352	Bonhams & Butterfields, Carmel Valley, CA	8/15/08
Allard				
1951 J2 Roadster	$308,000	67	Gooding, Pebble Beach, CA	8/17/08
1953 J2X Roadster	$258,500	68	Gooding, Scottsdale, AZ	1/17/09
1950 J2 Roadster	$253,000	169	RM, Phoenix, AZ	1/16/09
1950 J2 Roadster	$220,000	S721	Russo and Steele, Scottsdale, AZ	1/20/08
1951 J2 Roadster	$154,000	261	RM, Amelia Island, FL	3/14/09
Alpine Renault				
1969 A110 Coupe	$138,198	42	Artcurial, Paris, FRA	2/9/08
1973 A110 1600S Coupe	$101,324	38	Artcurial, Paris, FRA	6/28/08
1973 A110 1600 SC Prototype	$100,118	23	Artcurial, Paris, FRA	11/16/08
1969 A110 Coupe	$37,301	216	Coys, Brands Hatch, UK	5/25/08
1973 A110 Group 4 Coupe	$63,200	312	Coys, Essen, DEU	3/29/08
Alvis				
1937 4.3-Liter Short Chassis Vanden Plas Tourer	$295,020	89	H&H, Buxton, UK	4/16/09
1939 Speed 25 Tourer	$173,250	236	RM, Amelia Island, FL	3/14/09
1937 Speed 25 4-Door Tourer	$117,812		Barons, Surrey, UK	4/28/09
1939 Cadillac V16 Special Roadster	$102,850	27	H&H, Sparkford, UK	10/12/08
1934 Speed 20SC Vanden Plas	$85,410	264	Bonhams & Butterfields, Greenwich, CT	6/7/09
AMC				
1969 SC/Rambler 2-Door Hardtop	$61,600	936.1	Barrett-Jackson, Scottsdale, AZ	1/18/09
1969 SC/Rambler 2-Door Hardtop	$60,500	929	Barrett-Jackson, Scottsdale, AZ	1/20/08
1969 SC/Rambler 2-Door Hardtop	$49,500	462	Barrett-Jackson, Scottsdale, AZ	1/20/08
1970 Javelin Coupe	$48,950	TH245	Russo and Steele, Scottsdale, AZ	1/20/08
1969 SC/Rambler 2-Door Hardtop	$48,400	936	Barrett-Jackson, Scottsdale, AZ	1/18/09
Amphicar				
1964 770 Convertible	$71,500	SP43	RM, Ft. Lauderdale, FL	2/17/08
1967 770 Convertible	$71,400	T90	Mecum, Kissimmee, FL	1/26/08
1964 770 Convertible	$66,000	714	Barrett-Jackson, Scottsdale, AZ	1/20/08
1964 770 Convertible	$61,600	SP166	RM, Ft. Lauderdale, FL	2/17/08
1967 770 Convertible	$60,500	F466	Russo and Steele, Scottsdale, AZ	1/20/08
Armstrong Siddeley				
1960 Limousine	$75,600	750	Kruse, Huntsville, AL	3/15/08
1920 30hp Series E Open Drive Limousine	$39,848	540	Bonhams, Hendon, UK	4/21/08
1946 18hp Hurricane Drophead Coupe	$6,162	203	Bonhams, Oxford, UK	3/8/09
1934 12hp Sedan	$5,748	608	Bonhams, Harrogate, UK	11/19/08
1936 12hp Sedan	$5,072	657	Bonhams, Harrogate, UK	11/19/08

Sales from the SCM Platinum Database, recorded between 1/1/2008 and 6/15/2009

Model	Sold Price	Lot #	Auction Location	Date
Arnolt-Bristol				
1954 Bolide Roadster	$252,787	125	Coys, Nürburgring, DEU	8/9/08
1959 Deluxe Competition Roadster	$205,521	143	Coys, Nürburgring, DEU	8/9/08
1954 Bolide Roadster	$161,700	37	H&H, Stoneleigh, UK	3/14/09
1959 Deluxe Roadster	$135,000	7	Gooding, Scottsdale, AZ	1/17/09
Aston Martin				
1961 DB4GT Coupe	$2,115,820	345	Bonhams, Newport Pagnell, UK	5/17/08
1966 DB6 Short Chassis Volante	$642,510	30	H&H, Harrogate, UK	4/16/08
1968 DB6 Mk I Volante	$606,620	304	Bonhams, Newport Pagnell, UK	5/17/08
1970 DB6 Mk II Volante Convertible	$526,125	322	Bonhams, Sussex, UK	9/19/08
1961 DB4 SIII Coupe	$464,963	21	Artcurial, Paris, FRA	2/9/08
Auburn				
1932 V12 Boattail Speedster	$687,500	126	Gooding, Pebble Beach, CA	8/17/08
1935 851SC Boattail Speedster	$566,500	262	RM, Amelia Island, FL	3/14/09
1936 852SC Boattail Speedster	$533,500	423	RM, Monterey, CA	8/16/08
1936 852 Boattail Speedster	$396,000	146	RM, Phoenix, AZ	1/18/08
1934 Twelve Salon Phaeton Sedan	$319,000	154	RM, Phoenix, AZ	1/16/09
Austin				
1967 Mini Cooper S	$87,560	61	H&H, Cheltenham, UK	2/27/08
1949 A-90 Atlantic Convertible	$55,575	225	Bonhams & Butterfields, Greenwich, CT	6/8/08
1962 Mini Jolly	$53,900	996	Barrett-Jackson, Scottsdale, AZ	1/18/09
1952 Venturer 14-Seat Bus	$35,450	538	Bonhams, Sussex, UK	7/11/08
1965 Mini Cooper S 1275 Mk I 2-Door Sedan	$29,060	223	Coys, Monte Carlo, MCO	5/10/08
Austin-Healey				
1956 100M Le Mans Roadster	$165,000	250	RM, Amelia Island, FL	3/8/08
1956 100M Le Mans Roadster	$159,500	481	RM, Monterey, CA	8/16/08
1965 3000 Mk III BJ8 Convertible	$137,500	654	Barrett-Jackson, West Palm Beach, FL	3/30/08
1966 3001 Mk III BJ8 Phase II Sports Convertible	$128,700	674	Barrett-Jackson, Palm Beach, FL	4/11/09
1966 3000 Mk III Convertible	$115,500	986	Barrett-Jackson, Scottsdale, AZ	1/20/08
Avanti				
1988 Convertible	$19,250	696	RM, Novi, MI	4/27/08
1984 II 2-Door Sedan	$15,660	19	Silver, Portland, OR	9/27/08
1984 Coupe	$13,780	T7	Mecum, Kissimmee, FL	1/24/09
1970 II2-Door Sedan	$12,150	64	Silver, Ft. McDowell, AZ	1/19/09
1980 II 2-Door Hardtop	$11,016	418	Leake, Oklahoma City, OK	2/23/08
Avions Voisin				
1935 C25 Aerodyne	$757,178	8	Artcurial, Paris, FRA	2/9/08
1931 C14 Chartre	$667,000	323	Bonhams & Butterfields, Carmel Valley, CA	8/15/08
1921 OC1 Presidential Coupe	$359,000	321	Bonhams & Butterfields, Carmel Valley, CA	8/15/08
1935 C25 Clairi re Berline	$330,000	35	Gooding, Scottsdale, AZ	1/17/09
1939 C30 S Coupe	$166,500	326	Bonhams & Butterfields, Carmel Valley, CA	8/15/08
Bentley				
1931 8-Liter Open Tourer by Harrison	$2,200,000	263	RM, Amelia Island, FL	3/8/08
1931 4½-Liter Blower	$1,760,000	114	Gooding, Pebble Beach, CA	8/17/08
1937 4¼-Liter Fixed Head Sport Coupe	$1,320,000	62	Gooding, Scottsdale, AZ	1/17/09
1929 4½-Liter Tourer	$880,000	135	RM, Phoenix, AZ	1/18/08
1927 Speed Six 2-seater and Dickey	$568,000	354	Bonhams & Butterfields, Carmel Valley, CA	8/15/08
Benz				
1912 14/30 PS Touring	$216,000	752	Kruse, Phoenix, AZ	1/27/08
1886 Patent Motorwagen Replica	$66,000	20	Gooding, Scottsdale, AZ	1/19/08
1899 Patent Motorwagen Replica	$48,956	512A	Bonhams, Hendon, UK	4/21/08
1886 Patent Motorwagen Replica	$40,950	201	Bonhams & Butterfields, Greenwich, CT	6/7/09
1886 Patent Motorwagen	$39,780	204	Bonhams & Butterfields, Greenwich, CT	6/8/08
Bizzarrini				
1966 Strada 5300 Coupe	$572,000	S648	Russo and Steele, Monterey, CA	8/16/08
1967 5300 GT Strada Alloy	$517,000	124	Gooding, Pebble Beach, CA	8/17/08
BMW				
1937 328 Roadster	$685,100	134	Bonhams, Monte Carlo, MCO	5/10/08
1938 328 Roadster	$507,600	265	Bonhams, Monte Carlo, MCO	5/18/09

Model	Sold Price	Lot #	Auction Location	Date
1937 328 Cabriolet	$302,500	245	RM, Amelia Island, FL	3/14/09
1938 327 Roadster	$278,569	167	Coys, Nürburgring, DEU	8/9/08
1935 319 Sport	$193,879	324	Coys, Essen, DEU	3/29/08
Bricklin				
1975 SV-1 Coupe	$11,340	2842	Kruse, Scottsdale, AZ	1/25/09
1975 SV-1 Coupe	$10,395	S603	Russo and Steele, Hollywood, FL	3/30/08
1975 SV-1 Coupe	$10,000	F39.1	Mecum, Kissimmee, FL	1/24/09
Bristol				
1955 405 Drophead Coupe	$49,170	15	H&H, Buxton, UK	4/16/09
1966 409 Coupe	$19,723	80	H&H, Buxton, UK	6/10/09
1984 Beaufighter Convertible	$17,026	220	Bonhams, Oxford, UK	3/8/09
1966 408 SI Coupe	$16,180	420	Coys, London, UK	3/12/09
1951 401 Coupe	$16,200	583	Cox, Branson, MO	4/18/09
Bugatti				
1937 Type 57SC Atalante Coupe	$7,920,000	27	Gooding, Pebble Beach, CA	8/17/08
1937 Type 57S Atalante Coupe	$4,408,575	142	Bonhams, Paris, FRA	2/7/09
1932 Type 55 Super Sport Roadster	$3,251,125	147	Bonhams, Monte Carlo, MCO	5/10/08
2009 Veyron 16.4 Grand Sport	$3,190,000	134	Gooding, Pebble Beach, CA	8/17/08
1913 Type 18 Sports 2-Seater "Black Bess"	$3,131,475	114	Bonhams, Paris, FRA	2/7/09
Buick				
1996 Custom "Blackhawk"	$522,500	1303	Barrett-Jackson, Scottsdale, AZ	1/18/09
1953 Skylark Convertible	$264,000	137	RM, Phoenix, AZ	1/18/08
1935 67C Custom Convertible	$242,000	1276.1	Barrett-Jackson, Scottsdale, AZ	1/20/08
1954 Skylark Convertible	$242,000	121	RM, Phoenix, AZ	1/18/08
1954 Skylark Convertible	$220,000	267	RM, Dallas, TX	4/19/08
Cadillac				
1930 452A V16 Roadster	$693,000	128	Gooding, Pebble Beach, CA	8/17/08
1931 452A V16 Sport Phaeton	$632,500	13	Gooding, Scottsdale, AZ	1/17/09
1938 V16 Convertible Coupe	$616,000	158	RM, Anaheim, CA	6/29/08
1931 V16 Sport Phaeton	$522,500	251	RM, Amelia Island, FL	3/8/08
1935 V16 Imperial Convertible Sedan	$473,000	148	RM, Phoenix, AZ	1/16/09
Chevrolet Bel Air				
1956 Bel Air 2-Door Hardtop Custom	$280,500	1256	Barrett-Jackson, Scottsdale, AZ	1/20/08
1957 Bel Air Custom Convertible	$181,500	1333.1	Barrett-Jackson, Scottsdale, AZ	1/20/08
1957 Bel Air 2-Door Hardtop Custom	$165,000	1001	Barrett-Jackson, Scottsdale, AZ	1/20/08
1955 Bel Air Custom 2-Door Sedan	$165,000	1275	Barrett-Jackson, Scottsdale, AZ	1/20/08
1955 Bel Air Custom 2-Door Hardtop	$159,500	795	Barrett-Jackson, Las Vegas, NV	10/18/08
Chevrolet Camaro				
1969 Camaro RS ZL1 Coupe	$800,000	S99	Mecum, Indianapolis, IN	5/18/08
1969 Camaro RCR Series 3 Coupe	$632,500	1303	Barrett-Jackson, Scottsdale, AZ	1/20/08
1967 Camaro Yenko Coupe	$504,000	S105	Mecum, Indianapolis, IN	5/18/08
1969 Camaro ZL1 Coupe	$504,000	S109	Mecum, Indianapolis, IN	5/18/08
1969 Camaro RS/SS Custom "Project American Heroes"	$500,000	369.1	Barrett-Jackson, Palm Beach, FL	4/11/09
Chevrolet Chevelle				
1970 Chevelle SS 454 LS6 Convertible	$525,000	S103	Mecum, Indianapolis, IN	5/18/08
1970 Chevelle 454 LS6 Convertible	$397,500	S126	Mecum, Indianapolis, IN	5/17/09
1965 Chevelle SS Z16 2-Door Hardtop Prototype	$355,100	S122	Mecum, Indianapolis, IN	5/17/09
1969 Chevelle 2-Door Hardtop	$341,000	S711	Russo and Steele, Scottsdale, AZ	1/20/08
1969 Chevelle COPO 2-Door Hardtop	$328,600	S124	Mecum, Indianapolis, IN	5/17/09
Chevrolet Corvette				
1963 Corvette "Rondine" Concept Car	$1,760,000	1304	Barrett-Jackson, Scottsdale, AZ	1/20/08
1962 Corvette 327/360 Gulf Oil Race Car	$1,485,000	121	Gooding, Pebble Beach, CA	8/17/08
1963 Corvette Z06 Yenko "Gulf One" Race Car	$1,113,000	S110	Mecum, Kissimmee, FL	1/24/09
2009 Corvette ZR-1 Coupe	$1,100,000	1316	Barrett-Jackson, Scottsdale, AZ	1/20/08
1967 Corvette L88 Competition Convertible	$744,000	355	Bonhams & Butterfields, Carmel Valley, CA	8/15/08
Chevrolet Impala				
1958 Impala Convertible	$167,200	990	Barrett-Jackson, Scottsdale, AZ	1/20/08
1958 Impala Convertible	$165,000	1241	Barrett-Jackson, Scottsdale, AZ	1/20/08

Model	Sold Price	Lot #	Auction Location	Date
1959 Impala Convertible	$137,800	S174	Mecum, Indianapolis, IN	5/17/09
1959 Impala Convertible	$132,000	967	Barrett-Jackson, Scottsdale, AZ	1/20/08
1958 Impala Convertible	$132,000	658	Barrett-Jackson, West Palm Beach, FL	3/30/08
Chevrolet Nomad				
1955 Nomad Custom Wagon	$198,000	1255	Barrett-Jackson, Scottsdale, AZ	1/18/09
1955 Nomad 2-Door Sportwagon	$115,500	S612	Russo and Steele, Monterey, CA	8/16/08
1955 Nomad 2-Door Wagon	$110,000	935.1	Barrett-Jackson, Scottsdale, AZ	1/20/08
1957 Nomad 2-Door Wagon	$110,000	1257.1	Barrett-Jackson, Scottsdale, AZ	1/20/08
1956 Nomad 2-Door Wagon	$106,700	750	Barrett-Jackson, Scottsdale, AZ	1/20/08
Chevrolet Nova				
1970 Nova	$129,150	S173	Mecum, Kissimmee, FL	1/26/08
1966 Nova Custom 2-Door Hardtop	$110,000	999	Barrett-Jackson, Scottsdale, AZ	1/20/08
1970 Nova Yenko Deuce Coupe	$110,000	1276.1	Barrett-Jackson, Scottsdale, AZ	1/18/09
1966 Nova SS 2-Door Hardtop	$100,100	1057	Barrett-Jackson, Scottsdale, AZ	1/20/08
1966 Nova SS 2-Door Hardtop	$93,500	966.1	Barrett-Jackson, Scottsdale, AZ	1/18/09
Chrysler				
1941 Thunderbolt LeBaron	$1,320,000	140	RM, Phoenix, AZ	1/18/08
1941 Newport LeBaron	$748,000	141	RM, Phoenix, AZ	1/18/08
1941 Newport Dual Cowl Phaeton	$687,500	270	RM, Amelia Island, FL	3/14/09
1932 CL Imperial Convertible Roadster by LeBaron	$660,000	240	RM, Rochester, MI	8/2/08
1931 CG Imperial Dual Cowl Phaeton	$605,000	28	Gooding, Scottsdale, AZ	1/17/09
Cisitalia				
1948 202 Nuvolari MM Spyder	$313,925	123	Bonhams, Paris, FRA	2/9/08
Citroën				
1973 DS23 ie Cabriolet	$435,375	123	Bonhams, Paris, FRA	2/7/09
1974 SM "Opera" Sedan	$250,905	122	Bonhams, Paris, FRA	2/7/09
1966 DS21 "Palm Beach" Cabriolet	$222,525	117	Bonhams, Paris, FRA	2/7/09
1968 DS21 Convertible	$205,216	40	Artcurial, Paris, FRA	2/9/08
1963 DS19 Decapotable	$130,900	282	Coys, Monte Carlo, MCO	5/10/08
Cord				
1929 L-29 Hayes Coupe	$1,078,000	141	Gooding, Pebble Beach, CA	8/17/08
1937 812 SC Convertible Coupe	$484,000	180	RM, Phoenix, AZ	1/16/09
1937 812 SC Phaeton	$401,500	S713	Russo and Steele, Scottsdale, AZ	1/18/09
1937 812 SC Phaeton	$363,000	48	Gooding, Scottsdale, AZ	1/19/08
1937 812 SC Phaeton	$313,500	150	RM, Phoenix, AZ	1/18/08
Crosley				
1950 Gardner Special	$27,500	219	RM, Amelia Island, FL	3/8/08
1951 Super Station Wagon	$18,150	608	Barrett-Jackson, Scottsdale, AZ	1/20/08
1947 2-Door Sedan	$13,230	411	Leake, Tulsa, OK	6/8/08
1947 2-Door Coupe	$13,200	301	Barrett-Jackson, Scottsdale, AZ	1/20/08
1950 Hotshot	$6,480	142	Leake, Tulsa, OK	6/8/08
Daimler				
1932 40/50 Double Six Sport Saloon	$2,970,000	39	Gooding, Scottsdale, AZ	1/17/09
1985 DS 420 Limousine	$68,200	207	RM, Amelia Island, FL	3/8/08
1913 30hp Landaulette	$66,880	12	H&H, Buxton, UK	11/26/08
1951 DB18 Special Sports Convertible	$57,040	176	Bonhams, Monte Carlo, MCO	5/10/08
1961 SP250 Roadster	$56,405	367	Bonhams, Hendon, UK	4/20/09
Datsun				
1980 280ZX Coupe	$36,720	800	Kruse, Ft. Lauderdale, FL	1/6/08
1977 280Z Custom Coupe	$18,700	331	Barrett-Jackson, Scottsdale, AZ	1/20/08
1982 280ZX Coupe	$16,200	179	Auctions America, Raleigh, NC	12/6/08
1974 260Z Coupe	$15,900	F70	Mecum, Indianapolis, IN	5/17/09
1972 240Z Coupe	$14,040	314	Auctions America, Raleigh, NC	12/6/08
DeDion Bouton				
c.1904 8hp Model V Rear-Entrance Tonneau	$150,000	868	Bonhams & Butterfields, Owls Head, ME	9/27/08
1904 Model Y 6hp Rear-Entrance Tonneau	$130,331	304	Bonhmas, London, UK	10/31/08
c.1898 3½hp vis-à-vis	$119,328	11	Bonhams & Goodman, Annesbrook, NZL	9/14/08
1901 4½hp Vis-à-Vis Voiturette	$98,354	302	Bonhmas, London, UK	10/31/08
1913 Type DX Touring	$58,500	850	Bonhams & Butterfields, Owls Head, ME	9/27/08

Top 5 Sales of 2008–09 by Marque

Model	Sold Price	Lot #	Auction Location	Date
Delage				
1937 D8-120 Aerosport Coupe	$825,000	132	RM, Phoenix, AZ	1/16/09
1931 D8 4-Seat Sports Tourer	$480,500	136	Bonhams, Monte Carlo, MCO	5/10/08
1935 D8-85 Clabot Roadster	$407,000	30	Worldwide, Auburn, IN	8/30/08
1933 D8 4-liter Foursome Drophead Coupe	$139,629	330	Bonhams, Sussex, UK	9/19/08
c.1929 DMN Faux Cabriolet	$65,674	20	Artcurial, Paris, FRA	6/28/08
Delahaye				
1952 235 Drophead Coupe	$280,500	208	RM, Phoenix, AZ	1/16/09
1948 135 M Pennock Cabriolet	$211,457	20	Artcurial, Paris, FRA	2/8/09
1946 135M Cabriolet	$200,100	108	Bonhams, Paris, FRA	2/9/08
1959 Merk Moteur Perkins Rizla + Promotional Vehicle	$22,253	162	Bonhams, Paris, FRA	2/7/09
DeLorean				
1981 DMC-12 Coupe	$27,500	142	Barrett-Jackson, Las Vegas, NV	10/18/08
1983 DMC-12 Coupe	$25,300	TH211	Russo and Steele, Scottsdale, AZ	1/20/08
1983 DMC-12 Coupe	$23,793	T9	Carlisle, Carlisle, PA	4/24/09
1981 DMC-12 Coupe	$21,465	T186	Mecum, Kissimmee, FL	1/24/09
1981 DMC-12 Coupe	$19,688	498	McCormick, Palm Springs, CA	11/23/08
DeSoto				
1958 Firesweep Convertible	$187,000	1252	Barrett-Jackson, Scottsdale, AZ	1/20/08
1956 Fireflite Hemi Convertible	$154,000	379	Worldwide, Escondido, CA	4/4/09
1957 Fireflite 2-Door Hardtop	$104,500	1253.1	Barrett-Jackson, Scottsdale, AZ	1/20/08
1950 Custom Suburban Station Wagon	$96,250	327	RM, Anaheim, CA	6/29/08
1949 Custom Suburban Station Wagon	$82,500	132	RM, Anaheim, CA	6/29/08
DeTomaso				
1973 Pantera Custom Coupe	$110,000	806	Barrett-Jackson, Las Vegas, NV	10/18/08
1973 Pantera Custom Coupe	$110,000	1260	Barrett-Jackson, Scottsdale, AZ	1/18/09
1969 Mangusta Coupe	$99,241	535	Bonhams, Sussex, UK	7/11/08
1970 Mangusta Coupe	$91,850	209	RM, Phoenix, AZ	1/16/09
1974 Pantera L Coupe	$88,000	270	RM, Monterey, CA	8/16/08
Dodge				
1954 Firearrow III Sports Coupe Concept Car	$880,000	170	RM, Phoenix, AZ	1/16/09
Dodge Challenger				
2008 Challenger SRT8 Coupe #001	$440,000	1331	Barrett-Jackson, Scottsdale, AZ	1/20/08
1971 Hemi Challenger R/T 2-Door Hardtop	$390,500	F520	Russo and Steele, Scottsdale, AZ	1/18/09
1970 Challenger R/T 440/6 Convertible	$265,000	S181	Mecum, Indianapolis, IN	5/18/08
1971 Hemi Challenger R/T 2-Door Hardtop	$247,500	S702	Russo and Steele, Scottsdale, AZ	1/18/09
1971 Hemi Challenger 2-Door Hardtop	$231,000	32	Worldwide, Houston, TX	5/3/08
Dodge Charger				
1969 Charger 2-Door Hardtop "General Lee"	$495,000	1321	Barrett-Jackson, Scottsdale, AZ	1/20/08
1971 Hemi Charger R/T 2-Door Hardtop	$215,000	S173	Mecum, Indianapolis, IN	5/18/08
1969 Hemi Charger 500 2-Door Hardtop	$181,500	1270.1	Barrett-Jackson, Scottsdale, AZ	1/20/08
1969 Charger 2-Door Hardtop	$176,000	S687	Russo and Steele, Scottsdale, AZ	1/20/08
2007 Charger R/T Custom Nitro Funny Car	$143,000	1330	Barrett-Jackson, Scottsdale, AZ	1/20/08
Dodge Coronet				
1970 Hemi Coronet R/T Convertible	$404,250	S108	Mecum, Indianapolis, IN	5/18/08
1970 Coronet Hemi R/T 2-Door Hardtop	$156,750	226	RM, Monterey, CA	8/16/08
1966 Hemi Coronet 2-Door Hardtop	$123,200	661.1	Barrett-Jackson, West Palm Beach, FL	3/30/08
1970 Coronet R/T 2-Door Hardtop	$88,000	1362	Barrett-Jackson, Scottsdale, AZ	1/20/08
1967 Coronet R/T 2-Door Hardtop	$80,000	T154	Mecum, Indianapolis, IN	5/18/08
Dodge Daytona				
1969 Daytona 2-Door Hardtop	$206,700	S154	Mecum, Kissimmee, FL	1/24/09
1969 Daytona 440 2-Door Hardtop	$173,250	S108	Mecum, St. Charles, IL	10/5/08
1969 Daytona 440 2-Door Hardtop	$159,000	S150	Mecum, Indianapolis, IN	5/17/09
1969 Daytona 440 2-Door Hardtop	$150,150	S122	Mecum, St. Charles, IL	10/5/08
1969 Daytona 2-Door Hardtop	$131,250	S176	Mecum, Kissimmee, FL	1/26/08
Dodge Super Bee				
1969 Super Bee 2-Door Hardtop	$129,800	1336	Barrett-Jackson, Scottsdale, AZ	1/20/08
1969 Super Bee 2-Door Hardtop	$78,100	640.1	Barrett-Jackson, West Palm Beach, FL	3/30/08
1969 Hemi Super Bee 2-Door Hardtop	$77,380	S203	Mecum, Indianapolis, IN	5/17/09

Model	Sold Price	Lot #	Auction Location	Date
1970 Super Bee 2-Door Hardtop	$73,980	489	Leake, Tulsa, OK	6/14/09
1970 Super Bee 2-Door Hardtop	$71,500	390	Barrett-Jackson, West Palm Beach, FL	3/30/08
Dual-Ghia				
1958 Convertible	$319,000	63	Worldwide, Hilton Head, SC	11/1/08
1957 Convertible	$319,000	257	RM, Dallas, TX	4/19/08
1963 L6.4 Coupe	$275,000	258	RM, Dallas, TX	4/19/08
1958 Convertible	$209,000	254	RM, Amelia Island, FL	3/14/09
1957 Convertible	$176,000	168	RM, Phoenix, AZ	1/16/09
Duesenberg				
1931 Model J Convertible Coupe by Murphy	$2,640,000	241	RM, Amelia Island, FL	3/8/08
1929 Model J Dual Cowl Phaeton	$1,760,000	136	RM, Phoenix, AZ	1/18/08
1930 Model J Dual Cowl Phaeton	$1,760,000	441	RM, Monterey, CA	8/16/08
1933 Model SJ Phaeton	$1,688,500	242	RM, Hershey, PA	10/10/08
1929 Model J Convertible Coupe	$1,413,500	457	RM, Monterey, CA	8/16/08
Edsel				
1959 Corsair Convertible	$126,500	109	RM, Phoenix, AZ	1/18/08
1959 Corsair Convertible	$70,200	767	Kruse, Naples, FL	3/2/08
1958 Citation Convertible	$55,000	NR118	RM, Ft. Lauderdale, FL	2/17/08
1959 Corsair Convertible	$52,800	660	Barrett-Jackson, Scottsdale, AZ	1/20/08
1959 Corsair Convertible	$46,200	9	Worldwide, Houston, TX	5/3/08
Excalibur				
1982 Roadster	$30,780	549	Leake, Tulsa, OK	6/8/08
1981 Series IV Phaeton	$29,425	TH240	Russo and Steele, Scottsdale, AZ	1/20/08
1976 Series III Phaeton	$28,600	100	Worldwide, Houston, TX	5/3/08
1982 Phaeton	$24,420	TH211	Russo and Steele, Scottsdale, AZ	1/18/09
1972 SS Roadster	$21,000	S1	Mecum, Kissimmee, FL	1/26/08
Facel Vega				
1961 HK500 Coupe	$142,830	224	Bonhams, Monte Carlo, MCO	5/18/09
1961 HK500	$96,250	225	RM, Monterey, CA	8/16/08
1960 HK500	$69,501	71	H&H, Cheltenham, UK	2/27/08
Ferrari				
1957 250 Testa Rossa	$12,402,500	237	RM, Maranello, ITA	5/17/09
1961 250 GT SWB California Spyder	$10,894,400	328	RM, Maranello, ITA	5/18/08
1964 250 LM Sports Racer	$6,979,225	339A	RM, Maranello, ITA	5/18/08
1960 250 GT LWB California Spyder	$4,950,000	78	Gooding, Scottsdale, AZ	1/17/09
1961 250 GT SWB Berlinetta	$4,510,000	447	RM, Monterey, CA	8/16/08
Fiat				
1970 Dino 2400 Spider	$124,775	106	Bonhams, Monte Carlo, MCO	5/10/08
1937 1500/6 Touring Superleggera Berlinetta	$103,180	266	Coys, Monte Carlo, MCO	5/10/08
1959 Abarth 750 Coupe	$88,000	61	Gooding, Scottsdale, AZ	1/19/08
1961 Jolly Convertible	$70,400	SP103	RM, Ft. Lauderdale, FL	2/17/08
1959 Jolly 600	$68,750	477	RM, Monterey, CA	8/16/08
Ford				
1934 Model 40 Special Speedster	$1,760,000	252	RM, Amelia Island, FL	3/8/08
Ford Mustang				
2008 Mustang Shelby GT500 KR Coupe	$605,000	1300	Barrett-Jackson, Scottsdale, AZ	1/20/08
2009 Mustang FR500 CJ Prototype #1	$412,500	1333.1	Barrett-Jackson, Scottsdale, AZ	1/18/09
1970 Mustang Boss 302 TransAm Race Car	$407,000	87	Gooding, Scottsdale, AZ	1/17/09
1969 Mustang Boss 429 Fastback	$357,500	1269	Barrett-Jackson, Scottsdale, AZ	1/20/08
1969 Mustang Boss 429 Fastback	$330,000	1329	Barrett-Jackson, Scottsdale, AZ	1/20/08
Ford Thunderbird				
1957 Thunderbird F-code Convertible	$159,500	817	Barrett-Jackson, Las Vegas, NV	10/18/08
1957 Thunderbird F-code Convertible	$159,500	817	Barrett-Jackson, Las Vegas, NV	10/18/08
1957 Thunderbird F-code Convertible	$159,500	817	Barrett-Jackson, Las Vegas, NV	10/18/08
1957 Thunderbird F-code Convertible	$150,700	1340.1	Barrett-Jackson, Scottsdale, AZ	1/20/08
1957 Thunderbird Convertible	$143,000	1024	Barrett-Jackson, Scottsdale, AZ	1/20/08
Ford Lotus				
1965 Cortina Mk I Sedan	$61,921	45	Artcurial, Paris, FRA	6/28/08
1965 Cortina Mk 1 2-Door Sedan	$61,474	63	Artcurial, Paris, FRA	2/8/09

BY THE NUMBERS

81

Top 5 Sales of 2008–09 by Marque

Model	Sold Price	Lot #	Auction Location	Date
1965 Cortina 2-Door Sedan	$23,583	16	H&H, Harrogate, UK	4/16/08
1967 Cortina Mk II Rally Car	$20,544	329	Bonhams, Stoneleigh Park, UK	3/15/08
1966 Cortina Mk I 2-Door Sedan Replica	$19,530	23	Shannons, Sydney, AUS	2/18/08
Hispano-Suiza				
1936 J12 Convertible Victoria	$880,000	47	Gooding, Scottsdale, AZ	1/17/09
1930 H6C Boattail Speedster	$616,000	129	Gooding, Pebble Beach, CA	8/17/08
1928 H6B Sedanca deVille	$297,975	118	Bonhams, Paris, FRA	2/9/08
Holden				
1977 LX Torana A9X Sedan	$177,560	52	Shannons, Melbourne, AUS	3/10/08
1977 LX Torana A9X Sedan	$110,670	21	Shannons, Sydney, AUS	2/18/08
1968 HK Monaro GTS 307 Coupe	$66,030	15	Shannons, Sydney, AUS	2/18/08
1977 LX Torana SS 5 Hatchback	$50,140	53	Shannons, Melbourne, AUS	3/10/08
1982 HDT Commodore VH SS Group 3 Sedan	$49,840	9	Shannons, Brisbane, AUS	2/10/08
Hudson				
1954 Italia Coupe	$275,000	290	RM, Amelia Island, FL	3/14/09
1927 Super Six Supercharged Sports Tourer	$198,000	276	RM, Amelia Island, FL	3/14/09
1948 Commodore Eight Convertible	$181,500	266	RM, Dallas, TX	4/19/08
1931 Greater Eight Boattail Sport Roadster	$110,000	142	RM, Phoenix, AZ	1/16/09
1912 Model 33 Mile-a-Minute	$106,470	260	Bonhams & Butterfields, Greenwich, CT	6/7/09
Hupmobile				
1929 Model A Four Place Coupe	$24,840	2496	Leake, Tulsa, OK	6/14/09
1924 Series R Special Roadster	$21,060	2598	Leake, Tulsa, OK	6/14/09
1910 Model 20 2-Seat Runabout	$18,216	521	Bonhams, Hendon, UK	4/21/08
1922 Series R Touring	$17,280	2599	Leake, Tulsa, OK	6/14/09
1924 Series R Special Roadster	$16,500	302	RM, Rochester, MI	8/2/08
Iso				
1969 Grifo Coupe	$308,000	157	RM, Phoenix, AZ	1/18/08
1966 Grifo GL Coupe	$200,401	248	Coys, Essen, DEU	4/4/09
1970 Grifo Coupe	$85,250	268	RM, Hershey, PA	10/10/08
1964 Rivolta IR 340GT	$78,205	317	Coys, Essen, DEU	3/29/08
1972 Grifo Series II Coupe	$45,742	529	Bonhams, Sussex, UK	7/11/08
Isotta Fraschini				
1913 100-120 hp Tipo KM 4 Four-Seat Torpedo Tourer	$1,492,000	316	Bonhams & Butterfields, Carmel Valley, CA	8/15/08
1933 Tipo 8A Dual Cowl Sports Phaeton	$1,089,000	43	Gooding, Scottsdale, AZ	1/17/09
1930 8A Transformable Torpedo	$495,000	176	RM, Phoenix, AZ	1/18/08
1930 8A Convertible Sedan by Castagna	$467,500	253	RM, Rochester, MI	8/2/08
1908 Tipo FENC Semi Racer	$166,500	518	Bonhams & Butterfields, Brookline, MA	10/4/08
Jaguar				
1960 XKE E2A Prototype Sports Racer	$4,957,000	364	Bonhams & Butterfields, Carmel Valley, CA	8/15/08
1955 XKD-type Sports Racer	$4,378,343	523	Bonhams, Sussex, UK	7/11/08
1938 SS 100 Roadster	$317,250	235	Coys, Essen, DEU	4/4/09
1937 SS 100 2½-Liter Roadster	$313,925	124	Bonhams, Paris, FRA	2/9/08
1994 XJ 220 Coupe	$313,500	1291	Barrett-Jackson, Scottsdale, AZ	1/20/08
Jensen				
1974 Interceptor SIII Cabriolet	$71,300	145	Bonhams, Monte Carlo, MCO	5/10/08
1975 Interceptor Mk III Cabriolet	$44,723	15	Artcurial, Paris, FRA	4/13/08
15.9.66 Interceptor Mk I Coupe	$40,077	41	H&H, Surrey, UK	6/8/08
2003 SV8 Convertible	$32,959	57	H&H, Buxton, UK	7/23/08
1961 541S Coupe	$29,848	391	Bonhams, Beaulieu, UK	9/13/08
Kaiser-Darrin				
1954 Roadster	$176,000	1254	Barrett-Jackson, Scottsdale, AZ	1/18/09
1954 Roadster	$176,000	957	Barrett-Jackson, Scottsdale, AZ	1/20/08
1954 Roadster	$137,500	984	Barrett-Jackson, Scottsdale, AZ	1/20/08
1954 Roadster	$126,500	SP92	RM, Ft. Lauderdale, FL	2/17/08
1954 Roadster	$115,500	671	Barrett-Jackson, Palm Beach, FL	4/11/09
Lagonda				
1936 LG45R Rapide Sports Racing 2-Seater	$1,382,000	310	Bonhams & Butterfields, Carmel Valley, CA	8/15/08
1976 V8 Series I Saloon	$498,820	320	Bonhams, Newport Pagnell, UK	5/17/08
1933 3-Liter Tourer	$253,000	24	Gooding, Scottsdale, AZ	1/19/08

Model	Sold Price	Lot #	Auction Location	Date
1938 LG6 Drophead Coupe	$247,500	264	RM, Amelia Island, FL	3/8/08
1933 M45 Tourer	$197,580	609	Bonhams, London, UK	12/1/08
Lamborghini				
1972 Miura P400 SV Coupe	$891,000	433	RM, Monterey, CA	8/16/08
1970 Miura P400 S Series II Coupe	$484,273	577	Bonhams, Sussex, UK	7/11/08
1969 Miura P400 S Coupe	$464,963	39	Artcurial, Paris, FRA	2/9/08
1970 Miura S Coupe	$423,500	S655	Russo and Steele, Monterey, CA	8/16/08
1967 Miura P400 Coupe	$412,500	437	RM, Monterey, CA	8/16/08
Lancia				
1955 Aurelia B24S Spyder America	$572,000	118	Gooding, Pebble Beach, CA	8/17/08
1955 Aurelia B24 Spyder America	$505,600	334	Coys, Essen, DEU	3/29/08
1955 Aurelia B24 Spyder America	$420,750	55	H&H, Sparkford, UK	10/12/08
1955 Aurelia B24S Spyder America	$406,995	176	Bonhams, Paris, FRA	2/7/09
1955 Aurelia B24S Spyder America	$380,025	236	Coys, Monte Carlo, MCO	5/18/09
LaSalle				
1931 345-A Dual Windshield 7-Passenger Touring	$95,000	73	Worldwide, Hilton Head, SC	11/1/08
1933 Convertible Coupe	$93,500	143	RM, Phoenix, AZ	1/16/09
1927 Series 303 Roadster	$78,440	6128	G. Potter King, Atlantic City, NJ	2/26/09
1940 Series 52 Convertible Coupe	$77,000	326	RM, Anaheim, CA	6/29/08
1932 Custom Boattail Speedster	$68,750	283	RM, Rochester, MI	8/2/08
Lincoln				
1936 Model K "Howard Hughes" Boattail Speedster	$1,080,000	496	Leake, Tulsa, OK	6/14/09
1941 Continental "Raymond Loewy" Town Coupe	$451,000	39	Gooding, Scottsdale, AZ	1/19/08
1933 Model KB Dual Cowl Phaeton	$242,000	235	RM, Hershey, PA	10/10/08
1962 Continental "John F. Kennedy" Sedan	$209,000	812	Barrett-Jackson, Las Vegas, NV	10/18/08
1941 Continental Coupe	$209,000	151	RM, Anaheim, CA	6/29/08
Locomobile				
1913 Model M-48-3 4-Passenger Baby Tonneau	$357,500	245	RM, Hershey, PA	10/10/08
1911 Model M-48 Seven Passenger Touring	$302,500	142	RM, Phoenix, AZ	1/18/08
1925 Model 48 Sportif	$161,000	867	Bonhams & Butterfields, Owls Head, ME	9/27/08
1918 Model 48-2 Sportif Touring Car	$161,000	516	Bonhams & Butterfields, Brookline, MA	10/4/08
1907 Type E Touring Car	$128,000	855	Bonhams & Butterfields, Owls Head, ME	9/27/08
Lotus				
1962 25 Formula 1 Single-Seater	$988,524	58	Bonhams & Goodman, Sydney, AUS	11/16/08
1978/79 79 Formula 1 Single-Seater	$373,442	61	Bonhams & Goodman, Sydney, AUS	11/16/08
1966 39 Tasman Series Single-Seater	$234,317	59	Bonhams & Goodman, Sydney, AUS	11/16/08
1959 16 Formula 2 Single-Seater	$226,994	56	Bonhams & Goodman, Sydney, AUS	11/16/08
1976 Esprit Coupe "The Spy Who Loved Me"	$165,020	679	Bonhams, London, UK	12/1/08
Maserati				
2006 MC12 Corsa	$2,194,318	252	Coys, Monte Carlo, MCO	5/10/08
2008 MC12 Corsa	$1,058,750	203	RM, Maranello, ITA	5/17/09
1931 Tipo 8C-2800 2-Seat Competition Car	$445,605	308	Bonhams, Sussex, UK	9/19/08
1966 Mistral 4000 Spyder	$369,675	126	Bonhams, Monte Carlo, MCO	5/10/08
1970 Ghibli Spyder	$330,000	S662	Russo and Steele, Monterey, CA	8/16/08
Mercedes-Benz				
1928 26/120/180 S-Type Roadster	$3,360,375	155	Bonhams, Paris, FRA	2/9/08
1936 540K Special Cabriolet	$2,035,000	144	RM, Phoenix, AZ	1/18/08
1936 500K Cabriolet A	$1,286,875	162	Bonhams, Paris, FRA	2/9/08
1936 500K Cabriolet B	$1,045,000	112	Gooding, Pebble Beach, CA	8/17/08
1938 540K Sport Cabriolet	$946,000	90	Gooding, Scottsdale, AZ	1/17/09
Mercury				
1964 Comet Caliente A/FX 2-Door Hardtop	$238,500	S109	Mecum, Indianapolis, IN	5/17/09
1949 Eight Station Wagon	$198,000	174	RM, Anaheim, CA	6/29/08
1951 Monarch Convertible	$155,925	SP102	RM, Toronto, CAN	4/5/09
1969 Cyclone GT SCJR 2-Door Hardtop	$148,500	934	Barrett-Jackson, Scottsdale, AZ	1/20/08
1950 Custom Bob Hope Special	$148,500	186	RM, Phoenix, AZ	1/16/09
Messerschmitt				
1963 KR201 Roadster	$41,538	113	Bonhams, Paris, FRA	2/7/09
1957 KR200 Cabriolet	$28,050	NR90	RM, Ft. Lauderdale, FL	2/17/08

Top 5 Sales of 2008–09 by Marque

Model	Sold Price	Lot #	Auction Location	Date
1956 KR200 3-Wheel Coupe	$22,680	788	Kruse, Phoenix, AZ	1/27/08
1956 KR200 Roadster	$19,710	340	Silver, Fountain Hills, AZ	1/21/08
MG				
1949 TC Race Roadster	$313,500	819	Barrett-Jackson, Las Vegas, NV	10/18/08
1935 K-type to K3 Supercharged Specification	$176,000	167	RM, Phoenix, AZ	1/18/08
1934 PB Airline Coupe	$148,500	281	RM, Amelia Island, FL	3/8/08
1935 PB "Cream Cracker" Trials Roadster	$99,369	312	Bonhams, Sussex, UK	9/19/08
1932 F2 Magna Sports	$73,200	303	Bonhams, Sussex, UK	9/19/08
Morgan				
1934 Super Sport Barrelback	$56,292	3	Artcurial, Paris, FRA	6/28/08
1964 4/4 Series V Roadster	$52,250	323	RM, Anaheim, CA	6/29/08
1929 Aero Super Sports 1100	$48,404	310	Bonhams, Sussex, UK	9/19/08
1964 Plus Four Drophead Coupe	$46,200	360	RM, Anaheim, CA	6/29/08
1926 Standard Popular Runabout	$44,914	18	Artcurial, Paris, FRA	2/9/08
Morris				
1960 Minor Pickup	$28,600	930	Barrett-Jackson, Scottsdale, AZ	1/20/08
1932 Oxford Six	$26,514	21	Brightwells, Herefordshire, UK	7/2/08
1923 Oxford 11.9hp Bullnose Tourer	$23,261	373	Bonhams, Beaulieu, UK	9/13/08
1968 Mini Cooper S Mk I Saloon	$22,080	5	Shannons, Melbourne, AUS	3/10/08
1926 Oxford 13.9hp Three-Quarter Coupe	$20,424	659	Bonhams, London, UK	12/1/08
Nash				
1956 Ambassador Custom 4-Door Sedan	$49,500	195	RM, Anaheim, CA	6/29/08
1922 697 4-Door Sedan	$44,000	762	Barrett-Jackson, Scottsdale, AZ	1/20/08
1951 Rambler Custom Landau Roll-Top Convertible	$34,650	283	RM, Monterey, CA	8/16/08
1959 Metropolitan Coupe	$33,000	46	Barrett-Jackson, Scottsdale, AZ	1/18/09
1950 Ambassador Custom Sedan	$33,000	344	RM, Anaheim, CA	6/29/08
Nash-Healey				
1953 Roadster	$253,000	27	Gooding, Scottsdale, AZ	1/19/08
1953 Le Mans Coupe	$126,500	489	RM, Monterey, CA	8/16/08
1953 Roadster	$115,500	470	RM, Monterey, CA	8/16/08
1951 Le Mans Alloy Roadster	$67,100	240	RM, Amelia Island, FL	3/14/09
1953 Le Mans Coupe	$58,300	S725	Russo and Steele, Scottsdale, AZ	1/18/09
Oldsmobile				
1911 Autocrat Racing Car "Yellow Peril"	$660,000	260	RM, Amelia Island, FL	3/14/09
1953 Fiesta Convertible	$253,000	246	RM, Dallas, TX	4/19/08
1923 Custom Touring Roadster	$220,000	397.2	Barrett-Jackson, Scottsdale, AZ	1/18/09
1958 J-2 Super 88 Convertible	$209,000	24	Worldwide, Houston, TX	5/3/08
1970 442 W30 Convertible	$206,700	1789	G. Potter King, Atlantic City, NJ	3/2/08
OSCA				
1955 MT4 Roadster	$477,945	116	Bonhams, Paris, FRA	2/7/09
c.1961 1600GT Coupe	$68,614	215	Bonhams, Gstaad, CHE	12/20/08
1963 1600 S Coupe	$47,925	224	Coys, Monte Carlo, MCO	5/18/09
1957 1500 S Berlinetta	$42,957	246	Coys, Essen, DEU	4/4/09
Packard				
1934 Twelve Coupe	$2,035,000	163	RM, Phoenix, AZ	1/18/08
1932 Model 904 Custom Eight Convertible Victoria	$1,210,000	50	Gooding, Scottsdale, AZ	1/19/08
1954 Panther-Daytona Roadster Concept Car	$700,000	277	RM, Amelia Island, FL	3/14/09
1932 Twin Six Coupe Roadster	$660,000	143	RM, Phoenix, AZ	1/18/08
1934 Twelve Model 1107 5-Passenger Touring	$495,000	65	Worldwide, Auburn, IN	8/30/08
Peerless				
1910 Victoria	$469,000	844	Bonhams & Butterfields, Owls Head, ME	9/27/08
1912 Model 36 7-Passenger Touring Car	$368,500	464	RM, Monterey, CA	8/16/08
1913 Model 48-Six Roadster	$330,000	465	RM, Monterey, CA	8/16/08
1909 Model 19 Touring Car	$170,500	463	RM, Monterey, CA	8/16/08
Peugeot				
1984 205 Turbo 16 Group B Rally	$359,586	67	Artcurial, Paris, FRA	6/14/09
1914 145S Torpedo Tourer	$243,000	561	Cox, Branson, MO	4/18/09
1988 405 Turbo 16 Grand Raid	$198,139	60	Artcurial, Paris, FRA	6/14/09

Model	Sold Price	Lot #	Auction Location	Date
1988 Oxia Concept	$198,139	45	Artcurial, Paris, FRA	6/14/09
1914 145S Torpedo Tourer	$172,000	360	Bonhams & Butterfields, Carmel Valley, CA	8/15/08
Pierce-Arrow				
1910 Model 48 SS	$632,500	145	Gooding, Pebble Beach, CA	8/17/08
1917 Model 48 Touring Car	$385,000	267	RM, Hershey, PA	10/10/08
1935 12 Convertible Coupe	$374,000	158	RM, Phoenix, AZ	1/18/08
1917 Four-Passenger Touring Car	$324,500	170	RM, Phoenix, AZ	1/18/08
1913 48-B 7-Passenger Touring	$315,000	847	Bonhams & Butterfields, Owls Head, ME	9/27/08
Plymouth 'Cuda				
1970 Hemi 'Cuda 2-Door Hardtop	$440,000	S704	Russo and Steele, Scottsdale, AZ	1/18/09
1971 'Cuda 2-Door Hardtop	$396,000	F515	Russo and Steele, Scottsdale, AZ	1/20/08
1971 Hemi 'Cuda 2-Door Hardtop	$378,000	S175	Mecum, Indianapolis, IN	5/18/08
1971 Hemi 'Cuda 2-Door Hardtop	$341,000	F518	Russo and Steele, Scottsdale, AZ	1/18/09
1970 Hemi 'Cuda 2-Door Hardtop	$286,200	S170	Mecum, Indianapolis, IN	5/17/09
Plymouth Road Runner				
1969 Road Runner 440/6 2-Door Hardtop	$153,300	S112	Mecum, Indianapolis, IN	5/18/08
1969 Hemi Road Runner 2-Door Hardtop	$140,450	S132	Mecum, Indianapolis, IN	5/17/09
1969 Road Runner 440/6 2-Door Hardtop	$138,600	S180	Mecum, Indianapolis, IN	5/18/08
1968 Road Runner 2-Door Hardtop	$126,500	1246	Barrett-Jackson, Scottsdale, AZ	1/20/08
1969 Hemi Road Runner 2-Door Hardtop	$121,000	SP129	RM, Ft. Lauderdale, FL	2/17/08
Plymouth Superbird				
1970 Hemi Superbird 2-Door Hardtop	$318,000	S180.1	Mecum, Indianapolis, IN	5/17/09
1970 Hemi Superbird 2-Door Hardtop	$286,200	S90.1	Mecum, Indianapolis, IN	5/17/09
1970 Hemi Superbird 2-Door Hardtop	$253,000	29	Worldwide, Houston, TX	5/3/08
1970 Superbird 2-Door Hardtop	$220,000	1021	Barrett-Jackson, Scottsdale, AZ	1/20/08
1970 Superbird 2-Door Hardtop	$214,500	1277.1	Barrett-Jackson, Scottsdale, AZ	1/20/08
Pontiac Catalina				
1963 Catalina "Swiss Cheese" 2-Door Hardtop	$451,500	S88	Mecum, St. Charles, IL	10/5/08
1962 Catalina Super Duty 2-Door Hardtop	$412,500	SN825	Russo and Steele, Scottsdale, AZ	1/18/09
1959 Catalina Convertible "Pink Lady"	$247,500	1314	Barrett-Jackson, Scottsdale, AZ	1/20/08
1961 Catalina Convertible	$66,000	1055	Barrett-Jackson, Scottsdale, AZ	1/20/08
1959 Catalina Convertible	$65,340	726	Kruse, Ft. Lauderdale, FL	1/6/08
Pontiac Firebird				
1968 Firebird Custom Coupe	$50,600	1068	Barrett-Jackson, Scottsdale, AZ	1/20/08
1967 Firebird Convertible	$47,300	186.1	Barrett-Jackson, Las Vegas, NV	10/18/08
1969 Firebird Convertible	$47,300	696.2	Barrett-Jackson, Scottsdale, AZ	1/18/09
1968 Firebird Convertible	$44,550	509	Kruse, Phoenix, AZ	1/27/08
1969 Firebird Convertible	$40,150	169.1	Barrett-Jackson, Las Vegas, NV	10/18/08
Pontiac GTO				
1966 GTO Monkeemobile	$396,000	1297	Barrett-Jackson, Scottsdale, AZ	1/20/08
1970 GTO Judge Ram Air IV Convertible	$378,000	S113	Mecum, Indianapolis, IN	5/18/08
1970 GTO Judge Ram Air IV "Tin Indian" 2-Door Hardtop	$180,200	S116	Mecum, Indianapolis, IN	5/17/09
1965 GTO 389 Arnie Beswick Drag Car	$161,650	S148	Mecum, Indianapolis, IN	5/17/09
1966 GTO Convertible	$143,000	956.1	Barrett-Jackson, Scottsdale, AZ	1/20/08
Pontiac Trans Am				
1973 Trans Am 455 SD "Bill Mitchell" Coupe	$153,700	S162	Mecum, Indianapolis, IN	5/17/09
1973 Trans Am Coupe	$148,500	SP55	RM, Ft. Lauderdale, FL	2/17/08
1969 Trans Am 400 Coupe	$111,300	S215	Mecum, Indianapolis, IN	5/17/09
1969 Trans Am Coupe	$96,600	S80	Mecum, St. Charles, IL	10/5/08
1969 Trans Am 400 Ram Air III Coupe	$96,460	T260	Mecum, Indianapolis, IN	5/17/09
Porsche				
1954 550 Spyder	$1,090,841	234	Coys, Monte Carlo, MCO	5/10/08
1964 904 GTS Coupe	$888,465	326	Bonhams, Sussex, UK	9/19/08
1966 906 Endurance Racing Coupe	$782,325	256	Bonhams, Monte Carlo, MCO	5/18/09
1981 935/78 Moby Dick Race Car	$550,000	451	RM, Monterey, CA	8/16/08
1972 911 2.7 RS Prototype	$480,000	359	Bonhams & Butterfields, Carmel Valley, CA	8/15/08

BY THE NUMBERS

Top 5 Sales of 2008–09 by Marque

Model	Sold Price	Lot #	Auction Location	Date
Renault				
1912 Type CB Coupe de Ville	$269,500	139	RM, Phoenix, AZ	1/18/08
1901 4½hp Type D Series A Rear-Entrance Tonneau	$100,130	307	Bonhmas, London, UK	10/31/08
1912 Type CC Salamanca	$63,724	400	Bonhams, Beaulieu, UK	9/13/08
1969 R8 Gordini Competition Sedan	$50,985	17	Artcurial, Paris, FRA	4/27/09
1951 R2163 Le Nain Gourmand Promotional Vehicle	$47,472	160	Bonhams, Paris, FRA	2/7/09
Riley				
1934 MPH Roadster	$308,000	64	Gooding, Pebble Beach, CA	8/17/08
1935 "Dobbs Special" 2-Liter Offset Monoposto	$191,124	568	Bonhams, Sussex, UK	7/11/08
1935 9hp Imp Roadster	$133,590	363	Bonhams, Sussex, UK	9/19/08
1934 9hp Imp Roadster	$121,000	275	RM, Monterey, CA	8/16/08
1935 9hp Imp 2-Seater	$107,042	362	Bonhams, Beaulieu, UK	9/13/08
Rolls-Royce				
1933 Phantom II Special Town Car	$2,310,000	453	RM, Monterey, CA	8/16/08
1925 Phantom I Barker Boattail	$1,210,000	131	Gooding, Pebble Beach, CA	8/17/08
1914 40/50hp Silver Ghost Skiff Torpedo	$1,072,500	81	Worldwide, Houston, TX	5/3/08
1933 Phantom II Streamline Saloon	$852,500	72	Gooding, Scottsdale, AZ	1/19/08
1913 40/50hp Silver Ghost Roi-des-Belges Tourer	$832,000	836	Bonhams & Butterfields, Owls Head, ME	9/27/08
Shelby				
1963 Cobra 289 Competition Roadster	$1,732,500	152	RM, Phoenix, AZ	1/18/08
1966 Cobra 427 S/C Roadster	$1,234,900	F248.1	Mecum, Indianapolis, IN	5/17/09
1966 Cobra 427 Competition Roadster	$1,060,000	F246	Mecum, Indianapolis, IN	5/17/09
1966 Cobra 427 Roadster	$962,500	248	RM, Monterey, CA	8/16/08
1967 GT500 Convertible	$874,500	F248	Mecum, Indianapolis, IN	5/17/09
Siata				
1952 Daina SL Sport Coupe	$147,370	531	Bonhams, Sussex, UK	7/11/08
1937 750 Gran Sport	$106,470	353	Bonhams & Butterfields, Carmel Valley, CA	8/15/08
Stanely				
1911 Steamer 10 Horsepower Model 63 Toy Tonneau	$184,250	241	RM, Hershey, PA	10/10/08
1908 Model M 5-Passenger Touring	$298,500	864	Bonhams & Butterfields, Owls Head, ME	9/27/08
1922 Steamer Roadster	$78,721	447	Coys, London, UK	7/5/08
1922 Roadster	$74,250	153	RM, Phoenix, AZ	1/16/09
Studebaker				
1931 President Four Seasons Roadster	$188,100	SP176	RM, Ft. Lauderdale, FL	2/17/08
1932 President Four-Seasons	$187,000	23	Gooding, Pebble Beach, CA	8/17/08
1932 President Brougham	$110,000	SP177	RM, Ft. Lauderdale, FL	2/17/08
1951 2-Door Custom "Super Sonic"	$106,700	1247.2	Barrett-Jackson, Scottsdale, AZ	1/18/09
1932 91 President St. Regis Brougham	$90,000	284	RM, Amelia Island, FL	3/14/09
Stutz				
1914 Series E Bearcat	$1,375,000	45	Gooding, Pebble Beach, CA	8/17/08
1932 DV-32 Super Bearcat	$594,000	151	RM, Phoenix, AZ	1/16/09
1915 Model 4-F Bulldog Demi-Tonneau	$352,000	29	Gooding, Scottsdale, AZ	1/17/09
1920 Bearcat Roadster	$253,000	60	Worldwide, Auburn, IN	8/30/08
1928 Model BB Sports Tourer	$138,840	16	Shannons, Brisbane, AUS	2/10/08
Sunbeam				
1905 12/14hp 5-Seat Side-Entrance Tonneau	$482,130	535	Bonhams, Hendon, UK	4/21/08
1965 Tiger Custom Convertible	$115,500	F502	Russo and Steele, Scottsdale, AZ	1/20/08
1965 Tiger Convertible	$71,500	S675	Russo and Steele, Monterey, CA	8/16/08
1965 Tiger Convertible	$60,500	S737	Russo and Steele, Scottsdale, AZ	1/18/09
1953 Alpine Sport Roadster	$57,200	206	RM, Phoenix, AZ	1/16/09
Talbot-Lago				
1939 T150C SS Teardrop Coupe	$4,847,000	330	Bonhams & Butterfields, Carmel Valley, CA	8/15/08
1937 T150C SS Teardrop Coupe	$3,520,000	23	Gooding, Scottsdale, AZ	1/17/09
1950 T26 Record Grand Sport Cabriolet	$297,975	109	Bonhams, Paris, FRA	2/9/08
1947 T26 Record Cabriolet	$214,500	239	RM, Monterey, CA	8/16/08
1954 T26 Grand Sport Coupe	$205,000	362	Bonhams & Butterfields, Carmel Valley, CA	8/15/08

Model	Sold Price	Lot #	Auction Location	Date
Thomas				
1904 Model 27 Racer	$1,188,000	775	Kruse, Phoenix, AZ	1/27/08
1907 Flyer Model 36 60hp	$1,028,500	127	Gooding, Pebble Beach, CA	8/17/08
Triumph				
1958 TR3 Roadster	$56,569	135	Coys, Nürburgring, DEU	8/9/08
1961 TR3A Roadster	$53,900	TH346	Russo and Steele, Scottsdale, AZ	1/18/09
1962 Spitfire Hardtop Roadster	$48,010	223	Bonhams, Silverstone, UK	7/26/08
1963 TR4 Surrey Top Convertible	$44,000	38	Gooding, Scottsdale, AZ	1/19/08
1963 TR3B Roadster	$40,700	60	Worldwide, Houston, TX	5/3/08
Tucker				
1948 48 Sedan	$1,017,500	449	RM, Monterey, CA	8/16/08
TVR				
1995 Chimaera Coupe	$41,928	14	Artcurial, Paris, FRA	4/13/08
1991 Tuscan Challenge Racer	$25,766	211	Coys, Brands Hatch, UK	5/25/08
1996 Chimaera Convertible	$12,293	45	H&H, Buxton, UK	4/16/09
1990 280S Convertible	$9,325	219	Coys, Brands Hatch, UK	5/25/08
1981 Tasmin Convertible	$4,662	22	H&H, Buxton, UK	6/10/09
Vauxhall				
1928 20/60 Hurlingham Speedster	$139,000	211	Bonhams & Butterfields, Greenwich, CT	6/8/08
1923 Type OD 23/60hp Malvern Tourer	$74,354	130	Bonhams & Goodman, Melbounre, AUS	3/13/08
1924 23/60 OD Malvern Tourer	$61,600	44	H&H, Stoneleigh, UK	3/14/09
1926 25/70hp Ormonde Sporting Sedan	$49,404	363	Bonhams, Beaulieu, UK	9/13/08
1926 14/40 Princeton Tourer	$24,180	9	Shannons, Sydney, AUS	2/18/08
Vector				
1996 M-12 Coupe	$94,600	1346	Barrett-Jackson, Scottsdale, AZ	1/18/09
Volkswagen				
1944 Schwimmwagen Amphibious	$231,725	163	Bonhams, Monte Carlo, MCO	5/10/08
1958 Type 2 Samba Van	$89,154	205	Coys, Padua, ITA	10/25/08
1964 Type 2 21-Window Deluxe Microbus	$71,500	407	RM, Monterey, CA	8/16/08
1974 Karmann Ghia	$63,600	S27	Mecum, Indianapolis, IN	5/17/09
1966 Custom Bus	$60,500	698	Barrett-Jackson, Scottsdale, AZ	1/18/09
Volvo				
1962 P1800 Coupe	$29,900	40	Shannons, Melbourne, AUS	3/10/08
1964 122S Amazon Rally Car	$19,143	312	Bonhams, Stoneleigh Park, UK	3/15/08
2001 C70 Convertible	$18,360	47	Silver, Fountain Hills, AZ	1/21/08
1967 P1800 S Coupe	$17,600	335	Barrett-Jackson, Scottsdale, AZ	1/18/09
1964 544 Sport 2-Door Sedan	$17,550	2431	Leake, Tulsa, OK	6/8/08
Willys				
1951 Jeep Convertible	$104,500	943.1	Barrett-Jackson, Scottsdale, AZ	1/18/09
1941 Street Rod	$100,100	SP131	RM, Ft. Lauderdale, FL	2/17/08
1941 Cabriolet Coupe Street Rod	$89,100	F501	Russo and Steele, Scottsdale, AZ	1/18/09
1941 Custom 2-Door Street Rod	$83,160	2468	Leake, Dallas, TX	11/23/08
1941 Coupe	$75,600	729	Kruse, Honolulu, HI	2/9/08
Wolseley				
1904 8hp Twin-Cylinder 4/5-Seater Rear-Entrance Tonneau	$82,365	309	Bonhmas, London, UK	10/31/08
1921 10hp "200 Mile Race" Replica	$50,094	36	H&H, Harrogate, UK	4/16/08
1934 Hornet Daytona Special	$29,670	423	Coys, London, UK	3/12/09
1969 Hornet Mk III 2-Door Sedan	$24,225	44	Artcurial, Paris, FRA	4/13/08
1924 A9 Open Coupe	$20,378	94	Brightwells, Herefordshire, UK	7/2/08
Zimmer				
1983 Custom Coupe	$42,120	1071	Kruse, Ft. Lauderdale, FL	1/6/08
1982 Golden Spirit Convertible	$21,525	T6	Carlisle, Carlisle, PA	4/24/09
1982 Golden Spirit Custom "Log Splitter"	$16,500	1534	Barrett-Jackson, Scottsdale, AZ	1/20/08
1987 Quicksilver	$6,588	15	Motleys, Richmond, VA	4/18/08

BY THE NUMBERS

Top 100 Leaders of the Muscle Pack

Muscle car prices fell off somewhat from their boom of 2005–06, but good, right cars still command-ed top dollar.*

1963 Shelby Cobra 289 Competition Roadster

Rank	Model	Sold Price	Lot #	Auction Location	Date
1	1963 Shelby Cobra 289 Competition Roadster	$1,732,500	152	RM, Phoenix, AZ	1/18/08
2	1966 Shelby Cobra 427 S/C Roadster	$1,234,900	F248.1	Mecum, Indianapolis, IN	5/17/09
3	1966 Shelby Cobra 427 Competition Roadster	$1,060,000	F246	Mecum, Indianapolis, IN	5/17/09
4	1966 Shelby Cobra 427 Roadster	$962,500	248	RM, Monterey, CA	8/16/08
5	1967 Shelby GT500 Convertible	$874,500	F248	Mecum, Indianapolis, IN	5/17/09
6	1967 Shelby Cobra 427 Roadster	$829,250	S654	Russo and Steele, Monterey, CA	8/16/08
7	1969 Chevrolet Camaro RS ZL1 Coupe	$800,000	S99	Mecum, Indianapolis, IN	5/18/08
8	1966 Shelby Cobra 427 Roadster	$781,000	SP79	RM, Ft. Lauderdale, FL	2/17/08
9	1969 Shelby GT500 Convertible	$742,500	1287	Barrett-Jackson, Scottsdale, AZ	1/20/08
10	1967 Shelby Cobra 427 Roadster	$687,500	1281.1	Barrett-Jackson, Scottsdale, AZ	1/20/08
11	1966 Shelby Cobra 427 Roadster	$675,000	264	RM, Amelia Island, FL	3/14/09

Sales from the SCM Platinum Database, recorded between 1/1/2008 and 6/15/2009

Rank	Model	Sold Price	Lot #	Auction Location	Date
12	1967 Shelby Cobra 427 Roadster	$660,000	1301	Barrett-Jackson, Scottsdale, AZ	1/20/08
13	1969 Chevrolet Camaro RCR Series 3 Coupe	$632,500	1303	Barrett-Jackson, Scottsdale, AZ	1/20/08
14	1965 Shelby Cobra 289 Roadster	$605,000	438	RM, Monterey, CA	8/16/08
15	1964 Shelby Cobra 289 Roadster	$583,000	6	Gooding, Scottsdale, AZ	1/19/08
16	1970 Plymouth Superbird Custom Replica	$551,100	1289	Barrett-Jackson, Scottsdale, AZ	1/18/09
17	1963 Shelby Cobra 289 Roadster	$550,000	143	Gooding, Pebble Beach, CA	8/17/08
18	1970 Chevrolet Chevelle SS 454 LS6 Convertible	$525,000	S103	Mecum, Indianapolis, IN	5/18/08
19	1967 Chevrolet Camaro Yenko Coupe	$504,000	S105	Mecum, Indianapolis, IN	5/18/08
20	1969 Chevrolet Camaro ZL1 Coupe	$504,000	S109	Mecum, Indianapolis, IN	5/18/08
21	1969 Chevrolet Camaro RS/SS Custom "Project American Heroes"	$500,000	369.1	Barrett-Jackson, Palm Beach, FL	4/11/09
22	1969 Dodge Charger 2-Door Hardtop "General Lee"	$495,000	1321	Barrett-Jackson, Scottsdale, AZ	1/20/08
23	1964 Shelby Cobra 289 Roadster	$495,000	S700	Russo and Steele, Scottsdale, AZ	1/18/09
24	1965 Shelby Cobra 289 Mk II Roadster	$467,500	185	RM, Phoenix, AZ	1/16/09
25	1965 Shelby GT350 Fastback	$462,000	1293	Barrett-Jackson, Scottsdale, AZ	1/20/08
26	1963 Pontiac Catalina "Swiss Cheese" 2-Door Hardtop	$451,500	S88	Mecum, St. Charles, IL	10/5/08
27	1967 Chevrolet Camaro RS/SS Nickey Coupe	$446,250	S97	Mecum, St. Charles, IL	10/5/08
28	1970 Plymouth Hemi 'Cuda 2-Door Hardtop	$440,000	S704	Russo and Steele, Scottsdale, AZ	1/18/09
29	1962 Pontiac Catalina Super Duty 2-Door Hardtop	$412,500	SN825	Russo and Steele, Scottsdale, AZ	1/18/09
30	1970 Ford Mustang Boss 302 TransAm Race Car	$407,000	87	Gooding, Scottsdale, AZ	1/17/09
31	1970 Dodge Hemi Coronet R/T Convertible	$404,250	S108	Mecum, Indianapolis, IN	5/18/08
32	1970 Chevrolet Chevelle 454 LS6 Convertible	$397,500	S126	Mecum, Indianapolis, IN	5/17/09
33	1966 Pontiac GTO Monkeemobile	$396,000	1297	Barrett-Jackson, Scottsdale, AZ	1/20/08
34	1971 Plymouth 'Cuda 2-Door Hardtop	$396,000	F515	Russo and Steele, Scottsdale, AZ	1/20/08
35	1971 Dodge Hemi Challenger R/T 2-Door Hardtop	$390,500	F520	Russo and Steele, Scottsdale, AZ	1/18/09
36	1971 Plymouth Hemi 'Cuda 2-Door Hardtop	$378,000	S175	Mecum, Indianapolis, IN	5/18/08
37	1970 Pontiac GTO Judge Ram Air IV Convertible	$378,000	S113	Mecum, Indianapolis, IN	5/18/08
38	1964 Ford Galaxie 500 "Tobacco King" Rocket Car	$376,000	S139	Mecum, Indianapolis, IN	5/18/08
39	1967 Shelby GT500 Fastback	$363,000	1318	Barrett-Jackson, Scottsdale, AZ	1/20/08
40	1969 Ford Mustang Boss 429 Fastback	$357,500	1269	Barrett-Jackson, Scottsdale, AZ	1/20/08
41	1965 Chevrolet Chevelle SS Z16 2-Door Hardtop Prototype	$355,100	S122	Mecum, Indianapolis, IN	5/17/09
42	1969 Chevrolet Chevelle 2-Door Hardtop	$341,000	S711	Russo and Steele, Scottsdale, AZ	1/20/08
43	1971 Plymouth Hemi 'Cuda 2-Door Hardtop	$341,000	F518	Russo and Steele, Scottsdale, AZ	1/18/09
44	1969 Ford Mustang Boss 429 Fastback	$330,000	1329	Barrett-Jackson, Scottsdale, AZ	1/20/08
45	1969 Chevrolet Chevelle COPO 2-Door Hardtop	$328,600	S124	Mecum, Indianapolis, IN	5/17/09
46	1969 Chevrolet Camaro ZL1 COPO Coupe	$319,000	1277.1	Barrett-Jackson, Scottsdale, AZ	1/18/09
47	1970 Chevrolet Chevelle 454 LS6 2-Door Hardtop	$318,000	S127	Mecum, Indianapolis, IN	5/17/09
48	1970 Plymouth Hemi Superbird 2-Door Hardtop	$318,000	S180.1	Mecum, Indianapolis, IN	5/17/09
49	1965 Shelby GT350 Fastback "Final Prototype"	$299,450	F240	Mecum, Indianapolis, IN	5/17/09
50	1969 Chevrolet Camaro Yenko COPO Coupe	$297,000	1278	Barrett-Jackson, Scottsdale, AZ	1/18/09
51	1970 Chevrolet Chevelle SS 454 LS6 Convertible	$294,000	S111	Mecum, Indianapolis, IN	5/18/08
52	1969 Ford Mustang Boss 429 Fastback	$288,750	S101	Mecum, Indianapolis, IN	5/18/08
53	1969 Ford Mustang Boss 429 Fastback	$287,280	2481	Leake, Tulsa, OK	6/8/08
54	1970 Plymouth Hemi 'Cuda 2-Door Hardtop	$286,200	S170	Mecum, Indianapolis, IN	5/17/09
55	1970 Plymouth Hemi Superbird 2-Door Hardtop	$286,200	S90.1	Mecum, Indianapolis, IN	5/17/09
56	1969 Chevrolet Camaro Yenko Coupe	$280,900	S128	Mecum, Indianapolis, IN	5/17/09

BY THE NUMBERS

Top Muscle Car Sales

Rank	Model	Sold Price	Lot #	Auction Location	Date
57	1970 Plymouth 'Cuda 2-Door Hardtop	$280,500	S706	Russo and Steele, Scottsdale, AZ	1/20/08
58	1969 Chevrolet Camaro Coupe	$270,600	F516	Russo and Steele, Scottsdale, AZ	1/20/08
59	1969 Ford Mustang Boss 429 Fastback	$269,500	1280	Barrett-Jackson, Scottsdale, AZ	1/20/08
60	1970 Ford Mustang Boss 429 Fastback	$269,500	1319	Barrett-Jackson, Scottsdale, AZ	1/20/08
61	1970 Plymouth Hemi 'Cuda 2-Door Hardtop	$269,500	1254.1	Barrett-Jackson, Scottsdale, AZ	1/20/08
62	1970 Dodge Challenger R/T 440/6 Convertible	$265,000	S181	Mecum, Indianapolis, IN	5/18/08
63	1970 Plymouth 'Cuda 440/6 Convertible	$260,000	S178	Mecum, Indianapolis, IN	5/18/08
64	1969 Chevrolet Camaro RS/SS NASCAR Pace Car Convertible	$258,500	F524	Russo and Steele, Scottsdale, AZ	1/18/09
65	1969 Ford Mustang Coupe	$253,000	F518	Russo and Steele, Scottsdale, AZ	1/20/08
66	1960 Plymouth Fury Convertible	$253,000	242	RM, Dallas, TX	4/19/08
67	1970 Plymouth Hemi Superbird 2-Door Hardtop	$253,000	29	Worldwide, Houston, TX	5/3/08
68	1969 Chevrolet Chevelle Yenko 2-Door Hardtop	$252,000	S80	Mecum, Indianapolis, IN	5/18/08
69	1969 Chevrolet Camaro Yenko Coupe	$250,000	S173	Mecum, St. Charles, IL	10/5/08
70	1969 Ford Mustang Boss 429 Fastback	$248,000	83	Worldwide, Houston, TX	5/3/08
71	1971 Dodge Hemi Challenger R/T 2-Door Hardtop	$247,500	S702	Russo and Steele, Scottsdale, AZ	1/18/09
72	1965 Shelby GT350 Fastback	$247,500	269	RM, Monterey, CA	8/16/08
73	1968 Shelby GT500 KR Convertible	$247,500	S722	Russo and Steele, Scottsdale, AZ	1/20/08
74	1968 Shelby GT500 KR Convertible	$246,100	S114	Mecum, Indianapolis, IN	5/18/08
75	1970 Plymouth Hemi 'Cuda 2-Door Hardtop	$244,125	S177	Mecum, Indianapolis, IN	5/18/08
76	1970 Plymouth 'Cuda 2-Door Hardtop	$242,000	S720	Russo and Steele, Scottsdale, AZ	1/20/08
77	1967 Shelby GT500 Fastback	$242,000	S715	Russo and Steele, Scottsdale, AZ	1/20/08
78	1970 Plymouth Hemi 'Cuda 2-Door Hardtop	$241,150	S113	Mecum, Indianapolis, IN	5/17/09
79	1965 Chevrolet Chevelle Z16 2-Door Hardtop	$238,875	S112	Mecum, Kissimmee, FL	1/26/08
80	1969 Chevrolet Camaro COPO Coupe	$231,000	F459	Russo and Steele, Hollywood, FL	3/30/08
81	1968 Shelby GT500 KR Convertible	$231,000	1278	Barrett-Jackson, Scottsdale, AZ	1/20/08
82	1971 Dodge Hemi Challenger 2-Door Hardtop	$231,000	32	Worldwide, Houston, TX	5/3/08
83	1970 Ford Mustang Boss 429 Fastback	$231,000	231	RM, Monterey, CA	8/16/08
84	1969 Ford Mustang Fastback	$231,000	S700	Russo and Steele, Scottsdale, AZ	1/20/08
85	1969 Chevrolet Camaro COPO Coupe	$225,250	S149	Mecum, Indianapolis, IN	5/17/09
86	1970 Plymouth Hemi 'Cuda 2-Door Hardtop	$220,500	U106	Mecum, Indianapolis, IN	5/18/08
87	1970 Plymouth Superbird 2-Door Hardtop	$220,000	1021	Barrett-Jackson, Scottsdale, AZ	1/20/08
88	1969 Shelby GT500 Fastback	$220,000	1329.1	Barrett-Jackson, Scottsdale, AZ	1/20/08
89	1970 Chevrolet Chevelle Convertible	$220,000	S701	Russo and Steele, Scottsdale, AZ	1/20/08
90	1967 Plymouth Barracuda West Coast Customs 2-Door Hardtop	$220,000	1306.2	Barrett-Jackson, Scottsdale, AZ	1/18/09
91	1966 Shelby GT350 Fastback	$220,000	1271.1	Barrett-Jackson, Scottsdale, AZ	1/18/09
92	1968 Shelby GT500 Convertible	$220,000	SP47	RM, Ft. Lauderdale, FL	2/17/08
93	1966 Shelby GT350 Fastback	$220,000	F509	Russo and Steele, Scottsdale, AZ	1/20/08
94	1970 Dodge Challenger 2-Door Hardtop	$217,800	S696	Russo and Steele, Scottsdale, AZ	1/20/08
95	1964 Ford Galaxie 2-Door Hardtop	$217,300	S130	Mecum, Kissimmee, FL	1/24/09
96	1968 Shelby GT500 KR Convertible	$217,250	SP41	RM, Ft. Lauderdale, FL	2/17/08
97	1967 Shelby GT500 E "Gone in 60 Seconds"	$216,700	1317	Barrett-Jackson, Scottsdale, AZ	1/18/09
98	1971 Dodge Hemi Charger R/T 2-Door Hardtop	$215,000	S173	Mecum, Indianapolis, IN	5/18/08
99	1970 Chevrolet Chevelle LS6 COPO SS 2-Door Hardtop	$214,500	1279.1	Barrett-Jackson, Scottsdale, AZ	1/20/08
100	1957 Chevrolet Corvette LS7 Custom Convertible	$214,500	1276	Barrett-Jackson, Scottsdale, AZ	1/20/08

Top 100 Corvettes—Where the Big Money Went

Corvettes occupy a special place in the collector car world, and the industry witnessed some significant sales in 2008–09.*

1963 Corvette "Rondine" Concept Car

Rank	Model	Sold Price	Lot #	Auction Location	Date
1	1963 Corvette "Rondine" Concept Car	$1,760,000	1304	Barrett-Jackson, Scottsdale, AZ	1/20/08
2	1962 Corvette 327/360 Gulf Oil Race Car	$1,485,000	121	Gooding, Pebble Beach, CA	8/17/08
3	1963 Corvette Z06 Yenko "Gulf One" Race Car	$1,113,000	S110	Mecum, Kissimmee, FL	1/25/09
4	2009 Corvette ZR1 Coupe	$1,100,000	1316	Barrett-Jackson, Scottsdale, AZ	1/20/08
5	1967 Corvette L88 Competition Convertible	$744,000	355	Bonhams & Butterfields, Carmel Valley, CA	8/15/08
6	1971 Corvette ZR2 Convertible	$550,000	S107	Mecum, St. Charles, IL	6/28/08
7	1969 Corvette L88 Convertible	$435,750	S91	Mecum, St. Charles, IL	6/28/08
8	1969 Corvette 427/430 L88 Coupe	$412,500	S714	Russo and Steele, Scottsdale, AZ	1/20/08
9	1971 Corvette ZR2 Coupe	$357,500	1290	Barrett-Jackson, Scottsdale, AZ	1/20/08
10	1967 Corvette 427/400 Convertible	$336,000	S73	Mecum, St. Charles, IL	6/28/08
11	1955 Corvette Duntov EX-87 Test Mule	$328,600	F208	Mecum, Indianapolis, IN	5/17/09

Sales from the SCM Platinum Database, recorded between 1/1/2008 and 6/15/2009

BY THE NUMBERS

Top Corvette Sales

Rank	Model	Sold Price	Lot #	Auction Location	Date
12	1969 Corvette 427/430 L88 Convertible	$323,300	S142	Mecum, Kissimmee, FL	1/25/09
13	1989 Corvette DR-1 Convertible	$286,000	1218	Barrett-Jackson, Scottsdale, AZ	1/19/09
14	1959 Corvette 283/290 FI Competition Convertible	$275,000	260	RM, Amelia Island, FL	3/8/08
15	1955 Corvette Bubbletop Roadster	$270,000	753	Kruse, Phoenix, AZ	1/27/08
16	1957 Corvette 283/283 FI Convertible	$265,000	S138	Mecum, Kissimmee, FL	1/25/09
17	1953 Corvette Roadster	$264,000	182	RM, Phoenix, AZ	1/18/08
18	1953 Corvette Roadster	$249,900	S109	Mecum, Kissimmee, FL	1/26/08
19	1967 Corvette 427/435 Convertible	$246,750	X9	Mecum, St. Charles, IL	6/28/08
20	1958 Corvette 283/240 Convertible	$242,000	990.1	Barrett-Jackson, Scottsdale, AZ	1/20/08
21	1963 Corvette 327/360 Z06 Coupe	$233,625	B34	Mecum, Indianapolis, IN	4/5/08
22	1968 Corvette L88 Coupe	$231,000	S6	Mecum, St. Charles, IL	6/28/08
23	1990 Corvette ZR-1 Coupe (w/5 others, '91–'95)	$231,000	S32	Mecum, St. Charles, IL	6/28/08
24	1967 Corvette 427/435 Convertible	$220,000	1267	Barrett-Jackson, Scottsdale, AZ	1/20/08
25	1959 Corvette 283/245 Convertible	$220,000	1019	Barrett-Jackson, Scottsdale, AZ	1/19/09
26	1957 Corvette LS7 Custom Convertible	$214,500	1276	Barrett-Jackson, Scottsdale, AZ	1/20/08
27	1958 Corvette 283/290 FI Convertible	$198,000	1272	Barrett-Jackson, Scottsdale, AZ	1/20/08
28	1967 Corvette 427/435 Coupe	$198,000	1327	Barrett-Jackson, Scottsdale, AZ	1/20/08
29	1953 Corvette Roadster	$198,000	278	RM, Amelia Island, FL	3/14/09
30	1989 Corvette ZR-1 Coupe	$198,000	1230.4	Barrett-Jackson, Scottsdale, AZ	1/19/09
31	1960 Corvette 283/290 FI Convertible	$192,500	1045	Barrett-Jackson, Scottsdale, AZ	1/20/08
32	1954 Corvette Roadster	$192,500	1259	Barrett-Jackson, Scottsdale, AZ	1/20/08
33	1963 Corvette 327/360 Z06 Coupe	$192,500	287	RM, Amelia Island, FL	3/14/09
34	1968 Corvette 427/435 L89 Coupe	$192,500	F513	Russo and Steele, Scottsdale, AZ	1/20/08
35	1970 Corvette ZR1 Coupe	$189,000	S108	Mecum, St. Charles, IL	6/28/08
36	1967 Corvette 427/435 Convertible	$188,000	S135	Mecum, Kissimmee, FL	1/26/08
37	1958 Corvette LS2 Custom Convertible	$187,000	788	Barrett-Jackson, Las Vegas, NV	10/18/08
38	1958 Corvette 283/270 Convertible	$181,500	1231.1	Barrett-Jackson, Scottsdale, AZ	1/20/08
39	1964 Corvette Z06 Coupe	$180,600	S87	Mecum, St. Charles, IL	6/28/08
40	1967 Corvette 427/435 Convertible	$178,750	SP91	RM, Ft. Lauderdale, FL	2/17/08
41	1966 Corvette 427/425 Convertible	$178,200	F503	Russo and Steele, Scottsdale, AZ	1/20/08
42	1967 Corvette 427/430 Convertible	$176,000	1247	Barrett-Jackson, Scottsdale, AZ	1/19/09
43	1989 Corvette ZR-1 Coupe "Snake Skinner"	$176,000	396.1	Barrett-Jackson, Scottsdale, AZ	1/19/09
44	1959 Corvette 283/290 FI Convertible	$176,000	1238	Barrett-Jackson, Scottsdale, AZ	1/20/08
45	1967 Corvette 427/435 Convertible	$173,250	X10	Mecum, St. Charles, IL	6/28/08
46	1967 Corvette 427/435 Convertible	$172,250	F236	Mecum, Indianapolis, IN	5/17/09
47	1966 Corvette 427/390 Convertible	$170,500	795.1	Barrett-Jackson, Las Vegas, NV	10/18/08
48	1958 Corvette LT4 Custom Convertible	$170,500	688	Barrett-Jackson, West Palm Beach, FL	3/30/08
49	1957 Corvette 427/510 Custom Convertible	$170,500	1327.1	Barrett-Jackson, Scottsdale, AZ	1/20/08
50	1967 Corvette 427/435 Coupe	$168,000	B35	Mecum, Indianapolis, IN	4/5/08
51	1967 Corvette 427/435 Coupe	$167,500	603	RM, Ft. Lauderdale, FL	2/17/08
52	1968 Corvette 327/350 Convertible	$167,200	350.1	Barrett-Jackson, West Palm Beach, FL	3/30/08
53	1957 Corvette 283/270 FI Convertible	$165,375	S115	Mecum, St. Charles, IL	6/28/08
54	1963 Corvette 327/360 FI Coupe	$165,000	1260.1	Barrett-Jackson, Scottsdale, AZ	1/19/09
55	1967 Corvette LS7 Custom Coupe	$165,000	1318	Barrett-Jackson, Scottsdale, AZ	1/19/09
56	1967 Corvette 427/435 Convertible	$165,000	807.1	Barrett-Jackson, Las Vegas, NV	10/18/08

Rank	Model	Sold Price	Lot #	Auction Location	Date
57	1969 Corvette 427/435 Coupe	$165,000	646	Barrett-Jackson, West Palm Beach, FL	3/30/08
58	1957 Corvette 283/283 FI Convertible	$165,000	1266	Barrett-Jackson, Scottsdale, AZ	1/20/08
59	1959 Corvette LS2 Custom Widebody Convertible	$165,000	1009	Barrett-Jackson, Scottsdale, AZ	1/20/08
60	1954 Corvette Roadster	$165,000	980.1	Barrett-Jackson, Scottsdale, AZ	1/20/08
61	1967 Corvette 427 Convertible	$160,628	SP125	RM, Toronto, CAN	4/6/08
62	1967 Corvette 427/435 Convertible	$159,500	1263.1	Barrett-Jackson, Scottsdale, AZ	1/20/08
63	1959 Corvette LS7 Custom Coupe	$156,600	602	Silver, Reno, NV	8/10/08
64	1967 Corvette 427/435 Convertible	$155,400	S129	Mecum, St. Charles, IL	6/28/08
65	1967 Corvette 427/400 Convertible	$155,100	SP48	RM, Ft. Lauderdale, FL	2/17/08
66	1967 Corvette 427/390 Convertible	$154,000	1337	Barrett-Jackson, Scottsdale, AZ	1/19/09
67	1954 Corvette Roadster	$154,000	251	RM, Dallas, TX	4/19/08
68	1957 Corvette FI Convertible	$154,000	SP56	RM, Ft. Lauderdale, FL	2/17/08
69	1957 Corvette 427/554 Custom Convertible	$154,000	1317	Barrett-Jackson, Scottsdale, AZ	1/20/08
70	1966 Corvette 555/850 Custom Coupe	$154,000	1338.1	Barrett-Jackson, Scottsdale, AZ	1/20/08
71	1955 Corvette Roadster	$152,250	F4	Mecum, Indianapolis, IN	5/3/08
72	2009 Corvette ZR1 Coupe	$151,250	262	RM, Monterey, CA	8/16/08
73	1968 Corvette 427/435 L89 Convertible	$151,250	1273	Barrett-Jackson, Scottsdale, AZ	1/20/08
74	1990 Corvette Active ZR-1 Coupe Prototype	$150,700	82	Barrett-Jackson, Scottsdale, AZ	1/19/09
75	1959 Corvette LS3 Custom Convertible	$148,500	652.1	Barrett-Jackson, Palm Beach, FL	4/11/09
76	1962 Corvette 327/360 FI Convertible	$148,500	1012	Barrett-Jackson, Scottsdale, AZ	1/19/09
77	1967 Corvette 427/435 Convertible	$148,500	SP85	RM, Ft. Lauderdale, FL	2/17/08
78	1962 Corvette Convertible	$148,500	444	RM, Ft. Lauderdale, FL	2/17/08
79	1960 Corvette 283/290 FI Convertible	$148,500	1244.1	Barrett-Jackson, Scottsdale, AZ	1/20/08
80	1959 Corvette 283/270 FI Convertible	$146,590	S71	Mecum, St. Charles, IL	6/28/08
81	1958 Corvette 350/400 Convertible Resto Mod	$145,750	S33	Mecum, Indianapolis, IN	5/17/09
82	1957 Corvette 283/283 FI Convertible	$145,750	109	Gooding, Pebble Beach, CA	8/17/08
83	1967 Corvette 427/400 Coupe	$145,200	1261.1	Barrett-Jackson, Scottsdale, AZ	1/19/09
84	1967 Corvette 427/435 Convertible	$145,200	1339	Barrett-Jackson, Scottsdale, AZ	1/20/08
85	1959 Corvette 283/290 FI Convertible	$144,375	B41	Mecum, Indianapolis, IN	4/5/08
86	1962 Corvette 327/360 FI Convertible	$143,000	674.1	Barrett-Jackson, Palm Beach, FL	4/11/09
87	1967 Corvette 427/435 Convertible	$143,000	1327	Barrett-Jackson, Scottsdale, AZ	1/19/09
88	1958 Corvette 283/290 FI Convertible	$143,000	1258	Barrett-Jackson, Scottsdale, AZ	1/20/08
89	2008 Corvette Z06 Coupe	$143,000	1258.1	Barrett-Jackson, Scottsdale, AZ	1/20/08
90	1962 Corvette 327/360 Convertible	$141,750	B36	Mecum, Indianapolis, IN	4/5/08
91	1966 Corvette 427/390 Convertible	$139,700	1338	Barrett-Jackson, Scottsdale, AZ	1/19/09
92	1954 Corvette Roadster	$138,600	14	Worldwide, Seabrook, TX	5/2/09
93	1967 Corvette 427/435 Roadster	$138,600	S627	Russo and Steele, Monterey, CA	8/16/08
94	1967 Corvette 427/435 Convertible	$138,000	237	RM, Monterey, CA	8/16/08
95	1959 Corvette 283/290 FI Convertible	$138,000	205	Silver, Reno, NV	8/10/08
96	1963 Corvette 327/360 FI Coupe	$137,500	1263.1	Barrett-Jackson, Scottsdale, AZ	1/19/09
97	1958 Corvette LS2 Custom Convertible	$137,500	1255.1	Barrett-Jackson, Scottsdale, AZ	1/19/09
98	1967 Corvette 427/435 Convertible	$137,500	5	Gooding, Scottsdale, AZ	1/17/09
99	2009 Corvette ZR1 Coupe	$137,500	S99.1	Mecum, St. Charles, IL	10/5/08
100	1956 Corvette 265/225 Convertible	$137,500	960.1	Barrett-Jackson, Scottsdale, AZ	1/20/08

BY THE NUMBERS

And the All-Time Winners Are...

From November 1983 to June 2009, these are the top ten sales at public auction.

1

1957 Ferrari 250 Testa Rossa
$12,402,500—RM Auctions, Marnaello, ITA, 5/17/09

2

1961 Ferrari 250 GT SWB California Spyder
$10,894,000—RM Auctions, Marnaello, ITA, 5/18/08

3

1931 Bugatti Type 41 Kellner Coupe
$9,800,000—Christie's, London, UK, 11/17/87

4

1962 Ferrari 330 TRI/LM Sports Racer
$9,281,250—RM Auctions, Marnaello, ITA, 5/20/07

5

1937 Mercedes-Benz 540K Special Roadster
$8,235,112—RM Auctions, London, UK, 10/7/07

6

1937 Bugatti Type 57SC Atalante Coupe
$7,920,000—Gooding, Pebble Beach, CA, 8/13/08

7

1929 Mercedes-Benz 38/250 SSK
$7,443,070—Bonhams, Sussex, UK, 9/3/04

8

1904 Rolls-Royce 10hp 2-Seater
$7,254,290—Bonhams, London, UK, 12/1/07

9

1962 Ferrari 250 LM Sports Racer
$6,979,000—RM Auctions, Maranello, ITA, 5/18/08

10

1931 Bugatti Type 41 Berline de Voyager
$6,500,000—Kruse, Reno, NV, 6/15/86

BY THE NUMBERS

Sales Results by Vehicle Era

Collectible automobiles can be divided into seven chronological eras. For each, we offer an analysis by number of cars sold, total sales per year, and average dollar per car sold.

Categories

Antique: Pre–1905

Veteran: 1905–18

Vintage: 1919–30

Post-Vintage: 1931–45

Classic: 1946–64

Post-Classic: 1965–74

Modern: Post-1974

Antique
Pre-1905

Total Sales Amount of Antique Cars at Auction by Year

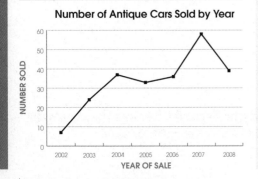

Number of Antique Cars Sold by Year

Average Cost of Each Antique Car Sold

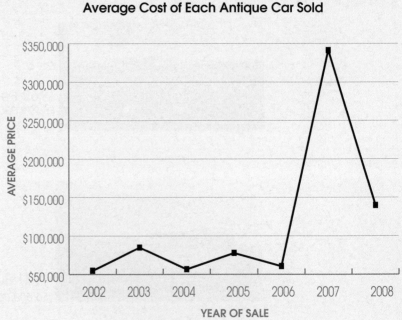

Veteran
1905–18

Total Sales Amount of Veteran Cars at Auction by Year

Average Cost of Each Veteran Car Sold

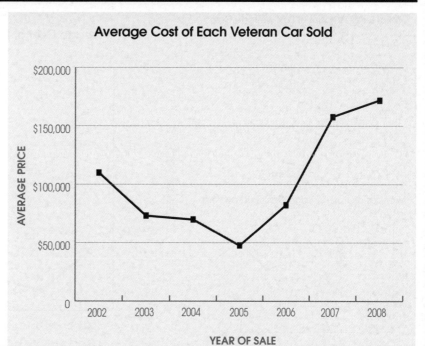

Number of Veteran Cars Sold by Year

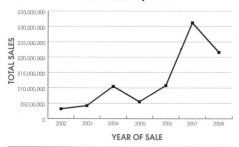

Vintage
1919–30

Total Sales Amount of Vintage Cars at Auction by Year

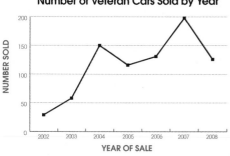

Average Cost of Each Vintage Car Sold

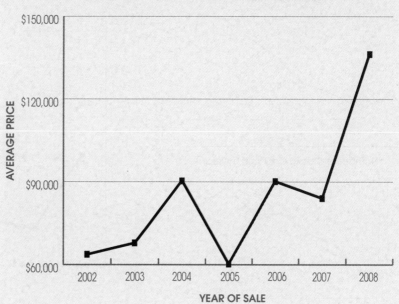

Number of Vintage Cars Sold by Year

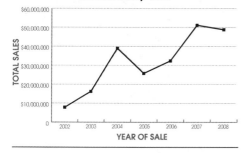

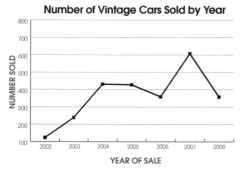

BY THE NUMBERS

Post-Vintage
1931–45

Total Sales Amount of Post-Vintage Cars at Auction by Year

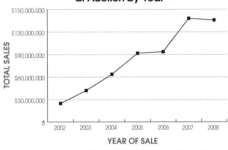

Number of Post-Vintage Cars Sold by Year

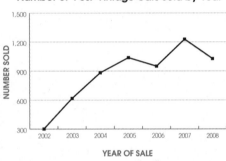

Average Cost of Each Post-Vintage Car Sold

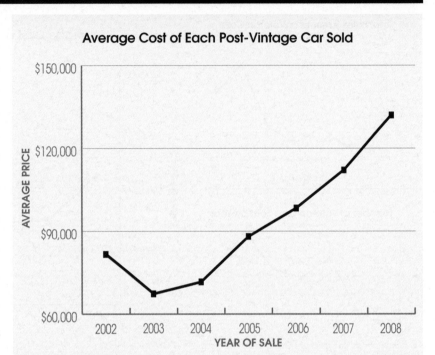

Classic
1946–64

Total Sales Amount of Classic Cars at Auction by Year

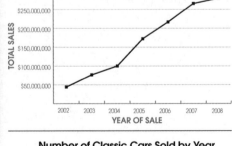

Number of Classic Cars Sold by Year

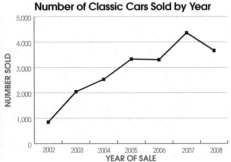

Average Cost of Each Classic Car Sold

Post-Classic
1965–74

Total Sales Amount of Post-Classic Cars at Auction by Year

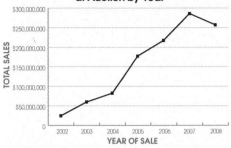

Number of Post-Classic Cars Sold by Year

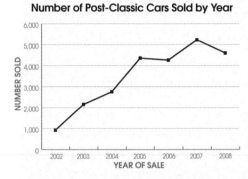

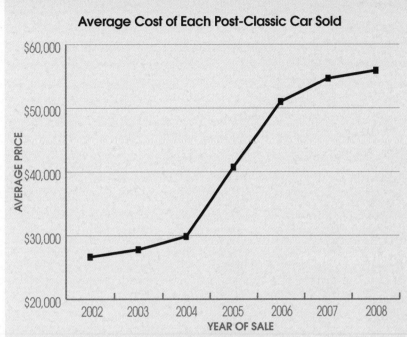

Average Cost of Each Post-Classic Car Sold

Modern
Post-1974

Total Sales Amount of Modern Cars at Auction by Year

Number of Modern Cars Sold by Year

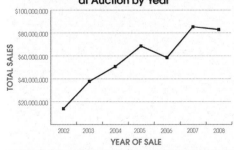

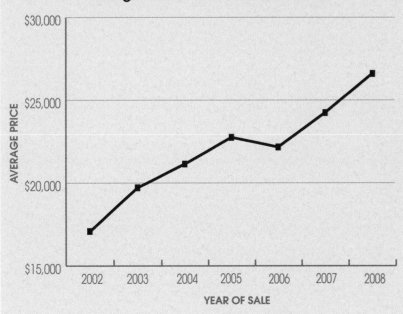

Average Cost of Each Modern Car Sold

BY THE NUMBERS

Market Reports

Now we have come to the real heart of what *Keith Martin's Guide to Car Collecting* is all about—actual prices of actual cars. The market reports in the following pages were compiled by a large cast of auction reporters from Sports Car Market magazine. Their job is a thankless one from many perspectives. They spend long hours examining cars at auction, sometimes in blazing sun, often in chilling rain, and generally far from home and family. Each evaluation of a collector car in this book represents time spent by one of Sports Car Market magazine's experts methodically going over the car from front to back, top to bottom. Their charge is to describe the car to you, in writing, as if you were interested in buying the car and they were talking with you on the phone.

"Nice car, shiny paint," doesn't really do it, does it? That's why you'll read sentences like, "Older restoration that is starting to come apart. Pitted chrome. Some rips and tears to seats. Yet overall, seems like an honest car, not tarted up for auction, but not horribly abused in a past life either." It takes a special kind of reporter to be able to look at one hundred cars a weekend and see the strengths and weaknesses in each, and these SCM reporters are indeed special.—*Keith Martin*

In This Section

Ferraris 101
British Cars.. 105
Porsches... 109
Muscle Cars 113
Corvettes 117
Pre-War Classics 121
Modern Day Supercars 125

Significant Ferraris Sold at Auction, 2008–09

No other automotive name conjures up more impossibly glamorous (and dangerous) imagery than that of Ferrari. From 1960s movie stars and tycoons picking up their cars at the factory in Maranello to dead racing heroes like Rodriguez, Parks, and Von Trips, Ferraris have history and swagger like no other marque. The early two-seater berlinettas and spyders have the greatest connection in the minds of collectors to the competition cars of the 1950s and 1960s, and consequently, these are the Ferraris most collectors covet. That isn't to say that great 2+2 GTs like the 250 GTE and 365 GT 2+2 don't have their merits; they just won't appreciate like the two-seater cars. Ferrari ownership, while potentially rewarding, also carries with it the risk of financial evisceration if the mechanicals misbehave. Choose wisely if you wish to survive—and enjoy—the Ferrari experience.

1991 FERRARI F40 coupe

Auction Infomation
SOLD AT $515,000. Lot #S104; Mecum, St. Charles, IL 10/07

Specs & Condition
S/N ZFFMN34A2M0089441. Red/red & black leather. Odo: 4,402 miles. As-new in all respects, as 4,400 miles would suggest. Excellent paint, glass, trim, leather, and alloy wheels. Tires show no wear, nose paint and spoiler show no chips or curb marks. Cond: 1.

Market Opinion
An as-new F40. Although these had an initial sticker price of $399,150, many buyers paid upwards of $700,000 to own one when they were new. For those who wanted one and missed out on a dealer-fresh example, here was their second chance. Expensive, but worth the price paid in this condition.

1967 FERRARI 275 GTB/4 coupe

Auction Infomation
SOLD AT $1,183,072. Lot #245; RM Auctions, London, UK, 10/07

Specs & Condition
S/N 10281. Eng. # 10281. Fly Yellow/black leather. Odo: 73,840 km. A two-owner car first in the U.S., then bought by Italian Giuseppe Prevosti in 1990. Paintwork most probably redone at some time, but still excellent, with only minor surface scratches visible. Chrome likely still original, interior definitely unrestored with leather still soft, engine bay also largely untouched and tidy. Cond: 1-.

Market Opinion
Blessed with iconic styling and capable of delivering tremendous performance, the 275 GTB/4 is aficionado-rated as being the ultimate front-engined Ferrari. This particularly fine and largely unmolested example duly raised just above top estimate money here.

Ferraris

1971 FERRARI 365GTB/4 Daytona coupe

Auction Infomation
SOLD AT $289,969. Lot #281; RM Auctions, London, UK, 10/07

Specs & Condition
S/N 14087. Rosso Corsa/black leather. Odo: 89,226 km. One of 530 of the first series Plexiglas-nose models. Knockoff wheels and a/c optioned from new. First Italian owned, then in France where restored. Panels, sills, and wide doors fit well, paint only slightly marked. Leather lightly worn, 4-cam engine bay presentation unexceptional. Original tool roll present. Cond: 2.

Market Opinion
Last seen at Bonhams Gstaad in December '06, where it sold at $233,253 (SCM# 43823). Happily for the seller, who had rather bravely consigned his motor car entirely without reserve, the hammer fell within the estimate band, correctly valuing this particular Daytona 4-cam for all concerned.

1985 FERRARI 288 GTO coupe

Auction Infomation
SOLD AT $616,000. Lot #4; Gooding & Company, Scottsdale, AZ, 01/09

Specs & Condition
S/N ZFFPA16B00005643. Red/black leather. Odo: 16,882 miles. Good panel fit, as per factory. Paint appears largely original and in good condition. Front spoiler shows some curb damage at bottom edge. Wheels good, but a bit soiled. Interior clean, with some wear on driver's seat side bolster and several scuffs on left door panel. Denon cassette radio fitted. Cond: 3.

Market Opinion
The last Ferrari "supercar" built during Enzo's watch, and as such, interest has steadily been rising. This was a good driving example, as it was both used and eminently usable. We'll see if the price can be repeated—for now, it's well sold.

1958 FERRARI 250 GT LWB CALIFORNIA spyder

Auction Infomation
SOLD AT $3,659,838. Lot #337; RM Auctions, Maranello, ITA, 05/08

Specs & Condition
S/N 0923GT. Eng. # 0923GT. Rosso Rubino/tan leather. Odo: 70,245 miles. Number three of 50 LWB cars built. A covered headlight example with known history and many owners. Mechanically original and overhauled in 2006, restored in the late '90s to its current non-original Rosso Rubino and tan configuration. Done to an excellent level all over and ready to be shown or enjoyed on the road. Cond: 1.

Market Opinion
Sold under the low estimate of $4m. To be compared with the yellow '59 at Gooding's first-time Scottsdale sale that brought $3.3m in January (SCM# 48791), the black covered headlight '59 that sold at $4.45m at Gooding's Monterey sale in August '07 (SCM# 46559), and the alloy '59 that sold for $4.95m at RM Monterey in August '07 (SCM# 46249). In 2000, they were $1m cars, but they returned 20% per year over the past eight years. Well bought, as long as the trend continues.

1987 FERRARI TESTAROSSA coupe

Auction Infomation
SOLD AT $79,200. Lot #F461; Russo and Steele, Monterey, CA, 08/08

Specs & Condition
S/N ZFFSG17A6H0073153. Rosso Corsa/tan leather. Odo: 6,734 miles. Original near-perfect body, paint, and interior. Complete with matching luggage, books, manuals, and tools. Appears as-new throughout. Cond: 1-.

Market Opinion
Values of Ferrari's '80s flagship are still suffering from not quite being back in fashion yet. This was claimed to be the lowest known mileage example, but many of these haven't seen much use. Still, for less than the price of a Boss 302 Mustang, you could have had this most impressive 12-cylinder Ferrari. A decent deal for condition and mileage.

1964 FERRARI 250LM sports racer

Auction Infomation
SOLD AT $6,979,225. Lot #339A; RM Auctions, Maranello, ITA, 05/08

Specs & Condition
S/N 5845. Eng. # 5845. Dark red/gray cloth. RHD. One of 32 built. Although 5845 had a busy racing life, with numerous owners all over the world, many colors, and some transformation including windows, nose, and interior (as it had been used as a New York City commuter), it was able to keep its original key components, chassis, engine, and gearbox. The pinnacle of its racing history was a win at the Austrian Grand Prix in 1965. Today restored back to its original racing specifications, it is a well-sorted example of a significant automobile. Cond: 2.

Market Opinion
First seen at the Tokyo Auction in March '92, where it failed to sell at $1,424,000 (SCM# 13130), later seen at World Classic's Monterey sale in August '93, where it failed to sell again at $800k (SCM# 15334). 250LMs rarely appear on the market, and they're both attractive and historically significant, as well as welcome at all events. This was a late consignment, but it was a right car. 5845 is ready for the track, and all parties should be happy with the price.

1961 FERRARI 250 GT Series II cabriolet

Auction Infomation
SOLD AT $851,125. Lot #338; RM Auctions, Maranello, ITA, 05/08

Specs & Condition
S/N 2381GT. Eng. # 2381GT. Black/black canvas/black leather. Odo: 72,560 km. Number 112 out of 201. Complete frame-off rebuild to very high standards. Panel fit, glass, rubber, and brightwork better than new, complete engine overhaul, new soft top. A few missed details include retrimmed dash top with some padding, non-original seat rails, and modern battery. A triple black car ready to be enjoyed, either by driving or show. Cond: 1-.

Market Opinion
A mid-estimate result, and a record price by far for a Series II. Most prefer the California's sporty style, which accounts for the higher price (rarity adding). I feel that the Series II cabriolets are equally appealing, trading sport for elegance. Less than 200 remain, as some were used for spares for other more expensive 250 models. Maybe bought a little too soon, but prices will catch up.

1963 FERRARI 250 GTL LUSSO coupe

Auction Infomation
SOLD AT $1,174,553. Lot #319; RM Auctions, Maranello, ITA, 05/08

Specs & Condition
S/N 5143GT. Eng. # 5143GT. Vernice Celeste/dark green leather. Odo: 29 km. Fresh out of a four-year, money-no-issue, rotisserie restoration by the best European specialists in each domain. Well done in every aspect from paint to custom dark green Connolly luggage. Complete known history, matching numbers, ready to drive or show. Provided with original handbook, sales brochures, and tool kit. Cond: 1.

Market Opinion
In August '07, Steve McQueen's Lusso in similar #1 condition sold for $2.3m at Christie's Monterey sale (SCM# 46176). SCM contributor John Apen's profile of this car in the November '07 issue estimated that most of this money was McQueen related, while an excellent Lusso is worth $400,000. The market has sped up on these cars since then, with excellent cars bringing close to this number. $1.2m seems over the top today, but there will always be buyers for the best.

1961 FERRARI 250 GT SWB coupe

Auction Infomation
SOLD AT $4,510,000. Lot #447; RM Auctions, Monterey, CA, 08/08

Specs & Condition
S/N 3087GT. Red/black leather. Odo: 53,802 miles. Coachwork by Scaglietti. Steel-bodied Lusso street version, and the 117th of 165 SWBs built between 1959 and 1962. Extensive restoration by Shelton Ferrari reportedly at the cost of $600,000, numerous prestigious awards won since. Four-wheel discs, owner's manual, warranty card, and tool kit. Cond: 1-.

Market Opinion
The high sale of the auction, and rightly so. A spectacular presentation, and although it may seem expensive at over the high estimate of $4.2m, it was not a bad deal in this appreciating Ferrari market.

Ferraris

1959 FERRARI 410 SUPERAMERICA Series III SWB coupe

Auction Infomation
SOLD AT $2,530,000. Lot #50, Worldwide Group, Auburn, IN, 08/08

Specs & Condition
S/N 1323. Eng. # 1323. Ruby Red/tan leather. Odo: 39,326 miles. Restored from 2002 through 2007 to better-than-new-condition. Presented as delivered, with covered headlights and Borrani wire wheels, yet with interior color change from gray to tan. Paint job so good and smooth that bugs don't even stick to it. Modern maintenance-free battery the only modern concession underhood. Some light road dust on undercoated chassis, black coated exhaust system, light fuel staining around carburetor base gaskets, clutch pedal rubber pad loose. Otherwise perfectly restored. Cond: 1.

Market Opinion
Number six of twelve Series III Superamericas built. To qualify my no bugs sticking comment, during the pre-sale gala, a June bug landed on the left front fender and promptly slid right off the front of the car while trying to skitter up toward the cowl. Overall, a very stunning restoration that had the look of being hosed down with money. The bidding started at a million, and when it hit $2.3m, the reserve was lifted. Given current market conditions for top-shelf Ferraris, this price was market-correct.

1977 FERRARI 308 GTB Vetroresina coupe

Auction Infomation
SOLD AT $63,336. Lot #211, Bonhams, Gstaad, CHE, 12/08

Specs & Condition
S/N 21025. Gray/black leather. Odo: 55,221 km. High-level Swiss restoration in 2006 with new paint, interior, and mechanical work. Flawless in all aspects. A close-to-perfect example of the "best" 308, with light fiberglass body, Euro-spec dry-sump engine, and attractive berlinetta design. Comes with tool kit and manuals. Cond: 1-.

Market Opinion
Sold at mid-estimate money. 12,000 308s were produced, but only 712 were molded in fiberglass, and quite a few of those have disappeared due to racing. Half the price of a Dino 246 or a 512 BBi. No major risk here.

1972 FERRARI 246 GT Dino coupe

Auction Infomation
SOLD AT $161,714. Lot #301, RM Auctions, Maranello, ITA, 05/08

Specs & Condition
S/N 03708. Red/camel leather. Odo: 25,398 km. Recent quality respray, panels straight and solid throughout. Chrome, glass, rubber, and Cromodora wheels all excellent. Original leather interior clean and supple but for the sagging door panels and lightly soiled carpets. Described with 62,000 km in 1984, so therefore probably 125,398 km today on the original engine. Underhood clean and tidy. Cond: 2.

Market Opinion
The color here was a welcome change from the more common red found on other 246 GTs. Price was correct, considering the potential cost of maintenance if the mileage was in fact over 100,000 km. Prices of Dino coupes in this condition seem to stay in the $150k–$180k range, so no risk and no harm here.

1960 FERRARI 250 GT SWB California spyder

Auction Infomation
SOLD AT $4,950,000. Lot #78, Gooding & Company, Scottsdale, AZ, 01/09

Specs & Condition
S/N 1963GT. Eng. # 1963GT. Red/black canvas/black leather. Odo: 69,560 km. Excellent door fit; hood and trunk lid off. Casual older paint is shiny but shows stress cracks, touched-in chips, and bubbling. Right side rear panel under trunk lid poorly profiled. Chrome is fair, with front bumper present but unmounted. Original interior has stiff seats with deep creasing and perished foam, some in-painting on console. With factory hard top. Cond: 4+.

Market Opinion
From the VanKregten Collection. The most desirable California Spyder, in SWB configuration with covered headlights. Not quite a time capsule worth preserving, but a superb base for a restoration. Sold at exactly the price we all thought it would (and should).

Significant Aston Martins and Other British Sports Cars Sold at Auction, 2008–09

Aston Martin's post-war history is illustrious to say the least, involving places like Le Mans and people like Roy Salvadori and Carroll Shelby. But who are we kidding? Astons were relatively unknown in the U.S. until Desmond Llewellyn—playing the acerbic head of "Q" branch in the movie "Goldfinger"—explained to an incredulous James Bond what the little red button under the gearshift lever on his DB5 did: "Ejector seat? You must be joking!" "I never joke about my work, 007!" So began the greatest bit of product placement from which any auto manufacturer has ever benefitted. Astons, unlike some fragile Italian exotics, have always seemed like a proper, sturdy car, and values have been consistently strong in the past five years.

On your way to such dizzying heights, there are plenty of other fun British sports cars to buy and enjoy. Start with an MG Midget or an Austin-Healey Bugeye Sprite, move up to an MG B or a Triumph TR4 or TR6, graduate to an Austin-Healey 3000 or Jaguar XK 120, and settle down—if you can call it that—with Jaguar E-type, before your inheritance comes in and you can buy a C-type (or a replica, if you're left out of the will). While wildly dissimilar in some ways, what all English cars have in common is a bulldog-like sturdiness of build and a springer spaniel-like desire to please.

1964 ASTON MARTIN DB5 coupe

Auction Infomation
SOLD AT $314,110. Lot #255; Bonhams, Sussex, UK, 08/07

Specs & Condition
S/N DB51441R. Eng. # 4001416. Silver/black leather. RHD. Odo: 2,168 miles. Original U.K. market car, repatriated in '03 from an Australian museum. Paint and interior changed twice before current 007 color and trim combo. 2005 Chris Shenton restoration included unleaded conversion, new clutch, alternator conversion, Harvey Bailey handling kit with Konis, and FM conversion for original Motorola radio. Cosmetically superb inside and out. Well-detailed engine bay likely to be mechanically super. Cond: 1.

Market Opinion
Last seen at Bonhams Sussex in July '06, where it sold at $257,331 (SCM# 42336). DB5s were the first of the DB Astons to take off price-wise, and the ever increasing sums paid for all the other Feltham and pre-V8 Newport Pagnell-made models reflect the now-cool status of the marque. This lovely example of arguably the prettiest Aston of them all duly achieved mid- to high-estimate money here.

1966 ASTON MARTIN DB6 Mk I coupe

Auction Infomation
SOLD AT $92,365. Lot #752; Bonhams, Beaulieu, UK, 09/07

Specs & Condition
S/N DB62740R. Eng. # 4002760. Silver/dark blue leather. RHD. Odo: 88,797 miles. U.K. home-market car driven until 1989, when shipped to British Columbia. Resident of Oregon by 1993, repatriated 1999. Recent repaint generally shiny with some chips and only fair in door jambs. Chrome, including wires, marked and worn. Still original leather soft but slightly shabby, headlining and carpets renewed 1998. Triple-carb-fed engine and bay unexceptional, wood wheel worn. Cond: 2-.

Market Opinion
A new owner could merely keep trying to use this car between continual repair bills, but the truly besotted might just tear it apart and start all over again. Hey, at this sort of money—which was inexpensive for a DB6—both would be appropriate. The rise in pre-V8 Aston prices, with more upside to come, one suspects, probably justifies the full makeover budget.

British

1967 AUSTIN MINI COOPER S Ex-Works Rally racer

Auction Infomation
SOLD AT $87,560. Lot #61; H&H Auctions, Gloucestershire, UK, 02/08

Specs & Condition
S/N CA2S71012033A. Red & white/black velour & leather. RHD. Odo: 11,500 miles. From the period when BMC moved from rallying to racing, this ex-Works Mini (raced by Hopkirk, finished 14th on '69 Tour de France) has been well restored. Split Webers rather than injection, eight-port head comes with car. Bolt-on Minilites, rear cage with new patches on floor under mounts, Halda Twinmaster, Moto-Lita wheel. MOT through Jan '09. Cond: 3.

Market Opinion
Ex-Works Minis are a minefield, and this was on the top estimate but under recent valuations of cars with good history. The price paid was about right for continuation of a known car in lesser specs that was reshelled at least once in period (as most were). Buyer and seller should both be happy.

1946 MG TC roadster

Auction Infomation
SOLD AT $48,400. Lot #78; Worldwide Group, Seabrook, TX, 05/08

Specs & Condition
S/N XPAG2287. Maroon & black/tan fabric/red leather. RHD. Odo: 44 miles. A U.S. version with sealed headlights, turn signals, and plated bumpers. Restored ten years ago to high standards, very little use since. Well maintained with minor fit issues. Attractive throughout. Cond: 2+.

Market Opinion
This TC sold for a market-correct price considering its condition. The only question would be the lack of use and whether it took a toll on engine seals. If no internal issues present themselves, then I hope the new owner gets rid of the whitewalls and drives the heck out of it.

1961 ASTON MARTIN DB4GT coupe

Auction Infomation
SOLD AT $2,115,820. Lot #345; Bonhams, Newport Pagnell, UK, 05/08

Specs & Condition
S/N DB4GT0145R. Eng. # 3700162GT. Green/buff leather. RHD. Odo: 18,273 miles. One of 75 built, 45 of which were supplied in RHD. Super order for a completely original 47-year-old car. Light surface rust under sills, window rubbers perished. Unmarked chrome, dash immaculate, heavy patina to seats. New carpets, but originals come with car. Looks almost untouched apart from brake caliper rebuild, new coils, and a stainless steel exhaust. A "reference car" for anybody restoring one. Cond: 3+.

Market Opinion
An expensive sale against a $1.3m–$1.5m estimate. Auctioneer Jamie Knight was heard saying, "I knew I had interest from a buyer in the room at $1.5m but he didn't even get his hand up before it went to the telephones." Rare in this original condition, and well bought and sold.

1989 ASTON MARTIN V8 Vantage Volante convertible

Auction Infomation
SOLD AT $261,660. Lot #308; Bonhams, Newport Pagnell, UK, 05/08

Specs & Condition
S/N SCFCV81VOKTL15794. Eng. # V5805794X. Black/cream cloth/cream leather. Odo: 8,284 km. Body straight and tidy, paint nearly perfect, good cream leather. Veneers spotless and alloys only marked where stick-on balance weights have been. Very clean throughout. One owner from new. Cond: 1-.

Market Opinion
$60k over top estimate. Originally sold by an Italian dealer, but has been in Switzerland and France since. Very collectible whether or not you can stand the plastic add-ons, and probably a shrewd buy at this time.

1965 JAGUAR XKE SI 4.2 coupe

Auction Infomation
SOLD AT $111,150. Lot #314; Bonhams & Butterfields, Carmel Valley, CA, 08/08

Specs & Condition
S/N 1E30680. Dark blue/biscuit leather. Odo: 130 miles. Excellent panel fit, but gaps not totally consistent. Very good paint shows polish swirl marks and a small scratch on left front fender, excellent chrome has no issues. Very good interior except for some soiling on driver's seat, worn armrest bases, and some fraying to left rear quarter panel trim. Two JCNA firsts, at 99.8+. Cond: 2+.

Market Opinion
A very high-level restoration of what is widely regarded as the most desirable E-type. Has fallen off a bit from its JCNA show wins, but would need very little to be a star again. Well bought and reasonably sold.

1956 AUSTIN-HEALEY 100M Le Mans roadster

Auction Infomation
SOLD AT $159,500. Lot #481; RM Auctions, Monterey, CA, 08/08

Specs & Condition
S/N BN2L229932. Eng. # 1B229932M. Old English White/tan fabric/red leather. Odo: 76,338 miles. One of 640 factory produced 100Ms, of which only about 150 are known today. British Motor Industry Heritage Trust certificate documents this as original 100M. Extensive restoration a few years back still showing well. Driver's door has wide gaps at bottom. Very well presented. Cond: 2.

Market Opinion
Many of the 100Ms offered were converted by their selling dealers, not the factory, so the Heritage Trust certificate makes all the difference here. With it the price paid was in line, and there was no major leap of faith.

1976 TRIUMPH TR6 convertible

Auction Infomation
SOLD AT $18,630. Lot #195; Auctions America, Raleigh, NC, 12/08

Specs & Condition
S/N CF55180U. Old English White/black vinyl/black vinyl. Odo: 53,663 miles. Older white paint features light swirl marks, chips, and edge wear. Excellent convertible top correct and could be original, interior likewise tidy with few flaws. Chrome and brightwork in very good nick with evidence of light overbuffing. Steel wheels with Redline tires and trim rings look correct. Engine compartment features an older restoration unwound from show quality but still in above-driver condition. Cond: 2-.

Market Opinion
Last seen at eBay/Kruse's Sunrise, Florida, sale in 2002, where it sold at $8,000 (SCM# 26715). If a well-preserved original, this was a remarkable car, although the consignor claims a full restoration was documented. Since no evidence of this was present, I'd venture a guess of something in between the two, with some elements obviously restored and other bits hardy and well-kept originals. An above-average driver example in cleanable, local British car show condition throughout, and a good price for both parties.

1959 JAGUAR XK 150S 3.4 roadster

Auction Infomation
SOLD AT $121,000. Lot #16; Gooding & Company, Scottsdale, AZ, 01/09

Specs & Condition
S/N S830418DN. Eng. # VS10249. Sherwood Green/green canvas/medium green leather. Odo: 28,497 miles. Excellent panel fit. Very good paint shows some light polish scratches. Nice chrome to bumpers, trim, and wire wheels. Excellent interior with no visible wear. Cond: 1-.

Market Opinion
A beautifully restored roadster with higher performance "S" equipment and wonderful colors throughout. Hard to fault. It stalled on the block at a $120k bid, but a deal was done before day's end to sell it. A great deal for the buyer at this price.

1965 TRIUMPH TR4A convertible

Auction Infomation
SOLD AT $25,300. Lot #62, Worldwide Group, Hilton Head, SC, 11/08

Specs & Condition
S/N CT63420. Black/white vinyl/red leather. Odo: 90,729 miles. High-quality black paint uniformly applied throughout. Body gaps good, driver's door would not open. Chrome and brightwork better than average although rear bumper shows some pitting. New interior kit fitted hastily and could use moderate tweaking; driver's door panel needs the most attention. Engine bay complete and in tidy driver condition. Cond: 2-.

Market Opinion
Although this was a TR4A, it was not an independent rear suspension car as cataloged. That said, it was rather nice throughout, and some minor tweaks would certainly bring the condition rating up a level. Market price.

1960 MG A Mk II roadster

Auction Infomation
SOLD AT $35,200. Lot #225, RM Auctions, Hershey, PA, 10/08

Specs & Condition
S/N HDK4372384. Eng. # 1866UH71788. Black/red leather. Odo: 2,914 miles. Former winner of Radnor Hunt Concours d'Elegance. Exhibits very slight mottling under lustrous paint, bodywork excellent throughout, chrome and brightwork without issue. Interior overdone in red leather, no top or bows present at this sale. Engine compartment exhibits similar but not visually identical MG B 1,800-cc engine and 4-speed transmission. Cond: 2+.

Market Opinion
Last seen at the Bonhams & Butterfields Greenwich sale in June '08, where it failed to sell at $25,000 (SCM# 116962). While an MG A resto-mod is not everyone's cup of tea, this was done better than most British Car Day concours-fanatic cars, and it likely gives considerably better performance than even one with a built 1,600-cc mill would. Perhaps there's a coming trend, but for now this was all the money and a bit more still.

1929 MORGAN AERO Super Sports roadster

Auction Infomation
SOLD AT $48,404. Lot #310, Bonhams, Chichester, UK, 09/08

Specs & Condition
S/N 1684A. Eng. # LTOWCS39377. Green/black leather. RHD. Odo: 4,774 miles. Original matching-numbers car. Tidy and usable, with no motor leaks, chains good and well lubed. Correct headlights, nice interior. Cond: 3.

Market Opinion
This example of the most desirable Morgan, with JA Prestwich rather than Matchless motor, fetched just over its lower estimate. With its matching numbers, it might have been expected to make a bit more, but it's the sub-$100k market that starts to look shaky first.

1936 LAGONDA LG45R Rapide roadster

Auction Infomation
SOLD AT $1,382,000. Lot #310, Bonhams & Butterfields, Carmel Valley, CA, 08/08

Specs & Condition
S/N 12111. Eng. # 12111. Dark red/black canvas/blue leather. RHD. Odo: 81,168 miles. Coachwork by Fox & Nicholl. Faded, lightly scratched, and somewhat chipped and mismatched paint with a plethora of event stickers. Replacement engine fitted, original comes with the car. Worn and scratched seats, new aluminum dash panel with what appear to be original gauges mounted inside. Extensive history file with scrapbooks and British log book included. Cond: 4+.

Market Opinion
A charismatic Lagonda racer with documented pre- and post-war track history. First rebuilt in 1974, then again in the '80s by Terry Cohn. Sold by Christie's in the U.K. in October 1983 at $95,000 (SCM# 9335). Worn, used, and fabulous. Worth every penny, and perhaps even a bit under the market at this price.

Significant Porsches Sold at Auction, 2008–09

Is there another marque that inspires the kind of devotion among the faithful, and consternation among the non-believers, than Porsche? The latter find them overpriced, underpowered, funny looking, and driven by recently divorced orthodontists bedecked in gold chains. The former, the true believers, consider them to be exquisitely engineered and assembled—beautifully balanced and like nothing else. Wherever you come down on them, there's no disputing Porsche's contribution to motorsport and the post-war sports car movement in the U.S. Vintage Porsches are prized because of their bulletproof reliability, faultless build quality, and all-around usability. In areas of the country with a mild year-round climate, a 356 coupe makes an ideal daily driver, capable of returning decent performance with excellent fuel economy. Any 911 adds significantly more performance and better visibility at the expense of a bit of vintage charm. Either way, you're a winner.

1964 PORSCHE 904 GTS coupe

Auction Infomation
SOLD AT $888,465. Lot #326; Bonhams, Chichester, UK, 09/08

Specs & Condition
S/N 021. Silver/black velour. Odo: 16,316 km. Good appearance for a former competition car, with just a few small areas where prep could have been more meticulous before paint. Fiberglass all good, Perspex OK, interior probably better than new. No engine leaks, nickel-plated exhaust shows well. Original flat-4 swapped out for a 6 after accident damage on the '65 Coupe des Alpes, later replaced by a 2.8 RSR motor. Lots of history, including '65 Le Mans. From the Bernard Consten Collection. Cond: 2.

Market Opinion
What we have here is a 904 in S2 904/6 spec with a later engine, and this very potent package brought mid-estimate money. However, it's not FIA eligible, even for HTP papers, and it would take a bit of work before assuming its suggested role as a concours queen. Well sold.

1952 GLÖCKLER-PORSCHE racer

Auction Infomation
SOLD AT $616,000. Lot #159; RM Auctions, Phoenix, AZ, 01/08

Specs & Condition
S/N 10447. Silver & yellow/black leather. Coachwork by Weidenhausen. The third Glöckler-Porsche Special built, ex-Max Hoffman/John Von Neumann. Very nicely detailed throughout. Excellent paint but for some small chips, very nice trim and brightwork. Plexiglass windows are clean and without major distortion. Clean interior is also well fitted, with good attention to detail throughout. Restored in New Zealand by Tempero Restorations with later engine, as the original unit and several subsequent others are thought to have been destroyed by alcohol fuel. Cond: 2+.

Market Opinion
First seen at Gooding's Palm Beach sale in January '06, where it didn't sell at $680,000 (SCM# 40352). Later seen at Worldwide's Hilton Head Island sale in November '06, where it failed to find new ownership at $630,000 (SCM# 43633). This car had both interesting history and a decent overall condition, and although it had suffered a little since its restoration, this was not a bad price to pay for a footnote racer with provenance.

Porsches

1962 PORSCHE 356B T-6 roadster

Auction Infomation
SOLD AT $170,500. Lot #245; RM Auctions, Monterey, CA, 08/08

Specs & Condition
S/N 89789. Red/black fabric/black leather. Odo: 16,925 km. One of just 248 "twin grille" roadsters built by D'Ieteren Freres of Belgium. Restored about ten years back with little use since. Swirls in paint along with a few chips and nicks, decent chrome and trim. Authenticated by Porsche AG. Cond: 2.

Market Opinion
Pricing Porsche's roadster is not an exact science of late, as they are moving faster than the price guides can be updated. The estimates of $75k–$100k here were well under the money, and the price paid was in line with the appreciating market.

1982 PORSCHE 928 coupe

Auction Infomation
SOLD AT $4,346. Lot #14; MidAmerica, Blaine, MN 09/07

Specs & Condition
S/N WP0JA0928CS822592. Gold metallic/brown leather. Odo: 88,275 miles. Fitted with sunroof, pw, and add-on rear spoiler. Decent quality older repaint, older aftermarket window tinting. 2004 Car Craft Summer Nationals participant sticker on left front windshield corner, Harley-Davidson sticker on rear hatch window below broken-off cell phone antenna mount. Used-car-grade engine bay and undercarriage, all original interior components. Heavier wear than would be expected to seats, far less to carpets. Trim around shift lever mostly missing, remaining pieces loose. Cond: 4+.

Market Opinion
Both stickers on this car—especially the Harley one—might as well have said "WARNING: DON'T BID ON ME." 928s aren't moving much in value, and they seem to be in the same league as run-down Rolls-Royce Silver Shadows. The new owner might get lucky enough to get 50k more miles out of it without issue, but it's more likely he'll just be waiting for something expensive to break every time he turns the key. Sold well.

1965 PORSCHE 356C coupe

Auction Infomation
SOLD AT $50,600. Lot #18; Worldwide Group, Hilton Head, SC, 11/08

Specs & Condition
S/N 218436. Gray/red vinyl. Odo: 50,272 miles. Older comprehensive restoration executed to a high standard just starting to come apart, numerous chips and touch-ups in driver's door and jamb. Passenger door adjustment slightly off, chrome and brightwork crisp but slightly dull. Interior uniform, with nice seats, carpet, and trim, although dash crash roll somewhat wavy. Engine compartment well if not recently detailed. Modern Michelin radials not in keeping with show-car appearance. Cond: 2.

Market Opinion
Like many past PCA 356 champions, which is what this likely once was, this car did the show circuit and then went out to pasture as a weekend driver. At the end of the day, it's just a late coupe in one of the least attractive colors—at least to my eye. Well bought and sold.

1983 PORSCHE 911SC convertible

Auction Infomation
SOLD AT $19,340. Lot #345; Auctions America, Raleigh, NC, 12/08

Specs & Condition
S/N WP0EA0918DS171636. Guards Red/black cloth/tan vinyl. Odo: 110,572 miles. Exterior repaint done to a high standard but does not extend far into jambs, which exhibit more than passable overspray. Broken driver door check a typical and normally cheap 911 repair. Black cloth top in good condition, tan vinyl interior and gauges faded, carpet appears fresh. Engine bay tidy and reflects claims of recent thorough overhaul. Cond: 3.

Market Opinion
This SC was just a typical driver example with plenty of cosmetic needs. This was huge money, and I was willing to bet it was bought by a couple of guys who were taken in by the brilliant red and a top that went down. All the money and more. Well sold.

1955 PORSCHE 356 Speedster

Auction Information
SOLD AT $137,500. Lot #159; RM Auctions, Phoenix, AZ, 01/09

Specs & Condition
S/N 82011. Eng. # 60669. White/black canvas/red leatherette. Odo: 60,669 miles. Numbers-matching with Kardex certificate of authenticity. Delivered with U.S. speedo and sealed beam headlights. Original condition with recent respray. Stated to have no rust or filler. A well-maintained, straight and solid 356. Cond: 3.

Market Opinion
Porsche 356s have been appreciating at a rapid rate, and some say the bloom is now coming off the rose. If this sale is any example, I think we have some way to go before we have to worry about any wilting here. Sold at the current going rate, even though the colors were not all that striking.

1973 PORSCHE 911 CARRERA RS coupe

Auction Information
SOLD AT $172,461. Lot #31; Artcurial, Paris, FRA, 02/09

Specs & Condition
S/N 9113600711. White/black leather. Odo: 92,187 km. Original 2.7 RS with Touring package rebuilt in 1995 from bare metal and extensively raced since then. In good condition today, with many upgrades. Externally looks stock. Interior with roll cage and all racing equipment, engine bay tidy. An efficient rally machine, but not a concours car. Cond: 2+.

Market Opinion
No longer an original car, and no historic racing results—the perfect tool for historic racing. Bonhams sold a perfect 2.7 RS Touring for $271,000 in August '07 (SCM# 46391), but this is the market price for a nice but imperfect RS today.

1986 PORSCHE 911 3.2 Carrera coupe

Auction Information
SOLD AT $19,074. Lot #45; H&H Auctions, Duxford, UK, 10/07

Specs & Condition
S/N WP0ZZZ91ZGS109622. Dark blue/gray leather. Odo: 87,192 km. Imported from Italy in 2006. Straight and clean, no bubbling in the usual places. Some lacquer lifting by the fuel filler, trunk floor straight, front bumper bolts unmolested. Motor clean and fitted with fresh heat exchangers. Some oil return pipes new, oil feed pipes in good shape, alloys unmarked. Dash clean, slightly discolored carpets and rear seats. Cond: 2.

Market Opinion
Prices of clean, low-mileage 3.2s are on the up in the U.K.—no doubt hauled on the bootstraps of the earlier cars—and it was interesting to see this LHD version go for a couple thousand under retail. As there were no real needs visible, this can be considered well bought.

1994 PORSCHE 911 Speedster

Auction Information
SOLD AT $51,840. Lot #552; Cox Auctions, Branson, MO, 10/07

Specs & Condition
S/N WP0CB2964RS455411. Red/black cloth/black leather. Odo: 7,420 miles. Very clean visually, seller claims all services are up to date. No repaint visible, all black trim nice. Excellent glass, back window plastic dirty but top remains good. Very clean interior speaks to the low miles. Cond: 2+.

Market Opinion
It won't be long before most all of the low-mile Speedsters—cars that were tough to give away a few years ago—will be gone, converted into drivers by those who forgot, or hopefully ignored, the "we hate these" credo by the self-serving Porsche people. Not cheap, but a good to excellent buy for the person who thinks long-term for his automotive horizon.

Porsches

1984 PORSCHE 911 Wide Body coupe

Auction Infomation
SOLD AT $26,950. Lot #328, Barrett-Jackson, Palm Beach, FL, 04/09

Specs & Condition
S/N WP0ZZZ91ZES103261. Black/black leather. Odo: 44,605 miles. Both doors out at bottom, hood fits tight at cowl. Paint is a budget respray and has been touched up since, matte black trim faded and weathered. Seat bolster well broken in, engine compartment looks weathered and worn. Cond: 4+.

Market Opinion
Porsche introduced the M491 option, also known as the Supersport, to resemble the 930 Turbo with wide wheelarches and the distinctive "whale" tail. It featured the turbo suspension, turbo braking system, and wide turbo wheels. This was a well-worn wide body, and in my opinion, one to stay away from. The paintwork was rough and obviously fluffed up for the sale, and if a guy doesn't take care of his car cosmetically, he often won't take care of it mechanically, either. Buyer beware here. Well sold.

1960 PORSCHE 356B coupe

Auction Infomation
SOLD AT $67,100. Lot #F547, Russo and Steele, Scottsdale, AZ, 01/09

Specs & Condition
S/N 112480. Black/red leather. Odo: 61,770 miles. Optional Blaupunkt multi-band radio and chrome wheels. Recent bare-body restoration performed by Classic Showcase. Superb body prep and panel fit, equally well done paint with a few polishing swirls. All original chrome replated, all original trim restored. No original glass left, including headlight covers and gauges. Engine compartment restored to concours standards. Expertly fitted seat upholstery, door panels, headliner, and dashpad. Authentic reproduction carpeting and dealer accessory rubber mat. Cond: 1-.

Market Opinion
Said to have been driven about 150 miles since it rolled out of rehab, and the light wear seemed to bear that out. On the auction block, things almost petered out at $50k, but after a bit the bidding got kick-started again, picking up momentum until the consignor pulled the reserve at this final market-correct bid.

1972 PORSCHE 911 2.7 RS Prototype coupe

Auction Infomation
SOLD AT $480,000. Lot #359, Bonhams & Butterfields, Carmel Valley, CA, 08/08

Specs & Condition
S/N 9113600012. Eng. # 6630022. Signal Yellow/black & white houndstooth cloth. Odo: 20,575 km. Excellent panel fit and paint. Otherwise excellent chrome has some small imperfections on side window base trim. Clean and well-fitted interior shows no wear. The first of the RS cars. Cond: 1.

Market Opinion
Superbly presented and outrageously desirable. During the preview, all the Porschephiles were salivating. Last crossed the block on the Peninsula in 2006, when Christie's sold it for $334k (SCM# 42513). Since then, it has been restored to a high level. Given the likely cost of the work, how much was the actual profit? A hard way to do it in my book. Market correct.

1956 PORSCHE 356 Super 1600 Speedster

Auction Infomation
SOLD AT $115,500. Lot #S665, Russo and Steele, Hollywood, FL, 03/08

Specs & Condition
S/N 81134. Eng. # 80050. Red oxide primer/primer hard top/tattered black vinyl. Odo: 48,225 miles. Numbers-matching 616.2 engine family, just the way you want it. Purchased in 1971, stored by the owner since 1989. Restoration started, most body work done. Originally white; all trim bits, extra badges and more included. Very desirable hard top and pedigree paperwork from the factory. Cond: 5.

Market Opinion
To do this right you'd have to plan on spending another $100k, but the finished product should be stunning—especially if done in its original livery. The price was about right for the condition, and I heard a rumor that the buyer was offered a profit on this before it was even paid for.

Significant Muscle Cars Sold at Auction, 2008–09

If sports and GT cars are like triathletes, able to excel at multiple tasks, muscle cars are like Pro Bowl offensive linemen—really good at one thing, flattening the opposition. And while the sports car crowd can bleat all day long about the indifferent quality control, bad handling, and iffy brakes of American iron, do one smokey burnout in a Hemi 'Cuda and see if you care about any of the above. When the bottom dropped out of the economy, muscle car prices took it on the chin. First the questionable cars—clones, non-original cars, and common stuff—fell, and then the really rare and desirable cars dropped as well. The muscle car market is almost certain to revive when the economy starts growing again, so the current bargain prices on Shelbys, COPO Camaros, and Chevelle LS6s may be short-lived.

1970 PLYMOUTH ROAD RUNNER Superbird 2-dr hard top

Auction Infomation
SOLD AT $132,300. Lot #S127; Mecum, St. Charles, IL 10/07

Specs & Condition
S/N RM23U0A178681. Lime Green/black vinyl/black vinyl. Odo: 18,388 miles. 440-ci V8, 4-bbl, auto. Original build sheet, Govier documents. New shiny paint shows no problems, lumps under vinyl top hint at sloppy glue or possible rust issues. Glass scratched, trim nice. Several interior paint issues to dash and column, interior chrome trim slightly pitted in places. Usual marginal nose fit, variable panel fit. New undercoating to chassis. Cond: 2-.

Market Opinion
New paint and a generally good interior showed a good start to this restoration, but the new owner still has some details to attend to. Expensive considering the needs noted, especially if the bubbles under the top turn out to be holes under closer inspection.

1970 CHEVROLET CHEVELLE SS 454 LS6 COPO 2-dr hard top

Auction Infomation
SOLD AT $214,500. Lot #1279.1; Barrett-Jackson, Scottsdale, AZ, 01/08

Specs & Condition
S/N 136370B144642. Daytona Yellow & black/white vinyl. 454-ci V8, 4-bbl, auto. The 2006 Goodguys Muscle Car of the Year. Loaded with options, including the ZL2 Cowl Induction system and the Z15 SS package. Paint shows some minor issues, chrome and trim excellent. Fitted with AM 8-track. Fully documented with two original build sheets. Close to perfection. Cond: 1-.

Market Opinion
Strong cars continue to bring strong money, and this was no exception, as it was fully documented with desirable options. A no-questions car, and while the buyer paid up to own it, he'll never need to explain why.

Muscle Cars

1969 CHEVROLET CAMARO RS/SS 396 coupe

Auction Infomation
SOLD AT $107,800. Lot #658.1; Barrett-Jackson, West Palm Beach, FL, 03/08

Specs & Condition
S/N 124379N610922. Black & white/white vinyl. Odo: 7 miles. 396-ci V8, 4-bbl, 4-sp. Variable panel fit probably near factory specs, but shows some issues. Trunk lid high, hood wide on right side, driver door out. Black paint shows every flaw in slightly wavy body. Slight cracking at rear window seams, minor scratches on bumper, single dent in window trim. Very nice interior shows little wear. New glass all around. Excellent overall, but paint and body is a let-down. Cond: 3+.

Market Opinion
I can't justify the price paid here no matter how optimistically I look at it. Granted, the black with white interior looked stunning, but the car appeared to have plenty of needs. There was no claim of matching numbers, which often means they don't, and there was no mention of documentation, either. This had plenty of desirable options, but the money spent was well over the top, and I'd call it very well sold.

1970 FORD MUSTANG Boss 302 fastback

Auction Infomation
SOLD AT $58,300. Lot #S125; Mecum Auctions, Kissimmee, FL, 01/09

Specs & Condition
S/N 0T02G163144. White & black/black vinyl. Odo: 39,680 miles. 302-ci V8, 4-bbl, 4-sp. Gaps per factory, driver's door out slightly along rear edge. Decent paint over average prep, with some masking issues and a few small drips. Rear blackout panel has overspray into taillights. Interior somewhat weathered, clutch pedal missing rubber pad. Engine bay well sorted and presents well. Could go up a grade with some minor fixes. Cond: 3+.

Market Opinion
The Boss 302 market has fluctuated lately, and sales have been hard to peg. This example had a few needs that wouldn't require a lot of heavy lifting. The white color, although not the most sizzling choice, was quite common for the Boss models. This is about spot-on in the current market, and both the buyer and seller should go away happy.

1966 FORD FAIRLANE 500 XL 2-dr hard top

Auction Infomation
SOLD AT $131,250. Lot #S147; Mecum Auctions, Indianapolis, IN, 05/08

Specs & Condition
S/N 6A47Z175140. Black/black vinyl. Odo: 60,319 miles. 427-ci V8, 2x4-bbl, 4-sp. Originally equipped with a 390 motor, but sent when new to Holman & Moody to install a SOHC 427-ci "cammer" engine for street use. Modified with relocated front spring towers, NASCAR-spec front suspension, revised steering geometry, and 9-inch full-floating rear axle. Restored in the late '80s and early '90s. Good but not exceptional repaint, decent door fit, good quality bumper replate. Detailed motor generally configured correctly. Original interior reused and somewhat musty. Cond: 3+.

Market Opinion
Built for one John R. Fulp, Jr., of South Carolina as the ultimate street sleeper. There was quite a bit of interest in the car, and after a bit of cajoling, the reserve was lifted after the bidding dried up at this amount. As a sum of its parts, including the "cammer" 427 (generally trading around $30k to $50k today), a big-block '66 Fairlane, a mess of vintage NASCAR suspension parts, and the Holman & Moody pedigree, this was bought well.

1970 BUICK GSX 2-dr hard top

Auction Infomation
SOLD AT $170,625. Lot #S107; Mecum Auctions, Indianapolis, IN, 05/08

Specs & Condition
S/N 446370H290161. Saturn Yellow & black/black vinyl. Odo: 48,843 miles. 455-ci V8, 4-bbl, 4-sp. Fast-ratio ps, pb, Rallye Ride Control suspension, full tinted glass, convenience group, and custom interior with mini console. Exquisite and authentic enough of a restoration to have earned 397 of 400 points in Buick Club of America concours judging. Shortly afterward, it was added to the Otis Chandler collection, which pretty much sums the car up. Since being acquired by Dave Christenholz, it has been exceptionally well maintained and has no signs of wear or use. Cond: 1+.

Market Opinion
Another Chistenholtz car, also acquired from the Otis Chandler collection. This price was high, but there were no excuses, and the new owner should be happy with his purchase.

1965 SHELBY COBRA 289 roadster

Auction Infomation
SOLD AT $605,000. Lot #438; RM Auctions, Monterey, CA, 08/08

Specs & Condition
S/N CSX2485. Guardsman Blue & white/black leather. Odo: 53,691 miles. 289-ci V8, 4-bbl, 4-sp. Unrestored with a known history from new. Has been authenticated and appears in the Shelby American World Registry. Shows all the nicks and bruises of time, with heavy wear to paint and aged interior and engine compartment. Cond: 4.

Market Opinion
A major shift in the car collecting world has seen interest in original cars grow, and that caused this 289 Cobra to sell well beyond its $350k–$500k pre-sale expectations. The question for the new owner is whether or not to restore... and with the market on cars like this still moving upward, I'd lean toward leaving it alone.

1966 SHELBY GT350 fastback

Auction Infomation
SOLD AT $108,000. Lot #556; Cox Auctions, Branson, MO, 09/08

Specs & Condition
S/N SFM6S2340. Red & white/black vinyl. Odo: 29,207 miles. 289-ci V8, 4-bbl, 4-sp. Originally green according to Shelby Registry. Excellent repaint looks nice, aside from hood that has more orange peel than rest of car. Some chrome has almost undetectable pitting but shows very well. Excellent interior aside from scratched sill plates and broken shift boot trim. Clean engine bay appears correct. No mention of matching numbers. A nice, fresh restoration of an early Shelby fastback. Cond: 2.

Market Opinion
This was a last-minute entry into the sale and was presented with a blank car card. It was presented with no Marti Report and no matching-numbers claims, and people were overheard asking if it was real. An excellent sale for both parties, and I would say the buyer had more information about the car than what was presented.

1970 FORD MUSTANG Boss 429 fastback

Auction Infomation
SOLD AT $209,000. Lot #1319; Barrett-Jackson, Scottsdale, AZ, 01/09

Specs & Condition
S/N 0F02Z110428. Grabber Blue/black vinyl. Odo: 27,984 miles. 429-ci V8, 4-bbl, 4-sp. Great paint and chrome, all gaps align better than factory. Fully detailed top to bottom to original specs. Photo-documented restoration. As-new in all respects. Cond: 1.

Market Opinion
The most impressive engine compartment of all production Mustangs, and at 375 hp, it was underrated by the factory. This car featured a solid restoration by a Mustang expert, and the price paid was fair for both buyer and seller.

1970 PLYMOUTH 'CUDA Hemi 2-dr hard top

Auction Infomation
SOLD AT $440,000. Lot #S704; Russo and Steele, Scottsdale, AZ, 01/09

Specs & Condition
S/N BS23R0B184309. Black/black vinyl/black vinyl. Odo: 66,009 miles. 426-ci V8, 2x4-bbl, 4-sp. Owned and consigned by actor Nicolas Cage. Wears California black license plates with current tags. Chrysler Registry confirms original equipment. Older high-quality authentic restoration. Repaint applied well, but now has several polishing swirls and light scratching. Replated bumpers also have light scuffing. Good but not spectacular door and panel fit and gaps, authentically restored engine compartment. Older reproduction soft trim shows minimal to no use or soiling. Cond: 2-.

Market Opinion
Based upon the sales of other 1970-71 E-body Hemis (and all of them consigned at this venue did sell), one can easily say that there was a 50% celebrity premium here. Whether Mr. Cage or an assistant made the decision ahead of time or if it was made live (Nicolas wasn't on site), it was cut loose at an overall market-defying price. Then again, the consignor didn't have to pay a celebrity premium when he bought the car.

1966 SHELBY COBRA 427 roadster

Auction Infomation
SOLD AT $766,500. Lot #S174, Mecum, St. Charles, IL 10/07

Specs & Condition
S/N CSX3304. Blue & white/black leather. Odo: 44,167 miles. 427-ci V8, 2x4-bbl, 4-sp. Original engine, chassis, and body. Talbot mirror glass flawed, large crack in windshield, Sidepipes nice, chrome and trim spotless. Sold with SAAC documentation. Cond: 1-.

Market Opinion
Prices for good Cobras are always strong, and this one was clean, with only very minor faults. Well bought and sold.

1968 AMC AMX coupe

Auction Infomation
SOLD AT $26,250. Lot #S91, Mecum Auctions, Kansas City, MO, 11/07

Specs & Condition
S/N A8M397X300580. Aqua Metallic & black/black vinyl. Odo: 66,850 miles. 390-ci V8, 4-bbl, 4-sp. Go Pack, ps, pb, & AM 8-track radio. Decent repaint shows some overspray on exhaust, front valance, wiring harness, and motor. Some orange peel in a few odd spots including trunk lid edge. Recently replated bumpers, mostly original emblems and trim. All original glass, backlight heavily scratched. Dingy engine bay and undercarriage. Generally well-preserved interior dull, with three cracks in simulated wood wheel and heavier wear to carpet. Cond: 3.

Market Opinion
The selling price here tracked with what we've seen on AMXs and other AMC muscle car prices as of late: gradual, non-dramatic increases. While not a pristine gem, you'll have to look quite a bit to find a better one than this for less. Well bought.

1969 DODGE DAYTONA 2-dr hard top

Auction Infomation
SOLD AT $206,700. Lot #S154, Mecum Auctions, Kissimmee, FL, 01/09

Specs & Condition
S/N XX29L9113390024. Orange & white/black vinyl. Odo: 20,323 miles. 440-ci V8, 4-bbl, 4-sp. Driver's door fit skewed, trunk gap tight on passenger's side. Other gaps look very good. Nice paint showing only light polishing marks and some micro-scratches. Heavily applied windshield sealant looks sloppy. Chrome and brightwork very nice but not show-ready. Clean and detailed engine bay with only minor cosmetic needs noted. Interior just a notch from number one condition. Cond: 2-.

Market Opinion
Claimed to have matching numbers. The winged Mopars have a long track record for holding value in most economic environments. In other words, you don't see a lot of fire sales on original Daytonas, so finding a bargain without a bunch of needs is not all that easy. This was a nice example, and I'd call the price market-correct for condition.

1969 PONTIAC GTO Judge 2-dr hard top

Auction Infomation
SOLD AT $49,500. Lot #379, Barrett-Jackson, Palm Beach, FL, 04/09

Specs & Condition
S/N 242379B165988. Orbit Orange/black vinyl. Odo: 30,340 miles. 400-ci V8, 4-bbl, 4-sp. Matching numbers. Paint very nice and shows few flaws, excellent panel gaps throughout. Brightwork very nice, with only some small dimples in trim. Chrome near show quality. Back glass scratched, interior shows some small cracks in hard plastic surfaces and a scratched steering column. Engine bay neat and tidy but could use some additional detailing. Cond: 2-.

Market Opinion
A very nice and well-sorted matching-numbers Judge. With so many fakes and clones, it is always refreshing to see the real deal with the documentation to prove it. Fitted with the 360-horse Ram Air III engine, a 4-speed, and finished in the most desirable Judge color, this was a great example to go after. If you were in the market for a quality Judge, your paddle should have been raised. Well bought.

Significant Corvettes Sold at Auction, 2008-09

A Corvette is the universal collector car—at least in the U.S. Nearly everyone fits in them, parts are widely available, and they were available with many powertrain options (2-speed automatics to beefy 6-speeds and engines making anywhere from 165 hp to over 600 hp), not to mention comfort features like truly effective a/c. Options and originality are what make the difference in Corvette values. Things like big-block engines, matching numbers, tank stickers, and Protect-O-Plates can make a difference of many thousands of dollars. Corvettes are also among the most liquid of collector cars; if and when you decide to move on, they trade in one of the widest markets imaginable.

1957 CHEVROLET CORVETTE convertible

Auction Infomation
SOLD AT $107,625. Lot #U78; Mecum, St. Charles, IL 10/07

Specs & Condition
S/N E57S104693. Onyx Black & silver/red vinyl. Odo: 536 miles. 283-ci 270-hp V8, 2x4-bbl, 4-sp. New paint, chrome, and interior. Some chrome pitted at taillights, other exterior brightwork servicable. Wonderbar radio, T-10 4-speed, off-road exhaust. NCRS Top Flight in 2001. Cond: 2+.

Market Opinion
A nice car inside and out, and although the restoration was an older one, it was still holding up well. Well bought.

1968 CHEVROLET CORVETTE L88 Competition convertible

Auction Infomation
SOLD AT $744,000. Lot #355; Bonhams & Butterfields, Carmel Valley, CA, 08/08

Specs & Condition
S/N 194678S405175. Blue & white/black vinyl. Odo: 4,696 miles. 454-ci 430-hp V8, 4-bbl, 4-sp. Ex-James Garner Team AIR/Dick Guldstrand FIA GT. A very well-known car, and driven onto the ramp and introduced by Guldstrand himself. Provenance from new, replaced engine. Recent vintage race and concours outings. Very well restored to better-than-new race car standards inside and out. Cond: 1.

Market Opinion
A reasonable price for an important piece of Corvette history, even if it wasn't very successful.

Corvettes

1962 CHEVROLET CORVETTE Gulf Oil racer

Auction Infomation
SOLD AT $1,485,000. Lot #121; Gooding & Company, Pebble Beach, CA, 08/08

Specs & Condition
S/N 20867S103980. Eng. # 2103980f1206RF. White & blue/black leather. Odo: 21,946 miles.
327-ci 360-hp fuel-injected V8, 4-sp. A true RPO 687 fuelie, delivered to Yenko's dealership
for the Gulf Oil racing team. Prepared and successfully raced, first place in the 1962 SCCA
A-Production Championship. Dismantled and sold in 1963 as a street car, college student's
daily driver in the '80s. Rediscovered and restored with original parts, including Motorola
2-way radio, Stewart-Warner gauges, and roll cage. First car to receive the NCRS American
Heritage Award, 2005 Bloomington Gold Hall of Fame. Cond: 1-.

Market Opinion
Sold above the high estimate of $1.2m. This is truly an important car within American racing history, and with so many original components fitted,
it's safe to say there's nothing else quite like it. Well sold at this price, but the new owner should have no complaints.

1954 CHEVROLET CORVETTE roadster

Auction Infomation
SOLD AT $63,800. Lot #F483; Russo and Steele, Scottsdale, AZ, 01/09

Specs & Condition
S/N E54S001808. Pennant Blue/beige cloth/beige vinyl. Odo: 68,396 miles. 235-ci 155-hp
straight 6, 3x1-bbl, auto. Purchased in 2007 from the second owner's estate. Cosmetically
restored on-the-frame in 2001, eight-year-old repaint and replating still look fresh. No-worse-
than-original door and panel fit and gaps. Once moderately well detailed motor now has
some light surface rust and oxidizing of radiator hoses. Interior soft trim has light wear but is
still very presentable. Dashboard repaint looks to have been done with a roller. Cond: 3+.

Market Opinion
Last seen at McCormick's Palm Springs auction in February '08, where it failed to sell at
$66,000 (SCM# 89935). The bidding started at $30k, and it took a while to get to $58k, when
the reserve was lifted. Maybe I'm somewhat biased because I like Pennant Blue the best of
all the '54 colors, but as this would be pretty easy to fluff up, I feel it was a decent buy.

2004 CHEVROLET CORVETTE Z06 coupe

Auction Infomation
SOLD AT $30,800. Lot #1536; Barrett-Jackson, Scottsdale, AZ, 01/09

Specs & Condition
S/N 1G1YY12S245117936. Silver/black leather. Odo: 35,300 miles. 5.7-liter 405-hp fuel-injected
LS6 V8, 6-sp. Features Head Up display, memory package, two remotes, window sticker,
and all books and manuals. Protective dashpad, driver's power seat, dual climate control,
Delco-Bose stereo. Lovely silver paint with one chip on driver's bump strip. Very nice interior.
Cond: 1-.

Market Opinion
Immaculate car and hard to fault—the way you'd want to find one. This price was $2,000
below low book, and it was a steal if you plan to drive it. C5s are a long way from making
you any money, so just hit the road. It's what they do best anyway.

1962 CHEVROLET CORVETTE convertible

Auction Infomation
SOLD AT $98,450. Lot #F540; Russo and Steele, Scottsdale, AZ, 01/09

Specs & Condition
S/N 20867S105350. Ermine White/black vinyl & white hard top/black vinyl. Odo: 32,887
miles. 327-ci 360-hp fuel-injected V8, 4-sp. All documentation from new. Options include
both tops, 4.11 Posi, Wonderbar radio, and Special Crankcase Ventilation. Mostly original,
achieved NCRS Second Flight with 89.5 points without even a car wash. Typical body wavi-
ness, good panel fit, paint with light polishing scratches and a few touch-ups. Good original
brightwork. Recently fluffed-up engine bay, rear axle retains original inspection paint mark-
ings. Light seat and carpet wear, original shift knob yellowing. Cond: 2-.

Market Opinion
Since the original owner (who was a founding member of Corvettes of So. Cal.) lived in Anaheim, he took it to the nearby shop of Bill Thomas
for maintenance, tuning, and the occasional performance part (such as a set of Koni shocks in 1965). There was very heavy interest in this car
on the auction block, and it went three bids past the $88k reserve without much trouble. Being a fan of originality over restoration, this was my
favorite Corvette of the weekend. Bought well, if just for the provenance and originality.

1963 CHEVROLET CORVETTE Z06 Yenko Gulf One coupe

Auction Infomation
SOLD AT $1,113,000. Lot #S110; Mecum Auctions, Kissimmee, FL, 01/09

Specs & Condition
S/N 30837S102227. White & blue/black vinyl. Odo: 4,173 miles. 327-ci 360-hp fuel-injected V8, 4-sp. One of 14 factory Z06 performance cars built specifically for competition. Outstanding gaps, better-than-factory build, very nice paint showing only minor polishing marks and light scratches. Paint is just right and not too glossy, limited chrome excellent. Period race tires. Interior restoration very nicely done but not over the top. The exhaust note is simply superb. Cond: 2+.

Market Opinion
This is the actual campaigned Z06 driven by Dr. Dick Thompson, AKA the Flying Dentist. Dr. Thompson presented the car while it was up on the block, and he stated that it was "in much better condition than when I drove it, and had it looked like it does today, I would have been able to drive it even faster." A pure piece of history. Expensive? I don't think so for such a historical piece. I'd call this well bought.

1967 CHEVROLET CORVETTE convertible

Auction Infomation
SOLD AT $336,000. Lot #S73; Mecum Auctions, St. Charles, IL, 06/08

Specs & Condition
S/N 194677S114190. Tuxedo Black & red/black vinyl hard & soft tops/black vinyl. Odo: 72,210 miles. 427-ci 400-hp V8, 3x2-bbl, 4-sp. Bloomington Gold Award in 2004, NCRS Top Flight in 2003. Fitted with sidepipes, a/c, and ps. Claimed to be matching-numbers and identified as a COPO car. 240 miles since restoration by Nabers Brothers. Fitted with four NOS Kelsey-Hayes bolt-on finned aluminum wheels and transistorized ignition. All documentation included. Cond: 1.

Market Opinion
Showroom new in all respects, and one of the top three earners in this year's sale for good reason. Well bought and sold.

1990 CHEVROLET CORVETTE ZR-1 coupe

Auction Infomation
SOLD AT $20,670. Lot #F24; Mecum Auctions, Kansas City, MO, 3/09.

Specs & Condition
S/N 1G1YZ23J2L5802560. Red/tinted Plexiglass/black leather. Odo: 38,244 miles. 350-ci 375-hp fuel-injected V8, 6-sp. Fitted with tinted roof panel and power leather sport seats. 1991-1993 alloys with fresh Sumitomo radials. Good original paint shows a few nicks and road abrasions. Used car undercarriage, heavily sooted exhaust outlets. Dealer-grade engine cosmetics, new Interstate battery. Upholstery wear commensurate with mileage. Dashboard lights extremely dim with car running. Cond: 3.

Market Opinion
Went past the reserve at $19,250 by one additional bid. A decent deal for all involved, as C4 sellers can't be too choosy if they really want to move their car. Buyer got a respectable deal on a low-mile driver ZR-1.

1966 CHEVROLET CORVETTE convertible

Auction Infomation
SOLD AT $108,150. Lot #S134; Mecum Auctions, Kissimmee, FL, 01/08

Specs & Condition
S/N 194676S114040. Tuxedo Black/black vinyl & hard tops/black leather. Odo: 30,013 miles. 327-ci 350-hp V8, 4-bbl, 4-sp. Even and deep black respray shows evidence of old gouges in small areas. Chrome and brightwork excellent, aside from scuffed trim on accessory hard top. Paint quality on the hard top also not uniform to the body, leading one to suspect it has not been with this claimed low-miles car the entire time. Interior near perfect throughout, new leather just a little too smooth. Engine bay correctly restored with little to fault. Factory a/c. Cond: 2+.

Market Opinion
Whether the black hard top was original to this car or not, the overall presentation was stunning—sidepipes, knockoffs on Goldlines, telescoping teak steering wheel, and luscious black leather rounding out the interior. The new owner certainly thought this as well, since he bid it squarely into six digits, no doubt pleasing the dealer consignor who brought it. Well sold, but not badly bought for an unusual piece.

1953 CHEVROLET CORVETTE roadster

Auction Infomation
SOLD AT $440,000. Lot #46, Worldwide Group, Hilton Head, SC 11/07

Specs & Condition
S/N E53F001103. Polo White/black cloth/red vinyl. Odo: 8 miles. 235-ci straight 6, 3x1-bbl, auto. Faultless paint and body to exceptional better-than-new quality throughout. Chrome and brightwork flawless. Top and interior not only well-executed but correct to NCRS standards. Engine bay likewise does not disappoint. An example comparable to or better than the 2007 restoration of a slightly later '53 by GM Heritage. Cond: 1.

Market Opinion
The car lost a few points with the NCRS due to overdoing some things... not missing details. Only three bids were cast in $100,000 increments, and the bidding closed with a sale at the low estimate. Maybe just under market today, but a few more years should see examples such as this appreciating at Gullwing speed. Well bought.

1971 CHEVROLET CORVETTE ZR2 convertible

Auction Infomation
SOLD AT $550,000. Lot #S107, Mecum Auctions, St. Charles, IL, 06/08

Specs & Condition
S/N 194671S117850. Ontario Orange/black vinyl. Odo: 21,020 miles. 454-ci 425-hp V8, 4-bbl, 4-sp. Good paint, chrome, and interior. Wiper door sits high, front cowl vent panel not screwed down tightly. Hood fit wide on left, hood release doesn't work. Looks to be body-off restored. Part of the 1999 Bloomington Gold Special Collection, the 2003 Bloomington Gold Hall of Fame, and the 2000 National Corvette Museum exhibit. Original factory Corvette Order Copy comes with car. Cond: 2+.

Market Opinion
With only twelve built and only two of them convertibles, the ZR2 cars are rare and highly sought by collectors. The ZR2 came from the factory with the LS6 V8, the M22 "Rock Crusher" 4-speed, transistor ignition, special radiator, and many special suspension parts. This was claimed to have the last build date of any known ZR2, which makes it the last car GM ever built with the LS6 big-block. Fast and rare, even though it will never be driven to its potential again. Although expensive, worth the money spent.

1981 CHEVROLET CORVETTE coupe

Auction Infomation
SOLD AT $26,500. Lot #F63, Mecum Auctions, St. Charles, IL, 06/08

Specs & Condition
S/N 1G1AY8762B5100072. Beige & dark bronze/camel leather. Odo: 2,998 miles. 350-ci 190-hp V8, 4-bbl, auto. Front and rear flex bumpers starting to change color as is typical in this generation of 'Vette. Light delamination starting on windshield at corners. Right headlight door sits high, other panel gaps to factory specs. Light paint chips on some interior trim, clean seats and carpet. The 72nd car to come from the Bowling Green plant after production moved from St. Louis in 1981. Cond: 2.

Market Opinion
This low-miles original must be rare because this a Corvette of this vintage wasn't often saved. I have always wondered why the factory quit doing two-tone color schemes as on the great '50s cars—perhaps color combos like this were the reason. Expensive, but find another low-mileage example in this condition.

2007 CHEVROLET CORVETTE Z06 coupe

Auction Infomation
SOLD AT $65,000. Lot #S254, Mecum, St. Charles, IL 10/07

Specs & Condition
S/N 1G1YY26E875104705. Black/red & black leather. Odo: 3,249 miles. 7.0-liter fuel-injected LS7 V8, 6-sp. A very clean used Z06 Corvette with low original miles. Several very light paint chips to nose, clean engine compartment and interior. Almost completely as-new. Cond: 1-.

Market Opinion
New Z06 sticker is $66,465, so even with its low mileage, this wasn't a bargain unless you just can't find one with a deal attached to it. Well sold.

Significant Pre-War Classics Sold at Auction, 2008–09

As recently as five or six years ago, many observers had given up the pre-war classic market for dead. The WWII generation—for whom Packards, V16 Cadillacs, and Duesenbergs resonated as the aspirational cars of their Depression-era youth—was fading from the car collecting scene, and the cars seemed destined for a quiet life in museums behind velvet ropes. And then a funny thing happened—Baby Boomers decided these magnificent cars, for which they had no cultural affinity, worked as art objects. Suddenly, every collector worth his or her salt had to have a big classic. As with anything else, originality and provenance are key here. Original sporting body styles bring a premium. Cars re-bodied out of period are penalized.

1937 BUGATTI TYPE 57SC Atalante coupe

Auction Infomation
SOLD AT $7,920,000. Lot #27; Gooding & Company, Pebble Beach, CA, 08/08

Specs & Condition
S/N 57511. Eng. # 17S. Olive green & cream/tan leather. RHD. Odo: 70,944 km. Converted to SC specs either by the factory or one of its early owners. Dry-sump supercharged 200-hp engine, lowered frame with rear axle passing through it. Known history, beautifully restored in 1974 with 100% of its original components. Thirty-five-year-old restoration has aged well, although some paint cracks are visible. Driver's door slightly off, interior with excellent patina and complete Jaeger dash. Some pitting inside headlights. Engine bay detailed. A 120-mph car in 1937. From the Williamson Collection. Cond: 2+.

Market Opinion
A "regular" Atalante is worth $1m, and rumor has it that $16m will be required to acquire Williamson's 57SC Atlantic—which is one of three built from new. Let's agree that a 57S Atalante with the compressor at $8m is reasonable.

1930 ROLLS-ROYCE SILVER GHOST roadster

Auction Infomation
SOLD AT $429,000. Lot #107; Gooding & Company, Pebble Beach, CA, 08/08

Specs & Condition
S/N 36PE. Eng. # M174. Dark green & black/tan cloth/dark brown leather. RHD. Odo: 3,649 miles. Coachwork by Barker. San Francisco "garage find" roadster with only two owners from new. Carefully placed on blocks in 1937 with oil in cylinders and fluids drained (maybe after an unfortunate encounter, as left side fender and running board are crushed), unused since then. Interesting design with seating for four in the back through pop-up seats. Obviously all original, including the underlayer of San Francisco dust below a layer of more modern dust. Stated to run well. Cond: 4-.

Market Opinion
Five large "DO NOT DETAIL" signs were posted in the car during the auction preview. I agree that there is nothing more rewarding than driving an unrestored, clean, carefully maintained automobile, but I don't understand the pleasure of driving a scruffy-to-the-extreme, smashed, and presumably unreliable car. This would be impossible to keep "as is" if you intend to use it, and it had too much original patina to restore. The market is still fascinated with preservation, but this was well sold at this price.

MARKET REPORTS

1930 DUESENBERG MODEL J Dual Cowl phaeton

Auction Infomation
SOLD AT $1,760,000. Lot #441; RM Auctions, Monterey, CA, 08/08

Specs & Condition
S/N 2270. Eng. # J243. Two-tone green/tan fabric/green leather. Odo: 23,324. Coachwork by LeBaron. Restored in the late '40s with known history from new. Desirable and rare "barrel-side" body, so called as top edge of body curves inward. Paint has held up well, with a few chips and nicks visible here and there. New leather interior and tan Haartz cloth top fitted. A striking Duesenberg that has been well maintained. Cond: 3.

Market Opinion
Sold by the Rick Carroll estate for $1,320,000 in 1990. It's difficult to state that a $1.7m Duesenberg was well bought, but this one was, as it could have easily approached the high estimate of $2.4m without question.

1937 MERCEDES-BENZ 540K Special roadster

Auction Infomation
SOLD AT $8,235,112. Lot #225; RM Auctions, London, UK, 10/07

Specs & Condition
S/N 4086. Eng. # 154086. Silver/black canvas/red leather. Odo: 37,237 miles. U.K.-owned before and during WWII, later refurbished by M-B. Spent 30 years in Brooks Stevens's Wisconsin museum, converted from RHD to current LHD, restored in the mid-1980s. Acquired by Ecclestone in '95. Panel fit good, chips to some edges, some localized shrinkage and minor bubbling, radiator shell and trim strip wavy. Underneath and engine bay spotless, interior apparently still period correct. Switch handles possibly original, retrimmed leather only lightly used. Cond: 1-.

Market Opinion
Of the 406 540Ks built, the 25 Special K models were rated as being the ultimate version to have both in period and ever since. Deservedly commanding pole position during viewing and given the power-plinth treatment to much audio-visual hullaballoo when its turn to cross the block came, Ecclestone's 540K Special Roadster was the undisputed star lot of the night. Inevitably, at such a high-profile auction as this, it cost the new owner more than the top estimate of $8m to take it home.

1937 DELAGE D8-120 Aerosport coupe

Auction Infomation
SOLD AT $825,000. Lot #132; RM Auctions, Phoenix, AZ, 01/09

Specs & Condition
S/N 50789. Eng. # 812041. Black/black pigskin. RHD. Odo: 1,894 km. Coachwork by Letourner et Marchand. The only notchback Aerosport Coupe thought to have survived. Excellent paint and panel fit, hand-tipped pigskin interior, Cotal pre-select transmission, Marchal lamps. Restored by RM. Brought Second in Class at 2006 Pebble Beach Concours. A stunning presentation. Cond: 1-.

Market Opinion
A rare and desirable coupe restored to perfection. Final and winning bid seemed a bit light and was well below the $1m low estimate, so I'll chalk this one up for the buyer.

1937 TALBOT-LAGO T150C SS Teardrop coupe

Auction Infomation
SOLD AT $3,520,000. Lot #23; Gooding & Company, Scottsdale, AZ, 01/09

Specs & Condition
S/N 90105. Eng. # 85019. Red/red leather. RHD. Odo: 7,269 km. Generally good panel fit, but hood somewhat variable. Older paint is presentable, but shows some bubbling, a few dings, and some prep issues. Chrome shows wear, fading, and light scratches. Original interior has a lovely patina, but torn seat top backrest on right side detracts. Cond: 4.

Market Opinion
Ex-Tommy Lee and Brooks Stevens. An example of the rarest of the teardrop designs, the "New York" variant. Largely untouched since a '70s repaint in the current red. The car was purchased by the seller at the Christie's Monterey sale in August '05 for $3.5m (SCM# 38879), and it sold here for the same amount. While it didn't make the seller any money, it was at least driven over 300 miles. Well bought.

1934 AUBURN TWELVE Salon phaeton sedan

Auction Infomation
SOLD AT $319,000. Lot #154; RM Auctions, Phoenix, AZ, 01/09

Specs & Condition
S/N 1066H. Eng. # BB248OU. Green/tan fabric/green leather. Odo: 33,490 miles. Last year for the Auburn Twelve, all of which were 1933 bodies with upscale Salon trim. Restored in 1990 and well maintained since, as are all the Atwood cars. Two-speed Columbia rear axle, Woodlites including very rare Woodlite parking lights. An exceptional example. Cond: 2+.

Market Opinion
An inexpensive car when new, these have continued to appreciate of late. The Woodlites gave this car a unique look, and the quality restoration still looked fresh almost 20 years later. Expensive, but well worth it.

1933 MARMON SIXTEEN Style 145 convertible sedan

Auction Infomation
SOLD AT $330,000. Lot #156; RM Auctions, Phoenix, AZ, 01/09

Specs & Condition
S/N 16145902. Yellow/black fabric/tan fabric. Odo: 31,070 miles. Coachwork by LeBaron. Once owned by Mrs. Marmon and D. Cameron Peck. From the Barbara Atwood collection. Class win at Pebble in 1988. Numerous other awards in the early '90s. Stored since. Good panel fit with presentable paint, right front passenger window not working properly. An impressive CCCA Full Classic, and the second of only 56 Marmons built in 1933. Cond: 2-.

Market Opinion
Marmons have an understated elegance combined with strong performance. Considering the distinguished ownership, limited production, and striking styling, this should be considered well bought, even though it sold above the $325k high estimate.

1929 STUTZ BLACKHAWK Rumble Seat roadster

Auction Infomation
SOLD AT $95,200. Lot #99; Worldwide Group, Hilton Head, SC, 11/07

Specs & Condition
S/N L64DA45D. Green & black/black cloth/tan vinyl. Odo: 3,204 miles. Offered at no reserve from the Walter B. Satterthwaite Estate Collection. Presentable older restoration with minor scratches and pitting to left front fender. Brightwork and chrome very good, paint finish quality well preserved. Driver's seat torn, older reupholstery shows its age. Newer black cloth top well-preserved. Engine compartment clean, detailing very old. Cond: 3+.

Market Opinion
Last seen at Kruse's Detroit sale in April '93, where it didn't sell at $35,500 (SCM# 21858). An unusual and rare car in need of slightly more than minor reconditioning to regain some past glory. While restored to the standards of the 1970s, it only added to the tattiness of the car's current appearance. Stutzes are rare, but this was about all the money for this one's condition. Well sold.

1932 DAIMLER 40/50 Double Six sport saloon

Auction Infomation
SOLD AT $2,970,000. Lot #39; Gooding & Company, Scottsdale, AZ, 01/09

Specs & Condition
S/N 32382. Eng. # 55628. Black/Aubergine wool. RHD. Odo: 58,199 miles. Coachwork by Martin Walter. Hood fit excellent, all four doors slightly out at front bottom edge. Excellent paint shows only a few polish scratches. Superb chrome, perfect interior shows only the barest traces of use. Cond: 1.

Market Opinion
1999 Pebble Beach Concours Best in Show, and still remarkable. It's hard to describe the presence of this car; it's massive and a bit evil. Wonderful. Was the price right? Of course—find another.

1932 PACKARD MODEL 904 Custom Eight convertible Victoria

Auction Infomation
SOLD AT $1,210,000. Lot #50, Gooding & Company, Scottsdale, AZ, 01/08

Specs & Condition
S/N 90471. Dark blue/beige canvas/beige leather. Odo: 469 miles. Coachwork by Dietrich. Excellent panel fit, right door slightly out at lower front edge. Nice paint and chrome, very good interior has a small scratch on right front seat cushion. Excellent wood trim, dash panel, and instrumentation. Cond: 1-.

Market Opinion
A stunningly lovely and rare Dietrich Victoria in great colors and with incredible presence. Stated to be one of only four known. A 2007 Pebble Beach class winner, and ready to win wherever you might take it. A market-correct price.

1931 CHRYSLER CG IMPERIAL Rumble Seat roadster

Auction Infomation
SOLD AT $172,500. Lot #57, Worldwide Group, Hilton Head, SC, 11/07

Specs & Condition
S/N 7802053. Brown & orange/tan cloth/brown vinyl. Odo: 100 miles. A common sedan as-new, rebodied many years ago with LeBaron coachwork. Panel fit good aside from hood alignment and passenger door bottom. Older high-standard repaint well-preserved, chrome wavy especially around windshield, headlights and steering linkage-controlled driving lights considerably better than flat trim. Aluminum rumble seat steps heavily corroded, newer cloth top in very good condition. Engine bay detailed to a high standard. Cond: 2.

Market Opinion
While a rebody of the period, this was not unacceptable to the CCCA, which awarded this car a National 1st some years ago. Brown and orange may yet become very much in style again, but for the moment, it merely dates this car more than cementing it in the period. A no-sale across the block, but efforts by the Worldwide Group managed to get this car sold later in the weekend. Well done by all parties concerned.

1939 LINCOLN MODEL K convertible

Auction Infomation
SOLD AT $79,920. Lot #571, Cox Auctions, Branson, MO, 04/08

Specs & Condition
S/N K9503. Eng. # 9503. Dark blue/tan cloth/brown leather. Odo: 59,095 miles. Alloy Brunn body with 14 coats of lacquer chipped and dented around hood hinges and latches. Interior is in salvageable condition but is dirty all over and has extra toggle switches under dash. Top needs replacement. Engine was show quality once but is now dirty and oily. Appears to have been unused for a long period of time. Cond: 3-.

Market Opinion
A beautiful example of a CCCA classic with patina. This car got more attention than the '42 Continental (lot 568, sold at $56,160) also offered at Branson. If the new owner has the paint issues fixed and has the car professionally detailed, it might bring even more at the right venue.

1937 CORD 812 SC convertible coupe

Auction Infomation
SOLD AT $220,000. Lot #238, RM Auctions, Amelia Island, FL, 03/08

Specs & Condition
S/N 32485F. Eng. # FC2399. Cigarette Cream/tan canvas/dark red leather. RHD. Odo: 2 miles. Five-month-old high level restoration shows well. Good panel fit aside from both doors sitting out at front edge and trunk lid slightly off from side to side. Excellent paint, chrome, and interior, show-detailed engine compartment. Replacement engine fitted. One of the last Cords built. Cond: 1-.

Market Opinion
Stunning in yellow with red interior, this just needed some final tweaking to be a show winner. The price was a bit on the low side, which was perhaps due to the bright color or the replacement engine. Either way, the buyer got a very good deal here.

MARKET REPORTS

Significant Modern Day Supercars Sold at Auction, 2008-09

More so than any vintage car, supercars are subject to the whims and caprice of the very well-heeled. It is axiomatic that anyone who can afford the price of admission can likely afford it on a regular basis to keep up with the latest in supercar fashion. Last year's models are often discarded like out-of-favor Christmas toys. Consequently, there is rarely a shortage of used late-model supercars on the market. Prices are often a fraction of what they were new, which frankly they have to be to entice someone to take on the risk of shocking maintenance costs. The few exceptions seem to be the McLaren F1, Porsche 959, and Ford GT. Buy these cars for the exhilarating performance they offer and the privilege of always been parked out front by the valet at your favorite restaurant. Ultimately, they will forever be a better image investment than financial one.

2004 FERRARI ENZO coupe

Auction Infomation
SOLD AT $1,319,244. Lot #318; RM Auctions, Maranello, ITA, 05/08

Specs & Condition
S/N ZFFCZ56B000136085. Eng. # 86766. Matte Titanio 20 Gloss/light brown leather. Odo: 2,762 km. As new and factory-original in every detail. Unique color combination of light blue with light brown interior suits the car very well and was exclusive to this example from new. Originally owned by a member of a Middle Eastern royal family. Cond: 1.

Market Opinion
Three years ago the new Enzos were million-dollar cars, and today eBay and land auctions put them at about $1.3m. Well bought, as this car's appealing color combination makes it unique and gives it a story to tell.

2001 FERRARI 550 BARCHETTA convertible

Auction Infomation
NOT SOLD AT $201,175. Lot #307; RM Auctions, Maranello, ITA, 05/08

Specs & Condition
S/N ZFFZR52B000124124. Rosso Corsa/black & red leather. Odo: 202 km. Nice throughout. Delivered to Germany in 2001, every component virtually as new. No hard top, matching pair of red helmets and all documentation since new come with car. Cond: 1.

Market Opinion
A similar example in black sold for $186,000 at Bonhams' Gstaad sale in December 2007 (SCM# 43812), so it might be safe to assume that the bottom of the depreciation curve for the 550 Barchetta is around $200,000. This seller was looking for more, but it'll be a while before anything more than this bid is forthcoming.

Modern Day Super Cars

1994 BUGATTI EB110 GT coupe

Auction Infomation
SOLD AT $315,115. Lot #135; Bonhams, Monte Carlo, MCO, 05/08

Specs & Condition
S/N ZA9AB01EOPCD39052. Silver gray/silver gray leather. Odo: 15,400 km. One of only 154 built over two years of production. As-new condition but for a few stone chips up front. Interior perfectly maintained with Nardi steering wheel and Nakamichi stereo. Engine bay clean. Cond: 1-.

Market Opinion
The same car was a no-sale here in 2006 at $229,500 (SCM# 41926). Two years later, with no change to the car, the hammer price shows a 10% annual return. A very similar "as-new" car sold here last year for $259,200 (SCM# 45708). This could be compared with a no-sale for the Ferrari equivalent F50 at $696k the following weekend at RM Maranello. Both cars were about the same price when new—around $500k—and both had 550 hp on tap. I'd call this market correct.

2006 NOBLE M400 coupe

Auction Infomation
SOLD AT $53,813. Lot #S70; Mecum Auctions, Des Moines, IA, 07/08

Specs & Condition
S/N DRMVB0000156612MO. Red/black leather & suede. Odo: 4,235 miles. State of Missouri-assigned VIN, current Missouri license tags. Near-new condition, with only minimal soiling to undercarriage and engine bay. 425-hp turbocharged 3.0-liter V6, 6-sp. No discernible paint nicks or wear. Some sidewall feathering on the tires from some exuberant cornering (big shock there). Equal light wear on suede side bolsters on driver's seat and driver's side carpets. Engine compartment and undercarriage wear commensurate with the miles indicated and about right for a "play-toy" car. Cond: 3+.

Market Opinion
I was probably just as surprised as everyone else when it was announced that the reserve was met at $50k. It then brought a couple more bids and become the top sale of the day. Since it was here, titled, and ready to go (some states get a little prissy about imported specialty cars—even this one with a good MO title), it was bought well.

2004 SALEEN S7 coupe

Auction Infomation
SOLD AT $260,700. Lot #805.1; Barrett-Jackson, Las Vegas, NV, 10/08

Specs & Condition
S/N 1S9SB18103S000026. Red/black leather. 7.0-liter fuel-injected V8, 6-sp. Numerous paint flaws around exhaust and rear wing. A few wear spots visible where leather rubs leather on interior. Fitted with a/c, power windows, and Lamborghini-style doors. Cond: 1-.

Market Opinion
Let's face it... nobody really drives these cars much, so they always look #2 or better. This looked very fast when parked and sounded extremely fast even when going slow. Well bought and sold.

2009 CHEVROLET CORVETTE ZR1 coupe

Auction Infomation
SOLD AT $137,500. Lot #S99.1; Mecum Auctions, St. Charles, IL, 10/08

Specs & Condition
S/N 1G1YRZ6R195800048. Red/black leather. Odo: 7 miles. 6.2-liter 638-hp supercharged V8, 6-sp. The 48th ZR1 built, still new in wrapper. Excellent paint, trim, and interior. Factory tag says 20 mpg. The "Blue Devil" has arrived. Cond: 1.

Market Opinion
On top of the $102,450 base price, the 3ZR premium equipment group adds $10,000, chrome wheels add $2,000, the gas guzzler tax tacks on $1,700, and the destination fee totals $850... bringing the total sticker to $117,000. This car went to $133k and it was stalled by the reserve until the bidder jumped his own bid to buy it at this price. While this might seem expensive, limited supply and high demand will likely keep prices high in the near future.

1997 MCLAREN F1 coupe

Auction Infomation
SOLD AT $4,058,120. Lot #275; RM Auctions, London, UK, 10/08

Specs & Condition
S/N 065. Silver/black & red leather & carbon fiber. Odo: 484 km. The last example built and sold of what many consider to be the best supercar ever. Practically as-new—sold from the showroom in 2004 and hardly driven since. No scuffs or scrapes, floorpan smooth and glossy, transmission tunnel signed by its designer, Gordon Murray. Comes with big service history, tool kit, and luggage. Unrepeatable. Cond: 1.

Market Opinion
This car brought about twice what was expected and set a new world record for the F1. One man in the room kept raising his stake against telephone bids until he owned this car. Determined and heroic stuff, but perhaps he could see the future.

2004 KOENIGSEGG CC8S targa

Auction Infomation
SOLD AT $254,560. Lot #617; Bonhams, London, UK, 12/08

Specs & Condition
S/N YT9M1GV8D2007006. Silver/gray suede & brown leather. Odo: 6,020 km. Almost like new with slight use evident on seats and small scuffs in sides that are hidden when rear clamshell is down. Only slight cosmetic issues include glue marks on leather top of windshield surround and bonding of roof glass—both hard to get right on low-volume composite cars. Motor clean and dry, no crash repair damage evident. Cond: 2.

Market Opinion
This had been the Spanish Koenigsegg importer's car and never before sold to a private owner. This price was near the top estimate, but looks like a total bargain compared with a McLaren F1, which it will outrun.

2006 SPYKER C8 spider

Auction Infomation
SOLD AT $148,500. Lot #8; Gooding & Company, Scottsdale, AZ, 01/09

Specs & Condition
S/N XL9AA11G36Z363102. Dark metallic blue/navy canvas/beige leather. Odo: 1,605 miles. Variable panel fit, presumably as per factory. Unmarked paint, very good bright trim, canvas top shows a few wear spots at fastening points. Very busy interior is clean, with some scuffing on kick panels and sill trim. Cond: 2+.

Market Opinion
A Dutch-built, Audi V8-powered "boutique supercar." The company motto is "Nulla tenaci invia est via," or "For the tenacious, no road is impassable." Perhaps, but the road's sure expensive. With an MSRP of $325k, the car had lost 55% in three years, with the 1,600 miles covered costing a mere $127 each. A good deal for the buyer here, that's for sure.

1997 LAMBORGHINI DIABLO VT roadster

Auction Infomation
SOLD AT $166,320. Lot #540; Cox Auctions, Branson, MO 10/07

Specs & Condition
S/N ZA9RU37P0VA12633. Black/tan leather. Odo: 2,348 miles. Paintwork appears all original and quite nice throughout. No trim issues found, excellent wheels and tires. Some light wear to the driver's seat and console, the rest is as new. Cond: 1-.

Market Opinion
A very solid sales result for a car that can't be a very easy impulse buy. One would think that a very large number of these cars are sold with financing behind them, but no such talk was heard here in Branson.

Modern Day Super Cars

1991 ACURA NSX coupe

Auction Infomation
SOLD AT $42,000. Lot #S55, Mecum Auctions, Kissimmee, FL, 01/08

Specs & Condition
S/N JH4NA115XMT002411. Red/black leather. Odo: 52,014 miles. Original red paint better than most similar-year Ferraris and Porsches. One rock chip in windshield, other glass excellent. Original leather appears a bit dry from an encounter or two with Armor All, very little entry wear apparent. Engine bay very clean, but rear struts no longer hold the hatch up. Cond: 2+.

Market Opinion
My friend (and SCMer) Bob Sinclair looked at a 1991 or 1992 NSX on his retirement from Saab USA's corner office. He drove it against a three-year-old Ferrari 328 GTS with a few thousand miles on it for the same price tag, and then bought the Ferrari. I asked him why, and he replied, "The Acura was just too perfect, it did everything right." Well, for the guy or gal who needs to have everything right, an NSX isn't a bad deal. Well sold, as the same money can get a newer car with fewer miles on the clock.

1988 LAMBORGHINI COUNTACH Quattrovalvole coupe

Auction Infomation
SOLD AT $119,543. Lot #212, RM Auctions, Maranello, ITA, 5/09

Specs & Condition
S/N ZA9CA05A4JLA12320. White/red leather. Odo: 18,512 km. U.S. model converted to Euro specs in 2007 with Euro small bumpers and some mechanical tuning. Shows well inside and out, with unmarked wheels and very clean engine bay. The '80s poster child with huge rear wing and fender flares. Cond: 2+.

Market Opinion
Sold above the high estimate. I witnessed a European model in similar condition but in a better suited bullish red color fail to sell in February '09 at Artcurial's Paris sale at $110,500 (SCM# 119672). This price was a little expensive in today's market, but I think the buyer will still do all right in the long run. Well sold.

2000 ASTON MARTIN DB7 Vantage coupe

Auction Infomation
SOLD AT $65,366. Lot #337, Bonhams, Newport Pagnell, UK, 05/08

Specs & Condition
S/N SCFAB1237IK301304. Eng. # AM201339. Blue/gray leather. RHD. Odo: 12,000 miles. Presented dirty, but almost as new. Alloys unmarked, interior good, engine compartment clean. Service history from new. Cond: 2.

Market Opinion
Sold at just over bottom estimate, or a third of its original purchase price, and a fair deal both ways. At this sale, only the older iron blew past presale high estimates. More recent fare such as this ran to normal retail money, and quite rightly, as there are plenty of others on the market.

1992 JAGUAR XJ 220 coupe

Auction Infomation
SOLD AT $150,700. Lot #805, Barrett-Jackson, Las Vegas, NV, 10/08

Specs & Condition
S/N N5327357. Blue/gray leather. Odo: 2,742 miles. Number 91 of 280 built. Lots of chips on front end paint, one bolt missing on each exhaust header. Heavy side bolster wear on driver's seat suggests many short trips. Cond: 2.

Market Opinion
Fitted with 6-27-01 engine emissions tag from Santa Monica, California. This looked like lots of wear for the miles indicated, but the selling price apparently took that into account.

Best Bets & Worst

This section of *Keith Martin's Guide to Car Collecting* is straightforward. We've got experts from Sports Car Market who are simply telling you, straight out and with no beating around the bush, exactly which cars are good buys and which ones are not.

You'll find everything from the Five Best Ferraris Over $1m to Nine Affordable Muscle Cars. You'll also find thoughtful advice on how to go about building a collection, and why buying something because "it's red and I saw one like it on TV" may not be the best way to fill your garage.

If you're hankering to purchase a collector car, this is the one section of the book you simply have to read, as it will help you narrow your choices down from a bewildering array of marques to just a handful, thoughtfully picked and presented. —*Keith Martin*

In This Section

Getting Started

Why Buy a Collector Car? 130

Starting Out: Buying Your First
Collector Car.. 131

Nine Exotics you Can Afford..................... 133

Fun Collectible Cars
Under $25,000.. 138

Italian

Eight Italian Sports Cars for the
First-Time Collector..................................... 141

Eight Ferraris for Under $100,000............... 145

Five Best Ferraris Over $1,000,000............. 148

12-Cylinder Ferraris You Can Afford......... 151

The Ferrari Market Today:
What's Really Going On............................. 154

British

English Convertibles Combining
Value and Fun... 156

How to Buy a Jaguar E-type..................... 159

Why Provenance Can Add 50%
to the Price 161

German

Entry-Level 356 and 911 Porsches 163

Porsches That Are on an Upward Trend... 165

Five Porsches to Avoid............................... 167

American

Buying Your First Collectible Muscle Car .. 169

How to Buy the Best Cobra and Tiger 171

Nine Muscle Car Sleepers......................... 173

How to Determine Legitimacy
in a Muscle Car 177

Corvettes

The Z-Code Option:
What Does It Mean?................................... 179

Top Ten Corvette Options for
Increased Value.. 185

Market Makers: Historical Corvettes
from the GM Fleet....................................... 187

Eight Corvettes to Run Away From 190

Why Buy a Collector Car

You can be fascinated by the sight, sounds, and smell of a particular car

by Donald Osborne

The reasons people become collectors of anything should be obvious. An enthusiasm, born of curiosity, leads to desire and acquisition. Whether it's vintage watches, rare books, baseball memorabilia, cut glass, or Beanie Babies, it is passion that drives the collecting. It's the same for collector cars.

There's an axiom in the hobby which holds that interest in cars and sometimes the prices they bring is based on a rolling curve. As financially secure adults, people seek those cars they coveted as impressionable teenagers but couldn't afford. So the group that grew up during the Depression, riding bicycles while seeing photos and film of Hollywood stars and wealthy industrialists driving Duesenbergs and Packards, made those cars the object of their affection in the 1960s. Kids who watched Armstrong walk on the moon in that same decade are the ones who are now making Detroit's muscle cars the top of the market today.

Exceptions exist, of course—there are certainly not many alive today who were teens when what we today call "brass-era" cars first hit the primitive roads in the early years of the 20th century. Yet today these cars are enjoying a much-deserved revival of interest. Why? Because of the basics of collecting—there are people today who see them as a remarkable expression of mechanical invention, ingenuity, and craftsmanship in steel, wood, brass, and leather. They are machines as art, and it doesn't matter that these collectors never knew them as new cars.

The cars people collect should be a reflection of who they are and what they love. Car collecting is sensuous. You can be fascinated by the sight of a car, by the sound of the engine's pull from idle to redline, by running your hand along a well-shaped fender, or by smelling hot oil, warm brakes, and a well-worn leather interior. It can be an incredibly stimulating experience.

There are also some people for whom the restoration process is the thrill. Finding a derelict car and using your own sweat and effort to return it to life is the most important thing for these folks. In fact, once the car is done, they will more often than not sell it, ready to attack their next project. For

Osborne with his Crosley (l) and Lancia

others, it's all about using their collector car. Whether it's in a national concours d'elegance, local "show-n-shine," or just parked in a lot at the local drive-in, polishing their pride and joy and showing it off to as many people as possible is why they collect.

Some couldn't imagine sitting next to their car on a lawn chair, but would rather be sitting behind the wheel. Vintage rallies, tours, and racing are where these collectors play. They will choose their cars based on the rules of the series or events they most want to run so they can have as much fun as possible.

While some people do collect cars for investment, it should never be the overriding factor in choosing a car. Unless you are very experienced in buying and selling cars, it can be difficult to predict what cars will appreciate most quickly, especially those not at the very top end of the market. It is also important to consider the costs of maintenance, repair, insurance, and storage when thinking about the possible financial return on a collector car. It's much better to buy a car you love, enjoy it in the way you like best, maintain it well, and take your profit in pleasure. ♦

Buying Your First Collector Car

Do you want a project, a driver, or a show car? Know what you want before you start looking

by Jim Schrager

The long and the short of your first acquisition

Remember your first date? Buying your first collector car can be just as intimidating—and turn out just as poorly—as that initial encounter with the opposite sex. But with a collector car, you have plenty of opportunity to do your homework and make your initial purchase both memorable and successful. There are three basic choices you need to consider to get you started in the right direction: Do you want a project car, a driver, or a museum piece? Figure this out and you'll be ahead of the game as you look for that perfect machine.

Project cars

Project cars appeal to those of us with lots of time on our hands, plenty of skill at doing odd (or even common) jobs, and the desire to work on a car for long periods of time rather than just get in and head to the malt shop. There are many significant upsides to buying a project car, including the often dramatically lower price you will pay, the intimate knowledge you will have inside and out when you are done restoring it, and the fact that all work will be done exactly to your standards (be they low or high).

The downsides are that you will have to commit to working rather than driving for some unknown—and in most cases, unforseeable—amount of time. Even with a running project car, much will be needed that will require you to take the car off the road for untold months. The big question before settling on a project car is to ask yourself if you have the skills needed to do the work and the discipline to really stay with the project. This last one is vital, as nothing sells more cheaply than a failed project. If you start it, you must either finish it or face long odds to come out even on the financial side.

Drivers

Take a step up in the collector world from a project car and you have a driver, a car that runs well enough to use and not leave you stranded too often. This category comprises the vast majority of cars you will see for sale, well above project car status, yet still quite far below the concours or museum-quality level.

The great fun here is that you have a car to enjoy and drive, and within reason, you can improve bits and pieces as smaller projects along the way. If the carpets are tatty, or you always wanted those upgraded fancy alloy wheels, a wood steering wheel, or a better radio—all those things are well within reach. Maybe it's going back to the stock carburetor or upgrading to a better distributor? That's fine, as you can do that in a weekend or two and be back on the road where you want to be.

The downside of the driver is that you will not have a real "show car." If you want to do local "show-n-shine" events you may get lucky, but for regional shows, be prepared to be outgunned by those with deeper trophy lust. Even regional car shows in the middle of nowhere can attract some amazingly well-preserved and -restored old cars. If you want to win trophies, then you'll need to step to the next level.

Show cars

Buying a show car is what many people first dream about when they think of buying their first collector car. It's kind of like dreaming about having your first date with Angelina Jolie. But buying a show car as your first collector car may not be a good idea. Do you really think you'll get anywhere with Angelina if it's your first time at bat?

For starters, if you have a true concours-winning car, don't plan on driving it much. Look around the parking lot of any serious car show—and some not-so-serious ones as well—and you'll see lots of trucks with covered trailers.

Show cars are too special, precious, and clean to drive to the show on their own power. The wildly competitive world of collector cars requires that your car be untouched by common road dirt, have no greasy fingerprints on the steering wheel, or, heaven forbid, show soot in the tailpipe!

You can drive the car, but realize that upon doing so, it will require many hours of cleaning. Most concours folks, even those with the best intentions to drive their cars, give up either on the driving part or the show part, as the punishment of cleaning is just too high a price to pay for using the car.

And I'm not talking about a wash job. True concours cars are as clean underneath as they are on top. The chassis and suspension parts have to be as immaculate as the interior. It's a tall order, and not many cars exist at this level of cleanliness.

Why it matters

You will find that the three different types of cars have three distinctly different owners, and you'll need a special approach for each type. Those selling a project car will be the easiest to deal with. They will be out of space, out of money, out of time—or all three—and generally will have a realistic price on their machine. In most cases, they will be serious sellers and you will be able to negotiate from a powerful position.

Those with drivers for sale may be a bit tougher. If their car doesn't sell right away, they can continue to use and enjoy it—unlike the project car owner whose car beckons for more time and money each time the owner walks by it. Of course, the owner of a driver may want to move on to other cars and can certainly be a motivated seller. But because his car runs, he simply has more options.

The concours guys are usually the toughest sellers, partly because they are often the wealthiest, partly because they feel their car is very special, and partly because they can afford to wait for that special buyer who will pay their price. They don't really use their car much anyway, and it needs no work, so it's no big deal to let it sit around awhile longer.

Think carefully about what kind of car is really best for you and you'll be better prepared to find a good one. Then point yourself in that direction and have at it. ♦

Nine Exotics You Can Afford

It's better to spend the money up front and buy a really good car than to buy a work in progress forever

by Rob Sass

1971 Aston DBS

The term "bargain exotics" seems like an oxymoron, since there is nothing cheap about these cars in the normal sense of car operative costs. However, the entry fee for a nice example of our picks is generally less than the cost of a loaded new Ford Explorer.

But here's the key: regardless of whether it's a quad-cam V12 under the hood or a pushrod Detroit V8, if you buy a fixer-upper, any of the cars on this list will cost the equivalent of several years of Ivy League tuition to put right. Repeat after me: It is never cheaper to buy a nasty exotic and try to make it nice than it is to buy a nice one.

The key to a happy life with any of these cars is to have your prospective car thoroughly inspected by someone who specializes in the marque and buy the best one you can find.

1967–72 Aston Martin DBS

Aston designed the DBS to take its new four-cam V8. The engine wasn't ready in time for production, so most DBSs made do with the straight-six from the outgoing DB6.

Still, in Vantage tune, the DBS is no sloth. While not as famous a James Bond ride as the silver DB5 that 007 drove in "Goldfinger" and "Thunderball," Bond did drive a DBS in the 1969 film "On Her Majesty's Secret Service." Although overshadowed by the earlier DB6 and later V8, the DBS is nonetheless handsome. It makes an ideal introduction to the marque, and to the very helpful and well-organized Aston Martin Owners Club. As with any Aston, poorly repaired accident damage and deferred maintenance are the major issues, especially in light of the fact that these expensive-to-maintain cars haven't been worth enough to justify top-flight care, at least on an economic basis. Buying one from an enthusiastic club member is the best bet.

SCM Price Guide: $50,000–$65,000

1968–78 Lamborghini Espada

Penned by Marcello Gandini, whose later efforts included the Countach and Diablo, the Espada was the fastest four-seater around at the time of its introduction. It was named

133

1972 Lamborghini Espada

1968–76 Jensen Interceptor

The Interceptor is a combination of Italian styling, courtesy of Vignale, British coachwork, and American Chrysler V8 power. This Anglo-Italo-American hybrid is similar in concept to the Aston Martin DBS, but free of the potentially ruinous drivetrain-related repair bills. Most are 2+2 coupes with the controversial fishbowl rear hatch; however, large auctions seem to have at least one of the undeniably handsome '74–'76 convertibles. Most Interceptors come fitted with every possible luxury item, some of which can even be found in working order. With the exception of the grievously rust-prone body panels, most parts are reasonably easy to source; you need look no further than your local NAPA for drivetrain items. Given the recent spike in anything Mopar, the notion of an Interceptor SP with a 440 Six Pack selling in the high teens, compared to a Coronet R/T with the same motor selling in the fifties, is downright absurd. I think there may be an upside for the Interceptor as the last of the cheap Mopar muscle.

SCM Price Guide: coupe $12,000–$24,000; convertible $14,000–$24,000.

1971–73 Maserati Indy

Maserati's answer to the Espada is slightly less roomy and more conventionally styled. With a V8 instead of a V12,

after the small sword used by bullfighters to dispatch the animal after ritually torturing it in the name of sport. There is no truth, though, to the rumor that Espada tool kits contain actual espadas for owners to dispatch themselves after being ritually tortured by their cars. This Lambo has a dramatic presence, but its broad, flat styling either appeals to you or it doesn't. Either way, this is a full four-seater car that goes like stink while making all of the appropriate Italian supercar noises. Aside from a Ferrari 400/412 and the Espada's stable mate, the Jarama, the Espada is the only Italian V12 that can be had for $47,000 or less.

SCM Price Guide: $28,000–$45,000

1975 Jensen Interceptor

1979 Porsche 930

the Indy is also a slightly less potent performer than the Espada. Nevertheless, it's extremely handsome in person, and Maserati nuts claim that these cars, once properly set up, are quite unfussy for an Italian exotic. Exercise extreme caution in selecting an example, as their values inspire maintenance and repair shortcuts; most four-seater Maseratis don't seem to have been loved by their owners. Like the Ghibli, its two-seat counterpart, the Indy is hideously rust-prone and parts are frighteningly expensive.

SCM Price Guide: $16,000–$24,000

1972 Maserati Indy

1976–79 Porsche 930

The 911 Turbo stretches the definition of exotic, in that basic service can be had at a Porsche dealer in almost any sizable town, and people drive these cars every day. Also, its styling is not terribly dramatic since, aside from the wide hips and famous whale-tail spoiler, the looks were similar to the "safety" 911 that Porsche introduced in 1974. Drama is, however, evident in the dynamics of these early Turbos. The first ones rode on relatively skinny tires mounted on 15-inch Fuchs wheels. The added power and wicked turbo lag accentuated the car's diabolical tail-wagging tendencies. Mastering one is an accomplishment. Brakes on the earliest cars, known as "Turbo Carreras," were also not up to the performance of the car. More than any other car on this list, the Turbo is an icon and bad to the bone. A word to the wise: Be careful of gray-market cars without proper EPA/DOT paperwork, or with ill-advised "performance" add-ons. Stock really is best here.

SCM Price Guide: $20,000–$36,000

1971–74 Citroën SM

If you subscribe to the definition of "exotic" as being something that is strange or striking in a way that is truly fascinating, this French oddity is the only true exotic on the list. A person who buys a less-than-mechanically-right example may think that "SM" stands for "sado-masochist;" it actually stands for Systeme Maserati, as the car shared the same V6 that powered the Maserati Merak. The engine, however, is probably the most mundane aspect of the SM. You want different? How about hydraulics that can raise a tire off of the ground without a jack, steering so ultra-quick that a sneeze can cause an unintended lane change, and brakes operated by a round, pressure-sensitive button on the floor. Some might argue that these features are just unnecessary complications, but that misses the point, which is simply that SMs are wildly different. Just make sure that the hydraulics, which power virtually everything on the car, have been attended to.

SCM Price Guide: $15,000–$30,000

1972 Citroën SM

1971–74 De Tomaso Pantera

The Pantera came to market so underdeveloped that a series of facilities had to be set up around the country to correct production and design flaws. In one legendary incident, Elvis pumped several .38 slugs into his when it let him down. The good news is that 30 years on, most cars have been sorted out and are now capable of driving down the road without overheating on a 60-degree day, spontaneously combusting, or provoking an owner into discharging a firearm into it. A 351 Ford Cleveland V8 and a ZF five-speed transaxle sit be-

hind the driver, and the noises coming through the dual ANSA exhausts will leave few people wanting anything more exotic. For those who aspire to a new Ford GT or an original GT40, but come up short in the fundage department, I have one piece of advice: Don't fool around with a GT40 repli-doodad. Buy a Pantera. You'll love it, and you'll have something of real value. Although official Pantera imports stopped in 1974, the car was actually produced for many years after that. Again, beware of gray-market imports without EPA/DOT papers, as well as those with extensive "boy-racer" modifications.

SCM Price Guide: $40,000–$65,000

1973 DeTomaso Pantera

1980 Ferrari 400

1976–89 Ferrari 400/412

No list of purported exotics would be complete without the obligatory Ferrari. My feeling is that if you're going to include one, make it a real one with a V12 in front, as God and Enzo intended. The 2+2s always bring up the rear in values, with the 400/412 as the current loss leader. I'm baffled as to the derision these cars take, as there is a lot to like here. With low beltline styling, five-spoke Cromodoras, and the classic Ferrari four-taillight rear treatment, these are fairly handsome cars in any color other than red or white. There's good headroom, a comfortable driving position, and some room in the rear. On the minus side, automatics outnumber five-speeds, and all are gray-market cars, often with bodged home-boy emission add-ons or non-existent federalization paperwork. Finally, these are tremendously expensive cars to maintain, with little potential for anything other than modest appreciation.

SCM Price Guide: $22,000–$30,000

1966–82 Avanti II

Easily the most practical car of the bunch, Avanti IIs were hand-made cars that were put together much better than the more collectible Studebaker-built cars. Early cars are best, with a Chevy 327 engine that was lighter than the Studebaker 289 lump it replaced. You could have an Avanti II in literally any color combination, which means that there are numerous cars running around that are legacies to their taste-challenged original owners. I personally witnessed, circa 1977, a metallic lime green car with silver leather being completed at the factory while my dad made his more subdued choices. No Avanti can be expected to handle like the European cars on this list, and they are particularly treacherous in the wet. However, their fiberglass bodies will never rust (frames are another story) and parts and service are a breeze. Try to hold out for a '66–'69 with a four-speed. They're rare, but they're out there.

SCM Price Guide: $13,000–$17,000 ♦

1980 Avanti II

Four Fun Collectible Cars Under $25,000

Buying a car that's fun to drive offers few challenges in parts or service, and it's easy to sell when you "move up"

by Donald Osborne

1967 Alfa Duetto

Multi-million dollar "Pebble Beach" restorations, race cars with Mille Miglia provenance, ex-Reggie Jackson muscle cars—there are plenty of ways to blow your wad if you're a super-rich collector. But what about the regular guy? Yes, you too can find something to put in your garage other than a lawn mower and all those cases of California Cabernet on which you got a great deal at Costco.

There are terrific cars in every price bracket, including many under $25,000. Some have a reasonable chance of appreciating, a few are even rare, and plenty can be more fun to own and drive than cars that cost ten times as much.

One of the most important things to consider when buying a collector car, regardless of price, is how it will be used. There's no point in "saving money" by purchasing a car that doesn't meet your needs or will present such a burden of own-

ership that the experience turns sour. If you stretch your budget to buy a car that has high maintenance costs, you may not be able to afford to own it. Keep in mind too, that someone is going to need to service the vehicle; get acquainted with a local mechanic before you buy a car that no one in your area can or will work on.

What follows is a list of five popular cars that are all fun to drive, offer few challenges in acquiring parts or service, and are relatively easy to sell when you want to "move up" in the collector car chain.

1966–69 Alfa Duetto, $15,000–$22,500

The Duetto debuted in the U.S. in 1967, with a radical "round tail" rear end that not everyone appreciated at first. Alfa heard the criticism, and in 1970 the Spider (as it had been rechristened) got a more conventional squared-off "Kamm tail." This change of heart means that 1966–1969 models were forever set apart from the many Spiders that followed through the end of production in 1993.

Immortalized in "The Graduate," the Duetto is what many people imagine when you say "Italian sports car," and the reality lives up to the hype. It is great fun to drive, with a free-revving 1,600-cc DOHC four and a slick five-speed transmission. The 1969 model (there was no 1968 U.S. model) received a bigger, 1,779 cc engine with a troublesome fuel injection system, making the 1967 model year the more desirable.

The biggest challenge to buying an old Alfa is a period of deferred maintenance that many went through when they were just cheap used cars. A weak second-gear synchro and head gasket are the chief areas of concern. Any sort of service history is a great bonus, although mechanicals in these cars tend to be robust and the cost of rebuilding an engine, which maxes out at around $4,000, is comparatively low compared to other Italian exotics.

The body, however, needs to be carefully maintained, as old Alfas rust with a vengeance. In addition, the pointed ends that make the car look so great tend to lose out in encounters with the "park by touch" crowd, and inevitably many hoods and trunk lids will have been repaired. Look carefully for a little raised ridge above the center of the grill; if it's not there, the car has been hit and ineptly repaired.

Alfa Spiders are as common as roaches, but the round-tail Duetto is a true classic, one of Alfa Romeo and Pininfarina's greatest accomplishments.

Pros: Sharp-edged, dramatic design; the top goes down; responsive, free-revving engine; slick transmission; great club support; easy parts availability.

Cons: Very vulnerable to parking dings and dents; deferred-maintenance issues; rust problems everywhere.

Bottom line: A famous open Italian sports car, a true classic for a very low price.

1965–67 MG B-GT, $8,500–$12,000

Following the successful introduction of the MGB roadster in 1962, a coupe version was planned. The Pininfarina design would share the roadster's front fenders and hood, but have a slightly taller windshield to allow more room inside. Thus, the well-proportioned MGB-GT was born in 1965, with a folding rear seat and a practical hatchback rear door.

1967 MG B-GT

The added weight of the roof somewhat compromised acceleration, but this was mitigated by enhanced aerodynamics and improved handling thanks to shifting more of the weight over the rear wheels. With genuine leather seats, wire wheels, and good build quality, the MGB-GT was sort of a poor man's Aston Martin.

Not surprisingly, when looking for a GT, rust is an important consideration. Due to the high quality of the original paint, MGBs usually rust from the inside out, caused by leaks and corrosion on the floors. Check to see that the seam between the front fenders and the footwells is solid, that the doors don't sag when opened, and check the condition of the rear spring hangers. A rust hole in the rocker panels is generally a terminal sign. Dented fenders, doors, and hatches, however, can be replaced with new items quite easily.

The optional overdrive is a real plus. Avoid cars from 1968 on, as the interior suffered from DOT "safety-itis," and the engine began to be smog strangled.

The engine, like that of most English cars, will likely show some signs of oil leakage—but not in the Exxon Valdez range. The B's 1,789-cc inline four is inexpensive to rebuild, less than $3,000 generally, and parts support for these cars is amazing.

For a true British grand touring experience at a fraction of the cost of a Jaguar, the MGB-GT is a great choice.

Pros: Fun to drive with an elegant style; practical coupe body; great parts availability and club support.

Cons: The top doesn't go down; more expensive to restore than a roadster, but worth less.

Bottom line: A real GT car with a pedigree, wire wheels, leather, and protection from the weather.

1965–66 Ford Mustang Coupe, $13,000–$19,500

The first-generation Mustang was enormously successful, with over 400,000 sold in its first year. Not only did the 'Stang go on to become one of the most beloved nameplates, but it spawned an entire segment, the "pony car."

In today's terms, Mustangs look sportier than they feel, but in period, the Ford Falcon-based sports car was certainly among the most fun-to-drive American cars on the road. Mustangs had vast options lists, allowing for everything from a quasi-economy car with a 120-hp six-cylinder, to a high-performance muscle car with a 271-hp, 289-ci V8, a four-speed manual transmission, and front disc brakes.

The most valuable Mustangs are original factory-built GT models, but as most of the package was available as dealer-installed pieces, it takes original build records to confirm a "real" GT. Cars that have such documentation, as well as convertible V8s, sell for well over $30,000, but the prices of coupes (and some fastbacks) are still hovering below the $25k mark, even with V8s.

If you just want to cruise down to the local ice cream parlor on a Sunday afternoon, a six-cylinder Mustang may suffice, but the V8 is far more desirable, even with the three-speed automatic transmission. Early Mustangs have great style, can be serviced at practically any gas station, and are supported by the hands-down largest network of parts suppliers in the country. These cars are easy to find, inexpensive to own and restore, and are not likely to depreciate.

There is no more iconic American car than the first-generation Mustang, a perfect first-time collector car.

Pros: Classic design; superb parts availability and ease of service; great club support; tremendous following.

Cons: Fairly common; coupes worth considerably less than convertibles; "fake" GT models abound; varying quality

1965 Ford Mustang

of many amateur restorations.

Bottom Line: A legend, practically as easy to own and drive as a new car.

1972–74 BMW 2002 tii, $10,600–$17,000

Although it was the homely Isetta bubblecar that saved BMW from almost certain extinction in the 1950s, it was the 2002 that put the automaker back on the map. Fitted with a 100-hp, 2-liter engine (from the 2000 sedan) and independent rear suspension, the two-door 2002 was the antithesis of the American idiom of big, brute power.

It was an instant hit in the U.S. market, causing David E. Davis to write in Car and Driver, "To my way of thinking, the 2002 is one of modern civilization's all-time best ways to get somewhere sitting down."

The ultimate 2002 variant was the Turbo of 1974, which was never officially imported to the U.S. But second in the pecking order is the tii (standing for Touring International Injection), introduced in 1972. The tii boasted higher compression, larger intake valves and brakes, wider wheels, and of course, a Kugelfischer mechanical fuel injection system. It had 25 more horsepower than the standard model, along with a much wider power band.

Mechanically, 2002s are very sturdy, but like most cars of the era, the real concern is in the body, which can, and does, rust. The key spots to check are the rear shock towers in the trunk, the spare tire well, the frame supporting the fuel tank, and the rocker panels (which are structural). Parts are readily available through an active network of suppliers and a large club.

A properly set-up 2002 tii provides a very modern driving experience with just enough vintage spirit.

Pros: Great to drive; outstanding original build quality; good parts availability.

Cons: Watch out for rust; needs high-octane fuel; '74 and later cars carry big federalized bumpers.

Bottom Line: The BMW reputation for performance, without the yuppie image. ♦

1973 BMW 2002 tii

Eight Italian Sports Cars for the First-Time Collector

These cars were designed by people who wanted every minute behind the wheel to be a passionate and unforgettable experience

by Donald Osborne

1965 Alfa Giulia Spider

1974 Alfa Spider 2000

Ferrari, Fiat, Maserati, OSCA, Lamborghini, Alfa Romeo. When people think of sports cars, they often think Italian. After all, take a red Alfa Romeo Duetto Spider, a sunny day, a pair of wrap-around shades, and even the nebbish Dustin Hoffman looks like Marcello Mastroianni. The reputation Italian cars have for mechanical unreliability and expensive maintenance can argue against one as a choice for a first-time collector. But with the right car and a good mechanic, Italian sports cars can be a reasonable and certainly enjoyable choice.

One of the most important things to consider when buying an older Italian car is its history. Because many became rather inexpensive used cars before they became collectible, maintenance may have been deferred, or the car serviced by a ham-handed, shade-tree mechanic. If one is well serviced by an experienced and knowledgeable technician, it should prove to be as reliable as any car.

Parts should not be a problem for anything on our list. A large and active roster of suppliers (though certainly not in the league of those supplying British cars) supports vintage Alfas, Fiats, and Ferraris. Although smaller, a network of sources also exists to support pre-1975 Lancias as well. As with any collector car, owners clubs are a crucial source of information about how to keep your Italian on the road.

The cars here are rather different in character, but they all share a uniquely Italian approach to driving, delivering the maximum involvement all the time. Whether being driven at nine-tenths on a track or at one-tenth on a leisurely Saturday evening cruise, the sounds they make, the way they handle, even the way you sit in them all tell you that they were designed by and for people who wanted every minute behind the wheel to be a passionate experience.

1964–66 Alfa Giulia Spider Veloce, $40,000–$52,000

The Giulia was introduced in 1963 as a successor to Alfa's first small sports car, the Giulietta. The differences were not great, but the engine was bumped up to 1,600 cc, making the car a more relaxed driver than its predecessor. "Veloce" denotes a higher state of tune for Alfas of the 1950s and 1960s. Twin-choke Weber carbs, hotter cams, and 129 hp (rather than 108 in the Normale) were part of the package.

Pros: Classic shape; great handling; SCCA racing heritage; good creature comforts for a '60s roadster

Cons: Rusty floors; cars out of long storage will likely need brake and steering work; watch out for "Abnormales"—Normales with Weber carbs and Veloce badging stuck on

Bottom Line: A true thoroughbred Italian sports car for the price of a new Mustang

1975 Ferrari 308 GT4

1971–74 Alfa 1750/2000 Spider, $6,750–$13,000

The successor to the Giulia Spider was the iconic 1,600-cc Duetto, or round-tail spider. The revised Kamm "square-tail" spider appeared in 1971 with a larger 1,779-cc engine, and was given the more evocative name 1750 to tie it to the legendary Alfa six-cylinder of the 1930s. A 2-liter engine arrived in 1972. It remained in production, continuously evolving (not always for the better) until 1993. For a collector, the pre-1975 cars are the ones to have, offering a classic feel, svelte chrome bumpers, and modern drivability and comfort. The bad reputation of their SPICA mechanical fuel injection is mostly a result of ignorant mechanics. Properly set up, it works well.

Pros: Clean lines; handling; sweet, direct-action 5-speed gearbox; superbly engineered top; active club and great parts support

Cons: Rust; values do not support full restorations; weak second-gear synchro; valve jobs good for 45,000 miles; dashes crack easily

Bottom Line: A Pininfarina-designed classic, fun to drive, great exhaust sound, an Italian convertible experience at a reasonable cost

1974–79 Ferrari 308 GT4, $23,000–$28,000

If you're willing to ignore the old adage "four seats is two seats too many for a Ferrari," the Bertone-designed GT4 has many charms for the first-timer. They were conceived as "everyday" cars and will typically have higher mileages than most Ferraris. If you can give up the style of the 308 GTB/GTS that followed, Ferrari performance and road holding can be yours for Camry money. The usual cautions about service apply: Be sure it has been serviced regularly, not just with respect to mileage, but also age, as the cam belts have to be replaced every five years, to the tune of $2,500–$5,000.

Pros: Room for small kids or big grocery bags; near everyday usability and dependability; total parts availability

Cons: Origami styling; four seats; parts and maintenance costs high relative to value; production volume (2,826) makes appreciation unlikely

Bottom Line: A great way to enter the Ferrari life at a reasonable price; above all else, buy only with documented history

1999–2004 Ferrari 360 Modena, $90,000–$120,000

When this successor to the 355 was introduced in 1999, it was hailed as a major step forward in the "basic" Ferrari.

2002 Ferrari 360 Modena

With its 400 hp engine, available paddle-shift F1 transmission, and clean lines, it was the ideal car to take Ferrari into the 21st century. Lessons were also learned from cars like the Acura NSX; it is agreed the 360 is the least idiosyncratic and easiest-to-live-with car ever to come from Maranello. Offering reasonable luggage space (room for the proverbial golf bag) and comfortable, yet supportive seats, it can be used far more often than you might think.

Pros: Easy to live with; factory support; modern conveniences; looks; performance

Cons: Still depreciating; fairly common; F1 transmission clutches can be short-lived

Bottom Line: Offers the Italian sports car experience with modern comfort and reliability

1969–72 Fiat Dino Spider, $39,000–$62,500

Ferrari's need to homologate a 2-liter V6 engine for Formula 2 competition resulted in two of the most interesting Fiats ever offered. The coupe, designed by Bertone, was attractive, but the Pininfarina-designed Spider was stunning. In spite of the superb engine and design, the car was a tough sell when it was new. Not many people (7,500 coupes and spiders made in six years) wanted to risk their lire on low Fiat prestige

1971 Fiat Dino Spider

with high Ferrari running costs. The cars were rushed into production, so early ones had problems with engine reliability and build quality.

A 2.4-liter version was introduced in 1969, when assembly was moved to Ferrari to improve quality. Look for these later cars, as they have more horsepower, a better gearbox, and an independent rear suspension. As with every Ferrari-powered car, as complete a service history as possible will minimize unpleasant surprises.

Pros: Flexible, tuneful Ferrari V6; stunning looks

Cons: Major engine repairs can approach the value of the car; Fiat badge gets no respect; cars were born with rust; crappy Fiat switchgear

Bottom Line: A great buy if you can manage the risk and don't have a bad case of Prancing Horse envy

1967–72 Intermeccanica Italia, Coupe $28,000–$45,000 / Convertible $35,000–$50,000

This is a car in the hybrid tradition: Italian style with American horsepower. The story is convoluted, so suffice it to say that the cars we're talking about here are the fifth iteration of the car, built from 1967–1972 and powered by a Ford 302 V8. Beautifully styled by Franco Scaglione, well-built and powerful, the cars found steady buyers until production was stopped by tightening U.S. emissions and safety standards in 1972.

1972 Intermeccanica Italia

Lancia Fulvia Coupe

Pros: Great performance; reliable, inexpensive-to-maintain mechanicals; rarity

Cons: Unobtainable trim; no "heritage"; thin market for resale

Bottom Line: Muscle car performance in a svelte Italian package

1965–76 Lancia Fulvia Coupe, $11,000–$18,000

The Lancia Fulvia was the successor to the Appia, the small-car offering of the innovative Italian firm. Introduced in 1965, the factory-designed coupe featured a narrow-angle, overhead-cam V4 engine, front-wheel drive, and a clean design. Beginning with 1.2 liters, the engine grew through 1.3 to 1.6 liters. The second-series cars, introduced in 1970 following Fiat's takeover of Lancia, added a five-speed gearbox to the mix. There was also a high-performance model called the HF, which formed the basis of the championship-winning Fulvia rally cars of the 1970s. The HF coupes will be at the higher end of the price range, with the most expensive being the 1.6-liter HF model. Any Fulvia is a great-handling, fun car to drive, and will set you apart from the crowd.

Pros: Superb design; racing history; rarity

Cons: Scarcity; parts availability; small resale market

Bottom Line: The individualist's choice, rewarding to own and to drive

1971–74 Pantera, $40,000–$65,000

Another Italo-American hybrid. Commissioned by the Ford Motor Company as a Corvette fighter for its Lincoln-Mercury dealers, the Pantera had all the right ingredients: a slick body designed by Tom Tjaarda for Ghia, the powerful Ford 351 Cleveland engine, and the backing of one of the world's largest automakers. The direct Ford connection lasted from the introduction in 1971 until 1974, though production continued until 1989 under the DeTomaso banner. Panteras offer ample interior room and amenities such as electric windows and air conditioning. Thanks to the tuneability of the high-performance Ford engines, many Panteras have been extensively customized. The best bets for a beginning collector would be one of the early (pre-'75) models, in stock or relatively stock form.

Pros: Creature comforts; performance; usual appeal; ease of service; club support

Cons: Difficulty in finding stock cars; loud, "street-racer" image

Bottom Line: An Italian alternative to the Corvette ♦

1974 DeTomaso Pantera

Eight Best Ferraris Under $100k

It's the magic number for a first-timer. It won't get you into trouble with your spouse, and it buys you a real Ferrari

By Michael Sheehan

1963 Ferrari 250 GTE

I get dozens of phone calls and emails from would-be first-time Ferrari buyers, and I always ask them the same questions: What's your "real" budget? Do you have any idea how much to expect for maintenance costs? Have you considered the pros and cons of old versus new? Are you prepared to pony up for the necessary pre-purchase inspection? What's your intended usage?

Most often, $100,000 tends to be the magic number for a first-timer, a sum that won't get you into too much trouble with your spouse but is still enough cash to buy a real Ferrari. What follows is a summary of the current market favorites in this price range, along with some considerations that can help identify which car might be right for you.

Best of the '60S

The standard-bearer of the early V12 Ferrari is the 1960–63 250 GTE. Built at a time when a high performance sports car meant user-cruel, it was surprisingly easy to drive. Road & Track, in its August 1962 issue, wrote, "Anyone can drive one and enjoy the experience, the connoisseur who can afford one wouldn't have anything else—this car is (almost) every sports car owner's dream."

With 954 built, the 250 GTE was Ferrari's first high-volume model and a major commercial success. A good driver-quality car will bring at least $100,000 today, up from $50k–$60k two years ago. Be sure to tack on at least $10,000 for the problems you will find if you buy a perfect one. Add $25,000 for repairs if you buy one with a few needs.

On to the '70S

While the 365 GTC/4 has its detractors, I feel the C/4 is the best buy under $100k. When new, these cars were more expensive than Daytonas, and with only 500 built, they are rarer as well.

At $100,000 and climbing for an exceptional example, the C/4 can even be rationalized as "an investment." A major

1972 Ferrari 365 GTC/4

service starts at about $5,000, but the "while-you're-at-its" of new clutches, cam chains, water hoses, a/c reseals, new synchros, suspension bushings, and shock rebuilds can (and will) quickly double or triple that amount. At least the C/4 is simple enough that it can be worked on by anyone who is reasonably familiar with a Weber carburetor—and you don't need a laptop to check anything.

The mid-'70s to mid-'80s

First in the line of Ferrari's new mid-engined supercars was the 365 GT4 BB, produced from 1973–76. With only 387 made, it remains the rarest of the Boxers, and the quickest, thanks to peaky cams and short transmission gearing. A good-running 365 Boxer is a rocketship, going through first, second, and third gears with amazing acceleration and the wonderful sound of a very busy flat-12 with lots of carburetors sucking air. A good example can still be found for less than $150,000, but don't hesitate if the right car comes along at a bit more, as this one is soon moving into six-figure territory.

The 512 BB came next, from 1976–81. With only 921 cars produced, carbureted 512s are relatively rare compared to Ferrari's current production numbers. While not as quick as the 365 through the first three gears, the extra 600 cc certainly makes a difference on the top end, making the carbureted 512 the king-of-the-hill fastest of the Boxers. With ever-toughening emissions controls worldwide, Ferrari added fuel injection to the 512, creating the 512 BBi in 1981. Tuned for more low-end and mid-range performance, but a weaker top-end, the injected Boxers are more tractable in around-town driving. Through 1984, a total of 1,007 512 BBis were produced.

With room for the tallest driver, adequate air conditioning, light steering, and excellent brakes, all Boxers are a driver's delight. On the downside, while the balance and handling are good, once the limits are reached the car will swap ends without much warning on an over-exuberant or unwary driver.

The rather bland styling and concerns with certification (Boxers were never sold new in the U.S.) have kept values below those of the more attractive but less refined Daytona. But with Daytonas selling for $250,000-plus, a 512 BB or BBi at $125,000-plus is still a supercar bargain. Bear in mind that an engine-out service on these cars starts at about $6,000, with typical ancillary work easily doubling that amount.

Fewer cylinders

The 1986–89 328 is relatively light and nimble to drive and beautiful to behold. Plus, it's instantly recognizable as a Ferrari, an important factor for most first-time buyers. A 328 will give years of reasonably priced and entertaining driving, but as the final evolution of the 308, it is a 30-year-old design with only adequate performance, braking, and HVAC. Prices range from $35,000 for a high-miler GTB up to $70,000 for a 1989 GTS with ABS, convex wheels, and low mileage. As the

1974 Ferrari GT4 BB

1999 Ferrari 355 F1 Spider

last of the V8 models that don't require an engine-out service, $4,000 should pay for your 30,000-mile checkup (as opposed to $7,000-plus for later 348s, F355s, and 360s).

The 348 replaced the 328 in 1989, the first mass-produced Ferrari with a longitudinally-mounted engine and unitized body. Unfortunately, the 348 had more than its share of teething problems but improved as it evolved, with viable electronics, great a/c, and a user-friendly cockpit. When 348 shopping, run fast and far from any car that hints at deferred maintenance. Coupes sell for under $50,000 now, while a great 1995 Spyder can be found for less than $75,000.

The F355 was the first Ferrari to feature a Formula One-inspired shifter, a desirable unit that has proven to be relatively bulletproof and makes the car a great daily driver. F355s have only two major problem areas: faulty exhaust manifolds and valve guides that tend toward rapid wear. For those not used to the world of Ferrari prices, an exhaust manifold for a 355 is $2,500, not including the labor to install it, and an engine-out valve job can run $10,000-plus. Expect to pay $50,000 for a 1995 Berlinetta with over 30,000 miles, while a 1999 Fiorano Spyder with F1 transmission and under 5,000 miles will take you outside this article's budget at $115k.

Enter the '90S

The 456 GT is a technological marvel and will provide a great ownership experience for the Ferrari buyer with small children and $75,000-plus to spend. With a 48-valve, 4-cam, 5.5-liter V12 putting out 442 hp, the 456 offers staggering performance, blasting through the quarter-mile in 13.4 seconds at 107 mph, and topping out at 186.

The quiet, user-friendly cockpit, luxurious seating, easy-to-read gauges and six-speed shifter make driving a pleasure, while the a/c and heater are more than adequate. While the 456 may lack the soulful exhaust sound of the C/4, its comfortable and quiet cockpit will make a 200-mile drive to your vacation spot a memorable experience, with no need to get out the aspirin or visit your chiropractor.

A major service on a 456 starts at about $5,000, but can go up if you add a new clutch, shocks, etc. These cars have now dropped from their new-in-1995 price of $225,000 to about $60k–$80k.

Overall, $100,000 should be plenty to get you a decent Ferrari, one that is a good first step on the ladder that ends up at $15,000,000 GTOs. If after you own one of the above cars, it turns out the Prancing Horse is not for you, you haven't risked much and can probably get most of your money back. If owning a 250 GTE makes you a 12-cylinder junkie, you've got the whole world of six- and seven-figure cars from Maranello just waiting for you to wave your wallet at them. ♦

Five Best Ferraris Over $1,000,000

The 512 hit 218 mph in fifth on the 3.5-mile Mulsanne Straight, the fastest piece of racing real estate on the planet

By Michael Sheehan

1957 250 TR

Before attempting to delineate the best seven-figure Ferraris, I called multiple collectors, dealers, and historians for their feedback, and I must admit to being surprised at how varied the opinions were. Of course, I had my own ideas on the subject, but it was made clear from my conversations that when you've got deep, deep pockets, you've got many, many choices. While there was little overall consensus among those I surveyed, some favorites emerged.

Best event car

The 250 Testa Rossa (1956–61) is eligible for literally every event on the planet, from the Roman roadways of the Mille Miglia to the highways of the Colorado Grand to the lawn at Pebble Beach. When vintage-raced, TRs are reasonably competitive, running at the front in Ferrari-only races and near the front in multi-marque competitions.

The 250 TR perfectly captures the look of the late 1950s sports racer with its swoopy lines and sexy pontoon fenders. Even better, TRs are robust, don't break, and parts are available. A TR is a very forgiving car to drive, giving lots of feedback and helping to make a bad driver look good and a good driver look busy.

The price to be in the game? Over $10m.

Best investment

While my crystal ball was recalled for defects around 1991, I still opine that a 250 GTO (1962–64) is a pretty safe investment today. While they have now hit their former 1989 peak prices, these values are still low when you factor in inflation. If stock market and interest rate uncertainties continue, owning a GTO certainly seems prudent compared to owning several million shares of any number of publicly traded companies whose self-serving managers make used-car dealers look like philanthropists.

Ferrari GTO ownership also guarantees you an invitation to almost any event, competition, or concours. It means you are a top player in the world of collector cars, and have the trophy in your garage to prove it. Besides, GTOs rarely sit alone in a one-car garage, with virtually every owner's car serving as the centerpiece of a substantial Ferrari collection.

The price to park one in your garage? Don't expect much change from today's $20m–$28m for a no-stories car.

Best serious vintage racer

Okay, I'll admit it, my choice for the ultimate hot ride, combined with the ultimate sound, are the 1970 512 S and the 1971 512 M. They were built to run flat-out for 24 hours at Le

250 GTO: An investment better than stocks

ers. Even so, a mildly tuned TdF was more than adequate to run away from virtually any competitor of its time, including Corvettes, 300SLs, and Jaguar XK 140s.

Nothing has changed in the last five decades, and the 250 TdF is still a great race car that rewards the skillful without punishing those of lesser talents. The soft suspension, skinny tires, live rear axle, and light weight give great driver feedback and make for a great event car, race car, and even user-friendly weekend street car.

The price to get started? About $2m and up.

Mans and are very durable and almost never break in today's 30-minute vintage races. With a factory rating of 600 hp and weighing only 1,800 pounds, their performance is staggering.

Before today's chicanes were installed at Le Mans, the 3.5-mile Mulsanne Straight was the fastest piece of racing real estate in the world, and 512 drivers shifted from fourth to fifth at 195 mph on the way to a 218-mph top speed. Not for the timid or those with limited racing experience, when set up properly, a 512 is a joy to drive, with massive torque, a power curve that seems to go on forever, and tolerable brakes.

The price to win the Ferrari-Maserati Historic series? Under $2m.

Best first Ferrari racer

In theory, the 250 Tour de France (1956–59) was available new to anyone with the ability to write a check to the local Ferrari dealer for $12,000. In fact, the best cars with the latest camshafts, pistons, and lightweight parts were reserved for the best-known, most talented, and well-connected driv-

Best all-around buy

The 1966 275 GTB/C is one of the lesser known Ferraris, often overshadowed by its predecessors, the 250 GT SWB and 250 GTO. As Ferrari's last purpose-built GT racer, the 275 GTB/C is a true race car that is the rightful successor to the GTO. Faster and more technically advanced than the GTO, the 275 GTB/C is also rarer, with only 12 produced versus 36 GTOs.

Ferrari built these cars between the end of the 275 GTB production run and the start of the 275 GTB/4 run, all of them fitted with a lightweight frame and body, powered by a three-carb, dry-sump 250 LM engine. The 275's tipo 213 engine was mistakenly homologated with three rather than six carbs, so this paperwork blunder was resolved by using three Weber 40 DF13 carburetors that gave over 300 hp at 7,500 rpm. These were the last competition GT cars designed and built from the ground up by Forghieri and the racing department at Maranello.

The price for this durable vintage racer? A great bang for the buck at about $2m.

512 S: Master of the Muslanne

1956 Ferrari 250 GT Tour de France

Where do we go from here?

All of these cars have now reached their 1989 high-water mark, but this is thankfully not because of a rush of speculators with too much money and too short a memory jumping on the bandwagon. Unlike the late 1980s, the Ferrari world of today is not one of Dutch tulip mania.

Vintage Ferraris are being bought by real people, with real money, and for real purposes. As this list shows, eligibility for events creates value, and there is a great deal of money out there willing to step up for personal satisfaction and entertainment. It's taken 15 years, but the Ferrari market is now strong across the board. As long as appreciation continues to be gradual and not led by greed, expect the market to remain strong and stable. ♦

1966 Ferrari 275 GTB/C

Three 12-Cylinder Ferraris You Can Afford

The 1986–89 Testarossa and 1992–94 512 TR are often the biggest bang for the buck in the Ferrari world

By Mike Sheehan

Boxer—user-cruel or driver's delight?

The majority of first-time, 12-cylinder Ferrari buyers have $50,000–$100,000 to spend, and while that won't buy you much more than a keyfob for a collectible vintage Ferrari, it's plenty for a modern flat-12 or V12.

Ferraris in this price range are bought for looks, performance, and pride of ownership, not as investments. Here's a summary of later-model favorites, one of which might be just right for you.

The Boxer still remains

You've missed the bus for a 365 BB, but the 1976–81 512 BBs are still under $120,000. With only 921 cars produced, carbureted 512s are relatively rare compared to Ferrari's current production numbers. Though the 365 trumps it through the first three gears, the 512's larger capacity certainly makes a difference on the top end, making the carbureted 512 the fastest of the Boxers.

To counter tougher emissions, Ferrari added fuel injec-tion to the 512 in 1981, creating the 512 BBi. Tuned for more low-end and mid-range performance, the injected Boxers are more tractable around town. Through 1984, a total of 1,007 512 BBis were produced.

Some would argue that Boxers are user-cruel. I beg to differ. With room for the tallest driver, adequate air conditioning, light steering, and excellent brakes, I find Boxers to be a driver's delight. Just remember that while balance and handling are good, once the limits are reached the car will treat you to unexpected tail swapping. Due to certification issues because they were never sold new in the U.S., and because the styling is fairly bland by Ferrari standards, values have stayed below those of the more attractive but less refined Daytona. However, Daytonas now sell for more than $275,000, so a 512 BB or BBi at $120,000 to $150,000 is a bargain.

Bear in mind that Boxers are now 20 to 30 years old, so they can run up stratospheric repair bills. An engine-out service on these cars starts at about $6,000, with typical ancillary work such as a new multi-plate clutch, water pump, starter and alternator rebuilds, cooling system work, and a full hose replacement doubling that amount.

The good news is that Boxers are fully depreciated and gained about $10,000 to $20,000 in the last year. Further appreciation will cover future maintenance costs, at best. So buy a car with a recent service and it should be a joy for the next five years. When the 30,000-mile service is due, get out your checkbook or wave bye-bye.

Boss Testarossa

The 1986–89 Testarossa and 1992–94 512 TR, in my opinion, offer the biggest bang for the buck in the Ferrari world. Both are big cars, and they have heavy-feeling controls under 15 mph—but who drives a Ferrari under 15 mph? They have acres of torque, effortless performance, and a cruising speed that will put you in jail in all 50 states.

The bold but "Miami Vice" dated styling makes them instantly recognizable—always important to first-time Ferrari buyers—and they are user-friendly, with excellent air-conditioning and heater. A 1986–87 TR with 25,000 miles and all services done can be bought at $50,000 or so, a late 1988–89 with about 10,000–20,000 miles will bring $75,000–$85,000, and a 1992–94 can be found for $115,000 or less. If you're a big guy—over 6'3"—the Testarossa is for you.

The Testarossa flat-twelve is a Boxer engine with four valves, so the same deferred and future maintenance costs apply. With over 7,000 built, Testarossas were a great buy when new and—if maintained—can be a great buy today. They aren't long-term investments, but with exotic performance and looks at a Lexus price, they get my value vote.

Maranello: Back to the Daytona

At the end of the TR series, Ferrari returned to front-engine technology and subdued styling with the 550 Maranello in 1996. The Maranello was the replacement for the 365 GTB/4. Like the Daytona, the 550 Maranello is aggressively styled with its cut-off tail and long-nosed good looks.

Fitted with a 5.5-liter, 48-valve V12 that pushes out 485 hp at 7,000 rpm, the 550 has a top speed of 199 mph and rips through a quarter-mile in 12.6 seconds. A total of 3,600 were built between 1996 and 2002. Today, a U.S.-legal European 1996 or 1997 Maranello is $75,000–$100,000, while mid–mileage 1997 or 1998 U.S. cars can be found for $95,000–$100,000.

As for pitfalls of ownership, early 550s run too much oil pressure and occasionally blow the oil filter apart, creating a major mess. Should the oil filter start to leak as an inattentive owner cruises down the freeway chatting on the cell phone, and he spins the bearings and scores the crank, the next stop

Dated "Miami Vice" styling, but supercar performance

550 Maranello: Engine contents under pressure

is the dealer and a new engine for $75,000. If he stops in time, a rebuild is only $25,000. Preventing the problem is simple: Remove a few spacers in the oil system (one hour's labor), which drops the oil pressure.

The circlip holding reverse gear to the gear cluster sometimes fails on earlier 550s, resulting in major transaxle repair bills. If your 550 pops out of reverse, truck it to your local Ferrari service center and have the transaxle pulled and the circlip and reverse gear replaced at a cost of about $3,500. Drive the car with the transaxle making ominous sounds and, after the reverse gear has bounced around in the transaxle like a ball in a squash court, the repair bill will climb to about $7,500. Clutches, traditionally a weak spot with novice Ferrari drivers, don't seem to be a problem.

In the engines, it's not uncommon to do a compression leak-down check on a low-mileage 550 and find poor ring seating and leaky valve seats. If the compression on a car you are considering is weak, keep looking. Also, cam and front seals tend to start leaking after about 10,000 miles, so most owners skip the 15,000 mile service and simply go to straight to the 30,000-mile service.

This includes cam seals, cam belts, tensioner bearings, and more for about $3,500. Check the records.

Life's too short to drive Hondas

Don't think about "Ferrari" and "investment" in this price range. There is no upside to any of these cars, other than to fulfill the dream of Ferrari ownership. But life is too short to drive Hondas—at least on weekends. If you take your family on a Caribbean or skiing vacation and spend $10,000, you don't expect to sell those memories and make a profit, do you?

So enjoy your Ferrari for the pride of ownership, the thrill of seeing it when you open the garage door, and the chance to take your wife or buddy to Sunday brunch in Italian style, savoring the admiring looks you get from those accountant-types in their Camrys.

But remember: Buy the right car, commit to spending $5,000 a year in maintenance, and don't look back. Buy the wrong car, and you'll put your mechanic's kids through college; pre-purchase inspection is a must. ♦

The Ferrari Market Today: What's Really Going On

The Ferrari market has returned to a refreshing level of liquidity, with cars selling again—although at 30% below last year's prices

by Michael Sheehan

1971 Daytona Spyder

The inspiration for this article occurred in March, when I returned from lunch to find an email from a Lusso owner who wanted us to sell his car and net himself $700,000—about $200,000 over the retail price for his Lusso in today's market. The very next email was from a client who had been web surfing and found an Indonesian site offering photos of a 275 GTB/4 (but with a 330 GTC serial number) for $400,000. He simply didn't "get it," or didn't want to "get it," that there were no bargain 275 GTB/4s for sale in Indonesia, and wanted to find a restored 275 GTB/4 for $400k—at least $500k under today's market.

Simply put, too many would-be sellers are lost in the ozone of last year's prices, using the 2008 peak-of-the-market numbers to gauge the value of their cars. Conversely, an equally large number of would-be buyers dwell in a fairy-land of Ferraris at 60% or more off. Neither is in touch with today's reality. So let's spell out current selling prices and percentage drops for an accurate picture of the market.

Real estate leads the way

Just as the real estate crash led the U.S., England, Spain, and Ireland into this recession, so a real estate recovery will ignite the long climb back to prosperity. As real estate begins to hit bottom, let's quantify the recession's effect on the Ferrari market. The Ferrari historians group I belong to agrees that RM's May 2008 auction at the factory in Maranello and the Monterey auctions of August 2008 were the high points of the 2003–08 Ferrari boom. So where are we now?

The numbers don't lie

One only needs to compare a few same-model, same-condition sales from the RM auctions at Maranello in 2008 with the RM auction at Maranello in 2009 for statistical answers. For example, 250 Lusso s/n 5143 was the subject of a five-year restoration and so brought "all the money" at the 2008 auction at $1,174,553. What a difference a year makes: 250 Lusso s/n 4405, also freshly restored (admittedly to a lesser standard), sold at the 2009 auction for $605,000, a drop of 49% in just one year.

Further up the food chain, 250 LWB California Spyder s/n 0923 sold for $3,659,838 at the 2008 auction, while 250 LWB California Spyder s/n 1487 sold for $2,911,563 at the 2009 auction, a drop of 21%. Shifting to newer cars, Euro model F40 s/n 89307 sold for $674,091 at the 2008 auction while Euro model F40 s/n 88835 sold for $393,250 at the 2009 sale. That's a drop of 39% for similar cars.

Ferraris of the 1970s, the Baby Boomer poster cars

Switching to the "poster child" cars of the 1970s, the cars that Baby Boomers relate to, we can compare the sales of a 246 GTS, a Daytona coupe, and a Daytona spyder for what is probably the best confirmation of the new market reality. A 246 GTS, s/n 6294, a red with black Euro model car, sold for $204,270 at the 2008 sale compared with 246 GTS, s/n 5104 GTS, also finished in red with black, which sold for $143,688 at the 2009 auction. That's down 30% for a comparable pair of nice, driver-level Dino spyders.

Moving to the poster child for the first supercar, a Daytona 365 GTB/4, s/n 14345, finished in red with tan and black, sold for $425,563 at the 2008 sale. At the 2009 sale, 365 GTB/4 s/n 13653, finished in silver with red and black interior, sold for $287,375, a drop of 33% for a relatively comparable pair of Euro-model Daytonas.

On the subject of Daytona spyders, 365 GTS/4, s/n 14415, a beautiful but older restoration in black with tan, sold for $1,489,469 at the 2008 sale. Fast forward to 2009 and s/n 14543, an ultra-detailed, time-warp, low-mileage Daytona spyder finished in white with black, was bid to $1,031,250 but not sold. I'd opine that the bid of $1,031,250 was indeed all the money in today's market, and it represents a drop of 31% in a year.

Bottom line, it's a 30% off sale

In a contango of rising Ferrari prices, the trend is your friend, until it ends. As the credit markets froze in late 2008, so did liquidity in the Ferrari market. Fed Chairman Ben Bernanke's "quantitative easing" (printing money) and massive bailouts have regreased the world's financial markets, real estate is hitting bottom, and the world's stock markets are rebounding. Likewise, the Ferrari market has returned to a refreshing level of liquidity, with cars again selling, although more or less 30% off last year's prices.

This too shall pass

It takes a lot of buying to move a market upward, but a mere lack of buyers creates a bear market. In the last year, the Ferrari market was negatively affected by a number of owners who had to sell their cars. Too many motivated sellers, too many cars, and too few buyers created today's lower prices. The "pig-in-the-python" problem of cars being squeezed slowly along to too-few buyers is behind us. Those owners who had to sell have sold. We are now back to price stability, but at 30% below previous prices and with no prospects of a speedy uptick.

Ferraris as a lagging indicator

Ferraris are a lagging indicator, as was clearly shown in 1989, when Ferrari prices remained strong long after U.S. real estate and the stock market had fallen off a cliff. Again last year, Ferrari prices continued to climb while Bear Stearns imploded, IndyMac was seized, Fannie Mae and Freddie Mac were nationalized, and Lehman Brothers sank into oblivion.

In only a year, the planet has experienced deleveraging on a breathtaking scale. The good news is that relative to banks and real estate, the drop in Ferrari prices has been modest—especially compared to the severe drops in the 1990–95 collector car price crash.

Ferraris remain liquid; buy-sell agreements can be made in a day, pre-purchase inspections effected in a few days. Ferraris have wheels, fit into trucks and cargo jets, and can be anywhere on earth within a week or two after purchase. Buyer demand—the arbitrage of weak dollars to strong euros and sterling, or vice-versa—will always provide buying opportunities. Once real estate rebounds, the stock markets revive, and employment picks up, Ferrari prices will again rise.

There's the best and the rest

The one thing we know about trends is that they are eventually going to end and collector car prices will rebound. But on the other hand, buyers do not wake up one morning and decide they will buy the highest-priced, least-documented car on the market. I'm still amazed how many sellers fail to grasp this simple concept. Regardless of where the market may be, it takes the best car, with the best documentation, best service history, best marketing, and best price to sell. ♦

Six English Convertibles Combining Value and Fun

If you're looking for the sheer thrill a classic car can bring, any of the following British roadsters will fit the bill

by Gary Anderson

1965 MG B

Dear Keith Martin on Collecting: I'm in the market for a British sports car. I would like to buy a very good, restored weekend driver. I've owned a Triumph TR4 and an MGA, but those were back in my college days. Now I'm just looking for something fun, something that will normally start and run, and something that may have some potential to keep its value.

I've been looking at Sunbeams, but I don't know much about them. I've thought about another Triumph or MGA, but I don't know if that is a good idea. Healeys are probably going to be more money than I want to spend. So I'm looking for suggestions on what model to buy, any special bits of information you could impart, and your thoughts on price and what to stay away from.—*J.P., via email*

I should start by noting that the phrase "a British car that will normally start and run" is considered an oxymoron in some circles.

However, if a British sports car is bought carefully, with advice from someone who knows the marque, then properly fettled by a specialist to make it safe and roadworthy, and after that given regular maintenance, it is certainly capable of dependable, long-term use. British cars from the 1950s and 1960s routinely complete coast-to-coast journeys today with few or no problems.

I put your question to a group of my British car friends, who suggested that your choice should meet the following criteria:

1. Your car should be capable of modern highway speeds and be in good enough condition to be rugged and reliable.
2. It should be easy to work on, with repair and maintenance parts readily available.
3. It should have a good regional club network on which you can rely for advice, technical assistance, and comradeship.

1972 Triumph TR6

1961 Triumph TR3

4. Good examples need to be generally available at reasonable prices.
5. You will probably want to restrict your search to cars built before 1973, so you don't need to worry about smog restrictions in the most restrictive states.

But before you even get this far, there's another question to ask. Bob Kinderlehrer, the former president of my local Triumph club and a long-time owner of a TR3, suggests that you ask yourself whether you are looking for a classic sports car to drive to fun places, or for a car to have fun with when you want to drive. If you're interested in vintage sports car driving for its own sake, for the sheer thrill a classic car can bring when you take it out for a bit of exercise regardless of where you are actually heading, then any of the following British roadsters should fit the bill.

1963–67 MG B

You mention Sunbeams. While they are nice enough cars, there aren't many around, and good examples are difficult to find. Not so for the MGB. These roadsters are everywhere, and as such, prices are more than reasonable. Good-to-excellent examples that don't require any major work can be found in most areas for $8,000 to $22,000, and in proper condition, they're almost trouble-free. No wonder a recent classic car magazine poll voted the mid-'60s MGB as the best sports car of all time. The most desirable models are the "pull-handle" chrome-bumper models from the mid-'60s, with piping-trimmed leather upholstery. While they built them through 1980, from 1968 on they became progressively less interesting due to smog and safety regulations.

1969–74 Triumph TR6

The six-cylinder Triumph, restyled from the TR250 by Karmann, is the most comfortable model of the Triumph line, far more so than the TR4. The clean lines and classic interior make a nice combination. In tests when it was new, magazines declared it the "last of the true sports cars." In terms of cost for condition and performance, the TR6 is probably the best bargain among British sports cars now. Look for one that has been restored to factory specs with relatively few upgrades, as many TR6s were ridden hard and put away wet. Good examples are pretty easy to find at $14,000–$22,000.

1955–61 Triumph TR3

The TR3 is a sports car for the real purist, with the distinctive quirkiness of styling and handling that set sports cars apart from the herd in the '50s. They're far more interesting than the TR4, with knuckle-dragger low doors, limited weath-

1958 MG A

1965 Austin-Healey 3000 Mk III BJ8

er protection, ox-cart suspension and heavy steering, making this car a true character builder. Still, they're in their element at highway speeds, especially if equipped with overdrive. These cars are treasured by their owners so they don't come on the open market very often, but excellent drivers can be bought for $19,000–$30,000.

1955–62 MG A

The MGA is attractive in an almost Italian way. Though limited in interior space, it is quite comfortable and very easy to work on. MGAs have built up their own strong support group, though they're not as common as Bs. Handling is exceptional, well beyond what would be required by the engine's unexceptional power. However, a well-done B engine swap is perfectly acceptable and makes the car into a great long-distance cruiser. MGAs are really beginning to come into their own and prices are starting to go up into Healey territory. Go for the plain vanilla 1500 or 1600, skipping the rare Deluxe and expensive, finicky Twin-Cam. Good drivers available for $18,000–$30,000.

1964–67 Austin-Healey 3000 Mk III (BJ8) Convertible

Yes, Austin-Healeys have recently been selling for record prices, but don't be deceived by the headlines. While pristine, just-restored cars from two or three top restorers get all the auction attention, there are always a reasonable number of good-looking, solid performers for sale in the club magazines for $50,000–$85,000. This is really everyone's ideal in sports cars, a great long-distance tourer capable of exceeding interstate speed limits for days on end but still fun on back roads. And the exhaust note is without compare. The purists like the true roadsters, with their pup-tent tops and sketchy side curtains, but your significant other will be happier with the convertibles. These were available in the last three years of production and have roll-up windows and more luxurious interiors.

1969–1971 Jaguar E-type SII

The Jaguar E-type is still the "ultimate crumpet-catcher." Sure, you can find examples selling in six digits, but if you want a driver instead of a collectible show piece, they're still affordable, more or less. Skip the numbers-matching trailer queens, and instead look for a good buy in a nice Series II. You'll give up the faired-in headlamps and dainty bumpers, but you'll get a solid 4.2-liter engine with all the performance you can handle, and the improved cooling system is really a plus. With some patience, a good-looking roadster can be found for $30,000–$45,000.

As general advice, no matter how realistic your dream of finding happiness and recapturing your youth in a British sports car, you should take your time looking. Wait until you find a car that satisfies all your criteria. Don't buy a car with needs just because it seems cheap. Trust me, the emotional heartache and financial heartburn that go into making a bad car good are something you just don't want to go through.

Join the local club for the marque you think you want and get to know as much as you can about what you're looking for. Join a marque-specific chat forum on the Internet and don't be afraid to ask questions that might seem naïve—you'll be surprised at how helpful other enthusiasts will be. Drive as many examples as you can. When you do find a possible candidate, get the expert assistance of a specialist to help you check it out. There are lots of ways these cars can be bad even when they look good, so a no-excuses car is well worth waiting for. ♦

1971 Jaguar E-type SII

Buying the E-type That's Right for You

They're not as temperamental as you've been led to believe, and a right car can be a reliable and rewarding driver

by Rob Sass

1962 Series I 3.8 coupe

Jaguar E-types are nearly everyone's favorite British sports car to look at, but as regular daily drivers, let's just say they're "misunderstood." While we've all heard the same thing said about pit bulls and the angsty motorcycle-riding kid who wants to date your daughter, in the case of certain versions of the E-type, it really is true. They're not as temperamental as you've been led to believe. A right car can offer a reliable and rewarding experience, both as practical transportation and as a rolling piece of collectible art.

Series I (1961–67)

The Series I E-types are the purest and prettiest cars of the lot. Distinguished by dainty bumpers, Plexiglas-covered headlights, small, above-the-rear-bumper taillights, and cool toggle switches on the dash, 3.8-liter cars (1961–64) were confounded by uncomfortable seats, mediocre brakes, and a devilish Moss gearbox with no first-gear synchromesh. Later (1965–67) cars gained an all-synchro box and better brakes but were still hampered by overheating in traffic, hot cockpits

with no a/c, and generally suspect items like alternators and fuel pumps made by Lucas and SU, respectively.

Body styles were convertible ("OTS" or "Open Two-Seater" in Jag-speak); coupe ("FHC" for Fixed Head Coupe) and 2+2. OTS cars are the most desirable, followed by the prettier FHC. 2+2s are largely unloved even in Series I form, since the longer wheelbase and roofline compromise the looks of the car. It doesn't help that a large percentage of these cars were also automatics.

Weak spots like the aforementioned fuel pump and alternator can be fixed by upgrading to modern items, including a Delco single-wire alternator conversion. An aluminum radiator and a large electric fan will cure the car's tendency to overheat in traffic (trust me, I know).

Series I½ (1968)

Not officially recognized by the factory as a separate series, the I½ was really an interim model that made way for the definitive Series II of 1969. In late 1967, the E-type lost its signature headlamp covers to U.S. headlight laws. Additionally,

1968 SI½ OTS

1969 SII coupe

in spite of no documented case of impalement by dashboard switches, the E dash became blander with the substitution of safety rocker switches for the toggles. Most significantly, the car lost its third carburetor and about 20 hp.

Series I½ cars can be a bargain in comparison to Series I cars. From a style standpoint, they're nowhere near as compromised as the Series II or Series III cars. With the exception of the dash switches, a committed owner could add most of the Series I bits like headlamp covers and three SU carburetors, and kits are available.

Series II (1969–71)

Series II represented the first major stylistic changes to the E-type. None was for the better. Bumpers grew, the recently uncovered headlights were pushed forward, the air intake was enlarged and tail lights were moved underneath the car. Still, all was not bad, as the changes made the E-type easier to live with and more fun to drive.

The massive new air intake forced enough air through the radiator to keep things cool while underway. The dual fan system helped keep the cars from overheating in traffic. More effective brake calipers and the addition of power steering and a/c made these among the most livable E-types. All three body styles outlined above were available in Series II form.

Series III (1971–74)

With the SIII, the Jaguar reputation for unreliability began in earnest. These were complex and none too well-assembled cars, with many of their flaws directly related to poorly thought out and meagerly funded responses to U.S. smog and safety regulations. Consequently, they are generally regarded as the most troublesome

of E-types. Indeed, one look under the bonnet with its miles of vacuum tubing is generally enough to scare someone into a 6-cylinder car—and they'll be grateful later.

Only the convertible (roadster) and 2+2 were offered in Series III form, and the convertible was built on the 2+2 chassis so it looked quite elongated, as well as awkward. An oversized, unattractive grille and fender flares did nothing for Malcom Sayer's original design.

Still, if you simply must have a V12 performance car, Jags certainly don't cost Ferrari money—either to buy or to maintain—and by virtue of their being E-types, they're welcome at nearly every event their more svelte predecessors are.

In conclusion, when the E-type first made its appearance, it was a superior car for its era. Over the years, the mechanical shortcomings it exhibited have been addressed by modern technology. If I were to rank these cars on a combination of style and reliability, the Series II would come first, the Series I second, and the Series III a reluctant last choice, only because their emission controls continue to be confounding and the number of specialists qualified to work on them dwindling. ♦

1973 SIII OTS

How Provenance Can Add 50% to the Price

This 1961 Aston Martin DB4 Series III was an exceptionally original car with a freshness that newly restored cars can lack

by Stephen Serio

Chassis number: DB4621L. Historical and condition introduction by the auction company.

The car pictured here is a DB4 Series III Aston Martin, which differs from the previous two series due to a better oil cooling system, including a bigger sump. The car condition is as exceptional as its history. On September 30, 1958, its future and sole owner, Mr. Claude Rouzaud, was invited by David Brown and Marcel Blondeau (the French importer) to the introduction of the new DB4 at the Garage Mirabeau, 71 Avenue de Versailles, in Paris.

On that very day, Claude Rouzaud was convinced by what he had seen and driven. While testing a DB4 belonging to the Garage Mirabeau, he found a four-leaf clover, which he carefully kept in a small envelope that is still clamped in the owner's manual.

Recognizing the qualities of the car, he ordered from the Garage Mirabeau a black DB4 with beige leather interior. This car, DB4621L, was delivered on March 28, 1961, and registered 6010 KZ 75 on April 7. More than 47 years later, this car is still the property of Mr. and Mrs. Rouzaud.

An Aston Martin is in any case a splendid automobile. The fact that this is a first-hand car with a well-documented history makes it highly desirable. What more can be said about a car that adds to these features an exceptional original and almost-new condition? The finish, the chrome-plated parts, and the light patina of the leatherwork are all proof of the good life enjoyed by the car, which shows a fresh condition that even many newly restored cars are lacking.

This DB4 had been overhauled recently, with new brakes and new stainless steel exhaust. It works very well, does not overheat, and shows good oil pressure. The steering wheel and gearshift show no wear.

It will be delivered with its owner's manual, tool set, and spare wheel, along with some documents, many of them coming from Aston Martin and signed by David Brown.

This is a rare opportunity to acquire such a superb Aston Martin and perhaps a unique one.

SCM Analysis *This car sold for $464,963 on February 9, 2008, at Artcurial's annual Paris sale.*

Visiting Rétromobile and the two coinciding auctions to perhaps gather some inventory was ultimately just a pipe dream. The nights were better spent dining out than in trying to buy an Aston Martin, as it turns out.

Hoping to score this car, lot 21, at the Artcurial auction was a real schooling in today's collector car climate. The combination of a weak dollar and rabid interest in original one-owner cars worldwide meant the car was completely unattainable at a price that would enable any dealer to remarket it. It set a record by a significant margin and blew the roof off the catalog estimate. Nevertheless, I say it was well bought.

Documents are all-important

The DB4 seemed unremarkable at first

Upon first inspection, this Series III DB4 seemed unremarkable on every level. I also admit that I hadn't yet read the catalog description (even with its quirky English translation), so I really didn't know what to expect, and I didn't know it was a one-owner car.

The car had very little visual "pop," plus the auction room was crammed with inventory; these cars were not displayed with any great forethought. Upon cursory inspection I noticed just the negative side. The original paint was dull, the steering wheel was from a DB2/4 Mk III (I'd have to see the build sheet to know if it was ordered as such), somehow DB5 Selectaride (just a bad idea) was added, two nasty non-original chrome strips were fitted to the rockers below the doors, the bumpers were pitted, two dings pocked the passenger door, and the whole thing needed detailing. And what's with the little hand-painted triangle on the doors? But like a little kid in a toy store, I was hooked.

With Tom Papadopoulos from Autosport Designs as my wingman, we agreed on one thing—it looked like an honest car. More a quiet golf clap than resounding approval.

Being a Series III car, it is arguably the red-headed stepchild of the five DB4 Series; it's neither fish nor fowl for looks. In 22 years, no one has ever asked me for a Series III car specifically. To me, that signifies something in the Aston Martin world. Series I and II cars are in many ways purer looking, and the later Series IV and V cars benefit from covered headlights or triple carb set-ups, or simply from being the much cooler Vantage version. The Series III is a bit of a yawn in my view, but nonetheless something kept grabbing me about the car.

I slowed down and took a long, hard look

I think it was my third pass when I slowed down and had a long, quiet look. It finally struck me that the whole ride was really original and unrestored (I blame jet lag for not picking up on this). The nose was perfect, the chassis unmolested, and the interior possessed that glorious old Connolly leather smell that cannot be replicated. The underside of the rear seat had the original chalk marks, the engine retained the original red paint around the serial number, the tools were all there, the manual was like new, it had warranty paperwork, the Avon Turbospeeds looked 30 years old, there was Indian jute under the carpet and trunk mat, and so on and so forth. Nice.

So mental midgets Tom and I happily concluded that it "could be" a $300,000 car back home. Hmmmm... let's try to buy it. What a laugh that turned out to be. I came, I nodded, I left empty handed, mon ami.

Suffice to say that the French auction arena that night may as well have been the bar scene from "Star Wars" compared to anything we were used to back home. The crowd was lifeless, the auctioneer incomprehensible, the auditorium was 98 degrees and getting warmer, and we weren't witnessing any real crazy numbers on the lots that were selling (we were foolishly lulled into thinking the French weren't paying attention).

And what about the bidding?

What really puzzled us was how folks were bidding. It was beyond subtle. A guide dog, night-vision goggles, and a Black Beret sniper would sure have been helpful. Okay, here comes lot 21. How do we get the auctioneer's attention? No need... this was a spirited lot, and the bidding exceeded by 50% any number we thought was sensible. $463,000! Sacre bleu! A minute later it was over, except for our slack-jawed reaction.

Our red-headed stepchild was the darling of the evening. However, this one sale does not constitute the re-jiggering of price guides. This anomaly can be explained easily. Savvy collectors are willing to chase down and pay for the car that is original only once.

In my (occasionally) humble opinion, I truly believe there is no price guide for something that has few or no peers with regard to originality.

If originality appeals to you—and the trend has gotten a lot stronger for that—you have to pay up, as someone is right there bidding with you and waiting for you to hiccup. Your other option is to go find another one at the used car factory. Good luck with that.

The DB4 that struck me as incredibly unremarkable was in fact "amazingly remarkable." To the new owner, I say well done. ♦

Entry-Level 365 and 911 Porsches

A 356 will provide maximum "style points" for the money, but an early 911 considerabley widens your choices

by Jim Schrager

1962 Porsche 356B T-6 coupe

Twenty thousand bucks doesn't seem to go far today, especially in our hot vintage market. After all, with Healeys at $60,000 and even some MG Bs hitting $30,000, how could you expect to buy an obviously superior car (at least in my opinion) for such a small amount? But you can. My picks balance the issues of appreciation potential, maintenance hassle, and ease of purchase. All the choices below offer excellent driving potential, as one of the great secrets of the vintage Porsche world is that these old cars, when you are behind the wheel, don't feel nearly as old as they really are.

The T-6 356B

My choice in a 356 for under $20,000 would be the best 1962–63 B coupe I could find. This model is the final body design for the 356 (the "T-6") and one of the better bargains. Values are quite stable, and a decent #2 car will just make our budget. It won't be perfect, but should have no big flaws, like significant rust, a noisy engine, or a clapped-out interior.

A 356 will provide the maximum "style points" for your

money. They are old and rare enough to attract lots of attention, as well as an almost unending supply of smiles and friendly questions. However, 356s do require a reasonable level of mechanical attentiveness. This is not to say they are fussy, as when new they were very reliable and still can be. But many 356s have been bodged over the years, and the result is often a poor-running and semi-reliable drivetrain. Unless you are highly knowledgeable, you'll need to find a wrench who knows 356s.

In the plus column for a 356 is one of the largest and most active model-specific clubs anywhere, the Porsche 356 Registry (for which I also write). They maintain a "talk list" that provides instant Internet access to a host of talented 356 folks. Visit their site at www.356registry.org; you don't need a 356 to join the club or the talk list. A good 356 is also an easy car to sell, with many people looking to enjoy its many virtues.

The early 911s

An early 911 (1965–73) is the other option. These provide a different set of trade-offs from the 356 and considerably widen your choices. For starters, you can still get an open car, the Targa. This is no longer possible in a 356, where a drivable but lousy open 356 starts at about $35,000. In addition, the mechanical sophistication and substantial performance increase of the 911 make this a rather different breed than the charming but old-technology 356.

The early 911 world splits into two factions—the original, short-wheelbase cars from 1965 to 1968, and the significantly improved long-wheelbase 911s from 1969 to 1973. For a first 911, unless you find a very nice SWB car at an excellent price, I'd advise you to get a LWB. Porsche made numerous improvements in 1969 that make owning a used one a generally lower-cost and much happier event. Not only did the longer wheelbase improve the car's handling, the drivetrain, body and interior were improved in many large and small ways.

You might be able to locate a sunroof coupe for under $20,000, but Targas are much easier to find. You won't have quite the rock-solid integrity of the coupe, but the trade-off for open-air motoring is worth it to many owners. In general, Targas cost about the same as coupes (other than the rare soft-rear window Targas, built mostly on the early short wheelbase cars, which command a premium).

The good news is that any well-sorted 911 is a great car to drive, and most are quite easy to make right. The engineering on the 911 engine and transmission are so far advanced over the 356 (and the 356-engined 912) that 911s can exist as sunny day cars almost forever. On 1969 and later cars, the main mechanical upgrade is Carrera-style chain tensioners. If the car you are looking at has these, there is a good chance the car has had good care.

Values

A 911, if selected carefully, will have every bit as much resale potential as a 356 coupe. But you'll have to move quickly—while 356 coupe values are well established and quite stable, early 911 prices have moved sharply in the last few years and seem destined to continue upward.

911 values are quite sensitive to model designation, unlike the 356s, where engine output has just a modest effect. A 911S can be worth twice what a 911T will bring, but most 911S cars will be out of your price range anyway. Don't despair, however, as the 911T or the mid-range 911E are great cars to drive, with their torquey engines and less-fussy specifications. You should find a decent 911T starting at about $15,000, with Es a few thousand more.

Style, performance, and options

For style points, the 911 is a much more familiar shape than the 356, although these early 911s have bright trim and quite different details than later cars. A good technician is always helpful for a 911, but the big difference, when compared to a 356, is the smaller chance that the 911 has been hacked together with non-original drivetrain pieces like Chinese-made pistons and cylinder sets, improper crankshafts, and incorrect carbs. The performance envelope of the 911 is a big step up from the 356, although those with both early 911 and 356 cars often report their 356s remain great fun to drive, within their own modest performance window. The 911 provides many more options as to road wheels (painted steel, chrome, Fuchs forged alloys in varying widths, Mahles and ATS cast wheels, just to name the stock offerings), modern radios, sports seats, and so on.

Under $20,000, you'll find a selection of 356 and 911 Porsches that will be fun to drive, reliable, and have good appreciation potential. You'll be entering an area of the Porsche hobby that is very active with plenty of fellow travelers. As far as fun for your dollar, these entry-level vintage Porsches can be one of the real sweet spots of the old-car hobby. ♦

1967 Porsche 911

Six Porsches That Are on an Upward Trend

Not every Porsche is going to the moon, but original-condition cars can still set records

by Jim Schrager

1957 Porsche 356A Speedster

1958 Porsche 356A Coupe

After a wild ride in Arizona in January 2006, there was little doubt we were in high times in the Porsche market. Few people remember bigger prices, including the dramatic and traumatic 1989–90 period. For some models, even vintage accessories have become unavailable, such as chrome horn rings for the 356B/C cars, Recaro Sport Seats for the 1967–73 911 cars, and the previously fairly common Les Leston wood steering wheels.

My favorite bit of nonsense I heard around the bar was that this time it was different because these were enthusiasts buying. Really? If it was an enthusiast who paid $135,000 for a decent but not special 356A Cabriolet, or $48,000 for an average 356B coupe, they had to be the most uninformed enthusiasts I'd ever heard of.

I'm not sure what to call these trend-setters, but because of their glorious ignorance of market prices, something most dyed-in-the-wool collectors are acutely aware of, the term enthusiast doesn't readily come to mind. For sure they've never read a single copy of the 356 Registry Magazine or SCM.

Yet not every special Porsche went to the moon, and even those moving up are doing so at differing rates. Here are a few bellwether examples in the current market.

1956–58 356A Speedsters

No report on the Porsche market can be complete without an update on the 356 icon. These cars are doing well,

with really special cars now topping $175,000, but they have slowed down a bit. Pre-A Speedsters, 1954–56, tend to bring less money due to their more fragile and lower-performance drivetrains and less-than-modern handling.

Speedsters are not rare, with over 4,000 built, so the acceleration of prices speaks of a broad increase in demand. Decent drivers that were $50,000–$60,000 five years ago now can reach $100,000. But the air gets pretty thin for six-figure Speedsters, and such a car needs to be an awfully nice example. We have seen the heady increases of the past few years slowing down in step with the depreciation of the Euro, which appeared to be driving much of the buying power.

1956–59 356A Coupes

These went wild a few years ago and special cars topped $55,000, but they have not continued to accelerate. They are far more numerous than Speedsters, and while original-condition cars can still set records, more common nice examples have tailed off, although prices have not dropped. Call this one sideways.

1973–76 914 2.0 Roadsters

As we have reported, these have been moving up nicely, although from a very low starting point. It takes about $8,000 to buy a very nice car, defined as one without chassis or body rust, with good cosmetics and a decent interior. Subtract about

1973 Porsche 914 2.0

1973 Porsche Carrera RS

$2,000 if the car has lost its fuel injection. 914s with carbs are far easier to maintain, but rarely run as strong.

The biggest shocker when you drive a good 914 2.0 is how much fun they are. It's not a 911, but they feel light, peppy, and nimble, in the best tradition of the 356 and 912 cars.

1969–73 911T Coupes and Targas

Over the ten years we have been writing about 911T values, our target for a decent car has slowly risen, from about $10,000 to $12,000, and now we set the bar at $20,000, which still buys a "decent" 911T of this vintage. By decent I don't mean a car to drive across the county or a show winner. But I mean a solid used car that you can enjoy with no fatal flaws such as substantial rust, a smoky engine, or a trashed interior.

The bigger price movements have been in the low-mileage, original 911T cars. It was unusual to see one of these sell in the low $20,000s five years ago, but today asking prices can reach $30,000 and even higher. To qualify for this price level they must have proof of low mileage beyond the odometer reading and original carpets, seats, and paint.

1973 Carrera RS (Touring)

These were the first 911s to shoot up into the stratosphere above $100,000, and exceptional cars continue to bring well into six figures, which is quite amazing for a used 911. Although far rarer than a Speedster, with about 1,500 built, these aren't a 904 (with 120 built). Prices have slowed down this year, but

have not fallen. This remains a seller's market not driven by the Euro, as most buyers are anxious U.S. enthusiasts.

Carrera GT

This is the highest performance street Porsche ever built. The car has powerful allure—many stars have one, and Jay Leno drove one to a new world record for a street-legal car. The design is breathtakingly beautiful and the finish quality, level of craftsmanship, and ultimate performance would make any 904 owner blush with envy. Yet Porsche had such difficulty selling the planned run of 1,500 that the production target has been lowered to 1,250.

Prices are soft on the exceptional supercar. How can this be, when 1,500 1973 Carrera RS cars were sold new without even trying? We tend to forget that everything, including exotic cars, has a price/volume relationship. The Carrera GT is the first production Porsche to sell at approximately five times the going rate for a standard 911. All earlier special Porsches sold at perhaps double production car prices.

Porsche discovered—as has Ford with the Ford GT—a car priced far above the standard price envelope for your marque makes demand very hard to estimate. If you're curious how strong the effect is, visit www.FordGTprices.com for a lively discussion of the effects of supply and demand on limited-production exotic GT cars.

And in the meantime, don't plan on making a killing with a quick flip on a Carrera GT. ♦

1973 Porsche 911T

Porsche Carrera GT

Five Porsches to Avoid

Remember, if you can't afford a good example of your favorite model, you REALLY can't afford a bad one

by Jim Schrager

What lurks beneath the rear hatch?

Excruciating tuition bills from the school of hard knocks have taught me that, no matter how fond I am of the cars from Stuttgart, some Porsches are best left unbought. Here's a rundown of those you should stay away from, lest you endanger your financial and mental health.

1. A 912 with a bad motor

I was recently called in to consult on the purchase of a 1967 912 that was for sale on eBay with a claimed "good" motor that just hadn't run in years. Of course, it was about as far from "good" as you can get; it was locked up solid. I wasn't surprised, as 912s far too often have major engine problems that are unable to be solved by simple tune-ups.

There are always those who have the "perfect" solution to this problem. Among the cars I've recently called on was a 1966 912 with a "funny noise" coming from the engine. It was a rust-free California car painted an incorrect color; the seller was asking $6,000. He was quick to volunteer that new big-bore kits were available for $300 and most any VW mechanic could easily rebuild the motor.

Longtime readers know where I stand on this sort of pseudo hot-rod modification. Not only do these cheapo rebuilds offend my sensibilities as a purist, but they usually result in a poorly performing engine that's impossible to keep in a correct state of tune. The result here is always the same: a largely undesirable car that doesn't drive like a vintage Porsche should.

When new, 912s were great. They were a real bargain, giving their owners much of the 911 experience at a 35% discount. But today, rebuilding a 912 engine to original standards with no excuses is about an $8,000 affair. When the values for these cars are going to top out at $7,000 for a nice #2, you just don't have any room left to work.

2. A 911 with a rusty chassis

I'm not a big fan of 911s with any rust at all. But if it's isolated in the front suspension pan area, it can be repaired for about $2,000 and you can still have a solid car. Rust at the rear of a 911 is a different matter. This is anything but easy to repair—if it can be done at all—and is often the talisman of a chassis that's beyond hope.

While the aficionados will say that Stoddard Porsche (www.stoddard.com) now sells special repair panels for the rear chassis, I would still be wary of undertaking such major surgery. If the car is a 911S in good colors with its original MFI engine, it's probably worth doing. Even so, this will be a long and painful journey. Unless you know your stuff, it's best to keep looking.

Lest you not believe me, here's an example of what you can expect. A local Porsche friend bought a 1971 911E, in the great period color of Signal Orange, for the modest sum of $4,800. (And yes, it ran.) There was just one slight prob-

Rust? What rust?

Beware the 944 with a bad engine

fun with it. Don't make an already tough job even harder by buying one with fake plastic bodywork. These cars just don't appeal to the hardcore Porsche folks, who tend to be more interested in finesse than flash, elegant engineering instead of raw horsepower.

A local dentist called me recently, desperately wanting to buy a 993 Turbo that was complete with Strosek bodywork, the full package that included tiny projector headlights. He was singing the praises of this machine, with its 600 hp and all the "fantastic" (his word) bodywork. At $125,000, he thought it was the bargain of a lifetime.

lem: The rear end had collapsed. Upon further inspection, it was clear that the rear torsion bar console had rusted through. Checkbook in hand, he started on his quest.

About $8,000 later, he had a $6,000 car on his hands. After he fixed the chassis, the rest of the car also needed work. After more than three tough years of trying to get the rust repair and chassis work correctly completed and the engine rebuilt due to its significant oil leaks, he cut his losses and sold the car for $6,000.

I took a look at the car, and I think the only original panel was the roof. I advised the would-be buyer to put away his checkbook and wait awhile. Sure enough, six months later the car was still for sale, at the radically reduced price of $85,000. I still think that's too much.

My rule on these cars is take the same car in stock configuration and subtract 25% for all the body mods. That means I'd value this one at about $50,000.

3. A 944 with a blown engine

Because 944 owners are often maintenance-averse, it's fairly common to find these cars with blown engines. This usually happens when their rubber-composite timing belts snap, unleashing an ugly cacophony of valves smashing into pistons.

Sure, these cars are dirt-cheap, and you can source another engine or even rebuild the one in the chassis. But resist the urge and buy a better car instead. The expense of getting and installing a new engine far outweighs the ease of simply buying a different 944. I recently saw a decent 1987 944 with good maintenance records trade hands for $3,000. They are both plentiful and inexpensive enough that a project 944 is only a good idea if you're extremely bored or someone gives you a couple of free cars.

5. All 924 Turbos

Turbo 924s don't rust, but that's cold comfort when it's parked at the end of your driveway, immobile. Any 924 is a troubled machine, but when you bolt a slapped-together turbocharger on that agricultural engine, you have a match made for masochists.

The truth is, these cars don't run for long. You may find a beautiful, low-mileage example, but I'll guess it's mostly because none of them racked up too many miles before trouble set in. This model is truly one of Porsche's darkest moments, a car to avoid even if you're given one as a gift. ♦

4. A fakey-doo 930

It's a Herculean task to sell a stock 930 once you've had your

924 Turbo—just walk away

Uh, sure it's a 930

Buying Your First Muscle Car

If renting a new Shelby for the weekend is a fling, buying a vintage muscle car is like getting married—for better or worse. Read on before saying "I do"

by John L. Stein

1971 Dodge Challenger

The attraction is undeniable: A rumbling V8 engine, decisive and unabashed styling, and an exciting and useful connection to simpler, braver times. Muscle cars of the 1950s through 1970s remain as alluring and compelling as rock music of the same era, but what should the newcomer buy – and where do you begin looking? Herewith, Sports Car Market's essential guide for first-time muscle-car buyers.

Authenticity first

Before answering an ad for a muscle car, or pursuing one online, get yourself mobilized—through friends, colleagues or a marque expert—to learn whether what you're looking at is real or an artful hoax. For instance, was that '62 Corvette fuelie really a fuelie from day one, or were its fuel injection and emblems added later? All that glitters is not necessarily gold.

Establishing authenticity is important because:
- You should get your money's worth when you buy
- You will derive more enjoyment, in both physical and emotional ways, from a "real" car than a fake
- A real McCoy is more worth maintaining and improving
- In an appreciating market, a real car will appreciate more than a clone
- It will also hold its value better in down times
- When it's time to sell, you can tell the truth rather than continuing a lie

The surest way of guaranteeing authenticity is an accurate paper trail, starting with the original dealer invoice and window sticker, build sheet, MSO, or whatever else came with the car in question. Service and mileage records can verify total mileage as well as establish the ownership history. Following up with previous owners by phone can add further assurance, but such dialogs aren't bankable like cold, hard paperwork.

Look for good bones

Top of the ladder is an original, unrestored, low-mileage, garaged vehicle. Unfortunately the term "original" is as meaningless today as a politician's promise, but it should mean "unmodified since new, with the exact same paint, interior, chrome and drivetrain that was installed at the factory—and no other!" I would rather buy a completely original car that's running, straight, and presentable than a shiny but hurried restoration.

Regardless of condition, you should create a worksheet and move around the car, recording your findings as you go. This is important for several reasons. Your discovery process may reveal items that need fixing down the road, and these faults can be used to negotiate a better deal with the seller. A close inspection will likewise help you determine whether the car has been expertly maintained or restored, or whether it's received only minimal attention.

Examining hard-to-reach areas can help determine the seller's true commitment to the vehicle. Put the car on a lift to see the cleanliness and quality of the undercarriage, exhaust, and suspension systems. A quick-and-dirty restoration usually won't pay much attention to out-of-the-way places. A good light source—and your reading glasses—can also reveal excellence or disrepute in the door openings, and underneath carpeting, fenders, and instrument panel. Be mindful of the quality of any restoration parts used, including replacement upholstery and carpeting and trim. Done cheaply, a claimed "concours restoration" may look little better than a cheap hooker up close.

Beside a frame-bending wreck, tin-worm is a muscle car's worst enemy. While it's possible to repair a rust-invested mess, do you really want to? It's one thing if you're dealing with a desirably optioned car or maybe your uncle Herb's actual '71 Challenger convertible which, when restored, would bring years of enjoyment and meaning to the family. But if it's just any '71 Challenger you're after, you're way ahead to pay fairly for a good car than to buy a cheap roach and then pay to restore it.

Audit the powertrain

A muscle car advertised as "numbers matching" may mean that the engine block and body VIN tag have matching numbers, but that's only half the battle. In many cases the cylinder heads, transmission, and differential cases, along with other components, should be correct for the year and model. This may not matter to you now, but when the time comes to sell, it may matter a lot to the guy writing you a check. A marque expert or competent book or web site will provide valuable guidance here. If an engine rebuild has been done, review the associated paperwork to determine the build quality—and note how many miles or years are on the new components.

Where to buy

The high-shine world of auctions is a good test for the strength of different market segments, and auctions do tend to attract desirable vehicles. However, auction catalogs often deliver lots of implied information that, when read critically, actually reveal very little about the car. Do your homework up front, inspect the car with a wary eye, and then set a price cap before bidding starts. Know your limit—and then stick with it.

EBay auctions are even more of a double-edged sword, because personally inspecting the vehicle is more difficult. If you can't go see the car, you'll be money ahead by finding an ally do it for you before you bid. Also, consider the seller's feedback heavily.

At day's end, your best chance to fully learn about any target car is through a private-party sale, or else via a broker who knows the car and seller. In this case, you also have the opportunity to negotiate, something that auctions don't allow—at least on the car's first trip across the block at an event.

Every experienced restorer, owner, or horse trader has probably learned a few "run away if" lessons the hard way. Here are a few common ones that clear thinking and forethought can help you avoid. Run away if:

- It's an unrestored, needs-everything barn find of a plentiful model
- There is evidence of substantial rust
- It's a half-finished project, with bits in boxes, and no guarantee that all the boxes are present
- Money has not been spent consistently in all areas
- Restoration work or replacement parts look cheap
- The seller cannot prove what model the car is and what options it originally had
- It hasn't been driven in many years
- The paperwork seems fishy

Follow these guidelines and you should enjoy years of fun. The worst decisions make the best stories later, but make sure you're roaring with laughter in the audience and not the storyteller. ♦

How to Buy the Best Cobra and Tiger

Read and study the registries of these cars and check with the clubs. Some have led very hard lives

by Colin Comer

427 Cobra

A s the rumble of Shelby auctions in Arizona and elsewhere fades away, it's time to look again at the Cobra market and include the underdog Sunbeam Tiger. The original CSX2000 leaf-spring 260-ci and 289-ci Cobras have shown enormous strength in the past five years. Prices seemingly vapor-locked in low six-figures are roughly $400,000 now.

With 515 "street" cars produced, these have always been desirable, but nowhere near as exclusive as a 250 GTO. However, few cars have captured the magic of the original wire-wheel, slab-sided Cobra.

Looking for drivers

While an admittedly crude creation, Shelby managed to combine the automotive equivalent of oil and water. This reason—along with the recent trend of collectors wanting cars they can drive—has sent leaf-spring Cobra prices to their current level.

I love leaf-spring Cobras, and will never be without one. They are usable, beautiful, and dead simple to maintain—all

with parts from your local NAPA outlet. But the best part is that nobody will ever mistake a leaf-spring Cobra for a "kit car." I think this contributes to the recent price surge.

Now for the big dog—the romping, stomping, CSX3000 427 Cobras—also known as the coil-spring cars. Always at the top of collectors' lists, they are far scarcer than the leaf-spring cars with just 260 "street" cars produced.

But while values have doubled from $300,000 five years ago to roughly $600,000 today, the 427 cars have not experienced the proportional increase of the earlier cars. A number of factors contribute to this: historically 427s have been twice as much as the leaf-spring cars, and buyers perhaps gravitated to the less-expensive car as an alternative.

While one cannot deny the pure automotive swagger of a 427, it has to contend with being the most replicated car of all time. The sheer number of 427 Cobra replicas—good, bad, and ugly—has weakened the market for original cars.

Shelby himself diluted the number of buyers by offering the new 4000 series Continuation cars, a very accurate replica of the originals. At roughly $100,000 for a Shelby-blessed

CSX4000 car, I'm guessing many people opted to go this route even though they could buy the real deal. As an original 427 Cobra owner, I contend there is no substitute, and I'm sure other purists agree.

Shelby's stepchild

The red-headed stepchild of the Shelby world is unquestionably the Sunbeam Tiger. It was produced by the Rootes Group in England when Ian Garrard hired Carroll Shelby to transform the anemic Sunbeam Alpine into a performance car.

Tiger, the Shelby stepchild

The addition of the 260-ci Ford V8 (similar to the Cobra, but the two-barrel, 164-hp version) made a car worthy of being called "Tiger"—after the 1926 Sunbeam land-speed record holder.

Never intended to be a stark sports car like the Cobra, the Tiger is a highly competent touring car. Fitted with a standard 2.88:1 rear axle ratio and BorgWarner T-10 4-speed, it's a relaxed and capable high-speed machine with better than 125 mph on tap.

Tigers aren't particularly rare, with over 7,000 produced from 1964 to 1967, but they've always had a loyal following. Production was split into three groups, consisting of 3,763 Mk I cars, 2,706 Mk IA cars, and 534 289-ci Mk II cars.

The problems with Tigers are modifications and abuse. Finding a stock Tiger that hasn't rusted out or been cobbled into an unrecognizable form is a challenge.

This makes it difficult to pin down an exact market value for an "SCM Approved" stock Tiger, as few of them change hands. I purchased a fantastic Mk IA example in the late 1990s for $11,000 and a one-owner Mk IA in similar condition in 2000 for $25,000, then a record price. The prevailing market today for a spectacular Mk I car is roughly $30,000 with a similar IA bringing $5,000–$10,000 over that.

The Mk II market is more difficult to peg. I've only seen six Mk II cars sell in the last ten years, and only one was spectacular. OK, I bought it, paying an out-of-the park record price of $59,000 on eBay Motors (item #4625301384).

I saw value in stepping up for a true 100% original, untouched, example of a Mk II—and I have since spent roughly $5,000 doing "might as well" maintenance and detailing. I don't regret it; these cars cost pennies on the dollar against anything else as interesting. I consider a great Tiger a solid buy.

What to look for

Buy the best Cobra you can find. Thanks to the *Shelby American World Registry*, details of every individual car's history are available. Production differences abound, so know what you are buying. Check for worm-and-sector or rack-and-pinion steering, and 260-ci or 289-ci engines. By the way, did you know 100 or so "427" Cobras left the factory with 428 engines?

Read and study the *Registry*, and before buying a car, join the club and contact Ned Scudder, Cobra Registrar, to ask if any new information is known about a particular car. Many Cobras led difficult lives, but seem to have more than the average cat. New bodies, new frames—some new cars have been built around little more than a serial number plate. So do your homework.

What might seem insignificant in the red-mist, pre-purchase euphoria can be a huge issue after your check clears. Paying a world-record price may get you teased, but not as much as if you buy a pig in a poke.

Tiger buyers have a more tedious path. Many cars have been cloned using the Alpine shells, and the resulting "Algers" are not always easy to spot. Specific details can help authenticate a real car, beyond VIN tags and data plates. The International Registry of Sunbeam Tigers is available online, as is the Sunbeam Tigers Owners Association (STOA) and their current list of "TAC'ed" (Tiger Authentication Committee) verified cars.

A few hours using Google to track down Tiger details may avoid a red face later. Another resource is the out-of-print *Book of Norman* by Tiger guru Norman Miller. It contains the complete list of original Tiger VINs and production details.

Where are they heading?

Since my crystal ball fell off the bookshelf and broke, I look back to predict market trends. Historically, leaf-spring Cobras have traded at about one-half coil-spring Cobra values. Demand for the leaf-spring cars far outstrips supply, leading me to predict great examples will be $500,000 in the near future.

Following this, the 427 cars will be next. Tiger values have been on a steady upswing for some time, as educated buyers seek out great examples. I see no reason that a 20% annual appreciation won't continue.

The bottom line is find the right car, make sure it *is* a right car, and buy it because you want it. Use it, enjoy it, and rest easy knowing that truly fine examples offer greater rewards to their owners than mere financial ones.♦

Nine Muscle Car Sleepers

Offering performance and a style all their own, these unsung muscle cars are heroes waiting to happen—and often at an affordable price

by John L. Stein

1975 Corvette

L ike the red-hot date possibilities for prom night, all the truly desirable muscle cars were laser-locked a long time ago, and their prices have soared accordingly. Mopar hemis, Corvette fuelies and big-blocks, and anything wearing Shelby badges quickly lunged to the top of the heap, with a long list of people constantly waiting to snap them up.

But lurking in the underbrush below these image leaders are plenty of second-tier muscle cars that have largely missed earning mainstream appeal. Offering style, performance and a certain *joie de vivre* all their own, these unsung muscle cars are heroes waiting to happen—and often at an affordable

price. Here are nine of them for your consideration. Like the Apple computer slogan says, "Think different."

1975 Chevrolet Corvette

Although it represents the low point of Corvette's horsepower rating, the 1975 model escapes smog inspections in California, which means you can reanimate it. Shunned by hard-line Corvette collectors thanks to its vinyl-skinned baby bumpers and underachieving 165-hp, 350-ci engine, these can be found relatively cheaply. Double the horsepower with a smart rebuild and find one with a paint code that doesn't make you gag (silver looks good), and you've got a winner

1960 Galaxie Sunliner

1965 Ford Mustang coupe

on a budget of $8,000 to $20,000. An additional attraction is that the '75 model was also the last Corvette convertible until 1986.

1962 Chrysler Newport

The two-door '62 Chrysler Newport coupe can still be bought for $2,500 to $15,000 tops, despite sharing under-pinnings with the vaunted 1961 Chrysler 300G, only with a smaller 265-hp, 361-ci V8 and no tailfins. The letter-series cars' other best features remain, including Chrysler's superb amphitheater-style instrument panel, "typewriter" transmission controls, and cantilevered headlights.

1960 Ford Galaxie

With gun sights on the front fenders, a "greenhouse" glass canopy, dramatic horizontal tailfins, and an Interceptor engine underhood, the 1960 Ford Galaxie was a stylish sleeper. A NASCAR racer back in the day and now a favorite of rat rod guys, the long and low Galaxie (and its cousin the drop top Sunliner) looks a bit like a lead sled even in stock condition.

1966 Barracuda

1969 AMC AMX

But nicely finished, it's a head turner with performance potential to match. Figure $5,000 to $15,000 for a solid car.

1964½–1966 Ford Mustang Coupe

Ford built over one million Mustangs in the first 18 months, and compared to the fastback and convertible, the notchback coupe was the homely sister. But while the fastback went to war against Cobras and Sting Rays in SCCA B Production, only the notchback got to race in the legendary Trans-Am championship when it began in 1966. In fact, one of the best-known of those racers actually began life as a lowly 6-cylinder model, the cheapest Mustang available at the time. Target one of the 260-ci or 289-ci V8 versions for better value (and resale value), and $2,500 to $15,000 will get you a respectable performer on a beer budget.

1964–66 Plymouth Barracuda

Generally ignored, the first-generation Barracuda has the makings of a muscle car—decisive and unique looks, available 235-hp, 273-ci V8 power, and legendary Mopar lineage. Historians will recall the wheel-standing Hemi Under Glass exhibition cars that frequented drag strips during the day. At $2,500 to $15,000, Barracudas sell well under other pony cars.

1968–70 American Motors AMX

For years American Motors was the black sheep of the U.S. auto industry, earning perennial ignominy for models like the Gremlin and Pacer. Fortunately for enthusiasts, however, there was also the 1968–70 AMX. Beautifully styled and motivated by a potent 315-hp 390-ci big block, then and now the AMX is a head turner and crowd pleaser—especially in its signature Big Bad Orange color. What's more, with AMC backing, Craig Breedlove set 106 speed records just prior to the car's introduction. Though coveted by AMC freaks, at $22,000 to $27,500 the AMX costs only a fraction of what some Camaros bring today.

1964–66 Dodge Dart

During the muscle car era, driving a Dodge Dart would pretty much brand you as a nerd. Until 1966 that is, when a V8-powered Dart won the first-ever Trans-Am race in the Over 2 Liter category. Although never hip enough to be considered a real pony car, today the 1964–66 Dart offers an excellent alternative to high-priced Challengers and 'Cudas with its homely yet endearing design, an available convertible, and a choice of 180- to 235-hp 273-ci V8 engines. Plan to spend $10,000 to $20,000 for a clean Dart GT, the one you want.

1965 Chevrolet Malibu SS

1964–65 Chevrolet Malibu

Crisply styled and modestly sized, available with a 327-ci V8 and carrying plenty of Bowtie street cred, the first-generation two-door Chevelle Malibu deserves a strong look as a Tier II muscle car. There were various models you don't want, such as a four-door with an inline-6 and a 2-speed Powerglide, but get a coupe or convertible with the SS package, bucket seats, a 4-speed manual tranny, and a 350-hp V8, and you've got a highly desirable little ride. Figure $10,000 to $45,000—and a ton more for the SS 396 model.

1964 Ford Falcon Futura Sprint Convertible

1964–65 Ford Falcon

Were it not for the second-generation Ford Falcon's bricklike body style, it coulda been a contender. Sharing much of its engineering with the red-hot Mustang, the Falcon never earned the following of the original pony car—or its value or credentials as a classic. That said, thanks to its tidy presentation, available 289- and 302-ci V8s, and genuine Trans-Am racing heritage, the Falcon nonetheless has genuine appeal, and at $5,000 up to $25,000 for a well-presented example, will always catch the eye of discerning enthusiasts. ♦

How to Determine Legitimacy in a Muscle Car

Learn how to decode VINs, know what "matching numbers" really means, and make sure all the dates check out

by Colin Comer

Technology has advanced to the point where almost any engine or VIN number can be recreated, and paperwork conjured up from thin air. Plus, as top muscle cars continue to hold strong values, with some in the seven-figure range, the sharks in the business smell the blood of the rubes just waiting to be fleeced. We lived through it once before in 1989–91, but then it was vintage Ferraris and Jaguar C- and D-types that were growing like weeds. Today, it's Hemi 'Cudas and COPO Camaros.

Luckily, decoding a car and figuring out exactly what it was when it left the factory are relatively simple tasks.

What follows is a beginner's guide for a basic muscle car "scratch-and-sniff" test, or preliminary inspection. It is not a comprehensive how-to, but rather a guide to help you determine with relative ease just what you are looking at.

Let's start by examining "matching numbers," a common term that is widely abused. Matching numbers implies that a car is exactly as it left the factory, with its original factory-installed engine, transmission, and rear axle. However, to the unscrupulous few, matching numbers can mean that the number they stamped on the engine block five minutes ago matches the number that was on the original one.

First, original paperwork is invaluable in determining if a car is real: window stickers, build sheets, dealer invoices, warranty cards, registration cards, owner history. The more you have, the easier it will be to document the car. I always look at every slip of paper with a car; even the most insignificant receipt may hold valuable information, such as a tune-up that noted engine size, a gas receipt with mileage and date noted, etc.

The best way to determine the legitimacy of numbers is to understand how these cars were built. As mass-produced cars, foundries cast engine blocks and heads, body plants stamped out body shells, and eventually all components formed a finished car. Simple. Every part has a casting number and date, the body has a build date, and the completed car was assigned a date when finished. Obviously, all parts must predate the

It's all in the numbers

completed car by a reasonable margin, usually one to three months.

Every part has a number

These time frames vary depending on the plant at which the car was built (engine blocks cast in Detroit were shipped by rail to a plant in L.A., as opposed to being at the factory in Detroit the day of completion), and time of year (Christmas shutdown, for example, slows production and widens the window). This is basic detective, work and I always look for consistency within dates on each car, rather than a set time frame. For example, if I find a block was cast in March 1969, I do not expect to find January 1968 cylinder heads. Remember, every part has a number and date on it, even window glass and bumper jacks.

Once you compile and compare all of the important date codes—for example, engine block, cylinder heads, intake manifold, body build date, and car completion date—it is time to look for the all-important "matching numbers."

Prior to 1968, many manufacturers did not have a VIN stamp on the block. This makes learning date codes and having concrete documentation that much more important. Certain high-performance cars, such as Corvettes and 1965–67 289 "K code"-equipped Fords and Shelbys, did have the VIN on their engine blocks. Post-1968, all cars have at least the last six digits of their serial number somewhere on the engine block and transmission case.

With the proper research, you can determine how "numbers-matching" your recent find is.

Just look it up

Many books exist on decoding numbers, including what casting numbers are correct, where to find them, and how to decode every component on the car. A decent book on any make you are considering is money well spent. The Internet is also a powerful research tool. Google "Chevrolet casting numbers" for instance, and look at what comes up. Numerous online communities exist for most popular cars. More often than not, these discussion boards can be very helpful with specific questions.

If considering a Pontiac GTO, the best $35 you will ever spend is ordering a Pontiac Historic Services report. These reports are worth their weight in gold. From the original factory records, Jim Mattison of PHS will provide you with copies of the original factory invoice and build card when provided with a VIN number. If you are in a hurry, for $10 extra PHS will fax you a copy immediately. Even though a seller may have his own PHS documents, as copies of originals, they are easily altered and I do not deem them reliable unless I obtain them myself. Go to www.phs-online.com and follow the instructions to order your report.

For Shelby shoppers, go to www.saac.com and order a copy of the *Shelby American World Registry*. In this 1,400-page monster is every Shelby ever built, with known history listed for each individual car. There are sections on each year, production changes, part numbers, and hints and tips. Do not buy a Shelby without looking it up in the *Registry*.

I also recommend joining the club to gain access to the registrars who can help you with additional information on particular cars. These guys are the best and the club support offered by SAAC is second to none.

Ford buyers can contact Marti Auto Works for a complete report on any Ford car from 1967–73. Kevin Marti has Ford's entire production database for these years. Please note these records also include all Shelby Mustangs produced from

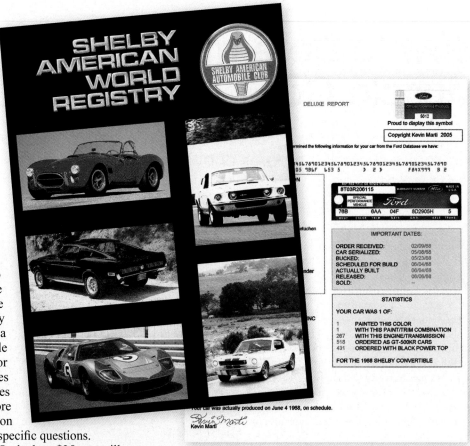

Hit the books

1967–70, and I highly recommend a Marti report in addition to checking the SAAC Registry. Marti Auto Works is on line at www.martiauto.com.

For Chrysler products, Galen V. Govier is the acknowledged authority. His company offers a wide range of services from basic decoding of cars over the phone to an on-site evaluation anywhere in the U.S. Govier also maintains The Chrysler Registry, which tracks all known examples of certain cars, at www.gvgovier.com

Above all, educate yourself on any car you are looking at and enlist the services of experts when needed. The time and expense of performing proper investigation is insignificant compared to the values of most cars. Chances are, you'll find that being a muscle car detective can have double rewards—first, in the knowledge you will gain, and second, by the sense of assurance you'll get knowing you've done your homework.

Of course, there are no guarantees, and even some of the world's top collectors are fooled by clones and air-cars now and then. But at least if you do your homework, you've got a running start on having the car you buy turn out to be what you thought it was, rather than a forger's delight. ♦

BEST BETS & WORST

The Z Code Option: What Does It Mean?

Zora Arkus-Duntov said, "Everyone tinks the Z stands for Zora. Dat ees nice. But eet actually meenz nutting"

by John Gunnell

Despite what you might suppose, Chevrolet "Z codes" were not named after the Corvette's first chief engineer, Zora Arkus-Duntov. Chevrolet expert Doug Marion asked Arkus-Duntov in 1983 if the Z meant anything. "He first smiled," says Marion, "then he said, 'Everyone tinks the Z stands for Zora. Dat ees nice. But eet actually meenz nutting.'"

Z packages weren't confined to Corvettes. Marion points out that the Z code was first used in 1963 for the Z11—a 427-powered Impala factory drag car. According to Marion, only 50 Z11s were built, although most sources say it was 57. (Marion has factory records to prove his number). "There are probably 50-plus Z code options, and they cover just about every Chevy model built since 1963, including vans," says Marion.

"Some Z code options are the same for every Chevrolet model, but other Z code options are totally different and go model to model," he points out. "There is a Z10 1969 Camaro Pace Car hard top, built as a special run for Texas or someplace. But there's a Z10 cargo van, too."

Buick also had Z code options, but they were two-character designations for individual extra-cost equipment for station wagons. Z2 designated a divided rear seat, Z4 indicated a power tailgate window, and Z5 was a "tailgate follower board," whatever that is. As most enthusiasts know, Oldsmobile high-performance packages were coded with a W. Pontiac used only three numbers to designate most of its options and three letters for most tire options.

Marion says he believes the letter Z was chosen because it was simply the next in line. With Chevy's larger range of models, it would be normal for Chevrolet Division to have a few more option groups than Oldsmobiles. Thus, the Chevy codes might run to Z, instead of W.

The following list shows 67 options offered between 1963 and 2005 that carried option codes (or model-option codes) that started with Z. The reason for the distinction between an option code and a model-option is that the ultra-high-

A badge to reckon with

performance, late-model Z06 hard top was merchandised much differently than the 1963 Z06 option, which was the first Z code Corvette package.

(Note: In 1963, the Z06 package was an option added to a car. Starting in 2001, the Z06 was a separate model that came only with the Z06 content.)

1963

RPO Z06: Special Performance Equipment package for Split-Window coupe ($1,818.45). Included special metallic power brakes, heavy-duty stabilizers, shock absorbers, and springs, 36½-gallon fuel tank, knockoff-type aluminum wheels, Positraction rear axle, 4-speed transmission, and 360-hp fuel-injection engine. (Later, the 36½-gallon fuel tank and knockoff aluminum wheels were rescinded, the price was cut to $1,293.95, and the package could be ordered for convertibles.) **Installs: 199**

1965

RPO Z01: Comfort and Convenience Group.

Included back-up lamps and inside day/night mirror ($16.15). **Installs: 15,397**

1969

RPO ZL1: Overhead-valve V8 of 427 ci, with bore and stroke of 4.251 x 3.76 inches, compression ratio of 12.50:1, 430 hp (actually over 500) at 5,200 rpm and 450 ft-lb at 4,400 rpm. Aluminum block. Five main bearings. Mechanical valve lifters. Special camshaft. Single Holley 850CFM four-barrel carb on aluminum manifold. ($4,718.25, and not available with radio and air conditioning). Required options K66 transistor ignition system, F41 special front and rear suspension, J56 special heavy-duty brakes, and G81 Positraction rear axle at extra cost. **Installs: 2**

1970

RPO ZQ3: Base overhead-valve V8 of 350 ci, with bore and stroke of 4.00 x 3.48 inches, compression ratio of 10.25:1, and 300 hp at 4,800 rpm. Five main bearings. Hydraulic valve lifters. Rochester type Quadra-Jet four-barrel carb, model 4MV. (Included in base prices). **Installs: 6,646**

RPO ZR1: Beginning in April 1970, the LT1 engine was a ZR1 option, part of Chevrolet's "Special Items" group. The ZR1 package included the LT-1 engine, M22 heavy-duty

4-speed manual transmission, J50/J56 dual-pin brakes with heavy-duty front pads and power assist, and F41 suspension consisting of special 89 lb/in ride rate front springs and 121 lb/in ride rate rear springs, matching shock absorbers, and a 0.75-inch front stabilizer bar. ($968.95) **Installs: 25**

1971

RPO ZR1: The ZR1 package included the LT-1 engine, M22 4-speed manual, J50/J56 brakes and F41 suspension. ($1,010). **Installs: 8**

RPO ZR2: The ZR2 Special Purpose LS6 engine package was a racing option like the ZR1, plus the RPO LS6 454-ci, 425-hp V8 ($1,747, and not available with automatic transmission). **Installs: 12**

1972

RPO ZR1: The ZR1 package included the LT-1 engine, M22 4-speed, J50/J56 brakes, transistor ignition, aluminum radiator, F41 suspension, and on some cars a rear stabilizer bar. ($1,010.05). **Installs: 20**

1973

RPO Z07: Off-road suspension/brake package with L82 or LS4 V8. Special front and rear suspension, heavy-duty brakes. Required J50 power brake assist, M21 4-speed manual transmission at extra cost. ($369, and not available with air conditioning). **Installs: 45**

1974

RPO Z07: Off-road suspension and brake package with L82 or LS4 V8. Special front and rear suspension, heavy-duty brakes. Required M21 4-speed manual transmission at extra cost. ($400). **Installs: 47**

1975

RPO Z07: Off-road suspension and brake package with L82 V8. FE7 special front and rear suspension, heavy-duty brakes. Required M21 4-speed manual transmission. ($400). **Installs: 144**

1977

RPO ZN1: Trailer package ($83). **Installs: 289**

RPO ZX2: Convenience group ($22). **Installs: 40,872**

1978

RPO ZN1: Trailer package ($89). **Installs: 972**

1971 ZR2 engine

RPO ZX2: Convenience group ($84). **Installs: 37,222**

1979

RPO ZN1: Trailer package ($98). **Installs: 1,001**

RPO ZQ2: Power windows and power locks ($272). **Installs: 28,465**

RPO ZX2: Convenience group ($84). **Installs: 37,222**

1980

RPO ZN1: Trailer package ($105). **Installs: 796**

1981

RPO ZN1: Trailer package ($110). **Installs: 916**

1984

RPO Z51: Performance handling package ($600.20). **Installs: 25,995**

RPO Z6A: Rear window and side mirror defoggers ($160). **Installs: 47,680**

1985

RPO Z51: Performance handling package ($470). **Installs: 14,802**

RPO Z6A: Rear window and side mirror defoggers ($160). **Installs: 37,720**

1986

RPO Z51: Performance handling package for coupe ($470). **Installs: 12,821**

RPO Z6A: Rear window and side mirror defoggers for coupe ($165). **Installs: 21,837**

1987

RPO Z51: Performance handling package for coupe ($795). **Installs: 1,596**

RPO Z52: Sport handling package ($470). **Installs: 12,662**

RPO Z6A: Rear window and side mirror defoggers for coupe ($165). **Installs: 19,043**

1988

RPO Z01: 35th Anniversary Special Edition package for coupe, included AQ9 leather sports seats, AC3

1998 Z4Z

power driver's seat, 24S removable blue-tinted roof panels, C68 electronically-controlled air conditioning, D74 illuminated driver side vanity mirror, Z52, and Z6A ($4.795). **Installs: 2,050**

RPO Z51: Performance handling package for coupe ($1,295). **Installs: 1,309**

RPO Z52: Sport handling package ($970). **Installs: 16,017**

RPO Z6A: Rear window and side mirror defoggers for coupe ($165). **Installs: 14,648**

1989

RPO Z51: Performance handling package for coupe ($575). **Installs: 2,224**

(Note: The ZR-1 model was due out this year, but delayed.)

1990

RPO Z51: Performance handling package for coupe ($460). **Installs: 5,446**

RPO ZR1: Special Performance package for coupe. Under the ZR-1's hood was a Lotus-designed 32-valve, dual-overhead-cam, 350-ci (5.7-liter) V8, built by Mercury Marine in Oklahoma. Although the displacement was identical to the standard Corvette V8, this was an all-new powerplant with different bore and stroke dimensions. Wider at the rear than a standard model

to contain huge 315/35ZR17 rear tires, the ZR-1 was easy to spot because of its convex rear end and rectangular taillights. Standard ZR-1 equipment included an FX3 Selective Ride adjustable suspension ($27,016). **Installs: 3,049**

In 1990, Corvette chief engineer Dave McLellan won the Society of Automotive Engineers Edward N. Cole Award for innovation for his work on the ZR-1.

1991

RPO Z07: Adjustable suspension package for coupe ($2,155). **Installs: 733**

RPO ZR1: Coupes with the ZR1 Special Performance Package again had different doors and a wider rear to accommodate 11-inch-wide rear wheels. Also, the high-mounted stop lamp went on the roof of the ZR-1, instead of on the rear fascia. All Corvettes, including the ZR-1, were again equipped with ABS II-S antilock braking and driver's side airbag, as well as an anti-theft system. The ZR-1 was again powered by the 32-valve DOHC 5.7-liter V8, matched with a 6-speed transaxle ($31,683). **Installs: 2,044**

1992

RPO Z07: Adjustable suspension package for coupe ($2,045). **Installs: 738**

RPO ZR1: Special Performance Package for coupe. The ZR-1 was basically a carry-over from the year previous, with new model badges above the rear fender vents ($31,683). **Installs: 502**

1993

RPO Z07: Adjustable suspension package for coupe ($2,045). **Installs: 824**

RPO Z25: Corvette marked its 40th Anniversary with an exclusive "Ruby Red" exterior and interior with color-keyed wheel centers, headrest embroidery, and bright emblems on the hood, deck, and side-gills. Optional equipment on all models ($1,455). **Installs: 6,749**

RPO ZR1: Special Performance Package for coupe. The ZR-1's 5.7-liter LT5 V8 was upgraded with improved air flow and valvetrain refinements to boost its rating from 375 hp to 405 hp. The 1993 Corvette also introduced GM's first Passive Keyless Entry system, whereby simply leaving or approaching the Corvette automatically locked or unlocked the doors. The 1993 Corvette was also the first U.S. car to use recycled body panels. Still with 6-speed transaxle ($31,683). **Installs: 448**

1994

RPO Z07: Adjustable suspension package for coupe ($2,045). **Installs: 887**

RPO ZR1: Special Performance Package for coupe. All Corvettes now had dual airbags, new carpeting, door trim panels, seats, steering wheel, a redesigned instrument panel, and a restyled console. Also new was an optional rear-axle ratio, revised spring rates, a convertible backlight with heated glass, and new exterior colors. The ZR-1 received new non-directional wheels for 1994 and again used the LT5 5.7-liter V8 with a 6-speed manual transmission ($31,258). **Installs: 448**

1995

RPO Z07: Adjustable suspension package for coupe ($2,045). **Installs: 753**

RPO Z4Z: Indy 500 Pace Car replica for convertibles only. For the third time (also 1978 and 1986), Corvette was the pace car for the Indianapolis 500. The 1995 Dark Purple Metallic over Arctic White Corvette was driven by 1960 Indy 500 winner Jim Rathmann ($2,816 over the price of a standard LT-1-powered Corvette convertible). **Installs: 527**

RPO ZR1: Special Performance Package for coupe. The big news of 1995 was the final appearance of the ZR-1 ($31,258). **Installs: 448**

1996

RPO Z15: The Collector Edition Package marked the final year of the C4 Corvette. The 1996 Collector Edition featured Sebring Silver paint, Collector Edition emblems, five-spoke aluminum wheels, and a 5.7-liter LT1 V8 fitted with a 4-speed automatic transmission. The LT4 V8 and 6-speed manual transmission were both optional ($1,250). **Installs: 5,412**

RPO Z16: Grand Sport Package. Admiral Blue Metallic Paint, white stripe, red "hash" marks on the left front fender and black five-spoke aluminum wheels. Powered by a 330-hp 5.7-liter LT4 V8 featuring a specially prepared crankshaft, steel camshaft, and water pump gears driven by a roller chain. Available only with 6-speed manual transmission ($2,880 for convertible or $3,250 for coupe). **Installs: 1,000**

RPO Z51: Performance Handling Package available on coupe and tuned for autocross competition ($350). **Installs: 1,869**

2002 Z06

1997

RPO Z51: Performance Handling Package for autocross competition ($350). **Installs: 1,077**

1998

RPO Z4Z: Indy Pace Car replica with purple exterior, black and yellow leather interior, and special trim ($5,039 with automatic transmission or $5,804 with manual transmission). **Installs: 1,163**

RPO Z51: Performance Handling Package with Bilstein adjustable Ride-Control system ($350). **Installs: 4,249**

1999

RPO Z51: Performance Handling Package with Bilstein adjustable Ride-Control system for coupe and convertible, standard with new hardtop ($350). **Installs: 10,244**

2000

RPO Z51: Performance Handling Package for coupe and convertible, standard with hardtop ($350). **Installs: 7,775**

2001

RPO 1YY37 + Z06: The all-new Z06 "model option" was merchandised as a separate model. The hard top included a 5.7-liter 385-hp Chevrolet LS6 V8 and a 6-speed manual transmission with overdrive. The Goodyear tires on the Z06 were an inch wider than standard but 23 lb lighter. The Z06 also featured a windshield and backlight made of thinner glass and a titanium exhaust system to reduce its weight by nearly 40 lb. The Z06 was equipped like the coupe, but with AM/FM cassette and radio optional and no automatic transmission option ($47,500 complete). **Production: 5,773**

RPO Z51: Performance Handling Package ($350). **Installs: 7,817**

2002

RPO 1YY37 + Z06: For 2002, a 20-hp boost made the Z06 the quickest production Corvette ever. This was the result of new hollow-stem valves, a higher-lift camshaft, a low-restriction mass air flow (MAF) sensor and a low-

2004 Z06

restriction air cleaner. The Z06-specific FE4 high-performance suspension system featured a larger front stabilizer bar, revised shock valving, a stiffer rear leaf spring, and different camber settings. The unique aluminum Z06 wheels were now cast rather than forged. The magnesium wheel option was discontinued. Hydroformed frame rails and a four-wheel independent front suspension with cast-aluminum upper and lower A-arms were other Z06 features.

The Z06 (and C5 Corvettes equipped with the Z51 package) now had aluminum front sway bar links and reduced weight. Now standard on Z06s, the Head-Up Display (HUD) system projected the speedometer and many other gauges digitally on the windshield, ahead of the steering wheel. New front pads reduced brake fade. Electron Blue replaced Speedway White as one of five Z06 color choices. As in 2001, an AM/FM cassette/radio was optional in the Z06; no automatic transmission was offered ($50,150 complete). **Production: 8,297**

RPO Z51: Performance Handling Package ($350). **Installs: 6,106**

2003

RPO 1YY37 + Z06: The Z06 Corvette continued unchanged and paced the Indy 500 again, though no Pace

Car package was produced ($51,155 complete). **Production: 8,635**

RPO Z51: Performance Handling Package ($395). **Installs: 2,592**

2004

RPO 1YY37 + Z06: 2004 model Z06 Corvettes featured revised chassis tuning. GM engineers refined the Z06's shock damping to improve handling and diminish the impact of yaw and roll. The Z06 was one of a handful of cars to break the eight-minute barrier for lap times over the 14-mile, 170-turn Nürburgring. Once again a Corvette paced the Indy 500 ($52,385 complete). **Production: 5,683**

RPO 1YY37 YY + Z06 + 1SB: The 2004 Commemorative Edition Z06 had Le Mans Blue finish and included a C5R-style Le Mans stripe scheme, special badges, polished Z06 wheels, and a lightweight carbon fiber hood. For 2004, the regular Z06 was given two performance-enhancing upgrades.

A lightweight, race-inspired carbon fiber hood was used on Z06s with the Commemorative Edition option, which weighed 20.5 pounds, 10.6 pounds less than the standard hood. Specifically developed for the Corvette, the Commemorative Edition Z06 hood achieved a higher level of exterior finish quality than previous automotive applications of carbon fiber ($4,335 over regular Z06). **Production: 2,025**

RPO Z51: Performance Handling Package ($395). **Installs: 3,672**

2005

The sixth-generation Corvette debuted in 2005, bringing back exposed headlights and a power top for the first time since 1962, plus a host of improvements. The car was five inches shorter and an inch narrower. The engine was punched out to 6 liters, redline went up 500 rpm to 6,500, horsepower went up to 400, and a 6-speed manual transmission was included in the car's base price. Options included OnStar, XM satellite radio, DVD-based navigation, heated seats, and side airbags. All Corvettes had keyless access and start. Once again, a Corvette paced the Indy 500, but there was no Z06.

RPO Z51: Performance Handling Package was significantly more expensive, reflecting more content—higher spring rates, cross-drilled brake rotors, engine, transmission, and power steering coolers ($1,495). **Installs: 15,345**

2006

RPO 1YY87 + Z06: The Z06 returned, based on the coupe body, with aluminum frame, magnesium-supported roof panel, and powered by a small-block 505-hp 7-liter LS7 V8 and 6-speed transmission. It also had an 8-quart dry-sump oiling system, titanium rods, 7,000-rpm redline, and

3.7-second 0–60 mph time on run-flat tires. The front facia was wider, with a cold-air intake, and there was much use of carbon fiber in the body. A Z06 paced the Indy 500 ($65,800). **Production: 6,272**

RPO Z51: Performance Handling Package included specific springs, shocks and sway bars, cross-drilled rotors, Goodyear Eagle F1 tires. Engine, transmission, power steering coolers. Available with 6-speed or automatic ($1,695). **Installs: 10,338**

2007

RPO 1YY87 +Z06: The Z06 continued relatively unchanged, though the price rose to $70,000. **Production: 8,159**

RPO 1YY87 Z33: One of two special editions, the Z33 package honored Ron Fellows, the American Le Mans Series racer. It was white with red front fender stripes and each one was signed ($7,500 over regular Z06). **Production: 399**

RPO 1YY87 Z4Z: The Indy Pace Car convertible was produced in Atomic Orange with a custom interior. It previewed some 2008 details, including wheels ($500 over regular Z06). **Production: 500.**

RPO Z51: Performance Handling Package included specific springs, shocks, and sway bars, cross-drilled rotors, Goodyear Eagle F1 tires. Engine, transmission, power steering coolers. Available with 6-speed or automatic

($1,696). **Installs: 10,338**

2008

RPO Z51: Performance Handling Package included specific spring, shocks and sway bars, cross-drilled rotors, Goodyear Eagle F1 tires. Engine, transmission, power steering coolers. Available with 6-speed or automatic ($1,695). **Installs: Still in production**

2009

RPO ZR1: Evoking the original high-performance packages of the '70s and the '90s, the all-new C6 ZR1 includes a 638-hp supercharged LS9 6.2-liter V8 and 6-speed manual with high-capacity dual-disc clutch. Specific suspension tuning with Magnetic Ride Control provides over 1g of lateral grip, while standard carbon-ceramic drilled brake rotors (15.5 inches in the front, 15 inches in the rear) and larger brake calipers help stop the car from its 200-plus-mph top speed.

Body features extensive use of carbon fiber, including fenders, roof panel, rocker moldings, front fascia splitter, and hood, with clear polycarbonate window over engine. Curb weight is approximately 3,350 lb. Only two options are available—chrome wheels and the "luxury" package. Without a doubt the fastest, most powerful Corvette ever produced, with a reported Nürburgring lap time of just 7:26.4 ($103,300). **Installs: Still in production** ♦

2008 Z06

Top Corvette Options

Rare performance options can multiply the value of a car but demand documentation, or the deal's off

by Tom Glatch

It can fairly be said that all Corvettes are created equal—it's the options that transform a them from country club cruisers into world class supercars. Unlike, say, Ferrari, where there is a huge difference between a Mondial and a Testarossa from the same era, all Corvettes are based on the same platform and share a common DNA. So when searching for a Corvette with the maximum investment potential, it's the option sheet that differentiates the deals from the duds. Here's what to look for:

Fuel Injected 1963 Chevrolet Corvette Z06

1. Fuel injection

John Dolza's Rochester "Ram Jet" Fuel Injection transformed the Corvette from wanna-be to world class. Introduced around April 1957, it became the performance option, making the Fuelie only the second American automobile to reach the magic one-horsepower-per-cubic-inch mark. The rarest of these are the 1957 RPO (Regular Production Order) 579E "Air Box" Corvettes, which included the 283-hp engine, mechanical tach, and special racing fresh-air intake. But all 1957 through 1964 Corvettes with the top horsepower fuel-injected engine are the most valuable of this era, while the 1965 FI and 396 cars are both of roughly equal value and collectibility. The complex mechanical fuel-injection systems have not been reproduced, though many components have been, so you are guaranteed a genuine unit, but there are many more fuel injection units out there than existing original cars, so demand documentation if you want maximum value.

From 1957 through 1960, Chevrolet made a lower horse-power FI version equipped with the 2-speed Powerglide automatic. It was a strange concept, which never sold well and should still be avoided. Also, in 1960–61 the Fuelie was available in both 285-hp and 315-hp versions. Again, only a small number of the lower-power cars were made. As always, the market wants the maximum-performance version.

2. Heavy-duty brakes/suspension

Hand-in-hand with fuel injection, the factory heavy-duty brake and suspension options transformed the street Corvette into a ready-racer. While many "big brake" cars were never raced, finding a 1957–62 Corvette with this option can be a tip-off to a car's racing past, or to an original owner who simply wanted the fastest, best handling American car of the era. In 1963, these options were rolled into the Z06 package, which is certainly the most desirable of the Split-Window cars.

3. Big-blocks

In 1965 Chevrolet phased out the Fuelie in favor of the all-new 396-ci. big-block. Built from 1965 through 1974, the monster motors were available in most years in multiple versions. Though the lower-horsepower cars were often better behaved on the street and available with air conditioning, the top-horsepower cars command the marketplace. The rare 1967–69 L88s, with 500-plus horses under the hood, are the stars of the group, while the equally rare aluminum-head

435-hp L89 is close behind. So is the 1971 LS6; these 454-powered, 425-hp coupes are the last of the monsters. The 1967–69 435-hp L71 Corvettes are more common and therefore somewhat less valuable, but no less desirable. Finally, the 1973–74 LS4 454s, though hardly high performance, are gaining in interest as affordable big-blocks. Any of these 396-427-454 cars are easy to fake, and at the height of the big-block boom" in the early 1990s, there were a number of prominent collections with cars of questionable pedigree, so demand documentation and get an expert opinion before investing.

4. The little things

Some Corvette options didn't increase the performance in any way, but make an individual automobile that much more desirable. The N32 Teakwood Steering Wheel option, available on the 1965–66 Corvette, is a perfect example. Only 6,200 Corvettes were originally equipped with this beautiful option, and reproductions exist, so finding a documented car with an original wheel is like icing on the cake. So is the N14 Side Mount Exhaust System, available from 1965–67 and on 1969 Corvettes. Many Corvettes have been fitted with after-market and reproduction side pipes, but finding one with original equipment can add a few thousand in value. Aluminum wheels are another desirable mid-year option. The 1963–66 RPO P48 Knockoff Wheel and 1967 N89 Cast Aluminum Bolt-On Wheel options complete the look, but again, demand documentation. It is thought that only a handful of 1963 Z06 cars—if any—were originally equipped with the alloy wheels, and there are many more 1964–67 Corvettes around today with these wheels than were originally built that way. It has to be documented, or all value disappears.

5. Corvette Challenge Cars

Most Corvettes built after 1972 generate little interest in the marketplace, with a few exceptions. The Corvette Challenge series in 1988 and 1989 pitted established and up-and-coming drivers in identical Corvettes, all on national TV. Chevrolet created the RPO B9P option to build these cars on the Bowling Green assembly line, then the cars were shipped to a subcontractor for roll cages and other safety equipment. In 1988 just 56 cars were assembled and 50 converted, while for the 1989 series 60 cars were assembled and 30 converted. Sadly, most of these cars are worth about as much today as their sticker price when new, although cars with exceptional race history, or raced by prominent drivers can command more. Why even consider a Challenge car, then? Simple—there's no other way you can own a piece of Corvette racing history for the cost of a used C5? They are even street legal.

6. Callaway Twin Turbo

After years of average performance, the 1987–91 RPO B2K Callaway Twin Turbo upgrade to the standard Corvette boosted power from 250 hp to a stunning 382 hp. The cars were shipped from Bowling Green to the Callaway shop in Connecticut, where the engine was removed and given the turbo upgrade. Later cars had 405 hp and the option of the Paul Deutschman-designed Aerobody package, and all carried the full GM warranty. 482 Twin Turbos were ordered through Chevrolet, and another 28 were upgrades to existing Corvettes. Most valuable are the ten Speedsters built at the end of the B2K program; other Twin Turbos sell for $20k–$60k or more. While other C4 Corvettes have elicited minimal market interest, including the mighty ZR-1 coupes, Callaways in above-average condition have slowly increased in value. ♦

RPO BK2

Market Makers: Historical Corvettes From the GM Fleet

Heritage Fleet Corvettes at Barrett-Jackson provided a fascinating insight into the ideas (good and otherwise) that surrounded the C4 and C5

by Thomas Glatch

1989 Corvette DR-1 Convertible—Lot 1218

General Motors captured the spotlight at the Barrett-Jackson Scottsdale Auction, January 11–18, 2009, when it released 252 cars from its Heritage Fleet for no-reserve sale. (The Heritage Fleet must be differentiated from GM's Heritage Collection; the former are surplus or less important cars, the latter are the milestone cars that represent GM's 100 years of contribution to automotive history.)

While many came with a scrap title (odd when you think who's selling the car), that was related to federal regulations, which don't have much to do with making a car work well. In the past, most of these vehicles would have been crushed, including 34 Corvettes, which provided a fascinating insight into dreams and ideas (good and otherwise) that surround the launch of a new model—in this case the C4 and C5.

You'll have to do your own research on the blown big-block 1987 Chevrolet Sprint, the 1999 two-millionth Saturn, and the 2001 Pontiac Aztek Daytona 500 Pace Car (we are not making this up). Here we analyze ten of the most important Corvettes from the fleet that came under the hammer.

1989 Corvette DR-1 Convertible—Lot 1218
Sold for $286,000 on Saturday, January 17, 2009

While Chevrolet never sold a ZR-1 convertible, the possibility was investigated. Two ZR-1 coupes were converted into convertibles by Lotus and Chevrolet for evaluation. Also, a standard 1989 L98 convertible with an LT5 engine installed was built for engineering executive Don Runkle, which became known as the DR-1. While hardly as well known as the Snake Skinners or the Big Doggie, the Ice Blue DR-1 was the highest selling Heritage Fleet Corvette. Why? No one has ever said auction results were the least bit logical, and this is one of those results. Besides, think of the bragging rights the new owner has.

1989 Corvette ZR-1 Coupe—Lot 1230.4
Sold for $198,000 on Saturday, January 17, 2009

Chevrolet built 83 pilot ZR-1 Corvettes in 1989, 25 of which were sent to France for the now-famous press introduction. Since the ZR-1 was officially released as a 1990 model, most of the '89 cars had to be destroyed. This was one of the survivors, which was loaned to the automotive press and

1989 Corvette ZR-1 Coupe—Lot 1230.4

1989 Corvette ZR-1 Coupe "Snake Skinner"—Lot 396.1

displayed at auto shows. Though this car, and most of the GM Heritage Fleet cars, can never be registered for street use, the new owner can proudly say he owns one of the few '89 ZR-1 Corvettes in existence, and its value can only increase in years to come. Well bought. And besides, between dealer plates and Alabama titles, never say never to getting a car on the street.

1989 Corvette ZR-1 Coupe "Snake Skinner"—Lot 396.1

Sold for $176,000 on Wednesday, January 14, 2009

The 1990 introduction of the Dodge Viper prototype stole some of the ZR-1's thunder. John Heinricy, Corvette engineer and racer, built the "Snake Skinner" as a response. Heinricy took one of the 83 1989 ZR-1 pilot cars, and using a Kevlar hood, Plexiglas rear window, and other tricks, pared its weight to 2,700 lb. Mercury Marine also built a special 475-hp LT5 engine. The result was very fast—Heinricy broke the long-standing 0-to-100-to-0 record of 14 seconds set by a 427 Cobra with a time of 12.8. I'm surprised this was not the high-selling Corvette of the Heritage Fleet cars, since it received press in almost every magazine at the time, but it was priced about right just the same. A second "Snake Skinner" was built by Heinricy in 1991; that car (lot 1302) sold for $73,700.

1989 Corvette ZR-2 "Big Doggie"—Lot 97

Sold for $71,500 on Monday, January 13, 2009

One thing the ZR-1 lacked was the unique, torque-heavy performance of a classic big-block V8. In response, engineer Scott Leon built the ZR-2, a 1989 Corvette powered by a modified 454 truck engine. It became known as the Big Doggie and was featured in many magazines and shown at Bloomington Gold in 1992. At a time when Corvette sales were dangerously low, GM considered building a production

version, but assembly concerns (the engine did not fit between the stock frame rails) and challenging CAFE standards killed the project. This was an outstanding buy of a well-known and shockingly fun-to-drive one-off Corvette.

1989 "Active" Corvette ZR-1 Coupe Prototype—Lot 82

Sold for $150,700 on Tuesday, January 13, 2009

Computer-controlled, hydraulically adjusted active suspension was developed in Formula One racing and was so successful in increasing cornering grip and controlling vehicle dynamics that it was ultimately banned. The "Active" Corvette was built by Chevrolet Engineering to test a similar setup on the Corvette. Road & Track magazine reported, "Bumps and dips are not in the dictionary of an active suspension. They cease to exist." It was predicted that active suspension would be in production in a few years, but it would have been a nearly $40,000 option, and it consumed as much as 40 hp, so it was never offered. A good buy on an important and unique engineering study.

1991 Corvette Convertible—Lot 907.2

Sold for $110,000 on Friday, January 16, 2009

In 1991, two ZR-1 convertibles were built on the Bowling Green assembly line. Adding the ZR-1's special wide bodywork and tires to a convertible would have required extensive re-engineering, so these cars were essentially stock L98 convertibles with the LT5 powertrain added. ZR-1 convertibles were considered to bolster sagging sales, but it was felt the convertible chassis was not strong enough for the LT5's additional power, and the project was cancelled. Vehicles used for engineering, testing, and marketing evaluation are normally destroyed, so this unique survivor was well bought and is sure to appreciate.

1989 Corvette ZR-2 "Big Doggie"—Lot 97

1989 "Active" Corvette ZR-1 Prototype—Lot 82

1991 Corvette Convertible—Lot 907.2

1990 Corvette Right-Hand Drive—Lot 1356

1989 Corvette "Splash" Custom—Lot 1599

1990 Corvette Right-Hand Drive—Lot 1356

Sold for $27,500 on Sunday, January 18, 2009

Bob Lutz has said the seventh generation Corvette would be developed in both left- and right-hand-drive versions. It wouldn't be the first time GM considered a right-hooker Corvette, since some RHD countries like Australia severely restricted the use of LHD cars (this has now relaxed somewhat). This 1990 Corvette was converted to RHD by Chevrolet Engineering, but the development, tooling, and certification required to produce such a car at Bowling Green were deemed too expensive for the limited market it would have served. While hardly a news-maker like the Snake Skinner or the Big Doggie, a one-of-a-kind engineering study for the price of a new Malibu is an excellent buy. And if you live in England, Australia, or the Maldives, here's the Corvette for you.

1989 Corvette "Splash" Custom—Lot 1599

Sold for $71,500 on Sunday, January 18, 2009

Chevrolet built 60 RPO R7F cars for the 1989 Corvette Challenge series. Of those, 29 were equipped by organizer Jim Powell for the series. This car was one of those 29, but it never raced. Instead it was used as a promo vehicle for the series and displayed at auto shows and other events. The paint scheme was designed by Corvette stylist John Cafaro. The Corvette Challenge cars are starting to show signs of life in the marketplace, and this one, with its unique history, may be one of the most desirable.

1997 Corvette "Alpha Build"—Lot 470.1

Sold for $41,800 on Wednesday, January 14, 2009

Long before the first C5 Corvette rolled off the Bowling Green assembly line, engineers racked up thousands of development miles in 14 "alpha" cars. Though crude compared to the final product, these cars helped refine the design. Preproduction cars rarely see the light of day, and most are destroyed either during development or after they are no longer needed. GM wisely kept one of the "alpha" cars, and the new owner has a piece of Corvette history that cannot be duplicated and may someday be as valuable as other one-of-a-kind Corvette prototypes.

1997 Corvette "Beta Build"—Lot 470

Sold for $41,800 on Wednesday, January 14, 2009

After extensive development of the "alpha" prototypes, the C5 team built about 30 "beta" cars that were even closer to the final design. Like the black "alpha" cars, the white "betas" were heavily camouflaged to protect them from automotive spies. Sold as a set with the "alpha" car, the new owner now has two of the most important development Corvettes ever shown to the public, much less sold to the public. General Motors did Corvette fans a huge favor by saving these special cars from the GM Heritage Fleet for future generations. ♦

1997 Corvette "Alpha Build"—Lot 470.1

1997 Corvette "Beta Build"—Lot 470

BEST BETS & WORST

Eight Corvettes to Run Away From

I had a hard time repressing the desire to crawl under my chair and plug my ears while this was on the block, as it had the look of a time bomb

1968 Convertible

1969 Convertible

1973 "Mud Bogger" Coupe

Years of study and expert advice can help you buy a correct Corvette you will be proud of. It takes time and effort, but it's worth it.

On the other hand… careless enthusiasm and a moment of weakness at an auction can find you way down a long, dark tunnel, with the only light being that of an approaching train.

1968 Convertible

427-ci 435-hp V8, 3x2-bbl, 4-sp. A resto-mod that reportedly had $80,000 worth of work completed, including powdercoated frame, Budnick wheels, Be Cool aluminum radiator, Wilwood brakes, Steeroid rack and pinion steering, and Vintage a/c. Glass replaced, chrome new, giant stereo installed. Headlights apparently not working. Hawaii plates. Cond: 3. **Sold at $88,000.**

This project felt like it was rode hard and put away wet, and it was further proof that money and good sense don't necessarily co-exist. If I was the seller, I'd have high-fived my way to the bar and bought a few rounds of Mai Tais. Well sold, regardless of the restoration cost.

1969 Convertible

350-ci 350-hp LT1 V8, 4-bbl, 4-sp. Rare M22 rock crusher, claimed 600 miles from new. Clearcoat over cracks in original paint, door jambs atypically smooth, top correctly finished. Amazingly original underneath, with cross-ply tires and expected finishes throughout. Driver's seat and pedals seem a bit worn for the mileage indicated, carpet looks newer. Cond: 2. **Sold at $80,000.**

This car drew interested buyers like moths to a flame. It was undoubtedly a very low-mileage car, but it's hard to say if the mileage was actually as low as was claimed. Perhaps the driver hopped in and out a lot in the garage and made vroom-vroom noises? Did the speedometer cable break early on? Regardless, this was very well sold.

1973 "Mud Bogger" Coupe

454-ci V8, 4-bbl, auto. Monster Garage "Mud Bogger" project car by Jesse James. Fitted with 12-inch lift, 4WD using chain-driven Toyota 4Runner front axle, nitrous, roll cage, zoomie pipes, Cobra seats, 9-inch Ford rear, and Mickey Thompson Baja Claw tires. 6-lug front wheels, 5-lug rear. No dash, scruffy paint. Cond: 4-. **Sold at $33,000.**

What did this poor old car do to deserve this? A classic case of "just because you can doesn't mean you should." Or as F1 champion James Hunt once said in color commentary at a Madison Square Garden Hot Rod show, "Looks like they all started with the wrong car." Well sold.

1963 Custom Convertible

454-ci V8, 4-bbl, 4-sp. Body modified with cut-out wheel-wells, fender flares, 1968 side vents, rear ducktail spoiler, and six taillights. Seller claims hood was a 1967 take-off big-block unit. Good quality older repaint starting to show light cracking at wheel well flares. Older replated bumpers, mostly replacement emblems. Aftermarket side exhaust, retrofitted 4-wheel power disc brakes. Older replacement top, quality new leather seating, typical reproduction door panels, dash pad, and carpet. Cond: 3. **Sold at $33,600.**

While somewhat radically modified, this wasn't quite the Nightmare from Route 66. Some of the assembly quality is all over the map (lazy, cheap person under the hood; well-off perfectionist at the upholstery shop), but it would be a bit hard to

1963 Custom Convertible

1969 Coupe

1987 Callaway Twin Turbo Coupe

get burned on this one. Anyone can tell it's a put-together special. The reserve was wisely lifted when the bidding ended.

1969 Coupe

502-ci V8, 4-bbl, 4-sp. Claimed to originally have been a 427/435 car, currently fitted with a 20-mile-old GM crate 502. Old body modifications done to flare out wheel openings not exceptionally noticeable but done rather well. Rear valance panel missing, but bits are included on the adjacent wooden pallet. Repaint dull with lots of nicks and scrapes. Both side mirrors missing. Declared while being sold to have inoperable front brakes. Moderate seat wear, but not worn though anywhere. Cond: 4-. **Sold at $18,750.**

The next-worst thing to a barn-find basket case. Actually worse, as a basket case may not have the body hacked apart. Besides, front brakes are overrated anyway—cars used to not have 'em until the mid-1920s. The only way one could come out even on this deal is to find the original motor on the parts pile pallet, and as I mentioned, you'll only likely keep up on the expenses, not making anything on it. Sold exceptionally well.

1984 Custom Coupe

350-ci 205-hp fuel-injected V8, 4+3 manual. Bizarre C5 body kit fitted to a first-year C4. Evidence that the driver's door was red suggests a profound rebuild took place. Paint quite good, marked wear to driver's seat. Wheel arches oddly proportioned. Cond: 3. **Sold at $9,180.**

This looked like David Byrne in the big, white suit from the Talking Heads' "Stop Making Sense" tour. It was a clumsy-looking conversion but it can't have been cheap. It does raise the question of how much of the original C4 body survived the likely crash. Was it a good buy? Who knows... Have you ever seen another?

1987 Callaway Twin Turbo Coupe

350-ci 345-hp twin-turbocharged fuel-injected V8, 4+3 manual. Buffed-out older repaint, with lots of scratches at driver's door. Exterior emblems rough, cloudy, and faded, right side Callaway emblem missing. Engine bay generally dingy and with dings in aftercoolers. Claimed to have recently rebuilt turbos. Aftermarket dash and steering wheel rim covers soiled. Heavily worn leather to seats on both sides. Uneven idle, offered at no reserve. Cond: 4. **Sold at $5,724.**

I had a hard time repressing the desire to crawl under my chair and plug my ears while this was on the block, as it had the look of a ticking time bomb. Sold cheap for scores of reasons, and none of them good. Be afraid, be very afraid.

1999 Convertible

5.7-liter 345-hp fuel-injected LS1 V8, auto. Sold on a salvage title due to collision repair. Good repaint finished commensurate to new build quality. Door, hood, and panel fit decent, rear fascia stretched. Power antenna won't fully retract, newer tires fitted. Heavy wear to convertible top, with some bow bite on passenger side and fraying at corners. Steering wheel rim glossy from wear, spokes dirty. Average used car undercarriage with equal wear and no indications of damage, overspray, or recent suspension alignment. Cond: 3. **Sold at $13,000.**

Sold between Kelley Blue Book's trade-in and private party values, but either of those numbers is too much for a Corvette with over 100k miles, collision repair work, and a salvage title. Most of the dealers had bailed out before it hit ten grand, so the buyer probably thinks he got a good deal. Unless you get it at a discount below dealer wholesale, a car like this will never be a good deal, as it will always tell a story no buyer wants to hear. ♦

1984 Custom Coupe

1999 Convertible

Buying & Selling Smart

There's no magic to buying a decent collector car. It takes thoughtfulness and a studied approach, one where you teach yourself about a marque before you buy, and where you carefully examine a car, with the help of experts when necessary, to determine what kind of shape it is really in.

Of course, few of us collect that way. I tend to prowl Internet classifieds looking for cars that are described as "perfectly restored" and at reasonable prices. Why should I spoil my fantasies by actually having a car examined, when I can pay for it, have it shipped thousands of miles to my door, and then discover it's a rusty pig that really would be happiest wallowing in iron oxide manure?

Selling one of your collector cars can be the best day of your life. Or the worst, depending on how you handle it. In this section, you'll find pithy advice on how to minimize the tax implications of selling a car, what your options are if the high bidder at an auction refuses to pay up, and the legalities you'll encounter if you bid on your own car at auction.

Car collecting begins and ends with passion, and we at Sports Car Market recognize that. However, at the same time, if we can help you interject just a bit of thoughtfulness and rationality into your collecting, we guarantee that you will be happier, much happier, with the types of cars you buy and sell.—*Keith Martin*

In This Section

What It's Worth

Does "Spare Parts Included" Really Matter.... 193

The Relationship Between Condition and Price 195

Why One High Sale Doesn't Mean All Cars are Worth More 197

Buying and Selling

Buying Collector Cars Online 199

What "Everything Works" Really Means 201

Buying Techniques That Work 203

Modify, Restore, or Preserve? 205

Avoiding the Taxes on the Sale of Your Collector Car 207

What "No Reserve" Really Means 209

Tax Consequences of Selling Your Car........... 211

When the High Bidder at an Auction Won't Pay Up........... 213

Finances

What is Collector Car Insurance? 215

What is an Agreed Value Policy?........... 217

How to Finance a Collector Car........... 219

Settling Insurance Claims........... 220

You and the Law

Lemon Laws........... 222

The Ferrari Enzo Crash in Los Angeles........... 224

"As Is" Disclosures........... 227

VIN Plate Transfers........... 229

Track Day Insurance 231

Barn Finds

The Famous Portuguese Barn Find........... 233

Unrestored 1911 Oldsmobile Sells for $1.65 Million........... 235

Does "Spare Parts Included" Really Matter

Look at the seller, not the parts. If the seller seems likely to make your life miserable, walk away

by Jim Schrager

I recently got a call from a long-lost 356 enthusiast, a fellow with twenty-some desirable cars, a few dozen motors, countless boxes of parts ,and a sizable literature collection. Due to a major life change, he will be moving to Europe, he said, and everything must go.

I made a few follow-up calls, and it was always the same story: Whenever asked how much he wanted for any particular item, he'd say: "I don't have any idea. I've been out of this too long to know."

After some discussion, I made a fair offer for the car I was interested in, a 1959 356A Sunroof. He agreed it was all the money and promised that I had first shot. I urged him to act as I was ready to send a check, but he said, "Nah, don't worry. I promise it's yours."

This has happened to many of us. As I hung up the phone, I realized there were many things that didn't make sense about this guy. For starters, a fellow this deep into the hobby clearly has some ideas about what stuff is worth. Just one issue of Hemmings is all it takes to get some rough bearings; SCM if he really wants to learn a bunch.

Next, anyone who keeps that much stuff, most of it unused, is generally doing it for one reason: to make money. Most of his cars were undriven, the engines disassembled. Why have an extra few dozen motors? Can anyone use that many even in a lifetime of driving?

The seller, not the car

Why give me, or anyone you don't know who hasn't even made a visit to your place, right of first refusal after just a phone call? This makes little sense.

Stack of gold or pile of junk?

So what gives? Well, the rest of the story is that this guy was just shopping, kicking the financial tires, and got out of my "right of first refusal" by simply changing his mind on what was for sale—for now. All in all, it was a total waste of time. How to avoid this in the future?

Look at the seller, not the car. That's really the secret to staying sane and having fun with the old car hobby. If the seller seems likely to make your life miserable, do your best to walk away.

Don't believe folks with big, deep experience who claim not to have the faintest idea of what their cars are worth. Serious sellers do their homework and come to the market with prices. Perhaps they need a call with a friendly buyer before revealing their price, but I have never yet found someone ready to sell who didn't have a number in mind.

I get worried when people tell too many non-car-related stories. Some people just need someone to talk to. A few off-topic sidebars are fine, but if you find that you, as a complete stranger, are being told someone's life story—repeatedly—be wary. By the end of these phone calls I heard what this guy's kids did for a living ... more than once.

Try to observe the seller in other ways. This seller told me he had promised a project Speedster to a "good friend." Okay, fair enough. He then offered this same car for sale, on a "bring all offers" basis, on the Internet. Several people came to his house, and he was able to coax ever-larger purchase offers. He then withdrew the car from all the buyers and offered it to me as part of a package—unpriced, of course.

Get a detailed list

Be wary if the seller won't provide a good, detailed list of what is for sale. I once did a deal for a large group of Porsche engines based on a pretty sketchy list. When the goods arrived, all were less than represented. Some "engines" were nothing more than cases; "roller cranks in excellent condition" were in fact suitable for use only as doorstops; "2-liter 911 engine being prepared for vintage racing" was a 1969

911T long block, dormant for dozens of years, that had apparently been prepared by storing it untouched in a damp environment. Needless to say, it wasn't a happy deal.

Our 356 seller got very specific when he was in the mood. For example, he asked how much disc brake conversions are going for. This is a desirable option, as it was provided only with the last two years of the 356 and can be used on almost any earlier A or B 356. He saw a set posted at $1,800 on a VW talk list. That's big money, but it's only an asking price. Of course it depends on condition, I told our secretive stash seller who claimed to know nothing. His response: "I've looked at the caliper bores in each of my seven sets, and there are no rust pits. These parts are in excellent condition!" This is the same guy who refused to write a list of what he had for sale. Seems a bit inconsistent, doesn't it?

So what's the game here? It's a classic mismatch of minds. The seller is looking for big money due to his hours expended in accumulating his outstandingly wonderful worldly possessions. Think of all the early Saturday morning swap meets, the miles spent on the road, the haggling with owners. The seller wants over retail to compensate for his Herculean efforts and the sheer majesty of his estate. He is looking for an emotional buyer who looks at the seemingly endless cache of parts and simply must possess them, damn the cost.

On the other hand, a thoughtful buyer is being forced to take lots of stuff he doesn't really want or need. To him, swap meets are fun, and he is glad to trade time for a lower price. He's looking for a discount to pay for his hassle in unloading what he doesn't want.

Most of the time, the twain never meet—or at least, not happily. Keep your checkbook in your pocket until you really know what you are getting. And be on the lookout for time-wasters masquerading as guys who "don't have a clue" what their merchandise is worth. ♦

Will you use any of these in your lifetime?

The Relationship Between Condition and Price

Price guides are never enough by themselves to accurately assess the value of a vintage Porsche, as there is no wholesale market

by Jim Schrager

Aetna Blue 356B Cabriolet

BUYING & SELLING SMART

Dear Keith Martin's Guide to Car Collecting: I am excited about a 1960 356B Roadster, repainted the original Aetna Blue (light, non-metallic blue/gray) with a gray interior and the 1600 Normal engine per the Kardex. Body panel gaps are very nice, although both doors are slightly out at their lower rear corners. No hard hits, pan has one section repaired properly, otherwise everything else is original and solid. All instruments rebuilt, Les Leston wood steering wheel, a jack and spare but no tool kit.

SCM says a current value of $60,000–$70,000, yet I've seen recent sales that seem quite a bit higher. Is the SCM guide behind the curve? What is your opinion of the range for cars in #1 condition? Some folks I have talked to are saying as high as $85,000. I am thinking the top end is about $75,000. Any input will be appreciated.—*Wray Brady, Pittsburgh, PA*

Price differences often involve condition. The SCM price guide is for a #2 condition car, and is an "aggressive" buying target. This means the buyer has to work a bit to find a car at this price.

Don't expect to visit your local collector-car dealer and find cars right at our numbers. There is no organized wholesale market for vintage Porsches. Dealers, who buy from the same folks we all do, have costs that must be recouped. So their prices, in deference to their work at finding and presenting cars for sale, may be higher than our guide. Of course, you spend your money or your time when buying a vintage car, and for many of us, the margin a dealer makes is money well spent.

A #1 condition 356 can be twice the price of a #2, due to the tremendous expense—and hassle—involved. Strictly by our price guide, we call a #1 Roadster $80,000–$100,000 and have reported sales in that range.

Regarding the Roadster you are looking at, it sounds like it is between #1 and #2 condition, with a price range of $40,000–$100,000. Disappointed with that huge range? Welcome to the world of collecting, where price guides are never enough by themselves to accurately assess the value of a vintage Porsche.

Dear Keith Martin's Guide to Car Collecting: I noticed Keith Martin commented on how hard his 911SC rode, and I have some thoughts and questions about my Porsches as well. I've disagreed with you for years, as I have always been a believer in getting the largest tires that will fit under the wheel wells of my various 911s. The more contact area I get on the ground, the higher the performance, in my mind. Plus it looks great with those big, fat meats in the wheel wells.

But now I have a 1974 911S Targa with stock six-inch wheels and original-type and -size tires, and I can't believe how nice it feels. The steering isn't heavy, and the ride isn't jarring anymore. I am now a believer in this idea that maybe Porsche does know more than I do about wheel and tire sizes.

But here are two technical talking points on which I can't agree with you:

1. You mention in your review of your 1976 912E (p.205) that the best tire for that car is a 185/65/15, as it is very close to the original 185/70/15 that was fitted to the six-inch wide wheels. I believe the better equivalent tire size is actually 195/65, as the diameter is essentially identical to the original 185/70 size.

2. I appreciate your affinity for the vintage look of steel wheels, but I believe that to lower the unsprung weight, a 911 really should have Fuchs alloys. In addition, with form following function and all that stuff, aren't the alloys more in keeping with the spirit of the original design?—***Philip Kahn, Denver, CO***

You are absolutely right that 195/65 tires approximate the rolling diameter of the original 185/70 size. But I am looking for more than just size—I am trying to rediscover that elusive "light yet connected" feel these cars had when new, the well-controlled ride without the harshness so often felt with high-performance tires. The same feeling you really like in your 1974 car is the feeling you will never have from a 911SC because of the wheel and tire sizes. Low-profile and high-performance tires are fatter and stiffer than the set-up on the earlier cars, and both translate directly into harshness.

Those 185/65/15 tires also have another advantage, in that the final gear ratio is slightly raised (numerically), so the car feels just a bit faster through the gears. Many people like the friskier feel brought by slightly smaller diameter tires, especially in our world of 70-mph speed limits.

On the unsprung weight issue, you are correct. The lower the unsprung weight, the better the theoretical handling. I simply like the looks of the steel wheels, and unless on the race course, the difference in handling is exceptionally hard to notice.

I have done many head-to-head wheel swaps, noting differences in handling and road feel with dozens of different wheel and tire combinations, including the rare and ultra-lightweight Mahle "gas burner" 911T wheels. I could not, by the seat of my pants, detect a difference in ride or handling feel on the street based on different wheels. Yet I can immediately—within ten seconds on the road—feel the harshness of a 195/60 or 205/55 set of high-performance tires.

A long time ago I realized just how smart the guys at the Porsche factory actually were, and that for general street use, they almost always had the right idea. I'm glad you are thinking along the same lines. ◆

Publisher Martin's lowered and consequently harsh-riding 911SC

Why One High Sale Doesn't Mean All Cars Are Worth More

The buyer had a "Gone in 60 Seconds" list from his boss that included a big Healey—and he was out of time

by Gary Anderson

Build it for $75k, or buy it done for twice as much?

Barrett-Jackson

On Saturday evening at the Barrett-Jackson Auction in Scottsdale in 2006, a 1967 Austin-Healey 3000 BJ8 convertible painted "golden beige metallic," an original Healey color for the year—but not original to this particular car—with red leather interior, and absolutely no historical significance, sold for $143,100.

This is the most expensive public sale of a production Austin-Healey ever (exceeded only by the limited-production 100S and Works Healeys). It tops the previous high by more than $50,000. Only five years ago, the sale of a Healey for anything over $40,000 was big news.

The question is: Should observers attach any market significance to this sale? The short answer is no.

This sale didn't just border on irrationality; it crossed that border at somewhere around $80,000. But in terms of free-market economics, why should we call any auction sale irra-tional—as each transaction clearly represents what a willing buyer, along with a nearly-as-willing underbidder, agrees to pay for a certain item at a certain time.

You could build this car for $75,000

Here's the biggest reason this sale falls outside of what I would call "reasonable": Anyone could go to the restorer who did the work on this car (or any of three or four other restorers with the same reputation for high-quality work) and ask him to create an identical car at a guaranteed price, and we suspect he wouldn't ask more than $75,000, tops. And that price would include the cost of the donor car. Would that be easy to do? Absolutely. There is no scarcity of 1967 Austin-Healey convertibles in restorable condition, and certainly no shortage of golden beige metallic paint or red leather.

As an aside, golden beige metallic was a shade that was selected for a small number of big Healeys in what was

197

expected to be the last year of their production. Until recently, original golden beige Healeys were rare enough to have their own registry, but this car wasn't originally that color, so aside from its inherent attractiveness, there's no particular significance here.

It wasn't an unusual color even when Healeys were new; Jaguar used the same formulation on their Mk IIs and E-types during the period, calling it "opalescent golden sand." Healeys with that exterior color could be ordered with either a black or a red interior, but red is definitely the more attractive of the two choices with the golden beige finish.

Tired of resale red

We don't know for sure, but it's possible that Kurt Tanner, the restorer of this car and a man who has managed to become a brand name in Healey restorations for auction sale, chose this color just because he was getting tired of building resale-red and bid-fetching-BRG convertibles.

Even considering the other Healeys that sold in January in the superheated air of Scottsdale, this sale wasn't in any ballpark we know. The real news at this auction was that there were eight other sales of Healeys in the $50,000 to $85,000 range. Two sold at $50,000, four more sold for under $75,000, and two sold for about $85,000.

Even those are historically stupendous prices for Healeys, but they're basically what it would cost to buy a solid project car with all its parts and good body panels, then pay a shop to restore it to show condition. But that would take nine months or so, and there are many buyers coming into the market today who aren't prepared to wait for what they want. Time is a valuable commodity to the Boomers that bid at these auctions, and they're happy to pay extra for immediate gratification.

Certainly it's good for Healey owners that newly restored Healeys have been bid up over the past five years to the point where one might pay for a decent restoration without being underwater at the end of the process.

Rising auction prices don't necessarily mean the prices of average, everyday cars will rise, but they certainly call attention to a marque. Decent Healeys in the club driver category are now recognized for the value that they provide. They're fast enough to hold their own on the freeway, they're instantly recognizable, and they have earned iconic status.

Boomers running out of time

More important, like '60s muscle cars, they fill the memory of Baby Boomers who have leisure time and discretionary income. We're now seeing decent drivers, which might have sold for a solid $25,000 five years ago, selling for $40,000.

As for the $140,000 sale, does it matter that a Healey has now sold for as much as an Aston-Martin DB5 or a Mulliner-bodied R-type Bentley? Is this sale likely to have any influence on the overall market value of Healeys?

We say no. If you can pay to have someone restore a Healey to your exact specifications for half what this buyer paid, even taking into account the time factor, then we must attribute that sale to something other than rationality.

If we had to invent a scenario to explain this transaction in any terms other than speed—or the Speed Channel-induced buyer's euphoria—here's one plausible story line.

Buyer had a "Gone in 60 Seconds" task

The buyer, who we know was buying cars on behalf of a wealthy car collector and museum developer, had perhaps a list of cars he was supposed to bring home—a "Gone in 60 Seconds" assignment—and at the end of the weekend, with only one Healey left to cross the block, he realized that a Healey was on that wish list and that he hadn't gotten one yet.

Whoops. Gotta have it. At any price. And with other bidders pretty much aware of his bidding style, there might even have been a game of chicken going on to push the bidding up.

Whatever the explanation, one golden beige metallic Austin-Healey went home for an incredible price, which made the restorer happy and had many owners calling their insurance agents the following week to bump their agreed-value policies up another $5,000 or $10,000.

But if you're thinking of selling your Healey in the near future (even if it is golden beige with red upholstery), don't expect to have a buyer knocking at your door any time soon with $140,000 in his pocket. Buyers like that don't come along very often. And if you want one just like it, and can wait a few months, you will have saved yourself $65,000. Which will probably be just about enough to buy a perfect MGB at the next Barrett-Jackson. ♦

How to Successfully Buy Collector Cars Online

If you can't eyeball your prospective purchase in person, or you don't feel qualified to do so, pay a professional appraiser or inspector to do it for you

by Rob Sass

Imagine trying to explain to someone ten years ago the notion of purchasing a car by wiring money to a perfect stranger hundreds or perhaps thousands of miles away for something you've never seen, except at 72 dpi resolution on a 17-inch computer monitor.

But what was a novelty ten years ago is now a fact of life—car buyers do it all the time, with varying degrees of success. Their reasons mirror Willie Sutton's explanation for why he robbed banks: Because that's where the money is—and online is where the cars are.

The biggest development in the online car buying world to take place since this book was last updated is the emergence of Craigslist as a credible companion to eBay Motors. Craigslist started in the Bay Area in 1995 as an email distribution system to keep the founder's friends apprised of local events. It turned into a web-based service the next year and began serving up local classifieds much like the old Trading Times classified papers did in local markets.

Cars were a natural for the no-frills website. Within the last several years, the number of cars posted on Craigslist seems to have increased exponentially. But Craigslist has several shortcomings compared with eBay Motors or other automotive classified web sites. The most significant is the fact that the seller, if he uses the standard Craigslist tool, can only post four photos, which cannot be enlarged by a viewer. Many listers get around this by posting unlimited numbers of photos of good quality on web sites like Flickr and Photobucket and linking to these in their Craigslist posting, but that's an extra step.

The other impediment (from the buyer's standpoint) is the fact that Craigslist isn't national. Each metro area has its own separate and distinct Craigslist site. Necessity being the mother of invention, several Craigslist aggregator sites have sprung up allowing one to search multiple Craigslists at once. One of many among these is Zimkiv.com.

The low-budget nature of Craigslist generally extends to

Craigslist

the listings—for the most part, the listings seem to occupy the bottom of the collector-car food chain. That's not a particularly bad thing, as there are many bargains to be found on Craigslist, and many savvy individuals I know swear that the new paradigm for bottom-feeders is to buy on Craigslist and sell on eBay.

The newest kid on the block is BringATrailer.com. The brainchild of Randy Nonnenberg, it's the site we all wish we'd come up with. In addition to exclusive ads, Nonnenberg scours other automotive web sites for the most interesting and unusual cars on the market. The user-generated comments are often quite helpful. If you're interested in the unusual, it's the site for you.

And if you want to know if the price is in line with what

BringATrailer.com

other people are asking, check out SCM's own www .collectorcarpricetracker.com and see what similar cars are have brought. A partnership between SCM Publisher Keith Martin and eBay Motors, it has nearly 600,000 confirmed collector car sales in its database, so you'll surely be able to find a car like the one you are looking at and find out what it sold for. It's also possible to figure out geographically where you ought to be buying and selling—though anybody who took high school geography knows to check rainfall and average temperatures.

The same rules that have always applied to on-line transactions still apply. The scammers haven't gone away, and they just keep getting more brazen.

1. Verify cashier's checks by calling an officer at the bank upon which it was drawn.

2. Never accept a check in an amount over the purchase price of the car or consent to refunding the overage. It's a popular scam—their check bounces, and yours doesn't.

3. Always insist on seeing a copy of the title, front and back, to verify that the VIN on the car matches the one on the title and that the seller has clear title. If there's a lien, it's best to deal directly with the lender rather than assuming the seller will take your money and pay off the loan. If he or she doesn't pay off the lien, you've bought nothing.

Buying sight-unseen has never been a good idea. If you can't eyeball your prospective purchase in person, or you don't feel qualified to do so, pay a professional appraiser or inspector to do it for you. A pre-purchase inspection from a mechanic is not duplicative and is also a good idea.

An appraiser is looking at the general condition of the car, particularly the body and interior, while a pre-purchase inspection from a reputable shop will focus on the mechanics of the car. In some cases, where the stakes are a bit lower, like looking at an MG or a Healey as opposed to a Ferrari, you might get by with having a knowledgeable local club member look things over.

Most successful online transactions culminate in the realization that you now own something too large to be mailed home. While I'm generally up for any adventure in an old car, I draw the line at a long road trip in an unproven car. Do yourself a favor and contact a reputable enclosed auto transporter.

To quote Ronald Reagan, if you use "trust but verify" as your guideline, chances are you will come out just fine. ♦

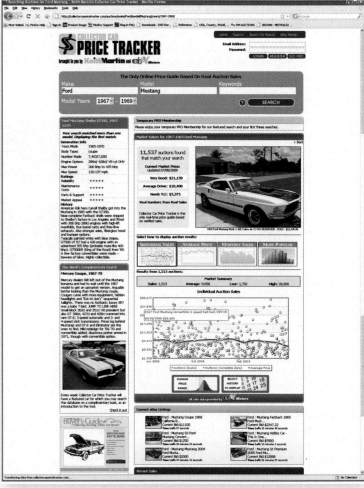

Collector Car Price Tracker

What "Everything Works" Really Means

Once all the repairs were completed, I asked the seller to compensate me and showed him the receipts. He told me to get lost

by John Draneas

1965 Corvette

Dear Keith Martin's Guide to Car Collecting: Six months ago I purchased a 1965 Corvette 327/375 Fuelie convertible from a well-known Corvette specialist dealer for $85,000. The car was reported in writing to be numbers-matching and completely operational, condition #2+. But after driving the car on the highway at 60 mph for 30 minutes and in traffic for 15 minutes, I discovered a large number of problems.

From serious overheating to fuel-injection problems, fuel leaks, oil leaks, and an inoperative wiper motor, the total repair bill was about $8,000. I informed the dealer of the problems, which took the better part of three months to correct. During that time, he said to save the receipts, and we would work something out.

Once the repairs were completed, I asked him to compensate me and showed him the receipts, whereupon he basically told me to get lost. I reminded him that when he sold me the car, he claimed that everything worked. He replied that the car worked for him every time he drove it around the block to get gas, and that the car was not supposed to be driven like I drive it.

I could not believe what I was hearing. "You mean to tell

me that when you said 'everything works,' you meant only to start it, drive it a couple of blocks, then put it away?" To which he answered, "Yes," and said something about collector cars being just to look at.

So what do I do? When a car is claimed to be fully operational, does that not imply operational for common driving conditions? Do I have any legal recourse to be compensated for the work performed to get the car operational for normal driving?—*B.C., Florida*

At first glance, this seems like a pretty simple situation, with little doubt that our reader is entitled to compensation for his stack of repair bills. But during my 30 years of legal practice, I have learned three important things. The first is that your clients never really tell you everything the first time. The second is that there are always at least two sides to every story. And finally, that the truth in any legal dispute usually lies somewhere in between the first two points.

More to the story

I asked the reader to send me a copy of the written report that he mentioned was a part of the sale. When he checked his sales documents, he found that the dealer had specified nothing in writing as to the condition of car. Nor was there a written warranty.

"I only have [the dealer's] verbal comments, with witnesses, that he said everything on the car works, and that it was a solid condition #2 car," the reader told me. "I believe the actual verbiage was, 'In complete working order.'" He went on to affirm that at no time, either verbally or in writing, did the dealer mention that there was anything wrong with the car.

The reader also told me that the dealer understood that he would probably rally the Corvette as well as take it to a race track.

A potential lawsuit

While this still looks like a pretty strong misrepresentation case, our reader has two problems, the most important being that he has nothing in writing.

The law does not require that representations or statements about the car be made in writing in order to be the basis of a claim. But it's a heck of lot easier to prove what was actually said if it's on paper, which is why my number-one mantra is to get everything in writing. While this usually means paying an attorney some money, it's cheap insurance against what in this case turned out to be an $8k disagreement.

Our reader states that he had witnesses present when the dealer described the condition of the Corvette, and this may be enough. Still, people hear and remember things differently, and the last thing you want at a trial is to get into a "Rashomon" retelling of the events.

Everything works, mostly

The second problem our reader faces in winning his case comes in what the law will interpret as the core of the contract. While the words the dealer used to describe the Corvette are simple enough, they are also capable of having more than one meaning. Just what does "everything works" mean?

"Working" does not necessarily mean working well, working perfectly, working under adverse conditions, or working for long. Nor does it mean not being in need of any repairs. Consider a motor that runs and drives but burns a quart of oil every 100 miles and needs a rebuild. Is it still "working"? Probably.

I don't think that the statement that the Corvette was a #2 car is a slam dunk, either. After all, SCM routinely rates auction cars as #2s without driving them. The 'Vette in question may have had a whole host of minor problems, but none of these were readily evident prior to the sale.

The verdict

Although this case could go either way, I still like our reader's chances. The context for considering any misrepresentation claim should be based on what the purchaser would be reasonably expected to believe as a result of the seller's statements. With the way this car was represented and the dealer knowing of our reader's intended use, I would think that a judge or jury would conclude that the dealer misled our subscriber into believing that this car was better than it was, and would hold the dealer responsible for at least a portion of the repairs.

The moral here is to avoid this sort of situation by not just relying on the seller's descriptions of the collector car. Always get a thorough pre-purchase inspection and perform an extensive test drive. These are old cars, and they aren't perfect.

Get everything in a sales contract clearly stated, avoiding generalizations like "everything works" or "needs nothing." A checklist that rates each significant component of the car for condition on a sliding scale will make it a lot harder for the seller to change his story later.

Don't be reluctant to spend some money to draw up a written contract that spells out the specific condition and terms of a sale, as legal fees will always be a small percentage of the purchase price of a car. Do the math and it's usually far less than the tax and license costs. That's really pretty affordable protection and certainly much less expensive than a lawsuit after the fact. ◆

Buying Techniques That Work

A flashlight is mandatory; use it to look for rust repair, panel replacement, and accident damage. Carry a magnet, too

by Colin Comer

Shelby American Automobile Club; www.saac.com

Have I got a deal for you

How do you keep a seller honest? Every seller has one goal in mind—getting your money—and even the most honest person can "forget" the truth. Over the years, I have developed a buying technique designed to catch Joe Isuzu, who wouldn't know the truth if it bit him. Herewith are some guidelines:

Read between the lines

Decipher what the seller's description really means. People have trouble putting a blatant lie in print for fear of getting caught or having it used against them. So what the description doesn't say is what you should worry about.

For example: "The 1969 Pontiac GTO Judge was equipped with a Ram Air III engine producing 366 hp." Guess what—I bet this Judge no longer has its original engine.

"Previous owner said it ran and drove very well." Call a tow truck if you buy this baby.

"Completely original, with freshly done interior, respray, and new drivetrain." Be afraid, be very afraid.

Ask tough questions, take notes

Once you have studied the description, make your list. Ask questions that clarify what is written, as well as what is left out. Write down the seller's answers, especially if dealing face to face. An honest seller won't mind you taking notes; a dishonest one will squirm.

Research the car you are buying and know important details, such as casting numbers on key components. Know what equipment was standard and what was optional.

Ask tough questions and keep asking until you are satisfied you get the truth. A "four-owner" car? Get the owners' names and ask if you may contact them. If the seller doesn't know the names, how does he know the car only had four owners? Such questions will help you decide if you should proceed.

Crawl all over the car

Check the seller's answers against the car. Have a flashlight and notepad, arm yourself with a book describing where the important numbers are located, and get dirty. Ever see buyers at auction wearing nice clean clothes, who never crack a hood or crawl under a car? They're asking for it. You'll see me in a T-shirt and jeans, with a pocket of greasy rags and a flashlight.

If you are not comfortable checking the numbers, get somebody who is—even if just to read them to you. Look for continuity among date codes and general appearance. If a 120,000-mile car has grease on everything except the serial number stamping and date-code casting on the engine block, look for a grinder and Home Depot stamp set under this seller's workbench.

How to find "original" sins

If the car appears to be real, start checking its condition. Your homework will have told you the trouble areas. For example, on early GTOs, the rear body mounts at the frame are the first place to look; these are the first place GTOs rust. It is also the last place anybody bothers to fix properly, and issues there are easy to spot.

If the car is reported to be unrestored, poke around for proof. Is the carpet original? Seat covers? Body panels? Paint? The desirability of unrestored cars has driven many to doll up tacky old dogs to look "unrestored."

Spend $300 and arm yourself with a digital paint-thickness gauge. This device, when held against paint, reports the thickness of the finish. Factory-applied paint is typically 2–5 mils; repaints will result in 8–10 mils or more.

At a recent auction, I was inspecting a car that proudly proclaimed "100% Original Factory Paint." Looking at it, I could see imperfections in the underlying prepwork—telling me the car had been repainted. Using my paint gauge, I walked around the car and checked surface thickness at various points.

The seller spotted this and quite defensively came over and barked, "What is that *thing* you are aiming at my car?" My reply: "It's a lie detector." Seller: "What does it tell you?" Me: "You're guilty." 10–15 mils everywhere.

A flashlight is mandatory. Use it to look for rust repair, panel replacement, and accident damage. Look in the trunk, under the rear window area, then all the way down the quarter panels forward to the doors. Body filler and paint guns can reach nearly everywhere without much effort, except these areas. Look closely at panel seams and spot welds.

Study original cars and apply this knowledge to restored ones. Be thorough, be educated, and make sure the seller sees you making this kind of inspection. The guilty ones won't stop talking, and the honest ones will let you look to your heart's content.

Get all claims in writing

Here's a tip for auction buyers: If the car passes these tests to your satisfaction, ask the seller to put in writing any claims he has made to you verbally that are not on the printed auction description. If the auction announces a car as "documented with the original build sheet" but it is not on the window card, have the seller and the auction company note on the block ticket that the original build sheet will be delivered with the car.

Take it slow, inspect the car, and verify the seller's claims. If you are short of knowledge or confidence, the best money you can spend is to hire a specialist.

However, don't fall prey to one of the "nationwide vehicle inspection services" that have grown up lately. These firms subcontract their orders to local insurance adjusters. I guarantee they will know less than you do about the car in question.

Instead, call restoration shops or clubs in the area and ask for recommendations. Ask the inspector for multiple pictures and to follow a pre-determined checklist. Have these sent to you upon completion. These techniques should help you get the car you thought you were buying into your garage, rather than one that keeps giving you one bad surprise after another. ◆

Modify, Restore, or Preserve

After a quick blast down the highway in a highly modified Speedster, some buyers won't care about the lack of correctness

by Jim Schrager

1970 Porsche 914 "V8"

Dear *Keith Martin's Guide to Car Collecting:* After reading about your silver 1976 912E, into which someone had put a 2-liter 911 engine, I began to contemplate the reality of what was done—the bastardizing of a rare Porsche model. Although I'm primarily a purist, I thought back to some of the Porsches that I've owned, and wondered if the alterations I made to them were merely small changes or if I had really bastardized them. There was the '58 Speedster fitted with a Super 90 engine and later transaxle, the 914/6 that was modified via a 2.6-liter 911S and short gears, and the 1981 911SC coupe that I converted to an all-steel Turbo body with a bi-wing rear spoiler.

Back when I modified it, the Speedster was just a $2,500 car. The 914/6, although already rare when "improved" by me, maintained a technically correct appearance; I just gave it the ability to match a 289 Cobra on acceleration. The SC, well, they're a dime a dozen, and I went racing with that car.

Your article made me think about adaptation parameters;

if there is such a thing, should there be? Of course, no one in his right mind would stuff a 993 engine into a 1967 911R, or transplant a 914 1.7-liter engine into a lightweight 1973 RS. Although those are extreme examples, with your 912/911s you have used a semi-precious engine as a replacement heart for a car that was, from birth, a slug. Yes, the new engine solved the issue of why the '76 was a slug, but couldn't a case be made for the early engine being better used in a 1969–73 period 911?

Are there cars out there that should be preserved? Will there ever be a shortage of 911SCs that is significant enough that I should have preserved my coupe? Because of my Speedster's robust engine, did that beautiful, white, rust-free example survive the last 35 years, or did the extra power cause it to be wrapped around a tree?

Your 912E is a rather pretty car, so using the SCM Price Guide, as a 912E, it would be worth about $8k. If it had been born a 1976 911S and was in similar condition, it would be worth about $10k. After the surgical implant of the early 911S engine, it has 180 DIN hp, compared to 165 DIN hp for a stock 2.7-liter 911S, and the modest 90 hp in its original four-cylinder form. What's it worth now? Or should a monetary result not be factored in?—*Pete Zimmermann, Bakersfield, CA*

Fire up the crystal ball

At one level, you are right about the engine swap in my 912/911 and similar modifications to other Porsches—they can easily offend. But let's dig a few layers deeper. If what I am doing does not hurt the value—or maybe even helps it and at the same time makes the car a better performer, then I'm in favor, purists be hanged. This philosophy made modifications of my 250k-mile well-used 912E a no-brainer. With its original, used-up four-cylinder running gear, the car was just plain worn out. I was lucky a previous owner had spent the time and money to fit a 2.0-liter 911 engine in there, and of course that was one of the big attractions for me. It meant that a lot of the hard work necessary for me to install a high-performance 2.2-liter 911S engine had already been done. Unless a stock 912E is a mint low-mileage example in great colors with original paint, I don't see any upside, no matter how long you wait.

But the values of our cars change over time, so to get things right requires a bit of crystal ball gazing. Since in general a car must be rare to be valuable, messing with cars with high production volumes is usually safe. However, in the Porsche world there are notable exceptions: Speedsters are not really that rare, with over 4,000 made, but are very valuable. Early 911S cars are not so rare, with a few thousand or so made each of seven years between 1967 and 1973, yet the values are very strong.

But 914-4 cars are not at all rare, with about 100,000 made, and neither are 911SCs, with production of over 60,000 units. I break this rule with the 912E, which is a rare car at just over 2,000 made. But like the "Notchback" 356B, any Sportomatic 911 (even an early 911S), the 911L, and the 912E, rarity does not always translate into value in the Porsche world.

There is another way to lose your shirt in this modification game, and that is to put too much in your upgrades. Examples include $50,000 914-4s made into fire-breathing 914-6 conversions, and 1973 911T cars made into near-perfect $75,000 Carrera RS clones. Keep an eye on what the market is for original vs. clone cars as you build your own ideal mongrel.

"Converted" cars newly collectible

One recent trend is that some highly desirable "converted" Porsches can bring as much as their stock counterparts, although not from the same type of buyer. For example, consider a beautiful silver 356A Speedster, with a later 912 engine, smooth-shifting SC gearbox, and more recent powerful disc brakes. After a quick blast down the highway, some buyers will be thrilled and not care about the lack of "correctness." They might not be interested in a Speedster with its original, more fragile running gear and modest performance, and might actually pay more for a "resto-mod" Speedster than for an original. Others will want nothing but the original parts, no matter how much they may interfere with the reliability or performance of the car, and will only shell out the big bucks for the real thing. The same holds for converted 914-6 cars and 911T cars made into RS replicas. So you might end up with the same market value for a correct car and a modified one, but from two very different types of buyers.

As to my 912E, it was surely not worth $10k when I bought it at about half that on eBay, and I felt everything done to the car was pure upside. As to putting the 2.2S engine in an earlier chassis, you'd be amazed at how this big-bumper car drives with this engine. All that high-rpm power feels just like it does in an earlier chassis, and the wheels and tires work together to deliver the compliant yet responsive ride we all remember from the early S cars. As to what it's worth today, I'd say about $10k.

But I admit I wasn't worried about that, as this car was made for driving. And in that category, it's a real winner. So long as your modifications make driving and aesthetic sense, and are within the budget you set, I don't see any reason to be a slavish adherent to "originality at all costs." ♦

1973 Porsche 914-errari

Avoiding Taxes on the Sale of Your Collector Car

How to use "like kind" 1031 exchanges to keep Uncle Sam from taxing the sale of your collector car. Pay no tax if you receive no cash

by John Draneas

1970 Hemi 'Cuda

Let's say you were smart enough or just lucky enough to buy a Hemi 'Cuda coupe a few years ago for $75,000. Let's also suppose that you think that its current $500,000 value is the top of the muscle car market, and that it's the perfect time to sell it and buy a four-cam Ferrari 275 GTB. Before you do that, you might want to give a little thought to how your income taxes are going to affect the deal.

Many of us have never made any real money on a collector car and haven't had to worry about paying taxes on these profits. But when you finally hit the jackpot on a car that's appreciated like mad, know that the IRS will be there to remind you that it is your silent partner—and it gets a pretty big share of your booty, too.

Depending on the tax rates in your state, the government's cut on a sale like the 'Cuda I've described could run about $140,000. That's the equivalent of buying Uncle Sam a nice new convertible 911 Turbo, and leaves you that much short for your Ferrari.

Sidestepping the taxman

So how do you avoid the tax collector, but still get to buy your Ferrari? By designing the transaction as what the tax law calls a "like-kind exchange." Under Section 1031 of the

Federal Tax Code, you can exchange one asset for another of a like kind and not pay tax on the gain, as long as no cash goes into your pockets.

But chances are, the owner of the Ferrari you covet isn't going to want your 'Cuda, so you can't just trade even-up. Fortunately, the law allows you to do what's called a deferred exchange, using a qualified accommodator or middleman.

Doing this is pretty easy. You start by finding the buyer for your car. Once you have a contract with him, you transfer the title and the sales contract to the accommodator, who sells the car and holds on to the money. Then you locate your Ferrari and instruct the accommodator to buy it for you, which he does, in turn transferring ownership to you. That completes the transaction, and you've legally traded cars without any money from the deal coming into your possession, and thus you don't owe any tax.

The fine print

While all this sounds pretty simple, there are a lot of devils in the details. Here are a few of them:

1. You have to pick the right middleman. The accommodator cannot be anyone who has been your agent (employee, attorney, accountant, etc.) within the last two years, or someone related to any of those people, or a business entity you control. One experienced accommodator is Classic Automobile Reserve (www.car1031.com, 877.218.7800). Managing member Steve Drake, who serves as the CPA for Barrett-Jackson in his spare time, says, "Most collectors don't even realize that they owe taxes on the sale of their collector car." Drake says that his firm's fees vary with the nature of the transaction, but are usually below 3% of the value of the car.

2. Once the accommodator sells your car, you have 45 days to identify up to three potential replacement cars. Make sure you give careful attention to this requirement, because this period can fly by. You cannot extend it, and you can't add more cars to the list if the ones you pick don't pan out. So you must both be careful with the cars you select, as well as being sure to actually select three in the hopes of bettering your odds if your first deal goes south.

3. You have 180 days from the sale of your car to actually take title to the replacement car from the accommodator. This is usually the easier deadline to meet, because once the car has been identified, the purchase usually moves pretty quickly. But that might not be the case when the replacement is a new car that has to be ordered. Something like a Porsche Carrera GT or a McLaren SLR might incur a wait. But remember, the accommodator has to be the one to buy the car, then transfer it to you—the car can't be sold directly to you. You need to factor this second transfer into your timeline as well.

4. Although I won't go into the details, it is worth mentioning that it is possible to do a 1031 exchange with multiple cars, like replacing your 'Cuda with a Daytona and a Porsche Speedster.

Financing

Liabilities can complicate the equation a little bit. For instance, if we go back to our original example, any money you owe on the 'Cuda is compared against what you borrow to buy the 275 GTB. If the money owed on the 'Cuda is greater, the excess is treated as though it were cash received by you, and you pay tax on that amount. Simply stated, you can't pull any cash out of the deal.

But there can be a way around this, too. First, you make the exchange using all the cash available from the sale. Then, some time after all the dust has settled, you can take out a loan against the Ferarri. How long after? That's hard to say, as it has to be long enough for the transaction to be completely finished in all aspects, long enough for the loan to be a separate deal from the exchange, and long enough to demonstrate that this wasn't what you were planning to do all along. You weren't, were you?

Before you ask, leases just don't work with 1031 exchanges, as you have to own the replacement car when all is said and done.

Reverse exchanges

Sometimes, the only reason you want to sell your car is because you found another one that you like better. What if the new car won't wait, it's a once-in-a-lifetime deal on that Ferrari, and you just have to buy it now and sell your Plymouth later? In these situations, it is possible to do a reverse exchange.

The way this works is you start by lending money to the accommodator to buy the Ferrari. The accommodator then stores the car until you find a buyer for your 'Cuda. (That's right, you can't drive the new car or keep it at your place during this time.) Then you transfer the 'Cuda and its sales contract to the accommodator, who sells it. You can then identify the Ferarri as the replacement car, which the accommodator will transfer to you, along with the cash from the 'Cuda sale that repays your original loan.

The IRS imposes similar timing rules on these reverse exchanges: You have 45 days from the purchase of the replacement car to sell the original one, and 180 days to finish the entire deal.

While 1031 exchanges can save you a lot of tax money, they do present lots of easy ways to go wrong, and any little missed detail can turn your deal into a taxable transaction. If you think you might be able to benefit from a 1031, it's best to get good advice, in advance, from a tax attorney or a competent CPA. ♦

What "No Reserve" Really Means

The traditional view is that a reserve affords protection to the seller, but in "no reserve," bidders know the car will sell

by John Draneas

Bidders should read their agreements so they know their rights—and those of the auction company

I hadn't even made it to the Phoenix airport on my way home when my cell phone started ringing with Arizona auction rumors. When I did get home, there were emails waiting for me with the same stories—cars sold to chandeliers, sellers buying their own cars back, buyers refusing to perform, you name it. The phony or chandelier bidding stories got my curiosity going. Several people asked me what the law says about this, so I decided to find out.

We are going to address only two issues here. One is the proverbial "chandelier bid," where the auctioneer calls out and recognizes a bid that no one seems to have made. The other is bidding on behalf of the seller on his own car, either by the seller himself, by a friend or agent of the seller, or by the auctioneer.

The law

Auctions are firmly covered in the Uniform Commercial Code, which is a commercial law adopted in all the states, although each state is free to make modifications to its version. Of interest to us is Section 2-328, which sets out the rules on auctions. Since individual states can modify the uniform rule if they chose to, I looked at Arizona's version as the most relevant to our situation. Arizona adopted UCC Section 2-328 without modification, likely the same law as in your state.

The meaning of the reserve

Under the law, auctions are considered to be "with reserve" unless it is made clear that the sale is being made without reserve. The reserve is the minimum price that the seller will accept for the car. For the seller's benefit, it is kept secret between the seller and auctioneer. A reserve auction carries one additional legal difference: The seller may withdraw the car from the auction at any time before the gavel falls. In a "no reserve" auction, once the first bid is made, the seller can no longer withdraw the car from the auction, and it sells to the highest bidder.

There are two schools of thought on reserves. The traditional view is that the seller is always better off with a reserve because it affords obvious protection against a horrible result if the high bid is woefully below the real value of the car.

The more modern view is that "no reserve" auctions work better because the bidders know the car is going to sell, and they are more motivated to bid. Proponents of this view point out that in a reserve sale, bidding frequently jumps once the auctioneer announces that the seller's reserve has been met. In a "no reserve" sale, this bidding heat begins as soon as the car is driven onto the block.

Whether or not the "no reserve" theory really brings higher sales prices is open for debate. But when things don't go as planned for proponents of the theory, there is plenty of incentive to "help" the real bidders reach the "right" price on the car; in other words, to protect the buyer against his car selling for far less than expected.

Chandelier bids

Chandelier (or phantom) bids are a well-recognized fact of auction life. In fact, at our SCM Insider's Seminars, we strive to teach attendees how to tell if there is "real money" on a car. But as common as the practice is, is it legal?

The answer is: No. Chandelier bids are misrepresentations and fraud. But you won't find any court cases on it. Not only is it hard to know when a chandelier is bidding, proving it in court is even tougher.

Chandelier bidding is often justified in reserve auctions on the "no harm, no foul" theory. That is, there won't be a deal struck until the reserve is met anyway, so no one is damaged when the auctioneer helps things along. But that misses one key point. As a seasoned negotiator, I like being the high bidder in a no-sale auction. That gives me the leverage to find the seller afterward and try to negotiate a deal off the block (but still with the auction company involved, obviously).

Seller bidding

The UCC is quite clear on the issue of sellers bidding on their own cars. It's generally illegal. The courts have cut some slack for sellers in reserve auctions, on the basis that no real

bid was going to take the car as long as the reserve had not been met. But "no reserve" auctions are an entirely different story.

In a "no reserve" auction, seller bids are illegal unless the real bidders have been given notice that the auctioneer will allow sellers to bid on their own cars. If notice is given, there is no legal problem, and "buyer beware" prevails. But if notice is not given and the seller buys the car, the legal situation gets very interesting. The UCC clearly states that the highest real bidder has the right to either cancel the purchase or to buy the car at the highest real bid made. And, in one court case involving intentional bid rigging, the highest real bidder was awarded punitive damages to boot.

What sort of notice is sufficient to validate seller bids? Obviously, an announcement made on the block by the auctioneer will do the trick, but no auctioneer really wants to do that. Curious, I checked my bidder's agreement from one of the recent Arizona auctions. There it was: The auction house reserved the right to accept bids from sellers, and even to make the bids for them. I had been warned in black and white, in unmistakable language. Is it legally sufficient? I would imagine that it is, since it has my signature on the bottom. Funny, though, it took me five years of registering as a bidder at this auction to notice that little sentence.

All of these rules apply equally to Internet-based auctions. The UCC is not limited to bricks-and-mortar auction houses. Oddly enough, Internet auctions may make it easier to prove phony bidding, even though the opposite may seem to be the case. The advantage is that Internet bids are made in writing, and there is a discoverable record of who made which bids.

Buyer beware

As illegal as many of these tactics are, bear in mind that they are common. Learn to know how to "read" the bidding, and how to know if there is real money on a car. Decide how much you are willing to pay before you even start to bid, and stop bidding when you get there. Not all auction houses bend the rules, and even the best ones have a hard time keeping the sellers from engaging in these practices. Read your bidder's agreement carefully, and see what the rules really are at that particular auction. ◆

Tax Consequences of Selling Your Car

In some cases, waiting a few weeks, or even a single day, to sell your car can result in substantial tax savings

by John Draneas

Collector car values are skyrocketing, and many of us have substantial gains in our collections. More and more collectors are wondering if the market is peaking, and whether they should sell. If they do sell, what are the tax consequences? Although many of us want to stay in denial about this, gains on collector cars are fully taxable, and failing to report them runs the risk of a tax fraud charge.

On the other hand, collectors who are new to the game are buying cars at today's rather feisty prices. Of course, if the market keeps going up, they will accrue substantial gains. But if the bubble bursts, as some expect, these investors could suffer losses. Are there any tax advantages to soften the blow?

Start with the right pigeonhole

You should begin by identifying the tax character of your collector car, which depends on the purpose behind your ownership and the way in which you use it. The various classifications, and their general tax characteristics, are as follows:

Personal use: This is the car that you drive for personal purposes; that is, your regular driver, not used in your business. You cannot depreciate the car. If you make money on it, the gain is taxable as a capital gain. If you lose money on it, there is no tax benefit afforded.

Investment: This is the car that you buy to make money on when it appreciates. It can be driven only in a limited manner; otherwise, it becomes a personal-use automobile. It can be a blue-chip collectible, but doesn't have to be. You cannot depreciate it. If you make money on it, the gain is taxable as a capital gain. If you lose money on it, the loss is a capital loss.

Business use: This car is driven as part of your business and you can depreciate it. If you make money on it, the gain is taxable as ordinary income to the extent of the depreciation that you have previously claimed on the car, and capital gain thereafter. If you lose money on it, the loss is deductible as an ordinary loss.

Inventory: This is the car that you own to sell to your customers in the ordinary course of your business. You cannot depreciate it. If you make money on it, the gain is taxable as ordinary income. If you lose money on it, the loss is deductible as an ordinary loss.

Which is better?

If you have a gain, it's best if it's a long-term capital gain. Long-term means you owned the car for at least a year. The result is that the profit is taxed at a maximum 28% federal tax rate (collector cars do not qualify for the 15% rate). A short-term capital gain is taxed the same as ordinary income, at your regular income tax rates up to 35%. Which means that in some cases, waiting a few weeks, or even a day, to sell your car can result in substantial tax savings (see sidebar).

1958 Porsche Speedster Tax Recap

ESTIMATED CAPITAL GAINS TAX IF PURCHASED AS AN INVESTMENT		
Length of Ownership	Under 1 Year	Over 1 Year
Purchase Price	$100,000	$100,000
Sold Price	$150,000	$150,000
Income	$50,000	$50,000
Tax	$17,500 (35%)	$14,000 (28%)
Net Profit	$32,500	$36,000

If you have a loss, an ordinary loss is best because it can be deducted against your ordinary income. Subject to various limitations, that can yield up to a 35% benefit. A capital loss can be offset against other capital gains, yielding a 15% or 28% benefit, or deducted against ordinary income at the rate of $3,000 per year. Any unused loss will carry forward.

State income taxation is generally the same as the federal treatment, although that differs in some respects in some states, and the tax rates vary widely.

A popular tax deferral technique for real estate is a "like kind" exchange. The same can be done with collector cars. If you meet the various rules that apply to the economics of the exchange, you can exchange one collector car for another without paying tax. This technique is available for collector cars held for investment and business use. It is not available for cars held for personal use or as inventory.

The IRS doesn't play fair

These distinctions were highlighted in a U.S. Tax Court case decided last year. This case dealt with the tax consequences of losses on the sale of collector cars by David Taylor Enterprises, Inc. after the death of its sole shareholder.

Taylor was a successful car dealer in the Houston area and one of the largest Cadillac dealers in the world. Taylor had a passion for classic cars and established an impressive inventory at his Galveston, Texas, facility. This effort began in 1979 with the purchase of a 1931 Cadillac Roadster for $40,000, and resulted in 80 car sales over 12 years.

All the classic cars were impeccably restored. They were stored in a temperature-controlled facility known as the David Taylor Classic Car Museum. The public was allowed to pay admission and tour the museum. All cars were available for sale at all times. They were kept on jack stands to protect the tires from leakage and flat spots, they were started every six weeks, and the oil was changed every six months.

In the years prior to Taylor's death, the corporation sold eleven cars, at gains of up to $143,000 on one car. It reported all gains as ordinary income from the sale of its inventory. After Taylor's death, it became necessary to raise cash to pay estate taxes, and 69 cars were quickly sold through a broker, not uncommon in this type of situation. The sales produced substantial losses, which the corporation deducted as ordinary losses, logical because the cars had always been treated as inventory.

The IRS challenged the deduction of the losses. They seized upon the storage of the cars in the museum, separate from the new car inventory, the admission fees charged to the public, the collector license plates on the cars, and the relative infrequency of sales (eleven) before Taylor's death. They also claimed the relatively long times the cars were owned (typically seven to ten years) and the lower level of marketing as compared to the new cars was proof that the cars were not held as inventory.

Rather, the IRS claimed, the cars were held for exhibition as museum pieces. As such, they were investment assets, and the losses were required to be treated as capital losses. With no capital gains against which to offset the capital losses, that produced a tax increase of about $545,000. Although not directly stated in the court's opinion, my estimate is that the sale of the 69 cars after Taylor's death generated a loss of over $1.5 million.

The tax court was not persuaded by the IRS. The judge couldn't understand the museum piece argument: "We question whether the dealership would expend effort to acquire, rebuild, and maintain the classic cars if the purpose was merely to display them, stationary, at a museum." Obviously, and luckily for the estate, the judge was not a car guy.

The court also criticized the IRS's lack of consistency. The IRS never objected when the corporation paid income tax at the higher ordinary rates on its profits when it sold the eleven cars in the years prior to Taylor's death. It reported the profit from those sales as ordinary income, and paid taxes at ordinary rates. But now that the pendulum had swung and the cars were being sold at losses and generating ordinary deductions, the IRS wanted to raise questions. That is true, but that's what they do.

Near total victory

The taxpayer won. Yet even though it seemed like the IRS didn't have much of a case, a contested audit was required, along with an appeal within the IRS and litigation in the U.S. Tax Court. I would guess that this entire exercise probably cost the corporation at least $100,000 in legal fees. But at least the legal fees are deductible as ordinary expenses, reducing their net cost by 30%–45%. Admittedly, that seems like little consolation, but when dealing with the IRS, you take any prizes you can, no matter how small. ♦

When the High Bidder at an Auction Won't Pay Up

The auction company informed the seller that the buyer apologized about having a change of heart

by John Draneas

Bidders may be qualified to buy, but that doesn't mean they'll go through with the deal

Our firm recently represented an SCM subscriber who had the seemingly impossible happen. He consigned his 1960 Porsche 356B Roadster to a very well-known auction company. At the end of spirited bidding, the hammer fell on a high bid of $95,000, and our client started buying champagne for all his friends. The bid seemed very high for a single-grille 356 Roadster, but this one had been expertly restored to all-original condition, carefully driven and maintained, and extremely well presented at the auction.

The next day, our client's jubilation turned to utter disbelief. The auction company informed him that the buyer came that morning to apologize about having a change of heart. He no longer wanted the car and refused to pay for it.

Faced with no better alternative, the auction company placed the Porsche in secure storage, engaged its attorneys to make the buyer fulfill his obligation, and assured the seller that all would be worked out. After many weeks of getting nowhere, the seller contacted our firm to sort out the mess.

Exactly what is guaranteed

"After all," our client asked, "the auction company pre-qualifies all bidders, and they all have provided proof of financial ability, haven't they?" Yes, but there is a practical limit to what they can do.

Auction companies routinely qualify their bidders in four ways: cash or cashier's check deposit; bank letter of credit; bank letter of guarantee; and authorized credit card. This situation would not have happened if either of the first two methods had been employed, but cash or cashier check deposits are very awkward at this level. So is the formal bank letter of credit: The issuing bank imposes a fee whether the letter of credit is used or not, and it is quite complicated to create. Thus, both these methods are uncommon.

The more common methods are the bank letter of guarantee, where the bank irrevocably commits to honoring a check written by its customer up to a specified amount, and the credit card. But both of these methods suffer from one very significant flaw: the buyer must write a check or sign a credit card charge slip. And if he or she just refuses to do so, there is nothing the auction company can do to force a signature.

Sold means sold—sometimes

Our client insisted, "Shouldn't that be the auction company's problem? Shouldn't they have to pay me because they approved this guy?" The first place to look for answers is the seller's contract with the auction company. This one seemed pretty good for our client; it did obligate the auction company to pay him once the car was sold. But in another section, the contract defined "sold" as when the auction company has received payment from the buyer. That left us at a dead end. Even though the Porsche was "sold" when the hammer fell, it was never "sold" for purposes of the seller's contract.

We next checked the bidder's contract with the auction company. It made it quite clear that the buyer was in default, but what was the recourse? Could the auction company force the buyer to complete the sale?

That is what the law describes as "specific performance"—forcing the buyer to do specifically what he agreed to do. But there are hoops to jump through before you can get this remedy. It will be allowed if the item is unique (this is where the "every piece of real property is unique" concept comes from), but this car was not unique. Otherwise, you have to show "irreparable harm," meaning that money damages cannot adequately compensate for your loss. But that doesn't work either, because we could simply sell the Porsche to someone else and sue the buyer for the sales price difference and any added sales expenses.

And there is yet another shortcoming with the bidder's contract—the seller is not a party to it, and doesn't have the legal ability to enforce it. Only the auction company can enforce it, and its damages would seem to be limited to its lost sales commissions.

When the hammer falls

So we look to a third contract, the one between the seller and the buyer. It was created the moment that the hammer fell. With the auctioneer acting as the agent for the seller, a meeting of the minds occurred, and a contract arose between the seller and the buyer, which the seller can enforce. But this contract has three practical shortcomings:

1. The court is unlikely to force the buyer to actually buy the car (see "specific performance" above), so to determine his actual losses, the seller will have to sell the car to someone else and then sue the buyer for his losses.

2. Say the seller lives in Seattle, the buyer lives in Atlanta, and the auction was held in Scottsdale. The seller can sue the buyer the buyer in Atlanta or Scottsdale, but not Seattle. That makes the seller's legal effort more expensive.

3. It is highly unlikely that the seller will be able to recover his attorney fees. That usually requires a specific contractual provision, and we don't have that. That makes the process expensive.

Making lemonade out of lemons

Faced with these contractual limitations, we worked with the auction company to minimize our client's losses as best we could. The second bidder on the car, at $90,000, was unwilling to buy the car, but said he would bid on it again if it ran through the next auction. The third bidder, at $85,000, wanted the car but thought that $75,000 was plenty under the circumstances.

Ultimately, I was able to convince the auction company to refund the seller's $1,500 in auction entry and transport expenses, agree to handle the seller's next sale at no commission, and just buy the car for $81,000.

That was actually a very fair deal for the seller. At the $95,000 high bid, the seller's net cash would have been $86,850. But if you give the auction company a little benefit of the doubt and dismiss the high bidder as a flake, the seller's net at the $90,000 underbid would have been only $82,200. The seller has a number of other collector cars, some more valuable than the Porsche, and the promised commission-free sale can even put him ahead of the game.

Protecting yourself

Clearly, this situation was a fluke. It is hard to believe that a qualified high bidder would refuse to write the check. But I doubt this was the first time it has happened. For instance, consider a high bidder who believes that he was snookered by auction or chandelier bidding, or one who simply had been hitting the bidder's bar a little too hard and got his zeros mixed up, deciding the next morning he just won't pay.

This auction company acted very responsibly, and with a little creativity the situation was resolved with minor losses for the seller. But you can't always count on that happening, and it makes sense to consider this situation before you consign your collector car to an auction. Much of your protection comes from the reputation and practices of the auction company. But if enough money is involved, it wouldn't hurt to have your attorney take a close look ahead of time at the auction company's bidder's contract, as well as its consignment contract, and advise what kind of legal situation you might end up in if the unexpected happens again. ♦

What is Collector Car Insurance?

The insurance company will produce its estimate of value based on comparable vehicles and will try to make the analysis appear as thorough and authoritative as they can. Don't believe it

by John Draneas

Get the right policy for the right car

When you finally get the car of your dreams, preparing for the total loss of it is hardly at the top of your list. Yet should some uninsured yo-yo run a light and T-bone your Hemi 'Cuda, it would be nice to know that you'll get back the $500,000 the car is worth, rather than the $35,000 a rusty six-cylinder coupe your insurance company has decided is a comparable.

There are two primary types of insurance, traditional "actual cash value" policies and the more modern "agreed value" policies. We'll discuss the former, although frankly, no collector in his right mind should use it.

You're offering me how much?

So let's suppose the unthinkable happens—your pride and joy is stolen, burned to a crisp, or totaled in a crash. Your collector car has become a statistic, and it's time to make an insurance claim. But many times, this process becomes an even bigger tragedy when the insurance adjuster offers you a sum that would barely cover the cost of a new set of wheels and tires.

The first thing to understand is exactly what is under dispute, which is the amount of your loss. Traditional insurance policies typically refer to this as the "actual cash value" of the vehicle, which is what it would take to buy another example of the same model, vintage and condition. While this seems simple enough, it rarely is.

The eye of the beholder

Establishing the pre-loss condition of your car is critical if you want to get the most out of your claim. Unfortunately, once the car is wrecked, this is much more difficult to prove. You can help yourself here by having detailed records of what has been done to the car, both in maintenance and improvements. That way, you can show that your car had three-year old paint, Rudge knock-offs, a high-end sound system, etc. If you've entered your car in a concours, keep the judging sheets and any awards. If your car appeared in a magazine article, keep a copy.

It's also helpful to have photos or video of the car, as the old adage about a picture being worth a thousand words holds true. The more recent, the better evidence they make. So get in the habit of taking detailed and comprehensive pictures or video once a year, just in case something happens and you need them.

You might even want to spend a few hundred dollars to hire an appraiser. While even a properly executed appraisal won't bind your insurance company, it will at least document the car's condition. The appraisal has to be current to impress an adjuster, so periodic updates are advised. One every few years should be fine, as long as you are still able to document that the condition of the car stayed the same since the date of the last appraisal. Even if the market has changed, your appraiser can adjust for that after the loss occurs.

Top 5 claims tips:

1. Check the comparables. The insurance company will produce its estimate of value based on comparable vehicles and will try to make their analysis appear as thorough and authoritative as they can. Here's my advice: Don't believe it. Ask for all available information on their "comparables," as many times you will find that these really aren't all that relevant. Even if they are for the same model and year, it's important to ask what condition these "comparables" are really in? Where are they? And when were the sales made?

2. Strip the car. If the car is a total loss, consider taking things off it before the adjuster sees it. I'm not advocating fraud here, but let's say the car has a high-end stereo system that you wouldn't mind keeping. The adjuster is only going to offer pennies on the dollar, so why not take it off and replace it with the factory system? The same goes for aftermarket performance equipment and other custom features.

3. Negotiate over the carcass. After the insurance company pays you off, they will own the wreck, which they will want to sell to someone to part it out or rebuild it. You can always negotiate over the ownership of the wreck and part it out or rebuild it yourself if this is the best way to get full compensation. Just be careful that any goodies that affect the value of the totaled car are included in the settlement in the first place, so you don't pay twice for the same stuff.

4. Get legal help. Even if you're the sort who's accustomed to negotiating business deals, get a lawyer anyway. It's a simple fact that I can probably negotiate your claim better than you can—as you would likely negotiate my claim better than I. This is because when it's your car, you tend to take the situation personally and frequently want to see its quick resolution. This gives the insurance adjuster an advantage in bargaining. Not to mention that an adjuster will take a lawyer more seriously, as this sends the message that you are serious about the claim. And don't be lulled into false comfort just because the adjuster is being nice and acts concerned. They're trained to act that way, as the insurance companies realize they can reduce their costs simply by being courteous. "Killing them with kindness" tends to make people think they are being treated fairly and keeps them from hiring attorneys.

5. File suit. Don't hesitate to file suit or institute arbitration. While this raises the potential that the litigation costs will exceed your ultimate recovery, statistics show that somewhere over 90% of lawsuits get settled before they go to trial—which is what you want to happen. Keep in mind that insurance is a nickel-and-dime business. If the insurance company can save a little bit of money on every claim, it adds up to a whole lot. But once a claim goes sideways, it's a loss that keeps getting bigger, and it's in the insurance company's best interests to settle.

Once you take this step, the case moves from the adjuster to the insurance company's attorney, which can bring a higher settlement offer. Just as your attorney is not emotionally involved in the case, neither is the insurance company's attorney. If your position has merit, the other lawyer is usually willing to recognize it and recommend a higher settlement. This lets the adjuster off the hook, since the higher settlement reflects on the outside attorney, rather than the adjuster's performance. ♦

What is an Agreed Value Insurance Policy?

To be smart and safe, cruise through the SCM price guide at least once a year and update your coverage

by John Draneas

Keep your classic covered appropriately, especially if you intend to drive it

We addressed the many ways that you and your insurance company can have differences of opinion about the value of your collector car after it has been stolen or totaled and how you might create sufficient evidence ahead of time to help win at that conflict. If you want to go this route, be our guest, but there's a much better way to avoid such disputes entirely: "agreed value" insurance policies.

These are different from traditional "stated value" policies that have been around for many years, as agreed value policies allow you to avoid a claims dispute by establishing the value of your car ahead of time. A stated value policy simply puts a limit on the amount that can be paid on your claim,

which is a good deal only for the insurance company. But under an agreed value policy, you're paid whatever value you set when the policy was written, without any squabble.

In other words, you don't have to prove that your all-original, numbers-matching, V8, four-speed '65 Mustang with Pony interior is worth more than a rusty six-cylinder "restoration project" after your car has been stolen—you do it up front when you set the value of your coverage.

Agreed value policies do impose some use restrictions, so you can't use your collector car as a daily driver. And you're not entirely immune to the claims process, as you'll still have to negotiate a partial loss, although you will likely still be better off if the insurance carrier knows that correctly repairing a collector car can be a much different process than respraying the fender of a minivan. The bottom line as a collector is that getting insurance from a company that specializes in collector cars is beneficial to both parties.

Setting the value

When you buy an agreed value policy, you can't just put any value you want on your car. The insurance company doesn't want you to have a financial incentive to lose your collector car, so the value has to reflect the market value of the car. As we all know, condition and provenance play an enormous role in determining the value of a particular collector car.

McKeel Hagerty, owner of Hagerty Insurance Co., explains that his firm requires photographs of every car they insure as a starting point. "Some collector cars, such as resto-rods, are very challenging to value," he says, so in these and other such situations, the insurance company may require an appraisal to confirm the value before the policy is issued.

Of course, the insurance company is going to be very careful about the value placed on a $2,000,000, Pebble Beach-winning Duesenberg, but they aren't going to be as critical with a $35,000 Porsche 356A coupe. With the Porsche, the numbers are small enough that any error isn't large enough to warrant the extra expense and hassle of investigation and appraisal. Most importantly, the insurers feel pretty secure because, even if a collector car is mildly over-insured, the insurance company has been adequately compensated for the risk, as the agreed value determines the premium.

How many miles and how old?

All agreed value policies restrict car usage in some way. Insurance companies that specialize in this sort of policy don't want to insure a daily-driver collector car, as that level of use presents a higher level of risk than is assumed in pricing such policies. Collector car policies have traditionally restricted mileage to about 2,500 per year, which is an adequate allowance for most of us. But Hagerty, for example, has relaxed that and now has no specific mileage limit, but does require that a car be given only "limited use" during the year. Be sure to ask about any limitations when you are getting a quote.

I was curious how the mainstream insurance companies played this game, so I consulted Rich Rogers, a friend and independent agent from AOA West Insurance in Tigard, Oregon. Rogers writes agreed value policies with Safeco Insurance, which actually offers two levels of agreed value coverage. One restricts usage to 2,500 miles per year, while the other has no mileage restriction but limits use to car shows and car club activities, with a correspondingly lower premium.

To be eligible for the Safeco policies, collector cars have to meet minimum age requirements, with a higher age required for the reduced premium. In contrast, Hagerty policies have no age requirement, and will cover relatively new cars that otherwise would qualify as collectibles.

The value in agreed value

My collector cars have been insured on an agreed value basis for some time now, and I recommend that you consider these policies as a way of reducing your insurance premiums. You might be amazed at the savings—hundreds of dollars per car, each year. When you're insuring five, 10, or 20 cars, that can add up to real money real fast.

Rogers supplied sample quotes from Safeco to illustrate exactly how much you stand to gain. Insuring a 1959 Porsche 356A coupe with an agreed value of $35,000, for example, costs $412 per year on a regular policy and $260 per year on the collector car policy. The corresponding premiums for a 1957 Alfa Giulietta Spider, with an agreed value of $20,000, are $406 and $194, an even bigger differential.

The reason that the savings are so huge is that the insurance companies know that their risk is minimal with a collector car. They know that we keep these cars garaged, we seldom drive them, we don't let them out of our sight when we do drive them, and we would prefer to lose an arm than to get the slightest scratch on our cars.

But with all of these positives, there is one critical issue to be aware of with agreed value policies. The agreed value is your coverage limit, and it doesn't change unless and until you change it. Meanwhile, the value of a particular collector car can change dramatically in a short period of time. So to be smart and safe, cruise through the SCM Price Guide and the other industry equivalents at least once a year, and update your coverage if necessary. ♦

How to Finance a Collector Car

Frankly, your local bank just doesn't understand that collector cars tend to rise in value rather than depreciate

by John J. Meldon

Drive today, pay over 15 years

Lease or buy? That's a choice that buyers of collector cars face. Each has its advantages, and, especially with six- and seven-figure cars, it's a decision that should be made after consulting with your financial advisors.

If, after doing this, you decide financing a purchase is what you want, let me say what you should be looking for. Using my company, J.J. Best, as an example, we make it possible to obtain fast, low-cost, fixed low-rate loans and long-term lending with up to 15-year financing terms. Most loans can generally be considered and processed for approval within three to five minutes with next-day check availability. In essence, J.J. Best provides customers with a complete financial solution, start to finish.

Classic car financing basics

Financial institutions our customers traditionally deal with would not lend on this automobile type. We understand the "precious collateral," and further understand the unique values underlying the classic car marketplace. Conventional lenders simply consider these types of vehicles as "used, worn-out cars." Frankly, your local credit union or bank most often just doesn't get that collector cars tend to rise in value rather than depreciate, and hence your 275 GTB/4 should be treated differently than a 2007 Escalade.

While interest rates have changed dramatically over the last two years and the Federal Funds Rate has escalated between 1% and 5% in the same period, you should look for a company that has maintained stable fixed rates and offers 15-year long-term loan opportunities for potential classic car customers.

In many cases, it may be more feasible and financially attractive to purchase on a long-term loan rather than lease, as many customers are accustomed to arranging on their new car financing. Bottom line—with purchasing, at the end of your term you actually own something.

How to start

In general, new classic car customers considering their first purchase will need to have the following available to secure financing on their vehicle:

• Established credit history and good credit rating
• Satisfactory debt-to-income ratio
• Valid state or country driver license
• Proof of insurance
• Copy of seller's title (front and back)

My company will lend up to 98% of the purchase price of the vehicle, including tax and title fees incurred. If the customer needs insurance, we can arrange that.

Once a customer's loan is completed, we also offer that customer access to Visa and MasterCard accounts that allow him to place a photo of his newly purchased vehicle on the front of his credit card.

Please use the above features and benefits as a checklist when you go shopping for classic car financing. Ask your friends where they have gotten their collector cars financed. At various auctions and shows, go to every finance company who has a booth—their very presence indicates that they are committed to the hobby.

And while we don't want to name names, you might ask the publisher of a well-known collector car magazine which company it was that helped him to arrange the financing of the silver 1963 Corvette from which he gets so much pleasure. ♦

Settling Insurance Claims

Owners make the mistake of believing that adjusters are supposed to be "fair" when settling a claim. "Good faith" is different

by John Draneas

You say it's worth $7,000, but most insurance companies won't agree

Dear Keith Martin's Guide to Car Collecting: I own a 99,000-mile 1971 MGB-GT that was in excellent condition and drove like new when it was hit by a negligent driver, who was clearly at fault and was cited by the police. I don't want to get my insurance company involved, so I have been trying to settle my claim with the other driver's insurance company, but seem to be getting nowhere. They made me a ridiculous offer of $2,500 to total the car, which I rejected outright.

Several months have passed, and I still get no contact from them. I wrote to the Ohio Insurance Board about a month ago. All I got back was a form letter, and still no contact from the insurance company. I hesitate to hire an attorney and start spending my own money when I am the victim entitled to due compensation. Can you suggest what I might be able to do?—*J.B., Canton, Ohio*

Insurance claims seem to be the continuing bane of collector car owners. Part of the problem is that insurance claims

adjusters are accustomed to dealing with damaged Dodge minivans, and often can't tell the difference between a collector car and just a very old used car. Their tendency is to assume that it's just an old used car, declare it totaled, write a small check, and move on to the next file.

Another part of the problem is that car owners make the mistake of believing that insurance adjusters are supposed to be fair when settling the claim. None of us expects a car dealer to be fair when selling us a car; why should we expect an adjuster to be fair when buying our wrecked car? The laws do require insurance companies to act in good faith, but "good faith" is quite a bit different from "fair." It leaves plenty of room for negotiation and difference of opinion about value, and also just plain ignorance.

It's not surprising that the state agency wasn't any help. They aren't consumer protection advocates who make sure you get full compensation. If they check into the situation and the insurance adjuster tells them that they are trying to settle the claim, but that you keep insisting on more money than your car is worth, it's usually enough for the agency to label it as a legitimate dispute and close their file.

Sorry, you need a lawyer

J.B.'s best course is to make an admittedly undeserved investment in an attorney. That will tilt the scale in several ways. It makes it clear that you are serious. It makes it clear that unwanted legal expense for the insurance company will likely follow if suit is filed. And, perhaps most important, it often brings the negotiations higher up the insurance company's ladder to a person who has broader authority to settle claims. But sometimes none of that happens until suit is filed. You have to be prepared for that, if it turns out to be the only way to get full compensation for your loss.

The SCM Price Guide indicates that J.B.'s MG is worth about $7,000. The difference between that and what the insurance company has already offered is $4,500. I hate to rub salt into the wound, but the attorney fees will easily become a significant erosion of the recovery, because one is legally unable to get reimbursement from the insurance company unless a specific state statute provides otherwise—which would be unusual.

But your attorney will know if there is any hope in this regard. For example, Oregon law allows the recovery of attorney fees for damage to personal property (cars fit that category) where the amount claimed is not more than $5,500. And you can be clever with that. Say your claim is $7,000. You might be better off suing for $5,500 and recover your legal fees than to sue for $7,000 and pay your own legal fees.

Call your insurer

J.B. may have made another mistake by not involving his own insurance company. He may be worried that his insurance premium might rise or his policy might get canceled if he made a claim against it, or perhaps he just feels that fairness dictates that the other driver's insurance pay the claim and he wants to assure that. But trying to do too much here might be working to his disadvantage.

Where the other driver is clearly at fault, there is no way that your insurance company is going to pay for the damage to your car. All they will do is negotiate the claim with you and the other company. Since they know that they are spending the other company's money, they will likely be more liberal about the value of the car. And they generally won't be able to penalize you for the claim when they didn't incur any loss.

Prevention is the best cure

Finally, J.B. is not dealing with a company that specializes in collectible cars and would be better off if he were. The specialty companies offer two advantages. One is that they know collector cars and are more willing to recognize their true value. The other is that they offer the opportunity to establish an agreed value for your car. If it is totaled, the agreed value is paid without further debate. And if, as here, the damage was the other driver's fault, your insurance company will pay your claim at the agreed value and then take on the other driver's insurance company to get reimbursement. At that point, what can the other company possibly say about the value of the car? ♦

Lemon Laws

The service advisor explained that the computer did not find any error codes, so there couldn't be anything wrong. The owner disagreed and went to court

by John Draneas

BUYING & SELLING SMART

Wisconsin attorney Bruce Tammi was a car guy from when he was a kid. His all-time favorites were Porsches, and he owned two of them—a 1978 911 Turbo and a 1999 Carrera. But one night his barn took a direct hit by lightning, and the resulting fire destroyed both Porsches.

Armed with an insurance settlement, Bruce leased a new, $133,000 2003 Turbo from one of the three Wisconsin Porsche dealers. He thought it an awesome car, but it developed an annoying glitch. Intermittently, after the rear spoiler had deployed at about 70 mph, Bruce would hear a loud whistling sound, and the dash light indicating a spoiler control failure would come on. Manual control wouldn't help. The only way to correct the situation was to pull over, shut the engine down, remove the key from the ignition, then restart the motor. The occurrences became more frequent.

He didn't warn his wife

Then he let his wife borrow the car without warning her about its quirk. He got a frantic phone call from the very dark side of the road, guided her through the "fix," and she was on her way, but presumably not very happy about the behavior of her husband's very expensive toy.

At the top of Bruce's list the next day was to take the car to the dealer for repair. But when Bruce picked up the car, the service advisor explained that the computer did not find any error codes, so there couldn't be anything wrong. "If it happens again, bring it back when it is broken."

The Porsche quit a few weeks later, and Bruce drove straight to the dealer. Sorry, they were too busy to look at it, and he would have to come back in three weeks.

He did that, and the diagnosis was the same—no error codes. But it failed on the way home. Bruce drove right back to the dealer, but when he got there the service department was closed.

Tried all three dealers

So Bruce went to another dealer... and another, who replaced the spoiler drive. That didn't fix it, either. Bruce was out of options, as he had been to all three Wisconsin Porsche dealers.

So Bruce boned up on the lemon laws. He found that the basis for this branch of the law is the 1975 federal Magnuson-Moss Warranty Act. Generally, if a consumer makes reasonable attempts to get a warranty item on a new car corrected (usually three to four tries), the consumer can bring legal action to receive either a refund of the purchase price (less a reasonable use allowance) or a replacement car. And, importantly, the consumer can recover his legal expenses.

The states have their own lemon laws—essentially

similar to the federal lemon law except that many of them give broader protection to the consumer. Thus, most lemon Llaw claims are brought in state court. That was Bruce's approach, as he learned that Wisconsin had a very tough lemon law.

Check your state's version

Under all of the lemon law variations, the first thing to do is to fully document the claim. You need a good record of your attempts to get the problem fixed, the work that was done by the dealer, and the outcome. Check your state law to determine how many attempts that requires. Next, you have to make written demand on the manufacturer to either refund your purchase price or to replace the car. When the manufacturer refuses to do that, procedural steps vary from state to state.

In Wisconsin, the manufacturer gets the option to force the dispute into an approved, non-binding arbitration program. If Porsche had done that, Bruce would have had to participate before he could sue. Instead, Porsche offered a different arbitration program. Bruce rejected that, then filed suit.

The litigation dragged on, and Bruce kept driving the Porsche, but the whistling problem had worsened to the point that he experienced a failure every ten minutes or so, which made it impossible to take any lengthy trip. Exasperated, he took the car back to the dealer, who commendably tried again to fix it. Bruce and the dealer learned that a microprocessor in the instrument cluster controls the spoiler and stores any error codes. This microprocessor didn't store any error codes, so the dealer replaced the instrument cluster. That helped a little—the problem wasn't solved, but at least now the error codes were being stored.

If you want something done...

When the dealer lost motivation, Bruce bought a shop manual and found a procedure to diagnose the problem. After eliminating everything that had already been tried, he decided the problem had to be in the fuse box. When he inspected it, he found that it was arcing between two fuses, and the problem was solved.

Soon after, Bruce's case came to trial. Both sides presented their witnesses, including experts. The Porsche was found to be a "lemon," and the focus turned to determining the measure of damages.

Wisconsin law gets fuzzy here. Since Porsche refused to replace the car, the recovery would be money damages—generally the cost of the car. When the car is leased, the cost clearly includes the total of the lease payments, but what about the cost of the buy-out at the end of the lease? In this case, the judge ruled that the buy-out was included in Bruce's damages, which made his damage claim the entire $133,000 cost of the Porsche.

Under federal lemon law, matters would have ended there. But the Wisconsin lemon law is much more favorable, and provides that the court must double this amount as a penalty, making the judgment $266,000. And, to add icing to the cake, the judge ruled that applicable Wisconsin legal precedent meant that Bruce did not have to give the car back. Bruce ended up with a 2003 Porsche Turbo and $133,000 in his pocket ($266,000 damages minus the $133,000 paid for the car).

Not a good deal for either side

Those are big numbers, but it's likely not a good deal for either side. Bruce invested several years of his life in difficult litigation. If he had paid for the legal services, the bill would have been well over $60,000 based on his time, and I think he was being more efficient than an independent attorney.

Porsche spent a lot of money defending the claim. It could have avoided the loss early by fixing the car. It could have settled the case at several points, but made only very modest settlement offers of $10,000 and $24,000. It could have tried to settle the case after the trial ended, but didn't even make an offer. Instead, it filed an appeal and will incur even more in attorney fees. And that will make it more costly for Bruce as well.

If your new car is acting up and you can't get it repaired, lemon laws can be strong friends. You can learn a lot about your state's lemon laws on the Internet, and many states' motor vehicle or transportation departments have helpful web sites and forms.

But all lemon laws are complicated, and there is a mind-numbing range of options and decisions. It is best to consult an attorney who is skilled in lemon law claims, and if you don't want to incur the full expense, at least hire an experienced attorney to coach you. But keep the attorney informed about your progress, and have him tell you when it's time to turn it over to professionals. ♦

The Infamous Ferrari Enzo Crash in Los Angeles

162-mph pileup, video by the missing "Dietrich," cars stolen from England, and a loaded gun under the seat

by John Draneas

At 6 a.m. on February 21, 2006, Malibu police Sergeant Phil Brooks answered what he thought was a routine call about a car crash on the Pacific Coast Highway. It would turn out to be anything but.

The script for this accident reads like "Mission Impossible": A car race between two stolen, foreign-registered, million-dollar cars ends at 162 mph, when one is cut in half by a phone pole.

Unhurt in the crash is a fugitive financier who claims someone else was driving. He's interviewed by mysterious "Homeland Security" officers, and the police trail uncovers millions in missing money, unregistered weapons, illegal drugs, and a "lost" yacht with other suspects aboard. The Internet has been buzzing ever since, and no West Coast cocktail party is complete without the subject being discussed.

Enzo in two pieces

At the crash site, Sergeant Brooks discovered a red 2005 Ferrari Enzo broken into two pieces immediately behind the passenger compartment—and the pieces were 600 feet apart. A concrete power pole was broken in two, with the bottom half lying on the ground and the upper half dangling from its wiring, which caused a power outage in the surrounding area. The Enzo's engine and other pieces were scattered along the road for 1,200 feet. Standing in the middle of the wreckage were Bo Stefan Eriksson and Trevor Karney.

Eriksson identified himself as a 44-year-old Swedish national and the owner of the Enzo. He said he was a passenger in the Enzo when the crash occurred. The driver was a German acquaintance named Dietrich (last name unknown), who fled the scene. Eriksson claimed that Dietrich had been racing a Mercedes SLR McLaren when he crashed. A breathalyzer test determined that Eriksson's blood alcohol level was above the legal limit. Karney said he was the passenger in the Mercedes, and corroborated Eriksson's story.

Homeland security?

A few minutes later, two men arrived and flashed badges, identifying themselves as officers from Homeland Security. They demanded to speak privately with Eriksson, and did so at length.

The police let Eriksson and Karney go. They called in a helicopter and a search-and-rescue team to search for "Dietrich," but gave up after three hours.

Further investigation uncovered a web of international intrigue.

Dietrich evaporated once police noticed that both airbags had deployed, but found blood only on the driver-side airbag. A DNA test proved that it was Eriksson's blood, and he then admitted that Dietrich did not exist.

199 mph when the tape stopped

Accident reconstruction determined the Enzo was traveling 162 mph when it became airborne and hit the power pole. Later, an anonymous witness told the police that Karney was the passenger in the Enzo and had a video camera. The witness claimed he had seen the video, which showed the speedometer registering 199 mph just before the tape stopped. He said Karney still had the video. The police went to Karney's address (a yacht moored at an exclusive marina), but the ship had sailed. It turned out to be registered to a Carl Freer. Freer, Karney, and the video remain missing.

Police discovered that the Enzo was owned by a Scottish bank and leased to Gizmondo Europe Ltd, a London-based company, of which Eriksson was an executive. Further research turned up a second Enzo—a black one—and a Mercedes SLR McLaren, which also belonged to banks who had leased them Gizmondo. The leases forbade the cars from being taken out of Great Britain, yet Eriksson had somehow managed to bring all three to the U.S.

None of the cars were registered for road use in the U.S., as Eriksson stated that they were only to be used for shows and off-road use. Nonetheless, many witnesses reported Eriksson caused quite a stir around normally blasé Los Angeles with his pair of Enzos.

The banks said payments on the leases stopped a few months after the cars came to the U.S. and have reported the cars stolen. The banks claim to be owed $1.15 million, including $566,000 on the wrecked Enzo.

Gizmondo goes wrongo

Eriksson has a storied past and many run-ins with the law. His first theft conviction netted him three months in jail, followed by another three and a half years for cocaine and arms-related convictions. Finally, he was convicted of fraud and counterfeiting and sentenced to ten years, but released after about five. In 2000, while working as a debt collector, he was assigned to find another Swede, Carl Freer, who had failed to deliver Ferraris to Sweden. The assignment developed into a friendship and the two formed Gizmondo to develop handheld video game systems to challenge Sony and Nintendo.

To raise capital, Eriksson, Freer, and several others acquired Floor Decor, Inc., a virtually defunct carpet retailer that had one significant asset—it was listed on the NASDAQ exchange. The name was changed to Tiger Telematics, and became the parent of Gizmondo Europe. The pair started raising cash by selling Tiger Telematics shares.

But Gizmondo couldn't sell many video game systems. Critics complained that they were more expensive than the competition, had numerous technological features of questionable utility, were rather ugly, and lacked one major element—games that could be played on them. Nonetheless, Gizmondo burned through an enormous amount of money, losing $263 million in its final year.

$1,500 lap dancers

Among the questionable expenditures: over $3.1 million in annual salary and bonuses for Eriksson, and over $3.4 million for Freer; over $500,000 in salary, bonuses, and automobile allowances for another executive's girlfriend, who worked for Gizmondo as a secretary; unspecified high consulting fees for Freer's wife; $1,500 lap dancers; company sponsorship of a Ferrari raced by Eriksson at Le Mans; $15 million in homes; a $10 million yacht; and millions in cars, diamonds, and other incidentals for executives.

Seeking a change of scenery, Eriksson, Freer, their wives, two Enzos, and a Mercedes left England and injected themselves into the L.A. social scene with a big splash. Then a Swedish newspaper ran a story connecting Eriksson and Gizmondo and describing his criminal past. Eriksson and Freer both resigned, and a few months later, Gizmondo filed for bankruptcy, listing debts in excess of $200 million.

Glock ammo under the seat

At the crash scene, Karney approached a motorist who had stopped to help and asked if he could borrow a cell phone. The motorist let Karney sit in his car to make the call, then later noticed a loaded Glock handgun magazine under his seat.

At the same time, Eriksson identified himself to police as the deputy commissioner of the anti-terrorism unit of the San

Gabriel Valley Transit Authority police department. Intrigued, police investigated the transit authority and discovered it is a non-profit agency founded by Yosuf Maiwandi that owns a "fleet" of five small buses used to provide transportation for disabled and elderly people.

The transit authority's main place of business was Homer's Auto Service, but it maintained its own police department, staffed by six volunteer officers. Eriksson was helping create a security system for the buses. You may wonder why such an agency would need a police force at all, but Maiwandi claims the police department was created to provide protection for riders and to run background checks on bus drivers.

Unimpressed, police raided the transit authority's offices and seized numerous documents, five firearms, police jackets, and many police badges. They also arrested Maiwandi on charges of perjury.

A further raid of Eriksson's Bel Air mansion netted several computers, a substance believed to be cocaine, and a .357 magnum Smith & Wesson that was registered to a businessman who served on the Orange County Sheriff's Advisory Committee as well as being a deputy in its services division. The sheriff has been criticized for giving deputy badges and concealed weapons permits to volunteers with no police training. Detectives are still wondering why the gun was at Eriksson's home.

Charges and still more charges

Eriksson was charged with embezzlement, grand theft, drunk driving, cocaine possession, and unlawful possession of a handgun. He faces 14 years in jail. He is in prison, unable to post bail because his assets are frozen. Eriksson pleaded not guilty to all counts and insists that he was in negotiations to pay off his banks when the crash occurred.

Charges against Eriksson were later expanded to include hit and run, driving without a license, and driving without insurance. Police say that on another occasion, Eriksson was driving a Porsche Cayenne when he rear-ended a Ford Explorer, then drove off. Police say he did not own the Cayenne, but did not elaborate as to how he came to be driving it.

Eriksson's associate, Carl Freer, was arrested and charged with perjury, impersonating a police officer in order to purchase a gun, and unlawful possession of a weapon. Police confiscated 12 rifles and four handguns from his home and yacht.

Then Eriksson's wife was pulled over while driving the SLR. She was cited for driving without a valid driver's license. The SLR was confiscated because it was unregistered, carried British license plates, was illegally exported from Great Britain, and had been reported stolen by the bank that owned it.

Not going anywhere soon

Eriksson's trial is scheduled to begin July 31. However, many motions have been filed by his attorneys, and that date is likely to change.

U.S. Immigration and Customs Enforcement continues to investigate how Eriksson and the cars got into the country and have placed an immigration hold on him, so that they can arrest him if he is released from jail. A spokeswoman stated, "He is potentially subject to deportation." Scotland Yard is also investigating.

Karney and Freer's yacht is believed to be sailing to Ireland, but has not been located. The Malibu Sheriff's Department is looking for the two "Homeland Security" agents, eager to question them.

Press and Internet buzz reflects amazement about the safety features of the Enzo. Many bloggers are amazed that Eriksson and Karney survived such a horrific crash without any injuries other than Eriksson's cut lip. A police officer at the scene was quoted with practically British understatment: "For a million dollars, you get a pretty good air bag system."

Ferraristi around the world are reported to be severely depressed about the sacrilegious loss of one of the 400 Enzos built by Ferrari. One fan even lit a rosary candle at the scene and tacked a picture of the Enzo to a cross. ("Get a life" might be an appropriate response here.)

And summing up neatly, Malibu Mayor Andy Stern suggests this case should serve as a warning to sports car drivers not to speed on Pacific Highway. Especially if they have a lot to lose. ♦

"As Is" Disclosures

Just inside the statute of limitations, the seller was served with a lawsuit claiming fraud, misrepresentation, and breach of warranty

by John Draneas

Have a comprehensive contract signed before it leaves the showroom floor

Here's another true story. We've given the subjects fake names, but the story is otherwise accurate. Let's call our dealer this month James. He had been doing quite well selling collector cars in the Northeast. Over 600 cars sold and, he says, "I had never even received a letter from an attorney." But his luck changed recently.

James acquired a real 1968 Camaro Z/28 some time ago. It was freshly painted the correct J-code Rally Green, with a vinyl top and black interior, power steering, power disc brakes, and in-dash tachometer. It had a matching-numbers engine, the rear end was the correct 3.73 ratio, and the transmission was correct, but not original to the car. The only negative was that it came in pieces. Jerry completed the restoration and sold it to a local customer. It changed hands a couple of times over the years, but was still in excellent condition when James reacquired it in early 2006 for $30,000.

He listed the Z/28 for sale on eBay. He described it as

above, and added that it "looks, runs, and drives strong like you would expect."

"Even nicer than I had thought"

A West Coast buyer beat him down to $33,500 over the phone. The buyer wouldn't buy the car on eBay, but came to James's dealership with an expert to inspect the car. At the end of the lengthy inspection, the buyer called his banker and said, "Send the man the money. This car is even nicer than I had thought it would be."

They signed James's short-form written contract, and the deal was done. It didn't occur to James to get the "as is" disclosures signed.

Buyer's remorse sets in

Buyer's remorse didn't take long to set in. A couple weeks later, the buyer called and said he "had a guy look at

227

the car and it had issues." The buyer mentioned rust under the dash. James pointed out that they all had a little rust there, as the factory didn't paint under the dash. A few days later, the buyer called again. He said that he "had another guy look at the car, he found a lot of poor work, and that '68 Z/28s in similar condition could be purchased for $15,000."

The buyer wanted his money back. Jerry declined, suggested that the buyer just put it up for sale, and that he could even make some money on it.

Almost two years went by without another contact. Toward the end of that time, the buyer had cut the roof, trunk, and outer wheel housings off the car and found hidden rust. He sent James a demand for $25,000 to correct the "deficiencies," accompanied by photographs of all the pieces and the hidden rust, plus a written appraisal that said the Camaro was worth only $7,000. Then—just before the statute of limitations expired—James was served with a lawsuit.

The lawsuit asserts liability for fraud, misrepresentation, and breach of warranty. The source for all of the claims seems to be the eBay listing statement that the Camaro "looks, runs, and drives strong like you would expect."

Oddly enough, there is no mention of the fact that the buyer and his expert inspected the car before he bought it. It suggests that the car was purchased on eBay and seen for the first time when it arrived at the buyer's home.

Lying about unknowns

In normal "Legal Files" style, let's take a look at the claims and predict their outcome.

To start with the obvious, how is the buyer ever going to prove that James misrepresented the car or tried to defraud him when he had to cut the car apart to find the rust? That one defies common sense. Fraud requires actual knowledge on James's part. To commit fraud, he would have had to know the car had rust and conceal it in some manner, which doesn't seem likely.

Misrepresentation is lesser conduct than fraud and can occur without actual knowledge. But before there can be a misrepresentation, there must first be a representation; in most states, silence is not a representation. The only statements identified are those made in the eBay listing, and none of them has anything to do with rust. "Looks, runs, and drives strong like you would expect" doesn't refer to rust. "All sheet metal work has been done to high standards," another statement in the listing, might connote that rust would have been repaired, but it misses the mark in two respects—the rust might have existed in areas that were not worked on, and the rust could have developed after the work was completed.

Also, a misrepresentation does not automatically create a warranty. A warranty is a specific term in a contract, and there are no facts alleged that the contract—oral or written—contained a warranty.

"Legal Files" would expect that motions will be filed to force the buyer to revise the complaint to be more specific about exactly what was represented and how it was inaccurate, and to eliminate the breach of contract claim.

The complaint alleges that the buyer had to repair numerous items that had been said to have been restored. This could establish a legitimate claim, as it alleges that something was specifically stated that turned out to be incorrect. But to establish misrepresentation, two added elements must be proven. The buyer must prove that he actually relied on the statements, and that it was reasonable for him to do so.

Defendant must know when he can win

If you are the defendant in a case like this, and even if you really believe you can win the lawsuit, you have to pay close attention to when in the legal process you can win. That is because the further into the legal process you go, the more it costs you to defend the case. And even if you win, you aren't going to recover your attorney fees. So unless you can win early, you could wind up losing by winning.

In this case, it will be important for James to try to knock out the rust claims at the earliest stage with legal motions. If the judge agrees that there is no valid legal claim stated, it can be tossed out right away.

James will undoubtedly point out that, since the buyer and his expert inspected the car before he bought it, he could no longer reasonably rely on James's statements. That is an excellent point, and it could be a winner, but it is considered a defense to the claim. The shortcoming of a defense is that the judge can't use it to throw out the case. Only the jury can do that, and that can't happen until the trial at the end of the expensive legal process.

Avoiding these problems

James is quick to kick himself for not getting the "as is" disclosures signed. That would have helped, but it still might not have been enough.

An agreement that a car is sold "as is" just means that no warranty is given. It does not eliminate claims that the seller misrepresented the car. To do that, the seller needs a contract that contains what is referred to as an "integration" clause. Such a provision would simply state that any representations and statements that may have been made about the car are not part of the deal unless they are specifically stated in the written contract. That would have prevented the buyer from making claims based on the eBay listing.

As "Legal Files" has said before, your best strategy is a good contract. That works both ways. This buyer is going to have a tough time winning, but both parties are going to spend a lot of money on lawyers. The more clearly the contract establishes what you are entitled to, the less likely it is you will end up in court.

This is an interesting case, and "Legal Files" will keep an eye on it as it unfolds, and if the ending turns out to be noteworthy, we'll be sure to update you. ♦

VIN Plate Transfers

The Shelby registry says that a rebodied Shelby is not an original Shelby, but has greater value than a replica or clone

by John Draneas

Original 1965 GT350

What do you do with your authentic, vintage Shelby GT350 when it's so rusty it's beyond repair? Some Shelby owners think the answer is pretty simple—just rebody it. But that can easily lead to confusion, fraud, criminal charges, and costly litigation, as we'll see below. Although this is an actual case, we'll do the guilty a favor and not disclose any real names.

Our rustbucket Shelby owner decides that his 1965 GT350 needs to be rebodied. To do this, carefully hold onto the Shelby VIN plate and cut away the rest of the car. Then take a donor Mustang body and carefully attach the Shelby VIN plate to it. Take all the Shelby parts off the old body and install them in the new body, and if you're attentive to detail, cut the body parts that hold the Ford VINs off the old body and attach them to the new body, and voila! You have a "refreshed" Shelby.

You might think this is the same process as just cutting the Shelby VIN plate out of the old body and attaching it to the donor Mustang body. But the California Highway Patrol considers that way of doing things a criminal alteration of a car's VIN. Read on for details.

What registry disclosures?

The Shelby American World Registry (www.SAAC .com) explains that, in their opinion, a rebodied Shelby is not really an original Shelby, but it has a greater value than a replica or a clone. Mustangs are unibody cars, so unlike many classic cars that have a separate body and frame, there is no frame that a new body can be attached to with the Mustang. So the Shelby registry carves out a compromise.

The registry view is that there is nothing inherently wrong with rebodying, and that the correct way to do so is to take all the body parts that carry Shelby and Ford VINs and graft them into the donor body. The registry finds it acceptable for the owner to keep this information secret while he owns the car.

If the registry is told that a Shelby has been rebodied, it's noted in the records but not published in the registry. However, the registry insists that it is fraudulent to sell a rebodied

1965 Ford Mustang, ready for Shelby bits?

Shelby without disclosing that fact. If a prospective purchaser calls to inquire about a particular Shelby, the registry will inform the purchaser that the car has been rebodied.

With friends like these...

Our rustbucket Shelby owner heeded this advice, and disclosed the rebody to our Culprit #1, an experienced Shelby enthusiast. Culprit #1 updated the Shelby records and informed the group of the rebody but asked that they not disclose it in the registry, so they simply noted the rebody in their files.

Along comes our Victim, who decides it's time to add a GT350 to his collection. He knows Culprit #2, a well-known Shelby expert and dealer, and asks him to find him a nice car. Culprit #2 presents the rebodied Shelby to our Victim. Victim sees that it is a high-condition car. Relying on his long relationship with Culprit #2, Victim does not make any inquiry with the Shelby registry, and pays an original-Shelby price for the rebodied car. The two Culprits split the profit.

The power steering bracket tells all

Victim enjoys the car for a number of years, and then decides it's time to sell it and buy something else. He consigns it to a well-known collector car dealer, who quickly finds a buyer. Per the buyer's request, the dealer sends the car to a well-known repair shop for a pre-purchase inspection. The shop owner immediately recognizes that the 1965 Shelby GT350 is a rebody, because he sees a mount on the firewall for the power steering that was used only on 1966 Mustangs.

As he explains this to an employee, the shop owner is overheard by another shop customer, a Shelby enthusiast who happens to be the head of the California Highway Patrol K-9 Unit. He launches an investigation, and pretty soon CHP impounds the Shelby because its VIN had been unlawfully removed, altered, or destroyed. During the investigation, Culprit #1 admits

his misdeeds, and CHP determines he is guilty of knowingly selling a vehicle with forged or counterfeit VINs. The CHP retags the car as a 1966 Mustang with its original VIN, and returns it to our Victim.

Two culprits equally at fault

Victim is chagrined that the district attorney won't prosecute Culprit #1 because his crimes are "too old." So he sues both Culprits and the original owner who sold the car to Culprit #1. The two Culprits tell varying stories about their involvement and knowledge. In a court-ordered, non-binding arbitration, the arbitrator rules in favor of Victim, finds the two Culprits equally at fault, finds the original owner innocent because he disclosed everything to Culprit #1, and orders the two Culprits to reimburse the original owner for his attorney fees because they caused him to be dragged into the lawsuit. Victim then settles with the Culprits, but the lawsuit still continues as to whether or not the Culprits have to pay the original owner's attorney fees, a result of the arbitration's non-binding status.

Moving a VIN makes an illegal car

This Legal File raises philosophical questions as to just what makes a "real" car. The unscrupulous think that all you need is an authentic serial number—probably not even the authentic VIN plate, as that can be recreated. Some classic car collectors think all you need is an authentic frame (or even a piece of it).

The Shelby registry apparently thinks all you need are the portions of the original body that hold all of the VINs, plus all (perhaps most?) of the unique Shelby parts from the original Shelby. But California law thinks that creates a car with a fraudulently altered VIN. The law believes, quite simply, if you move a VIN from one car to another, it's an illegal car.

As collectors, we pay substantial premiums for authenticity and originality because they define the rarity and form the bridge to the past that creates value. But just what does it take to keep the soul of an original car alive?

If you add a complete assortment of Shelby parts to a Mustang, you have a clone. If those Shelby parts came from a real Shelby, is it something different? If not, does adding a Shelby VIN plate make a difference? The market seems to think so, because a rebodied Shelby will sell for less than an original Shelby, but for more than a clone.

Perhaps this Legal File prompts us to reflect that rarity and authenticity have separate effects upon value. But on a more practical level, it demonstrates another way that the unscrupulous can victimize the innocent, and adds another item to the car buyer's due diligence checklist.

Meanwhile, the rebodied Shelby is in Colombia, South America, being enjoyed by a savvy collector who knows its entire story and is completely satisfied with what he paid and what he ended up with in his garage. ♦

Track Day Insurance

High Performance Driver Education coverage insures bad things don't happen to good people (that's you) during track days

by John Draneas

Here's a man-bites-dog twist to track day crash liability concerns, resulting from a crash at a Dodge Viper Owners Invitational track event at Las Vegas Motor Speedway. Dodge sponsors such events periodically and invites Viper owners to participate. The sessions include classroom instruction, track time, and professional driving school instructors.

According to reports from knowledgeable sources, here is the surprising story. A novice (never before on any track) Viper owner, who just happened to be a state court judge, was paired up with an instructor from a professional racing school. Everyone involved signed a full release of liability. After the first couple of laps, the instructor insisted that the student was braking too early for the turns, and told him to stay on the throttle until the instructor told him to hit the brakes.

Whether it was a communication problem or reaction problem, the end result was that the student braked too late, sending the Viper into a spin and into the concrete wall. The student was unhurt, but the instructor's foot was tangled up in the mangled floorboard, trapping him in the car. He was cut out of the car and rushed to the hospital. In addition to less permanent physical injuries, he lost a toe that the doctors were unable to reattach.

In a twist to the usual track liability claim, the instructor sued the student, claiming he was to blame for the injuries because he didn't follow instructions. The instructor's claims include medical costs, pain and suffering, loss of the toe, lost wages, impairment of his ability to properly heel-and-toe downshift, and loss of marital relations from his resulting feelings of inadequacy without the toe. He has demanded $1.5 million in damages, and the case is presently scheduled for trial in October 2009.

This is not the first time "Legal Files" has reported on track liability and the fact that most automobile insurance policies now specifically exclude racetrack claims from coverage, but many track day participants still don't understand or believe that.

Brake... brake... BRAKE!

Problems beget opportunities

Fortunately, a new industry has developed to fill the need. An Internet search under "track day insurance" will identify a number of insurance agencies that offer coverage specifically designed to protect you and your car from financial ruin. These policies typically cover damage to your vehicle only, but some offer liability protection as well. Some are single-event policies, while others are annual policies. There are too many to list and detail, so "Legal Files" reviewed three companies' offerings to give readers an overview.

Steve Katz, of Jacob J. Katz and Company (www.ontrackinsurance.com), worried about his own lack of coverage when driving his Viper ACR at track days. He searched around for an insurance company that would be interested, and eventually paired up with Great American Insurance Company to offer High Performance Driver Education (HPDE) coverage. Instant price quotes and online applications are easy to use. Maximum available coverage is $100,000, but Katz expects that to increase substantially very soon. Premiums are typically about 0.56% of the value of the car. The deductible is 5% of the value of the car, with a $1,500 minimum. Coverage is afforded for an entire event, whether it is one or two days in length, with a 50% discount for a third day of an event.

For example, say you are driving a $50,000 Porsche Boxster S. Your premium will be about $280 for the first two days, with a deductible of $2,500. $15,000 of crash damage costs you $2,500 to repair. Total the car, and you get a check for $47,500.

Your premium is refundable, except for the modest service fee, if you don't participate in the event after buying the policy. Damage caused by you, your designated co-driver, or your instructor is all covered. Applications are virtually automatically accepted if the event is listed on their calendar (most club events are). Other events are individually reviewed. Coverage is denied for race events and race cars, defined as those incapable of being registered for street use, for those who have had a previous HPDE claim (subject to review), and for those with poor driving records.

Katz explains, "We are looking to insure competent drivers who are willing to obey the rules established at well-managed track events. We don't care so much about a ticket or accident or two, but 'habitual traffic offenders' display a lack of willingness to follow the law and are likely to not follow track rules either."

Katz assures readers that HPDE coverage is sorely needed. "The days of racing exclusions requiring 'speed contests' or 'timed events' are long gone. So are the days of insurers that will cover you once before they cancel you. Every auto policy I've seen over the last few years has contained a very broad exclusion that denies coverage for just about anything that happens on a racing surface."

Register and insure

Many track day sponsors have signed on with Motorsport reg.com to handle their event registrations. In a very logical pairing, Motorsportreg.com teamed up with Lockton Infinity Insurance Company to provide HPDE coverage that is a mouse-click away. The program is very similar to the Katz program, with instant price quotes and online applications. Maximum available coverage is $100,000, and premiums are typically about 0.6% of the value of the car.

The deductible is 5% of the value of the car, with a $1,000 minimum. Coverage is afforded for an entire event, whether it is one, two, or three days in length, and your premium is refundable, except for the modest service fee, if you don't participate. Damage caused by you, your designated co-driver, or your instructor is all covered. Applications are virtually automatically accepted if the event is listed on their calendar (most club events are). Other events are individually reviewed. Coverage is denied for anyone who has had a previous HPDE claim within three years, and for any racing or competitive event, including time trials.

The other way to go

Anthony Bevilacqua, of Anthony & Company, Inc. (www .anthonycompany.com), has taken a different course. Teaming up with Lloyd's of London, Bevilacqua offers annual policies that will cover you for up to ten events per year. Each policy is individually underwritten, based upon numerous factors such as skill, claims, experience, etc. Bevilacqua gave an example of a recent quote for a 2000 Ferrari 360 Challenge Car valued at $100,000. The premium was $4,000, with 100% coverage after a $10,000 deductible. If you do all of the ten allowable events,

that comes out to $400 per event, or a rate of only 0.04% of the value of the car.

But what really sets Anthony & Company apart is that they offer liability coverage as well as property damage coverage. Standard coverage is $1 million, with typical premiums of $1,500–$2,000 per year for up to ten events. Higher limits, up to $5 million, are available in the $5,000–$7,000 range. Coverage is quite broad, including any third party liability for anything that arises from a track incident, and can insure you, anyone driving your car, and any specifically designated others.

Bevilacqua agrees with Katz that most every auto policy now excludes anything that happens on a racetrack, and he stresses that the policies extend that exclusion to the liability coverage in your policy, not just the property damage provisions. He adds, "Most people agree that the liability waivers signed by participants are not enough to give complete peace of mind. There are many ways they might be unenforceable. They might not be properly signed, for example. Also, if a death occurs, the waiver might not restrict the legal claims of the person's survivors, depending on the law of the particular state. These policies are pretty cheap ways to sleep at night."

"Legal Files" agrees wholeheartedly. You are really very foolish if you think nothing bad will ever happen to you at a track event, or if you assume that your auto policy will protect you. These specialized policies are affordable, especially when you consider the cost of your entry fees, tires, brakes, fuel, and wear and tear on your car. If you participate in track events, check out these and other carriers to find the best policy for you.

A key warning

But there is a potentially huge downside here. Keep in mind that these are all agreed-value policies. Also, they contain the typical auto insurance policy provisions that damage in the range of 70% or so of the car's value will result in it being declared a total loss. When that happens, you get paid the amount of your agreed value, and the insurance company becomes the owner of the wrecked car.

So, say you want to insure your $450,000 Porsche Carrera GT. You make the mistake of thinking you can buy $100,000 of coverage and self-insure the rest. You have an incident that results in $80,000 of damage (not hard with this car), and the insurance company has the right to pay you $100,000, the amount of your agreed-upon coverage, and own the wrecked car. Even if you can talk them into selling the wrecked car back to you cheaply, you might still end up with a salvage title and a greatly diminished value.

Katz says they really have no interest in such a situation. They don't want to end up with hard feelings if this result arises, and they don't want to take the risk of partially insuring a $450,000 car. Consequently, they pay very close attention to the values placed on the cars, and refuse to provide coverage when this sort of situation is possible.

But readers shouldn't rely on the insurance company to protect them, because they stand to lose a lot of money if a loss situation falls through a crack in the policy. It's far better to know exactly what you are getting into. ♦

The Famous Portuguese Barn Find

Huge collections like the one in Portugal don't just happen. Cars are accumulated by someone with a purpose—someone like a dealer

by Tom Cotter

One day this January, I received at least ten forwarded email attachments to a web site that featured photos of an eclectic collection of old cars in a decaying building. For the next week it seemed the web was literally blanketed with these images, each giving a similar story:

"Imagine moving into an old farmhouse in the Portuguese countryside, and, while walking around the lower 40 of your new investment, you come across an old building. Curious as to what may be inside, you pry open the rusted door and for the first time in decades, one of the largest hordes of old cars ever discovered is exposed to sunlight."

I didn't believe that story for a moment.

Huge collections of cars don't just happen. Cars are accumulated—sometimes lovingly, sometimes not—by someone with a purpose. I was sure this collection was not assembled by accident; nobody would simply sell an old farm and fail to mention to the new owners the stash of old cars in the barn.

I decided to investigate. I searched the web and ultimately came to an English-language dead end at the Mazda Miata Club Norway web site. But I kept going, sending emails in English and hoping that some kind recipient would take a few moments to answer some questions. All indications were that the cars were hidden somewhere in Portugal, so that's where I focused my investigation.

Through a Cobra buddy, Don Silawski of Washington, DC, I contracted with a Portuguese translator, Clara Dixon. Dixon would be my tour guide and try to unearth some of the naked truth regarding this huge stash. Dixon also checked the Internet for news stories that may have been written in Portuguese newspapers about the cars. I was beginning to feel like a CIA sleuth.

I must admit that for me, a lifelong barn-finder, a collection this large would be the discovery of a lifetime. My 15-year-old son, Brian, even tried to convince me to hop a flight to Portugal

Portuguese barn houses 180 cars, all covered with decades of dust

to see if I could actually find the collection myself.

I was eventually able to contact the photographer who was contracted by the cars' owner to shoot the photographs that would ultimately appear on millions of car-guy computer monitors beginning on January 20, 2007.

The story behind the story

Manuel Menezes Morais shot the photos, but he was sworn to secrecy about the cars' location and the owner's name. However, he was able to obtain permission from the elusive owner to give me the following information:

The owner of the cars was a car dealer in the 1970s and 1980s, who decided to save the more interesting cars that came through his doors. When the barn was full, he padlocked and "soldered" the doors shut. (Perhaps welding was too permanent.)

Web sites varied on the number of cars: 58, 100, and 180 were speculated. According to Morais, there are 180 cars in the barn.

And, aw shucks, none of the cars is for sale

Dixon was able to determine that the cars are located somewhere in the area of Sintra, near Lisbon.

I asked Morais if he could ask the owner if he had a favorite car. "He has lots of good cars in very good condition," he said, "but he loves the Lancia Aurelia B24. He has two."

I would ask that a European-based SCM subscriber pick this story up and help fill in the blanks. And let me know what you find (tomgcotter@roadrunner.com). I'd like to include the true story in a future *In the Barn* book, as well as in SCM.♦

So, What's In There?

All the cars are dusty and the lighting is pretty poor, but searching through photos of these cars on various web sites, I was able to identify a fair number. Here is a partial list:

1950s Alfa Giulietta, 1960s Sprint Speciale, 1950s Nash Metropolitan

Dozens of American sedans, from a 1932 Ford 2-door sedan to 1970s Olds Cutlasses

Dozens of 1950s and 1960s Mercedes sedans; a couple of Formula race cars.

Abarth 1300 Scorpione
Alfa GTV
Alfa 1900 SS
Alfa Bertone
Alfa Giulietta
Alfa Giulietta Sprint
Alfa Giulia Sprint Speciale
Alfa Sud 1.5
Austin A30
Austin A40 Somerset
Austin Healey Sprite
Austin Mini Cooper

Austin Mini Cooper S
BMW 2002
BMW 1800
BMW 501 V8 Sedan
BMW Isetta
Bristol 404 Saloon
Chrysler CD
Citroën Traction Avant
Datsun 240Z

1970s Abarth Scorpione

DKW 1000SP
Fiat Cabriolet
Fiat Topolino
Fiat 500
Fiat 508 Balilla
Ford Cortina
Ford Taurus
Hillman Californian
Lancia Aurelia B20 2+2
Lancia Aurelia B24
Lancia Appia

1950s Lancia B20

Lancia Flaminia Zagato
Lancia Flaminia Coupe
Lotus Elan DHC
Lotus Elan FHC
Lotus Elan +2
Lotus Europa
Lotus Super 7 Series IV
MG Midget
MG Magnette
Matra Djet

Maxwell
Mini Moke
Nash Metropolitan
Opel GT
Opel Rekord
Porsche 356B
Porsche 356C
Peugeot 202
Peugeot 404 Cabriolet
Peugeot 505 Cabriolet
Renault Dauphine
Rover P5 Saloon
Rover P6
Saab 93
Simca Coupe de Ville
Singer Gazelle
Steyr Puch
Triumph TR4
Volvo PV444
VW Beetle

1931 Chrysler CD roadster

* Note: More than one car may exist for each model listed above.

Unrestored 1911 Oldsmobile Sells for $1.65 Million

Without evidence of time, what does a real object offer the collector that a perfect replica does not? Cars are lining up with guns, clocks, and furniture

by Miles Collier

Engine number: 64128. Historical and condition description by the auction company.

RM Auctions

Oldsmobile made its name with the tiny single-cylinder "curve dash" buckboard in the early years of the 20th century, but went on to produce one of the most significant and largest early American cars.

Based on the earlier Model Z, the 1910 Limited rode on the same 130-inch wheelbase with massive 42-inch wheels. The following year the wheelbase was stretched to 138 inches and the engine was expanded from the Z's 505-ci 6-cylinder to a massive 707-ci unit. A roadster, a touring car, a four-passenger "tourabout," and a limousine were offered, at prices from $5,600–$7,500, competing with Packard, Peerless, and Pierce-Arrow.

Oldsmobile built only 159 7-passenger touring cars in 1911, so finding one in any condition is unlikely. This car was bought new by the president of the Brewyn-White Coal Company in Cambria County, Pennsylvania. It is one of three known and the only one never restored.

The car was discovered by collector William Swigart in the 1950s and he resisted urges to restore it, though he did find a set of new tires. It presently carries incorrect headlights, though the right Solarclipse 950 units are available with a bit of hunting. The Olds also lacks a top or top bows, though they were optional. Oldsmobile sold only 140 Limiteds in 1912, the last year for the model.

SCM Analysis *This car sold for $1.65 million at RM's Hershey, Pennsylvania, sale on October 12, 2007. There are a number of interesting issues to which this transaction gives rise.*

The subject car is a passably preserved barn find. It is com-

plete in most respects but shows signs of distress and deterioration and has largely unplumbed mechanical systems to boot.

I examined the 1912 Limited that sold at the Otis Chandler estate sale a year ago and felt it lived up to its "finest and most desirable in existence" billing. When the hammer fell, that car sold for $1.25 million. So why did our barn find do so much better?

We are beginning to see the emergence of a trend among collectors wherein wholly unmolested cars—with all the wear, tear, and shabbiness that implies—command significant premiums over beautifully restored examples.

Are these signs the collector car world is starting to fall in line with other areas of antiquarian collecting—some varieties of furniture, silver, porcelain, firearms, clocks, scientific instruments, and so on—where originality is everything?

Diametrically opposing demands

Yes and no. Let's take a look at the two diametrically opposing demands on collectible cars—perfect operating capa-

bility versus historical integrity.

Unlike other antique objects, save for perhaps musical instruments, collectible cars are required to operate at, and sometimes beyond, their original design limits. In the past, this operating ethos has been so pervasive that the vehicle's integrity as a "historical document" was customarily subordinated to the demand for perfect operation.

Hence we are used to the ubiquity of the "total restoration," which erases any evidence of historical age in order to create the simulacrum of newness. Two factors contributed to the drive to restore—the collector's personal relationship to the car and the recent nature of the automobile collecting movement.

The collector's personal relationship to his car is often based on its ability to connect him to his own specific past. Nostalgia causes him to see the car not as a historic object, but, like the collector himself, as an inhabitant of the present with the right to be reinvented according to whim, even if that be restoration at the expense of erasing the object's historical nature.

The second factor that contributes to the "perfect operation at all costs" philosophy is the immaturity of the field. Collecting cars started as an activity for enthusiasts to own some valueless old crocks that represented a piece of history they cared about.

Experiencing the cars as they were

As the cars were essentially valueless, much of the focus of these ur-collectors was on the salvaging and rehabilitation of these objects by the collectors themselves in order to experience the cars as they were when the hobbyist remembered them.

Indeed, that was the point of the hobby. Today, however, at one end of the collecting continuum lie automobiles that by virtue of their exceptional qualities and historical significance command prices on a par with rarefied objects in other fields.

In this arena, minor differences in condition (of which originality is by far the most important), provenance, original specification, etc., have enormous repercussions on value. So this is no longer a hobby; it is connoisseurship.

The two opposing factors, use versus history, conspire to create a major disconnect in our field: We desire (and price) these objects as masterpieces of the past, yet we treat them as modern artifacts without regard to history. With total restoration, we erase patina, the historic evidence of the object's travel through time to the present day.

By erasing the evidence of history, the car loses its identity as a historical object, which is the only real value in the first place. Without evidence of time, what does a real object offer the collector that a perfect replica does not?

A replica would serve better

Indeed, for many uses to which collectible automobiles are being put, a perfectly executed replica would serve better.

We truly could experience our car as it was when new. The conventional response to this statement is that people don't want modern copies; they want "real" cars.

This response raises a major epistemological question, however. If an antiquarian object manifests no signs of history, how do we know it's real? Indeed, what makes it real? We need only consider the countless examples of fraudulent works from our own as well as other fields that have fooled experts.

So returning to our subject car, I would suggest that the Olds's primary property is that its historical reality is absolutely verifiable. The very bones of its legitimacy are there for all to see. Some insightful collectors have realized that, like collectors in other fields, history should trump function.

The unrestored historic automobile offers us a direct connection to the people and times of a past era, whether distant or recent. We can sit on the same leather, touch the same finish, and operate the same vehicle despite its quirks of age and decay. Such surviving cars are the rarest and purest of all collectible automobiles redolent with the fascination of historical reality. Collectors who share that appreciation will pay accordingly.

However, limited if not marginal operation has drawbacks, because unrestored cars are remarkably fragile, deteriorating to nothing if subjected to significant use or exposure. That's why there will always be a demand for restored "good drivers," no matter where this original car trend goes. Clearly, based on price, the buyer of this Olds plans neither to restore nor use this car extensively once the mechanical conservation and rehabilitation is performed.

The buyer's risk in this deal lies in the revelations of a detailed exploratory examination—whether the body's wood frame, its body skins, its major mechanical components have sufficient integrity to allow conservation of the visual elements and the successful resuscitation of its original mechanicals.

Barn-find prices allow no room for error

Barn-find price premiums allow no room for error. And this is the major difference between the barn-find purchase—a piñata of potential unpleasant surprises—and the purchase of a known, original car that aged gracefully in the public eye. Because of the unknowns, the barn find should be priced below a comparably original car that has demonstrated its structural integrity over years of use and exposure.

How did our buyer do in this deal? Assuming the car has sufficient integrity to permit conservation alone, I think he's okay. I would guess that in today's market, the Chandler car would be worth the same as this one. So, pricing equal to the best restored example for the only untouched, reference-quality, original Oldsmobile Limited may well prove to be a deal as this trend develops. Fairly bought. ♦

Restoration Today

The heartbreak of restoration is something every collector must come to grips with at one time or another. We buy a car that just needs "paint and upholstery," and three years and $125,000 later, we've got a completely restored car worth $75,000 on the best day of its life.

The articles in this section won't stop you from making irrational, emotion-driven decisions concerning the slightly decrepit car in the garage you're thinking of making into a concours prize winner, but hopefully they will slow you down a bit.

Go to restorers who know what they are doing and who have restored cars like yours before. Don't go to someone who will end up going to school on your car. Be aware that doing anything to old cars is expensive, and if you don't want to pay, don't play in the first place.

Like a straight shot of single-malt whiskey, the advice in this chapter—all from experts who have been through the restoration process many times—will rock you back on your heels. And save you tens, if not hundreds of thousands, of dollars.

Before you start to restore any car, read this chapter. And then read it again. And then decide if you really want to pull the trigger. If you do, at least you can comfort yourself that you thought it all through before you began. You may still have to take out a home equity loan to get the restoration finished, but at least this way you'll be planning on it from the start, rather than trying to explain to your significant other half way through why, instead of remodeling the kitchen, you're putting a new engine in the Ferrari.—*Keith Martin*

In This Section

Restoration Types:
Street, Show, and Race 238

Restoring Your Dream Car 240

Odometer Replacement and Value 242

Restoration to True Concours Standard 244

Seven Ways to Make your British Car
More Reliable 246

Restoration Types: Street, Show, and Race

Sports car restorations can take one of three paths. Once you've headed in one direction, it's hard to change course

by Gary Anderson

Chuck Blakeslee in his daily-driver MG B

So you've found a classic British car—an MG B or Triumph TR4, perhaps—in someone's barn or an old garage where it was parked many years ago. The rust is superficial, the body is in good shape, and all the parts are there. The price is good, in line with the price guide for "project cars." This could be your dream car after you restore it. But restore it to do what?

What kind of a dream do you have for that classic car? What you do with it when it's finished will make a major difference in what you'll spend to restore it and the process you'll follow.

Three key questions

Let's break down the possibilities into three categories.

1. Fun daily driver: Take the car on club tours and out to meet friends on a Saturday morning.

2. Show car: Draw admiring glances from concours d'elegance judges and other club members.

3. Race car: You're sliding into the seat, pulling on your helmet, buckling the shoulder and lap belts, and heading onto the track in a vintage race.

In today's classic car hobby, those are three different ends to the journey, and the forks in the road come pretty quickly. Once you've headed in one direction, it's hard to change course, and the cost differences are dramatic.

To illuminate the road map, we talked to Kent Prather, six-time SCCA national champion in MGAs and one of the most respected builders of racing MGs in the country. Then we spoke with Jim Perell, an organizer of concours events in the Sacramento area and the proud builder and owner of an MG B show car that's been featured in several national magazines. Finally we asked our buddy Chuck Blakeslee, who owns an attractive MG B that he drives two or three days a week and takes on tours with local car buddies.

Prather reckons a nice MG B, or similar British roadster of the '50s and '60s, will cost $10,000 to $15,000 to take from "ran-when-parked" to a fun driver. If you want to show the car in judged events, plan on spending $25,000 to $40,000. And if you want to go racing, pony up $35,000 to $60,000.

Baby, you can drive your car

For a daily driver, plan a basic rebuild on the engine and transmission, and while the engine is out redo the brakes and shocks, replace the interior upholstery with a ready-made kit, and get a reasonable paint job at a local shop without dismantling the car and after doing the prep work yourself. If you're lucky and don't need pricey parts for the engine or any major bodywork, you should get by with $5,000 for mechanicals and $5,000 for paint and trim. Your money will be pretty safe. If you build a good driver, somebody else will appreciate that, too.

However, if the car is going to be shown at local concours for a season or two before you start to drive and enjoy it, then take it down to the frame. Every part needs to be stripped, cleaned, refurbished, and refinished. It's got to look better than original.

Since you're putting serious money into the cosmetics, have a good engine shop do the engine. Jim Perell rebuilt his engine to exact original specs (called "blueprinting") and went through the mechanicals. The cost sheets for his MG B show he has $17,000 into drivetrain, suspension, and electrics.

Paint and bodywork costs real money in a show car. Be very clear with your body shop about what you want and how much you can spend. It takes hours to smooth a surface so that it will reflect straight lines, and each hour can add $50 to $75 to the bill. Perell invested over $20,000 in his paint and bodywork. A good (but not great) job might have cost half that; on the other hand, if he had been after a "best in the country" paint job, he could easily have spent another $10,000.

Why concours is costly

Interiors are another issue. Upholstery kits are fine for a driver, but on a show car, the pleats have to be exactly equal and straight, the welts smooth, and the stitches exact. Perell spent over $8,000 having a correct-style interior custom-made for his MG B and a good top hand-fitted.

Then there's the question of replacement parts. A lot of catalog stuff will fit fine and work dependably. But anyone who knows what the original part looks like can spot the difference in finish, shape, logo, or color between a new-old-stock (NOS) part and a reproduction.

Patience and the miracle of eBay can unearth good original parts, but always at a price more expensive than "repops." Perrell figures he spent about $5,000 to find the right replacement trim and other cosmetic components. He's got an MG B on which he's spent over $50,000, but he's won several shows, and feels he's getting good value from his investment.

However, he will frankly admit it takes a real effort to drive it down to the ice cream parlor or park it on the street while running an errand. He can't help thinking about all the effort he's invested and how easy it would be to get a scratch or a dent.

Do you want to race—or win?

Perhaps you'd prefer hot laps to hot wax, and your idea of a parade is a pace lap, not Main Street. Maybe you're dreaming of racing.

Here Kent Prather is very clear. Before you go down that road, be sure you're going to enjoy racing, because a car prepared to be safe in current vintage racing—not only for the driver but for other drivers around him—is undriveable on the street. And it's the most expensive alternative of the restoration options we are examining here.

Speed costs money; how fast do you want to go? You can install a roll bar, safety belts, catch tanks, and a fuel cell in your street car, replace the wheels with safe racing wheels and tires, and buy a suit, shoes, and helmet for about $3,000 to $5,000. That gets you into track schools, where you can drive at speed but can't actually race.

But at this level of preparation, your car won't be competitive, even though it might get through the technical and safety inspection. You won't be as fast, nor will your car be as responsive and predictable, as your competition. You'll be a moving chicane.

If you really want to race—even at the polite vintage level—you'll strip the interior for weight and safety and install a racing seat for support. You'll need to completely rebuild the engine and transmission with racing-quality components and replace the entire suspension with new or excellent original components.

And if you want to be competitive, you're easily in Prather's estimate of $35,000 to $60,000. At the lower price, you'll be safe, have a car that will challenge your ability, and teach you to race. But if you want to be at the front of the grid, count on the top of the range. And the car will be noisy, uncomfortable, difficult to drive at low speeds, and probably illegal on the highway. ◆

1962 Sebring MG B race restored by Butch Gilbert

Restoring Your Dream Car

Although bias-ply tires look great, they'll make your car wander like a drunken hound on the scent of fifty rabbits

by Colin Comer

Don't be afraid to sacrifice strict originality for everday usability

So you just bought your high school dream car at auction—that Plum Crazy 1970 Hemi Road Runner with a four-speed.

Now it's time to drive it and—holy smoke! The belted tires follow every crack in the road; it doesn't want to turn or stop; the engine's spinning at 4,500 rpm at 70 mph; and you can't hear yourself think.

Maybe Thomas Wolfe was right—you can't go home again. And if you do, you'll find Peggy Sue isn't your 100-pound high school sweetheart any more. But maybe she moved out to California and had herself nipped and tucked? That's what you need to do with your dream car: Upgrade it and give it a chance to fulfill your high school fantasies.

There have been huge technological advances in the 40 years since the first muscle cars rolled out of Detroit. They've raised our expectations of how a car should drive. Perhaps it's time to make that perfectly restored muscle car behave as good as it looks.

Having four-wheeled garage art is only half the fun. Weather permitting (I do live in Wisconsin), I drive an old car every day.

Unless you are satisfied with a trailer queen or a limited-use concours car, improvements can peel away the years from that old Detroit iron.

First make sure the car will actually get from point A to point B. Although British car owners know driving shoes must also be comfortable walking shoes, there is no need for that here.

Concentrate on basics: spark, fuel, cooling, starting, and charging.

1. Ignition: Conversion kits exist to rid your distributor of its breaker points and replace them with reliable solid-state electronics. It's completely hidden; I like the PerTronix brand. For under $100, you can't go wrong.

2. Fuel: Make sure everything is absolutely perfect from the fuel tank forward, including having factory-specified fuel line diameters. I have seen lots of big blocks with small block line sets and sending units. Get the car on a chassis dyno with an exhaust gas analyzer to make sure the carburetor jetting, timing, and distributor advance curve are spot-on. I've seen increases of over 50 hp from a proper "super tune." A properly set-up, carbureted V8 will run nearly as well as a fuel-injected one. At this point we have a car that really runs and still looks bone-stock. Be thorough, though, and inspect, calibrate, and change everything from the ignition wires to the idle jets—the devil is truly in the details.

3. Cooling System: Put the original date-coded radiator in storage and buy a stock-appearing, high-performance version—either brass or aluminum painted black. Install the right thermostat and make sure the cooling fan is correct and the shroud is in place. If equipped with a fan clutch, check that it works.

4. Starting System: Buy a modern sealed battery with more juice than stock, and no more acid leaks. Have the starter rebuilt correctly, and make sure all cables are tight and insulated properly. Invest in a high-output rebuild of your stock alternator, and if equipped, hide a solid-state external regulator under the cover of an original points-style version.

5. Transmission: Now that we have this baby humming, let's make her dance. Steep gears and four speeds sound great on paper, but in reality, nobody wants to be spinning 4,500 rpm at 70 mph. Bolt-in five-speed conversions are readily available for all domestic cars—and if that doesn't appeal to you, calculate your overall tire diameter and what rear axle ratio you'll need to put your engine around 3,000 rpm at 70 mph. For automatic transmission cars, four-speed automatic overdrive transmission conversions are available—again, bolt in and swap back to stock if you ever need to. Have the driveshaft balanced. Measure and correct the rear differential pinion angle to minimize vibration, if needed. A car that can go down the freeway effortlessly is more useful than one that is a half-second faster in the quarter mile, but makes you feel like you're stuck in a Mixmaster when you're on a cruise.

6. Tires: Although correct bias-ply tires look great, they'll make your car wander like a drunken hound on the scent of fifty rabbits. Calculate the overall diameter and width of the OEM tire and find a suitable radial replacement. For suspension, install improved bushings, establish proper ride height using good aftermarket springs painted and detailed to look stock, and add a good set of gas shocks painted the OE color. Blueprinted and quick-ratio steering boxes rival the best rack-and-pinions. Research aftermarket companies to learn correct alignment settings or your suspension won't work properly. Most suspensions were fairly well engineered when new, and only become ineffective after many years of Joe Bob Cooter deciding he "knows better than all them fancy engineering types in Dee-troit."

7. Brakes: Bolt-on disc brake kits are available and the change is easily reversible. Updated lining material is available for both factory and aftermarket systems. On cars prior to 1967, it's a good idea to incorporate a dual-circuit master cylinder in place of the stock single-circuit. Make sure all rubber parts and hoses are new and that the lines and hoses are properly routed where they won't be cut by other components or melted by the exhaust. Brake upgrades such as vented rotors, bigger calipers, and even bigger rear drums are available, but they're not necessary for the street if the stock system is fresh. Remember to use a high quality DOT 4 fluid and change it every year.

8. Gremlins: Lastly, have a competent mechanic chase out the "bugs." If your lights or wipers don't work, you surely won't find out until 10:00 pm about 300 miles from home on a deserted country road. Your car functioned reliably when new and should do so now. There is no excuse for a car that doesn't work.

Following this program, I've built some super-reliable and thoroughly enjoyable old muscle cars. There's nothing like a thousand-mile road rally or showing your 40-year-old taillights to a Honda festooned with more wings than a Wright Brothers experiment. ◆

Odometer Replacement and Value

If the odometer is replaced, and the replacement does indicate the actual mileage of the car, then no further disclosure is required

by John Draneas

Dear Keith Martin's Guide to Car Collecting: I enjoy and appreciate your "Legal Files" column, but any SCMer who has been on the wrong end of an odometer discrepancy should be offended by your March 2005 article on replacement odometers. You went to great lengths to portray the situation as a minor legal inconvenience for the seller, with no mention of a moral dilemma. Would you feel the same if it was the dealer doing the misrepresenting?

You also stated that you wouldn't be inclined to accept the proposition that the odometer repair requires the dealer to represent the vehicle as "True Mileage Unknown." Please look a little more closely at the federal laws concerning odometers—if the car rolls into the repair facility with the odometer not turning, by law it is TMU and must be disclosed as such. Failure to do so by a dealer can cost him his license and earn him prison time.

The question that was asked of the Ferrari 348 owner was, "Has the odometer ever been tampered with, rolled back, or disconnected?" You say that the owner's answer of "no" was technically correct. Really? Is it actually possible to replace an odometer without disconnecting it?

The owner made a moral judgment when he stated that the odometer reading on his car was correct. The fact that you speak not of right or wrong but simply of liability is troubling to anyone who has been a victim of odometer fraud, either by a dealer or a private party.—*M.B., Laguna Beach, CA*

First, a quick refresher. My March column dealt with a reader who owned a 348 that had had its defective odometer replaced. The work was done by his local Ferrari dealer, which reset the new unit to reflect the actual miles on the car. The owner had all the paperwork to back this up, which he gave to the guys at a different Ferrari dealership, along with all the other service records, when he traded in his car on a 360 Modena.

While completing the transaction, one of the documents he filled out asked him if the odometer on his car had ever been tampered with. He replied "no." A couple of days later, the dealer called him, reduced the trade-in allowance for the 348, and demanded more money to make the deal work, as the 348 had been misrepresented and the dealer was now going to have to list the car as TMU.

Turning back the clock can land you in prison

Curbing fraud

The actual law in question here is the Federal Odometer Act (FOA), which was enacted to curb odometer fraud, and to a great extent it has. Of interest to us is that it makes two specific things illegal. The first is driving a vehicle when you know the odometer is disconnected or inoperable, with the intent to defraud. The second is altering or tampering with the odometer with the intent of changing the actual mileage shown.

The FOA also imposes the now familiar disclosure requirements on everyone who transfers a title on a car that is less than 10 years old. You must state one of the following:

1. The indicated mileage is the actual mileage.

2. The indicated mileage is the actual mileage over the odometer's mechanical limit. (For example, 13,000 indicated miles is actually 113,000 when you have a five-digit odometer.)

3. That the indicated mileage is not the actual mileage.

Repairs are covered, too

Odometer repairs are also covered by this statute. If an odometer is repaired and it is impossible to register the actual mileage of the car, the odometer must be reset to zero and a sticker explaining the discrepancy must be attached to the left front door frame of the car. Thereafter, the inaccuracy of the odometer reading must be disclosed when transferring title.

However, if the odometer is replaced and the replacement odometer does indicate the actual mileage of the car, then no sticker or further disclosure is required. In this case, the owner is able to certify the mileage as actual when he transfers the title.

This is precisely what our reader did and thus his answering "no" to the dealer's disclosure form is not a misrepresentation. He stated the odometer reading reflected the actual mileage of his car, which it did. As the reader described the situation to me, the defective odometer was replaced with a new one that had been adjusted to reflect the actual mileage of the car. There is nothing in the FOA that treats the odometer being physically disconnected for repair as any sort of violation, at least not unless the car is driven while it is disconnected. The reader had the old odometer and the signed documents to prove it—what more could he be expected to do?

Similarly, I do not see how the dealer has a problem with this Ferrari. The indicated mileage is the actual mileage of the car and can be represented as such.

Fraud abounds

I don't mean to minimize odometer fraud by any means. The National Highway Traffic Safety Administration recently published a study that determined odometer fraud occurs in as many as 3.47% of cars less than 10 years old, and costs consumers over $1 billion per year, or about $2,336 per case. These are pretty big numbers.

Odometer fraud is a hot topic. An Internet search readily linked me to numerous web sites maintained by lawyers who handle these types of cases and to many state-sponsored sites that alerted people to the problem and gave tips about how to detect it.

Odo resetting, just sign here

But I found the most interesting sites were the ones that offered digital odometer reprogramming services. These operations all offer legal disclaimers to advise that tampering with the mileage is illegal, and that they will do their work only on the basis of your promise that you aren't going to do anything illegal with the odometer after its displayed mileage is adjusted. I saw one shop that even requires an agreement to reimburse it for any liability it might incur for having adjusted your odometer.

Which brings us to a point we have made time and time again in SCM. The best way to have confidence in an odometer reading is for the seller to provide service bills that stretch back several years, with each representing an odometer reading that is in sync with the use the car is represented to have had. Anything else is really just wishing on an odometer and hoping for the best. ♦

Ferrari 348

Restoration to True Concours Standard

A restoration is like a war-planning exercise, coordinating multiple teams of specialists working at insanely expensive prices

by Michael Sheehan

Detailing the suspension is just the beginning

Over the years, the term "restoration" has had evolving meaning in the Ferrari world. Back in the 1970s, it meant new paint, clean leather, maybe a valve job or an engine rebuild, some non-original chrome work and a great detail. Today, however, it implies much more.

The assumption now is that a restored Ferrari is one worthy of a place on the lawn at Cavallino, Concorso Italiano, or even Pebble Beach. As this standard and the times have changed, so have the costs, which have escalated dramatically.

More work

In the 1980s and early 1990s, a "Pebble Beach-quality" restoration was usually estimated at about 2,000–2,500 hours labor, plus parts, machining, sublet, and materials. Today, the same car would be subjected to 3,000–3,500 hours, and a whole new world of peripheral expenditures would be tacked onto the bill for things like research, logistics, and presentation.

This is because when a restored Ferrari is finally ready to show, a full support staff is needed. These people cover detailing upon delivery, show setup, and most importantly, prepping the owner for presentation. The car's owner must be briefed such that he can understand the entire restoration and become familiar with every aspect of the work. Hopefully he can convince the judges of the veracity of the work, not only by knowing the answers to their questions, but by anticipating potential questionable areas before being asked.

A restoration is like a war-planning exercise, coordinating multiple teams of specialists who disassemble, store and itemize, sublet, fabricate and finish, rebuild and repair, paint and polish, retrim, and reassemble insanely expensive and usually unique pieces at a price and with a firm deadline. In the small world of concours entrants, miss your target date for Cavallino or Pebble Beach, and you lose your client.

The shops

Today, I believe there are only four large total-service restoration shops with ten or more employees in the U.S. These are Motion Products in Wisconsin, Bobby Smith in Texas, Dennison Motor Sport in Washington, and Paul Russell and Co. in Massachusetts. All are located in the suburbs or farther removed from the expenses of the big cities.

There are several smaller shops such as CAROBU Engineering and F.A.I. in Southern California, and Patrick Ottis and Perfect Reflections in the San Francisco area, or David Carte in Virginia. All have had Ferraris at Concorso Italiano or Pebble Beach in August.

Sadly, there are no large restoration-only shops left in California. While California may be car-crazy, it is also one of the most litigious places on the planet, and a large, high-profile shop filled with top-end Ferraris is simply a target for every lawyer fresh out of law school who believes a law degree guarantees a house at the beach and a paid-for BMW.

Overhead and regulations

It costs a lot of money to keep the doors open at a restoration shop. There are many costs, such as hazardous material disposal, that have gone sky-high in the past 20 years. From painting, plating, and powder coating to machining and sand blasting, all of these processes have become increasingly regulated due to the environmental implications of the materials involved. The effect on the cost of a restoration has been huge. While it once cost $10k to do the chrome on a 275 GTB, the same job is $35k today.

For a further example, in 1989 I outfitted my expanding restoration shop with a brand-new, industry-standard paint booth and the latest piston-type compressor and air drier. It cost me $30k for the booth and $15k for the compressor, installed and ready to go.

When I re-leased the same building in 1998, the new tenant had to install a new downdraft paint booth and a new rotary air compressor with a dryer system. Cost? About $225k for the booth and $50k for the rest, all to comply with newer regulations. Undoubtedly today you're looking at an even bigger bill.

Labor costs are another factor. In the mid-1980s, a top mechanic or painter might make $50k a year, while today the same top-level technicians can expect a healthy six figures. I know some shop managers that could literally name their salary.

Think this run-up in costs is crazy? Consider the cost of insurance. All restoration shops now insist their customers carry their own insurance, as the cost to insure a facility filled with a dozen or more Ferraris, all valued at over $1m, is simply unobtanium.

The ever-raising bar

There are no more barn-find 375 MMs or 250 GTOs, so today's restoration is almost always the recycling of last decade's Pebble Beach contender, but to an ever-higher standard. The factors driving this start with the general competitiveness of the Ferrari industry.

In the 1970s, restoring old cars, even Ferraris, usually meant hot-rodding them and chroming everything in sight. But not anymore. Today it is not enough to complete a world-class restoration, but the result must be documented in voluminous photo albums that are used to convince skeptical judges that every detail is absolutely correct. The wrong trim, the wrong fasteners, the lack of a photo to show how something was done, and you just dropped a point further away from the podium.

There are many anal-retentive trainspotters, including most of the top judges in the hobby, who take this stuff very seriously. Some judges are professional restorers themselves. These guys dedicate massive hours of research and documentation to their craft, scanning in old photos and linking up online to more clearly define the standards for concours excellence.

Cuteness doesn't count

Cars are usually judged at concours by starting at 100 points and then subtracting points for flaws. Only Motion Products has scored 100 points at Pebble Beach, and it has done so five different times, making it the standard bearer for both top quality and research in the world of restorations.

The paradox of restoration is that the big collectors, those with multiple best-of-the-best Ferraris who can hire the very best shop and can afford the best presentation, expect to win. So the reality is such that a lesser car requires even more work and higher standards to beat the big guys at their game and bring home a trophy.

While I was able to do a quality restoration on a four-cylinder 1930 BMW cabriolet for about $35,000, and my eleven-year-old twins brought home a third-place podium finish in a mini-car class based more on "cuteness" than presentation, the highly competitive Ferrari world is a bit different.

Just as speed costs money in racing, the same applies to restoration. To gain that extra point, that extra edge, it is always extra-expensive. When you're up against the most desirable and unique Ferraris in the world, competing against the best shops and some of the wealthiest men in the world, winning is an expensive art form. ♦

Seven Ways to Make Your British Car More Reliable

Original starters were heavy, drained the power supply when they turned the engine, and had a bad habit of burning out bearings

by Gary Anderson

L et's face it, our beloved British cars aren't perfect. Perhaps by standards of the period they were pretty good, but when compared to modern cars, they're really not very safe, certainly not as reliable, and you're not going to find one that has the 100,000-mile service intervals we've come to expect from new cars.

Yet despite these shortcomings, we specifically buy these old cars today to take on 1,000-mile tours and other fun-time events. So in the spirit of tweaking for comfort and safety without changing the character of your old car or detracting from its value, here are seven changes for you to consider (of course, most of these apply to all old cars, not just those from England). Where applicable, we have included a representative web site. But this is a situation where Google is truly your friend.

Spin-on oil filter

Most older British cars came equipped with an elaborate cartridge system that makes changing the oil filter a challenge. The original filters had bolts, washers, spacers, gaskets, and O-rings. Leave any part off, install it crooked or backwards, and you can easily wind up with oil all over your garage floor.

Adapters are readily available from British car parts suppliers that allow you to use a standard modern spin-on oil filter from the nearest Pep Boys. Better, this change is simple to reverse. $150 (www.mossmotors.com)

Multi-bladed fans help to keep temperatures—and repair bills—down

Lightweight multi-blade fan

Overheating is a standard problem with British cars. If you look at the rudimentary and crudely made two-blade or four-blade fans that were original equipment, this isn't surprising. Also, these old cast or pressed fan blades occasionally break free and spin into the radiator or body work. An easy solution is to replace the original fan with a modern, lightweight plastic six-blade fan. You can usually find a suitable one in an auto parts store or through car clubs. $45–$75 (www.ntahc .org for Healey version, others at www.napaonline.com)

Alternator

The original generators were just about adequate to power the headlights, taillights, and heater while recharging the battery, and they were big and heavy to boot. Your best bet is to replace it with a modern alternator. They're small, lightweight, and produce two or three times the power of the original generator. A bonus is that an alternator will power everything you could want to mount on the car, including those neat rally lights, your discretely installed audio system, and a power point for your cell phone and computer. $100–$150 (Installation info can be found at www.mgaguru.com/mgtech/ electric/ac101.htm)

High-ratio starter

Original starters were exceptionally heavy, put a huge drain on the power supply when they turned over the engine, and had a bad habit of burning out bearings. They also use a Rube Goldberg arrangement of springs and gears to engage the ring gear, another typical source of starter problems.

Fortunately, the Japanese have come up with small, lightweight gear-reduction starters that draw much less power to spin up the engine, will spin it faster, and are a bolt-in replacement. $269 (www.aptfast.com), or buy a rebuilt 1988–91 Isuzu Trooper starter for your MGA/MGB and similar models for $85. (www.autoexpress.safeshopper.com)

12-volt battery

Many British cars came with two six-volt batteries mounted on the frame behind the seats that were only accessible after you'd removed the dog, the luggage, the carpet, and the access door.

Though you're probably still stuck with the original location, at least you can pull out the two old six-volt batteries, and replace them with one good deep-cycle, low-maintenance 12-volt battery the same size as one of the old six-volt jobs. $65–$85 at any auto parts supplier.

Modern fuse panel

Nearly all British cars came with two fuses. Typically one fused the horn and the other fused most of the other electrical circuits. This setup has led to long, learned treatises on what happens when the smoke escapes from the electrical circuit of a British car.

A good idea is to add some inline fuses—for example, to the rear light circuit and the front light circuit—so that a short doesn't result in total loss of lights or complete incineration of the entire electrical system.

A better idea is to install a modern fuse panel in some discrete but accessible place in the interior or engine compartment, and run each of the separate circuits through its own fuse. This change isn't easily reversible, but it costs less than $25, improves the car's reliability and in many cases enhances its value. (A good list of instructions that apply to almost every British Car can be found at www.mgaguru.com/mgtech/ electric/et201b.htm)

5-speed transmission

Though this improvement is expensive, substitution of a 5-speed transmission from a Japanese junker or English Ford for the original transmission, using one of the readily available conversion kits on the market, is a good thing in most British marques.

A modern 5-speed will provide smoother shifting, generally better intermediate gearing, and a nice top gear for 70-mph cruising. You won't be able to accelerate any faster, but at least you won't be terminally uncomfortable at cruising speed. $2,500–$3,000 (www.quantumechanics.com) ♦

RESTORATION TODAY

Price Guide

In the end, it's all about money. Sort of. One of the first questions asked about a collector car is, "What's it worth?"

In this section, we address that question head on, telling you what over 2,000 models of collector cars are worth in today's market.

You'll find two numbers by each car, which represent a buy-sell range for good, condition #2 cars. The first number is what we are comfortable telling you to pay, and the second is what we think you should ask when you go to sell. You may find some cars for less, and sell others for more, but overall we think the range is representative of the market.

By the time you finish this chapter, you'll know how much you'll have to spend to get what you want.

So within two weeks of finishing Keith Martin's Guide to Car Collecting, we expect that you will have gone out and hunted down the car of your dreams, paid the right price for it, and hauled it home to your garage.—*Keith Martin*

Investment Grade:

Note: This is not a value appreciation guide. Rather, it is an overall ranking of the desirability of the car, regardless of current market conditions.

A Grade: Cars that will always have a following and will always bring strong money when they are offered for sale. They embody the attributes of style, performance, historical significance, rarity and competition history that often typify first-rank collectibles. Examples are the Ferrari SWB, the Mercedes-Benz 300Sc Roadster and the Alfa Romeo 8C 2300 Monza.

B Grade: Cars that have something special about them, often technical innovation, style or competition provenance—but normally not all three. They were generally produced in far larger numbers than the A-tier cars. Examples are the Austin-Healey 100/4, the Ferrari 512 BB Boxer and the Lotus 7.

C Grade: Cars that have some inherent interest, but had few special or desirable characteristics. Examples are the Porsche 914, the Saab Sonett II and the Triumph TR4.

D Grade: Cars that had the potential to be interesting but failed to be successful in the collector car marketplace, often due to design, engineering or styling flaws. Examples include the Ferrari 400 2+2, the Acura NSX and the Alfa 2600 Sprint.

F Grade: Cars with few if any redeeming characteristics, that are consequently hopeless in nearly every way. Examples include the Alfa Romeo Alfetta sedan, the Iso Lele and the Lotus Eclat.

Key to Appreciation Ratings:

★★★★★ Value likely to increase much more than the market at large, perhaps as much as 25% in the next 12 months.

★★★★ Will outperform the market at large; perhaps 10% gain in 12 months.

★★★ Fully priced at the current time. Will appreciate or depreciate along with the market at large.

★★ Somewhat overpriced today, or a car that is slightly out of favor. May represent a good buying opportunity if you think the market's opinion of the car will change.

★ Often a recent production car that is still depreciating heavily, or a vintage car whose maintenance costs far outweigh its market value and appeal. These collector cars are only good buys if you can do work yourself and love orphans.

1 Year % Change Notes:

NL Indicates new listing

n/c Indicates no change

Mkt. Adj. Indicates market adjustment of 75% or more

	Yrs. Built	No. Made	Buy-Sell Price Range Low	High	Grade	Rating	1 Yr. % Change
ABARTH							
207A Boano Spider	57	12	$160,000	$190,000	B	★★★★	9%
Zagato 750 Double Bubble	58–61	n/a	$52,500	$87,500	B	★★★	30%
Record Monza	59–62	n/a	$62,000	$90,000	B	★★★	29%
(Add $15k for correct twin-cam engine; $40k–$60k for 850-cc twin-cam; $80k–$100k for 1000-cc twin-cam bialbero.)							
850 TC 2+2	62–66	n/a	$16,500	$25,000	C	★★	27%
AC							
Ace roadster	53–63	226	$140,000	$230,000	B	★★★	38%
Aceca coupe	54–63	319	$75,000	$110,000	C	★★★	22%
Ace Bristol roadster	56–63	466	$170,000	$240,000	B	★★★	n/c
(36 cars, mostly RHD, were fitted with Ford Zephyr 6-cylinder engine, Rudd alloy head, and triple Webers. Add $20k.)							
428 coupe	67–73	58*	$40,000	$70,000	C	★★★	n/c
428 convertible	60–73	20*	$75,000	$125,000	D	★★★	n/c
ACURA							
NSX coupe	91–99	19,000	$30,000	$45,000	D	★	7%
NSX coupe	00–05	inc.	$40,000	$70,000	D	★	n/c
(Add 5% for T-top. Deduct 15% for automatic.)							
ALFA ROMEO							
RL Normale/Turismo	22–25	1,702	$100,000	$150,000	C	★★★	18%
RL Sport/Supersport	25–26	987	$200,000	$250,000	B	★★★★	42%
RL Targa Florio	23–24	4	$650,000	$1,000,000	A	★★★★	27%
6C 1500 Normale	27–29	864	$120,000	$190,000	C	★★★	31%
6C 1500 Sport	28	181	$250,000	$350,000	B	★★★	56%
6C 1500 SS Supercharged	28	13	$500,000	$750,000	A	★★★	38%
6C 1750 Turismo	29–33	1,100	$110,000	$170,000	C	★★★★	9%
6C 1750 Gran Touring	30–32	526	$300,000	$400,000	B	★★★★	46%
6C 1750 GS SC 2+2	30–33	inc.	$475,000	$700,000	B	★★★★	45%
6C 1750 GS SC Zagato	30–33	inc.	$875,000	$1,250,000	A	★★★★	27%
6C 1750 GS Touring	30–33	inc.	$850,000	$1,300,000	A	★★★★	28%
(For previous two models, deduct up to $100k for non-matching engines.)							
8C 2300 long chassis	31–34	80	$2,300,000	$3,500,000	A	★★★	16%
"Le Mans" Team Cars	31–34	12	$5,000,000	$7,000,000	A	★★★★	25%
8C 2300 short chassis (all)	31–34	48	$5,000,000	$7,000,000	A	★★★	n/c
8C 2300 "Monza"	31–34	39	$5,000,000	$7,000,000	A	★★★	n/c
Tipo B Monoposto (P3)	32–34	15	$3,000,000	$4,000,000	A	★★★★	14%
Tipo C Monoposto (8C-35)	35–36	6	$4,500,000	$5,500,000	A	★★★★	10%
6C 2300 saloon coachwork	34–39	858	$80,000	$100,000	C	★★★	17%
6C 2300 Sp. coachwork	34–39	748	$300,000	$400,000	B	★★★★	43%
6C 2300 Mille Miglia	38	101	$500,000	$725,000	A	★★★★	24%
8C 2900 short chassis	35–39	10	$10,000,000	$15,000,000	A	★★★	12%
8C 2900 long chassis	36–39	32	$9,000,000	$11,000,000	A	★★★	10%
(2,594 6C 2500 chassis of all types were built. Numbers below are included in that figure.)							
6C 2500 SS (coachbuilt)	39–43	50–100	$350,000	$500,000	B	★★★	29%
6C 2500 SS Corsa	39–40	10*	$500,000	$700,000	B	★★★	21%
6C 2500 cabriolet (coachbuilt)	39–53	50*	$350,000	$550,000	B	★★★★	21%
6C 2500 SS (coachbuilt)	46–53	383	$325,000	$425,000	B	★★★	15%
6C 2500 Frec. D'Oro	46–50	680	$75,000	$110,000	C	★★	16%
6C 2500 Villa D'Este	49–53	25	$400,000	$525,000	B	★★★	22%
1900 5-window coupe	51–54	949	$100,000	$140,000	B	★★★	27%
1900M 4WD	52–57	2,076	$10,000	$15,000	D	★	n/c
1900 3-window coupe	55–58	854	$115,000	$150,000	B	★★★	15%
1900 cabriolet	52	91	$75,000	$100,000	B	★★	10%
1900 Zagato (SSZ)	55–57	28*	$550,000	$750,000	A	★★★★	27%
(6C and 1900 sedans are easily converted to MM or Zagato-bodied cars; provenance is critical.)							

	Yrs. Built	No. Made	Buy-Sell Price Range Low	High	Grade	Rating	1 Yr. % Change
2000 Spider	58–62	3,443	$35,000	$42,000	C	★★	6%
2600 Spider	62–65	2,255	$37,000	$55,000	C	★★★	12%
2600 Sprint	62–66	6,999	$15,000	$23,000	D	★★	1%
2600 Sprint Zagato	65–67	105	$70,000	$95,000	B	★★★	Mkt. Adj.
750 Sprint Normale	54–59	7,000*	$26,000	$34,000	C	★★★	3%
750 Spider Normale	55–59	7,000*	$27,000	$35,000	C	★★★	n/c
750 Spider Veloce	56–59	2,300*	$45,000	$65,000	B	★★★	9%
750 Sprint Veloce	56–59	1,100*	$55,000	$75,000	B	★★★	15%
(For '56–'57 Veloces, add 50% for event eligibility.)							
750 Sprint (lightweight)	56–57	100*	$100,000	$130,000	A	★★★	4%
750 SS (low-nose)	57–58	100*	$75,000	$100,000	B	★★★	4%
101 1300 Spider Normale	59–62	7,800*	$28,000	$36,000	C	★★★	11%
101 1300 Spider Veloce	59–62	500*	$42,000	$62,000	B	★★★	4%
101 1300 Sprint Normale	59–62	17,000*	$22,000	$30,000	C	★★★	n/c
101 1300 Sprint Veloce	59–62	1,900*	$38,000	$48,000	B	★★★	-5%
101 1300 Sprint Speciale	58–62	1,366	$38,000	$48,000	B	★★★	-5%
SZ-1	60–61	169	$225,000	$275,000	A	★★★	n/c
SZ-2	61–62	44	$200,000	$235,000	A	★★★	9%
TZ-1	63–64	101	$550,000	$650,000	A	★★★	4%
TZ-2	64–65	12	$2,500,000	$3,500,000	A	★★★	n/c
(Note: TZs and SZs are easy to fake. Prices are for authentic cars with paperwork.)							
101 1600 Spider Normale	62–65	9,250	$22,000	$33,000	C	★★★	n/c
101 1600 Spider Veloce	64–66	1,091	$40,000	$52,000	B	★★★	13%
101 1600 Sprint Normale	62–64	7,107	$18,000	$28,000	C	★★★	n/c
101 1600 Sprint Speciale	63–66	1,400	$43,000	$62,000	B	★★★	7%
Giulia Sprint GT	63–66	21,452	$14,000	$22,000	C	★★★	n/c
Giulia Sprint GT Veloce	66–68	14,240	$16,000	$30,000	B	★★★	4%
Giulia GTC	64–66	1,000	$30,000	$40,000	B	★★★	20%
Giulia TI Super	63–64	500	$58,000	$75,000	B	★★★	6%
Giulia Super	65–72	124,590	$9,000	$15,000	B	★★★	n/c
4R Zagato	66–68	92	$45,000	$60,000	B	★★★	n/c
1600 GTA Stradale	65–67	560	$100,000	$125,000	B	★★★	n/c
1600 GTA Corsa	65–67	inc.	$120,000	$150,000	A	★★★	n/c
1300 GTA Jr. Stradale	68–71	447	$80,000	$100,000	B	★★★	n/c
1300 GTA Jr. Corsa	68–71	inc.	$90,000	$115,000	A	★★★	n/c
1750 GTAM	68–72	40	$110,000	$130,000	A	★★★	2%
(Note: GTA prices are especially affected by originality, completeness, and history.)							
TT 33/2 Stradale	67–69	18	$2,000,000	$2,500,000	A	★★★	n/c

1930 Alfa Romeo 6C 1750 Gran Sport spyder

1970 AMC Rebel Machine 2-dr hard top

	Yrs. Built	No. Made	Buy-Sell Price Range Low	Buy-Sell Price Range High	Grade	Rating	1 Yr. % Change
TT 33/2 (2-liter)	67–69	30	$650,000	$800,000	A	★★★★	14%
TT 33/3 (3-liter)	69–72	20	$700,000	$850,000	A	★★★★	27%
TT 33 12-cylinder	75	12	$425,000	$600,000	B	★★★	15%
TT 33 SC 12 (Supercharged)	77	2	$500,000	$700,000	B	★★★	29%
Duetto	66–67	15,047	$15,000	$22,500	B	★★★	n/c
Spider 1750 (Roundtail)	68–69	inc.	$14,000	$20,000	B	★★★	n/c
GTV 1750	69	44,265	$14,000	$24,000	B	★★★	11%
1300 Junior Zagato	68–72	1,108	$18,000	$24,000	B	★★★	n/c
1600 Junior Zagato	72–75	402	$26,000	$32,000	B	★★★	n/c
Montreal	72–75	3,925	$21,000	$30,000	C	★★★	12%
Berlina 1750/2000	69–74		$3,500	$5,000	D	★★★	26%
GTV 1750/2000	70–74	37,459	$14,500	$24,500	C	★★★	13%
Spider 1750/2000	70–74	n/a	$6,750	$13,000	C	★★★	22%
Spider 2000	75–81	n/a	$6,000	$10,500	D	★★★	15%
Alfetta sedan	75–79	n/a	$3,000	$4,500	F	★	n/c
(Deduct $500 for automatic.)							
Alfetta GT (U.S.)	75–79	13,715	$3,450	$5,150	F	★	16%
Spider 2000	82–84	n/a	$7,750	$12,000	D	★	39%
GTV-6 coupe	81–83	n/a	$4,250	$5,750	D	★★	10%
GTV-6 Balocco coupe	82	350	$4,750	$5,750	C	★★	5%
GTV-6 coupe	84–86	n/a	$4,750	$7,000	C	★★	2%
GTV-6 Maratona coupe	84	n/a	$5,500	$7,500	C	★★	4%
GTV-6 Twin Turbo coupe	85	n/a	$13,500	$17,000	B	★★★	14%
Spider 2000	85–86	n/a	$4,650	$6,500	D	★	4%
Milano sedan	87–89	n/a	$2,100	$4,000	D	★	10%
(Deduct $1,000 for automatic.)							
Milano Verde sedan	87–89	n/a	$2,750	$5,500	C	★	7%
Spider 2000	87–90	n/a	$3,650	$6,000	D	★	-1%
Zagato ES-30	90–92	1,020	$26,000	$34,000	C	★★	23%
164/164L sedan	91–95	n/a	$3,150	$6,000	F	★	-1%
164S sedan	91–95	n/a	$5,250	$7,400	C	★	-3%
(For '94–'95 164, add $2,000 for 4-cam on "L" and "LS" models. For '95 164Q, add $3,000.)							
Spider 2000	91–92	n/a	$6,750	$11,000	D	★★	13%
Spider 2000 (com. ed.)	93	n/a	$7,500	$13,250	D	★★	6%
(Deduct $1,500 for automatic.)							
ALLARD							
K2	51–52	119	$90,000	$135,000	B	★★★	47%

	Yrs. Built	No. Made	Buy-Sell Price Range Low	Buy-Sell Price Range High	Grade	Rating	1 Yr. % Change
K3	52–54	62	$80,000	$125,000	B	★★★	41%
J2X	52–54	83	$220,000	$285,000	B	★★★★	38%
AMC							
SC/Rambler	69	1,512	$20,000	$36,000	C	★★	-12%
Rebel "Machine"	70	2,362	$17,000	$27,000	C	★★	-11%
AMX	68–70	20,187	$18,000	$32,000	B	★★	-10%
(Add 30% for 390 engine; 10% for GoPack, Big Bad colors, or Shadow Mask paint. Deduct 20% for automatic; 20% for 1968 models.)							
Javelin SST	68–70	69,027	$11,000	$16,000	C	★★	-11%
(Add 20% for 390 engine; 10% for Big Bad colors.)							
Javelin "Mark Donohue"	70	2,501 (inc)	$16,000	$25,000	C	★★	-12%
Javelin "Trans Am"	70	100 (inc.)	$25,000	$36,000	B	★★	-11%
Javelin AMX	71–74	16,961	$11,000	$16,000	C	★★	-7%
(Add 25% for 401 engine.)							
AMPHICAR							
770 convertible	61–68	3,878	$40,000	$60,000	C	★★	5%
ARNOLT-BRISTOL							
Bolide roadster	54–59	142	$117,500	$167,500	C	★★★	58%
DeLuxe roadster	54–59	inc.	$122,500	$172,500	C	★★★★	49%
Mk II coupe	54–59	3	$287,500	$362,500	B	★★★	31%
ASTON MARTIN							
For all Aston serial production cars through current, deduct 25% for RHD in U.S. only.							
DB2 coupe	50–53	302	$85,000	$175,000	C	★★★★	17%
DB2 DHC	50–53	102	$125,000	$200,000	B	★★★★	15%
DB3 coupe	51–53	10	$700,000	$1,250,000	A	★★★★	23%
DB2/4 coupe	53–55	492	$75,000	$150,000	C	★★★★	22%
DB2/4 DHC	53–55	73	$150,000	$275,000	B	★★★★	35%
DB2/4 Bertone Spyder	53–55	3	$850,000	$1,250,000	A	★★★★	12%
DB3S Team car	53–56	11	$3,750,000	$5,000,000	A	★★★★	9%
DB3S Customer car	53–56	10	$2,250,000	$3,500,000	A	★★★★	13%
DB2/4 Mk II coupe	55–57	199	$90,000	$135,000	C	★★★★	7%
DB2/4 Mk III coupe	55–57	551	$100,000	$190,000	C	★★★★	7%
DB2/4 Mk III DHC	55–57	inc.	$175,000	$300,000	B	★★★★	11%
DB2/4 Mk III Notchback	55–57	inc.	$90,000	$130,000	B	★★★★	5%
DBR1	56–60	5	$6,000,000	$10,000,000	A	★★★★	47%
DBR2	57	2	$11,000,000	$13,000,000	A	★★★★	47%
DB4 Series I–IV coupe	58–63	925	$150,000	$225,000	B	★★★★	7%
DB4 Series V coupe	61–62	185	$225,000	$275,000	B	★★★★	5%
DB4 DHC (I–V)	58–63	inc.	$325,000	$500,000	B	★★★★	6%
(For Series IV–V SS triple-carb engine, add $10,000; Series V covered headlights, add $10,000.)							
DB4GT	59–63	75	$900,000	$1,500,000	A	★★★★	6%
DB4GT Zagato	60–63	19	$3,000,000	$4,000,000	A	★★★★	n/c
(For factory team race cars—1VEV and 2VEV—add up to 50%.)							
DB5 coupe	63–65	886	$225,000	$325,000	B	★★★★	9%
DB5 coupe Vantage	63–65	inc.	$250,000	$350,000	B	★★★★	11%
DB5 DHC	64–65	123	$325,000	$450,000	A	★★★★	10%
DB5 Shooting Brake	64–65	12	$225,000	$275,000	C	★★★★	n/c
DB6 Volante Mk I (short chassis)	65–66	37	$375,000	$525,000	B	★★★★	6%
DB6 coupe	65–69	1,321	$150,000	$215,000	B	★★★★	8%
DB6 Vantage coupe	65–69	inc.	$175,000	$250,000	B	★★★★	16%
DB6 Shooting Brake	65–69	6	$200,000	$300,000	C	★★★★	1%
DB6 Volante Mk II (long chassis)	66–69	140	$250,000	$350,000	B	★★★	10%
DBS (6 cyl.)	67–72	857	$50,000	$65,000	D	★★★	9%
DB6 Mk II coupe	69–70	240	$195,000	$250,000	B	★★★	7%
DB6 Mk II Volante	69–70	38	$400,000	$600,000	B	★★★	18%
(Add $15,000 for Vantage.)							

	Yrs. Built	No. Made	Buy-Sell Price Range Low	High	Grade	Rating	1 Yr. % Change
DBSV8	70–72	399	$50,000	$65,000	C	★★★	9%
AM Vantage	72–73	70	$50,000	$65,000	C	★★★	9%
AMV8 Series II/III	74–79	1,259	$50,000	$70,000	C	★★★	4%

(AMV8 Series II/III pre- "Oscar India" V8s have leather dashes. Production for SIII Vantages was 43.)

	Yrs. Built	No. Made	Low	High	Grade	Rating	1 Yr. % Change
AMV8 Volante	79–82	350	$50,000	$75,000	C	★★★	4%

(All Volantes had "Oscar India" wood dashes.)

	Yrs. Built	No. Made	Low	High	Grade	Rating	1 Yr. % Change
AMV8 Series IV (carb.)	79–85	299	$70,000	$125,000	C	★★	n/c

("Oscar India" Series IVs can be identified by their wood dashes.)

	Yrs. Built	No. Made	Low	High	Grade	Rating	1 Yr. % Change
AMV8 Series IV (inj.)	86–89	4	$100,000	$150,000	C	★★	n/c
Lagonda saloon	83–85	645	$25,000	$40,000	D	★★	n/c
Volante	83–86	inc.	$55,000	$85,000	C	★★	n/c

(Injection became standard in late '86.)

	Yrs. Built	No. Made	Low	High	Grade	Rating	1 Yr. % Change
Vantage Volante	87–89	58	$70,000	$120,000	B	★★	-3%
Lagonda saloon	85–87	inc.	$20,000	$45,000	D	★★	n/c
Volante (inj.)	86–89	n/a	$55,000	$85,000	C	★★	n/c
Lagonda saloon	88–89	inc.	$35,000	$60,000	D	★★	n/c
Virage coupe	91–92	370	$30,000	$60,000	C	★★	n/c
Virage Volante	92–93	134	$70,000	$100,000	C	★	n/c
Virage Volante (Wide-body)	93	13	$100,000	$150,000	C	★	n/c
DB7 coupe	97–03	n/a	$35,000	$75,000	C	★	-9%
DB7 Volante	97–03	n/a	$40,000	$85,000	C	★	-4%
DB9 coupe	04–	n/a	$95,000	$165,000	C	★	-8%
DB9 Volante	04–	n/a	$105,000	$175,000	C	★	-11%
V12 Vanquish coupe	02–07	n/a	$90,000	$145,000	C	★	-6%
V12 Vanquish S coupe	05–07	n/a	$160,000	$195,000	C	★	-10%

AUBURN

Custom/Standard Eight

	Yrs. Built	No. Made	Low	High	Grade	Rating	1 Yr. % Change
Boattail speedster	31–34	est. 56,000	$160,000	$250,000	B	★★	4%
Phaeton	31–34	inc.	$90,000	$150,000	B	★★	n/c
Cabriolet	31–34	inc.	$100,000	$175,000	C	★★	n/c
Sedan	31–34	inc.	$27,000	$40,000	C	★★	n/c
Coupe	31–34	inc.	$32,000	$50,000	C	★★	n/c

Custom/Salon Twelve

	Yrs. Built	No. Made	Low	High	Grade	Rating	1 Yr. % Change
Boattail speedster	32–34	est. 2,000	$220,000	$350,000	B	★★★	12%
Phaeton	32–34	inc.	$150,000	$200,000	B	★★	n/c
Cabriolet	32–34	inc.	$115,000	$175,000	B	★★	n/c
Sedan	32–34	inc.	$30,000	$45,000	C	★★	n/c
Coupe	32–34	inc.	$35,000	$50,000	C	★★	n/c

851/852 Supercharged

	Yrs. Built	No. Made	Low	High	Grade	Rating	1 Yr. % Change
Boattail speedster	35–36	est. 500	$320,000	$450,000	A	★★★	6%
Phaeton	35–36	inc.	$140,000	$200,000	B	★★★	7%
Cabriolet	35–36	inc.	$120,000	$160,000	B	★★★	7%
Sedan/Coupe	35–36	inc.	$55,000	$105,000	C	★★★	13%

AUDI

	Yrs. Built	No. Made	Low	High	Grade	Rating	1 Yr. % Change
Quattro coupe	90–91	n/a	$3,500	$5,000	D	★	n/c
TT coupe	00–07	n/a	$14,000	$23,000	D	★	-8%
TT convertible	00–07	n/a	$16,000	$25,000	D	★	-10%

AUSTIN/MORRIS

	Yrs. Built	No. Made	Low	High	Grade	Rating	1 Yr. % Change
Mini Cooper	62–64	30,000*	$11,000	$23,000	C	★★	-9%
Mini Cooper S	64–66	13,922	$17,000	$30,000	B	★★	-2%

(Model years and non-S production numbers for U.S. models only.)

AUSTIN-HEALEY

	Yrs. Built	No. Made	Low	High	Grade	Rating	1 Yr. % Change
100-4 (BN1, 3-sp)	53–55	10,010	$30,000	$45,000	B	★★	n/c
100-4 (BN2, 4-sp)	55–56	4,604	$35,000	$50,000	B	★★	n/c
100S	55	50	$400,000	$600,000	A	★★★★	48%
100M	55–56	640	$75,000	$150,000	B	★★★	36%
100 w/ Le Mans kit	55–56	n/a	$50,000	$80,000	C	★★★	27%

	Yrs. Built	No. Made	Buy-Sell Price Range Low	High	Grade	Rating	1 Yr. % Change
100-6 BN4 (2+2)	56–59	11,294	$30,000	$45,000	C	★★	n/c
(For BN6 2-seat, add $10,000)		4,150					
3000 Mk I (BT7) 2+2	59–61	10,825	$30,000	$45,000	B	★★★	n/c
(For BN7 2-seat, add $10,000)		2,825					
3000 Mk II BT7 (2+2) tri-carb	61–62	5,096	$30,000	$50,000	B	★★★	n/c
(For BN7 2-seat, tri-carb, add $15,000)		355					

(For 100-6/3000, add $2,000 for factory 2-seat hard top; $1,000 for 4-seat hard top. Deduct $2,000 for disc wheels.)

	Yrs. Built	No. Made	Low	High	Grade	Rating	1 Yr. % Change
3000 Mk II BJ7 (roll-up windows)	62–63	6,113	$40,000	$65,000	B	★★★	19%
3000 Mk III (BJ8)	63–67	17,712	$50,000	$85,000	B	★★★	n/c
BJ8 factory-built rally cars	63–67	7	$150,000	$300,000	B	★★★	22%
Bugeye Sprite	58–61	48,987	$13,000	$25,000	B	★★★	5%
Sprite	61–71	80,360	$4,500	$10,000	C	★★	14%

BENTLEY

(For all pre-war chassis types add up to 100% for original or exceptional coachwork, matching numbers, or racing provenance.)

	Yrs. Built	No. Made	Low	High	Grade	Rating	1 Yr. % Change
3-Liter, closed	22–25	1,622	$93,500	$160,000	C	★★★	5%
3-Liter, closed	22–25	inc.	$130,000	$260,000	A	★★★	4%
3-Liter Speed Model (Red Badge), closed	23–29	inc.	$130,000	$260,000	B	★★★	22%
3-Liter Speed Model (Red Badge), open	23–29	inc.	$260,000	$415,000	B	★★	4%
3-Liter Speed Model Super Sports (18 built)	22–25	inc.	$275,000	$425,000	A	★★★	NL†
6½-Liter, closed	25–30	545	$415,000	$625,000	A	★★★	4%
6½-Liter, open	25–30	inc.	$520,000	$780,000	A	★★★	4%
4½-Liter, closed	27–31	665	$208,000	$340,000	B	★★	4%
4½-Liter, open	27–31	inc.	$520,000	$1,300,000	A	★★★	4%
6½-Liter Speed Six, open or closed	28–30	inc.	$625,000	$1,300,000	B	★★★	4%
4½-Liter Supercharged	29–31	55	$780,000	$2,080,000	A	★★★	4%
8-Liter, open or closed	29–31	100	$575,000	$1,300,000	A	★★★	4%
4-Liter, open or closed	31–32	50	$125,000	$175,000	A	★★★	n/c
3½-Liter, closed	33–36	1,177	$52,000	$78,000	B	★★★	4%
3½-Liter, open	33–36	inc.	$156,000	$312,000	C	★★	4%
4¼-Liter, closed	36–39	1,234	$73,000	$120,000	B	★★★	4%
4¼-Liter, open	36–39	inc.	$210,000	$420,000	C	★★	5%

(1938–39 MR/MX series, add 15%. Cars with unusual and/or exceptional coachwork may be worth multiples of these amounts.
Deduct 25%–50% for RHD to LHD conversions.)

	Yrs. Built	No. Made	Low	High	Grade	Rating	1 Yr. % Change
Mk V	1939	35	$80,000	$160,000	C	★★	n/c

1935 Auburn 851 SC Boattail Arlington speedster

1998 Bentley Arnage saloon

	Yrs. Built	No. Made	Buy-Sell Price Range Low	High	Grade	Rating	1 Yr. % Change
Corniche	1939	4	$500,000	$1,000,000	C	★★	NL†
Mk VI standard steel saloon	46–52	5,368	$31,000	$57,000	C	★★	3%
(Add 40% for 4.6-Liter engine.)							
Mk VI coachbuilt, closed	47–52	inc.	$56,500	$92,000	C	★★★	2%
Mk VI coachbuilt, open	47–52	inc.	$87,000	$153,000	D	★★★	2%
R-type standard steel saloon	52–55	2,486	$30,500	$56,500	B	★★★	2%
R-type coachbuilt, closed	52–55	inc.	$42,000	$75,000	C	★★★	10%
R-type coachbuilt, open	52–55	inc.	$90,000	$160,000	B	★★	NL†
R Continental	52–55	208	$357,000	$510,000	B	★★★★	2%
S1 standard steel saloon	55–59	3,107	$27,000	$46,000	B	★★★	n/c
S1 Continental, non-MPW coachwork	55–58	431	$179,000	$306,000	A	★★★	2%
(LHD cars will likely bring a 25% premium in the U.S.)							
S1 Continental (PW)	55–58	inc.	$87,000	$130,000	B	★★	3%
S1 Continental DHC/LHD	55–59	inc.	$305,000	$410,000	B	★★★	2%
S1 Continental DHC/RHD	55–59	inc.	$153,000	$179,000	A	★★★	2%
S1 Continental Flying Spur	58–59	inc.	$102,000	$153,000	D	★	2%
S2 Continental (M/PW)	59–62	388	$41,000	$77,000	D	★	3%
S2 Continental DHC	59–62	inc.	$90,000	$150,000	D	★★★	17%
S2 standard steel saloon	60–62	1,922	$15,500	$28,500	C	★★★	2%
S3 standard steel saloon (LHD)	62–65	1,318	$51,000	$77,500	B	★★	3%
S3 Continental Harlequin Headlights, closed	62–66	312	$61,500	$97,000	D	★★	2%
S3 Continental Harlequin Headlights, open	62–66	inc.	$127,500	$178,500	D	★★	2%
S3 Continental Flying Spur	63–66	inc.	$97,000	$168,500	C	★★	2%
T standard steel saloon	65–76	1,721	$7,000	$17,500	C	★★	-6%
T1 MPW closed	66–70	98	$20,000	$35,000	C	★★	n/c
T1 MPW open	66–70	77	$41,000	$51,000	D	★★	2%
Continental Flying Spur	77–81	433	$30,000	$45,000	D	★	n/c
Continental Turbo	81	8	$38,000	$57,000	C	★	-5%
T2 standard steel saloon	77–81	568	$11,500	$27,500	C	★★	-3%
Corniche closed	77–80	63	$25,000	$35,000	C	★	n/c
Corniche open	77–80	45	$42,000	$77,500	C	★	n/c

	Yrs. Built	No. Made	Buy-Sell Price Range Low	High	Grade	Rating	1 Yr. % Change
Mulsanne standard steel saloon	80–87	533	$14,500	$24,000	C	★	-4%
Mulsanne LWB	80–87	18	$15,000	$25,000	C	★★	NL†
Mulsanne Turbo	82–85	498	$17,000	$27,000	C	★	-5%
Continental convertible	85–89	429	$42,500	$70,000	C	★	n/c
Continental convertible	90–92	inc.	$52,000	$107,000	C	★★	n/c
Continental convertible	93–95	inc.	$85,000	$115,000	C	★	n/c
Turbo R (includes LWB)	85–98	5,864	$22,000	$64,000	C	★	-2%
Continental coupe	85–87	inc.	$28,000	$47,500	C	★	-5%
Eight	84–92	1,736	$14,000	$36,000	C	★	-5%
Mulsanne S (includes LWB)	87–92	970	$14,000	$28,500	C	★	-6%
Turbo RT LWB	97–98	216	$25,500	$64,000	C	★	-14%
Continental R	91–92	1,290	$64,000	$88,500	C	★	-2%
Continental S	94–95	37	$65,000	$85,500	C	★	NL†
Continental R Mulliner	99–02	46	$67,000	$88,000	C	★	NL†
Brooklands (includes LWB)	92–98	1,380	$27,500	$47,000	C	★	-2%
Brooklands R	97–98	339	$31,000	$60,000	C	★	-3%
Turbo S	94–96	60	$32,500	$51,500	C	★	-2%
Azure	95–02	1,098	$75,000	$100,000	B	★	-40%
Azure Mulliner	99–02	154	$90,000	$125,000	C	★	NL†
Continental T / Continental T Mulliner	97–02	557	$65,000	$120,000	C	★	-24%
Arnage Red Label	97–02	2,273	$68,000	$120,000	C	★	-34%
Arnage R	02–	n/a	$63,750	$150,000	C	★	-8%
Arnage RL	01–	n/a	$63,750	$265,000	C	★	NL†
Arnage T	02–	n/a	$65,000	$245,000 (MSRP)	C	★	NL†
New Azure	05–	n/a	$175,000	$330,000 (MSRP)	C	★	NL†
Continental Flying Spur	04–	n/a	$108,750	$150,000 (MSRP)	C	★	-14%
Continental GT	04–	n/a	$75,000	$180,000 (MSRP)	C	★	-12%
Continental GTC	05–	n/a	$115,000	$195,000 (MSRP)	B	★	-10%

BITTER

	Yrs. Built	No. Made	Buy-Sell Price Range Low	High	Grade	Rating	1 Yr. % Change
SC coupe	83–84	n/a	$10,000	$16,000	F	★	23%
SC coupe	85	n/a	$12,000	$21,000	F	★	21%

BIZZARRINI

	Yrs. Built	No. Made	Buy-Sell Price Range Low	High	Grade	Rating	1 Yr. % Change
5300 GT & Strada	65–69	100*	$400,000	$575,000	B	★★★★	18%
(Deduct 25% for fiberglass "America" models.)							

BMW

	Yrs. Built	No. Made	Buy-Sell Price Range Low	High	Grade	Rating	1 Yr. % Change
328	37–39	465	$200,000	$300,000	A	★★★	11%
Isetta 250/300	55–62	158,728	$15,000	$30,000	C	★★	n/c
Isetta 600 2+2	57–59	34,813	$12,000	$16,000	D	★★	n/c
507 roadster	56–59	253	$300,000	$550,000	A	★★★★	6%

(Add $15k for Rudge knock-offs; $15k for factory hard top. Deduct $15k if car has sedan replacement block.)

Note: Most serial production BMWs should be regarded as "used cars." Condition is the prime determinant of value.

	Yrs. Built	No. Made	Buy-Sell Price Range Low	High	Grade	Rating	1 Yr. % Change
2800CS	68–71	9,399	$8,200	$12,300	C	★★	n/c
Bavaria 4-door	71–74	39,056	$3,500	$5,500	D	★★	n/c
3.0 CSL	71–72	1,039	$20,000	$30,000	C	★★★	n/c
3.0 CS	72–74	11,063	$8,900	$15,200	C	★★★	n/c
1600 coupe	67–70	277,320	$5,600	$7,200	C	★★★	n/c
2002 coupe	68–71	339,084	$6,600	$9,200	C	★★★	n/c
2002 coupe	72–73	inc.	$6,800	$9,600	C	★★	n/c
2002 tii coupe	71–75	38,701	$10,600	$17,000	B	★★★	n/c
2002 turbo	73–75	1,672	$12,000	$18,000	B	★★★	n/c
2002 coupe	74–76	inc. 2002	$4,400	$6,900	C	★★	n/c
320i coupe	77–80	389,101**	$2,400	$3,800	F	★	n/c

	Yrs. Built	No. Made	Buy-Sell Price Range		Grade	Rating	1 Yr. % Change
			Low	High			
320i coupe	81–83	inc.	$2,800	$4,000	F	★	n/c
318i coupe	84–85	192,566*	$2,000	$3,500	F	★	n/c
325e coupe	84–87	17,756	$2,000	$4,000	F	★	n/c
325i coupe	87–88	352,993**	$2,500	$4,500	F	★	-20%
325i convertible	87–89	inc.	$3,000	$5,000	D	★	-23%
325i convertible	90–91	inc.	$3,500	$5,500	D	★	-13%
630 CSi coupe	77	n/a	$4,800	$6,400	D	★★	n/c
633 CSi coupe	78–82	32,292	$5,000	$6,500	D	★★	n/c
(3-Series production totals are worldwide.)							
633 CSi coupe	83–84	5,332	$5,200	$6,800	D	★★	n/c
635 CSi coupe	85–87	17,354	$6,500	$8,500	D	★★	n/c
635 CSi coupe	88–89	4,241	$7,500	$10,500	D	★★	n/c
750iL 4-door	88–89	23,721	$3,500	$5,500	F	★	-16%
750iL 4-door	90–91	15,318	$5,500	$8,000	F	★	-6%
850i coupe	91–92	11,932	$12,000	$18,000	D	★	n/c
840i coupe	94–97	5,808	$14,000	$24,000	D	★	n/c
M1 coupe	79–80	450	$75,000	$125,000	B	★★★	-10%
(M1 production numbers include Group 4 & 5 competition models.)							
M3 coupe	86–91	17,970	$9,500	$12,500	C	★★	-5%
M5 4-dr. (Euro)	85–86	2,145	$8,500	$12,000	D	★	n/c
M5 4-dr.	87–96	12,254	$8,500	$13,500	D	★	-9%
M6 coupe	87–88	5,803	$14,000	$18,000	D	★	n/c
L7 4-dr.	86–87	209	$5,000	$6,500	D	★	n/c
L6 coupe	87	1,300*	$6,500	$9,000	D	★	n/c
M3 coupe	95–97	22,597	$10,000	$16,000	C	★	n/c
Z3 roadster (4-cyl.)	96–97	263,887	$9,000	$12,000	D	★	n/c
Z3 roadster (6-cyl.)	97–02	inc.	$11,000	$21,000	C	★	-5%
(Add $4,000 for M coupe/roadster.)							
Z8	00–03	5,703	$75,000	$105,000	C	★	n/c

BRICKLIN

	Yrs. Built	No. Made	Low	High	Grade	Rating	1 Yr. % Change
SV1 coupe	74–75	2,897	$12,000	$20,000	D	★	-25%

BUGATTI

	Yrs. Built	No. Made	Low	High	Grade	Rating	1 Yr. % Change
Type 35	24–30	100*	$800,000	$1,300,000	B	★★★★	7%
Type 35A	25–30	100*	$650,000	$1,000,000	B	★★★★	n/c
Type 35B/C	27–30	40*	$1,000,000	$2,750,000	B	★★★★	n/c
Type 37A Grand Prix	25–29	291	$300,000	$550,000	A	★★★★	12%
Type 43/43A	27–31	160	$750,000	$1,300,000	B	★★★★	12%
Type 44 cabriolet	27–30	1,250	$180,000	$250,000	A	★★★	26%
Type 50 coupe sur-profilée	30–34	10	$1,000,000	$2,500,000	B	★★★	n/c
Type 50 Tourer	30–34	65	$800,000	$1,500,000	B	★★★★	4%
Type 51	31–35	40	$1,100,000	$3,250,000	B	★★★	20%
Type 57 Atalante coupe	35–38	40	$550,000	$900,000	A	★★★	-3%
Type 57/57C Stelvio cabriolet	34–39	100	$375,000	$800,000	A	★★★	19%
Type 57S Atalante coupe	36–38	40	$3,500,000	$7,000,000	A	★★★	38%
Type 57SC Atalante coupe	36–38	2	$4,000,000	$8,000,000	A	★★★★	29%
Type 57SC Atlantic coupe	36–38	4	$15,000,000	$20,000,000	A	★★★★	NL†
EB110	92–95	139	$180,000	$275,000	B	★★	-1%
Veyron	06	300	$1,100,000	$1,200,000	B	★★	n/c
Veyron 16.4 Grand Sport	09	n/a	$1,500,000	$2,000,000	B	★★	NL†

BUICK

	Yrs. Built	No. Made	Low	High	Grade	Rating	1 Yr. % Change
Skylark convertible	53	1,690	$150,000	$195,000	B	★★★	NL†
Skylark convertible	54	836	$115,000	$150,000	B	★★★	NL†
Skylark GS 400	65–67	23,442*	$12,500	$17,500	C	★★	-10%
Convertible	65–67	6,122	$16,000	$21,500	C	★★	-19%
Skylark GS 400	68–69	17,009*	$16,000	$21,000	C	★★	-11%
Convertible	68–69	4,230	$20,000	$26,000	C	★★	-20%
(Add 20% for 4-sp. Deduct 20% for 1968 models.)							
Skylark GS 400 Stage 1	69	1,256	$26,000	$36,000	B	★★	-19%
Convertible	69	212	$46,000	$60,000	B	★★	-14%
Skylark GS 455	70	8,732	$23,000	$29,000	B	★★	-12%
Convertible	70	1,416	$32,000	$42,000	A	★★	-8%
Skylark GS 455 Stage 1	70	8,732	$45,000	$55,000	B	★★	-10%
Convertible	70	1,416	$85,000	$100,000	A	★★★	-14%
Skylark GSX 455	70	678	$50,000	$60,000	A	★★	-9%
(Add 20% for 4-sp; 50% for Stage 1.)							
Skylark GS 455	71–72	15,991*	$20,000	$25,000	B	★★	-12%
Convertible	71–72	1,754	$27,000	$36,000	B	★★	-11%
Skylark GS 455 Stage 1	71–72	1,529	$30,000	$37,000	B	★★	-9%
Convertible	71–72	162	$72,000	$86,000	A	★★★	-11%

CHEVROLET

Camaro

	Yrs. Built	No. Made	Low	High	Grade	Rating	1 Yr. % Change
SS 350	67–68	36,469	$21,000	$32,000	C	★★	-9%
Convertible	67–68	inc.	$23,000	$36,500	C	★★	-9%
SS 396	67–68	23,068	$26,000	$48,500	B	★★	-15%
Convertible	67–68	inc.	$27,500	$58,000	B	★★	-11%
Z28	67	602	$52,000	$75,000	A	★★	-18%
Yenko Camaro	67	107*	$275,000	$350,000	A	★★★	-8%
Z/28	68	26,213	$40,000	$50,000	A	★★	-10%
(Add 20% to '67–'69 Z/28 for RS option.)							
Yenko Camaro	68	64*	$315,000	$350,000	A	★★★	-9%
SS 350 Pace Car	69	3,675	$26,000	$50,000	C	★★	-9%
Convertible	69	inc.	$32,000	$54,000	B	★★	-10%
SS 396 Pace Car Convertible	69	inc.	$35,000	$60,000	B	★★	-19%
Yenko Camaro	69	200*	$250,000	$300,000	A	★★★	-9%
Z/28	69	20,302	$45,000	$75,000	B	★★	-25%
Z/28	70–73	27,744	$18,500	$29,000	B	★★	-20%
(Add 10% to '70–73 Z/28 for RS option.)							
SS 396	70–72	27,415	$23,000	$38,000	C	★★	-7%
Z/28	74	13,802	$15,000	$23,000	D	★★	-8%
Z/28	77–78	69,256	$6,500	$12,000	D	★★	-8%
Z/28	79–81	173,286	$6,500	$13,500	D	★★	-10%
Pace Car	82	6,360	$6,500	$10,000	D	★	-12%
Pace Car	93	633	$11,000	$17,500	D	★	-9%

Chevelle

	Yrs. Built	No. Made	Low	High	Grade	Rating	1 Yr. % Change
SS 396 (360-hp)	65	81,112	$22,500	$31,000	B	★★	-12%
SS 396	66–67	135,218	$21,000	$48,000	B	★★	-16%

1928 Bugatti Type 37A Grand Prix

1954 Chevrolet Corvette roadster

	Yrs. Built	No. Made	Buy-Sell Price Range Low	High	Grade	Rating	1 Yr. % Change
Convertible	66–67	inc.	$30,000	$58,000	B	★★	-14%
SS 396	68–69	149,915	$22,000	$48,000	B	★★	-14%
Convertible	68–69	inc.	$31,000	$58,000	B	★★	-12%
Yenko Chevelle	69	99*	$200,000	$300,000	A	★★★	-10%
SS 396 (402/454)	70	62,372	$26,500	$52,000	B	★★	-15%
Convertible	70	inc.	$30,000	$60,000	B	★★	-11%
SS 454/360-hp LS5	70	4,298	$40,000	$50,000	B	★★	-11%
Convertible	70	inc.	$42,000	$70,000	B	★★	-5%
SS 454/450-hp LS6	70	4,475	$55,000	$95,000	A	★★	-20%
Convertible	70	inc.	$200,000	$300,000	A	★★★	-30%
(Add 25% for 4-sp.)							
SS 396	71–72	82,000	$18,000	$28,500	C	★★	-18%
Convertible	71–72	inc.	$21,500	$36,000	C	★★	-13%
SS 454 LS5	71–72	14,835	$26,000	$48,000	C	★★	-15%
Convertible	71–72	inc.	$29,000	$55,000	C	★★	-19%

Corvette

C1

	Yrs. Built	No. Made	Low	High	Grade	Rating	1 Yr. % Change
235/150 Roadster	53	300	$125,000	$275,000	A	★★★★	3%
235/150 Roadster	54	3,640	$65,000	$108,000	B	★★★	-3%
235/155 Roadster	55	7	$62,000	$125,000	B	★★★	-1%
265/195	55	693	$65,000	$122,000	A	★★★	-1%
265/210 Convertible	56	387	$45,000	$85,000	B	★★★	n/c
265/225	56	3,080	$50,000	$90,000	B	★★★	-2%
283/220 Convertible	57	1,633	$45,000	$90,000	B	★★★	-1%
283/245	57	2,045	$50,000	$95,000	B	★★★	n/c
283/250 FI	57	284	$60,000	$115,000	A	★★★	1%
283/270	57	1,621	$50,000	$97,000	B	★★★	-3%
283/283 FI	57	756	$70,000	$126,000	A	★★★	n/c
283/230 Convertible	58	4,243	$40,000	$78,000	B	★★★	-3%
283/245	58	2,436	$45,000	$88,000	B	★★★	-1%
283/250 FI	58	504	$53,000	$105,000	B	★★★	n/c
283/270	58	978	$48,500	$87,000	B	★★★	-4%
283/290 FI	58	1,007	$68,000	$125,000	B	★★★	-1%
283/230 Convertible	59	5,487	$39,000	$72,000	B	★★★	-6%
283/245	59	1,417	$44,000	$83,000	B	★★★	-3%
283/250 FI	59	175	$53,000	$100,000	B	★★★	n/c
283/270	59	1,846	$48,000	$87,000	B	★★★	-1%
283/290 FI	59	745	$67,000	$124,000	B	★★★	1%
283/230 Convertible	60	5,827	$40,000	$78,000	B	★★★	-2%
283/245	60	1,211	$45,000	$86,000	B	★★★	-2%

	Yrs. Built	No. Made	Buy-Sell Price Range Low	High	Grade	Rating	1 Yr. % Change
283/250 FI	60	100	$53,000	$100,000	B	★★★	-2%
283/270	60	2,364	$49,000	$90,000	B	★★★	-1%
283/290 FI	60	759	$68,000	$125,000	B	★★★	n/c
283/230 Convertible	61	5,357	$41,000	$74,000	B	★★★	-3%
283/245	61	1,175	$46,000	$84,000	B	★★★	-1%
283/270	61	2,827	$50,000	$88,000	B	★★★	n/c
283/275 FI	61	118	$56,000	$100,000	B	★★★	-1%
283/315 FI	61	1,462	$67,000	$122,000	B	★★★	-1%
327/250 Convertible	62	4,907	$45,000	$80,000	B	★★★	-4%
327/300	62	3,294	$48,000	$88,000	B	★★★	-1%
327/340	62	4,412	$52,000	$93,000	B	★★★	-1%
327/360 FI	62	1,918	$75,000	$138,000	B	★★★★	n/c

(1956–62, add $2k–$4k for auxiliary hard top.)

C2

	Yrs. Built	No. Made	Low	High	Grade	Rating	1 Yr. % Change
327/250 Split-Window Coupe	63	10,594	$40,000	$75,000	A	★★★	-2%
327/300 L75	63		$43,000	$78,000	A	★★★	-1%
327/340 L76	63		$47,000	$83,000	A	★★★	-1%
327/360 FI L84	63		$72,000	$125,000	A	★★★	-1%
327/360 Z06	63		$125,000	$185,000	A	★★★★	3%
327/250 Convertible	63	10,919	$35,000	$63,000	B	★★★	-2%
327/300 L75	63		$36,000	$66,000	B	★★★	-2%
327/340 L76	63		$39,000	$72,000	B	★★★	-2%
327/360 FI L84	63		$64,000	$118,000	B	★★★	1%
Grand Sport	63	5	$6,000,000	$10,000,000	A	★★★★	New
327/250 Coupe	64	8,304	$32,000	$53,000	B	★★★	-5%
327/300 L75	64		$34,000	$59,000	B	★★★	-2%
327/365 L76	64		$36,500	$65,000	B	★★★	n/c
327/375 FI L84	64		$55,000	$95,000	A	★★★	1%
327/250 Convertible	64	13,925	$35,000	$60,000	B	★★★	n/c
327/300 L75	64		$37,000	$64,000	B	★★★	n/c
327/365 L76	64		$39,000	$68,000	B	★★★	-1%
327/375 FI L84	64		$56,000	$97,000	A	★★★	-1%
327/250 Coupe	65	8,186	$39,000	$71,000	B	★★★	n/c
327/300 L75	65		$39,000	$70,000	B	★★★	n/c
327/350 L79	65		$41,000	$75,000	B	★★★	-1%
327/365 L76	65		$43,000	$78,000	B	★★★	-2%
327/375 FI L84	65		$63,000	$114,000	A	★★★	-1%
396/425 L78	65		$65,000	$125,000	A	★★★	1%
327/250 Convertible	65	15,378	$39,000	$75,000	A	★★★	-2%
327/300 L75	65		$39,000	$75,000	B	★★★	n/c
327/350 L79	65		$42,000	$80,000	B	★★★	-1%
327/365 L76	65		$43,000	$85,000	B	★★★	-1%
327/375 FI L84	65		$64,000	$121,000	A	★★★	1%
396/425 L78	65		$70,000	$125,000	B	★★★	-1%
327/300 Coupe	66	9,958	$38,000	$75,000	B	★★★	-2%
327/350 L79	66		$43,000	$77,000	B	★★★	-2%
427/390 L36	66		$56,000	$102,000	B	★★★	-1%
427/425 L72	66		$68,000	$125,000	A	★★★	n/c
327/300 Convertible	66	17,762	$40,000	$80,000	A	★★★	-2%
327/350 L79	66		$45,000	$83,000	B	★★★	-1%
427/390 L36	66		$58,000	$107,000	B	★★★	-1%
427/425 L72	66		$70,000	$127,000	A	★★★	-1%
327/300 Coupe	67	8,504	$45,000	$80,000	B	★★★	-2%
327/350 L79	67		$48,000	$85,000	B	★★★	-1%
427/390 L36	67		$62,000	$109,000	B	★★★	n/c
427/400 L68	67		$72,000	$130,000	B	★★★	n/c

Model	Yrs. Built	No. Made	Buy-Sell Price Range Low	High	Grade	Rating	1 Yr. % Change
427/430 L88	67		$1,200,000	$2,000,000	A	****	n/c
427/435 L71	67		$95,000	$175,000	A	***	n/c
327/300 Convertible	67	14,436	$48,000	$94,000	B	***	-1%
327/350 L79	67		$50,000	$100,000	B	***	-1%
427/390 L36	67		$65,000	$121,000	B	***	n/c
427/400 L68	67		$75,000	$143,000	A	***	n/c
427/430 L88	67		$1,200,000	$2,000,000	A	****	n/c
427/435 L71	67		$99,000	$190,000	A	***	1%

(For 1963–67, add $2k–$3k for side exhaust; $2k–$4k for auxiliary hard top; $4k–$6k for a/c; $5k–$8k for knockoff wheels; $6k–$10k for aluminum wheels.)

C3

Model	Yrs. Built	No. Made	Buy-Sell Price Range Low	High	Grade	Rating	1 Yr. % Change
327/300 Coupe	68	9,936	$18,000	$36,000	C	***	n/c
327/350 L79	68		$20,000	$41,000	C	***	n/c
427/390 L36	68		$25,000	$50,000	C	***	n/c
427/400 L68	68		$28,000	$58,000	C	***	1%
427/430 L88	68		$225,000	$315,000	A	***	3%
427/435 L71	68		$40,000	$72,000	B	***	n/c
427/435 L89	68		$54,000	$95,000	B	***	1%
327/300 Convertible	68	18,630	$24,000	$47,000	C	***	-1%
327/350 L79	68		$26,000	$52,000	C	***	-1%
427/390 L36	68		$36,000	$61,000	C	***	n/c
427/400 L68	68		$35,000	$69,000	C	***	n/c
427/430 L88	68		$275,000	$350,000	A	****	n/c
427/435 L71	68		$46,000	$83,000	B	***	n/c
427/435 L89	68		$59,000	$106,000	B	***	n/c
350/300 Coupe	69	22,129	$18,000	$39,000	C	***	-1%
350/350 L46	69		$21,000	$43,000	C	***	-1%
427/390 L36	69		$25,000	$52,000	C	***	-1%
427/400 L68	69		$29,000	$60,000	C	***	n/c
427/430 L88	69		$250,000	$325,000	A	***	n/c
427/435 L71	69		$38,000	$69,000	B	***	n/c
427/435 L89	69		$50,000	$93,000	B	***	-1%
427/430 ZL1	69		$2,000,000	$3,000,000	A	****	n/c
350/300 Convertible	69	16,633	$23,000	$50,000	C	***	n/c
350/350 L46	69		$24,000	$55,000	C	***	-1%
427/390 L36	69		$30,000	$63,000	C	***	-1%
427/400 L68	69		$34,000	$70,000	C	***	-1%
427/430 L88	69		$275,000	$325,000	A	****	n/c
427/435 L71	69		$45,000	$80,000	B	***	1%
427/435 L89	69		$57,000	$105,000	B	***	1%
350/300 Coupe	70	10,668	$18,500	$39,000	C	***	n/c
350/350 L46	70		$22,000	$40,000	C	***	-3%
350/370 LT1	70		$28,000	$56,000	C	***	n/c
454/390 LS5	70		$27,000	$58,000	B	***	n/c
350/300 Convertible	70	6,648	$24,000	$50,000	C	***	n/c
350/350 L46	70		$25,000	$55,000	C	***	n/c
350/370 LT1	70		$33,000	$68,000	C	***	n/c
454/390 LS5	70		$33,000	$70,000	B	***	1%
350/270 Coupe	71	14,680	$18,000	$36,500	C	***	n/c
350/330 LT1	71		$25,000	$53,000	C	***	-1%
454/365 LS5	71		$25,000	$55,000	B	***	n/c
454/425 LS6	71		$64,000	$130,000	A	***	3%
350/270 Convertible	71	7,121	$25,000	$48,000	C	***	-1%
350/330 LT1	71		$31,000	$65,000	C	***	-1%
454/365 LS5	71		$33,000	$67,000	B	***	n/c
454/425 LS6	71		$70,000	$150,000	A	***	6%
350/200 Coupe	72	20,496	$18,500	$40,000	C	***	n/c
350/255 LT1	72		$26,500	$55,000	C	***	n/c
454/270 LS5	72		$27,500	$56,000	C	***	n/c
300/250 Convertible	72	6,508	$25,000	$51,000	C	***	n/c
350/255 LT1	72		$35,000	$66,000	C	***	2%
454/270 LS5	72		$33,000	$67,000	C	***	-1%

(1968–72, add $1k–$2k for auxiliary hard top; $2k–$3k for a/c.)

Model	Yrs. Built	No. Made	Buy-Sell Price Range Low	High	Grade	Rating	1 Yr. % Change
350/190 Coupe	73	25,521	$13,000	$24,000	C	***	n/c
350/250 L82	73		$15,000	$28,000	C	***	n/c
454/275 LS4	73		$17,000	$33,000	C	***	4%
350/190 Convertible	73	4,943	$20,000	$33,000	C	***	2%
350/250 L82	73		$22,000	$40,000	C	***	5%
454/275 LS4	73		$24,000	$42,000	C	***	5%
350/195 Coupe	74	32,028	$11,000	$23,000	C	***	3%
350/250 L82	74		$14,000	$28,000	C	***	5%
454/270 LS4	74		$15,000	$30,000	C	***	3%
350/195 Convertible	74	5,474	$19,000	$32,000	C	***	4%
350/250 L82	74		$21,000	$36,000	C	***	2%
454/270 LS4	74		$22,000	$40,000	C	***	4%
350/165 Coupe	75	33,836	$10,000	$19,000	C	***	3%
350/205 L82	75		$12,500	$23,000	C	***	2%
350/165 Convertible	75	4,629	$18,000	$33,000	C	***	4%
350/205 L82	75		$20,000	$37,000	C	***	4%
350/180 Coupe	76	46,558	$9,000	$16,000	C	***	4%
350/210 L82	76		$11,000	$20,000	C	***	n/c
350/180 Coupe	77	49,213	$9,500	$18,000	C	***	4%
350/210 L82	77		$12,000	$22,000	C	***	1%
350/185 Coupe	78	24,991	$10,000	$18,000	C	***	n/c
350/220 L82	78		$13,000	$23,000	C	***	3%
350/185 Silver Anniversary	78	15,283	$13,000	$25,000	C	***	6%
350/220 L82	78		$16,000	$30,000	C	***	7%
350/185 Pace Car	78	6,502	$20,000	$35,000	C	***	5%
350/220 L82	78		$20,000	$40,000	C	***	1%
350/195 Coupe	79	53,807	$10,500	$19,000	C	***	1%
350/225 L82	79		$13,500	$24,000	C	***	4%
350/190 Coupe	80	40,614	$12,000	$20,000	C	***	6%
350/230 L82	80		$14,000	$24,000	C	***	3%

1971 Chevrolet Corvette

1995 Chevrolet Corvette coupe

	Yrs. Built	No. Made	Buy-Sell Price Range		Grade	Rating	1 Yr. % Change
			Low	High			
305/180 (California only)	80		$10,000	$18,000	D	★★★	4%
350/190 Coupe	81	40,606	$12,000	$21,000	C	★★★	5%
350/200 Coupe	82	18,648	$12,000	$22,000	C	★★★	1%
350/200 Collector Edition	82	6,759	$17,000	$30,000	C	★★★	1%

(1973–82, add $750 for aluminum wheels, $1,250 for auxiliary hard top. 1978–82, add $650 for glass top.)

C4

	Yrs. Built	No. Made	Low	High	Grade	Rating	1 Yr. % Change
Coupe	84	51,547	$5,500	$9,000	D	★★	-7%
Coupe	85	39,729	$6,000	$9,000	D	★★	-14%
Coupe	86	27,794	$6,500	$10,500	D	★★	-6%
Convertible	86	7,315	$9,500	$16,000	D	★★	n/c
Malcolm Konner Comm. Coupe	86	50	$10,000	$20,000	D	★★	8%
Coupe	87	20,007	$7,500	$11,500	D	★★	n/c
Convertible	87	10,625	$10,000	$16,000	D	★★	n/c
Callaway Cpe/Cvt	87	188 inc.	$20,000	$32,000	D	★★	4%
Coupe	88	15,382	$7,500	$11,000	D	★★	-8%
Convertible	88	7,407	$10,000	$16,000	D	★★	n/c
35th Anniversary coupe	88	2,050 inc.	$13,000	$22,000	D	★★	n/c
Challenge Racer	88	56 inc.	$26,500	$40,000	D	★★	2%
Callaway Cpe/Cvt	88	125 inc.	$20,000	$31,000	D	★★	n/c
Coupe	89	16,663	$7,500	$12,000	D	★★	-10%
Convertible	89	9,749	$11,000	$17,000	D	★★	n/c
Challenge Racer	89	60 inc.	$26,000	$40,000	D	★★	2%
Callaway Cpe/Cvt	89	67 inc.	$21,000	$32,000	D	★★	1%
Coupe	90	12,967	$8,000	$13,000	D	★★	-5%
ZR-1 coupe	90	3,049	$22,000	$32,000	C	★★	-6%
Convertible	90	7,630	$10,000	$18,000	D	★★	-7%
Callaway Cpe/Cvt	90	58 inc.	$21,000	$32,000	D	★★	n/c
World Challenge Racer	90	23 inc.	$24,000	$35,000	D	★★	n/c
Coupe	91	12,923	$9,500	$13,000	D	★★	n/c
ZR-1 coupe	91	2,044	$20,000	$32,000	C	★★	-8%
Convertible	91	5,672	$12,000	$18,500	D	★★	-2%
Callaway Cpe/Cvt	91	71 inc.	$21,500	$32,000	D	★★	n/c
Coupe	92	14,102	$10,000	$14,000	D	★★	n/c
ZR-1 coupe	92	502	$21,000	$33,000	C	★★	-7%
Convertible	92	5,875	$12,000	$18,500	D	★★	-3%
Coupe	93	15,396	$10,000	$14,000	D	★★	-8%
ZR-1 coupe	93	448	$22,000	$36,000	C	★★	-25%
Convertible	93	5,692	$13,000	$19,000	D	★★	-3%
40th Anniversary coupe	93	6,749 inc.	$15,000	$22,000	D	★★	-4%
40th Anniversary convertible	93	inc.	$19,000	$27,000	C	★★	n/c
40th Anniversary ZR-1 coupe	93	inc.	$34,000	$48,000	C	★★	-1%
Coupe	94	17,536	$11,000	$16,000	D	★★	-6%
ZR-1 coupe	94	448	$32,000	$44,000	C	★★	n/c
Convertible	94	5,346	$15,000	$20,000	D	★★	n/c
Coupe	95	15,323	$12,000	$17,000	D	★★	-5%
ZR-1 coupe	95	448	$32,000	$45,000	C	★★	-4%
Convertible	95	4,444	$15,000	$20,000	D	★★	-6%
Pace Car convertible	95	527	$25,000	$33,000	D	★★	-7%
Coupe	96	12,326	$13,500	$18,000	D	★★	-6%
Convertible	96	2,798	$16,000	$21,500	D	★★	-7%
Collector Edition coupe	96	4,031	$17,000	$25,000	D	★★	6%
Collector Edition convertible	96	1,381	$19,000	$30,000	D	★★	8%
Grand Sport coupe	96	810	$25,000	$40,000	C	★★★	4%
Grand Sport convertible	96	190	$30,000	$55,000	C	★★★	5%

(1984–96, add $1,300 for auxiliary hard top, $600 for 6-sp, $3,000 for LT4 in 1996.)

C5

	Yrs. Built	No. Made	Low	High	Grade	Rating	1 Yr. % Change
Coupe	97	9,752	$16,500	$21,500	D	★★	n/c
Coupe	98	19,235	$17,000	$22,500	D	★★	n/c
Convertible	98	10,686	$21,500	$28,500	D	★★	n/c
Pace Car convertible	98	1,163	$29,000	$38,000	D	★★	n/c
Coupe	99	18,078	$19,000	$24,000	D	★★	n/c
Convertible	99	11,161	$22,900	$29,000	D	★★	n/c
Hard top	99	4,031	$18,000	$23,000	D	★★	n/c
Coupe	00	18,113	$20,500	$26,000	D	★★	n/c
Convertible	00	13,479	$24,000	$29,000	D	★★	n/c
Hard top	00	2,090	$19,000	$24,000	D	★★	n/c
Coupe	01	15,681	$23,500	$28,000	D	★★	n/c
Convertible	01	14,173	$26,000	$32,500	D	★★	n/c
Z06 hard top	01	5,773	$26,000	$33,000	C	★★	n/c
Coupe	02	14,760	$25,000	$31,500	D	★★	n/c
Convertible	02	12,710	$29,000	$36,000	D	★★	n/c
Z06 hard top	02	8,297	$27,500	$36,900	C	★	n/c
Coupe	03	8,727	$27,000	$32,900	D	★	n/c
Convertible	03	6,475	$32,000	$38,000	D	★	n/c
Z06 hard top	03	8,635	$29,000	$37,000	C	★	n/c
50th Anniversary coupe	03	4,085	$31,000	$39,000	D	★	n/c
50th Anniversary convertible	03	7,547	$34,000	$44,000	D	★	n/c
Coupe	04	13,950	$28,000	$34,000	D	★	-1%
Convertible	04	9,557	$33,000	$40,000	D	★	-1%
Z06 hard top	04	3,658	$33,000	$38,000	C	★	-1%
Commemorative coupe	04	2,215	$29,000	$36,000	D	★	-2%
Commemorative convertible	04	2,659	$34,000	$39,000	D	★	-3%
Z06 Commemorative hard top	04	2,025	$32,000	$40,000	C	★	-5%

C6

	Yrs. Built	No. Made	Low	High	Grade	Rating	1 Yr. % Change
Coupe	05	26,278	$33,000	$42,000	D	★	-3%
Convertible	05	10,644	$40,000	$45,500	D	★	-5%
Coupe	06	16,598	$37,000	$43,000	D	★	-4%
Convertible	06	11,151	$43,000	$50,000	D	★	-5%
Z06 coupe	06	6,272	$54,000	$60,000	C	★	-6%

	Yrs. Built	No. Made	Buy-Sell Price Range Low	High	Grade	Rating	1 Yr. % Change
Coupe	07	21,484	$38,000	$43,000	D	★	-4%
Convertible	07	10,918	$58,000	$65,000	D	★	-3%
Pace Car convertible	07	500	$58,000	$65,000	D	★	-3%
Z06 coupe	07	8159	$58,000	$62,000	C	★	-8%
Ron Fellows Z06 coupe	07	399	$68,000	$72,000	C	★	-1%
Coupe	08	n/a	est. MSRP	$46,000	D	★	New
Convertible	08	n/a	est. MSRP	$54,000	D	★	New
Z06 coupe	08	n/a	est. MSRP	$71,000	C	★	New

(Note: Bloomington Gold, NCRS certification, or racing history can add significantly to the value of a Corvette.)

Impala

	Yrs. Built	No. Made	Low	High	Grade	Rating	1 Yr. % Change
Impala SS	94	6,303	$7,000	$11,500	F	★	-14%
Impala SS	95	18,649	$7,500	$12,000	F	★	-18%
Impala SS	96	25,000*	$8,500	$13,000	F	★	-16%

Nova

	Yrs. Built	No. Made	Low	High	Grade	Rating	1 Yr. % Change
Nova SS	62-65	62,108	$12,000	$22,000	C	★★	-12%
Nova SS	66-67	20,200	$17,000	$36,000	C	★★	-23%
Nova SS 327 L79	66-67	5,487	$24,000	$40,000	B	★★	-33%
Nova SS 396/375-hp L78	68-70	5,618	$22,000	$34,000	B	★★	-54%

(Add 25% for 4-sp—must have authenticating paperwork.)

Nova SS 350	68-72	49,340	$12,500	$19,500	C	★★	-22%
Yenko Nova 427	69	23*	$350,000	$425,000	A	★★★	-16%
Yenko Nova Deuce	70	120*	$80,000	$110,000	B	★★★	-18%
Nova SS 350	71-72	19,324	$11,000	$15,000	C	★★	-3%
Nova SS 350	73	35,542	$6,500	$9,800	D	★★	-13%

CHRYSLER

300

	Yrs. Built	No. Made	Low	High	Grade	Rating	1 Yr. % Change
300 coupe	55	1,725	$35,000	$60,000	C	★★	-5%
300B coupe	56	1,102	$35,000	$58,000	C	★★	-2%
300C coupe	57	1,918	$30,000	$43,000	C	★★	-3%
Convertible	57	484	$100,000	$150,000	B	★★★	34%
300D coupe	58	618	$35,000	$45,000	C	★★	n/c
Convertible	58	191	$110,000	$150,000	B	★★★	13%
300E coupe	59	550	$55,000	$65,000	C	★★	n/c
Convertible	59	140	$100,000	$125,000	B	★★★	9%
300F coupe	60	964	$45,000	$55,000	C	★★	n/c
Convertible	60	248	$115,000	$150,000	B	★★★	21%
300G coupe	61	1,280	$45,000	$55,000	C	★★	n/c
Convertible	61	337	$110,000	$150,000	B	★★★	23%

(Add 25% for 4-sp.)

300H coupe	62	435	$19,000	$25,000	C	★★★	n/c
Convertible	62	123	$60,000	$85,000	C	★★★	17%
300J coupe	63	400	$25,000	$30,000	C	★★★	n/c
300K coupe	64	3,022	$13,500	$19,000	C	★★★	n/c
Convertible	64	625	$25,000	$45,000	C	★★★	15%
300L coupe	65	2,405	$13,000	$16,000	C	★★★	n/c
Convertible	65	440	$25,000	$40,000	C	★★★	15%

CISITALIA

	Yrs. Built	No. Made	Low	High	Grade	Rating	1 Yr. % Change
D46	46-48	36	$75,000	$110,000	A	★★★	14%
202MM (Spyder Nuvolari)	47-51	30	$350,000	$475,000	A	★★★	18%

(For incorrect engine, deduct 25%. Beware, as Cisitalias are a fake du jour. The replicas never used Cisitalia chassis numbers. They generally have a Simca engine, look brand new—because they are—and have no paperwork or history.)

202 coupe	47-54	153	$185,000	$265,000	A	★★★	17%
202 Spyder Vignale	47-54	17	$150,000	$225,000	A	★★★	19%

CITROËN

	Yrs. Built	No. Made	Low	High	Grade	Rating	1 Yr. % Change
DS21 Decapotable	64-71	1,246	$125,000	$165,000	C	★★★	14%
SM	70-75	12,920	$15,000	$30,000	C	★★★	22%

CORD

L-29

	Yrs. Built	No. Made	Low	High	Grade	Rating	1 Yr. % Change
Sedan	29-32	5,010	$65,000	$100,000	B	★★★	7%

	Yrs. Built	No. Made	Buy-Sell Price Range Low	High	Grade	Rating	1 Yr. % Change
Brougham	29-32	inc.	$85,000	$110,000	B	★★★	n/c
Convertible sedan	29-32	inc.	$150,000	$200,000	B	★★★	n/c
Cabriolet	29-32	inc.	$175,000	$225,000	B	★★★	8%

810

Sedan	36	1,764	$45,000	$66,000	B	★★★	n/c
Phaeton	36	inc.	$112,000	$160,000	A	★★★	n/c
"Sportsman" convertible	36	inc.	$160,000	$225,000	A	★★★	4%

812

Sedan	37	1,066	$44,000	$68,000	B	★★★	n/c
Phaeton	37	inc.	$120,000	$175,000	A	★★★	n/c
"Sportsman" convertible	37	inc.	$170,000	$240,000	A	★★★	7%
SC Phaeton	37	inc.	$175,000	$250,000	A	★★★	n/c
SC "Sportsman"	37	inc.	$185,000	$270,000	A	★★★	7%

DAIMLER

SP250	59-64	2,650	$18,000	$28,000	C	★★	13%

DATSUN

1600 convertible	66-70	31,350*	$6,500	$16,000	C	★★★	n/c
2000 convertible	68-79	14,450*	$8,000	$18,000	C	★★★	n/c
240Z	70	16,215	$10,000	$20,000	C	★★★	n/c
240Z	71-73	131,900	$9,000	$15,000	D	★★★	n/c
260Z	74-75	101,479	$5,000	$9,000	D	★★	n/c
280Z	75-78	182,385	$4,000	$9,000	D	★	-12%
280ZX	79-83	603,627	$4,000	$9,000	D	★	-9%

DELAGE

D-6 65 cabriolet	34-35	est. 250	$60,000	$130,000	B	★★★	n/c
D-6 70 coupe	37-39	inc.	$70,000	$165,000	B	★★★	n/c
D-6 70 cabriolet	38-39	inc.	$90,000	$205,000	B	★★★	n/c
D-6 75 coupe	38-39	inc.	$75,000	$125,000	B	★★★	n/c
D-6 75 cabriolet	38-39	inc.	$75,000	$155,000	B	★★★	n/c
D-6 (3-liter) coupe	46-49	inc.	$55,000	$100,000	B	★★★	n/c
D-8 Torpedo	29-31	est. 200	$175,000	$450,000	A	★★★	n/c
D-8C cabriolet	29-33	inc.	$175,000	$250,000	A	★★★	n/c
D-8S cabriolet	30-33	inc.	$175,000	$300,000	A	★★★	n/c
D-8 15 coupe	32-34	inc.	$100,000	$205,000	A	★★★	n/c
D-8 15 cabriolet	34-35	inc.	$95,000	$200,000	A	★★★	n/c
D-8 105 cabriolet	34-35	inc.	$150,000	$250,000	A	★★★	n/c
D-8 120 cabriolet	36-39	inc.	$400,000	$800,000	A	★★★	n/c
D-8 120 Aerosport	36-39	inc.	$350,000	$1,200,000	A	★★★	n/c

(Prices are for factory coachwork. Cars with unusual and/or exceptional coachwork may be worth multiples of these amounts.)

1947 Cisitalia 202

1967 Dodge Coronet RT convertible

	Yrs. Built	No. Made	Buy-Sell Price Range Low	High	Grade	Rating	1 Yr. % Change
DELAHAYE							
135MS coupe	35–39	n/a	$275,000	$500,000	B	★★★	10%
135MS cabriolet	35–39	n/a	$275,000	$450,000	A	★★★	14%
135M coupe	46–53	n/a	$100,000	$200,000	B	★★★	10%
135M cabriolet	46–53	n/a	$165,000	$275,000	A	★★★	9%
135MS cabriolet	46–53	n/a	$200,000	$275,000	A	★★★	19%

(Prices can vary greatly depending on coachwork and history; est. $850k–$2m for Figoni et Falaschi.)

	Yrs. Built	No. Made	Low	High	Grade	Rating	Change
DELOREAN							
DMC-12	81–83	8,583*	$17,500	$30,000	C	★★	-9%

(Includes 3 gold-plated cars.)

DETOMASO							
Vallelunga	67	50*	$100,000	$150,000	B	★★★	36%
Mangusta	67–71	400*	$75,000	$110,000	B	★★★	16%
Pantera	71–74	5,629	$40,000	$65,000	B	★★★	n/c
Pantera GT/L, GTS	75–89	3,500*	$45,000	$65,000	B	★★★	5%

(For true GT5, add $10,000.)

DODGE							
Challenger							
Coupe (340 or 383)	70–71	83,009	$22,000	$32,000	C	★★	-11%
Convertible	70–71	5,388	$32,000	$44,000	C	★★	-12%
T/A	70	2,399	$49,000	$80,000	B	★★★	-12%
R/T	70–71	36,505	$30,000	$40,000	C	★★	-14%
w/Six Pack (440)	70–71	1,890	$65,000	$85,000	B	★★★	-7%
w/Hemi	70–71	418	$100,000	$150,000	A	★★★	-30%
R/T Convertible	70	2,737	$60,000	$90,000	B	★★★	-17%
w/Six Pack (440)	70	90	$150,000	$275,000	B	★★	-41%
w/Hemi	70	9	$450,000	$650,000	A	★★★	-23%

(Add 25% for R/T 440; add 40% for factory Shaker hood.)

Rallye (340)	72	6,902	$18,000	$22,500	C	★★	-11%
Rallye (340)	73–74	18,256	$16,500	$20,000	C	★★	-18%

(For all Challengers, add 25% for 4-sp.)

Charger							
Charger (440)	66–67	53,088	$19,000	$25,000	C	★★	-9%
w/Hemi	66–67	586	$45,000	$75,000	B	★★	-17%
R/T	68–70	46,472	$35,000	$45,000	C	★★	-13%
w/Six Pack (440)	70	684	$50,000	$80,000	B	★★	-15%
w/Hemi	68–70	116	$100,000	$150,000	A	★★	-38%
Charger 500	69–70	500	$58,000	$70,000	C	★★	-13%
w/Hemi	69	52	$160,000	$225,000	B	★★★	-10%
Daytona (440)	69	433	$150,000	$200,000	B	★★	-14%

	Yrs. Built	No. Made	Buy-Sell Price Range Low	High	Grade	Rating	1 Yr. % Change
w/Hemi	69	70	$400,000	$600,000	A	★★	-30%
R/T	71	3,118	$26,000	$57,000	C	★★	-14%
w/Six Pack	71	178	$65,000	$80,000	B	★★	-14%
w/Hemi	71	63	$80,000	$140,000	A	★★★	-25%

(For all Chargers, add 25% for 4-sp.)

Coronet							
Coronet Hemi	66	714	$50,000	$75,000	B	★★★	-16%
Convertible Hemi	66	27	$90,000	$150,000	B	★★★	-56%
Coronet R/T	67	9,553	$20,000	$35,000	C	★★	-4%
Convertible	67	628	$30,000	$45,000	C	★★	-7%
R/T w/Hemi	67	283	$90,000	$150,000	B	★★★	-54%
R/T (440)	68–70	n/a	$35,000	$50,000	B	★★	-12%
w/Six Pack	70	194	$55,000	$75,000	B	★★	-15%
w/Hemi	70	330	$80,000	$125,000	B	★★	-20%
R/T Convertible w/Hemi	68–70	20	$200,000	$300,000	A	★★★	-25%
w/Six Pack	70	16	$100,000	$200,000	A	★★★	-33%

(For all Coronets, add 25% for 4-sp.)

Super Bee							
Super Bee	68–70	48,221	$30,000	$40,000	B	★★	-14%
w/Six Pack	69–70	3,175	$45,000	$65,000	B	★★★	-18%

(Add 50% for 1969.5 M code; 25% for 4-sp.)

w/Hemi	68–70	383	$80,000	$125,000	A	★★★	-24%
Super Bee	71	4,144	$22,500	$35,000	C	★★	-13%
w/Six Pack	71	99	$68,000	$95,000	B	★★	-10%
w/Hemi	71	22	$150,000	$200,000	B	★★★	-36%

(For all Super Bees, add 25% for 4-sp.)

Dart							
GTS 340	68–69	15,447**	$18,000	$24,000	C	★★	-10%
GTS 383	68–69	inc.	$32,000	$59,000	C	★★	-10%
GSS 440	68	50	$125,000	$165,000	A	★★★	-21%
Convertible 340	69	760	$21,000	$35,000	C	★★	-16%

(Add 30% for 383.)

Demon							
Demon 340	71–72	10,798	$17,000	$24,000	C	★★	-13%
Other							
Super Stock Hemi	68	80	$175,000	$275,000	B	★★★	-33%

DUAL-GHIA							
Convertible	56–58	117	$175,000	$250,000	B	★★★	24%
L6.4 Coupe	61–63	26	$125,000	$200,000	C	★★★	38%

DUESENBERG							
Model J							
Convertible Sedan	29–37	est. 480	$700,000	$1,000,000	A	★★★	n/c
Tourster	30–35	inc.	$750,000	$1,200,000	A	★★★	n/c
Phaeton	29–37	inc.	$700,000	$1,200,000	A	★★★★	11%
Murphy open sedan	29–32	inc.	$700,000	$950,000	A	★★★	n/c
Murphy convertible coupe	29–34	inc.	$750,000	$1,100,000	A	★★★	n/c
Murphy torpedo convertible	30–34	inc.	$850,000	$1,250,000	A	★★★	n/c
Murphy sedan	29–34	inc.	$500,000	$675,000	B	★★★	n/c
Murphy town car	29–34	inc.	$675,000	$800,000	B	★★★	-5%
Rollston town car	30–37	10	$500,000	$625,000	B	★★★	-7%

(Add 25% for original supercharger. Exceptional or rare coachwork can command higher prices.)

FACEL VEGA							
HK500	59–61	500	$45,000	$97,000	B	★★★	n/c
Facel II	62–64	184	$85,000	$125,000	C	★★★	n/c
Facel III	62–64	1,500	$15,000	$23,000	C	★★	n/c

FERRARI							
166 Spyder Corsa	47–48	8	$950,000	$1,200,000	A	★★★	n/c
166 MM Berlinetta	48–50	12	$1,200,000	$2,000,000	A	★★★	n/c

	Yrs. Built	No. Made	Buy-Sell Price Range		Grade	Rating	1 Yr. % Change
			Low	High			
166 MM Barchetta	48 50	25	$2,000,000	$2,750,000	A	★★★	11%
166 Inter	48-51	37	$700,000	$900,000	B	★★★	n/c
195 Inter	50-52	25	$500,000	$700,000	B	★★★	n/c
340 America Closed	51	12	$600,000	$2,000,000	A	★★★	n/c
340 America Open	51	13	$1,000,000	$3,000,000	A	★★★	n/c
340 Mexico	52	4	$2,500,000	$3,500,000	A	★★★	n/c
342 America Berlinetta	52-53	3	$600,000	$750,000	A	★★★	n/c
342 America cabriolet	52-53	3	$1,100,000	$2,000,000	A	★★★	n/c
212 Export (closed)	51-52	9	$750,000	$1,200,000	B	★★★	n/c
212 Export (open)	51-52	8	$1,300,000	$1,800,000	B	★★★	n/c
212 Touring Barchetta	51-52	7	$800,000	$1,400,000	A	★★★	n/c
212 Inter	51-52	84	$550,000	$1,000,000	B	★★★	n/c
225 Sport	52	22	$1,000,000	$1,800,000	A	★★★	n/c
166 MM Berlinetta S2	52-53	4	$1,200,000	$1,600,000	A	★★★	n/c
166 MM Spyder S2	52-53	9	$1,300,000	$1,700,000	A	★★★	n/c
250 MM	52-53	13	$2,000,000	$2,700,000	A	★★★	n/c
250 MM Berlinetta	52-53	16	$1,800,000	$2,500,000	A	★★★	n/c
340 MM	53	9	$3,000,000	$3,800,000	A	★★★	n/c
500 Mondial	53-54	33	$1,200,000	$2,000,000	A	★★★	n/c
375 MM	53-54	16	$3,800,000	$4,800,000	A	★★★	n/c
375 MM Berlinetta	53-54	7	$3,800,000	$5,000,000	A	★★★	n/c
250 Europa Series I	53-54	18	$600,000	$900,000	B	★★★★	20%
375 America	53-54	12	$600,000	$1,200,000	A	★★★	n/c
375 MM+	54	6	$5,000,000	$5,500,000	A	★★★	n/c
250 Monza	54	4	$3,000,000	$4,000,000	A	★★★★	n/c
750 Monza	54-55	33	$1,300,000	$1,800,000	A	★★★	n/c
250 Europa Series II	54-55	34	$600,000	$800,000	B	★★★	n/c
410 Sport Spyder/ coupe	55	4	$4,200,000	$6,500,000	A	★★★	n/c
860 Monza	55-56	2	$2,500,000	$3,000,000	A	★★★	n/c
500 TR	56	17	$1,400,000	$1,750,000	A	★★★★	n/c
410 Superamerica	56-59	37	$1,250,000	$1,750,000	A	★★★★	23%
250 GT Boano/Ellena	56-58	130	$350,000	$475,000	B	★★★★	n/c
250 GT Tour de France	56-59	77	$1,400,000	$2,700,000	A	★★★	n/c

(Early Pininfarina-bodied "roundtail" TdFs ('56) will command a premium.)

	Yrs. Built	No. Made	Buy-Sell Price Range		Grade	Rating	1 Yr. % Change
			Low	High			
*14-louver competition car		8 (inc.)	$2,200,000	$3,000,000	A	★★★	n/c
*Zagato-bodied		5 (inc.)	$4,000,000	$5,000,000	A	★★★★	n/c
500 TRC	57	19	$2,000,000	$2,400,000	A	★★★	n/c
250 Testa Rossa (all)	56-61	34	$7,000,000	$16,000,000	A	★★★	n/c
250 GT PF cabriolet Series I	57-59	40	$1,500,000	$2,500,000	A	★★★	13%
250 GT PF cabriolet Series II	59-62	200	$375,000	$500,000	B	★★★★	n/c
250 GT California Spyder LWB	57-60	42	$3,500,000	$4,000,000	A	★★★★★	20%
*Alloy-bodied		9	$5,000,000	$7,000,000	A	★★★	29%
250 GT California Spyder SWB	60-63	51	$4,000,000	$5,500,000	A	★★★★★	7%
*Alloy-bodied		3	$5,500,000	$7,500,000	A	★★★★★	23%
250 GT Interim Berlinetta	59	7	$1,200,000	$2,000,000	A	★★★★	n/c
250 Pininfarina coupe	59-62	350	$225,000	$250,000	B	★★★	23%
250 GT SWB (steel)	60-62	90	$2,600,000	$3,600,000	A	★★★	11%
*Alloy-bodied w/no stories		75	$4,000,000	$5,000,000	A	★★★	n/c
*SEFAC variant	61	Inc.	$6,500,000	$7,500,000	A	★★★★	25%
400 Superamerica Coupe	60-64	36	$750,000	$1,400,000	A	★★★	n/c
400 Superamerica Cabriolet	60-64	11	$900,000	$2,200,000	A	★★★	n/c
250 GTE 2+2	60-63	955	$100,000	$150,000	C	★★★	-20%
250 GTO	62-64	39	$20,000,000	$28,000,000	A	★★★★★	33%

	Yrs. Built	No. Made	Buy-Sell Price Range		Grade	Rating	1 Yr. % Change
			Low	High			
250 GTL Lusso	62-64	350	$500,000	$700,000	B	★★★	13%
330 LM Berlinetta	63	4	$6,000,000	$7,500,000	A	★★★	n/c
330 America	63	50	$135,000	$150,000	B	★★★	4%
330 GT 2+2 (4-headlight)	63-65	1,080	$70,000	$100,000	C	★★★	-9%
330 GT 2+2 (SII 2-headlight)	65-68	inc.	$75,000	$115,000	C	★★★	-13%
250 LM (no stories)	64-65	32	$4,500,000	$5,000,000	A	★★★	n/c
500 Superfast	64-66	36	$600,000	$800,000	A	★★★	n/c
275 GTB/2 SN	64-66	450	$600,000	$900,000	A	★★★★	13%

(Add $100k for longnose; $50k for 6 carbs; $100k for alloy body; $25,000 for outside filler cap.)

	Yrs. Built	No. Made	Buy-Sell Price Range		Grade	Rating	1 Yr. % Change
			Low	High			
275 GTB/C Series I	65	11	$1,800,000	$2,200,000	A	★★★★	n/c
275 GTB/C Le Mans	65	3	$5,000,000	$7,500,000	A	★★★★	n/c
275 GTS	65-66	200	$450,000	$575,000	B	★★★★	17%
275 GTB/C Series II	66	12	$2,000,000	$2,700,000	A	★★★★	n/c
275 GTB/4	66-68	280	$900,000	$1,400,000	A	★★★★	17%

(Add $500k for alloy body.)

	Yrs. Built	No. Made	Buy-Sell Price Range		Grade	Rating	1 Yr. % Change
			Low	High			
275 GTB/4 NART Spyder	67-68	10	$5,000,000	$7,000,000	A	★★★★	21%
330 GTC	66-68	600	$180,000	$235,000	B	★★★	-16%
330 GTS	66-68	100	$550,000	$700,000	A	★★★	16%
365 California Spyder	66-67	14	$850,000	$1,300,000	A	★★★	n/c
206 GT Dino	67-68	144	$130,000	$160,000	B	★★★	7%
365 GTC	68-70	168	$200,000	$275,000	B	★★★	n/c
365 GT 2+2	68-71	800	$75,000	$115,000	C	★★★	-11%
365 GTB/4 Daytona coupe	68-73	1,301	$275,000	$375,000	B	★★★★	5%
365 GTS	69	20	$550,000	$650,000	B	★★★	n/c
365 GTB/4C (Fact. Daytona Comp.)	71-73	15 (inc.)	$3,000,000	$3,500,000	A	★★★	8%
Non-factory Daytona Comp.	71-73	5 (inc.)	$1,500,000	$1,800,000	B	★★★★	9%
365 GTS/4 Daytona Spyder	72-73	123	$850,000	$1,250,000	A	★★★	n/c
365 GTC/4	71-72	500	$85,000	$120,000	C	★★★	5%
246 GT Dino coupe	69-74	2,609	$130,000	$150,000	B	★★★★	11%
246 GTS Dino Spyder	72-74	1,274	$165,000	$210,000	B	★★★★	3%

(Add $15,000 for "chairs and flares.")

	Yrs. Built	No. Made	Buy-Sell Price Range		Grade	Rating	1 Yr. % Change
			Low	High			
365 GT4 2+2	72-76	470	$25,000	$35,000	D	★★	-25%
365 GT4 BB Boxer	74-76	387	$140,000	$175,000	B	★★★	11%
308 GT4 2+2	74-79	2,826	$23,000	$28,000	C	★★	-22%
308 GTB (fiberglass)	75-77	712	$40,000	$60,000	C	★★	-5%

(Add $5,000 for dry sump.)

	Yrs. Built	No. Made	Buy-Sell Price Range		Grade	Rating	1 Yr. % Change
			Low	High			
308 GTB (steel)	75-79	2,089	$30,000	$38,000	C	★★	12%
308 GTS	77-79	3,218	$32,000	$38,000	C	★★	14%

1963 Ferrari 250 GTL Lusso coupe

1981 Fiat Spider 2000 convertible

	Yrs. Built	No. Made	Buy-Sell Price Range Low	High	Grade	Rating	1 Yr. % Change
512 BB	76-81	929	$120,000	$140,000	B	★★★	11%
400 2+2 carbureted	76-80	502	$22,000	$30,000	D	★★	-6%
(Add $2,500 for 400/400i with manual shift.)							
512 BB LM	79-80	25	$1,000,000	$1,200,000	B	★★★	n/c
308 GTBi	80-82	494	$27,000	$37,000	D	★★	27%
308 GTSi	80-82	1,743	$29,000	$39,000	D	★★	31%
400i	80-84	1,308	$20,000	$27,000	D	★★	6%
Mondial 8 coupe	81-82	708	$18,000	$24,000	D	★★	5%
512 BBi Boxer	82-84	1,007	$125,000	$150,000	B	★★★	9%
308 GTB QV	83-85	748	$34,000	$42,000	C	★★	5%
308 GTS QV	83-85	3,042	$34,000	$42,000	C	★★	5%
Mondial coupe QV	83-85	1,848	$25,000	$33,000	D	★★	19%
Mondial cabriolet QV	83-85	629	$25,000	$35,000	C	★★	15%
288 GTO	84-85	272	$500,000	$600,000	B	★★	20%
Testarossa	85-87.5	7,200	$50,000	$65,000	C	★★	13%
Testarossa	87.5-91	inc.	$55,000	$70,000	C	★★	4%
412	85-89	576	$30,000	$38,000	D	★★	12%
Mondial 3.2 coupe	86-88	987	$28,000	$32,000	D	★★	7%
Mondial 3.2 cabriolet	86-88	810	$33,000	$38,000	C	★★	15%
328 GTB	86-88	1,345	$45,000	$55,000	B	★★★	13%
328 GTB	89	inc.	$54,000	$61,000	B	★★★	16%
328 GTS	86-88	6,068	$45,000	$58,000	B	★★★	8%
328 GTS	89	inc.	$54,000	$63,000	B	★★★	6%
F40	88-91	1,315	$400,000	$550,000	A	★★★★	18%
Mondial t coupe	89	840	$35,000	$44,000	C	★★	3%
Mondial t cabriolet	89-91	1,010	$38,000	$48,000	D	★★	-2%
348 tb	90	2,895	$48,000	$55,000	D	★★	8%
348 ts	90-92	4,230	$50,000	$57,000	D	★★	11%
512 TR	91-95	2,280	$75,000	$115,000	C	★★	n/c
456 GT	92-03	1,548	$45,000	$65,000	C	★★	-18%
456 GTA	95-03	inc.	$45,000	$65,000	C	★★	-27%
456M GT/GTA	98-03	403	$75,000	$125,000	C	★★	8%
348 Spider	93-95	1,090	$57,000	$67,000	B	★★	-1%
F512 M	94-96	500	$100,000	$120,000	C	★★	-20%
F355 Berlinetta	94-99	3,938	$50,000	$75,000	B	★★	-8%
F355 GTS	96-99	2,048	$70,000	$77,000	B	★★	-2%
F355 Spider	95-99	2,663	$70,000	$90,000	B	★★	-9%
(Add $5,000 for F1 transmission.)							
F50	95-97	349	$800,000	$900,000	A	★★★	12%
550 Maranello	96-03	1,600	$75,000	$100,000	C	★	-26%

	Yrs. Built	No. Made	Buy-Sell Price Range Low	High	Grade	Rating	1 Yr. % Change
355 Serie Fiorano	99	100*	$75,000	$115,000	B	★★	3%
360 Modena	99-05	8,800	$90,000	$120,000	B	★	-19%
360 Modena Spyder	00-05	7,565	$125,000	$150,000	B	★	-27%
(Add $7,500 for F1 transmission. Deduct $25k for gray-market cars.)							
360 Modena Challenge	00-05	inc.	$75,000	$95,000	B	★	-9%
430	05-	n/a	$175,000	$225,000	B	★	-11%
430 Spyder	05-	n/a	$200,000	$265,000	B	★	-30%
(Add $7,500 for F1 transmission.)							
550 Barchetta	01	448	$185,000	$210,000	C	★	-10%
Enzo	03-04	400	$1,100,000	$1,300,000	B	★★	21%
575M Maranello	02-05	2,100*	$110,000	$150,000	C	★	-10%
575 Superamerica	04-05	559	$250,000	$295,000	C	★	-5%
FXX	05-06	30	$1,800,000	$2,200,000	B	★★★	n/c
612 Scaglietti	05-	n/a	$175,000	$235,000	C	★	-6%
599 GTB Fiorano	06-	n/a	est. MSRP	$295,000	B	★	-5%

*Concerning "cut-cars": non-factory, non-NART Spyder conversions are valued primarily by the quality of workmanship. In today's market, rarely is a cut car valued more than the coupe from which it is derived.

Formula One Cars

	Yrs. Built	No. Made	Buy-Sell Price Range Low	High	Grade	Rating	1 Yr. % Change
312 "Spaghetti Exhaust"	'60s	12	$1,000,000	$1,500,000	A	★★★	20%
70-80 312 B & T series	68-70	40*	$450,000	$600,000	A	★★	n/c
Turbocharged	81-88	36*	$225,000	$275,000	A	★★	n/c

Ferrari Sports Prototype Racers

	Yrs. Built	No. Made	Buy-Sell Price Range Low	High	Grade	Rating	1 Yr. % Change
Front-engined V6 (Dinos)	57-60	6*	$2,750,000	$3,750,000	A	★★★	n/c
(Includes 196, 206, 246, 296 S without stories.)							
Rear-engined V6 & V8 Dino racers	61-67	25*	$1,450,000	$1,850,000	A	★★★	n/c
(Includes 166, 196, 246, 286, 268 SPs without stories.)							
Rear-engined V12 racers	63-67	22*	$4,000,000	$9,500,000	A	★★★	n/c
(Includes 250 P, 275 P, 330 P, 330 P2, 275 P2, 365 P, 330 P3, 365 P2/3, 330 P4, 330 P3/4 (412 P) without stories.)							

FIAT

	Yrs. Built	No. Made	Buy-Sell Price Range Low	High	Grade	Rating	1 Yr. % Change
8V (body by Rapi)	53-55	114 total	$350,000	$550,000	B	★★★	17%
Body by Zagato (28)		inc.	$525,000	$750,000	A	★★★	12%
Show Cars/Other Coachwork		inc.	$200,000	$300,000	B	★★★	n/c
(Correct 8V engines are difficult to find. Deduct 70% for incorrect type or no engine. Add 25% for significant, documented history.)							
1100/1200 TV roadster	57-58	n/a	$18,500	$28,500	C	★★	19%
1200/1500 roadster	59-67	n/a	$10,500	$14,000	D	★★	14%
Fiat Dino Spider	66-72	1,989	$39,000	$62,500	B	★★	19%
Fiat Dino coupe	66-72	5,814	$16,000	$26,500	D	★★	34%
850 Spider	67-74	124,660	$4,625	$7,125	D	★★	2%
124/2000 Spider	68-85	150,000*	$6,375	$9,750	C	★★	10%
X1/9	74-90	150,000*	$3,250	$4,900	F	★	20%

FORD

Fairlane and Torino

	Yrs. Built	No. Made	Buy-Sell Price Range Low	High	Grade	Rating	1 Yr. % Change
Fairlane GT/GTA	66-67	51,685	$14,000	$21,000	C	★★	-3%
Convertible	66-67	6,444	$18,000	$28,000	C	★★	-13%
(For 390 engine, add $7,500.)							
Talladega 428	69	748	$22,000	$32,000	C	★★	-7%
Torino Cobra 428	68-69	14,000*	$16,000	$24,000	C	★★	-13%
Torino GT 429 CJ	70-71	88,560	$16,000	$24,000	B	★★	-13%
Convertible GT CJ	70-71	5,552	$18,000	$26,000	B	★★	-36%
Torino Cobra 429	70-71	10,749	$15,000	$24,500	C	★★	-9%

Mustang

	Yrs. Built	No. Made	Buy-Sell Price Range Low	High	Grade	Rating	1 Yr. % Change
V8 convertible	65-66	15,000**	$24,000	$35,000	B	★★	-18%
GT convertible	65-66	inc.	$27,500	$37,500	B	★★	-23%
(Add 40% for K code; 20% for 4-sp.)							
Coupe	65-66	909,011**	$13,000	$19,500	B	★★	-15%

	Yrs. Built	No. Made	Buy-Sell Price Range Low	High	Grade	Rating	1 Yr. % Change
2+2 fastback	65–66	145,231**	$17,500	$28,000	B	★★	-19%
(Add 40% for K code; 20% for 4-sp.)							
V8 convertible	67–68	n/a	$18,000	$24,000	C	★★	-10%
GT convertible	67–68	n/a	$21,000	$27,500	C	★★	-10%
GT fastback	67–68	113,367	$22,000	$26,500	C	★★	-24%
GTA fastback	67–68	inc.	$22,500	$27,000	C	★★	-23%
(Add 20% for 390 engine; 40% for 428 CJ in 1968.)							
Mach 1 351	69–70	113,428	$22,000	$32,000	C	★★	-9%
Mach 1 428 Q code	69–70	15,864	$32,500	$48,000	B	★★	-18%
428 CJ convertible	69–70	inc.	$45,000	$70,000	B	★★★	-22%
(Add: 20% for 4-sp.)							
Boss 302	69–70	8,252	$36,000	$55,000	A	★★★	-18%
(Add 20% for 1969 model.)							
V8 convertible	69–70	inc.	$21,000	$28,000	C	★★	-14%
(Add 15% for SCJ; 25% for SCJ code with Drag Pak; $2,000 for Shaker hood on 428 CJ and Boss 302.)							
Boss 351	71	1,806	$33,000	$45,000	C	★★	-15%
Mach 1	71–73	99,564	$16,000	$24,000	C	★★	-20%
Mach 1 429 CJ	71	1,255	$30,000	$40,000	B	★★	-16%
V8 convertible	71–73	n/a	$14,000	$22,500	C	★★	-21%
Mustang II Cobra	76–78	23,919	$4,500	$7,750	D	★★	-14%
Boss 429	69–70	1,359	$190,000	$250,000	B	★★★	-14%
(Add 10% for 1969 model.)							
SVO	84–86	9,502	$4,500	$7,500	D	★★★	8%
Saleen	85–86	341	$6,750	$9,500	D	★★★	n/c
Saleen	87–88	988	$9,000	$11,000	D	★★	-13%
Saleen	89–90	977	$11,000	$13,500	D	★★	-12%
Saleen	91–92	109	$11,000	$15,000	D	★★	-13%
GT							
GT	05–06	4,000	$135,000	$160,000	C	★	-8%
SHELBY							
Cobra 260	62–63	75	$375,000	$500,000	A	★★★	6%
Cobra 289	63–65	580	$500,000	$650,000	A	★★★★	11%
(Deduct 10% for worm-and-sector steering.)							
Cobra 427	65–67	348	$675,000	$825,000	A	★★★★	3%
(Deduct 10% for 428; chassis # 3200–3300, approx.)							
Daytona coupe	64–65	6	$6,000,000	$8,000,000	A	★★★★	n/c
GT350	65	521	$225,000	$300,000	A	★★★	-10%
GT350 R	65	34	$800,000	$850,000	A	★★★	n/c
GT350	66	1,368	$110,000	$150,000	A	★★★	-13%
GT350 H	66	999	$105,000	$145,000	A	★★★	-18%
(Deduct 10% for automatic.)							
GT350	67	1,175	$80,000	$100,000	A	★★★	-14%
GT500	67	2,048	$120,000	$150,000	A	★★★	-24%
(Deduct 10% for automatic.)							
GT350	68	803	$60,000	$75,000	A	★★★	-7%
Convertible	68	404	$80,000	$100,000	A	★★★	-8%
GT350 H	68	224	$60,000	$75,000	A	★★★	-7%
GT500	68	1,044	$70,000	$90,000	A	★★★	-6%
Convertible	68	402	$95,000	$125,000	A	★★★	-7%
GT500 KR	68	1,053	$90,000	$125,000	A	★★★	-9%
Convertible	68	517	$160,000	$200,000	A	★★★	-13%
GT350	69–70	935	$50,000	$65,000	B	★★★	-9%
Convertible	69–70	194	$75,000	$90,000	B	★★★	-11%
GT500 Fastback	69–70	1,534	$65,000	$85,000	B	★★★	-13%
Convertible	69–70	335	$100,000	$125,000	B	★★★	-11%
(Add 25% for Drag Pak. Deduct 10% for automatic.)							
Thunderbird							
Convertible	55–57	53,166	$28,000	$42,500	C	★★★	-10%
E-code Convertible (dual carbs)	57	inc.	$45,000	$60,000	C	★★★	3%

	Yrs. Built	No. Made	Buy-Sell Price Range Low	High	Grade	Rating	1 Yr. % Change
F-code Convertible (supercharged)	57	194	$85,000	$130,000	B	★★★	2%
(Deduct $1,000 for only one top.)							
Coupe	58–60	173,891	$12,000	$20,000	C	★★★	-11%
Convertible	58–60	24,255	$21,000	$34,000	C	★★★	-17%
(Add 25% for 430-ci J-code in '59–'60.)							
Coupe	61–63	173,468	$11,000	$21,000	C	★★★	9%
Convertible	61–63	26,273	$17,500	$28,000	C	★★★	-27%
(Add $1,000 for 390-ci M-code.)							
Sports Roadster	62–63	1,882	$28,000	$42,000	C	★★★	n/c
(Add $5,000 for 390-ci M-code.)							
GT40							
Mk I–IV	64–69	102*	$1,500,000	$2,000,000	A	★★★	n/c
(Includes road and race cars from original phases of production. Prices will vary greatly for cars with significant history.)							
FRAZER NASH							
Le Mans Replica	48–56	34	$500,000	$700,000	B	★★★	n/c
GORDON-KEEBLE							
GK1 coupe	64–68	99	$25,000	$45,000	D	★★	14%
GRIFFITH							
Series 400 coupe	65–66	36	$30,000	$50,000	C	★★	n/c
HISPANO-SUIZA							
H6, open	19–24	n/a	$600,000	$2,000,000	A	★★★★	Mkt. Adj.
H6, closed	19–24	n/a	$300,000	$1,000,000	A	★★★★	60%
H6B, open	24–28	n/a	$600,000	$2,000,000	A	★★★★	Mkt. Adj.
H6B, closed	24–28	n/a	$300,000	$1,000,000	B	★★★★	62%
H6C, open	28–31	n/a	$600,000	$2,000,000	B	★★★★	67%
H6C, closed	28–31	n/a	$300,000	$1,000,000	B	★★★★	12%
J12 Type 56 (9-liter)	31–38	n/a	$800,000	$2,000,000	A	★★★★	Mkt. Adj.
J12 Type 68 (11-liter)	31–39	n/a	$1,500,000	$2,500,000	A	★★★★	Mkt. Adj.
K6, open	33–39	n/a	$300,000	$550,000	A	★★★	54%
K6, closed	33–39	n/a	$200,000	$350,000	B	★★★	29%
(All H-S are custom-bodied; prices depend on coachwork and history.)							
HONDA							
S800	67–70	11,536	$8,000	$12,000	D	★★	-18%
(Add 25% for convertible.)							
HUDSON							
Italia	54	26	$250,000	$325,000	B	★★★	NL†
INTERMECCANICA							
Italia coupe	67–72	411	$28,000	$45,000	C	★★★	16%
Italia convertible	67–72	inc.	$35,000	$50,000	B	★★★	-6%

1956 Ford Thunderbird convertible

1930 Isotta Fraschini 8A convertible sedan

	Yrs. Built	No. Made	Buy-Sell Price Range		Grade	Rating	1 Yr. % Change
			Low	High			
ISO							
Rivolta coupe	63–70	799	$40,000	$60,000	C	★★★	30%
Grifo	65–74	412	$200,000	$300,000	B	★★★★	38%
(Add $7,000 for 427 V8; $2,500 for long-nose model. Deduct $2,500 for 351 V8.)							
Lele	69–74	317	$20,000	$35,000	F	★★	18%
ISOTTA FRASCHINI							
Tipo 8 Touring	19–24	n/a	$450,000	$675,000	A	★★★	n/c
Tipo 8A cabriolet	30–32	n/a	$580,000	$780,000	A	★★★	n/c
Tipo 8A convertible coupe	25–32	n/a	$560,000	$765,000	A	★★★	n/c
Tipo 8A S cabriolet roadster	25–32	n/a	$620,000	$820,000	A	★★★	n/c
Tipo 8A SS dual cowl phaeton	25–32	n/a	$735,000	$945,000	A	★★★	n/c
Tipo 8A SS roadster cabriolet	25–33	n/a	$800,000	$1,100,000	A	★★★	n/c
(Prices can vary greatly depending on coachwork. For Castagna coachwork, add 15%.)							
JAGUAR							
SS I coupe	31–36	4,200*	$35,000	$45,000	C	★★	n/c
SS II coupe	31–34	inc.	$33,000	$43,000	C	★★	n/c
SS 90	35–36	22	$150,000	$200,000	B	★★	n/c
SS 100 2 1/2-Liter	36–40	190	$165,000	$200,000	B	★★	n/c
SS 100 3 1/2-Liter	38–40	118	$225,000	$350,000	A	★★★	n/c
SS Jaguar saloon	35–40		$20,000	$30,000	D	★★	n/c
SS Jaguar DHC	38–40		$43,000	$50,000	B	★★	n/c
Mk IV saloon (1.5-, 2.5-, 3.5-liter)	45–49	11,378	$22,000	$30,000	D	★★	n/c
Mk IV DHC (1.5-, 2.5-, 3.5-liter)	47–49	664	$45,000	$65,000	B	★★	n/c
Mk V saloon (2.5-, 3.5-liter)	49–51	9,462	$18,000	$27,000	D	★★	9%
Mk V DHC (2.5-, 3.5-liter)	49–51	1,001	$45,000	$60,000	B	★★	n/c
XK 120 roadster (alloy)	49–50	240	$185,000	$295,000	A	★★★	6%
XK 120 roadster	51–54	7,391	$75,000	$110,000	B	★★★	16%
XK 120 coupe	51–54	2,678	$50,000	$80,000	C	★★★	n/c
XK 120 DHC	53–54	1,769	$75,000	$100,000	B	★★★	17%
(Add $10,000 for SE option—dual exhausts, spoke wheels, cams, etc.)							
XK 140 roadster	54–57	3,347	$75,000	$110,000	B	★★★	14%
XK 140 DHC	54–57	2,740	$70,000	$85,000	B	★★★	13%
XK 140 coupe	54–57	2,797	$65,000	$85,000	C	★★	7%
(Add $10,000 for MC option—C-type head, cams, suspension, and spoked wheels.)							
XK 150 3.4 roadster	58–61	1,339	$55,000	$90,000	B	★★★	n/c

	Yrs. Built	No. Made	Buy-Sell Price Range		Grade	Rating	1 Yr. % Change
			Low	High			
XK 150 3.4 DHC	58–61	2,489	$65,000	$85,000	B	★★	17%
XK 150 3.4 FHC	58–61	4,101	$55,000	$75,000	C	★★	15%
(Add $5,000 for 3.8L engine.)							
XK 150S 3.4 roadster	59–61	1,466	$85,000	$135,000	A	★★★	n/c
XK 150S 3.4 DHC	59–61	inc.	$65,000	$95,000	B	★★★	n/c
XK 150S 3.4 FHC	59–61	inc.	$55,000	$75,000	B	★★★	19%
(Add $15k for 3.8L 150S FHC and DHC; $50k for 3.8L 150S roadster.)							
Mk VII saloon	51–56	20,939	$18,000	$23,000	F	★★	15%
Mk VIII saloon	57–58	6,332	$14,500	$22,000	F	★★	n/c
Mk IX saloon	59–69	10,005	$17,500	$24,000	F	★★	n/c
Mk X/420G	62–64	11,234	$11,000	$16,000	F	★★	n/c
Mk II saloon 2.4	56–59	25,173	$10,000	$12,000	D	★★	n/c
Mk II saloon 3.4	60–66	28,663	$18,000	$20,000	D	★★	n/c
Mk II saloon 3.8	60–67	30,140	$28,000	$45,000	B	★★★	n/c
(Deduct $2,000 for disc wheels; $2,000 for automatic; $1,500 for no overdrive.)							
XK C-type	50–53	54	$2,000,000	$2,750,000	A	★★★★	9%
XK D-type	53–55	77	$3,000,000	$4,500,000	A	★★★★	33%
XK-SS	56–57	18	$3,000,000	$4,500,000	A	★★★★	33%
(Price ranges for XK C, D, and SS Jaguars are determined by provenance, completeness, and originality. A car with all of its original parts and no stories will bring three to four times that of a "bitsa" with only a few authentic parts.)							
XKE Factory Lightweight (SI)	61–62	16	$1,250,000	$1,600,000	A	★★★★	n/c
XKE 3.8 convertible (flat floor) (SI)	61–62	7,827	$60,000	$90,000	B	★★★	n/c
XKE 3.8 coupe (flat floor) (SI)	61–62	7,669	$40,000	$60,000	B	★★★	n/c
XKE 3.8 convertible (SI)	62–64	inc.	$50,000	$80,000	B	★★★	n/c
XKE 3.8 coupe (SI)	62–64	inc.	$40,000	$50,000	B	★★★	11%
XKE 4.2 convertible (SI)	64–67	9,548	$65,000	$110,000	B	★★★	9%
XKE 4.2 coupe (SI)	64–67	7,770	$40,000	$60,000	B	★★★	5%
XKE 2+2 coupe	66–67	4,220	$25,000	$50,000	D	★★★	13%
(Deduct $3,000 for automatic.)							
XKE 4.2 convertible (SII)	68–71	8,627	$50,000	$75,000	B	★★★	8%
XKE 4.2 coupe (SII)	68–71	4,855	$30,000	$45,000	C	★★★	13%
XKE 2+2 coupe (SII)	68–71	5,326	$25,000	$40,000	D	★★★	5%
(Add $1,000 for a/c. Deduct $3,000 for automatic.)							
XKE V12 convertible (SIII)	71–74	7,990	$45,000	$80,000	C	★★★	8%
XKE V12 coupe (SIII)	71–74	7,297	$30,000	$50,000	B	★★★	6%
(For SIII, deduct $3,000 for automatic; $2,000 for disc wheels; $1,000 for no a/c. Add $3,000 for factory hard top.)							
XJ 220	91–93	300	$165,000	$200,000	B	★★★	8%
(Due to changes in U.S. DOT laws, XJ 220s can now be brought into the U.S.)							
XK8 coupe	97–04	n/a	$22,000	$55,000	D	★	10%
XK8 convertible	97–04	n/a	$30,000	$65,000	D	★	21%
XKR coupe	97–04	n/a	$35,000	$65,000	D	★	10%
XKR convertible	97–04	n/a	$35,000	$70,000	D	★	10%
JENSEN							
Interceptor II/III FHC	66–76	6,387	$12,000	$24,000	D	★★	n/c
Interceptor FF coupe	67–71	inc.	$14,000	$24,000	C	★★	n/c
Interceptor III DHC	74–76	inc.	$30,000	$50,000	C	★★★	38%
JENSEN-HEALEY							
Convertible	72–76	10,453	$5,400	$10,000	D	★★	-6%
GT	76	473	$5,700	$9,000	F	★★	n/c
LAGONDA							
M45 saloon	34–35	70	$90,000	$125,000	B	★★	n/c
M45 Tourer	34–35	inc.	$100,000	$145,000	A	★★★	n/c
LG6 DHC	36–40	n/a	$62,000	$125,000	B	★★★	n/c
LG6 Tourer	36–40	n/a	$85,000	$100,000	B	★★★	n/c
V12 Rapide roadster	38–40	25	$175,000	$225,000	A	★★★	n/c
V12 Touring	38–40	278	$65,000	$90,000	A	★★★	n/c
2.6-Liter DHC	48–53	517**	$22,000	$35,000	C	★★	n/c

PRICE GUIDE

	Yrs. Built	No. Made	Buy-Sell Price Range Low	High	Grade	Rating	1 Yr. % Change
3.0-Liter DHC	53–58	256**	$24,000	$40,000	C	★★	n/c
LAMBORGHINI							
350 GT	64–66	143	$150,000	$225,000	B	★★★★	15%
400 GT 2+2	66–68	244	$150,000	$200,000	B	★★★★	33%
Miura P400	66–69	465	$250,000	$350,000	B	★★★★	29%
400S	69–71	138	$300,000	$400,000	B	★★★★	21%
400SV	71–72	148	$650,000	$925,000	A	★★★★	21%
Espada	68–78	1,223	$28,000	$47,000	C	★★	n/c
Islero (400 GT version)	68–69	125	$85,000	$135,000	D	★★	36%
"S" version	69	100	$85,000	$135,000	D	★★	30%
Jarama (both versions)	70–76	327	$27,000	$42,000	D	★★	n/c
(Add $7,500 for "S".)							
Urraco P250	72–76	525	$15,000	$25,000	D	★★	n/c
P200	75–77	66	$15,000	$23,000	D	★★	n/c
P300	75–79	198	$25,000	$35,000	D	★★	n/c
Countach LP400 (Periscopo)	74–76	110	$250,000	$350,000	B	★★★★	42%
Countach LP400	77	40	$125,000	$200,000	B	★★★★	37%
LP400 S	76–82	235	$85,000	$105,000	B	★★★	n/c
LP5000 S	82–85	323	$85,000	$110,000	B	★★★	n/c
LP5000 QV	85–88	610	$100,000	$125,000	B	★★★	n/c
25th Anniversary	89	657	$110,000	$130,000	B	★★★	n/c
Silhouette	76–78	52	$35,000	$58,000	C	★★	n/c
Jalpa P350	82–88	410	$20,000	$47,000	D	★★	n/c
LM002	87–90	300	$50,000	$67,000	C	★★	n/c
(For American version, add $15k.)							
Diablo	90–93	n/a	$80,000	$100,000	D	★	-1%
Diablo VT	94–99	n/a	$100,000	$125,000	D	★	-2%
Diablo	96–01	n/a	$100,000	$125,000	D	★	-4%
Diablo VT roadster	96–99	466	$120,000	$150,000	D	★	-7%
Murcielago	02–	n/a	$170,000	$210,000	D	★	-9%
Murcielago roadster	05	n/a	$250,000	$290,000	D	★	-6%
Murcielago LP640	07–		est. MSRP	$335,000		★	-7%
Gallardo	04–	n/a	$135,000	$165,000	D	★	-5%
Gallardo Spyder	06–	n/a	$210,000	$245,000	B	★	-4%
LANCIA							
Appia GTZ, GTE (Zagato)	57–62	n/a	$60,000	$110,000	B	★★★	9%
Appia Sport (Zagato)	61–63	200	$70,000	$105,000	B	★★★	11%
Aurelia B20GT coupe S1-6	51–58	3,121	$70,000	$135,000	B	★★★	22%

(Note: S1, 2, & 3 were all RHD, and are valued higher in Europe than S4, 5, & 6 due to racing history. In the U.S., add $1,000 for Nardi steering wheel; $1,500 for Nardi floor shift; $5,000 for Nardi carb kit; $2,500 for period Webasto sunroof; $7,500 for Borrani wires.)

	Yrs. Built	No. Made	Buy-Sell Price Range Low	High	Grade	Rating	1 Yr. % Change
Aurelia B22 sedan	52–53	1,074	$55,000	$85,000	B	★★	18%
Aurelia B24 Spider America	54–55	240*	$350,000	$575,000	A	★★★★★	32%
(*Factory number, but probably optimistic.)							
Aurelia B24 convertible	55–59	521	$185,000	$250,000	A	★★★	-3%
(Add $5,000 for Nardi carb kit; $2,500 for factory hard top; $5,000 for Borrani wires.)							
Aurelia B50/B51 cabriolet	50–51	585**	$150,000	$250,000	B	★★★	19%
Aurelia B51 woody	50–51	47	$200,000	$300,000	B	★★★	35%
Flaminia GT Touring	60–65	1,703	$40,000	$60,000	C	★★	5%
GTL 2+2 Touring coupe	63–65	303	$40,000	$65,000	D	★★	5%
Flaminia convertible	60–64	847	$90,000	$110,000	B	★★★	40%
Flaminia Sport (Zagato)	59–67	599	$120,000	$150,000	A	★★	4%

(Four variations: Covered headlight 2.5L; open headlight 2.5L; double bubble sport with 2.8L; super sport with chopped tail. Add for all Flaminias: $5,000 for added triple Weber carbs; $4,000 for original 2.8L, 3C model.)

	Yrs. Built	No. Made	Buy-Sell Price Range Low	High	Grade	Rating	1 Yr. % Change
Flavia Sport (Zagato)	62–67	1,643	$25,000	$35,000	D	★★	33%
Flavia Vignale convertible	62–67	640	$25,000	$38,000	D	★★	8%
Fulvia coupe	65–73	104,679	$11,000	$18,000	C	★★	5%

	Yrs. Built	No. Made	Buy-Sell Price Range Low	High	Grade	Rating	1 Yr. % Change
Fulvia 1.2/1.3 HF coupe	65–68	1,317	$25,000	$40,000	B	★★★	5%
Fulvia 1.6 HF coupe	69–76	4,948	$22,000	$45,000	D	★★★★	25%
(For genuine early "Fanalone" cars, add 100%.)							
Fulvia Sport (Zagato) alloy	65–67	909	$17,000	$32,000	C	★★	6%
Fulvia Sport (Zagato) steel	67–72	6,193	$15,000	$31,000	C	★★	8%
Stratos Stradale	73–76	495	$185,000	$240,000	A	★★★★★	26%
Stratos Competizione	74–76	inc.	$175,000	$350,000	A	★★★★★	14%
LOTUS							
Six	53–58	110	$30,000	$40,000	C	★★	n/c
Seven SI	57–60	242	$28,000	$35,000	B	★★★	n/c
Seven S2	60–68	1,350	$30,000	$37,000	B	★★★	n/c
Seven S3	68–70	350	$20,000	$25,000	B	★★★	n/c
Seven S4	70–73	625	$11,000	$14,500	B	★★★	n/c
Caterham 7	74–82	n/a	$12,000	$17,000	D	★★	n/c
Lotus Eleven (S1 & S2)	56–60	270	$65,000	$90,000	A	★★★	n/c
Elite S1&2 (Climax eng)	58–63	1,076	$35,000	$50,000	B	★★★	n/c
(This number represents "complete body units" finished or not. Actual production number runs from 1,029 to 1,076.)							
Elan SI convertible	62–64	9,053	$18,500	$26,000	B	★★★	n/c
Elan S2 convertible	64–66	inc. SI	$21,500	$26,500	B	★★★	n/c
Elan S3 convertible	65–68	inc. SI	$17,000	$22,000	B	★★★	n/c
Elan S3 coupe	66–68	inc. cvt.	$13,000	$18,000	B	★★★	n/c
Elan Plus 2	67–74	4,798	$9,000	$12,500	D	★★	n/c
Elan S4 convertible	68–74	inc. SI	$19,000	$25,000	B	★★★	n/c
Elan S4 coupe	68–74	inc. cvt.	$11,000	$16,000	C	★★	n/c
Europa S1	67–68	8,969	$4,500	$7,700	C	★★★	n/c
Europa S2	69–72	inc.	$7,000	$11,000	C	★★★	n/c
Europa Twin Cam / Special	72–74	inc.	$12,000	$15,000	B	★★★	n/c
(217 TC/Specials were numbered; the rest were decaled and stickered.)							
Elan 26R (S1 & S2)	65–66	97	$95,000	$125,000	A	★★★	n/c
Europa 47	68–70	55	$65,000	$85,000	A	★★★	n/c
Cortina Mk I	62–66	2,894	$20,000	$30,000	C	★★	n/c
Cortina Mk II	67–70	4,032	$10,000	$11,500	D	★★	n/c
Elite S1	74–80	2,225	$5,500	$9,000	F	★★	n/c
Eclat S1 Sprint	75–80	1,302	$6,000	$10,000	F	★★	-3%
Esprit S1	76–78	718	$6,500	$10,000	D	★★	n/c
Esprit S2	78–81	1,045	$10,000	$14,500	D	★★	n/c
Esprit Turbo/Carbs (Giugiaro)	80–82	378	$8,250	$11,000	D	★★	-5%
Turbo	83–85	1,023	$11,000	$19,000	D	★★	-5%
Turbo/Inj. (Giugiaro)	85–87	506	$12,000	$19,000	C	★★	-3%

1959 Lotus Elite coupe

1972 Maserati Bora 4.7 coupe

	Yrs. Built	No. Made	Buy-Sell Price Range		Grade	Rating	1 Yr. % Change
			Low	High			
Turbo (new style/220-hp)	88	495	$15,000	$21,000	C	★★	-3%
Turbo (SE gearbox, 230-hp)	89	121	$15,000	$23,000	C	★★	n/c
Turbo SE (intercooled, 264-hp)	89–93	1,608	$15,000	$30,000	C	★★	n/c
Turbo S4 (264-hp)	94–95	385	$24,000	$35,000	B	★★	n/c
Turbo S4 (300-hp)	95	64	$25,000	$35,000	B	★★	n/c
Elan M100	90–91	3,855	$11,000	$16,000	D	★★	n/c
Elan S2	94	800	$11,000	$15,000	D	★★	n/c

Elan S2s were built for U.K. and R.o.W. only.)

	Yrs. Built	No. Made	Low	High	Grade	Rating	1 Yr. % Change
Esprit V8	97–03	3,500*	$30,000	$51,000	C	★	-5%
Elise (U.S. model)	05–		$35,000	$42,000	D	★	-8%

MASERATI

	Yrs. Built	No. Made	Low	High	Grade	Rating	1 Yr. % Change
A61500	46–50	61	$200,000	$400,000	B	★★★★	17%

(60 PF coupes, 1 Zagato)

A6GCS	47–53	16	$800,000	$1,000,000	A	★★★★	n/c
A6GCS/53	51–53	52	$1,200,000	$1,800,000	A	★★★★	22%
A6G54/A6G2000 Allemano coupe	54–57	21	$275,000	$450,000	B	★★★★	17%
A6G54/A6G2000 Frua Spyder	54–57	12	$650,000	$750,000	B	★★★★	18%
A6G54/A6G2000 Zagato coupe	54–57	20	$1,000,000	$1,600,000	A	★★★★	23%

(Also 6 Frua coupes, 1 Zagato Spyder built.)

150S	55–57	24	$850,000	$1,500,000	A	★★★★	n/c
200S, Si	55–58	30*	$1,500,000	$2,500,000	A	★★★	n/c
300S	55–58	28	$4,000,000	$4,500,000	A	★★★	n/c
450S	56–58	10	$5,000,000	$6,000,000	A	★★★	n/c
3500 GT, GTi	57–65	1,991	$75,000	$125,000	C	★★★	28%
3500 GT Vignale Spyder	59–64	227	$155,000	$285,000	B	★★★★	16%

(3500 add $5,000 for wires, $3,500 for 5-sp.)

5000 GT Allemano coupe	59–64	32	$400,000	$600,000	A	★★★★★	38%

(Prices vary considerably for special coachwork by Touring, Michelotti, Frua, Pinin Farina, Ghia, and Bertone.)

Birdcage Tipo T 60/61 front engine	59–61	22	$1,700,000	$2,800,000	A	★★★★	n/c
Birdcage Tipo 63/64 rear engine	60–61	6	$650,000	$900,000	B	★★★★	n/c
Sebring coupe SI	62–65	346	$50,000	$90,000	C	★★	21%
Sebring coupe SII	65–66	98	$45,000	$70,000	C	★★	14%
Quattroporte I	63–69	776	$12,000	$17,000	D	★★★	n/c
Mistral coupe	64–70	828	$35,000	$60,000	C	★★★	n/c
Mistral Spyder	64–69	120	$100,000	$200,000	B	★★★	35%
Mexico 4.2	65–68	250	$22,000	$32,000	D	★★★	n/c

	Yrs. Built	No. Made	Buy-Sell Price Range		Grade	Rating	1 Yr. % Change
			Low	High			

(Add $2,000 for 4.7 version.)

Ghibli 4.7L coupe	67–70	1,149	$55,000	$80,000	B	★★★	12%
Ghibli SS 4.9L coupe	70–73	inc.	$65,000	$100,000	B	★★★	12%
Ghibli Spyder 4.7L	69–71	100	$175,000	$275,000	B	★★★	11%
Ghibli SS Spyder 4.9L	71–72	25	$300,000	$400,000	B	★★★	29%
Indy	69–74	1,136	$16,000	$24,000	C	★★★	n/c

(Add $2,000 for 4.7L or 4.9L engine.)

Bora	71–80	571	$35,000	$55,000	B	★★★	13%
Merak	72–76	1,832	$15,000	$23,000	D	★★★	n/c
Khamsin	74–80	421	$18,500	$50,000	C	★★★	29%
Merak SS	76–80	277	$18,000	$25,000	C	★★★	n/c
Kyalami	77–82	150	$16,000	$26,000	C	★★★	n/c
Quattroporte II	73–75	13	$15,000	$50,000	C	★★	n/c
Quattroporte III	78–87	2,155	$15,000	$20,000	D	★	n/c
Biturbo coupe	84–94	18,895**	$7,500	$14,000	F	★	n/c
Biturbo Spyder	84–89	1,325**	$3,000	$6,000	F	★	n/c
Biturbo Spyder (Inj.)	86–94	1,331**	$6,500	$10,000	F	★	n/c

(For all Biturbos, deduct $2,000 for automatic.)

228	86–92	469	$6,500	$10,000	D	★★	n/c
430	87–94	995	$6,500	$10,000	D	★★	n/c
Spyder	02–04	n/a	$50,000	$70,000	C	★	n/c
Coupe	02–04	n/a	$55,000	$75,000	C	★	n/c
Quattroporte V	05–	n/a	$80,000	$95,000	D	★	n/c

MAZDA

RX-7	79	72,692 *	$4,000	$6,000	D	★★	20%
RX-7	80–85	435,000*	$3,500	$6,500	D	★★	30%
RX-7	93–95	14,000*	$10,000	$16,000	D	★★	8%

MCLAREN

F1	94–98	106	$2,500,000	$3,500,000	A	★★★★	38%

MERCEDES-BENZ

K Sedan Custom	26–30	150	$200,000	$300,000	B	★★★	n/c
K Tourer	26–30	inc.	$350,000	$525,000	A	★★★	n/c
S Rennsport	27–30	146	$3,000,000	$4,000,000	A	★★★★	n/c
S tourer	27–30	n/a	$1,800,000	$2,500,000	A	★★★★	n/c
SS tourer	28–35	107	$3,000,000	$4,000,000	A	★★★★	n/c
SS roadster	28–35	n/a	$750,000	$1,200,000	A	★★★★	n/c
SSK roadster	28–32	33	$7,000,000	$10,000,000	A	★★★	n/c
290 cabriolet	34–36	n/a	$125,000	$250,000	B	★★	n/c
380 cabriolet	33–34	154	$325,000	$460,000	A	★★★	n/c
500K Tourer	34–36	325	$1,300,000	$1,900,000	A	★★★	n/c
500K cabriolet b	34–36	inc.	$375,000	$560,000	A	★★★	n/c
500K Special roadster	34–36	29	$3,000,000	$5,000,000	A	★★★	n/c
540K coupe	36–39	419	$275,000	$350,000	A	★★★	n/c
540K cabriolet	36–39	inc.	$750,000	$1,250,000	A	★★★★	n/c
540K Special roadster	36–39	inc.	$3,000,000	$5,500,000	A	★★★★	n/c

190SL/300SL

190SL convertible	54–63	25,881	$35,000	$90,000	B	★★★	20%

(Add $1,500 for factory hard top.)

Gullwing (Steel body, Type 198.040)	54–57	1,371	$400,000	$650,000	A	★★★★★	12%
Gullwing (Alloy body, Type 198.043)	55–56	29	$1,000,000	$1,400,000	A	★★★★★	8%

(Add $20k for Rudge wheels; $5,000 for factory luggage. Deduct $8,000 for no belly pans.)

Roadster (drum brake, T. 198.042)	57–61	1,377	$400,000	$550,000	A	★★★★★	13%
Roadster (disc brake)	61–62	269	$475,000	$625,000	A	★★★★★	2%
Roadster (disc brake, alloy engine)	62–63	210	$500,000	$650,000	A	★★★★★	2%

(Disc brakes from S/N 2780 on, alloy engine block from S/N 3049 on. Add $25k for Rudge wheels; $5,000 for factory luggage; $5,000 for factory hard top.)

230/250/280SL

230SL	63–67	19,831	$30,000	$65,000	C	★★★	21%
250SL	67–68	5,196	$30,000	$55,000	C	★★★	n/c

	Yrs. Built	No. Made	Buy-Sell Price Range Low	High	Grade	Rating	1 Yr. % Change
280SL	68–71	23,885	$35,000	$80,000	C	★★★	4%

(Add $1,500 for 4-speed; $5,000 for ZF 5-speed. Deduct $2,500 for no hard top.)

(Note: '74 and later SLs and SLCs should be regarded as "used cars" without much collector potential. Condition is the prime determinant of value.)

	Yrs. Built	No. Made	Low	High	Grade	Rating	1 Yr. % Change
350SL / 450SL convertible	71–73	15,304	$11,000	$30,000	D	★★	2%

(Add %5 for chrome bumpers.)

	Yrs. Built	No. Made	Low	High	Grade	Rating	1 Yr. % Change
450SLC coupe	72–77	20,619	$10,000	$15,000	F	★★	n/c

(Add $3,000 for 1972–73 450SLC.)

	Yrs. Built	No. Made	Low	High	Grade	Rating	1 Yr. % Change
450SL convertible	74–79	45,097	$10,000	$18,000	D	★★	11%
450SLC 5.0 coupe	77–79	1,470	$15,000	$30,000	D	★★	11%
450SLC coupe	78–80	11,120	$10,000	$15,000	F	★★	14%
450SL convertible	78–80	21,201	$12,000	$20,000	D	★★	n/c
350SLC coupe	71–80	13,925	$7,500	$15,000	F	★★	n/c
380SLC coupe	81	1,991	$8,000	$12,000	F	★★	n/c
380SL convertible	80–83	24,083	$8,000	$15,000	D	★★	n/c
380SL convertible	84–85	19,805	$10,000	$20,000	D	★★	n/c

(Note: 380SL and 380SLC production numbers are for U.S. sales.)

	Yrs. Built	No. Made	Low	High	Grade	Rating	1 Yr. % Change
560SL convertible	86–87	49,347	$20,000	$30,000	D	★★	n/c
560SL convertible	88–89	inc.	$25,000	$40,000	D	★★	n/c
300SL convertible	90–92	n/a	$12,000	$18,000	D	★★	-10%

(Add 15% for 5-sp.)

	Yrs. Built	No. Made	Low	High	Grade	Rating	1 Yr. % Change
500SLC coupe	80–81	1,299	$20,000	$35,000	D	★★	9%

(Note: 450SLC 5.0 and 500SLC were produced in Europe only.)

	Yrs. Built	No. Made	Low	High	Grade	Rating	1 Yr. % Change
500SL convertible	90–92	n/a	$14,000	$20,000	D	★★	-9%
500E sedan	92–93	1,131	$22,000	$35,000	C	★★	9%
E500 sedan	94	374	$25,000	$40,000	C	★★	12%

(Note: 500E and E 500 production numbers are for U.S. sales.)

	Yrs. Built	No. Made	Low	High	Grade	Rating	1 Yr. % Change
C43 sedan	99–00	1,500	$13,000	$24,000	D	★	n/c
SLK roadster	97–04	n/a	$15,000	$28,000	D	★	-12%
SLR McLaren	04–07	3,500	$300,000	$400,000	D	★	-29%

Other Collectible Mercedes-Benz

	Yrs. Built	No. Made	Low	High	Grade	Rating	1 Yr. % Change
170S cabriolet A	49–51	2,394	$35,000	$50,000	C	★★★	6%
220 cabriolet A	51–55	1,167	$42,000	$100,000	B	★★★	12%
220 cabriolet B	51–55	950	$30,000	$50,000	B	★★★	n/c
220 coupe	54	83	$40,000	$75,000	B	★★★	22%

(13 hard top coupes w/sunroof, 70 w/o; production number includes A,B,C models.)

	Yrs. Built	No. Made	Low	High	Grade	Rating	1 Yr. % Change
300S (2-door) cabriolet	52–55	203	$175,000	$235,000	B	★★★	2%
300S coupe	52–55	216	$90,000	$140,000	B	★★	-4%
300S roadster	52–55	141	$175,000	$235,000	B	★★★	2%
300b 4-door sedan	51–55	6,214	$20,000	$30,000	D	★★	n/c
300b 4-door cabriolet B	51–55	91	$80,000	$125,000	B	★★★	20%
300c 4-door cabriolet C	55–56	51	$85,000	$145,000	B	★★★	4%
300c Sedan	55–58	1,432	$20,000	$35,000	D	★★	9%
300Sc coupe	55–58	98	$175,000	$220,000	B	★★★	3%
300Sc cabriolet A	55–58	49	$350,000	$475,000	A	★★★	3%
300Sc roadster	55–58	53	$350,000	$475,000	A	★★★	3%
220S cabriolet	56–59	3,290	$50,000	$75,000	C	★★★	8%
220S coupe	57–60	2,081	$22,000	$35,000	D	★★	5%
300d cabriolet D (Adenauer)	58–62	65	$125,000	$225,000	B	★★★	9%
300d 4-door sedan	57–62	3,077	$25,000	$40,000	D	★★	-8%
220SE coupe	58–60	n/a	$30,000	$50,000	C	★★★	25%
220SE cabriolet	58–60	n/a	$70,000	$150,000	B	★★★	5%
220SEb coupe 2-dr.	60–65	16,902	$20,000	$40,000	C	★★★	17%
220SEb cabriolet	60–65	inc.	$35,000	$60,000	B	★★★	11%
300SE cabriolet	62–67	3,127	$42,000	$72,000	B	★★★	8%
600 Limousine	63–81	2677	$55,000	$100,000	B	★★★	NL[†]
250SE coupe	66–68	6,213	$20,000	$30,000	C	★★★	n/c
250SE cabriolet	66–68	inc.	$40,000	$65,000	B	★★★	5%
300SEL 6.3	67–72	6,525	$25,000	$60,000	C	★★★	n/c
280SE coupe (high grille)	68–69	inc.	$25,000	$40,000	C	★★★	8%

	Yrs. Built	No. Made	Buy-Sell Price Range Low	High	Grade	Rating	1 Yr. % Change
280SE cabriolet (high grille)	68–69	5,187	$40,000	$68,000	B	★★★	3%
280SE coupe (low grille)	70–71	inc.	$30,000	$50,000	C	★★	6%
280SE cabriolet (low grille)	70–71	inc.	$60,000	$105,000	B	★★★	12%
280SE 3.5 coupe	70–71	3,270	$35,000	$70,000	C	★★	10%

(Add $3,000 for factory sunroof. Air conditioning standard on 808 U.S. sales; deduct $5,000 for no a/c.)

	Yrs. Built	No. Made	Low	High	Grade	Rating	1 Yr. % Change
280SE 3.5 cabriolet	70–71	1,232	$100,000	$175,000	B	★★★	-4%

(Add $1,000 for console shift automatic. Air conditioning standard on 801 U.S. sales; deduct $5,000 for no a/c.)

	Yrs. Built	No. Made	Low	High	Grade	Rating	1 Yr. % Change
450SEL 6.9	75–80	7,380	$15,000	$33,000	F	★	23%
190E-16 valve	86–87	2229 U.S.	$12,000	$20,000	F	★★	19%
C36 sedan	95–97	n/a	$10,000	$18,000	F	★	n/c

MERCURY

Cougar

	Yrs. Built	No. Made	Low	High	Grade	Rating	1 Yr. % Change
Coupe	67–70	320,496	$12,500	$18,000	C	★★	-15%
XR-7	67–68	59,933	$14,000	$21,000	C	★★	0%
XR-7G (Gurney)	67	37	$28,000	$38,000	C	★★	-6%
GT 390	67	8,444	$18,000	$28,000	C	★★	-13%
GT-E	68	602	$24,000	$28,000	C	★★	-6%
Eliminator	69–70	4,611	$14,000	$23,000	C	★★	-8%
Convertible	69–70	8,118	$15,000	$19,500	C	★★	-1%
XR-7 convertible	69–70	6,001	$17,000	$23,500	C	★★	-6%
Cougar convertible	71–73	4,247	$9,000	$14,000	D	★★	-7%
XR-7 convertible	71–73	6,811	$12,500	$17,500	D	★★	-18%

(For Eliminator, add $4,000 for Boss 302 engine; $6,000 for 428 CJ.)

Cyclone

	Yrs. Built	No. Made	Low	High	Grade	Rating	1 Yr. % Change
Cyclone GT	66–67	17,231	$13,500	$21,000	C	★★	10%
Convertible	66–67	2,536	$19,000	$28,000	C	★★	3%

(Add $7,500 for 390 engine.)

	Yrs. Built	No. Made	Low	High	Grade	Rating	1 Yr. % Change
Cyclone CJ	69	3,261	$16,000	$22,500	C	★★	-12%
Spoiler II	69	519	$16,500	$23,000	C	★★	-1%
Cyclone GT	70–71	12,457	$12,000	$18,500	C	★★	-8%
Spoiler	70–71	1,984	$12,500	$19,500	C	★★	-8%

(Add 50% for 429 CJ or SCJ.)

MG

	Yrs. Built	No. Made	Low	High	Grade	Rating	1 Yr. % Change
NA Magnette roadster	34–36	745	$35,000	$45,000	B	★★★	n/c
PA Midget roadster	34–35	1,900	$30,000	$43,000	C	★★★	n/c
PB Midget roadster	34–36	526	$42,000	$80,000	C	★★★	n/c
NB Magnette roadster	35–36	98	$37,000	$52,000	B	★★★	n/c
SA drophead coupe	36–39	300*	$36,000	$50,000	C	★★★	n/c
TA drophead coupe	36–39	3,000**	$25,000	$40,000	B	★★★	n/c
VA drophead coupe	37–39	576	$34,000	$62,000	B	★★★	n/c

1969 Mercedes-Benz 280SL convertible

1962 MG A Mk II roadster

	Yrs. Built	No. Made	Buy-Sell Price Range		Grade	Rating	1 Yr. % Change
			Low	High			
WA drophead coupe	38–39	51	$30,000	$40,000	B	★★★	n/c
TB roadster	39–40	379	$20,000	$40,000	C	★★★	n/c
MG TC	45–49	10,000	$30,000	$45,000	B	★★★	n/c
MG TD	49–53	29,664	$20,000	$28,000	B	★★★	-8%
MG TF 1250	53–54	6,200	$25,000	$35,000	B	★★★	n/c
MG TF 1500	55	3,400	$28,000	$40,000	B	★★★	n/c
MG A 1500 roadster	55–59	58,750	$25,000	$35,000	B	★★★	n/c
MG A 1500 coupe	55–59	inc. rdstr.	$20,000	$26,000	C	★★★	n/c
MG A Twin-Cam roadster	58–60	2,111	$35,000	$45,000	B	★★★	n/c
MG A Twin-Cam coupe	58–60	inc. rdstr.	$30,000	$35,000	B	★★★	n/c
MG A 1600 roadster	59–61	31,501	$23,000	$35,000	B	★★★	-17%
MG A 1600 coupe	59–61	inc.	$20,000	$30,000	C	★★★	8%
MG A DeLuxe roadster	60–61	82	$30,000	$40,000	B	★★★	n/c
MG A 1600 Mk II roadster	61–62	8,719	$25,000	$35,000	B	★★★	n/c
MG A 1600 Mk II coupe	61–62	inc. rdstr.	$25,000	$35,000	C	★★★	n/c
MG A Mk II DeLuxe roadster	61–62	313	$30,000	$45,000	B	★★★	n/c
MG B convertible Mk I	62–67	387,675	$15,000	$22,000	B	★★★	n/c
MG B (chrome bumper)	68–74	inc.	$12,000	$17,000	B	★★★	n/c
MG B (rubber bumper)	75–80	inc.	$3,000	$8,000	D	★★★	-18%

(For MG B, add $1,000 for factory hard top; $500 for overdrive. For MG A/B, deduct $2,000 for disc wheels, except on Twin-Cam and DeLuxe.)

	Yrs. Built	No. Made	Low	High	Grade	Rating	1 Yr. % Change
MG B-GT	65–67	125,597	$8,500	$12,000	B	★★★	n/c
MG B-GT	68–74	inc.	$7,500	$10,000	C	★★★	n/c
MG B-GT V8	73–76	2,591	$13,000	$17,000	B	★★★	n/c
MG C convertible	67–69	4,552	$12,000	$24,000	B	★★★	n/c
MG C-GT	67–69	4,457	$10,000	$19,000	C	★★	-3%

(Deduct $1,000 for automatic.)

	Yrs. Built	No. Made	Low	High	Grade	Rating	1 Yr. % Change
Midget	61–64	16,080	$6,000	$10,000	D	★★★	n/c
Midget	64–66	22,601	$5,000	$7,500	D	★★★	n/c
Midget	66–74	99,896	$5,000	$7,500	D	★★	n/c

(1967 model is the highest valued, at up to $1,000 more.)

	Yrs. Built	No. Made	Low	High	Grade	Rating	1 Yr. % Change
Midget	74–79	73,899	$4,800	$7,000	D	★★	-4%

MORETTI

	Yrs. Built	No. Made	Low	High	Grade	Rating	1 Yr. % Change
GS Bialbero (750-cc)	54–56	96	$190,000	$275,000	B	★★★	20%
Barchetta Bialbero (750-cc)	63–69	n/a	$300,000	$400,000	B	★★★	29%

(Spare engines are non-existent. Cars w/o engines have marginal value at best. Add 25% for documented, significant history.)

MORGAN

	Yrs. Built	No. Made	Low	High	Grade	Rating	1 Yr. % Change
Flat radiator models	45–53	750*	$30,000	$40,000	B	★★★	n/c

	Yrs. Built	No. Made	Buy-Sell Price Range		Grade	Rating	1 Yr. % Change
			Low	High			
Plus 4 (Triumph powered)	54–68	3,390	$30,000	$50,000	B	★★★	n/c
4/4 (Ford powered)	54–90	n/a	$20,000	$35,000	B	★★★	n/c

(Prices are for 4-seat models. For 2-seat and DHC models, add $4,000. For SS, add $4,000.)

	Yrs. Built	No. Made	Low	High	Grade	Rating	1 Yr. % Change
SS	60–69	102	$75,000	$100,000	A	★★★	n/c

(Factory-built only, matching numbers.)

	Yrs. Built	No. Made	Low	High	Grade	Rating	1 Yr. % Change
Plus 8	68–90	2,500	$40,000	$60,000	C	★★★	n/c

MUNTZ

	Yrs. Built	No. Made	Low	High	Grade	Rating	1 Yr. % Change
Jet	51–54	394	$50,000	$85,000	C	★★	n/c

NASH-HEALEY

	Yrs. Built	No. Made	Low	High	Grade	Rating	1 Yr. % Change
Roadster (Healey)	51	105	$120,000	$170,000	B	★★	NL†
Roadster (Pininfarina)	52–53	252	$160,000	$220,000	B	★★★	NL†
LeMans Coupe	53–54	150	$65,000	$95,000	C	★★	NL†

NISSAN

	Yrs. Built	No. Made	Low	High	Grade	Rating	1 Yr. % Change
300ZX	84–89	219,076	$2,500	$4,250	F	★	n/c
300ZX Turbo	84–89	44,966	$2,750	$4,500	F	★★	n/c
300ZX Twin Turbo	89–90	6,896	$3,000	$6,000	F	★★	n/c
300ZX Twin Turbo	91–93	9,187	$5,000	$8,500	F	★	-4%
300ZX Twin Turbo	94–96	2,191	$6,000	$10,000	F	★	-13%

(Deduct $1,000 for 2+2 body style.)

OLDSMOBILE

	Yrs. Built	No. Made	Low	High	Grade	Rating	1 Yr. % Change
442	64	2,999	$14,000	$22,000	C	★★	-8%
442	65	25,003	$13,500	$21,000	C	★★	-6%
442	66–67	46,826*	$14,000	$23,500	C	★★	-11%
Convertible	66–67	5,933	$18,000	$27,500	C	★★	-19%
442	68–69	36,642	$14,000	$22,500	C	★★	-10%
Convertible	68–69	9,437	$18,000	$28,000	C	★★	-24%
W-30	68–69	2,300	$33,000	$48,000	B	★★	1%

(Add 25% for 4-sp.)

	Yrs. Built	No. Made	Low	High	Grade	Rating	1 Yr. % Change
Hurst 442	68–69	1,421	$33,000	$47,500	C	★★	-37%
442	70–71	27,189	$22,500	$31,000	C	★★	-10%
Convertible	70–71	4,237	$24,000	$34,500	B	★★	-24%
W-30	70–71	4,020	$52,000	$62,000	B	★★	-14%
Convertible	70–71	374	$160,000	$325,000	B	★★★	-8%

(For '70–71 442 and W-30, add 25% for 4-sp.)

	Yrs. Built	No. Made	Low	High	Grade	Rating	1 Yr. % Change
Rallye 350	70	3,547	$19,000	$27,500	C	★★	-29%
SX 455	70–71	9,374	$18,000	$25,000	C	★★	-12%
Convertible	70–71	inc.	$21,500	$26,000	C	★★	-43%
442	72	9,845	$12,500	$20,000	C	★★	-14%
Convertible	72	1,171	$15,000	$24,000	C	★★	-23%
W-30	72	772	$30,000	$35,000	C	★★	-12%
Convertible	72	113	$38,000	$55,000	B	★★	-40%
Hurst	72	499	$21,000	$30,000	C	★★	-6%
Pace Car convertible	72	130	$27,500	$40,000	C	★★	-10%

OPEL

	Yrs. Built	No. Made	Low	High	Grade	Rating	1 Yr. % Change
GT	69–73	n/a	$4,500	$8,500	D	★★	19%

OSCA

	Yrs. Built	No. Made	Low	High	Grade	Rating	1 Yr. % Change
MT4 1100	48–56	35	$650,000	$850,000	A	★★★★	23%
MT4 1350	49–50	8	$700,000	$900,000	A	★★★★	24%
MT4 1450	53–55	8	$850,000	$950,000	A	★★★★	26%
MT4 1500	54–56	27	$950,000	$1,100,000	A	★★★★	25%
TN 1500	55–56	2	$950,000	$1,100,000	A	★★★★	25%
F2/S 1500	57–58	4	$850,000	$1,000,000	A	★★★★	24%
FS 1500	58	4	$600,000	$800,000	A	★★★★	23%
Type J	59–64	15	$120,000	$160,000	A	★★★★	14%
750S	56–60	17	$400,000	$500,000	A	★★★★	14%
950S	56	1	$450,000	$500,000	A	★★★★	12%
1100S	57–59	5	$500,000	$550,000	A	★★★★	9%
1500S	57	3	$800,000	$1,000,000	A	★★★★	15%
1600S	60	2	$550,000	$800,000	A	★★★★	29%

Model	Yrs. Built	No. Made	Low	High	Grade	Rating	1 Yr. % Change
1000S	61	1	$450,000	$550,000	A	★★★★	30%
2000S	54-60	5	$850,000	$1,050,000	A	★★★★	12%
1600 GT	60-65	128	$190,000	$300,000	B	★★★★	-4%

(1600 GT price is for Zagato Berlinetta. Deduct $100k for Fissore or Boneschi body.)

PEGASO

Model	Yrs. Built	No. Made	Low	High	Grade	Rating	1 Yr. % Change
ENASA coupe	50-52	14	$350,000	$540,000	A	★★★★	33%
Saoutchik coupe	52-55	14	$350,000	$450,000	A	★★★★	31%
Saoutchik cabriolet	52-54	4	$350,000	$450,000	A	★★★	9%
Touring coupe (flat windshield)	53-57	30	$350,000	$450,000	A	★★★	25%
Touring coupe Panoramica	55-57	8	$400,000	$500,000	A	★★★	11%
Serra roadster	55-56	3	$300,000	$400,000	A	★★★	32%

PLYMOUTH

Barracuda

Model	Yrs. Built	No. Made	Low	High	Grade	Rating	1 Yr. % Change
Barracuda	64-65	88,039	$9,500	$13,000	C	★★	n/c
Formula S	65-66	14,695	$14,000	$19,250	C	★★	n/c
Barracuda	67-69	139,993**	$8,000	$11,500	C	★★	-15%
Formula S	67-69	65,000*	$18,000	$25,000	C	★★	-9%
Convertible	67-69	8,510	$15,500	$22,000	C	★★	-12%
Formula S 383	67-69	37,317	$28,000	$37,500	C	★★	-15%
Cuda 440	69	360	$50,000	$68,000	C	★★	-10%
Super Stock Hemi	68	70	$200,000	$250,000	B	★★★	-22%
Gran Coupe	70-71	9,798	$18,000	$23,000	C	★★	-10%
Convertible	70-71	2,568	$31,000	$40,000	C	★★	-13%
Cuda 340/383	70-71	n/a	$40,000	$50,000	C	★★	-22%
Cuda 440	70-71	952	$40,000	$60,000	C	★★	-10%
Cuda 440 Six Pack	70-71	1,992	$65,000	$85,000	B	★★	-17%
Cuda Convertible	70-71	1,009	$50,000	$75,000	C	★★	-12%
Cuda Six Pack Convertible	70	29	$200,000	$250,000	B	★★★	-17%
Cuda Six Pack Convertible	71	17	$250,000	$275,000	B	★★★	-19%

(For previous four models, add 25% for 4-sp; 10% for Track Pak, 25% for Shaker hood; additional 40% for 1971 model year.)

Model	Yrs. Built	No. Made	Low	High	Grade	Rating	1 Yr. % Change
AAR 'Cuda	70	2,724	$55,000	$90,000	B	★★★	-10%
Hemi 'Cuda	70	652	$125,000	$200,000	A	★★★	-23%
Hemi 'Cuda convertible	70	14	$900,000	$1,500,000	A	★★★	-25%

(Add 25% for 4-sp; 10% for Track Pak.)

Model	Yrs. Built	No. Made	Low	High	Grade	Rating	1 Yr. % Change
Hemi 'Cuda	71	107	$325,000	$500,000	A	★★★	-33%
Hemi 'Cuda convertible	71	7	$1,300,000	$1,800,000	A	★★★	-13%

(Add 25% for 4-sp.)

Belvedere

Model	Yrs. Built	No. Made	Low	High	Grade	Rating	1 Yr. % Change
Belvedere Hemi	66-67	64*	$55,000	$75,000	B	★★	-27%

GTX

Model	Yrs. Built	No. Made	Low	High	Grade	Rating	1 Yr. % Change
GTX	67	11,429	$21,000	$30,000	C	★★	-18%
Convertible	67	680	$24,000	$34,000	C	★★	-38%
Hemi	67	720	$75,000	$95,000	B	★★	-15%
Convertible	67	inc.	$175,000	$225,000	B	★★★	-25%
GTX	68-70	1,651	$29,000	$58,000	C	★★	-15%
Convertible	68-70	inc.	$49,000	$58,000	C	★★	-12%
Hemi	68-70	729	$85,000	$105,000	B	★★★	-18%
Convertible	68-70	47	$200,000	$300,000	B	★★★	-25%
Six Pack	70	678	$60,000	$75,000	C	★★	-7%
GTX	71	2,538	$29,000	$39,000	C	★★	-18%
Six Pack	71	135	$65,000	$80,000	C	★★	-10%
Hemi	71	30	$100,000	$150,000	B	★★★	-40%

Road Runner

Model	Yrs. Built	No. Made	Low	High	Grade	Rating	1 Yr. % Change
Road Runner	68-70	2,952	$20,000	$35,000	C	★★	-36%
Convertible	69-70	inc.	$45,000	$65,000	C	★★	-18%
Six Pack	69-70	3,929	$45,000	$65,000	B	★★	-23%
Hemi	68-70	1,938	$95,000	$125,000	B	★★★	-25%

(Add 50% for 1969.5 Six Pack M-code; add 25% for Hemi 4-sp; deduct 20% for 1968 model.)

Model	Yrs. Built	No. Made	Low	High	Grade	Rating	1 Yr. % Change
Road Runner	71	7,952	$26,000	$36,000	C	★★	-13%
Six Pack	71	246	$65,000	$90,000	C	★★	-16%
Hemi	71	55	$125,000	$175,000	B	★★★	-25%
Road Runner/GTX	72-74	38,239*	$17,000	$20,000	C	★★★	-14%

*(*indicates Road Runner only)*

Satellite

Model	Yrs. Built	No. Made	Low	High	Grade	Rating	1 Yr. % Change
Hemi	66-67	817	$55,000	$75,000	C	★★★	-31%
Convertible	66-67	27	$125,000	$145,000	B	★★★	-28%

Superbird

Model	Yrs. Built	No. Made	Low	High	Grade	Rating	1 Yr. % Change
Superbird (440)	70	1,069	$85,000	$120,000	B	★★★	-17%
Six Pack	70	716	$140,000	$200,000	B	★★★	-10%
Hemi	70	135	$250,000	$300,000	B	★★★	-13%

(Add 25% for 4-sp.)

PONTIAC

Firebird

Model	Yrs. Built	No. Made	Low	High	Grade	Rating	1 Yr. % Change
V8 coupe	67-69	200,752	$12,000	$16,000	C	★★	-14%
Convertible	67-69	39,069	$15,000	$19,500	C	★★	-28%
400 coupe	67-69	inc.	$17,500	$23,000	C	★★	-23%
Convertible	67-69	inc.	$24,000	$33,000	C	★★	-16%
Trans Am (Ram Air IV add 75%)	69	697	$65,000	$100,000	B	★★★	-18%
Formula	70-73	30,926	$16,000	$22,000	C	★★	-3%
Trans Am	70-73	11,400	$19,000	$28,000	C	★★	-13%
Trans Am SD-455 ('73 add 50%)	73-74	1,155	$35,000	$55,000	B	★★	-11%
Formula SD-455 ('73 add 50%)	73-74	101	$38,000	$52,500	B	★★	-2%

(For all 1967-74, add 25% for 4-sp.; add $4,000 for Ram Air III on 400 engine; $1,000 for Formula; $1,000 for 455 engine.)

Model	Yrs. Built	No. Made	Low	High	Grade	Rating	1 Yr. % Change
Trans Am	74-76	84,230	$14,000	$21,000	D	★★★	23%
Trans Am 455	75-76	73,975	$15,000	$22,000	D	★★★	25%
Trans Am	77-78	162,086	$10,000	$18,000	D	★★★	9%
Trans Am 10th Anniversary	79	7,500	$14,500	$22,500	D	★★★	3%
Trans Am	79-81	201,497	$9,500	$16,000	D	★★★	4%
Turbo Pace Car	81	2,000	$11,500	$18,000	D	★★	-12%
Trans Am 15th Anniversary	84	55,374	$8,250	$11,500	F	★★	-1%

GTO

Model	Yrs. Built	No. Made	Low	High	Grade	Rating	1 Yr. % Change
Coupe	64	24,806	$21,000	$32,000	C	★★	-9%
Convertible	64	6,644	$24,000	$37,500	B	★★	-17%
Coupe	65	64,041	$29,000	$38,000	C	★★	-10%
Convertible	65	11,311	$35,000	$45,000	B	★★	-25%

1978 Pontiac Trans Am

1964 Porsche 356C coupe

	Yrs. Built	No. Made	Buy-Sell Price Range Low	High	Grade	Rating	1 Yr. % Change
Coupe	66	84,148	$21,000	$28,000	C	★★	-14%
Convertible	66	12,798	$32,000	$43,000	B	★★	-13%
Coupe	67	72,205	$27,500	$34,000	C	★★	-6%
Convertible	67	9,517	$38,000	$50,000	B	★★	-14%
Coupe	68	77,704	$17,000	$23,000	C	★★	-23%
Convertible	68	9,980	$22,500	$32,500	B	★★	-13%
Coupe	69	58,126	$23,000	$30,000	C	★★	-9%
Convertible	69	7,328	$27,500	$35,000	C	★★	-9%
Judge	69	6,725	$55,000	$75,000	B	★★	-12%
Judge Convertible	69	108	$125,000	$145,000	B	★★★	-20%
GTO	70	32,737	$22,000	$27,500	C	★★	-17%
Convertible	70	3,615	$27,500	$35,000	C	★★	-16%
Judge	70	3,629	$50,000	$70,000	C	★★	-13%
Judge Convertible	70	168	$130,000	$140,000	C	★★★	-13%
Coupe	71	9,497	$18,000	$22,000	C	★★	-10%
Convertible	71	357	$22,000	$29,500	C	★★	-18%
Judge	71	661	$70,000	$90,000	C	★★	-13%
Judge Convertible	71	17	$150,000	$190,000	C	★★★	-54%
Coupe	72	5,807	$12,500	$15,000	C	★★	-16%
Coupe	73	4,806	$11,000	$14,000	C	★★	20%

(For all GTOs, add 20% for 4-sp.)

(For 1964–66, add 35% for Tri-Power. For 1967–69, add 40% for Ram-Air III; 75% for Ram-Air IV.)

(For 1970–72, add 15% for 455 V8; 50% for 455 HO V8.)

PORSCHE

356

	Yrs. Built	No. Made	Buy-Sell Price Range Low	High	Grade	Rating	1 Yr. % Change
356 coupe "pre-A"	50-55	7,627	$45,000	$55,000	B	★★★	n/c

(Two-piece windshield until April '52. One-piece "bent" window until Oct. '55. Standard one-piece curved from then on.)

356 cabriolet	50-55	1,685	$75,000	$90,000	B	★★★★	15%
356 Speedster	54-55	1,233	$115,000	$160,000	B	★★★★	35%
356A coupe	56-59	13,010	$45,000	$55,000	B	★★★	n/c
356A cabriolet	56-59	3,367	$65,000	$75,000	B	★★★	n/c
356A Speedster	56-58	2,911	$125,000	$175,000	B	★★★★	37%
356A convertible D	59	1,330	$80,000	$90,000	B	★★★★	15%

(For 356 and 356A, add $5,000 for Super engine.)

356A Carrera GS coupe	56-59	541	$175,000	$200,000	A	★★★★	13%

(This is total production for all GS and GT cars. Numbers below included.)

356A Carrera GS cabriolet	56-59	140	$175,000	$200,000	A	★★★	13%
356A Carrera Speedster	56-59	75	$200,000	$225,000	A	★★★★	7%
356A Carrera GT coupe	56-59	n/a	$180,000	$200,000	A	★★★	1%

	Yrs. Built	No. Made	Buy-Sell Price Range Low	High	Grade	Rating	1 Yr. % Change
356A Carrera GT Speedster	56-59	72	$250,000	$285,000	A	★★★	2%

(There were 7 pushrod GT Speedsters built.)

356B coupe (T-5 body)	60-61	8,556	$25,000	$35,000	C	★★	18%
365B cabriolet (T-5)	60-61	3,091	$40,000	$55,000	B	★★★	n/c
356B roadster (T-5)	60-61	2,649	$70,000	$85,000	B	★★★	-3%
356B Notchback (T-5)	60-61	1,048	$19,000	$23,000	D	★★	17%

(Spotter's Note: T-5 body has gas filler cap inside trunk; T-6 has external gas filler cap.)

(For 356B, add $5,000 for Super engine; $7,000 for Super-90.)

356B coupe (T-6)	62-63	6,289	$28,000	$38,000	C	★★★	n/c
356B cabriolet (T-6)	62-63	3,096	$55,000	$65,000	B	★★★	n/c
356B "twin-grille" roadster (T-6)	1962	248	$100,000	$120,000	B	★★★	n/c
356B Notchback (T-6)	1962	697	$20,000	$27,000	D	★★★	-2%
Carrera 2 GS	62-65	360	$170,000	$200,000	A	★★★★	3%
Carrera 2 cabriolet	62-64	88	$200,000	$230,000	A	★★★★	2%
356C coupe	63-65	13,507	$28,000	$40,000	C	★★★	n/c
356C cabriolet	63-65	3,174	$55,000	$75,000	B	★★★	n/c
356 coupe SC	63-65	inc. coupe	$30,000	$48,000	B	★★★	n/c
356 cabriolet SC	63-65	inc. cab	$60,000	$80,000	B	★★★	n/c

(For all 356, add sunroof, $5,000; Rudge wheels, $12k; cabriolet hard top, $3,000; Speedster hard top, $6,000. Deduct 15% of value for wrong engine per Kardex; 25% of value for improper exterior color for model year.)

911: Small Bumper, Short Wheelbase

911 2.0 coupe	65	235	$50,000	$65,000	B	★★★	4%
911 2.0 coupe	66-68	10,399	$22,000	$37,000	B	★★★	7%
911 2.0 Targa	67-68	1,427	$27,000	$41,000	B	★★★	15%
911S 2.0 coupe	67-68	4,689	$44,000	$74,000	A	★★★★	41%
911S 2.0 Targa	67-68	1,160	$52,000	$82,000	A	★★★★	48%
911L 2.0 coupe	68	1,169	$20,000	$35,000	B	★★★	n/c
911L 2.0 Targa	68	307	$20,000	$35,000	B	★★★	n/c

911: Small Bumper, Long Wheelbase

911T 2.2 coupe	69-71	13,019	$20,000	$35,000	B	★★★	n/c
911T 2.2 Targa	69-71	7,303	$25,000	$38,000	B	★★★	13%
911E 2.2 coupe	69-71	5,027	$22,000	$37,000	B	★★★	n/c
911E 2.2 Targa	69-71	935	$25,000	$39,000	B	★★★	8%
911S 2.2 coupe	69-71	1,430	$40,000	$70,000	B	★★★★	27%
911S 2.2 Targa	69-71	2,131	$50,000	$80,000	A	★★★★	38%

(Add 15%–30% for Soft-Window Targa. Deduct 15% for 1969 2.0L cars.)

911T 2.4 coupe	72-73	9,964	$20,000	$30,000	B	★★★	n/c
911T 2.4 Targa	72-73	7,968	$22,000	$33,000	B	★★★	9%

(Add $2,000 for 1973.5 911T w/ CIS injection.)

911E 2.4 coupe	72-73	2,490	$22,000	$32,000	B	★★★	n/c
911E 2.4 Targa	72-73	1,916	$22,000	$32,000	B	★★★	n/c
911S 2.4 coupe	72-73	3,180	$40,000	$60,000	A	★★★★	16%
911S 2.4 Targa	72-73	1,914	$44,000	$66,000	A	★★★★	24%

(Add $1,000 for sunroof. Deduct $1,000 for 4-speed transmission.)

Carrera RSL "Touring"	73	1,360	$165,000	$200,000	A	★★★★	18%
Carrera RS "Light-weight"	73	200	$250,000	$350,000	A	★★★★	n/c

911: Federalized Bumper

Carrera 2.7 Euro coupe	74-75	16,977	$30,000	$35,000	B	★★★	n/c
911S 2.7 coupe	74-77	17,124	$8,000	$13,000	D	★★★	n/c
911S 2.7 Targa	74-77	inc.	$8,000	$13,000	D	★★★	n/c
Carrera 2.7 coupe (U.S.)	74-75	3,353	$10,000	$15,000	C	★★★	n/c
Carrera 2.7 Targa (U.S.)	74-75	inc.	$10,000	$15,000	C	★★★	n/c
Carrera 3.0 coupe (Euro)	76-77	3,691	$15,000	$17,000	C	★★★	n/c
Carrera 3.0 Targa (Euro)	76-77	inc.	$15,000	$17,000	C	★★★	n/c

911SC: Federalized Bumper, Wide Body

911SC coupe	78-83	35,607	$11,000	$15,000	C	★★	-15%
911SC Targa	78-83	27,678	$11,000	$15,000	C	★★	-15%
911 "Weissach" Edition	80	408	$14,000	$18,000	B	★★	n/c

	Yrs. Built	No. Made	Buy-Sell Price Range Low	High	Grade	Rating	1 Yr. % Change
911 Ferry Porsche Edition	82	200	$14,000	$18,000	B	★★	n/c
911SC cabriolet	83	4,187	$14,000	$17,000	B	★★	-3%
930 Turbo							
930 Turbo 3.0 coupe	75	284	$22,000	$32,000	B	★★	30%
930 Turbo 3.0 coupe	76–77	2,596	$26,000	$36,000	B	★★	34%
930 Turbo 3.3 coupe	78–85	10,004	$26,000	$36,000	B	★★	26%

(2,918 U.S. legal production. All '75 and '80-'85 930s are gray-market. Deduct 35% for gray-market, 50% if no EPA/DOT papers.)

	Yrs. Built	No. Made	Low	High	Grade	Rating	1 Yr. % Change
Carrera and Speedster							
Carrera	84–86	36,834	$15,000	$18,000	C	★★	-3%
Carrera Targa	84–86	19,502	$15,000	$18,000	C	★★	-3%
Carrera cabriolet	84–86	22,283	$16,000	$19,000	C	★★	-3%
Carrera	87–89	inc.	$17,000	$23,000	C	★★	-5%
Carrera Targa	87–89	inc.	$17,000	$23,000	C	★★	-5%
Carrera cabriolet	87–89	inc.	$21,000	$25,000	C	★★	n/c

(Add for factory wide-body appearance group, $5,000; factory Turbo-look, $5,000.)

	Yrs. Built	No. Made	Low	High	Grade	Rating	1 Yr. % Change
(Add for factory wide-body appearance group, $5,000; factory Turbo-look, $5,000.)	86–89	4,363	$26,000	$32,000	C	★★	17%
911 Turbo 3.3 cabriolet	87–89	2,002	$30,000	$37,000	C	★★	6%
911 Turbo 3.3 slantnose	87–89	675	$28,000	$35,000	C	★★	10%
911 Turbo 3.3 Targa	87–89	657	$25,000	$32,000	C	★★	n/c
Carrera Club Sport	88	340	$25,000	$29,000	C	★★★	n/c
25th Anniversary coupe	89	875	$21,000	$25,000	C	★★	n/c
25th Anniversary cabriolet	89	inc. above	$23,000	$27,000	C	★★	n/c

(For U.S., 120 coupes, 100 cabs, 80 Targas. Deduct 25% for any gray-market Turbo.)

	Yrs. Built	No. Made	Low	High	Grade	Rating	1 Yr. % Change
Speedster	89	2,065	$50,000	$60,000	C	★★★	9%
964							
Carrera 2	90–94	n/a	$20,000	$24,000	C	★★	-5%
Carrera 2 Targa	90–94	n/a	$20,000	$24,000	C	★★	-5%
Carrera 2 cabriolet	90–91	n/a	$20,000	$26,000	C	★★	n/c
Carrera 4	89–94	n/a	$20,000	$24,000	C	★★	-5%
Carrera 4 Targa	90–94	n/a	$20,000	$26,000	C	★★	n/c
Carrera 4 cabriolet	90–91	n/a	$20,000	$26,000	C	★★	n/c
C2 Turbo coupe	91–93	5,125	$35,000	$43,000	C	★★	n/c

(Add 20% for 1992 380-hp S models, 80 built.)

	Yrs. Built	No. Made	Low	High	Grade	Rating	1 Yr. % Change
America roadster	92–93	n/a	$40,000	$50,000	B	★★★	6%
Carrera 2 Speedster	93–94	925	$45,000	$50,000	B	★★	6%
993							
Carrera	95–97	46,919	$25,000	$40,000	C	★	-12%
Carrera 4	95–96	inc.	$25,000	$40,000	C	★	-12%
Carrera cabriolet	95–98	inc.	$25,000	$40,000	C	★	-12%
Carrera 4 cabriolet	95–98	inc.	$25,000	$40,000	C	★	-12%
Carrera Targa	96–98	inc.	$25,000	$40,000	C	★	-12%
Carrera 4S	96–98	inc.	$31,000	$45,000	C	★	-9%
Carrera S	97–98	inc.	$31,000	$45,000	C	★	-9%
993 Twin Turbo	96–97	n/a	$65,000	$75,000	B	★	-14%
993 Turbo S	97	180	$75,000	$100,000	B	★	-14%
996							
Carrera	99–04	n/a	$22,000	$45,000	C	★	-12%
Carrera 4	99–04	n/a	$22,000	$45,000	C	★	-12%
Carrera cabriolet	99–04	n/a	$22,000	$45,000	C	★	-12%
Carrera 4 cabriolet	99–04	n/a	$22,000	$45,000	C	★	-12%
Carrera Turbo	02–04	n/a	$50,000	$80,000	C	★	-8%
Carrera Targa	02–04	n/a	$40,000	$60,000	C	★	-10%
GT3	99–01	n/a	$58,000	$85,000	B	★	-8%
GT2	02–04	n/a	$135,000	$150,000	B	★	-11%
997							
Carrera	05–	n/a	$55,000	$65,000	C	★	-13%
Carrera 4	05–	n/a	$60,000	$70,000	C	★	-12%

	Yrs. Built	No. Made	Buy-Sell Price Range Low	High	Grade	Rating	1 Yr. % Change
912							
912 coupe (1.6L)	66–69	29,212	$6,500	$9,000	D	★★★	-6%
(Add $500 for Targa, $2,500 for Soft-Window Targa.)							
912E coupe (2.0L)	76	2,099	$6,500	$9,000	D	★★★	-6%
914							
914-4 (1.7L)	70–73	114,479	$6,000	$9,000	C	★★★	13%
914-6	70–72	3,351	$25,000	$30,000	B	★★★	42%
914-6 GT	71	11	$95,000	$170,000	A	★★★	15%
914 R	72	4	$75,000	$125,000	A	★★★	n/c
916 (2.7 RS spec engine)	72	20	$75,000	$125,000	A	★★★	n/c
914S (aka 914-8)*	72	2	$100,000	$150,000	A	★★★	n/c
*(*Custom built for Porsche family members.)*							
914-4 (2.0L)	73–76	inc. abv.	$7,000	$10,000	B	★★★	n/c
914-4 (1.8L)	74–76	inc. abv.	$5,000	$7,500	C	★★★	n/c
924							
924	77–82	122,304	$3,200	$4,500	F	★★	n/c
924 Turbo	78–83	12,356	$3,300	$5,500	D	★★	n/c
924 S	87–88	n/a	$4,500	$6,000	D	★★	n/c
928							
928	78–82	n/a	$6,000	$8,000	D	★★	n/c
928 S	83–86	n/a	$9,000	$12,000	D	★★	n/c
928 S4	87–88	n/a	$11,500	$13,500	D	★★	n/c
928 S4	89–90	n/a	$17,500	$22,500	D	★★	n/c
928 S4	91–92	n/a	$20,000	$25,000	D	★★	-7%
(Add $1,500 for 928 GT.)							
928 GTS	93–95	n/a	$30,000	$46,000	D	★★	n/c
944							
944 coupe	83–85	n/a	$4,000	$6,500	F	★★	n/c
944 coupe	86–87	n/a	$5,000	$7,000	F	★★	n/c
944 coupe	88–89	n/a	$5,700	$8,200	D	★★	n/c
(Add $750 for "S"; $2,000 for Turbo; $2,500 for "S" Turbo.)							
944 S2 coupe	89–91	n/a	$7,000	$11,000	D	★	-22%
944 S2 cabriolet	90–91	n/a	$10,000	$15,000	D	★	-28%
968 coupe	92–93	n/a	$11,000	$16,000	D	★	-17%
968 cabriolet	92–93	n/a	$15,000	$20,000	D	★	-13%
Boxster							
Boxster roadster	97–04	n/a	$13,000	$19,000	C	★	-41%
Boxster S roadster	00–04	n/a	$16,000	$25,000	C	★	-41%
Carrera GT							
Carrera GT	04–05	n/a	$275,000	$325,000	B	★★★	-8%
959							
959 "Komfort"	86–88	200*	$200,000	$235,000	A	★★★	n/c

(Some 959s were built up from parts, and VIN numbers higher than 290 have been observed. "Komfort" street models were equipped with power leather seats, a/c, p/w, etc.)

1981 Porsche 928 coupe

1965 Rolls-Royce Silver Cloud III saloon

	Yrs. Built	No. Made	Buy-Sell Price Range		Grade	Rating	1 Yr. % Change
			Low	High			
Competition Cars							

Note: Price ranges for competition Porsches are determined by provenance, completeness, and originality. A car with all of its original parts and no stories will bring three to four times that of a "bitsa."

	Yrs. Built	No. Made	Low	High	Grade	Rating	1 Yr. % Change
550	54–55	90	$750,000	$1,000,000	A	★★★	n/c
550A	56–57	39	$1,200,000	$1,500,000	A	★★★	n/c

(Includes Le Mans coupes. Most 550As were sold in the U.S. and have only SCCA history. Add at least 25% for documented international provenance. Factory team FIA cars add 60%.)

	Yrs. Built	No. Made	Low	High	Grade	Rating	1 Yr. % Change
RSK	58–59	34	$750,000	$850,000	A	★★★	n/c
695GS Abarth Carrera	59–62	21	$750,000	$850,000	A	★★★	n/c
RS 60/RS 61	60–61	35	$750,000	$850,000	A	★★★	n/c
904 GTS	63–64	122	$600,000	$800,000	A	★★★	n/c

(Production includes 104 four-cylinder 904s, 12 six-cylinder 904s, 6 eight-cylinder 904s.)

	Yrs. Built	No. Made	Low	High	Grade	Rating	1 Yr. % Change
906 Carrera 6	66	65	$500,000	$700,000	A	★★★	n/c
910	67–68	34	$700,000	$900,000	A	★★★	n/c
908-01/908-02/908-03	68–69	62	$650,000	$1,300,000	A	★★★	n/c
917 LH/K/10/20/30	69–71	70	$2,000,000	$4,000,000	A	★★★★	n/c

(25 FIA non-turbo endurance cars, 20 Can-Am type open cars.)

	Yrs. Built	No. Made	Low	High	Grade	Rating	1 Yr. % Change
Carrera 3.0 RSR	73–74	60	$375,000	$475,000	A	★★★★	n/c

(15 3.0 RSRs were built in 1973 for IROC.)

	Yrs. Built	No. Made	Low	High	Grade	Rating	1 Yr. % Change
Carrera 2.8 RSR	73	43	$350,000	$45 0,000	A	★★★	n/c
907	67–68		$1,000,000	$2,000,000	A	★★★	n/c
RENAULT							
R5 Turbo	83–86	3,576	$25,000	$35,000	D	★★★	42%
ROLLS-ROYCE							

(For all pre-war chassis types add up to 100% for original or exceptional coachwork, matching numbers, or racing provenance.)

	Yrs. Built	No. Made	Low	High	Grade	Rating	1 Yr. % Change
Silver Ghost (British)	07–25	6,173	$104,000	$1,400,000	A	★★★★	27%
Silver Ghost (Springfield)	21–26	1,703	$104,000	$1,400,000	A	★★★★	27%
Phantom I (British)	25–29	2,258	$130,000	$470,000	B	★★★	4%
Phantom I (Springfield)	26–31	1,241	$130,000	$520,000	B	★★★	4%
Phantom II, closed	29–35	1,681	$78,000	$140,500	B	★★	4%
*Rare/open coachwork		inc.	$156,000	$286,000	A	★★★	4%
Phantom II Continental, closed	31–35	inc.	$83,500	$182,000	B	★★	4%
*Rare/open coachwork		inc.	$235,000	$520,000	A	★★★	4%
Phantom III, closed	36–39	719	$39,000	$90,000	C	★★	5%
*Rare/open coachwork		inc.	$130,000	$235,000	A	★★★	4%
Twenty, closed/formal w/ div.	22–29	2,940	$25,500	$47,500	C	★★	1%
*Other coachwork		inc.	$47,500	$77,500	C	★★★	n/c
20/25hp saloon	29–36	3,827	$25,000	$45,000	D	★★	n/c

	Yrs. Built	No. Made	Buy-Sell Price Range		Grade	Rating	1 Yr. % Change
			Low	High			
*Other coachwork		inc.	$47,500	$87,500	C	★★★	n/c
25/30hp, closed	36–38	1,201	$20,000	$40,000	D	★★	n/c
25/30hp, open	36–38	inc.	$25,000	$47,000	C	★★	NL†
Wraith, all coachwork	38–39	491	$27,500	$77,500	C	★★★	n/c
Silver Wraith (SWB)	46–58	1,244	$32,500	$65,000	C	★★	n/c
Silver Wraith (LWB)	46–58	639	$32,500	$55,000	C	★★	-11%
Silver Wraith "S"	56–59	inc.	$62,500	$125,000	C	★★	n/c
(Includes 4.9L engine and power steering.)							
Phantom IV	50–56	18	$520,000	$1,145,000	A	★★★	4%
Silver Dawn standard steel saloon	49–55	761	$35,500	$66,500	C	★★★	2%
Silver Dawn, coachbuilt (64 coachbuilt)	49–55	inc.	$75,000	$125,000	C	★★★	NL†
Silver Cloud I standard steel saloon	55–59	2,238	$33,000	$54,500	D	★★★	3%
Silver Cloud I standard steel saloon (LWB)	55–59	122	$36,000	$61,500	C	★★★	3%
Silver Cloud II standard steel saloon	55–59	inc.	$280,000	$415,000	B	★★★	3%
Silver Cloud II standard steel saloon (LWB)	59–62	2,418	$20,500	$36,500	D	★★★	4%
Silver Cloud II coachbuilt, open or closed (LHD)	59–62	299	$23,000	$38,250	D	★★★	2%
Silver Cloud II HJM DHC (LHD)	55–59	inc.	$255,000	$362,500	B	★★★	3%
Phantom V, Park Ward	60–62	inc.	$150,000	$200,000	B	★★★	n/c
Phantom V, James Young	59–68	832	$92,000	$125,000	B	★★★	6%
Silver Cloud III standard steel saloon	62–65	2,555	$56,000	$92,000	D	★★★	2%
Silver Cloud III standard steel saloon (LWB)	62–65	254	$56,000	$92,000	C	★★★	2%
SCIII coachbuilt, open or closed (LHD)	62–65	*50	$300,000	$410,000	B	★★★	3%
(Deduct up to 50% for RHD or non-factory conversions. Factory-built DHCs are properly termed "adaptations.")							
Silver Shadow standard steel saloon	66–76	16,717	$9,500	$19,000	D	★★	-5%
Silver Shadow coachbuilt, closed (LHD)	67–70	571	$17,500	$24,500	D	★★	-2%
Silver Shadow coachbuilt, open (LHD)	67–70	505	$35,000	$50,000	B	★★★	n/c
(Rebadged as Corniche in 1971, with 6.75-liter engine.)							
Corniche S1, closed	71–76	780	$22,000	$27,000	D	★★	n/c
Corniche S1, open	71–76	1,233	$35,500	$46,000	B	★★★	2%
Camargue	75–86	514	$25,000	$45,000	C	★★	n/c
Corniche S2, closed	77–81	310	$25,000	$35,000	D	★★	n/c
Corniche S2, open	71–76	1,595	$35,500	$51,000	B	★★★	2%
Silver Shadow II	77–80	8,980	$14,500	$24,000	D	★★	-4%
(Silver Shadow II production number includes Bentley T2.)							
Silver Wraith II	77–80	2,154	$22,000	$39,000	D	★★	-2%
Corniche DHC	78–85	3,239	$28,000	$48,500	D	★★	2%
Corniche	81–87	8,129	$11,500	$21,000	D	★	-6%
Silver Spirit / Silver Spur	81–90	14,468	$21,000	$44,000	D	★	-4%
Corniche II	86–89	1,226	$46,000	$76,500	C	★★	2%
Corniche III DHC	90–91	425	$86,500	$112,000	C	★★	2%
Silver Spirit II	91–92	1,152	$27,000	$39,000	D	★	-2%
Silver Spur II	91–93	1,658	$29,500	$44,000	D	★	-2%
Silver Spirit III / Silver Spur III	93–94	641	$34,300	$49,000	D	★	-2%
Corniche IV	92–95	219	$82,000	$112,000	D	★★	2%
Silver Dawn	95–98	237	$31,200	$51,000	D	★★	-2%
Silver Spirit	95	122	$28,000	$39,500	D	★	NL†
Flying Spur and Touring Limousine	95–98	507	$61,200	$83,000	C	★★	-2%
Corniche S	95–96	25	$85,000	$115,000	D	★	NL†
Park Ward I	95–98	44	$50,000	$65,000	D	★	NL†
Silver Seraph	98–02	1,570	$80,000	$100,000	C	★	NL†

Model	Yrs. Built	No. Made	Low	High	Grade	Rating	1 Yr. % Change
Corniche	00–02	374	$140,000	$175,000	D	★	NL†
Park Ward II	00–02	127	$125,000	$140,000	D	★	NL†
Phantom	03–	1,000/yr	$175,000	$225,000	D	★	-19%
Phantom DHC	07–	n/a	est. MSRP	$400,000	D	★	NL†
SAAB							
GT-750	58–62	400*	$12,000	$20,000	C	★★★	n/c
GT-850	63–65	1,650*	$13,000	$22,000	C	★★★	14%
Monte Carlo 850	65–67	2,500*	$13,000	$25,000	C	★★★	11%
Sonett II (2-stroke)	67	258	$15,000	$28,000	C	★★★	33%
Sonett II V4	67–69	1610	$9,000	$15,000	C	★★★	15%
Sonett III	70–74	8351	$5,000	$12,000	C	★★★	29%
99 EMS	72–78	n/a	$4,500	$9,500	C	★★★	NL†
99 Turbo	77–81	n/a	$5,000	$12,000	D	★★★	NL†

(Add 25% for 1977 test car; add 15% for 79-81 and all non-U.S. models with higher performance.)

Model	Yrs. Built	No. Made	Low	High	Grade	Rating	1 Yr. % Change
SIATA							
300BC	49–52	70	$750,000	$150,000	C	★★★★	Mkt. Adj.

(Deduct $7,500 for Fiat 1100 engine.)

Model	Yrs. Built	No. Made	Low	High	Grade	Rating	1 Yr. % Change
Daina cabriolet	51–55	80	$75,000	$110,000	C	★★★	30%

(Add $20,000 for Grand Sport (twin Webers); $50,000 for alloy body.)

Model	Yrs. Built	No. Made	Low	High	Grade	Rating	1 Yr. % Change
208 coupe (Farina & Balboa)	52–55	25*	$400,000	$600,000	B	★★★★	30%
208S America roadster	52–55	36*	$450,000	$650,000	A	★★★★	39%

(Correct 8V engines are difficult to find. Significant deduction for incorrect type or no engine. Examples with exceptional and fully documented history can command exceptional prices.)

Model	Yrs. Built	No. Made	Low	High	Grade	Rating	1 Yr. % Change
STANGUELLINI							
1100	47–56	60	$175,000	$275,000	B	★★★	22%

(Price for OHC or DOHC engines. Deduct $40k for pushrod engine; $20k for 750 engine.)

Model	Yrs. Built	No. Made	Low	High	Grade	Rating	1 Yr. % Change
Formula Junior	59	120	$40,000	$50,000	B	★★★	n/c
STUDEBAKER							
Avanti R1 Coupe	63–64	4,647	$16,000	$28,000	C	★★	n/c
Avanti R2 Supercharged Coupe	63–64	inc.	$20,000	$32,000	C	★★	n/c
Avanti II	65–83	2,241*	$13,000	$17,000	C	★★	n/c

(The Avanti II was not built by Studebaker, but by former dealer Nathan Altman.)

Model	Yrs. Built	No. Made	Low	High	Grade	Rating	1 Yr. % Change
SUNBEAM							
Alpine roadster (early style)	53–55	3,000	$11,000	$20,000	C	★★	n/c
Alpine roadster	60–67	69,251	$7,500	$11,000	C	★★★	n/c
Tiger Mk I/IA (260-ci)	64–67	6,498	$30,000	$45,000	B	★★★	7%
Tiger Mk II (289-ci)	67	536	$40,000	$55,000	B	★★★	5%
TALBOT-LAGO							
T150C coupe	34–39	51**	$200,000	$300,000	B	★★★	30%
T150 SS teardrop coupe	36–39	inc.	$3,500,000	$5,500,000	A	★★★★	28%
T150C SS Figoni cabriolet	36–39	inc.	$1,500,000	$3,000,000	A	★★★★	31%
T150C convertible	34–39	inc.	$250,000	$300,000	A	★★★	-5%
T26 Record sedan	47–56	750**	$100,000	$150,000	B	★★★	n/c
T26 Record cabriolet	47–56	inc.	$200,000	$400,000	A	★★★	38%
T26 Grand Sport coupe	53–54	inc.	$300,000	$600,000	B	★★★	19%
T26 Grand Sport cabriolet	53–54	inc.	$300,000	$600,000	A	★★★	17%

(Examples with exceptional coachwork and fully documented history can command exceptional prices.)

Model	Yrs. Built	No. Made	Low	High	Grade	Rating	1 Yr. % Change
TOYOTA							
2000GT	67–70	351	$400,000	$425,000	B	★★★★	39%
MR2	85–87	166,104	$1,800	$3,000	F	★★	n/c
MR2	88–89	inc.	$2,200	$3,500	F	★★	n/c

(Add $1,500 for Supercharger.)

Model	Yrs. Built	No. Made	Low	High	Grade	Rating	1 Yr. % Change
MR2	91–95	19,082	$3,000	$5,000	F	★	n/c

(Add $2,000 for Turbo.)

Model	Yrs. Built	No. Made	Low	High	Grade	Rating	1 Yr. % Change
TRIUMPH							
1800/2000 roadster	46–49	4,501	$20,000	$30,000	C	★★	n/c
TR2 (long door)	53–54	8,628	$23,000	$32,000	B	★★★	-11%
TR2 (short door)	54–55	inc.	$21,000	$30,000	B	★★★	-14%
TR3 (small mouth)	55–57	13,378	$21,000	$30,000	B	★★★	-4%
TR3A (large mouth)	57–61	58,236	$19,000	$30,000	B	★★★	-4%
TR3B	62–63	3,331	$20,000	$32,000	B	★★★	-8%

(TR2/3 add $750 for overdrive; $1,000 for factory hard top. Deduct $2,000 for disc wheels.)

Model	Yrs. Built	No. Made	Low	High	Grade	Rating	1 Yr. % Change
TR4	61–64	40,253	$14,000	$23,000	C	★★★	-8%
TR4A	64–68	28,465	$17,000	$22,000	C	★★★	-10%

(Add $500 for IRS; $1,000 for surrey top (TR4/TR250); $750 for overdrive. Deduct $1,000 for disc wheels.)

Model	Yrs. Built	No. Made	Low	High	Grade	Rating	1 Yr. % Change
TR250	68	8,484	$17,000	$24,000	B	★★★	-5%
TR5 (Europe only)	67–68	2,947	$20,000	$26,000	B	★★★	NL†
TR6 (small bumpers)	69–74	94,619	$14,000	$22,000	B	★★★	-14%
TR6 (rubber bumpers)	75–76	inc.	$13,000	$20,000	B	★★	-6%
TR7	76–81	112,368	$4,000	$6,500	F	★★	n/c
TR7 convertible	79–80	inc.	$4,000	$6,500	D	★★	n/c
TR8 coupe	80–81	2,497	$5,000	$9,000	D	★★	n/c
TR8 convertible	80–81	inc.	$7,500	$11,000	D	★★	-8%
Stag	70–77	25,877	$10,000	$13,500	D	★★	n/c
Spitfire Mk I/II	62–67	82,982	$6,000	$9,000	C	★★★	n/c
Spitfire Mk III	68–70	65,320	$6,000	$8,500	C	★★★	n/c
Spitfire Mk IV	70–74	70,021	$5,000	$8,000	D	★★	n/c
Spitfire 1500	75–80	95,829	$5,000	$8,000	C	★★	n/c
GT6 coupe (Mk I)	67–68	15,818	$6,000	$9,000	C	★★★	n/c
GT6+ coupe (Mk II)	69–70	12,066	$6,000	$8,500	C	★★	n/c
GT6 coupe (Mk III)	70–74	13,042	$5,500	$8,000	C	★★	n/c
TUCKER							
Torpedo	48	51	$500,000	$750,000	A	★★★★	32%
TVR							
Griffith	63–66	300	$35,000	$42,000	B	★★★	9%
Tuscan	67–71	n/a	$30,000	$46,000	B	★★★	-3%

(For Griffith and Tuscan, add $2,000 for 271-hp V8.)

Model	Yrs. Built	No. Made	Low	High	Grade	Rating	1 Yr. % Change
2500 coupe	71–73	n/a	$7,500	$10,500	C	★★	n/c
2500M coupe	72–77	n/a	$6,500	$10,000	C	★★	n/c
Taimar	76–79	395	$6,500	$10,000	C	★★	n/c
Taimar roadster	78–79	258	$10,000	$15,000	C	★★	n/c
Tasmin	83	n/a	$6,500	$10,000	C	★★	n/c
280i	84–87	n/a	$7,000	$10,000	C	★★	-3%
VECTOR							
W8	85–92	18	$200,000	$275,000	C	★★★	57%
M12	95–99	17	$100,000	$150,000	D	★★	NL†
VOISIN							
C3C/C3L	21–27	1,940	$250,000	$400,000	A	★★★	NL†
C5	23–27	500	$300,000	$600,000	A	★★★	NL†
C11	26–28	2,180	$200,000	$400,000	B	★★★	NL†
C11 Lumineuse coach	26–28	inc.	$300,000	$450,000	A	★★★	NL†
C14	28–32	1,795	$200,000	$400,000	B	★★★	NL†
C14 Lumineuse coach	28–32	inc.	$500,000	$600,000	A	★★★	NL†
C14 Chartre 2-door coach	28–32	inc.	$450,000	$650,000	A	★★★	NL†
C14 Chartreuse 4-door coach	28–32	inc.	$350,000	$500,000	B	★★★	NL†
C14 Chartrain limousine	28–32	inc.	$200,000	$400,000	C	★★★	NL†
C23/C24	31–36	455	$200,000	$400,000	C	★★★★	NL†
C25/C28	34–37	89	$400,000	$550,000	A	★★★★	NL†
VOLVO							
P1800	61–63	6,000	$7,500	$12,000	C	★★	n/c
1800S	63–69	23,993	$6,000	$12,000	C	★★	n/c
1800E	70–72	9,414	$7,500	$12,500	C	★★	n/c
1800ES	72–73	8,078	$7,500	$13,000	C	★★	2%
1800ESi	74	n/a	$7,500	$13,500	C	★★	2%

PRICE GUIDE

Resources

It's not what you know, it's where to find what you need to know.

In this chapter, the experts at Sports Car Market have pulled together a listing of car clubs. If you want to get into collecting, car clubs are a great place to start. They can give you great insight and answer all of your questions. Whatever your vintage automotive needs, the chances are good you'll find a path, or at least some help to move along your path, here.—*Keith Martin*

In This Section

Clubs..273
Glossary of Car Terms 281

Car Clubs

There's no better source of information than talking with another owner of the same type of car you have or are thinking of buying.

Club Name	Location	Web site
20th Century Chevy, Inc. Founded: 1970	PO Box 371 Washington, IN, 47501	www.20thcenturychevy.com
356 Registry Inc. Founded: 1974	PO Box 356 Stillwater, MN, 55082	www.356registry.org
912 Registry Founded: 1997	PO Box 862219 Los Angeles, CA, 90086	www.912registry.org
AACC-UK Association of American Car Clubs UK Founded: 1993	PO Box 2222 Braintree, CM7 9TW	www.motorvatinusa.org.uk
Adirondack Corvettes Inc. Founded: 1989	PO Box 716 Glens Falls, NY 12801	www.adirondackcorvettes.com
Alaska Sports Car Club Founded: 1959	PO Box 220254 Anchorage, AK, 99522	www.aksportscarclub.org
Alfa Romeo Owners Club - USA	PO Box 12340 Kansas City, MO 64116	www.aroc-usa.org
All American Corvette Club	PO Box 8063 Paramus, NJ, 07653	allamericancorvetteclub.com

RESOURCES

Allante Owners Association Founded: 1991	17327 Via Del Campo San Diego, CA 92127	www.allante.com
Aloha Mustang & Shelby Club of Hawaii Founded: 1979	PO Box 10161 Honolulu, HI, 96816	www.alohamustang.org
Altoona Corvette Club Founded: 1969	PO Box 2346 Altoona, PA, 16601	www.altoonacorvetteclub.com
AMC Rambler Club Founded: 1980	6 Murolo Road North Grosvenordale, CT, 06255	www.amcrc.com
AMC World Clubs Founded: 1972	7963 Depew St Arvada, CO, 80003-2527	www.amx-perience.com
AMCA, American Motors Club of Alberta Founded: 1994	919 114th St NW Edmonton, AB T6J 6Z6	clubs.hemmings.com/frameset .cfm?club=amcalberta
American Bugatti Club Founded: 1960	600 Lakeview Terrace Glen Ellyn, IL, 60137	www.americanbugatticlub.org
American Chevelle Enthusiasts Society ACES Founded: 1995	900 Conference Dr Ste1-B #222, Goodlettsville, TN 37072	www.chevelles.com
American MGB Association Founded: 1975	PO Box 11401 Chicago, IL, 60611-0401	www.mgclub.org
American Motors Owners Association, Inc. Founded: 1973	10791 Sprinkle Road Vicksburg, MI 49097	www.amonational.com
Antique Automobile Club of America AACA Founded: 1935	501 Governor Rd; PO Box 417 Hershey, PA, 17033	www.aaca.org
Appalachian British Car Society Founded: 1992	2324 Brandon Lane Kingsport, TN, 37660	www.britcars.net
Aston Martin Owners Club Founded: 1960	Drayton St Leonard, Wallingford, Oxfordshire OX10 7BG, UK	www.amoc.org/
Avanti Owners Association International	PO Box 1743 Maple Grove, MN, 55311-6743	www.aoai.org
Belgium Federation of Old Vehicles	PB 48, Begijnendijk, 3130	www.bfov.be
Bentley Drivers Club Founded: 1936	Ironstone Lane, Wroxton, Banbury, Oxfordshire, OX15 6ED	www.bdcl.co.uk
Bloomington Gold Corvettes USA	705 E. Lincoln W Suite 201 Normal, IL, 61761	www.bloomingtongold.com
Bloomington/Normal Corvette Enthusiasts Club Founded: 2002	PO Box 1552 Bloomington, IL, 61702-1552	www.blnlcorvetteenthusiasts.homestead.com
Blue Ridge Corvette Club Founded: 1977	PO Box 1 Stuarts Draft, VA, 24477	www.blueridgecorvetteclub.com
Blue Ridge Land Rover Club Founded: 1978	181 Anderson Rd Davisville, WV 26142	www.brlrc.org
Bluebonnet Region #6 VCCA Founded: 1995	720 Falling Leaves Dr Adkins, TX, 78101	www.geocities.com/funstarz
BMW Car Club of America	640 South Main Street Suite 201, Greenville, SC, 29601	www.bmwcca.org
Boss 429 Owners Directory Founded: 1974	PO Box 8035 Spokane, WA 99203	www.bossperformance.com
Brampton Corvette Club Founded: 1971	45 Franklin Ct Brampton, ON, L6T 3Z1	www.bramptoncorvetteclub.com
Bridgehampton Historical Society Founded: 1950	PO Box 977 Bridgehampton, NY, 11932	historicalsociety.hamptons.com
Buick Club of America	PO Box 360775 Columbus, Ohio 43236	www.buickclubofamerica.org
Cadillac and LaSalle Club	PO Box 360835 Columbus, OH 43236-0835	cadil3.securesites.net

California Association of Sunbeam Tiger Owners	2950 Calle Grande Vlsta San Clemente, CA 92672	www.catmbr.org
Chevrolet Nomad Association Founded: 1989	10405 Miller Rd Johnstown, OH, 43031	www.chevynomadclub.com
Chrysler 300 Club International	PO Box 40 Benson, MD 21018	www.chrysler300club.com
Citroën Car Club Inc Founded: 1956	PO Box 743 Hollywood, CA, 90078	www.citroens.org
Classic Car Club of America / CCCA Founded: 1952	1645 Des Plaines River Rd, Suite 7A Des Plaines, IL, 60018	www.classiccarclub.org
Classic Car Club of Southern California, Inc.	30 Hackamore Lane, Suite 1, Bell Canyon, CA, 91307-1065	www.socalccca.org
Classic Corvette Club Founded: 2002	PO Box 682 Moorestown, NJ, 8054	www.classiccorvetteclub.com
Continental Mark II Association Founded: 1965	13533 Hitt Road Apple Valley, CA, 92308	www.markii.com/markii/cma
Cooper Car Club Ltd Founded: 2001	Bryn Ymenyn Bach, Butter Hill, St Ishmael's, Pembs. SA62 3SR	www.coopercars.org
Corvette Club of America/ NCCC Founded: 1956	PO Box 3355 Gaithersburg, MD, 20885-3355	www.corvetteclubofamerica.org
Corvette Club of Illinois NCCC Founded: 1970	309 South Main Box 153 Oakwood, IL 61858-0153	www.ccofi.org
Corvette Club of Manitoba, Inc. Founded: 1971	Box 42032 RPO Ferry Rd Winnipeg, MB, R3J 3X7	www.corvettemanitoba.com
Corvette Club of Michigan NCCC Founded: 1958	PO Box 510330 Livonia, MI, 48151	www.corvetteclubmi.com
Corvette Club of Northeast Pennsylvania	PO Box 3415 Scranton, PA, 18505-0415	www.ernccc.org/ccnepa
Corvette Club of Northern Delaware Founded: 1973	PO Box 10103 Wilmington, DE, 19850-0103	www.vetteclub.org
Corvette Club of Nova Scotia Founded: 1974	R.R. # 2 Wentworth, NS, B0M 1Z0	nscorvette.chebucto.org
Corvette Club of Ontario Founded: 1962	PO Box 53062, 10 Royal Orchard Blvd., Thornhill, ON L3T 7R9	www.ontariovettes.com
Corvette Club of the Palm Beaches	132 VanGogh Way Royal Palm Beach, FL, 33411	www.corvetteclubpalmbeach.com
Corvette Marque Club of Seattle Founded: 1963	PO Box 534 Kirkland, WA, 98083	www.corvettemarqueclub.com
Corvette Owners Club of San Diego Founded: 1956	8130 La Mesa Blvd #184 La Mesa, CA, 91941	www.cocsd.com
Crosley Automobile Club, Inc. Founded: 1969	307 Schaeffer Road Blandon, PA 19510	crosleyautoclub.com
Cross Flags Corvettes	231 Hillbrook Dr. Spartanburg, SC, 29307	www.crossflagscorvetteclub.com
Cruisin' Buddies Rod Custom Classic Founded: 2000	7 Kress Street Binghamton, NY, 13903	www.cruisinbuddies.com
Cruisin' Tigers GTO Club Founded: 1989	PO Box 695 Westmont, IL, 60559	www.cruisintigersgto.com
Cruzin' Few Unique Vehicle Club Founded: 1993	356 Frankfort Road Monaca, PA 15061	www.geocities.com/cruzinfew
DeLorean Owners Association Founded: 1983	15023 Eddie Drive Humble, TX 77396	www.delorean.com
Dino Register Founded: 1981	Meisenburger Weg 22 D-42659 Solingen	www.dinoregister.com

RESOURCES

Early Ford V-8 Club of America	PO BOX 1715 Maple Grove, MN, 55311	www.efv8.org
Edsel Owners Club, Inc.	1740 NW 3rd Street, Gresham, OR, 97030	www.edselclub.org
ELVA Owners Club Founded: 1979	Unit 3, Gaugemaster Way, Ford Road, Ford, Arundel, West Sussex. BN18 0RX. UK	www.elva.com
Facel Enthusiasts USA Founded: 2001	PO Box 6142 San Pedro, CA, 90734	www.geocities.com/motorcity/show/2564/facel-vega.html
Fairlane Club of America Founded: 1981	340 Clicktown Rd Church Hill, TN, 37642	www.fairlaneclubofamerica.com
Falcon Club of America	PO Box 113 Jacksonville, AR, 72078-0113	www.falconclub.com
Falls City Mustang Club Founded: 1995	PO Box 12, Nab, IN, 47147	www.fallscitymustangclub.com
Ferrari Club Argentino Founded: 1996	3 de Febrero 312, Rosario Sta Fe, 2000	www.ferrariclub.com.ar
Ferrari Club of America, Inc. Founded: 1962	PO Box 720597 Atlanta, GA, 30358	www.ferrariclubofamerica.org
Florida West Coast Region AACA Founded: 1964	14968 Imperial Point Drive N. Largo, FL, 33774	www.aaca.org/fwcr
Flywheels Car Club Founded: 1961	404 S Second St Silverton, OR, 97381	silvertonflywheels.org
Ford Galaxie Club of America Founded: 1983	PO Bx 429 Valley Springs, AR 72682	www.galaxieclub.com
Ford Mercury Restorers Club of America Founded: 1969	PO Box 2938 Dearborn, MI, 48123	www.fmrcoa.org
Gateway Z Club Founded: 1975	PO Box 3694 Ballwin, MO, 63022-3694	www.gatewayzclub.com
Golden Gate Lotus Club Founded: 1973	PO Box 117303 Burlingame, CA, 94011	www.gglotus.org
GTO Association of America	PO Box 213 Timnath, CO, 80547	www.gtoaa.org
Intermeccanica Enthusiasts Club Founded: 1998	PO Box 1868 West Chester, PA, 19380	www.intermeccanica.org
International Amphicar Club Founded: 1993	1926 Princeton Avenue Camp Hill, PA, 17011	www.amphicar.com
International Edsel Club	108 S. Oak Street Russellville, KY, 42276-2355	www.internationaledsel.com
International Ford Retractable Club Founded: 1971	PO Box 157 Spring Park, MN, 55384	www.skyliner.org
International Mercury Owners Association Founded: 1991	PO Box 1245 Northbrook, IL, 60065-1245	www.mercuryclub.com
Jaguar Clubs of North America	234 Buckland Trace Louisville, KY, 40245	www.jcna.com
Kustoms of America Founded: 1949	4427 Ginger Drive Gastonia, NC, 28056	www.kustomsofamerica.com
L.A. Roadsters Founded: 1957	PO Box 6639 Burbank, CA, 91510	www.laroadsters.com
Lincoln & Continental Owners Club Founded: 1953	POBox 1715 Maple Grove, MN, 55311-6715	www.lcoc.org
Lincoln Highway Association	136 N. Elm St. PO Box 308, Franklin Grove, IL, 61031	www.lincolnhighwayassoc.org
Lotus Ltd Founded: 1973	PO Box L College Park, MD, 20741	www.lotuscarclub.org

Manx Dune Buggy Club Founded: 1994	PO BOX 233 Ringwood, IL, 60072-0233	www.manxclub.com
Mazda Club Founded: 1988	PO Box 11238 Chicago, IL, 60611	www.mazdaclub.com
Mercedes-Benz Club of America Founded: 1956	1907 Lelaray Street Colorado Springs, CO, 80909-2872	www.mbca.org
Mercedes-Benz Owners' Association Founded: 1989	Langton Road Langton Green, UK, TN3 0EG	www.mercedesclub.org.uk
Mercedes-Benz Veteranen Club Deutschland (MVC) Founded: 1971	Flurrstr. 76, 44145 Dortmund, 44145	www.mvconline.de
MG Drivers Club of North America Founded: 1997	18 George's Pl Clinton, NJ, 08809-1334	www.mgdriversclub.com
MG Octagon Car Club Founded: 1969	Unit 1/2 Porchfields Enterprise ParkColton Rd, Trent Valley, Rugeley, Staffs, WS15 3HB	www.mgoctagoncarclub.com
MG Owners Club Founded: 1973	Octagon House1 Over Road Swavesey, Cambridge, CB4 5QZ	www.mgownersclub.co.uk
MGCC of Toronto Founded: 1955	PO Box 64Station R Toronto, ON, M4G 3Z3	www.geocities.com/motorcity/shop/6055/index.htm
MGs of Baltimore Founded: 1977	5237 Glen Arm Rd Glen Arm, MD, 21057	www.mgsofbaltimore.com
Model A Ford Club of America	250 South Cypress La Habra, CA, 90631-5515	www.mafca.com
Music City Mustang Club	7612 Drag Strip Road, Fairview, TN, 37062	www.musiccitymustangclub.org
Mustang 428 Cobra Jet Registry Founded: 1998	Box 247 Burke, VA, 22009-0247	www.428cobrajet.org
Mustang Club of America Founded: 1976	4051 Barrancas Ave. PMB102 Pensacola, FL, 32507	www.mustang.org
Nash Car Club of America Founded: 1970	1 N 274 Prairie Glen Ellyn, IL, 60137	www.shcarclub.org
Nash Car Club of America/PNW Region Founded: 1999	17839 Wallingford Ave N Shoreline, WA, 98133	www.pnwnash.org
Nashville British Car Club Founded: 1991	364 Dandridge Drive Franklin, TN 37067	www.nashvillebritishcarclub.org
National Association of Antique Automobile Clubs of Canada Corporation NAAACCC Founded: 1964	3512 Marine Ave. Belcarra, BC, V3H 4R8	www.naaaccc.ca
National Capital Mustang Association Founded: 1991	2446 Bank Street, Suite 363 Ottawa, ON, K1V 1A8	www.ncma.cc
National Capital Region Mustang Club	4222 Fortuna Center Plaza, #224, Dumfries, VA, 22025-1515	www.ncrmc.org
National Chevy Association Founded: 1985	947 Arcade St. Paul, MN, 55106	www.tiolchevyassoc.com
National Corvette Museum	350 Corvette Dr. Bowling Green, KY, 42101	www.corvettemuseum.com
National Corvette Owners Association Founded: 1975	900 S Washington St #G-13 Falls Church, VA, 22046	www.ncoa-vettes.com
National Corvette Restorers Society Founded: 1974	6291 Day Rd Cincinnati, OH, 45252-1334	www.ncrs.org
National Council of Corvette Clubs NCCC Founded: 1960	492 Meadowlark Way Clifton, CO 81520-8811	www.corvettesnccc.org
National Firebird and Trans Am Club Founded: 1984	PO Box 11238 Chicago, IL, 60611	www.firebirdtaclub.com
National Historic Route 66 Federation Founded: 1994	PO Box 1848, Dept. WS Lake Arrowhead, CA, 92352-1848	www.national66.com

National Impala Association Founded: 1980	5400 43rd Ave So Minneapolis, MN, 55417	www.nationalimpala.com
National Monte Carlo Owner's Association, Inc. Founded: 1986	204 Shelby Drive Greensburg, PA, 15601-4974	www.montecarloclub.com
National Motorists Association Founded: 1982	402 W 2nd St. Waunakee, WI, 53597-1342	www.motorists.org
National Nostalgic Nova Founded: 1982	PO Box 2344 Your York, PA, 17405	www.nnnova.com
National Woodie Club	3733 W. Surrey Avenue Phoenix, AZ, 85029	www.nationalwoodieclub.com
New England MG T Register Ltd Founded: 1963	PO Box 1957 Cary, NC, 27512-1957	www.nemgt.org
North American Subaru Impreza Owners Club, Inc.	141 Newburyport Tnpk #215 Rowley, MA, 01969	www.nasioc.com
Oldsmobile Club of America	PO Box 80318 Lansing, MI, 48908	www.oldsclub.org
Packard Automobile Classics, Inc. Founded: 1953	PO Box 360806 Columbus, OH, 43236-0806	www.packardclub.org
Packard Club Founded: 1953	420-S Ludlow St Dayton, OH, 45402	www.packardclub.org
Packards of Chicagoland	PO Box 1031 Elmhurst, IL, 60126-9998	www.geocities.com/chicagopackard

Pantera International Founded: 1973	330 Central Avenue, #25 Fillmore, CA, 93015	www.panteracars.com
Pantera Owner's Club of America (POCA) Founded: 1973	PO Box 3574 San Dimas, CA, 91773-0574	www.poca.com
Pierce-Arrow Society, Inc. Founded: 1957	PO Box 2636 Cedar Rapids, IA, 52406-2636	www.pierce-arrow.org
Police Car Owner's of America	172 CR 136 Eureka Springs, AR, 72631	www.policecarowners.com
Porsche 356 Club	4865 Via del Corral Yorba Linda, CA, 92887	www.porsche356club.org
Porsche Club of America Founded: 1955	PO Box 1347 Springfield, VA, 22151-0347	www.pca.org
Renault Alpine Club International Founded: 1998	Friedrich Ebert Strasse 51, 63512 Hainburg, Deutschland	www.renault-alpine.com
Renault Owners Club of North America Founded: 1991	13839 Hwy 8 Business El Cajon, CA, 92021	www.renaultclub.us
Rolls-Royce Enthusiasts' Club Founded: 1957	The Hunt House, Paulerspury, Towcester, Northants, NN12 7NA	www.rrec.co.uk
Rolls-Royce Owners Club Founded: 1951	191 Hempt Road Mechanicsburg, PA, 17055	www.rroc.org
Roskilde American Bil Club	Kampstrupsti 2, 4000 Roskilde	www.roskilde-abc.dk
Route 66 Association of Illinois Founded: 1989	110 W Howard St Pontiac, IL, 61764	www.il66assoc.org
Saab Club of North America Founded: 1973	30 Puritan Drive Port Chester, NY 10573	www.saabclub.com
Saddleback Mustang Association Founded: 1985	PO Box 790 Lake Forest, CA, 92609	www.saddlebackmustang.org
San Diego Jaguar Club Founded: 1959	8009 Avenida Secreto Carlsbad, CA 92009	www.sdjag.com
San Diego Pontiac Club Founded: 1990	6778 Cibola Rd San Diego, CA, 92120	www.sdpoci.com
San Diego Saab Owner's Group	10559 Lansford Ln San Diego, CA, 92126-5902	www.annexus.com/sdsog
Shelby American Automobile Club SAAC Founded: 1975	PO Box 788 Sharon, CT, 6069	www.saac.com
Sports Car Club of America	PO Box 19400 Topeka, KS, 66619-0400	www.scca.com
Studebaker Drivers Club, Inc. Founded: 1962	Box 1715 Maple Grove, MN, 55311-7615	www.studebakerdriversclub.com
The Maserati Club Founded: 1986	PO Box 5300 Somerset, NJ, 08875-5300	www.themaseraticlub.com
The Milestone Car Society Founded: 1971	626 N Park Ave. Indianapolis, IN, 46204	www.milestonecarsociety.org
The Skyscrapers International Car Club Founded: 2002	4552 Camellia Ave Studio City, CA, 91602	www.cadillacworld.net
The Super Stock AMX Registry Founded: 1986	748 Pine Eagle Lane San Antonio, TX, 78260	www.ssamx.com
Tigers East - Alpines East Founded: 1977	PO Box 1260 Kulpsville, PA, 19443	www.teae.org
Toyota Land Cruiser Association Founded: 1976	PO Box 186 Evergreen, CO, 80439	www.tlca.org
Toyota Mr2 MK1 Club Founded: 1995	10 Chestnut Grove, Barnton, Northwich, Cheshire, CW8 4ST	www.mr2mk1club.com

RESOURCES

RESOURCES

TrabantUSA Founded: 2001	17527 Troyer Rd, White Hall, MD, 21161	www.geocities.com/trabantusa
Triumph Standard Motor Club Founded: 1985	57 Main St, Meriden, Coventry, CV7 7LP England	www.standardmotorclub.org.uk
Tucker Automobile Club of America Founded: 1973	9509 Hinton Dr Santee, CA, 92071-2760	www.tuckerclub.org
United Council of Corvette Clubs Founded: 1978	PO Box 532605 Indianapolis, IN, 46253	www.unitedcouncil.com
United Kingdom Buick Club	PO Box 2222 Braintree, Essex, CM7 9TW	www.motorvatinusa.org.uk
Vintage Car Club of Canada Founded: 1958	PO Box 3070 Vancouver, BC, V6B 3X6	www.vccc.com
Vintage Chevy Van Club Founded: 1998	107 Avenue E, Metairie, LA, 70005	www.vcvc.org
Vintage Mustang Club of Kansas City Founded: 1985	PO Box 40082 Overland Park, KS, 66204	www.mustangclubofgreaterkc.com
Vintage Mustang Owners Association	PO Box 5772 San Jose, CA, 95150	www.vintagemustang.org
Vintage Rallies Founded: 1991	80 Jackson Hill Rd Sharon, CT, 06069	www.vintagerallies.com
Vintage Sports Car Club of America VSCCA Founded: 1958	170 Wetherhill Road Garden City, NY, 11530	www.vscca.org
Vintage Sports Car Drivers Assoc.	9780 Rolling Hills Drive Alto, MI, 49302	www.vscda.org
Vintage Thunderbird Club International Founded: 1968	1304 Greenwood Schertz, TX, 78154	www.vintagethunderbirdclub.org
Vintage Triumph Register	PO Box 655 Howell, MI 48844	www.vtr.org
Voitures Anciennes du Quebec, Inc. Founded: 1974	270, Rue des Oeillets, Otterburn Park, QC J3H 6G4 CAN	www.vaq.qc.ca
Voitures Anciennes et Classiques de Montreal Founded: 1956	217, Rue Capri, Repentigny QC J6A 5L1 CAN	www.vacm.qc.ca
Volkswagen Type 181 Thing Registry Founded: 1993	700 SE Crescent Drive Shelton, WA, 98584-8665	www.type181registry.com
Volvo Club of America	Box 16, Afton, NY 13730	www.vcoa.org
Willys-Overland Jeepster Club Founded: 1964	255 Thompsonville Road McMurray, PA, 15317	www.jeepsterclub.com
Yenko Sportscar Club Founded: 1997	PO Box 375 Alton, MO, 65606	www.yenko.net

Glossary of Car Terms

Gearheads have a language all their own, and most of it is printable. Here is an automotive Rosetta Stone to help you on your way.

Barn Find	A car found in long-term storage in highly original although not necessarily orderly or complete condition.
Base Coat/Clear Coat	A paint system that consists of several coats of a "base" color and several coats of hardened "clear." It is the clear coat that produces the depth and gloss.
Bias Ply Tires	Tires in which the cords or plies are wrapped around the tire in a diagonal overlapping manner. Produces higher rolling resistance and more heat than a radial design.
Big Block	Any large displacement optional engine. Usually over 400 ci.
Black Plate Car	A car still registered with its original black and yellow California license plate issued in the 1960s. Indicative of a car that has always been in California.
Blue Plate Car	A car still registered with its original blue and yellow California license plate issued in the 1970s. Indicative of a car that has always been in California.
Body-Off Restoration	A comprehensive restoration during which the body is actually removed from the chassis and every component is either replaced or renewed. Chassis and undercarriage should show to a high standard in a proper body-off restoration.
Bored	Method of increasing the displacement of an engine by enlarging the cylinder bores.
Brightwork	Shiny metal on the exterior of a car. Either chrome, polished stainless steel, or polished aluminum.
Cabriolet	Usually a two-door open car with a lined convertible top and four or five seats, often with external landau irons; also "cabro." Origin: a light, two-wheeled carriage with a folding leather top and side irons.
Chandelier Bid	An auctioneer tactic used to advance bidding that has not reached the reserve in the absence of activity on the part of an actual bidder. Not used by reputable auction houses.
Classic	A trademarked term of the Antique Automobile Club of America. Refers to a limited number of significant pre-war (and several post-war) cars designated as "Full Classics."
Clone	A car that has been altered to appear as though it is a more desirable model than it actually is. A clone can easily become a counterfeit depending on the seller's representations. Also called replica, tribute, or recreation.
Coachbuilder	Firm that was commissioned to build bodies for bare chassis. Karrosserie in German, carrozzeria in Italian and carrosserie in French.
Concours	Short for concours d'elegance, a judged showing of finely restored cars. Also a statement of condition. "Concours" condition is synonymous with a car in show-worthy condition.
Continuation car	A type of replica usually very accurate and involving some of the original parts and constructors. Often serial numbered consecutively with the originals.
Convertible	Any open car with roll-up windows.
Convertible Coupe	An open two-door bodystyle with a well-finished and lined convertible top. Europeans refer to it as a "drop-head coupe."
Convertible Sedan	An open four-door bodystyle with a well-finished and lined convertible top. Europeans refer to it as a "drop-head sedan."
COPO	Acronym for Central Office Purchase Order. Most commonly applied to 427-ci Camaros ordered "straight from the assembly line."
Coupe	Two-door, fixed-roof, seating either two or two with occasional rear passengers (called a 2+2); pronounced in Europe and England as "coo-pay" (also known as fixed head coupe). Origin: four-wheeled horse-drawn carriage for two persons inside with an outside front seat for the driver.
Detailing	The process of cleaning and light refurbishing of an automobile often in preparation for show or sale.
Displacement	Total of the volume of each cylinder of an internal combustion piston engine. Denoted as cubic inches (ci), cubic centimeters (cc), or liters (L).
DOHC	Double overhead cams. A cylinder head design where the cams are located in the head and actuate the valvegear directly rather than by pushrods. Driven by chains or a belt.
Drophead Coupe	From England; convertible with roll-up windows and a soft top with an internal lining. Usually, but not always, without cabriolet landau irons.
Driver Quality	A car that is a deteriorated older restoration or a cosmetically freshened but not restored car. Not showorthy, but suitable to be driven and enjoyed without worry. Also referred to simply as "a driver" or "everyday driver."
Electronic Fuel Injection	Fuel injection system where fuel is metered by means of an electronic computer.
Enamel	Generally an acrylic-based paint that produces a durable high-gloss finish with minimal rubbing. Two-stage or "base coat/clear coat" enamels produce an even glossier, more durable finish. Extremely toxic when mixed with catalyzed hardeners.

Glossary

Etceterini	Originally a term describing Italian cars other than Fiat, Ferrari, and Maserati. Now shorthand for any oddball make or model.
Flat-6 or Flat-4	Denotes engine architecture where the cylinders are horizontally opposed and separated by a centrally located crankshaft. "Boxer" or "pancake" are synonyms. Porsche is the most frequent proponent of this design.
Four-door Sedan	A four-door built with a structural B-pillar extending from the sill to the roof; the doors also carry structural frames around the side windows. The most common bodystyle. Also "saloon" (British).
Fright Pig	A car that is in unusually poor conditon. Implies a certain level of dishonesty to the condition, as if an attempt has been made to make the car appear better than it actually is or includes poorly executed modifications or "upgrades."
Hard Top	Body style that does not use a B-pillar, creating a continuous open area when both side windows are rolled down.
Kardex	The certificate of authenticity issued by the Porsche factory to the owner of a Porsche. States the original colors and options.
Lacquer	A cellulose-based automotive paint favored by manufacturers until the late 1950s. Multiple coats and hand or machine rubbing produced a high gloss. Lacquer finishes are fragile and crack and check with age.
Landaulet	Usually a formal body design, with top divided betwteen a fixed roof in front and a soft top section over the rear passengers, which can be lowered to create an open compartment. Origin: four-wheel carriage with a top divided into two sections that can be let down, thrown back, or removed, and with a raised seat outside for the driver.
Limousine	Large, luxurious, usually chauffeur-driven sedan that often has a glass partition separating the front seat from the rear passenger compartment.
Matching Numbers	A matching-numbers car is one that has all of its original numbered components intact so that they match precisely those numbers recorded by the factory in its records.
MB Tex	Or "Tex." Trade name of a high quality leatherette used by Mercedes-Benz.
Mechanical Fuel Injection	Early type of fuel injection where mixture was determined and fuel metered by means of mechanical pump rather than electronics. Common makers were SPICA, Bosch, Bendix, and Kugelfischer.
Muscle Car	Intermediate-sized vehicle with a large-displacement, large-horsepower engine. Pontiac GTO created by John Z. DeLorean was among the first muscle cars. Popular in U.S. and Australia in the 1960s and '70s.
NART	Acronym for North American Racing Team, applied to Ferraris campaigned by American distributor Luigi Chinetti. The NART Spyder was shorthand for a very limited run of 275 GTB street cars specially commissioned by Chinetti as open cars.
Nut-and-Bolt Restoration	A comprehensive restoration in which every component is either replaced or renewed, whether "body-off" or "rotisserie," in the case of a unibody car.
Original	In the strictest sense of the word, all mechanical components and surfaces of the car are unaltered from the way the car left the factory, as opposed to "restored as original," in which factory finishes and surfaces are replicated as part of the restoration process.
Overhead Cam	Cylinder head design where the valve gear is actuated by chain- or belt-driven cams located in the top of the cylinder head rather than by pushrods. Design generally allows higher maximum revs.
Panel Fit	Refers to the quality of eveness in the gaps on the opening surfaces of an automobile body, ie., doors, hood, trunk lid, etc.
Phaeton	Open four-door body style that lacks roll-up side windows. Dual-cowl phaetons have two windshields.
Provenance	An automobile's documentable history or pedigree. Always refers to a specific example rather than a marque or a model.
Radial Tires	Tires in which the cords or plies are wrapped around the tire at a ninety-degree angle.
Redline	Maximum safe revolutions per minute recommended by the manufacturer. Usually indicated by a red marking on the tachometer.
Replicar	An amalgam of the words "replica" and "car." A modern recreation or simulation of any historic or collectible car. Most replicars are sold as what they are with no attempt to deceive.
Retractable Hard Top	Non-removable hard top that can be lowered into a compartment at the rear of the car, creating a convert-ible.
Roadster	An open two-seater, generally with side curtains instead of roll-up windows.
Roof Pillars	Structural posts between the roof and the body of a car named in alphabetical order from front to rear: the windshield post is the A-pillar, the mid-roof post is the B-pillar, and the rear quarter post is the C-pillar.
Rotisserie Restoration	Restoration usually undertaken on a unibody car in which the bare tub is attached to a rotating "rotisserie" so that the underside can be refurbished to the same standard as the upper sufaces of the car.
RPM	Revolutions per minute. A measure of engine crankshaft speed.
Sedanca/Sedanca deVille	Top divided between an open section in front and a covered section over the rear passengers, with either a removable soft or hard top section that can be placed over the front compartment.
Shill Bid	A bid procured by a seller at an auction solely to increase the price paid by the sucessful bidder. Strictly illegal.

Side Curtains	Weather protection on an open car in lieu of roll-up windows that consists of removable plastic sliding windows attached via sockets in the tops of doors.
Skiff	Wood body with pointed tail, taking the reverse form of a nautical skiff, which is a flat-bottomed boat with a pointed bow and square stern. Many by coachbuilder Labourdette.
SOHC	Single overhead cam.
Speedster	Open car body style that usually has a rudimentary top, low windshield, and limited weather protection.
Spider/Spyder	Lightweight, open, two-seat sporting car with minimal comfort features; most often the spelling with the "i" is used for Italian cars, with a "y" for the German cars, but not exclusively. Origin: a carriage that was a lighter version of a phaeton, with narrower wheels, two seats, and a basic top.
Station Wagon	Utility vehicle derived from sedan or light truck chassis with an enclosed, windowed, rear cargo area; originally served as a method to transport guests from railroad stations to country hotels or homes (also "estate" and "shooting brake"). Originally wood-boodied and known as "woodies" from 1920–1952. Later models have plastic applique on the sides.
Stroked	Method of increasing the displacement of an engine by increasing the stroke of the piston.
Tonneau	Veteran car with open rear seating compartment, usually with a rear entry door; in modern usage, a removable cover for the passenger compartment. Origin: French, meaning container or cover.
Tourer	Open car with two rows of seats, four doors, and a convertible top. Disappeared by the 1950s.
Tourster	First used to refer to an early Ford "tourer" sold without doors; later used by U.S. coachbuilder Derham for what is actually a dual cowl phaeton body.
Town Car	Formal design, with a top divided between an open section in front and a covered section over the rear passengers with a divider window between; there may be a removable soft top that can be placed over the front compartment.
Trailer Queen	A car usually restored to a very high standard that is seldom driven and most often trailered to shows.
Turbo	Short for "turbosupercharger" or simply "turbocharger." An exhaust gas-driven forced-induction system designed to increase horsepower without increasing displacement or fuel consumption.
Two-door Hard top	Two-door built without a structural B-pillar, in which the side windows roll completely into the doors leaving an open space from A-pillar to C-pillar (see "roof pillars").
Two-door Sedan	Two-door built with a structural B-illar extending from the sill to the roof; the doors also carry structural frames around the side windows.
Unibody	A car constructed in a manner where the body and floorpan form a single structural unit as opposed to a separate body and frame car.
Whale Tail	Aerodynamic device appended to the engine lid of a Porsche 911 Turbo. Also called a rear spoiler.
Wire Wheels	Road wheels that consist of a rim and center hub laced with wire spokes. Ususally secured by a single center lock nut or "knockoff."
Yenko	Don Yenko, a legendary Pennsylvania Chevrolet tuner famous for his Camaro and Chevelle Specials.

British to American

Bonnet	Hood
Boot	Trunk
Cellulose	Lacquer
Fender	Bumper
Five Star Petrol	Leaded Premium Gasoline
Hood	Convertible Top
Hood Sticks	Convertible Top Frame
MoT	Safety Inspection
Punter	Bidder or Buyer (connotes one who is somewhat uninformed)
Scuttle	Cowl
Shunt	An accident, usually racing related
Spanner	Wrench
Tappets	Valves
Two-pack Paint	Base Coat/Clear Coat Paint
Windscreen	Windshield
Wing	Fender

RESOURCES

 YOU FOLLOWED YOUR HEART WHEN YOU BOUGHT IT. USE YOUR HEAD WHEN YOU INSURE IT.

Trust your car with a company that really "gets it" when it comes to handling insurance claims for passionate car enthusiasts. Trust your "baby" with Chubb.

Our great coverages and features include Agreed Value, choice of body shop and no deductibles — all backed by our great people.

At the time of a covered loss, they're empathetic, fair and polite. Above all, they're knowledgeable and resourceful. So when you need a flawless paint job, or a hard-to-find part, you can get it.

To learn more about Chubb and our decades of experience with collectors, call us at 1-877-60CHUBB (1-877-602-4822). Or visit us on the Web at chubbcollectorcar.com.

Because anything else could be a real heartbreaker.

 **CHUBB PERSONAL INSURANCE**

Financial Strength and Exceptional Claim Service

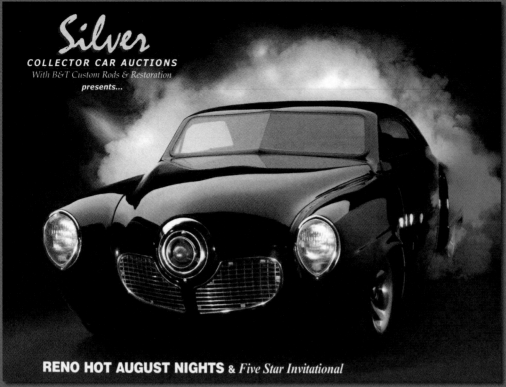

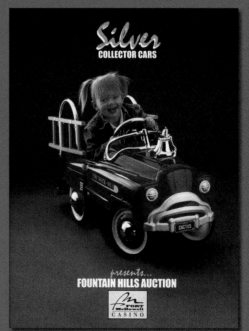

Classic Showcase

Where Great Cars Achieve Perfection

Finally!
The Perfect
Rear End.

For the Discerning Jaguar Collector

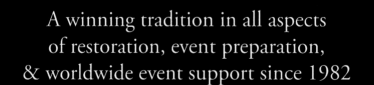

Offering the
World's Finest
Motor Cars

AUCTION BUILD SHEET

Since 1971

Ident. Number	Model	Date Received
2nd Annual	Las Vegas, Mandalay Bay	Oct 7-10, 2009

Paint	Number of Cars Offered	Dealer
Red & Black	500 plus	Only Barrett-Jackson

Standard Features

- Experienced & passionate management team

- Total auction transparency

- Highest standard of business ethics

- Real buyers

- Real sellers

- Level playing field

- Vehicles offered reflecting diverse market

- Live SPEED television coverage

For nearly four decades, the Barrett-Jackson Auction Company has been recognized throughout the world for offering a unique selection of collector vehicles, outstanding professional service, and unrivaled sales success. From classic and one-of-a-kind cars to exotics and muscle cars, Barrett-Jackson offers something for everyone. Our auctions have captured the true essence of a passionate obsession with cars that extends to collectors and enthusiasts throughout the world.

Introducing Barrett-Jackson Endorsed Collector Car Insurance
Get Your Quote Online at: www.Barrett-Jackson.com/insurance

Barrett-Jackson

THE WORLD'S GREATEST COLLECTOR CAR AUCTIONS

LAS VEGAS · OCT 7-10, 2009

MANDALAY BAY RESORT AND CASINO

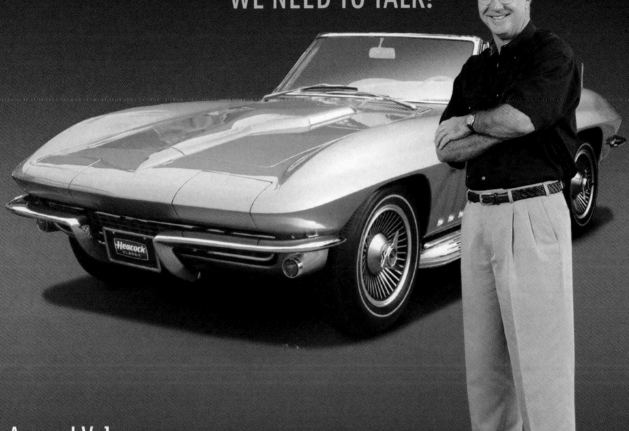

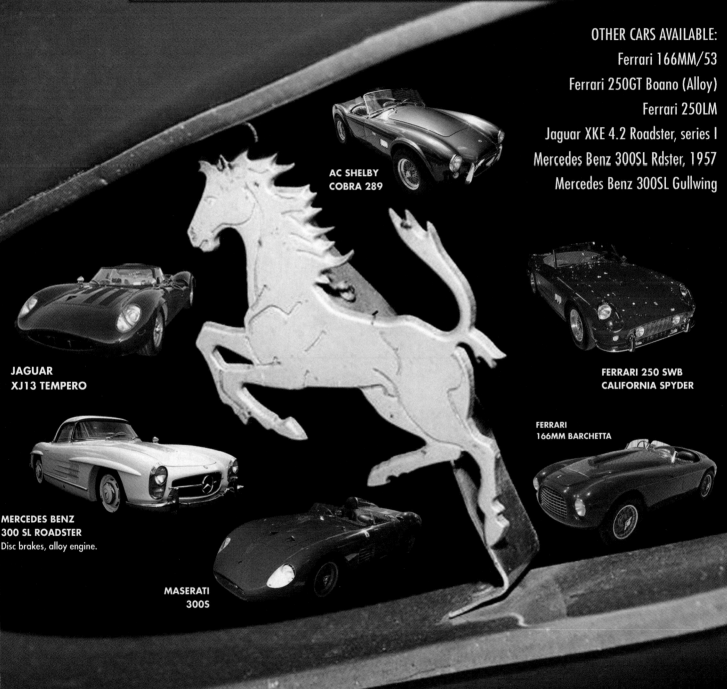

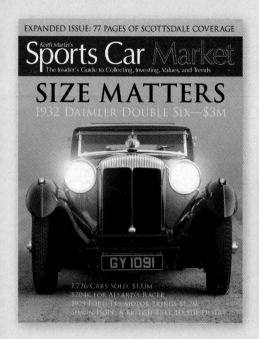
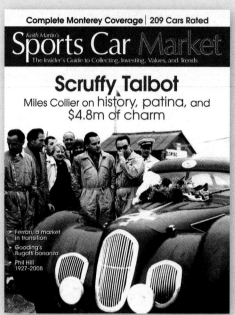

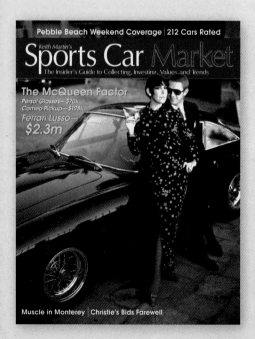

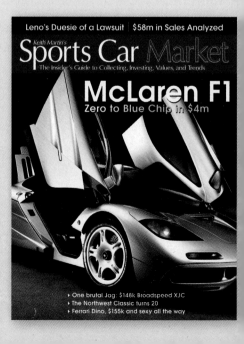